BLOOMSBURY GUIDES TO ENGLISH LITERATURE

Romantic Literature

BLOOMSBURY GUIDES TO ENGLISH LITERATURE

Romantic Literature

A Guide to Romantic Literature: 178   18
Edited by Geoff Ward

BLOOMSBURY

This edition published in 1994
by Bloomsbury Publishing Plc
2 Soho Square, London WIV 5DE

The moral right of the authors has been asserted.

Copyright © Bloomsbury 1993

A copy of the CIP entry for this book is available from the British Library.

ISBN 0 7475 1952 8

Typeset by Hewer Text Composition Services, Edinburgh
Printed in Britain by Cox & Wyman Ltd, Reading, Berks

Contents

Acknowledgements

General Editor

Marion Wynne-Davies, Keele University

Editor

Geoff Ward, University of Liverpool

Originator

Christopher Gillie

Authors of Essays

Edward Burns, University of Liverpool
Alison Milbank
Philip Shaw, University of Leicester

Contributors to Entries
Janet Barron (Eighteenth-century Prose)
James Booth (Romantic Poetry), University of Hull
Catherine Byron (Irish Literature), Loughborough College of Art and Design
Gail Cunningham (Nineteenth-century Prose), Kingston Polytechnic
John Drakakis (Critical Theory), University of Stirling
Lesley Johnson (Medieval Literature), University of Leeds
David Nokes (Eighteenth-century Prose), King's College, London University
John O'Brien (French Literature), University of Liverpool
Val Pedlar (Context of Literature), Open University
Jonathan Sawday (Renaissance Literature), University of Southampton
Eva Simmonds (Eighteenth-century Drama)
Mercer Simpson (Welsh Literature)

Editorial
Editorial Director Kathy Rooney
Project Editor Tracey Smith

General Editor's Preface

The Bloomsbury guides to English literature derive directly from *The Bloomsbury Guide to English Literature* (1989), and are intended for those readers who wish to look at a specific period or genre, rather than at the wide-ranging material offered in the original text. As such, the guides include material from the larger and earlier work, but they have been updated and supplemented in order to answer the requirements of their particular fields. Each individual editor has selected, edited and authored as the need arose. The acknowledgements appropriate for the individual volumes have been made in the respective editor's prefaces. As general editor I should like to thank all those who have been involved in the project, from its initial conception through to the innovative and scholarly volumes presented in this series.

Marion Wynne-Davies
University of Keele

Editor's Note

Cross References

A liberal use of cross references has been made. In both the essays and the reference entries, names, titles and topics are frequently marked with an arrow (▷) to guide the reader to the appropriate entry in the reference section for a more detailed explanation. Cross-reference arrows appear both in the text and at the end of entries.

Dates

Dates after the names of people indicate their life spans, except when they follow the names of monarchs, when they show the length of the reign.

Editor's Preface

Most of the *Bloomsbury Guides to English Literature* cover periods of at least a century. The bulk of the material covered by this particular Guide was written between the late 1790s, when English Romanticism may fairly be said to have begun, in the early poems of Wordsworth and Coleridge, and the early 1820s, when the deaths of Keats, Shelley and Byron brought the activities of the 'second generation' of Romantic poets to an abrupt and premature end. The brief span of both these writers' lives and of the period itself take nothing away from the achievements of English Romanticism. Indeed, an acute apprehension of both the urgency of writing and the proximity of death is one of the hallmarks of the period, and one that recalls the Renaissance, the only phase of English literature to rival the Romantic period in the variety and intensity of its poetry. This is a time in which massive historical and external forces, exemplified by the French Revolution, guide the subject matter of literature in particular directions; yet it is an age of radical individualism, in which personal psychology and emotions receive an unprecedented level of attention. These apparent contradictions are exhibited in full by a writer such as Lord Byron. From a twentieth-century perspective, his work may appear extravagantly self-centred, and yet it covers an extraordinary range of settings, themes, and historical and social changes, delivering its findings to a mass audience. Contemporary poetry appears nervous and parochial by contrast.

Shocking as Wordsworth's early poems seemed (and, arguably, should still seem), Romanticism did not spring out of nowhere, but expresses a climactic intensification of, as well as a series of arguments with, eighteenth-century forms of thought. Nor is it the case that the movement died with Byron and Sir Walter Scott, to be neatly and entirely superceded by Victorian literature. The interested reader will find a number of pathways in this Guide through which to explore the origins, the byways and the ultimate destinations of Romanticism, manifestations of which may be said to continue up to the present day. Hence, the Guide includes alphabetically organized entries on writers such as Tennyson, who carry on a Romantic tradition in English poetry. And, although English literature of the period has its own distinct attributes, Romanticism was a thoroughly European development: to P.B. Shelley, for example, German literature, French politics and the Italian landscape had a more immediate importance than the English scene from which he was voluntarily exiled for most of his adult life. The entries in the Guide reflect this international networking, and help to show how a massively influential writer such as Baudelaire was able to both prolong and offer a critique of the Romantic stress on the primacy of imagination.

As with other periods, those who wrote are not all named in the roll-call of those who published at the time, and, as in other periods, the gender of the writer can be a factor in her exclusion. Re-publication and critical analysis of the neglected or previously undiscovered writing by women in the Romantic period is beginning to happen now, and this Guide is both up-to-date and comprehensive in terms of keeping pace with these developments. I have taken care both to draw a recognizable map of the period, giving due emphasis to canonical landmarks, while sketching in enough new territory for the reader to be able to draw his or her own new map, including feminist, European, philosophical or modernist dimensions.

This multiplicity of approaches is reflected in the four essays, each of which was commissioned for this book, and each of which takes on a distinct topic within the period: drama, on the page and in performance; literature as, and as interpreted through, philosophy; women and the Gothic: and an Introduction that seeks to provide a possible overview of the period.

I would like to thank the authors of these essays. Edward Burns is Senior Lecturer in English at the University of Liverpool. His books include *Restoration Comedy: Crises of Desire and Identity* (1987) and *Character: Acting and Being on the Pre-modern Stage* (1990), and he is currently working on Romanticism and Tragedy. Philip Shaw is Lecturer in the English Department at the University of Leicester. Co-editor with P.J. Stockwell of *Subjectivity and Literature from the Romantics to the Present Day* (1991), he is currently writing a book on Byron and Wordsworth. Alison Milbank lives and teaches in Cambridge. She is the author of *Daughters of the House* (1991). I owe a particular debt to her, as I do to Tracey Smith of Bloomsbury for her efficient and sympathetic editing. My association with this series of Bloomsbury Guides is unusually close, in that, although this was nowhere stipulated in either of our contracts, I married my General Editor during the early stages of work on the book. To Marion Wynne-Davies I owe a huge debt of thanks for her wisdom and skilfulness in editing, as well as loving support and encouragement that stretch far beyond the call of duty.

Geoff Ward
University of Liverpool

Essay section

The Persistence of Romanticism

1

Geoff Ward

I

Introduction

'With what eyes these poets see nature!' ▷ William Hazlitt's exclamatory and admiring verdict on meeting ▷ William Wordsworth and ▷ Samuel Taylor Coleridge, (and, as importantly, hearing them read their poetry aloud), encapsulates in precise and immediate terms the categories of pleasure and instruction through which 'these poets' entered and remain within the canon of English verse. The 'chaunt', the note of bardic exaltation which Hazlitt heard in Coleridge's voice in particular, sounded the liberation of poetry from the shackles of eighteenth-century convention. Henceforth, the tight couplets of Alexander Pope's verse, and his focus on 'What oft was thought, but ne'er so well expressed', would seem complacent and narrowly technical. The age of Pope and Samuel Johnson had been characterized by a self-doubting and frequently pessimistic retraction of artistic ambition, leaving satire as the only poetic channel for a relatively unfettered expression of energy. But now the ambition of poetry seemed limitless. The next thirty years would see the revival of ▷ blank verse, the ▷ epic, the ▷ ode, borrowed forms such as the Italianate ▷ *terza rima* and ▷ *ottava rima*, as well as more or less freshly invented forms such as Coleridge's conversation poem. Indeed, a poem such as ▷ *Frost at Midnight*, with its blend of philosophical complexity and everyday vocabulary, is emblematic of the confidence and range of English poetry in the period from 1798 to the deaths of Shelley and Byron in the early 1820s.

In his pathbreaking poem ▷ *Lines Composed a Few Miles Above Tintern Abbey*, the closing meditation of the collection written in collaboration with Coleridge, ▷ *Lyrical Ballads* (1798), Wordsworth wrote about landscape, and of its powers of healing and secular redemption through memory, in ways that paid more homage to both the workings of subjectivity and the features of Nature than the 'official', London-based poetry of the Augustan age would have thought either sane or desirable. Recreating a visit to the banks of the River Wye after a lapse of 'five summers', the poem's questing voice moves from description of 'mountain springs', 'lofty cliffs' and 'plots of cottage-ground' to more conceptualized sensations of being able to 'connect/ The landscape with the quiet of the sky', and hence connect it with the mind. This is done with what may strike readers of today as a perfectly musical and smooth modulation. (In a not dissimilar way, the landscape paintings of John Constable, once so radical and startling, now form a suburban cliché as mass-market prints.) But Wordsworth's poetry – at least in this early stage of his career – is above all a poetry of exploration and experiment, and even his most apparently premeditated disquisitions on the nature of identity are rarely without moments of surprised self-discovery and encounter:

These beauteous forms,
Through a long absence, have not been to me
As is a landscape to a blind man's eye:
But oft, in lonely rooms, and 'mid the din
Of towns and cities, I have owed to them,
In hours of weariness, sensations sweet,
Felt in the blood, and felt along the heart;

Gaining in both poignancy and potency from the lapse of years, the 'beauteous forms' of cliffs, woods and water become not so much ambiguous as multi-directional, existing not only in the outer world but 'in the blood', and 'along the heart', as if that organ had its own mysterious coastline. The novelty of these lines (and of many key poems by Wordsworth) lies in their proposition that the inner, personal world of bodily experience and subjective recollection matches the outer world in its complexity, beauty and depths. With this in mind, the statement by Hazlitt with which this essay begins can now be seen to be a formulation as much about 'eyes' as about 'Nature', as much about perception as landscape. This double focus animates Wordsworth's lines, and may indeed be a feature common to all Romantic poetry.

The shock of the new in Wordsworth's poetry may be hard to register in the 1990s, when nostalgia for an unspoiled rural England, and the commercialization of that sentiment by the heritage industry, have co-opted the poet, as Constable's painting has been co-opted. The nostalgic and conservative reading of a painting such as *The Haywain* (1821) views it as the faithful representation of a real and beautiful scene from England's rural past, of a kind which has had to be sacrificed to the advances of industrialization and urbanization, but which can still be visited by car at weekends, and which proposes certain values (moderation, calm, respect for continuity and ritual) which serve the interests of our political masters, particularly at a time of economic instability and underlying disquiet. This kind of interpretation of English landscape painting brings its own agenda to bear on the work, but it is not conjured out of thin air; any viewer of Constable's paintings, like all readers of Wordsworth, must respond to a rendering of Nature so vibrant as to be empathetic, deciding in consequence whether that empathy has materialist, metaphysical or social implications.

Sometimes what we see or read here are examples of what John Ruskin would term in *Modern Painters* (1834) the 'pathetic fallacy', the attribution of human feelings or aspects to non-human subjects. A painting of an English elm by Constable, done around 1821, is structured as if it were a portrait. An even more dramatic humanization of Nature can be found in the paintings of Caspar David Friedrich, or Johan Christian Claussen Dahl, about whose evocation of a birch tree in a storm the art critic Robert Rosenblum observed that 'branches almost appear to be the exposed nerves of a suffering creature'. Equally ecstatic and empathetic conjurations abound in Wordsworth's poetry, as in these famous lines from Book VI of ▷ *The Prelude*:

> *The rocks that mutter'd close upon our ears,*
> *Black drizzling crags that spake by the wayside*
> *As if a voice were in them, the sick sight*
> *And giddy prospect of the raving stream,*
> *The unfettered clouds and region of the Heavens,*
> *Tumult and peace, the darkness and the light –*
> *Were all like workings of one mind, the features*
> *Of the same face, blossoms upon one tree;*
> *Characters of the great Apocalypse,*
> *The types and symbols of Eternity,*
> *Of first, and last, and midst, and without end.*

The first wave of English Romantic poetry, and the northern European landscape painters, share a tendency to return or even relegate human figures to the sphere of Nature, whose wild storms, immeasurable vistas of sky and sea, ceaselessly changing effects of light and cloud, down to the most delicately microscopic intricacies of leaves or the colours of flowers, announce cosmic and possibly God-given mysteries beyond the constrictions – the lack of *vision* – permitted by religious orthodoxy. Yet notice how in the case of these lines from *The Prelude*, the pathetic fallacy, the attribution of human speech to the non-human 'rocks' and 'crags', undoes and reverses its own ambition of harmonization and the reintegration of humanity into Nature. It is, after all, only by the imposition of the utterly human and linguistic notion of signifying meaning through 'Characters', 'types' and 'symbols' that the wild and incoherent landscape seen by Wordsworth in the Alps can be made to cohere. The strong biblical echoes of the climactic 'first, and last, and midst, and without end' speak of what is infinitely larger than human comprehension, but do so using terms that are perfectly humanly recognizable, and so supply a satisfactory and resonant 'end' to what was alleged to be endless.

Similarly, Friedrich's Romantic evocations of the beauty or endlessness of Nature, *Monk by the Sea* (1809) for example, or *Two Men Contemplating the Moon* (1819), depict distinct consciousnesses, at least as firmly as they stage the re-entry of the human into the maternal embrace of Nature. To return John Constable's *Haywain* to this context is to divest it of late twentieth-century nostalgia, to turn it from commodified culture back into art, but then to see in it a contradiction, or at least a doubleness, that links it to both Friedrich and to Wordsworth. Constable's brushwork – exploratory, conspicuous, and variously textured – appeared shockingly modern – unfinished, as it were – in its time. It is precisely that quality that is most lost by mass reproduction, and that acts to separate both the painter and the viewer from any premature reinsertion of solitary human consciousness into the wider frame of Nature. Wordsworth had written in *Tintern Abbey* 'of all the mighty world/ Of eye, and ear, – both what they half create,/ and what perceive;' and Constable's brushwork reminds us likewise of the primacy of perception, and the degree to which reality is given significance by human creativity and attention, an attention that may, finally, be solitary. The larger and more idealistic projects of Romanticism co-exist with the risk that any form of search for a larger frame than the single consciousness may undo itself, unmasked as a consolatory strategy in a world that ultimately begs questions, but does not supply answers.

And so there is much in the poetry of the English Romantic movement that is new, and that has to be granted its unconventionality and even its built-in contradictions, if it is to be read with clarity after the lapse of almost two hundred years. Yet, if the poetry is shockingly new, it is important to note in passing certain ways in which Romanticism draws for its intellectual resources on a partial return to previous models and procedures. These are frequently not only non-Augustan, but anti-Augustan in spirit. For example, by combining the hypnotic and driving rhythms of the ▷ ballad with luridly colourful imagery drawn from Gothic tales and his own more feverish imaginings, Coleridge took English poetry forward by taking it back. His early poem ▷ *The Rime of the Ancient Mariner* (1798), like ▷ *Kubla Khan* and ▷ *Christabel* (both 1816), gained its novelty partly from a revivification of neglected and popular (that is, culturally low-grade) materials. Likewise, the rhetorical grandeur of Wordsworth's writing drew to some extent on the blank verse of ▷ Milton's ▷ *Paradise Lost* for its scope and intensity, leavening it with what Coleridge termed the 'divine chit-chat' of a less prophetic and more conversational poet, ▷ William Cowper.

In order to fashion itself, each age tends to denigrate the previous period; this is as true of Renaissance impatience with the benighted Middle Ages, or modernist disdain for Victorian pieties, as of the Romantic reaction against the supposed limitations of the eighteenth century. However, there has never been a major period of English literature in which the availability of literary forms drawn partly from the past coincided with the furious energies of a revolutionary present to produce a poetry so suddenly bold in scope, and wide-ranging in style. Hazlitt's reaction to the new poetry of Wordsworth and Coleridge is therefore one of the Edenic moments in English poetry and criticism. Wordsworth's lines from Book X of *The Prelude*, 'Bliss was it in that dawn to be alive,/ But to be young was very heaven', may likewise stand both for his recollection of reactions to the ▷ French Revolution in its early, inspiring phase, and as a motto for the Romantic moment.

The term 'Romanticism' has a clear etymological proximity to the word 'romance', and, although there will be much in this Introduction and in the book as a whole to complicate and darken any too simple understanding of Romanticism as the literary expression of idealism, it is worth beginning by paying heed to one of this period's dominant tones, the revolutionary hope for a better world, articulated in a visionary poetry that asks us to look at the old world through new eyes.

II

Paradises Lost and Found

All the major poems of the Romantic period, from ▷ William Blake's ▷ *The Marriage of Heaven and Hell* (c 1790–93) to ▷ Lord Byron's picaresque epic

▷ *Don Juan* (1818–24), are concerned with the accessibility or otherwise of a paradise. However, the Romantic paradise is only rarely identifiable as the Christian heaven. To Wordsworth, the paradisal perception which poetry strives to investigate and hopefully revive is closely tied to an understanding of childhood as Edenic, but blurred and progressively less available to consciousness as time and decreasing energy take their toll. His ▷ *Ode: Intimations of Immortality from Recollections of Early Childhood* asks 'Whither is fled the visionary gleam?/ Where is it now, the glory and the dream?' Such a privileging of the state of childhood runs quite contrary to eighteenth-century perceptions. It also diverges from, while using, Christian allegories and symbolism.

Wordsworth's relationship to Christianity appears to have been easy, in his own mind at least. Although his poetry constantly utilizes the vocabulary of redemption and the healing of the soul through submission to a higher force, it does so through a secular version of the Protestant tradition of introspection, with its plain but confessional rhetoric of self-transformation; the poet wrote cheerfully to a clergyman who had questioned his devotion to Christ that he felt no particular need for a redeemer.

It is clear that Coleridge, by contrast, strove in both his writing and his work as a lay preacher for an accommodation of his experience and his philosophical learning to orthodox Christianity, an accommodation severely undermined by the intellectual discoveries of his poetry, no less than by his opium addiction. The introduction of the deity into the phenomenology of poems such as *Frost at Midnight* (1798) and *The Eolian Harp* (1796) seems dutiful and superfluous; Coleridge's most vital perceptions are coloured by fear, guilt and nightmare. Poems such as *The Ancient Mariner* and *Kubla Khan* are so rich in symbolism as to repudiate any attempt to tie their meaning down to a single set of symbols. Coleridge's poetry is less successful when the poet is, paradoxically, most able to formulate his beliefs clearly. This was certainly noticed by ▷ P.B. Shelley, whose poem ▷ *Mont Blanc* is (among its other activities) a critique of the belief-system underpinning an earlier poem by Coleridge, *Hymn Before Sun-Rise, in the Vale of Chamouni*.

Both poems are set in the vicinity of Mont Blanc, and take as their subject the relationship between the awe-inspiring turbulence of the landscape, and the human mind, searching for clues to the organization and purpose of existence in a scene that seems to promise revelation while dwarfing the individual observer. In the case of Coleridge, exclamatory and strained rhetoric becomes the platform for a hierarchical and conventional, almost Sunday School, understanding of the mountainous earth reaching upward towards a deity in the sky:

> *Thou too again, stupendous mountain! thou*
> *That as I raise my head, awhile bowed low*
> *In adoration, upward from thy base*
> *Slow travelling with dim eyes suffused with tears . . .*
> *Great Hierarch! tell thou the silent sky,*
> *And tell the stars, and tell yon rising sun*
> *Earth, with her thousand voices, praises GOD.*

By contrast, Shelley visits the same scene to produce, in *Mont Blanc*, a text as complex, volatile and dense with activity as the landscape itself. Shelley has none of the guilt and anxiety that pushed Coleridge into acquiescent piety. Instead, his poem is a subtle but extraordinarily self-possessed disquisition on the nature of the relationship between human perception and the 'universe of things around', which in a sense masters the landscape by using it to illustrate what are in effect a series of philosophical positions:

> *The everlasting universe of things*
> *Flows through the mind, and rolls its rapid waves,*
> *Now dark – now glittering – now reflecting gloom –*
> *Now lending splendour, where from secret springs*
> *The source of human thought its tribute brings*
> *Of waters, – with a sound but half its own,*
> *Such as a feeble brook will oft assume*
> *In the wild woods, among the mountains lone,*
> *Where waterfalls around it leap for ever,*
> *Where woods and winds contend, and a vast river*
> *Over its rocks ceaselessly bursts and raves.*

Mind and landscape mirror and echo each other, bring each other significance, as in Wordsworth's phenomenology. But if Wordsworth was led to muse reflectively on what is felt in the blood and felt along the heart, Shelley presents perception as a maelstrom. The individual mind may be 'a feeble brook', but the collective unconscious, the 'One Mind' as it would be conjured in ▷ *Prometheus Unbound*, is not only the equal of the external landscape, but what finally gives it significance. There is no God to Shelley, and the poem is atheist. (A more protracted analysis might show that even Shelley's most vehemently materialist writing is never without a mystical inflection; but it is never one that conforms to religious orthodoxy, *á la* Coleridge.)

Yet Coleridge's strongest poetry is very far from reaching definite conclusions about the nature of existence, let alone firm religious belief. Doubly sub-titled 'A Vision in a Dream' and 'A Fragment', *Kubla Khan* is best read as a collage of delightful and unfathomable mysteries, in which the reader-interpreter can wander at will without ever reaching a conclusion. As with much of the engaging literary work from this period, open-endedness or multiple, even undecideable meaning, becomes an attraction and a virtue – perhaps even a form of realism, as the world after the French Revolution seemed less fathomable and more malleable than before.

> *In Xanadu did Kubla Khan*
> *A stately pleasure-dome decree:*
> *Where Alph, the sacred river, ran*
> *Through caverns measureless to man*
> > *Down to a sunless sea.*
> *So twice five miles of fertile ground*

With walls and towers were girdled round:
And here were gardens bright with sinuous rills,
Where blossomed many an incense-bearing tree;
And here were forests ancient as the hills,
Enfolding sunny spots of greenery.

The Orient in English literature (see ▷ Orientalism) tends to have been viewed ambiguously as despotic and barbarous, and therefore simpler than the West, and yet intricate, appealing to the senses, a canvas on which desires repressed by occidental culture and morals could be luridly brought to life. Do the Khan's decrees issue therefore from an absolute power, used on this occasion for benign purposes related to art and the imagination? Is it significant that X stands at the end of the alphabet, A at the beginning, and K in the middle, when the poem appears to be concerned with the origins, ending and centre of life? Does the Khan's miniature world of walls and towers and gardens symbolize the compartments of the mind? (And if so, why 'twice five miles of fertile ground'? Does 'five' have occult significance?)

Although the poem is only fifty-four lines long, what follows this – already exceedingly complex – opening takes the text in too many labyrinthine directions to be susceptible of neat analysis, in an essay of this length at least. Coleridge did nothing to solve the poem's mysteries by adding an account of its composition in an opium-reverie, in 'a lonely farmhouse between Porlock and Linton' in the West Country, after reading a seventeenth-century travel volume, *Purchas's Pilgrimage*, and in particular these phrases: 'Here the Khan Kubla commanded a palace to be built, and a stately garden thereunto. And thus ten miles of fertile ground were inclosed with a wall.' So, that might account for the twice five miles. Coleridge stated that he composed (mentally) a poem between 'two to three hundred lines' in length, of which the fragment we have is all that he could commit to paper before some nameless 'person from Porlock' distracted the poet with mundane business, driving the delicate imagining of gardens of oriental delight clean out of his head. Unfortunately for Coleridge, modern scholarship has uncovered more than one draft of the poem, and the narrative has been proved untrue in other respects.

The poem, however, is in itself concerned with the fugitive and slippery nature of truth and knowledge, the disappearance of hard fact in fiction and dream, the inability of the wandering mind to envision a paradise other than in glimpses. All that Coleridge's explanatory narrative proves, finally, is that he did not know what he had got hold of. His poem had (whether through opium or not hardly matters) written itself; and no recourse to church and scripture could possibly accommodate its sinuous, oneiric puzzles, walled gardens and blind alleys. Just as Wordsworth's project to reintegrate human life into the larger world of Nature foundered on the very agent of reintegration, perception, stressing the reality of a solitary consciousness, so in Coleridge's poem the dreams dissolve into the pathos and vulnerable isolation of the single mind, haunted by dissolving palaces. 'A damsel with a dulcimer/ In a vision once I saw': could the poet hear her song once more, he would construct the Khan's dream-dome and get back to the Garden, the oriental Eden of imagination released from moral stricture:

> Could I revive within me
> Her symphony and song,
> To such a deep delight 'twould win me,
> That with music loud and long,
> I would build that dome in air,
> That sunny dome! those caves of ice!
> And all who heard should see them there,
> And all should cry, Beware! Beware!
> His flashing eyes, his floating hair!
> Weave a circle round him thrice,
> And close your eyes with holy dread,
> For he on honey-dew hath fed,
> And drunk the milk of Paradise.

The final images convey great beauty in their figure of the Poet as the incarnation of capable imagination, a construction lent considerable pathos and in a sense undone by the tenses of these magnificent final lines: "twould', 'would', 'should'. They signify wistfulness, incapability, impotence. The vitality and effectiveness of the poem are complicated but far from diminished by the tragic shadow cast over its visions of paradise. This time it was Shelley's turn to tread the same ground, but produce a weaker poem than Coleridge. His 'West Wind' ode uses key Coleridgean terms such as 'dome', 'vaulted', 'burst' and 'towers', and seeks to elevate the prophetic figure of the Poet to an unprecedented degree, but lacks the emotional dimension which is brought to *Kubla Khan* precisely through its failure to complete the projects it initiated. It might be concluded that while the paradise motif is, in some form or other, a feature of all key Romantic poems, the shadows cast over its attainability are as much the poetry's final subject as its more positive, visionary and revolutionary elements. The explosion of creativity in English poetry at this period involves the articulation of dream, doubt and vertigo, at least as much as it does the expression of optimism and achievement.

It was Coleridge's mixed gift and curse to be able to best illuminate the workings of human psychology through the drama of his own self-estrangement and baulked creativity. If the most affecting moments in Coleridge's poetry are to do with glimpsing visionary paradises and psychological hells (see *Christabel* in particular), his experience of writing was frequently purgatorial, a career of procrastination, unworkable projects and a reliance on the verbatim incorporation of the work of others that amounts to plagiarism. (The fullest treatment of these matters is still Norman Fruman's *Coleridge: The Damaged Archangel*, 1972. For an authoritative examination of Romantic poetry in relation to religious frames of thought, see M.H. Abrams's *Natural Supernaturalism*, 1971.)

▷ Thomas De Quincey's conjurations of a visionary paradise are similarly unorthodox, and similarly conditioned by an unshakeable addiction to opium.

As the author of ▷ *Confessions of an English Opium Eater* (1821; revised 1856), De Quincey has become the most celebrated drug-user in the canon of English literature. In fact he drank the drug in the form of laudanum, a solution of opium in wine or brandy. It was hard to judge the dosage; editors who complained of the illegibility or absence of certain words in De Quincey's manuscripts were not alluding to his mental state, directly; laudanum spilled from the wine glass he would have by him while writing was sufficiently acidic to burn through the ink. The author of the *Confessions* knew Coleridge well, though their relationship soured as De Quincey's fortunes declined. Discussion of their shared addiction was circumspect, and coloured by self-delusion as well as incomplete knowledge; opium was commonly available in the nineteenth century as a panacea for a wide range of conditions, but its addictive properties were not properly understood. Curiously, and again like Coleridge, De Quincey defines his sense of self through the textuality of hallucination to a degree that suggests the author would have been a hypersensitive dreamer, had he never touched drugs. Texts and the life outside them chase each other at speed in the Romantic period, and it is impossible to establish whether De Quincey wrote a drug-induced literature, now called Romantic, or whether the literary influences he followed (being a devoted and early admirer of Wordsworth and Coleridge) would have pushed his writing in certain directions with or without the drug.

Either way, his conjurations of paradisal flights of imagination in *Confessions of an English Opium Eater* are apt to turn hellish in an instant. The book is indebted to religious structures of thought, but the debt is complex and ironic. The daily ritual of opium-taking may have opened the doors to memory and imagination, but it was also a sinful and debilitating indulgence. The *Confessions*, as the title immediately suggests, both echo, parody and exceed in intellectual complexity those narratives of conversion such as those produced by sects like the Clapham Saints, of which the writer's mother was a member: 'Thou hast the keys of Paradise,' intones De Quincey, 'oh, just, subtle, and mighty opium!' Darkly witty, pedantically scholarly, suddenly acute in its proto-Freudian intuition of the importance of dreams, as labyrinthine and sonorous as a seventeenth-century sermon, revised and yet interminable, De Quincey's most important book is as orchidaceously peculiar as it is vital. In its way a spiritual autobiography, it resembles *The Prelude*, and in the mixture of drug-related orientalia, the terrors of the night and the pathos of the dreamer, it may be read as a prose sibling to Coleridge's more adventurous poems. The quotation that follows is long, of necessity:

Many years ago, when I was looking over Piranesi's Antiquities of Rome, Mr Coleridge, who was standing by, described to me a set of plates by that artist, called his Dreams, and which record the scenery of his own visions during the delirium of a fever. Some of them (I describe only from memory of Mr Coleridge's account) represented vast Gothic halls: on the floor of which stood all sorts of engines and machinery, wheels, cables, pulleys, levers, catapults, &c, &c, expressive of enormous power put forth and resistance overcome. Creeping along the sides of the walls, you perceived a staircase; and upon it, groping his way upwards, was Piranesi himself: follow the stairs a little further, and you perceive it come to a sudden abrupt termination, without any balustrade, and allowing no step onwards to him who had reached the extremity, except into the depths below. Whatever is to become of poor Piranesi, you suppose, at least, that his labours must in some way terminate here. But raise your eyes, and behold a second flight of stairs still higher: on which again Piranesi is perceived, by this time standing on the very brink of the abyss. Again elevate your eye, and a still more aerial flight of stairs is beheld: and again is poor Piranesi busy on his aspiring labours: and so on, until the unfinished stairs and Piranesi both are lost in the upper gloom of the hall – With the same power of endless growth and self-reproduction did my architecture proceed in dreams. In the early stage of my malady, the splendours of my dreams were chiefly architectural: and I beheld such pomp of cities and palaces as was never yet beheld by the waking eye, unless in the clouds.

The central allusion is to the eighteenth-century engraver, Giovanni Battista Piranesi. The plates referred to as the 'Dreams' were in truth entitled 'Imaginary Prisons', and they show classical dungeons, rather than the distinctly Gothic architecture described by De Quincey. This is in the literary sense a heavily ▷ Gothic passage, however: it resembles the currently fashionable puzzle-drawings and *trompe l'oeil* labyrinths of M.C. Escher, as the figure of poor Piranesi appears and reappears in constant aspiring labour, but it has none of the cool interest in mathematics and draughtsmanship that underpins Escher's eyecatching conundrums. The passage is full of self-directed pathos, and the figure of Piranesi is clearly intended to reflect on the figure of Coleridge, both standing finally as versions of De Quincey, trapped in his own mind between paradisal flights of aspiring imagination, and the Gothic 'malady' of his addiction to drugs and the fleeting dreams they bring. The mixture of orotundity, pathos, a sense of claustrophobic imprisonment coupled with sudden and dizzying release into the fantastic, is typical of his writing. But so is the psychological and analytical acuity: the *Confessions* is in many ways a theoretical work on the nature and importance of dreams.

De Quincey is a 'second generation' Romantic writer, who as a teenager had written an admiring letter to his hero, Wordsworth, and who in sense would always write within the parameters that the first generation had laid down. The next section will be concerned with the poets of the second generation, who variously prolonged, modified and questioned the tenets of Wordsworth and Coleridge.

III

The second generation

The importance of paradises lost and found runs through the major poetry of the three chief figures in what might be termed the second generation of Romantic poets, ▷ John Keats, Percy Bysshe Shelley, and George Gordon, Lord Byron. Racking up phenomenal scores as a fornicator with both sexes in that earthly paradise, Venice, 'mad, bad, and dangerous to know' in the words of his equally wild ex-lover Lady Caroline Lamb, and the partial source for literary vampires from Polidori's Lord Ruthven to Stoker's Count Dracula, it was Byron whose conduct most publicly and flagrantly departed from Christian norms and ideals. Yet it is Byron whose poetic questionings of the beginnings and ends of human life are most apt to leave the door open to religious answers, though not to a religious faith. The rhetorical mode of *Don Juan* is of a predominantly comic scepticism, tinged with moments of sober doubt. His paradises tend to be exotic and geographical, such as the island in the poem of that name (a reworking of the story of Fletcher Christian's mutiny on 'The Bounty') or the far-flung locations of parts of *Don Juan*. (For a rereading of Byron's poetry that lays more stress on the proto-religious nature of his thinking, see Bernard Beatty's *Don Juan*, 1984.)

Byron was made famous by ▷ *Childe Harold's Pilgrimage* (1812–18), a long and often sprawling poem in four Cantos, whose exotic locations and Hamlet-like musings on passion and mutability appealed by virtue of a turbulent self-centredness, characteristic of the time. As an image of alarm and fascination to the English imagination, the collective upheaval of the French Revolution had been replaced by the egotism and expansionist aims of ▷ Napoleon Bonaparte. Byron, the only Romantic poet to have a first-hand knowledge of armed conflict, was half-drawn to a figure he saw as fated, as tragic, yet as mastering a world of hard political actualities and the struggle for power. The more floridly rhetorical and dandyish passages in Byron have served to conceal a more sober and historically analytical intelligence with a distinctively British (and rather eighteenth-century) respect for hard fact. The ideological conflicts of his age are expressed through Byron's writing and his conduct; a libertine who had his daughter educated in a convent, a Regency fop with a liking for physically dangerous escapades, an aristocrat who backed popular uprisings. Most paradoxical of all, although the persona of the writing is the most bluff and British of the Romantic poets, it is Byron who immersed himself in European politics and culture and who has had perhaps more influence on the course of European writing than any other English poet from ▷ Shakespeare to the present day.

Byron's writing is inseparable from the figure of the man himself – or, rather, the man he invented as the Lord Byron he wished people to see. Darkly glamorous (if club-footed), exuding sexual magnetism (including an incestuous relationship with his half-sister Augusta), he was a product as well as a producer of literary genres: part Gothic, part neo-Augustan wit. Nothing in the world of *Don Juan* is safe from bathetic deflation, yet the hectic pace and love of the incongruous are tied to a sense of life's limitations and frailty:

> *I would to heaven that I were so much clay,*
>   *As I am blood, bone, marrow, passion, feeling –*
> *Because at least the past were pass'd away*
>   *And for the future – (but I write this reeling,*
> *Having got drunk exceedingly today,*

> *So that I seem to stand upon the ceiling)*
> *I say – the future is a serious matter –*
> *And so – for God's sake – hock and soda-water!*

Byron was the most doubtful of the Romantic poets as to the value of what the first generation had done. Canto Three of *Childe Harold* does (as Wordsworth indignantly complained) rely in part on a Wordsworthian view of Nature; but this was due to Shelley's (temporary) influence. Byron was sceptical about revolution, and about any kind of ecstasy beyond the momentary loss of self in sex. More heartfelt than *Childe Harold*'s verdict on Wordsworthian landscape are these cutting lines from *Don Juan*:

> *And Wordsworth, in a rather long 'Excursion'*
> *(I think the quarto holds five hundred pages)*
> *Has given a sample from the vasty version*
> *Of his new system to perplex the sages;*
> *'Tis poetry – at least by his assertion,*
> *And may appear so when the dog-star rages –*
> *And he who understands it would be able*
> *To add a story to the tower of Babel.*

This is wonderfully accomplished satire, however (deliberately) flip and callow; but it is also instructive, in a cautionary way. If we could go back in time, to interrogate Byron or Wordsworth, neither would understand the label 'Romantic'; the term stands for a historical-cum-critical mapping operation, that has more to do with the twentieth century than the highly individualistic standpoints from which these authors felt themselves to be writing at the time. But then individualism is the cardinal tenet of Romanticism.

Not so much famous as infamous, P.B. Shelley was Byron's friend but in many respects his antitype. Shelley prided himself on the observational accuracy of his poetry, be it in the meteorological aspect of his paean to revolution, *Ode to the West Wind* (1819), the domestic bric-à-brac of the urbane *Letter to Maria Gisborne* (1820), or the stormy landscape of *Mont Blanc* (1816). However, Shelley's preferred things are things on the move: wave-effects, clouds, dawn, things captured just as they are about to turn into something else:

> *Maidens and youths fling their wild arms in air*
> *As their feet twinkle; they recede, and now*
> *Bending within each other's atmosphere,*
>
> *Kindle invisibly, and as they glow*
> *Like moths by light attracted and repelled,*
> *Oft to their bright destruction come and go,*
>
> *Till like two clouds into one vale impelled,*
> *That shake the mountains when their lightnings mingle*
> *And die in rain – the fiery band which held*

> *Their natures, snaps – while the shock still may tingle;*
> *One falls and then another in the path*
> *Senseless – nor is the desolation single,*
>
> *Yet ere I can say where – the chariot hath*
> *Passed over them – nor other trace I find*
> *But as of foam after the ocean's wrath*
>
> *Is spent upon the desert shore . . .*
>   (*The Triumph of Life*)

In one sense this is a delicate but mordant evocation of the basic human narrative of attraction, courtship, sexual union, down to the last sad stains of exchanged bodily fluids ('foam after the ocean's wrath/ Is spent') in the miniature death that follows sex . . . before the whole cycle starts up again. Shelley's is a world-weary yet compassionate summary of the most pleasant aspect of humanity's animal side; and, as always, the writing reflects on language itself and the capacities and limitations of poetry, which also allows a wild dance and copulation of verbal energies – leaving little more than spent foam behind. *The Triumph of Life* was Shelley's last, unfinished poem, and although its last line – '"Then, what is life?" I said' – would stand as a motto for all his work, the earlier work is frequently more sanguine, and convinced of the rightness of political struggle along proto-socialist lines.

The genial *Letter to Maria Gisborne* attempts, as the poetry of Wordsworth often does, to offer an Edenic perception of things seen as if for the first time. However, the brilliant quirkiness and rapidity of movement in the verse are as distant from Wordsworth's meditative steadiness as they are from Byron's tolling rhetoric. Where Byron, typically, works from things out to a larger world-view, and Wordsworth sets self and landscape in a rolling phenomenological circularity, Shelley's world-view is more radically intellectualized and conceptual; things, in Shelley, are there to illustrate ideas. That may make him sound curiously eighteenth century, and a poem such as the *Letter* does put a quasi-Augustan urbanity and tact back into poetic circulation. In crucial respects, however, the relationship of image to idea in Shelley breaks new ground in English poetry, while utilizing in altered form the innovations of the first generation Romantics. Specifically, it is important to see that neither the 'things', the poetic images, nor the ideas they illustrate, are static. Language misses its mark, that of static representation, but in so doing generates new ideas: indeed, this is the theme of *Epipsychidion* (1821), consequently one of Shelley's most frantic yet intensely reasoned poems.

The poem is concerned with a beautiful teenage girl of the Shelleys' acquaintance, one Emilia Viviani, locked up in a convent by her parents while they sought out a suitable huband-to-be. Whatever the depths or shallows of the poet's affection for her, Emilia certainly made the ideal subject for a Shelley poem, bearing in her incarceration the related scars inflicted by church, class, gender, parents and marriage. Shelley loved to scandalize, and *Epipsychidion* contains some of his most acrid satire on the condition of wedlock. A reader might have expected it to contain a portrait of Emilia, but – and here the poem's central and more theoretical concerns come into view – the poem is partly about the failure of words to do their author's bidding. Words can describe, sketch, characterize, depict; do anything but actually *be* what they refer to. And yet the act of writing or speaking lets words develop their own life, on the page or in the mouth. Within the space of fifty lines, Emilia is called 'Seraph of Heaven', 'Sweet Benediction', a 'Moon', a 'Star', a 'Wonder', a 'Mirror', a 'Lute' and many other things, until the speaker concludes, 'I measure the world of fancies, seeking one like thee,/ And find – alas! mine own infirmity.' Emilia's humanity dissolves under the impact of 'failed' language, until she becomes a part of it, and is resurrected as achieved metaphor:

> *A Metaphor of Spring and Youth and Morning;*
> *A Vision like incarnate April, warning*
> *With smiles and tears, Frost the Anatomy*
> *Into his summer grave.*

The mutability and uncontrollable fluidity of language has become a virtue. Nothing in Shelley comes nearer the concept of paradise than this, the condition of metaphor itself.

Shelley's is a deceptive and difficult poetry. Early editions of this poem were small – 100 copies or so – and he had few admirers outside the immediate circle of Byron, ▷ Mary Shelley, and the other members of the 'Pisan Circle'. With the honourable exception of ▷ Swinburne, poets of the next generation would fail to rise to the challenge of his work. His Victorian successors disliked Shelley's morals, ignored his politics, and wilfully misread his fiery lyricism as ardent but insubstantial. To Matthew Arnold, famously, Shelley was 'a beautiful and ineffectual angel, beating in the void his luminous wings in vain'. That unfortunate and prejudiced assessment was effectively perpetuated by T.S. Eliot and F.R. Leavis in the earlier part of this century. The poet's reputation would only rise again in the 1930s, when Shelley's atheism, pacifism, call for universal suffrage and free love found sympathetic ears in the Auden generation. The proto-socialist Shelley, with whom Paul Foot's book *Red Shelley* (1984) is concerned, shows through clearly in a poem such as ▷ *The Mask of Anarchy* (1819), with its unique mixture of political allegory and the aggressive simplicity of cartoon.

A more comprehensive assessment of Shelley's achievements that takes account of his subtlety and range begins with the post-1945 generation of American critics – Earl Wasserman, M.H. Abrams – and reaches a kind of apotheosis in Shelley's adoption by the Yale Deconstructionists (▷ Jacques Derrida, ▷ Paul de Man, ▷ Harold Bloom, J. Hillis Miller and ▷ Geoffrey Hartman) who took Shelley's *The Triumph of Life*, unfinished at the time of his death, as the catalyst for a collection of essays on the (by these critical lights) interconnected topics of absence, death and writing (Harold Bloom, ed., *Deconstruction and Criticism*, 1979). This book contains a remarkable essay by the late Paul de Man, whose writings on Romanticism, collected in *Blindness and Insight* (1983) and *The Rhetoric of Romanticism* (1984), are among the most incisive pieces of criticism on the subject to have appeared in recent years.

De Man's model of Romantic literary practice is set down in a crucial essay of 1969, 'The Rhetoric of Temporality' (collected in *Blindness and Insight*). All of his subsequent writing on poetry would make a modified return to the postulates of this essay. The argument, too subtle and full to be susceptible to paraphrase on this occasion, identifies symbolism with the Romantic urge towards idealism, and towards an organicist world-view. Wordsworth's drive to reintegrate the human self into Nature, or Coleridge's divinizing of poetic utterance, would be examples of this. Allegory, the expression in rhetoric of temporality, undercuts the symbol and undoes Romantic ambition. As death, loss, change, meaninglessness – summarized by the word 'temporality' – are unavoidable forces in human existence, so even the most idealist literary text will disclose them on the page in spite of its intentions. In Wordsworth's case, for example, it is precisely a form of idealism that deconstructs his leanings towards pantheism, the attempted immersion of the self into a wider, cosmic Self. A basic contradiction runs through Wordsworth's presentation of the self, and other selves. The urge to lose discrete identity in something larger is countered by a radical prioritization of the ego, and so, to return to the admiring exclamation of Hazlitt's with which this essay began, we can see that what appeared to be a statement about Nature and then seemed to be as much a statement about perception, may finally be an egotistical statement about one man's perceptions. The lines from the *Tintern Abbey* poem quoted earlier may similarly be seen to deconstruct their own phenomenology of integrated subject – object relations by a stress on the self-centredness of experience. As de Man notes, 'Since the assertion of a radical priority of the subject over objective nature is not easily compatible with the poetic praxis of the Romantic poets, who all gave a great deal of importance to the presence of nature, a certain degree of confusion ensues.'

It will be clear that my own readings of Romantic texts are far from unfriendly to the kind of literary deconstruction that Paul de Man theorized and practised; the essay by Philip Shaw in this volume offers a more committed enquiry along de Manian lines. However, it may be worth taking issue with de Man's term 'confusion', perhaps suggesting that contradiction of meaning in Romantic texts may be a part of their conscious rather than unconscious activity. Deconstruction, like many schools of literary theory, produces its most startling results on texts which can be shown to be innocent of its approach; the nineteenth-century novel, for example. Problems arise with texts from two periods – the Romantic, and the contemporary. Contemporary literature may be written by the university-educated individual below a certain age, who may have studied literary theory, and be capable of meeting its approach forewarned and forearmed. Without suggesting that the English Romantic poets anticipated recent literary theory and braced themselves to meet it a couple of hundred years *avant le lettre*, it could still be argued that a strongly self-reflexive element in the poetry indicates that deconstruction might be viewed as a modern development of Romanticism, rather than as its anatomist.

The linguistic self-consciousness shown by ▷ Keats, for example, is hardly less than that shown by the Yale Deconstructionists (and some of his puns are as bad as Derrida's). Of all the poets from the period covered by this guide, John Keats is the writer who registers with the most lyrical poignancy the discrepancy between a paradise glimpsed, and a paradise attained. The idealistic urge to break through the confining fabric of the everyday to reach a higher or an eternal realm recurs in his poetry at all levels. It operates in miniature in Keats's use of synaesthesia – that is, the expression of experience by one of the senses in the language of one or more of the others. Examples abound, and include such lines from ▷ *Hyperion* as 'Let the rose glow intense and warm in the air', a relatively gentle conflation of the visual and the tactile. Conflation turns to deliberate confusion in these lines from *Isabella*, a poem that skirts the ludicrous in other respects: 'O turn thee to the very tale,/ And taste the music of that vision pale'; here taste, sound and sight are pushed into a weird overlap. Keats is not above a feverish and discordant levity, as in the redundant puns that are scattered throughout the *Ode on a Grecian Urn* (▷ Odes, Keats's), or the mixture of an arch tone and rabidly Gothic material that we see elsewhere. (Readers searching for a rationale behind the oddities in Keats's poetry should consult Christopher Ricks, *Keats and Embarrassment*, 1984.) But something more purposeful seems to underpin even the strangest of his synaesthetic conjunctions; for, after all, if the reader is able to stretch and bend habitual ways of seeing in order to accommodate an intensified or novel sensation at the level of metaphor, he or she may be prepared to do so in other spheres of life. Unlike Shelley or Byron, Keats had no real interest in political theory beyond the general openness to radical and libertarian thought that was current among intellectuals of his time. His idealism is centred on not the external world but the world of the senses, and the degree to which experience may or may not empathize or give itself over to what is outside itself, and with what consequences. Some theoretical reflections on this propensity for extreme and creative self-abandon that marks out the 'chameleon poet' were set down in a letter by Keats, from which the phrase 'negative capability' has come to summarize this vital aspect of his practice as a poet:

> . . . *several things dovetailed in my mind, and at once it struck me, what quality went to form a Man of Achievment especially in Literature & which Shakespeare possessed so enormously – I mean Negative Capability, that is when man is capable of being in uncertainties, Mysteries, doubts, without any irritable reaching after fact and reason . . .*

The poet should be prepared at all times to surrender to the instant of experience, without allowing the limitations of rationality or morality to get in the way of imaginative immersion in the instant. Here can be seen Keats's utter rejection of the precepts of Augustanism, and his leaning towards an art for art's sake, promoted after his death by Pre-Raphaelite and related spirits:

Dante Gabriel Rossetti, or A.C. Swinburne. The association of ▷ Shakespeare with Negative Capability is very much in tune with a series of lectures on the English poets given by Hazlitt, at the Surrey Institution, at which Keats was a keen attender. He would certainly have heard Hazlitt say of Shakespeare that 'He was nothing in himself . . . He had only to think of anything in order to become that thing . . .'

Empathy is then a crucial factor in Keats's attempts to construct or find a paradise, as is clear from a brief survey of certain of the Odes. In the *Ode on a Grecian Urn*, the speaker is held by the propensity of art to keep in a frozen eternity what would otherwise die:

> *Fair youth beneath the trees, thou canst not leave*
> *Thy song, nor ever can those trees be bare;*
> *Bold lover, never, never canst thou kiss,*
> *Though winning near the goal – yet do not grieve:*
> *She cannot fade, though thou hast not thy bliss,*
> *For ever wilt thou love, and she be fair!*

The melancholy paradox on which the poem turns is that while positive experiences held for eternity constitute paradise, negative experience held for eternity spells death: for example, the garlanded heifer about to be slaughtered, later in the poem, may spend eternity in that odd condition, and the 'little town', emptied of its inhabitants, will be silent 'for evermore'.

The urn is not the subject so much as the catalyst of the poem; it could not be 'shifted round', turned in the hand like the marble urn of the *Ode on Indolence*. Rather it is the trigger for a flight into Negative Capability, into which (to return to Keats's original definition) an 'irritable reaching after fact and reason' necessarily intrudes, puncturing the ideal with logic. Keats, regretfully, leaves the world of the urn to its 'Cold pastoral'. A 'friend to man?', it is still non-human despite being a product of human creativity in an idealist mode: in the urn's frieze, nothing can die, whereas in the larger world over which mortality holds sway, death is everywhere; and yet paradoxically it is our knowledge of death that quickens a more intense appreciation of life. The poem's closing motto 'Beauty is truth, truth beauty', has been the recipient of an untoward amount of competitive excavation by critics, but we should remember that this is the urn talking. A poem from the mid-1970s, John Ashbery's *Self-Portrait in a Convex Mirror*, exists in a Romantic tradition descending partly from Keats, and also concerns a work of art whose lessons for the living present are both profound and partial:

> *This is what the portrait says.*
> *But there is in that gaze a combination*
> *Of tenderness, amusement and regret, so powerful*
> *In its restraint that one cannot look for long.*
> *The secret is too plain. The pity of it smarts,*

> *Makes hot tears spurt: that the soul is not a soul,*
> *Has no secret, is small, and it fits*
> *Its hollow perfectly: its room, our moment of attention.*

As with Wordsworth and John Keats, the questing gaze that seeks in artwork or anything else outside the self an empathetic negation of the ego that might be the key to some larger understanding finds itself returned to itself. The Renaissance self-portrait by Parmigianino which triggers Ashbery's meditation has no reality outside 'our moment of attention', and art, it is conceded, proposes only consolatory strategies for dealing with the fight against time and mortality. Much has changed in the history of poetry between Keats's time and Ashbery's, but a certain transhistorical continuity, a persistence of Romanticism, suggests that the break between modernist and Romantic poetry is still not as great as the historical and epistemological rupture between Augustan verse and the activities of Wordsworth and Coleridge.

Where a negation of the ego in life may be fraught with problems, death may provide the ultimate abandonment of self to what is other. In Keats's *Ode to a Nightingale*, what might be termed death's analogue, death as a seductive narcotic causing loss of consciousness, is imaged in the speaker hearing the nightingale's song:

> *Darkling, I listen; and, for many a time*
> *I have been half in love with easeful Death,*
> *Called him soft names in many a mused rhyme,*
> *To take into the air my quiet breath;*
> *Now more than ever seems it rich to die,*
> *To cease upon the midnight with no pain,*
> *While thou art pouring forth thy soul abroad*
> *In such an ecstasy.*

Here the very attention to natural detail which had characterized Wordsworth's poetry or the paintings of Friedrich and Constable is wilfully abandoned in preference for a condition of not-seeing, again a Negative Capability, a resting in uncertainties. Eventually the dream is broken and the poetic voice returned to earth, as if from a drug-experience: 'Was it a vision, or a waking dream?/ Fled is that music . . . Do I wake or sleep?'

The speaker of the 'Nightingale' ode is left at last in a twilight zone, neither the realm of the everyday, nor quite the realm of the nightingale's song. Rather this is a borderline state of consciousness, arrived at by accident, but resembling what a later generation of writers, in the 1890s, would aim for on purpose; a state where, to excerpt from Arthur Symons's manifesto for a *Decadent Movement in Literature* (see ▷ Nineties Poets), 'the unseen world is no longer a dream, and the visible world no longer a reality'. Suppose however that consciousness were to be trapped in a twilight zone which was as repetitively circular as that of the urn, as close to death as the world of the 'Nightingale' ode, and yet without any of the consolations of either poem? To depict a world where the unseen is no longer a dream and the visible no longer a reality, is exactly the world of one of Keats's most important poems, *La Belle Dame sans Merci*. The speaker of most of the poem's stanzas, the knight-at-arms, may be read not as a proponent but as a victim of Negative Capability:

I

O what can ail thee, knight-at-arms,
    Alone and palely loitering?
The sedge has withered from the lake,
    And no birds sing.

II

O what can ail thee, knight-at-arms,
    So haggard and so woe-begone?
The squirrel's granary is full,
    And the harvest's done.

III

I see a lily on thy brow,
    With anguish moist and fever-dew,
And on thy cheeks a fading rose
    Fast withereth too.

IV

I met a lady in the meads,
    Full beautiful – a faery's child,
Her hair was long, her foot was light,
    And her eyes were wild.

V

I made a garland for her head,
    And bracelets too, and fragrant zone;
She looked at me as she did love,
    And made sweet moan.

VI

I set her on my pacing steed,
    And nothing else saw all day long,
For sidelong would she bend, and sing
    A faery's song.

VII

She found me roots of relish sweet,
    And honey wild, and manna-dew,
And sure in language strange she said –
    'I love thee true'.

VIII

She took me to her elfin grot,
　　And there she wept and sighed full sore,
And there I shut her wild wild eyes
　　With kisses four.

IX

And there she lullèd me asleep
　　And there I dreamed – Ah! woe betide! –
The latest dream I ever dreamt
　　On the cold hill side.

X

I saw pale kings and princes too,
　　Pale warriors, death-pale were they all;
They cried – 'La Belle Dame sans Merci
　　Thee hath in thrall!'

XI

I saw their starved lips in the gloam,
　　With horrid warning gapèd wide,
And I awoke and found me here,
　　On the cold hill's side.

XII

And this is why I sojourn here
　　Alone and palely loitering,
Though the sedge is withered from the lake,
　　And no birds sing.
　　　　(La Belle Dame sans Merci. A Ballad)

Like a number of poems of this time – Shelley's ▷ *Ozymandias* and Coleridge's *Ancient Mariner*, for example – *La Belle Dame* begins with a feint, the inclusion of a speaker who will not be the poem's real subject. The shared rationale for this might lie in stressing the depth of the gulf that can stretch between one human consciousness and another, with only language as the tightrope between; that, certainly, is the miserable lesson the knight has learned, or perhaps refuses to learn, but is still condemned to reiterate. He has been struck a devastating psychic blow, by the being drawn up from the real world and, as it were, shot into paradise by an erotic obsession with a woman who may be a lamia, a vampire, a *femme fatale*, and therefore false. He is now trapped in a typically Keatsian twilight zone, alone and palely loitering, the onset of winter in the external world in effect an attribute of his wintry consciousness. Still half in love, he cannot go forward and resume his place in the real world; but he cannot go back, as paradise has turned into brutal awakening on the cold hill's side. Of all Keats's protagonists and voices, the knight in this poem is most a victim.

In a horrible and ironic sense, he is a victim of Negative Capability; he is *compelled* to rest in mysteries and uncertainties, and has no fact or reason for which to reach, irritably or otherwise. No reasons are given for La Belle Dame's conduct, and nothing we are told helps either the knight or the reader. Unlike Coleridge's Mariner, Keats's knight may leave the reader sadder, but no wiser. The view of the world implied by this text is darkly ironic, to say the least: we have freedom to act as individuals, but that may signify the chance to become ensnared. The experience of falling into the paradise of love is common – the hillside is littered with courtly predecessors to the knight – but each must travel through peril alone, and none may truly help another. Peril lies in unexpected places. Perhaps the image of a knight is a fanciful externalization of exactly that state of consciousness; armed to the teeth, except against the one weapon that can penetrate armour, loss of self-possession. That abandonment of the self to empathy with the other, be it the lover or Nature, that began with Wordsworth and Coleridge, is here brought to its most vertiginous and ironic potential for danger, in the poetry of Keats.

IV

William Blake

That these matters did not entirely originate with Wordsworth and Coleridge, to be passed on to the second generation, is clear from an examination of the poems of William Blake, barely known in his own lifetime. To be sure, Blake's poetry is thoroughly perfused with Christian narrative and symbolism, but his revision of orthodox morality is as rigorously corrosive as the acid that he would apply to metal plates to fashion his engravings, while his liking for subversive epigrams and dialectical play runs as contrary to conventional reasoning as the skill in writing backward that Blake had to develop in order to incorporate his poetry onto the plates.

The early twentieth-century tendency to view Blake as an artist working in different media, literary and pictorial, undermines his intention to produce one multiform, prophetic art which would operate in the verbal and visual fields simultaneously. For example, the interplay of signification between the poems and the engravings in his ▷ *Songs of Innocence and of Experience* (1789, 1794) is often complex and ironic. The lyric beginning 'Tyger, tyger, burning bright,/ In the forests of the night' is a common anthology piece, resonating for most readers with a sense of Romantic lyricism as celebrating the more frightening and beautiful forms of life and Nature; yet the accompanying picture of the Tyger shows a sheepish and oddly diffident little beast. A similar restlessness and deployment of reversed logic inhabits all of Blake's thought, from the shocking 'Proverbs of Hell' in ▷ *The Marriage of Heaven and Hell*, such as 'Sooner murder an infant in its cradle than nurse unacted desires', to his snarling attacks on church and clergy, as in *The Garden of Love* from the *Songs of Innocence and of Experience*:

> *I went to the Garden of Love,*
> *And saw what I never had seen:*
> *A Chapel was built in the midst,*
> *Where I used to play on the green.*
>
> *And the gates of this Chapel were shut,*
> *And 'Thou shalt not' writ over the door;*
> *So I turn'd to the Garden of Love*
> *That so many sweet flowers bore,*
>
> *And I saw it was filled with graves,*
> *And tomb-stones where flowers should be;*
> *And Priests in black gowns were walking their rounds,*
> *And binding with briars my joys & desires.*

In this case, the thrust of Blake's argument is, by his standards, relatively direct. The lost paradise of *The Garden of Love* is an Edenic vision of happily promiscuous sexuality ('so many sweet flowers'), and the agents of repression are identified as the uniformed priesthood, 'walking their rounds' to police human desire. It is possible to argue not so much against this reading of the poem, as against the attitudes held by its speaker. Blake is a provocative poet, who wants the reader to argue back. It could be pointed out that no flowers last forever, and that the whole world is 'filled with graves': not even the most resolute libertarian can stave off mortality; and isn't it death that most forcefully binds our 'joys & desires', rather than the church, which does at least address itself to life-and-death matters? But in that case it might be pardonable to gather rosebuds, or 'sweet flowers', while ye may, and the case for a Romantic insurrection that pits natural desire against institutionalized repression asserts its paradisal energy once more. Such a revolving spectrum of argument is characteristic of Blake's restless engagement with ideology.

The generation of meaning in texts by Blake is generally less straightforward, however, and his investment in contrariety on principle results in lines as multidirectional as Wordsworth's, but so supercharged with possible significations as to become gnomic and opaque. The final lines of *London* are superbly resonant, but hard to pin down:

> *But most thro' midnight streets I hear*
> *How the youthful Harlot's curse*
> *Blasts the new born Infant's tear,*
> *And blights with plagues the Marriage hearse.*

Are the effects of the prostitute's curse good or bad? Perhaps infected herself with a sexually transmitted 'plague', does she 'blast' her own child's chances of a future by passing on the disease; or is the blasting away of a tear a cleansing, symbolically bracing, even a revolutionary rousing of the underclass to political action? This last reading seems to be confirmed by the attitude to the priesthood shown in *The Garden of Love*. Here can be seen a paradox central to the operations of Romantic poetry from Blake to Shelley: the greater the scope of the poetry in terms of topic, the more distant its language from customary usage. (This was something that troubled Byron: the drift of linguistic experiment into solipsism was something he debated on the page and in person with Shelley, patronized in Keats, and diagnosed in Wordsworth and Coleridge, the butts of satire in *Don Juan*.) In the twentieth century, such tendentious obscurity and a multiplication of meaning as we find in Blake has alternately been thought pleasurable and intrinsic to poetic practice, and a sign of alienation or bad writing. T.S. Eliot undervalued Romantic poetry, preferring the allegedly more unified expressiveness of the ▷ Elizabethan and ▷ Jacobean periods. F.R. Leavis followed him in undervaluing Shelley, and indicted Blake for manifesting the estrangement of an auto-didact, cut off from the nurturing influence of a literary community. This echoes Eliot's nostalgia for an age when writing counted. However, Eliot's diagnosis of a 'dissociation of sensibility', a Fall from this organic community around the time of ▷ Milton, is ironically itself a Romanticization of a historical change in the relationship between writer, audience, patronage and the means of production, which might be more accurately understood through materialist analysis of the period concerned, rather than idealized as an expression of being.

One revaluation of the Romantics begins in the 1940s, itself a period in which a form of Romanticism – dubbed the school of the 'New Apocalypse' – flourished briefly in the work of such British poets as David Gascoyne and George Barker. Critically, revaluation reached its apogee with the work of literary theorists such as Harold Bloom, Geoffrey Hartman and Paul de Man, whose writing from roughly 1960 to 1980 moves from ▷ New Criticism to deconstruction. This move, mediated by the impact of ▷ psychoanalytical, ▷ Marxist and ▷ structuralist theory on American teaching of English literature, involved a shift from viewing the generation in a poem of multiple or undecideable meaning as intentional, to seeing it as an inevitable side-effect of linguistic expression. It may be that in the Fall from various versions of paradise conjured in Romantic poetry can be seen the imagistic expression of what is at root a linguistic Fall, the slippage of expression from intention, of signifier from signified. It may be that literary criticism has now caught up with Romantic poetry, by showing how language, like all human dream-forms, is condemned to make and break itself.

V

The persistence of Romanticism

An historically limited view of Romanticism would declare it to be a bounded movement, that began (with influences as diverse as the French Revolution and the German tale of terror) with the early poetry of Wordsworth and Coleridge, and concluded with the death of ▷ Sir Walter Scott in 1832. By these lights, Victorian literature, with the burgeoning primacy of the novel, would be thought to move into a new era of ethical rather than egotistical writing, the question as to how we should live replacing the Romantic agony of who we are. The novels of ▷ Jane Austen, with which this Introduction has not dealt, might therefore be seen as important precursors of what was to come, given their emphasis on marriage and social positioning, actualities rather than dreams and desires. And yet the Victorian period, from the frequently luscious and oneiric poetry of ▷ Tennyson, Swinburne and the Pre-Raphaelites through to the Decadent poets of the 1890s, is replete with the kind of concerns that exercised Keats. The professions of artistic impersonality that accompany the seminal modernist works by T.S. Eliot, Wyndham Lewis and others by no means account for texts such as *The Waste Land* in their entirety; and the high modernist period was succeeded by literature of the 1930s, where dreams of a socialist utopia, as well as an interest in ▷ Freud, maintain a line of descent from the writing of Shelley and his generation. The bardic lyricism of the 1940s, the bulk of modern American poetry, and the 1960s cult of the self all confirm the persistence of Romanticism. The literature of Romanticism was persistent in conjuring ways through which the articulate self could empathize with something or someone outside, and was as persistently driven back into ironies and paradoxes that questioned that intention, while providing some of the most recurrently engaging and vital writings of the last two hundred years. As readers and writers of the 1990s, we are still situated in important ways within the questions that body of writing has posed.

Death Strolls Between Letters: Romantic Poetry and Literary Theory

2

Philip Shaw

I

But where has art led us? To a time before the world, before the beginning. It has cast us out of our power to begin and to end; it has turned us towards the outside where there is no intimacy, no place to rest. It has led us into the infinite migration of error. For we seek art's essence, and it lies where the nontrue admits of nothing essential . . . It ruins the origin by returning to it the errant immensity of directionless eternity.
(Maurice Blanchot, *The Space of Literature*, 1955)

What does it mean to speak 'before the beginning'; to be out of power; to be placed in exile; to have no truth beyond the sorrow of straying?

I will answer with a further question. Do we approach the 'essence' of art from the direction of literature or of philosophy? In this essay I will assume the necessity of both, not because the paths of literature and philosophy are indistinguishable – they are not, and we would be wrong to remove the distinctions that separate them – but because in the poetry of the Romantic period the two are often dangerously intertwined. The dream of Romanticism is a discourse that will encapsulate both. On the one hand, as ▷ S.T. Coleridge puts it, we see the technical process of 'just distinction' belonging to philosophical method; on the other the 'spirit of unity' characteristic of the creative Imagination (▷ *Biographia Literaria*, 1817). What the 'synthetic' power of Imagination effects, however, is far removed from this dream. The clash of unity with distinction, 'of sameness, with difference, of the general with the concrete, the idea with the image', is not resolved in the Romantic enterprise. And Coleridge is painfully aware of this fault. His imagination reveals itself in the flawed words and stubborn sounds of the philosophically imperfect.

To think through literature, therefore, we run the risk of repeating a great Romantic error. But that, I would argue, is our fate; for in a sense we are still Romantics, still subjects of an epoch whose 'essence lies where the nontrue admits of nothing essential'. In this sense to repeat is to err; but it is also to remind ourselves that our authenticity has its origin in what is useless, indefinite and nontrue. The Romantic epoch is 'born', to adapt ▷ Byron, 'from the knowledge of its own desert' (▷ *Manfred*, 1817). Here the key terms are wandering, anarchy and exile. In Romanticism, we encounter the world not as our home but as a nomadic labyrinth; a space that is truly infinite, without *arche* or *telos*, beginning or end. If truth depends on limits, on the assumption of foundations and of regulated and well-defined boundaries, then to think in this space is to commit thought to the inevitability of error. No wonder that Byron, in common with many Romantic poets, is derided for his lack of clarity, since to support this view one must cease to think in terms of the rational and the real.

One must commit oneself to an event over which critical thought no longer has any control.

But from whence do we derive this rhetoric of ambiguity? In a highly influential essay, 'Literature and the Right to Death' (1949) (collected in *The Gaze of Orpheus*, 1981), Maurice Blanchot presents an analogy between literature and revolutionary action. What literature and revolution share, he argues, is a desire for the absolute: the absolute of history, the absolute of knowledge, the absolute of subjective experience – the ultimate expression of which is the absolute purity of annihilation. Literature and revolution therefore accomplish themselves in the 'freedom' of death. For Blanchot, this is the meaning of the ▷ French Revolution. The subject is liberated from external bonds (the law of tutelage); critical thought is urged on by the giddiness of the event. The modern age begins.

Two impulses are born here: on the one hand the Kantian ideals of human progress and subjective autonomy (freedom from external control through the exercise of reason); on the other hand the eruption of systematic violence allied to the bloodlust of the emergent collective (freedom from reason itself, an act of pure will). The theatre of modern consciousness begins, so to speak, with the affirmation of a convulsive duality. It stages this dualism in the tensional relation between literature and philosophy. As reason finds its justification in the progressive impulse of revolution, artistic activity is confirmed in the liberation of terror. The task in this essay, therefore, will be to unleash the latent violence of the Romantic poem so that reason may be forced to a confrontation with a range of excluded others: the random, the aberrant, the mystical and the absurd.

If philosophy attempts to explain the world in terms of unity, cohesion and universals, Romantic poetry helps us to think the unthinkable. To do so, however, requires an act as irrational as the fall of a blade; a revolt that commits thought to the infinite migration of (t)error.

II

Whence that completed form of all completeness?
Whence came that high perfection of all sweetness?
(▷ Keats, ▷ *Endymion*, 1, 606–7, 1818)

Why a theory of Romanticism? On the back cover of *The Literary Absolute: The Theory of Literature in German Romanticism* (1988), the authors Philippe Lacoue-Labarthe and Jean-Luc Nancy make the following statement:

> *Romanticism is first of all a theory. And the invention of literature. More precisely, it constitutes the inaugural moment of literature as production of its own theory – and of theory that thinks itself as literature. With this gesture, it opens the critical age to which we still belong.*

With the epoch of Romanticism we reach the stage where literature becomes the perpetual positing of its own question. Henceforth literature, ceaselessly deferred and dissembling, can never be perfected or closed in on itself: 'This is why Romanticism, which is actually a moment (the moment of its question) will always have been more than a mere "epoch", or else will never cease, right up to the present, to incomplete the epoch it inaugurated.' We are, as I have suggested, Romantics. Or rather we are not yet Romantic. For if the Romantic epoch is interminable and incomplete it can never reach the status of a 'thing'. It is more true to say that it is 'nothing'. Thus, in answer to the question what is the essence of art we might do better to reply that Romanticism, or literature, 'is that which has no essence, not even its own inessentiality'.

Because the answer to the question 'what is Romanticism' is endlessly deferred, Romantic texts through their very dispersion demonstrate the impossibility of essence – and thus of being itself. For, as the writers of *The Literary Absolute* would claim, an epoch that begins with theory is an epoch that founds itself on the loss of being: on the supplement or the perfection of the work of art rather than with the completed work of art.

In an important sense, therefore, the question of Romanticism continues to haunt criticism. Who, for example, would deny that a correlation exists between Romanticism and ▷ deconstruction? One has only to consult the enormous variety of works on Romantic topics published in the United States in the last twenty years to find confirmation of this. A canonical book such as *Deconstruction and Criticism* (1979), with contributions by some of the most eminent theorists of deconstruction – ▷ Harold Bloom, ▷ Jacques Derrida, ▷ Geoffrey Hartman, ▷ Paul de Man and J. Hillis Miller – makes the connection between Romantic loss and postmodern absence explicit by adopting ▷ Shelley's *Triumph of Life* (1822) as a common reading text. Not the least of their concerns in treating Shelley is the problematic relation between language, literature and thought. In Derrida's essay, 'Living on: Borderlines', the problem focuses on the concept of genre. Why does the poem overflow its limits? What is it that prevents the text from maintaining the rigorous determinations of authorship, historical specificity and generic type?

The 'answer', common to Hillis Miller and de Man, is that language is a radically unstable construct. It cannot help but 'deconstruct' the imposition of borders, whether these are conceived in terms of the identity of the author, the priority of voice over writing, or the specificity of genre. If deconstruction derives this notion from the study of Romantic texts it is because Romanticism tends to demonstrate its own apparent contradictions clearly. How, for example, does one classify a 'theoretical' text such as ▷ Wordsworth's *Essay Upon Epitaphs* (1810)? As speculative meditation, prose poem, text book, autobiography or elegy? The list is potentially endless. If, on the one hand, we seek its essence in a literary genre we are led to the place where the law of genre, to recall Blanchot, 'admits of nothing essential': the text is what it is only on the condition that it excludes all of the others. Unfortunately Wordsworth's essay is incapable of such exclusion. Like all Romantic writing – here let us include the unfinished epics of Byron, Keats and Shelley; the encyclopaedic 'projects': Schlegel's *Fragments* (1798–1800), Wordsworth's *The Recluse*, Coleridge's *Biographia Literaria* (1817) – the *Essay Upon Epitaphs* struggles between comprehension and fragmentation. It wants to say everything – to reflect on the 'truth', including the truth of its own production – but it remains a fragment and 'as yet', Schlegel argues, 'no genre exists that is fragmentary both in form and in content' (*Athenaeum Fragments*).

The key phrase here is 'as yet' for the sense of the unfulfilled present strikes at the very heart of the Romantic concept of genre. Rather than to the idea of an assemblage or union the work of Romanticism points to the undefined and the illimitable: 'something evermore about to be', as Wordsworth writes in ▷ *The Prelude* (1805, 6, 542). To comprehend this fecundity, however, the energy of Romanticism must be directed toward the production of a 'literature . . . that would be a great, thoroughly connected and organized Whole, comprehending many worlds of art in its unity, and being at the same time a unitary work of art' (Schlegel, 'On the Combinatory Spirit', 1804). The Romantic work must be 'capable of containing its own reflection and of comprehending the theory of its "genre"' (*The Literary Absolute*). Literature and criticism, in other words, must become one. This prescriptiveness and conditionality, however, ultimately disfigure this aim, for if the 'essence' of Romanticism is 'that it should forever be becoming and never be perfected' (*Athenaeum Fragments*) then the process of infinite self-generation is one that is perpetually in excess of the ability of the genre to reflect and unify. The essence of the Romantic genre is therefore radically unstable. On the one hand it is fragmentary and limitless: 'No theory can exhaust it, and only a divinatory criticism would dare to characterize its ideal'; on the other encyclopaedic and holistic: 'It embraces everything' (*Athenaeum Fragments*).

But how can the essence of something not comprise a particular manifestation in space and time, with the coincidence of form and content necessary for any self-relation? Moreover, if Romantic poetry is, in some sense, the genre of genres (see again *Fragments*) what does this tell us about the relationship between literature and identity? To understand the background to this thought it is necessary to re-examine the conceptual antinomies of Enlightenment philosophy, particularly within the work of ▷ Immanuel Kant.

III
I feel I am; – I only know I am

(▷ John Clare, *I am*, c 1845)

From Descartes to Hegel philosophers have created systems of thought predicated on the autonomous existence of the thinking subject: *res cogitans*. According to this view the only thing of which we can be certain is our own capacity to doubt; *res cogitans* is that which remains when all else has been dismissed: the body, the external world and God. But the consequence of this is isolation. Like the narrator in Clare's sonnet *I am*, or the spectre of Coleridge's *This Lime-Tree Bower My Prison* (1797) the subject is deprived of its connection with 'otherness'. It has lost

> *Beauties and feelings, such as would have been*
> *Most sweet to my remembrance even when age*
> *Had dimmed mine eyes to blindness!*

The Cartesian solution to this 'problem' is to insist that the subject's relationship with *res extensa* – with material space, or 'nature' – is constructed by and issues from the subject's relationship to itself. Henceforth, to quote Mark C. Taylor, 'modern philosophy becomes a philosophy of the subject. The locus of certainty and truth, subjectivity is the first principle from which everything arises and to which all must be reduced or returned' (*Deconstruction in Context*, 1986).

In the history of ideas, Descartes marks the shift from a theocentric world view to a humanist one. Humanism, however, does not imply the negation of God. For even as the conceptual significance of the divine suffers a displacement, its structural function is preserved, and possibly reinforced, by its relocation in consciousness. The subject, in other words, *is* God. And like God it possesses the ability to produce itself, to create a world and to exist alone. For Taylor, this last point is crucial. Since the subject 'relates only to what it constructs . . . What seems to be a relationship with otherness – be that other God, nature, objects, or subjects – always turns out to be an aspect of mediate self-relation that is necessary for self-consciousness'. There is, in other words, no 'other' that is not already an aspect of subjectivity. Nothing can appear to consciousness that does not confirm the subject's self-relation, constructive power and sovereign solitude.

The Cartesian subject therefore transforms the other into a mirror for itself. Like the figure of ▷ Dorothy in Wordsworth's ▷ *Tintern Abbey* (1798), the other is present in the poem as the basis of the poet's capacity to sustain her as a mirror figure. Through catching in the sister's voice 'the language of my former heart', by reading 'my former pleasures in the shooting lights / Of thy wild eyes' (117–20), the identity of the creating subject is maintained over time. That of the sister, however, has been reduced to a creative foil; her difference has been incorporated within the circle of subjectivity's full knowledge of itself.

Discussions of Cartesian subjectivity lead, inevitably, towards a consideration of the status of knowledge. Given that in the distinguishing of the *cogito* a rift is driven between subject and object how are we to gain knowledge of anything that exists beyond the 'fact' of consciousness? If the other – which may be experienced in sensory phenomena, or felt as pleasure and pain – can never be present except as an aspect of mediated self-reflection how can we be said to have knowledge of the other? The problem is addressed by Kant in the *Critique of Pure Reason* (1781) (readers should again consult Taylor's excellent summary of the Kantian position in *Deconstruction in Context*). In brief, Kant argues that knowledge is the product of a marriage between reason and experience. The human subject makes sense of the raw data of sense experience by imposing a priori forms of intuition (*eg* the concepts of space and time) and categories of understanding (*eg* relations of cause and effect, unity and diversity and so on). In Kant's synthesizing of Cartesian and empiricist theories, to know is to exercise reason so that difference may be reduced to identity, the manifold to the one.

This still leaves unanswered the question of how the subject relates to otherness. If reason, as Kant claims, *imposes* form upon matter, does this not mean that subject and object, reason and nature, are ineluctably separate? That there was not, at some time, an original unity of theoretical and practical reason? A solution, of sorts, is offered in Kant's third *Critique*, the *Critique of Judgement*

(1790). Here it is suggested that the unity of subjectivity and objectivity can be recovered in the practice and form of 'fine art'. The argument is based on the identification of two concepts of constructive activity: the work of natural organic engendering (standing for the object or other) and the work of artistic production (standing for the subject or consciousness). Kant therefore grants the art work a privileged status. If ordinary experience is random and chaotic, marked by fragmentation and loss, artistic experience is self-determining and unified, unaffected by external forces or governed by anything other than itself. Through the work of art or *poiesy* – art that is considered as 'pure' production, without use or purpose – the creating subject realizes its freedom from outside determination. Its 'finality', Kant writes, 'appears just as free from the constraint of arbitrary rules as if it were a product of mere nature'. In this way, subjectivity and objectivity – artistic activity and natural production – are related and come to completion within and through each other. Nature can only be realized through art; and art can only be realized through nature.

At this point it may be helpful to draw a further connection with Romantic verse. To take a previously cited example: in Coleridge's lime-tree bower 'the friends' who enable the poet to break out of his Cartesian isolation are both constructs of the mind and products of nature. The act of imaginative projection into the gaze of the other – 'to contemplate . . . the joys we cannot share' (67) – thus creates a reciprocal relation between subject and object, a reciprocity figured in the image of 'the solitary humble-bee' singing in the bean-flower (58–9). The solitary bee signifies the self-autonomy and constitutive labour of authentic subjectivity as well as the idealized union of natural and artistic forms of making.

This, at least, is how Coleridge (and Kant) might wish us to read the poem. And many critics have been willing to follow this tack. M.H. Abrams, for example, writes of the poetic strategy in which 'nature is made thought and thought nature both by their sustained interaction and seamless metaphorical continuity' ('Structure and Style in the Greater Romantic Lyric' in *From Sensibility to Romanticism*, 1965). Similarly, Earl Wasserman has cited Coleridge as the reconciler of 'the phenomenal world of understanding with the noumenal world of reason' ('The English Romantics, The Grounds of Knowledge' in *Studies in Romanticism*, 4). It is, however, equally arguable that in the act of synthesizing subject and object through the structures of art the poet has merely confirmed the 'natural' priority of the one over the other. As Paul de Man argues, commenting on Abrams and Wasserman in 'The Rhetoric of Temporality' (1969, collected in *Blindness and Insight*, 1983), the claim for a reconciliation of self and other in Coleridge is based on the assertion of 'affinity' or 'sympathy', terms which only make sense in the context of a relationship between subjects, not in the relationship between a subject and an object. An example of this effect occurs in the opening of ▷ *Frost at Midnight* (1798):

> the thin blue flame
> Lies on my low-burnt fire, and quivers not;
> Only that film, which fluttered on the grate,
> Still flutters there, the sole unquiet thing.

> *Methinks, its motion in this hush of nature*
> *Gives it dim sympathies with me who live,*
> *Making it a companionable form,*
> *[With which I can hold commune.]*
>
> (13–19)

To escape the solitude and silence that 'vexes meditation' the poet must find an object in nature analogous to the movements of his own mind. The fluttering film provides this function. But the assertion of unity between mind and nature is not entirely convincing, as Coleridge's manuscript revisions make abundantly clear. From a reading of these revisions it could very well be argued that the concept of organic inter-communion is meaningless without the translation of objectivity into subjectivity. Coleridge himself seems uneasily aware of the sort of paradoxes that emerge from this process:

> *Idle thought!*
> *But still the living spirit in our frame,*
> *That loves not to behold a lifeless thing,*
> *Tranfuses into all its own delights,*
> *Its own volition, sometimes with deep faith*
> *And sometimes with fantastic playfullness.*
>
> (20–25; added in 1828)

Does the living spirit proceed from the self or from nature? If consciousness predominates then the relationship with otherness will turn out to be 'an intersubjective, interpersonal relationship that, in the last analysis, is a relationship of the subject toward itself'. Should, however, the subject fail to convert lifeless nature into an echo of infinity then consciousness is placed in bondage to the supremacy of the finite. The mind is a slave to external forms and thus to time. Whichever course is chosen, the supposed inter-communion of subject and object turns out to be a deceitful construct, a will-o'-the-wisp confirming consciousness in its mortal isolation.

If the link between subject and object is placed in jeopardy the fault can be traced to the dependence of speculative idealism on the structures of art. Despite Coleridge's insistence on the identity of art and nature – 'such as the life is, such the form' – the resemblance between them remains purely formal. It is possible for the work of art and the work of nature to coincide only because they have been made to partake of the same set of categories – and here the relationship is not one of subject and object, it is a relationship of signs. To put this again in Kantian terms: since, as Lacoue-Labarthe and Nancy argue, the work of auto-formation can only occur through art, the individual can only come to itself as *artifax* or, worse still, *ars*. Paradoxically then it is the very dependency on artistic form that effectuates the break between the *bildende Kraft* (creative force) of the artist and the archetype of natural organic production.

The fundamental insight of Romanticism, therefore, against Kant, is that artistic creativity predominates over the organic and the natural. Here, the subject is not transcendental, but becomes instead an effect of the art work. And in the work-of-art (to recall Blanchot) the process of auto-formation is one whereby consciousness both creates and becomes self-consciously aware of itself in creation. This, however, is a process of unfolding rather than control. Here we lose the notion of identity, of a Cartesian substratum underlying meaning. To exist in the act of writing is to commit thought to 'a non-transitive language whose task is not to speak of things . . . but to speak (itself) in letting (itself) speak, without however making itself the new object of this language without an object'. In terms, therefore, that directly anticipate the contemporary discourse of post-structuralism, the 'I' of Romanticism is one that effectively reveals and confronts its status as a linguistic 'effect'. In writing it is no longer the subject but language that speaks. The text ceaselessly unworks 'itself'.

> *Woe is me!*
> *The winged words on which my soul would pierce*
> *Into the heights of Love's rare Universe,*
> *Are chains of lead around its flight of fire –*
> *I pant, I sink, I tremble, I expire!*
> (Shelley, *Epipsychidion*, 587–91, 1821)

If the deconstruction of the subject seems alien to the official message of Romanticism – Paul de Man, for example, has been accused of the most formalistic 'misreading' of Romantic poetry – we have only to read the pronouncements of the Romantics themselves to correct this view. Schlegel, for instance, points out 'that words often understand themselves better than do those who use them' and that a certain ghost within writing will 'bring everything into confusion' ('On Incomprehensibility', 1800). Even Wordsworth, quite often miscast as the self-assured father figure of English Romanticism, seems distrustful of the claim for organicity:

> *Words are too awful an instrument for good and evil, to be trifled with; they hold above all other external powers a dominion over thoughts. If words be not . . . an incarnation of the thought, but only a clothing for it, then surely will they prove an ill gift; such a one as those possessed vestments, read of in the stories of superstitious times which had the power to consume and to alienate from his right mind the victim who put them on. Language, if it do not uphold, and feed, and leave in quiet, like the power of gravitation or the air we breathe, is a counter-spirit, unremittingly and noiselessly at work, to subvert, to lay waste, to vitiate, and to dissolve.*
> (*Essays Upon Epitaphs*. 3)

Wordsworthian ontology unfolds into an ethical imperative to maintain a rigorous defence against corruption. There is in this impassioned rhetoric a feeling that language will not incarnate thought, that the transparency of the word will turn into ghostly matter, revenging itself on the passive spirit of mind.

Romantic theory, then, in a prefiguring of modern thought, encounters language as a force from elsewhere. It becomes a 'counter-spirit' to the mastery of the self. In this connection, Wordsworth's thought is very close to that of

Heidegger: 'Man acts as though he were the shaper and master of language, while in fact language remains the master of man. When this relation of dominance gets inverted, man hits upon strange manoeuvres. ('. . . Poetically Man Dwells . . .', in *Poetry, Language, Thought*, 1971). In response to this inversion, Romanticism marshals a number of strategies, the most significant of which is the valorization of symbol.

For Coleridge, the symbol 'always partakes of the Reality which it renders intelligible; and while it enunciates the whole, abides itself as a living part in that Unity, of which it is the representative' (*The Statesman's Manual*, 1830). With the emphasis on the relationship between part and whole, the structure of symbol resembles that of synecdoche. The symbol, in other words, is always 'a living part' of the totality that it stands for. The vengeful revenant is returned to the silence of the tomb. But not even the organic coherence of synecdoche can escape the effects of the inversion that Heidegger relates. As Coleridge's *The Eolian Harp* (1796) illustrates, within the alien realm of poetry, the displacement of symbolic language occurs at precisely those moments where the unity of consciousness and community, part and whole, is most needed. Throughout the poem, language draws attention to its own status as an artificial construct. In lines 3–5, for example, the symbolic significance of the 'white-flower'd Jasmin' and 'broad-leav'd Myrtle' – natural objects that would unite reason and experience – is undercut by the following parenthesis: '(Meet *emblems* they of Innocence and Love!)' (lines 4–5; my emphasis). As Tilottama Rajan suggests ('Displacing Post-Structuralism: Romantic Studies After Paul de Man', *Studies in Romanticism* 24), by bracketing the moral qualities that are meant to subsist in the landscape, reminding us that the flowers are only 'emblems', the poem discredits the claims of the symbolic style to be the 'living educt of the imagination'. It becomes, like any other trope, a supplement to the actualization of the real. By foregrounding artificiality – the synaesthesia of lines 26–7; the formal, neo-classical conceit of 32–3 – *The Eolian Harp* suggests that the work of inter-communion has more to do with aesthetic tinkering than with natural engendering.

Strangely, however, it is through the work of the aesthetic that the poem is returned to what de Man refers to as 'an authentically temporal destiny' – though time, in this case, has nothing to do with what is normally associated with authenticity, the ability to coincide, to unify and to reflect on one's self; rather, time is that which leads the subject away from itself, putting it in a relation to pure anteriority, the *outside* of selfhood. A poem such as *The Eolian Harp*, therefore, works on two levels: first to convert the violence of time into the passivity of literary or mental space; secondly, to disrupt this space through the return of time.

In the first movement the temporality of nature is reduced to metaphors of stillness and silence. These metaphors reinforce the tendency of symbol to postulate states of organic inter-fusion:

> *and the world* so *hush'd!*
> *The stilly murmur of the distant Sea*
> *Tells us of silence.*
>
> (10–12)

The suspension of movement and duration at this point dissolves the 'I' into a state of oneiric repose. Consciousness slows down. The subject is spaced out. With the return to the meditation on the subject lute, however, the flaunting of artificiality translates the poem back onto the plain of time. The temporality that the second movement of poetry restates, therefore, is the temporality of tropes, a difference signified, in this case, in the shift from a symbolic to an allegorical mode of discourse.

According to Paul de Man, language is an ▷ allegory of its own deconstruction. He bases this claim on the ▷ structuralist distinction between the synchronic and diachronic poles of language. According to this view, formulated by ▷ Roman Jakobson, tropes such as symbol belong to the synchronic axis. Their structure is spatial in kind. Tropes such as allegory, on the other hand, partake of the diachronic axis. Their structure is durational and thus, in a sense, 'authentically temporal'. Before going further, it is worth quoting de Man's definition of these forms:

> *Whereas the symbol postulates the possibility of an identity or identification, allegory designates primarily a distance in relation to its own origin, and, renouncing the nostalgia and the desire to coincide, it establishes its language in the void of this temporal difference.*

('The Rhetoric of Temporality')

Allegory in *The Eolian Harp*, whilst not explicitly presented as a theme of the poem, is nevertheless present in the necessarily temporal relationship that exists between signs. The symbol is no exception. Despite the appeal to organicity, the symbol, like any other sign, is able to recapture or reflect upon itself. To echo the philosophy of Merleau-Ponty, this turn of the symbol 'recuperates everything [art, nature and so on] except itself as an effort of recuperation, it clarifies everything except its own role' (from *The Visible and the Invisible*, 1968). Something, in other words, always escapes, translating the symbol back onto the plain of the diachronic, opening a gap in the text that no act of existential faith can close.

Therefore, by formulating the symbol in terms of synecdoche (part for whole), Coleridge has attempted to spatialize an essentially temporal experience. But more than this, he has attempted to exclude the time of the other. The other returns, however, in the final movement of the poem through the dialogical interference of Sara Coleridge, the wife to whom the poem has been addressed. Like Dorothy in *Tintern Abbey*, Sara can be seen as a rhetorical 'excess', an unrecuperable isotope that emerges from the failure of poetic language to realize itself. Her look of 'mild reproof' (49) subverts the poem's founding trope: the idea that the antimonies of art and nature, consciousness and the world, can be overcome through an appeal to visionary correspondence. Against the 'half-clos'd eye-lids' (36) of mental seeing, Sara's 'more serious eye' (49) is a timely reminder of corporeal limits. The darting look pierces the infinite gaze, and Coleridge is returned to the body, the mortal body in which we find our home or not at all.

Following from this, the closing address to God 'The Incomprehensible' (59) is perhaps the most moving and most pathetic statement of the entire Romantic movement. Having eschewed the symbol as a medium for self-determination, God is accepted, beyond signs, beyond temporality, as the unrepresentable horizon of a lost totality. God is what remains when all else has been closed. Faced with this knowledge, the poet's subjective freedom reverts to the pre-Enlightenment condition of tutelage, defined by Kant as 'man's inability to make use of his understanding without direction from another'.

From start to finish, therefore, the conversation poem is an allegorical disruption of the pursuit of knowledge. But Coleridge, like Kant, cannot escape his Cartesian inheritance: trapped within the *cogito*, the desired reciprocity of man and nature, self and other, turns out to be a chimera, an escape that confirms the fact of its own imprisonment. And it is one that must be repeated, like the 'rime' of the ▷ Ancient Mariner, over and over again.

V

'*violence from within*'
(Wallace Stevens, 'The Noble Rider and the Sound of Words')

Within Western thought temporality is habitually excluded from the creation of systems. Time cannot be rationalized. Time is absolutely other. Given, then, that the subject through his or her relation to mortality is locked in time, how can we conceive of subjectivity as part of a system? Once again, to think the unthinkable we must look beyond philosophy toward the impure thought of poetry. Here, we may even 'see as a god sees' (Keats, *The Fall of Hyperion*, 1, 304, 1819), exchanging our mortal bodies for the immortality of mind.

But god-like vision comes at a price. To take the depth of things the self must not only pass beyond the bonds of temporality, it must also withstand the effects of human memory:

> *Without stay or prop*
> *But my own weak mortality, I bore*
> *The load of this eternal quietude*
> (*The Fall of Hyperion*, 1, 388–90)

In Keats's unfinished epic, the self undertakes a journey into the realm of the divine. One would therefore expect a rhetoric of self-empowerment. But Keats booby-traps the poem with pockets of irony. In the example of the lines quoted above, by juxtaposing the 'I' of 'mortality' against the 'eternal quietude' of a god, we are forced to confront what is really at stake in the dream of transcendence. Since time escapes knowledge, and since the human subject is in a perpetual process of becoming, our knowledge of the world remains partial and incomplete. This is something that the Kantian thesis, with its spatializing of human thought, cannot accept. But it is also the source of its subversive potential. For if the art work is free and indeterminate, unbounded by conceptual certainty, how can we presuppose the integrity of self-consciousness? Evermore about to be, the temporality of artistic activity denies the stability of a transcendent 'I'.

To see as a god sees, therefore, the subject must renounce its connection with process and change; it must, as Keats writes in the earlier ▷ *Hyperion* (1819) 'Die into life' (3, 130). Only in this way can the subject attain the closure necessary for complete self-consciousness and total knowledge. ·

But if death closes, it does so on the condition that it closes all. For to live beyond death is a scandal that no philosophical system can bear. Philosophy, however, endeavours to preserve this fantasy by converting the absolute negativity of death into the positive reserve of a temporal dialectic. This idea is presented by Hegel in a famous passage from *The Phenomenology of Spirit* (1807). 'The life of the Spirit', he writes, 'is not the life that shrinks from death and keeps itself untouched by devastation, but rather the life that endures it and maintains itself in it. It wins its truth, only when, in utter dismemberment, it finds itself.' For Hegel, self-realization entails absolute knowledge. But this can only occur if the subject incorporates the knowledge of its own dissolution. Death, in other words, must be included as a structural element within the progressive unfolding of a temporal dialectic. To do this, however, requires an act of repression – for Hegelian thought cannot tolerate a negative that fails to preserve a kernel of positivity. Through the process of *Aufhebung* (literally a raising and suspending), therefore, death is itself negated and turned into profit. In a direct allusion to the Christian myth of death and resurrection, the subject 'dies' only to be reconstituted as historically transcendent, omnipotent and omniscient. Nothing escapes this process. The random, the senseless, the stubbornly material – in Hegel's philosophy everything is assimilated into the economics of self-realization.

This includes the Kantian concept of art. What Hegel cannot accept in the Kantian thesis is an unforeseen reliance on the irrational and the incoherent. For Hegel, art is an insufficient ground for the realization of self-consciousness. Art can never be transparent in the way that pure thought requires. What occurs in the Romantic work is a form of death that cannot be converted into profit. It retains, so to speak, the force of an absolute negativity; a pure otherness that escapes the systematic totality of dialectical reason. To maintain its integrity, therefore, Hegel's philosophy must sublimate the radical imperfection of Romantic art. It must move beyond the instability of poetic representation to the pure reflection of conceptual thought. Hegelianism must, in short, pronounce the end of Romanticism.

VI
Death Strolls Between Letters
(Jacques Derrida, 'Edmund Jabes and the Question of the Book', in *Writing and Difference*, 1978)

What happens, then, when Romantic poetry experiments with the radical negativity of death; with death considered as a literary absolute? The link between the work of the creative artist and the power of the negative may be more intimate than we might at first suppose. Take the example of *The Prelude*. For a vast majority of readers the key note of the poem is a heartfelt belief in

> *the life*
> *Of all things and the mighty unity*
> *in all which we behold, and feel, and are*
>
> (13, 253–5)

Unity, blending, interchange; the 'filial bond' between man and nature – such is the dream of Romantic perfection. But against the grain of this assumption, Romantic writing inscribes a transgressive language: a rhetoric of failure, non-sense and irreducible absence. As Geoffrey Hartman comments, within this language 'the Imagination [which] usually . . . vitalizes and animates . . . stands closer to death than life' (*Wordsworth's Poetry*, 1965). Hence the Romantic interest in disaster; its thirst for annihilation – as in ▷ Cowper's *Castaway* (1799), Shelley's *Alastor* (1817) and Byron's ▷ *Cain* (1821), poems of despair, enervation and paradoxical pride which tease the borderline between self-affirmation and self-abnegation. The otherness of death, when it appears in these poems, is an event that cannot be accounted for, still less converted into profit. And not even Wordsworth can escape this force. When the imagination, rising 'like an unfather'd vapour' in Book 6 of *The Prelude*, releases the self from subjection to mortality, the assertion of a-temporality is made dependent on the dangerous equation of death as denial and death as possibility. At this moment, literature opens itself up 'to a time before the world, before the beginning'; to an 'outside where there is no intimacy, no place to rest' (Blanchot). This irreducible and unrepresentable 'past' opens a fissure in the text that makes presence – the assertion of the god-like, transcendent 'I' – impossible. Not even the restoration of time, through the punctual 'now' ('Halted, without a struggle to break through. / And now recovering', 530–1) can restore the integrity of self. 'Now' belongs to the space-time of literature, not of the world; it is an interruption that does not unify. Literary time announces the recommencement of the exodus away from self.

Perhaps this last point explains why Romantic writing continues to elicit our interest. The more philosophy struggles to attain a comprehensive view of the world, the greater the faithfulness of Romanticism to the call of the irrational and the absurd. Whether that call is heard in the cold pastoral of Keats's *Ode to a Grecian Urn* (1819), the warped lament of ▷ Thomas Hood's *Silence* (1823), or in the sorrows of ▷ Frankenstein's monster (1818), it speaks of what cannot be grasped except in fragmentary or unfinished form. But to cross the void, to forsake perfected truth for the sake of broken authenticity is a perilous, even impossible, task. In Keats, like Wordsworth, it leads to a space of pure difference; without beginning or end; without any purpose except the ceaseless affirmation of error:

> *No stir of life*
> *Was in this shrouded vale, not so much air*
> *As in the zoning of a summer's day*
> *Robs not one light seed from the feather'd grass,*
> *But where the dead leaf fell there did it rest:*
> *A stream went voiceless by, still deaden'd more*

> *By reason of the fallen divinity*
> *Spreading more shade*
> (*The Fall of Hyperion*, 1, 309–16)

The difference between Keats and Wordsworth lies in their response to this void. With Keats's work, unlike *The Prelude*, the death of nature is welcomed as a source of negative inspiration. The poet draws a perverse energy from self-destroying enthralments. In the realm of Saturn, in a grotesque parody of Hegelian self-consciousness, everything comes to a productive halt. 'But where the dead leaf fell there did it rest'. A sense of immobility threatens to paralyse the poem. The subject dissolves into silence and shade. When, at last, time is restored, one would expect the syntheses of the *Aufhebung*: the subject 'dies' in order to be reborn on the altar of rational knowledge. But time in Keats's poem

> ... *works a constant change, which happy death*
> *Can put no end to; deathwards progressing*
> *To no death*
>
> (1, 259–61)

Thus, rather than 'a-mortizing' death, Keats has made death immortal; a process to which there is no end and from which it is impossible to derive sense. Death has become useless, unworkable within any system of dialectical reason.

It is for this reason that the incompletion of the poem is so piquant and attractive. The shade of the fallen divinity is darkness *in extremis*. Thus, at the 'end', it is not the enlightenment of Apollo but the 'blank splendour' of Saturn's gaze that has most force. We are no longer faced with the desire for presence but the passivity of absence. The black hole of these eyes ('Half-closed, and visionless entire they seem'd/ Of all external things') drains the enkindled gaze of the poet so that the dawning of the ephebe ('Knowledge enormous makes a God of me', *Hyperion*, 3, 113) is stymied, halted without a power to break through.

In the place of the dream of absolute knowledge, therefore, Keats has offered the birth of a more terrible beauty: the affirmation of death, not as mastery and endurance, but as 'Life's high meed' (*Why did I laugh to-night*, 14). In making this claim, Keats perhaps more so than any other Romantic poet points the way to a space purged of self-consciousness. As he writes in a famous letter: 'As to the poetical Character itself . . . it is not itself – it has no self – it is everything and nothing – it has no character . . . A poet is the most unpoetical of any thing in existence: because he has no Identity'. To achieve this destiny – the will to give up self – Keats utilizes the substitutions and displacements inherent in poetic language. With Keats, unlike say Wordsworth, Byron, Shelley or Coleridge, words are embraced as forces of dispersal. Here language coincides with that which does not coincide; it leads, in advance, to the *détournement* of all unity. The result is an achieved dearth of meaning; the opening of a positive void. The provocation of a time before history.

What these fragments unwittingly celebrate, therefore, is the 'power' of uselessness and failure: 'I have left / My strong identity, my real self' (*Hyperion*,

1, 114). And in leaving the 'real self', the poet has escaped the utilitarian world of subject-making and self-mastery. Art, to paraphrase Blanchot, has deprived the writer of the power to say 'I' – the birth of Apollo will not take place – but it has enabled him to pronounce on the nature of the other. It has allowed him to accept his death.

VII

Nothing, whether deed, word, thought, or text, ever happens in relation, positive or negative, to anything that precedes, follows, or exists elsewhere, but only as a random event whose power, like the power of death, is due to the randomness of its occurrence.
(Paul de Man, 'Shelley Disfigured', in *Deconstruction and Criticism*)

only nomadic affirmation remains
(Maurice Blanchot, *Le Pas au-delà*, 1973).

How does Romanticism manifest itself in the present age? I have argued in this essay that Romanticism continues because of the Romantic fragment's affirmation of incompletion. We must understand, however, that the fragment does not affirm its lack of perfection in relation to a lost totality. Despite the perceived official message of Romantic poems, Romanticism is not, in essence, nostalgic. As Timothy Clark notes, whilst for Schlegel 'every part can be a whole' and conversely 'every whole can be a part', the truth of Romanticism does not reside in the recovery of an original unity or lost totality but in the moment of its interruption; the moment, that is, where the fragment 'maintains a singularity that both exceeds and resists subsumption, yet by this same token this singularity falls short of a determined identity and constitutes a lack in any putative totality.' What Romanticism affirms, therefore, is its ceaseless failure to present itself in a completed form. This is why Romanticism continues, right up to the present, to unwork the possibility that human knowledge may be articulated as a unified or total 'system'.

Where do we measure this effect in our time? One could trace it in any of the major avant-garde movements of this century: in Dada, ▷ Surrealism, Abstract Expressionism, postmodernism and so on – wherever the random or the aleatory speaks of a lack beyond the insistence of being. For the purpose of this essay I will focus on a prose fragment by the poet Paul Celan (1920–70) entitled 'Conversation in the Mountains' (1959). At the start of this text an unnamed Jew steps out of his hut to take an evening walk. The Jew, it emerges, is blind. As he shuffles along, tapping his stick on the stone, a first person stutters into life. The voice comes to us unannounced, babbling, as if from nowhere: 'Do you hear . . . here I am I, I am, I am here'. It could be the voice of the Jew, of the author, or of something entirely 'other', something at odds with the confidence and supreme virility of the eloquent 'I' – the authentic, integrated self of much Romantic literature. But whoever owns this voice and wherever it comes from, the ontological certainty of 'Here I am', the phrase with which Abraham responds to the call of God, is put into a position of extreme jeopardy. No one replies, night falls, and the voice stutters: 'I, I, I', broken and alone. Presently, another person approaches; it is the Jew's cousin, equally blind, equally uncertain. For a long time there is silence but 'it's just a pause, just a hiatus, an empty space'. At last the dialogue begins:

> 'You came from far away, came here . . .'
> 'So I did. I came. I came like you.'
> 'I know that.'
> 'You do know. You know what you see: The earth has folded up here, folded over once, then twice, then three times, and split open in the middle, and in the middle there is water, the water is green, the Green is white and the White comes from still further on high, comes from the glaciers, one could say, but shouldn't, that this is a language for the here and now, the Green with the White within, a language for neither you nor me – for I ask, for whom is it meant, this earth, for I say it is not meant for you or for me – a language to be sure, without I or Thou, merely He, merely It, do you understand, merely She and nothing more'.

In general terms, what this obscure and beautiful text acknowledges is the condition of its own belatedness. Without nostalgia and without pathos Celan draws attention to the persistence of a certain way of thinking, the presence/absence of an epistemology that might, for want of a better word, be called 'Romantic'. This is manifested in several ways. To begin with the mountainous landscape is haunted by the ghosts of Romantic agony: with Shelley's ▷ *Mont Blanc* (1816); Wordsworth's *Simplon Pass*; Büchner's *Lenz* and Byron's ▷ *Manfred*. But where, for example, in *Lenz*, the failure of the idealized unity of unity and difference, self and other, propels the 'I' into suffering and madness, here Celan manages to find a way of *affirming* that very failure in such a way that it is the voice of the overwhelming 'other' rather than of the isolated ego that has priority. By emphasizing 'babble' over eloquence, 'borrowed' language over original speech, the Green language of the 'here and now' over the White language of the timeless and transcendent, a 'Conversation in the Mountains' presents an ethical challenge to the ontological drama of Romanticism. Where Byron's ▷ *Childe Harold* expresses a hopeless desire for ownership of the 'one word' (3, 97), the unnamed Jew speaks of a language 'without I or Thou'; in so doing he enables us to welcome difference: a difference between ascent and descent, origin and anarchy, activity and passivity, mastery and subjection.

For Celan, drawing on the unacknowledged insights of Romanticism, language cannot be owned, or grasped; it comes from elsewhere, like the power of death. And like death, to adapt the words of Emmanuel Levinas, the 'He', 'She' or 'It' of language 'announces an event over which the subject is not master, an event in relation to which the subject is no longer a subject' ('Time and the Other', 1987); yet only in relation to this can the subject come into being. To signify, therefore, one must begin with annihilation, with death. I say 'a flower', and magically the concept flower appears – separated or split from the material flower. In many ways Romantic poetry 'begins' by recording this original violence – the way in which language creates meaning by negating the internal essence of things. When Celan writes, however, we are moved by silence rather than by words, by what is not there rather than by what is. The breaks and pauses in his writing gesture towards a region saturated with non-sense – a non-sense which turns out, paradoxically, to be the radical sense of poetry. Here we cannot help but supply the relations that the random event of language would deny. Death inhabits language; it is we who signify.

'I could a tale unfold': Women, Romanticism and the Gothic

Alison Milbank

Until recently the prose fiction of the Romantic period – least of all the ▷ Gothic genre – would have scarcely merited a mention in a volume such as this. Poetry at the end of the eighteenth century was considered a higher form than prose, while the novel still had many years of struggle ahead before gaining equal intellectual respectability. In a letter to ▷ Wordsworth concerning ▷ Walter Scott's narrative poem ▷ *Marmion*, Coleridge centres his criticism precisely in a perceived similarity to prose romances: it is a 'novel versified'. *Marmion* reminds him particularly of the Gothic, and he proceeds to classify the qualities of the latter form:

> *I amused myself a day or two ago in reading a Romance in Mrs Radcliffe's style with making out a scheme which was to serve for all Romances a priori; only varying the proportions. A baron or baroness, ignorant of their birth and in some dependent situation; castle on a Rock; a sepulchre – at some distance from the Rock – Deserted Rooms – underground passages – Pictures – a Ghost, so believed – or a written record – blood in it – a wonderful Cutthroat, etc. etc.*

Coleridge's reductive account of Gothic tropes makes them seem like a cumbersome set of stage machinery, and has the effect of distancing himself and his correspondent from the sort of literature described, even though many of the same motifs would find their way into mainstream Romantic verse, not least Coleridge's own productions. ▷ *Christabel* (1816) is in essence a medieval romance, complete with baron, ancient castle, haunted dog, and a mysterious lady who claims to have been captured by strange warriors, and exerts seemingly magical powers, while the ▷ *Rime of the Ancient Mariner* (1798) would itself have an influence on later Gothic writing.

However, Coleridge's scheme does fit many a Gothic tale in which the same elements are continually re-articulated, and the pleasure of repetition is itself a quality of Gothic fiction. The form was already well-established by the turn of the century, the first 'modern' Gothic fable, ▷ *The Castle of Otranto* by ▷ Horace Walpole, having been published thirty-six years before. For, in contrast to the ordered neo-classicism of the earlier eighteenth century ran an equally strong strain of interest in the 'Gothic' feudal past, in graveyard melancholy, and in human passions and extreme emotional states. At first, Walpole's tale was indeed presented as an authentic medieval account, so that its supernatural machinery of a giant helmet and the rapacious lusts of the tyrannical owner of the Castle were seen as of a part with a less enlightened, though fascinating, age. When its contemporary authorship was revealed, Walpole still sought to cast an aura of distance and privilege about his tale by locating its origin in a dream. (▷ Mary Shelley was to do the same in relation to ▷ *Frankenstein*, as Coleridge too with *Kubla Khan*, which remains unfinished because of the interruption to his opium-induced dreams by the importunate 'person from Porlock'.) Whereas Walpole – and later ▷ William Beckford, author (in French) of the exotic *Vathek: An Arabian Tale* (1786) – were aristocrats with archeological interests and the money to realize their architectural and historical fantasies in Strawberry Hill's Gothic turrets and the excesses of Fonthill respectively, soon women writers began to essay 'Gothic' fables.

▷ Clara Reeve's *The Champion of Virtue* (1777), which was later revised as *The Old English Baron*, and went through many editions, was described by its author as 'the literary offspring of *The Castle of Otranto*'. However, quite deliberately, this novel eschews the spectacular supernatural effects of its fictional parent. Edmund, the true heir to the Baron Fitz-Owen's castle, does indeed evoke ghostly presences when he spends the night in a haunted room, but the visitants are his own parents, and, as in the case of Hamlet, the reader is at some liberty to interpret the haunting as an inner vision rather than an external apparition. An early specimen of the historical novel, Sophia Lee's *The Recess: A Tale of Other Times* (1783–5), charts the tragic adventures of two daughters of Mary Queen of Scots, to escape the jealous ire of Elizabeth I. The novel's historical setting and the subterranean dwelling of its sister heroines, who live immured in the underground chambers of a Tudor great house which had formerly been a convent, makes it as engendered, as it were, Gothically. As Chris Baldick's introduction to *The Oxford Book of Gothic Tales* indicates, it is the centrality of an ancient, ruinous house – imprisoning the protagonist and mediating the baleful presence of the past over all its inhabitants – which makes a novel or short story Gothic. The house in a tale like Edgar Allan Poe's 'The Fall of the House of Usher' is itself a protagonist.

So before the arrival of ▷ Ann Radcliffe's first novel *The Castles of Athlin and Dunbayne* in 1789, all the Gothic tropes that Coleridge lampooned were current and operating with different degrees of effectiveness. Radcliffe's novel already seems implicitly parodic of the genre it presents with its warring barons, plethora of captives, ambushes and secret passages, and a low-born young man who saves the life of a chief and marries the latter's sister after his nobility and heroism is finally established. Yet in the four novels which succeeded this first attempt, Radcliffe took the Gothic novel to new heights, and helped establish it as the most popular form of fiction until the 1820s.

Women writers of Gothic tended to turn away from interest in the guilty (male) tyrant and usurper towards his victims: in *The Recess* women become, as they were to remain, the central focus, so that Ellen Moers can describe the whole Gothic phenomenon as 'a device to send maidens on journeys'. At a time when the picaresque novel was becoming virtually extinct, the errant heroines of Sophia Lee – whose travels take them all over England, to the Continent and even to the Americas – seemed evidence of a new form, the episodic journey tale. The glamorous foreign locations were, how-ever, merely changes of background to enable ever grosser treacheries and extreme dangers to assault the heroine. There is no attempt in *The Recess* to bring the settings to imaginative life as elements themselves in the story.

It was Ann Radcliffe who, in a series of novels published between 1789 (the year of the ▷ French Revolution) and 1797 (the year before Coleridge and Wordsworth's ▷ *Lyrical Ballads*), brought together these various elements of the Gothic, combining Lee's historicism and interest in enclosed spaces with Walpole's *Otranto*, with its castle and the central feud, and blending with these a strong emphasis on the natural landscape. Up to that time, in England, only the poet and novelist ▷ Charlotte Smith had employed extended natural description as a part of her fiction, though in her *Emmeline, The Orphan of the Castle* (1788) the sea-shore reveries of the eponymous heroine are but a small part of a conventional romance plot. In Radcliffe's tales, however, the landscape itself increasingly takes the part of an actor in the plot; indeed, ▷ Keats (who likened titles of two of his own poems to 'Mother Radcliffe's' style) commented on this feature in a letter recording an 1819 visit to a friend in Devon 'whence I intend to tip you the Damsel Radcliffe – I'll concern you, and grotto you, and Waterfall you, and wood you, and water you, and immense rock you, and tremendous sound you, and solitude you'. The nouns here become verbal in the same manner that the Radcliffe landscape precipitates human action. One typical example of this phenomenon occurs in *A Sicilian Romance*, when Madame de Menon, governess to the lost heroine, enjoys an evening stroll:

> *The evening was remarkably fine, and the romantic beauty of the surrounding scenery invited her to walk. She followed the windings of a stream, which was lost at some distance amongst luxuriant groves of chestnut. The rich colouring of evening glowed through the dark foliage, which spread a pensive gloom around, offered a scene congenial to the present temper of her mind, and she entered the shades. Her thoughts, affected by the surrounding objects, gradually sunk into a pleasing and complacent melancholy, and she was insensibly led on.*

Giving herself up to the rhythms and impulses of the scene, Madame de Menon seems to sleep-walk as she is 'moved' in her emotions and the windings of the stream to find a solitary figure, who proves to be her lost pupil. Others who see the girl and violate the intentions and shapes of the landscape are continually misled. They fail to notice the beauty of nature, so are unable to be helped by her benign presence or 'read' her secrets.

The locations of Radcliffe's novels are (with the exception of her first, which is set in Scotland) in continental Europe, principally France, Switzerland and Italy. It is usual to argue that the reason for the foreign nature of her locations was the more exotic terrain, the prevalence of Catholicism and the likelihood of violence and political instability. All this may be true, but it is also clear that Radcliffe had read and absorbed ▷ Rousseau's novels *Emile, ou L'Education* (1756) and *Julie, ou la nouvelle Héloïse* (1760) with their depictions of the Alps and lakes, woodlands and pastoral retreats. Several of Radcliffe's novels describe the upbringing of her heroines away from the corruptions of urban upper-class life, where parents devote themselves to the education of their children in the arts and in the appreciation of nature. Rousseau's privileging of the 'natural' over the civilized, and his theories of childhood innocence were enormously influential all over Europe in the development of Romanticism. Wordsworth is often credited with bringing these ideas into the mainstream of English poetry, but Radcliffe before him, especially in *The Romance of the Forest* (1791) and *The Mysteries of Udolpho* (1794), explored the educational ideas, as well as the social vision of little quasi-familial groups in rural retreat that are found in Rousseau's two novels. *The Romance of the Forest* includes a Swiss pastor, La Luc, whose family dispense charity, nurse the sick of their village, and teach its children, taking their pleasure in rambling among the scenic wonders of their Alpine home. The landscape provides simultaneously secure protection from outside influences and imaginative and religious expansion through the aesthetic power of mountain scenery. Similarly, *Udolpho* opens with a description of Emily St Aubert's childhood home, La Vallée:

> *on the nearest banks of the Garonne, in the province of Gascony, stood, in the year 1584, the chateau of Monsieur St Aubert. From its windows were seen the pastoral landscapes of Guienne and Gascony, stretching along the river, gay with luxuriant woods and vines and plantations of olives. To the south, the view was bounded by the majestic Pyrenées, whose summits veiled in clouds, or exhibiting awful forms, seen, and lost again, as the partial vapours rolled along were sometimes barren, and gleamed through the blue tinge of air, and sometimes frowned with forests of gloomy pine, that swept downward to their base. These tremendous precipices were contrasted by the soft green of the pastures and woods that hung upon their skirts; among whose flocks, and herds, and simple cottages, the eye, after having scaled the cliffs above, delight to repose. To the north, and to the east, the plains of Guienne and Languedoc were lost in the midst of distance; on the west Gascony was bounded by the waters of Biscay.*

This protective environment of the heroine is as safely enclosed as the Garden of Eden itself, with its 'luxuriant' vegetation 'bounded' on the south by mountains, and on the west by 'the waters of Biscay'. Conversely, 'the eye' – which is the prime mover of the scene rather than the ambulant human – has its gaze extended into a seeming infinity to the north and east, in which direction the plains are 'lost in the mist of distance'. The Edenic motif continues in the precise historical dating of the narrative in 1584, the year of the renewal of the Catholic League, which aimed to defeat French Protestants under Henry of Navarre, the next heir to the throne, and also the time when Philip of Spain's 'Catholic Enterprise' to depose Elizabeth was becoming known in Britain. Navarre is within the Pyrenees, so that all the force of Protestant religious 'purity' is enclosed in this region of natural sublimity, while the River Garonne on which the Aubert chateau is built had been the site of an earlier battle in the same Wars of Religion. Moreover, Aubert, the heroine's surname, recalls that of Navarre's mother, Jeanne d'Albret, whose lands were in Gascony. So La Vallée holds its 'repose' precariously on the Huguenot frontier, at risk from Catholic invasion, as Adam and Eve were from the serpent's grateful incursion. This admixture of the historical religio-political with the stately procession of aesthetic contrasts of an ideal landscape gives a new intensity to picturesque landscape, and energizes its portrayal. Emily St Aubert, the novel's young heroine, is soon to leave this pastoral retreat for a journey among the Pyrenees to restore the health of her bereaved father, and then for further travel, after his death among the mountains, for the gaieties of Venice, a setting which Radcliffe uses as a lovely but mystifying place of absence and false sentiment, in contrast to the stark, awful heights of the Pyrenees. Venice causes the visitor to look down, not up, as to 'the lower world', to see narcissistic reflections in the waters, rather than a presence in nature that takes one beyond the self: 'a new heaven and trembling stars below the waves, with shadowy outlines of towers and porticos'.

The Venetian scenes of *Udolpho*, with their plangent music that so moved ▷ Byron in ▷ *Childe Harold* are, in the context of the novel's aesthetic and moral scheme, ominous. Venice's physical lowness, as well as its fairy-tale illusionism, makes it a place dangerous to the imagination. For although Radcliffe anticipates the place of the mental landscape and the concept of the sublime in Romantic poetry, she is far from sharing the latter's boundless trust in the imagination. The sublime in the poetry of Wordsworth becomes a moment of direct imaginitive and moral expansion; indeed, it is the imagination itself which is sublime, as it acts to break down categories, and to unite disparate elements. But in the eighteenth-century tradition which culminates in Radcliffe and finds its most cogent expression in ▷ Edmund Burke's *Essay on the Origin of the Sublime and Beautiful* (1757), it is objects extraneous to the self that are sublime, such as great natural phenomena, mountains or cataracts, great poetry and art, architectural size and longevity, powerful heroes, and, most of all, the Divine. The awful greatness of such as these overwhelms the viewer; first, the viewer is made aware of her own littleness, her subjection to forces beyond her own control, and only then, through this very negation, is a sense of imaginative access possible. So Ellena, the heroine of *The Italian*, who has been imprisoned in an Apennine convent by her aristocratic lover's powerful mother, has her prison both confirmed and yet transcended by the power of the view from her turret window:

> *Here, gazing upon the stupendous imagery around her, looking, as it were, beyond the awful veil which obscures the features of the Deity, and conceals him from the eyes of his creatures, dwelling as with a present God in the midst of his sublime works; with a mind thus elevated, how insignificant would appear to her the transactions, and the sufferings of this world.*

She concludes that her enemy was therefore 'unable to chain her soul, or compel her to fear him, while he was destitute of virtue'.

The result of this aesthetic communion is not a quietist acceptance of destiny – all Radcliffe heroines show considerable fortitude, dignity and resourcefulness under hosts of murderous attacks. But the communion is the means by which the heroine is able to maintain a sense of her value as a person by, as it were, a mental dramatization of her actual life-threatening situation, which is projected into an imaginative *agar* or conflict, where the spectator's self-hood is almost annihilated, only to be re-established on a re-ordered footing as holding its place in God's providential order. 'Thus man, the giant who now held her in captivity, would shrink to the diminutiveness of a fairy,' thinks Ellena.

This trope of the entrapped woman fleeing the sexual or murderous attentions of a male attacker is one of the most potent devices of the Gothic genre, and survives right up to literature and film of the present day. Walpole uses it in *Otranto*, but the woman writers of the 1790s and after gave it a central focus. In one sense it is a universal story, and one, in the more realist setting of contemporary seduction that formed the matter of Samuel Richardson's novels *Pamela* (1740–1) and *Clarissa* (1747–8) as well as many novels of sensibility. Despite feeding from that tradition, the Gothic novel generally gives the predatory attacks an exotic architectural setting, so that the woman is pursued through the labyrinthine passages of the tyrant's castle, monastery, or actual prison. But just as Richardson is making a mainly bourgeois critique of aristocratic ethical codes of honour and shame, Radcliffe and her host of imitators filling the lists of the ▷ Minerva Press inevitably place their villains among the relics of a decayed aristocracy. *Udolpho's* Montoni is further and further confined to his own estates and castles as his only field of force (the Byronic hero owes his pride and sense of damnation to such figures, as they owe theirs to Milton's portrayal of Satan in *Paradise Lost*). In charting the escape of women from confinement, the Gothic aligns itself to the Enlightenment project itself, though its potential political radicalism is tempered by the fact that the heroine and her associates generally go on to live a retired *Emile*-like existence in *private* life only; the public realm is eschewed for a pastoral retreat consisting of the polite arts and the social joys of the sublime.

This kind of 'female' Gothic is not necessarily to do with the gender of the author. ▷ William Godwin writes an interesting version of 'female' Gothic in *Caleb Williams, or Things as they Are* (1794), in which the hero, having found evidence of his aristocratic master's crime, is pursued by agents of that noble but flawed Falkland the length and breadth of Britain. Finally brought to account for a supposed crime against Falkland, Caleb abandons attempts to assert his innocence in favour of a version of sublime discourse dramatizing his own destitution and the impossibility of escape; the hero finally triumphs. 'Male' Gothic writers include the ▷ Marquis de Sade, M.G. Lewis (▷ 'Monk' Lewis), ▷ Charles Maturin, Francis Latham and the youthful ▷ Shelley. Their works are characterized by a doomed and guilt-ridden hero, such as Ambrosio in Lewis's *The Monk*, who breaks endless taboos by committing murder, incest and fratricide (amongst other sensational things), in a careless desire for mastery and forbidden knowledge. Ambrosio is in some ways the archetypal 'male' Gothic hero, who assaults barriers to penetrate inwards, whether into bodies, locked chambers or castles, in contrast to the female protagonists of the Radcliffean mode who seek to move beyond the 'bounds', whether of room, castle, or limited subjection as women.

In ▷ Mary Wollstonecraft's tale *Maria: or, The Wrongs of Woman* (1798) feminism and the 'female' Gothic form come together overtly in a contemporary setting, with the following opening:

Abodes of horror have frequently been described and castles, filled with spectres and chimeras conjured up by the magic spell of genius to harrow the soul, and absorb the wondering mind. But, formed of such stuff as dreams are made of, what are they to the mansion of despair, in one corner of which Maria sat, endeavouring to recall her scattered wits.

The 'mansion of despair' referred to is a lunatic asylum, where Maria has been incarcerated by her husband for pecuniary gain, separating her from her young children. The story quickly develops beyond the usual confinement-escape plot: Maria falls in love with a fellow inmate, with whom she elopes, and although the loves remained unfinished at Wollstonecraft's death, her notes indicate a subsequent disillusioned parting, regret and sad decline. This is far removed from the Radcliffean 'female' Gothic, and indeed none of the three women writers most closely associated with the Romantic poets – Wollstonecraft herself, ▷ Dorothy Wordsworth and Mary Shelley – embraces the 'female' Gothic plot described above (Dorothy Wordsworth was in fact the recipient of the Coleridge letter mocking Radcliffe). Mary Shelley's powerful *Frankenstein* in particular declares its status as 'male' Gothic in its subtitle 'The Modern Prometheus', this mythological figure being the stealer of fire from the gods, and tied to a rock in eternal agonies, the archetypal damned hero of dark Romanticism. Frankenstein also transgresses the divine order in trying to create in his own image, and is explicitly associated with ▷ Milton's Satan. The story is, of course, a powerful critique of the creation of a being without mothering, without any associates, no Eve for his Garden of Eden, nor friendly angels to advise.

The prevalence of Miltonic elements in Mary Shelley's *Frankenstein* is often attributed to the influence of her husband's reading of ▷ *Paradise Lost* while she was writing her novel. There is, I believe, quite another reason why Milton's epic of the destruction of perfect human relations and the fall of nature provides a common source for Mary Shelley and for the hundreds of Gothic tales imitating Ann Radcliffe. In the late twentieth century, we may miss the radical elements in Milton's portrayal of sexual relations, being aware only of the hierarchy that makes Eve for Adam, while he is made for God – 'He for God only, she for God in him'. However, eighteenth-century feminists, reading Milton in the context of a history of extreme misogyny, latched onto the dignity and intelligence of Milton's Eve; there were even editions of *Paradise Lost* that changed the line quoted above to 'He for Gŏd only, she for God *and* him' (my emphasis). In the context of this positive reading of Milton, the 'female' Gothic plot of entrapment of the heroine by a villain whose grandeur, pride and superhuman qualities mark him as a descendant of Milton's heroic Satan takes on a new resonance. It is a re-narrating of the scene of Eve's temptation by Satan in such a way that she is freed from guilt (because it is through no fault of her own that she is in his power), and also triumphs, she escaping her persecutor's clutches and he bringing him to justice. The scene in Radcliffe's *Romance of the Forest* in which Adeline is taken by the ruffians of a Marquis to his luxurious villa, where attempts on her virtue take the form of delicious fruits and ices, sweet music, delightful smells, the arts of poetry, oratory and the vanity of mirrors, parallels the wiles of the serpent tempting Eve to eat the fruit of the tree of knowledge. Several references to the tempter of Milton's *Comus* point the moral.

The many references to the works of Milton, Shakespeare – which indeed exceed those of the later poet in frequency – and Collins, Thomson and other eighteenth-century poets suggest the literary ambitions of the Gothic novel. At a time when Romantic poetry, notably the *Lyrical Ballads*, seeks to represent the rhythms of ordinary speech and the concerns of the countryman and peasant, the Gothic novel seeks a different, and elevated, poetic expression. Novels such as Radcliffe's and Charlotte Smith's contain many verses by their authors, put into the mouths of their characters, by which their heroines reach towards literary expression of their feelings of awe and delight. Tags from the English poets furthermore seek to situate Gothic writing in a specifically native tradition, which was only beginning to enjoy the status of 'classic' awarded primarily to Greek and Latin literature. Classical learning in this sense is denied most female Gothic writers, so they reach out to an alternative genealogy. Many Gothic tales were published in *The Lady's Magazine*, and despite its subtitle – *Or, Entertaining Companion for the Fair Sex Appropriated Solely to their use and Enjoyment* – which stressed entertainment, the frontispiece engraving showed a serious intent. It shows the Goddess of Wisdom, Minerva, pointing, with a lady in a well-stocked library reading *The Lady's Magazine*, towards a Pantheon, or 'Temple of Wisdom'. The publishing house that poured out most Gothic tales was also called The Minerva Press.

The quotation in the title of this chapter is from Act I, Scene v of Shakespeare's *Hamlet*, and sounds a note of self-confidence in authorship when it heads Ann Radcliffe's *A Sicilian Romance*. Its context in the original play, however, gives it a darker meaning. The speaker is the ghost of Hamlet's father:

> But that I am forbid
> To tell the secrets of my prison-house
> I could a tale unfold whose lightest word
> Would harrow up thy soul, freeze thy young blood,
> Make thy two eyes like stars start from their spheres,
> Thy knotted and combined locks to part,
> And each particular hair to stand on end
> Like quills upon the fretful porcupine.

The most obvious effect of the Gothic novel is its ability to arouse fear and terror in its readers. Indeed, Joanna Baillie's play on the passion of fear, *Orra* (1815), concerns a girl who goes mad through giving herself up to superstitious terror, which has been fed by reading Gothic romances. In these tales, episodes of country rambling and delightful exploration of ruined abbeys which arouse elevated meditations are followed by terrifying discoveries of murdered corpses, or attacks by murderous monks. Although ghosts haunt the pages of the Gothic tale they are quite often explained away as natural phenomena. The view of critics like Coleridge (who renders the supernatural real in his own work) is that such a move to demystify shows a lack of confidence on behalf of Gothic authors, so that the whole plot collapses like a fairy palace into the air. This is, however, to miss the point of the terrific fears of the Gothic heroine, which are a form of testing. In ▷ *Northanger Abbey* (1818), ▷ Jane Austen's credulous heroine expects all the horrors of Udolpho to come true when she stays with the Tilneys in their ancient house; and she casts the General as a Montoni in wickedness, believing him to have murdered his former wife. Of course, he is nothing of the sort, and a great deal of comedy is extracted from Catherine's mistake. Yet, although her more exotic accusations are wrong, she is proved right in that Tilney is a tyrant – if a petty one – who unceremoniously throws her out of the house when he learns that she is not an heiress.

Northanger Abbey is a parody of a Gothic story, but in many ways it also possesses a true Gothic plot, in which the supernatural fear is removed only in order to reveal an actual bodily threat or deception. The castle around which ghostly sighs are expended in *A Sicilian Romance*, terrifying its inhabitants, is indeed haunted, but not by a spectre. Instead, its vaults contain the living person of the Marquis's first wife, who was immured there years before, so that he could remarry. The supernatural is demystified in order to reveal the unjust and demonic character of the Marquis, and of his order. There is an inherent feminism in the Gothic of the entrapped heroine, which is not to be found in the 'male' Gothic of Lewis and Maturin, in which the supernatural is an unquestioned reality. The heroines of 'female' Gothic learn to eschew the thrills of terror over dark passages and ghostly knocks in favour of religious awe and fear in the power of God's creation, to forego their fears of the seemingly sublime tyrant for the transposed power of the sublime. It is perhaps here that the form shows most clearly its critique of Romanticism. The heroines who become the true heirs of the tyrant's castle do not go on to inhabit their possession, but leave it to become even more ruined. There are moves today in post-structuralist literary criticism to deconstruct the claims of the Romantic poet to universality and harmony of vision and to elucidate instead an awareness of loss and the indeterminacy of meaning. This process is akin to the demystification of the sublime villain and his supernatural castle by the Gothic novel which acts to 'ruinate' his image. Perhaps we may even come to see the Gothic now not as some clumsy articulation of tropes that merely anticipates a glorious Romanticism, but rather see Romantic poetry itself, with its omnivorous claims and egotistical sublime, as merely a variation on the 'male' Gothic.

'The Babel din': 4
Theatre and European Romanticism

Edward Burns

The Romantic period seems like the last place one might look for drama, at least if what one is looking for are durable dramatic texts. As far as the literary history of English drama is concerned, the period is a kind of hiatus between the comedy of manners of the ▷ Georgian stage and its revival in the ▷ Victorian period in conjunction with a new realism and the importation from France of the well-made play. At the same time, theatricality is very much a part of Romanticism, as even our cultural stereotypes of the period reveal. We imagine Romantic poets in theatrical and cinematic clichés; we *picture* them, enjoying a flamboyant self-presentation, or we cosily enshrine their quietism. Poets of no other period are dramatic characters in this sense. Behind the clichés is an intuition of the importance of theatre to the period. Yet it is a paradoxical importance, in which a distrust of and revulsion from theatre is as important as a belief in the medium, and in which the results of the writers' worrying at, subverting, deconstructing the processes of theatrical communication can be seen as fully in other forms of writing as on the stage itself.

In Britain in the late eighteenth and early nineteenth centuries, the theatre as an institution moves decisively from the position of cultural centrality it had occupied from the late Middle Ages onward. This is in sharp contrast to the role theatre played in the development of European Romanticism. The riot that took place at the first performance of ▷ Victor Hugo's *Ernani* is often seen as a pivotal moment in French culture, as a break away from classical tradition and the establishing triumph of Romantic form and feeling. The critic and philosopher Madame de Staël in *Germania* analyses the difference between northern and southern Europe in terms of opposing trends in drama, and, writing in the aftermath of the ▷ French Revolution argues that the invention of a new form of tragedy is a necessary response to the historical moment. Germany saw a revolution in standards of theatrical production and design under the patronage of the provincial courts, and the transition from classicism was again played out on the stage – in the late classical works of ▷ Goethe, in the historical plays of Schiller, and in the exploration of extremes of feeling and situation in the ironic tragedy of Kleist, and Buchner. Both in Germany and in Italy opera was the medium of politically engaged Romanticism and of the bourgeois Romanticism of private feeling – in the pathos of Donizetti's *Lucia di Lammermoor* or the popular and nationalist propaganda of Verdi's *Nabucco*, the political mythopoeia of Wagner's *Ring*, or the picturesque pathos of Weber's *Der Freischütz*. The development of theatre in Europe is very much a product of its direct engagement with political and social change. In European culture the idea of a 'theatre revolution' is by several degrees less absurd than in England.

In Britain in this period, theatre occupies a culturally marginal position, seemingly more escapist than engaged. Theatrical activity tended to the condition of pantomime, ▷ Gothic melodrama or farce. One can see this in the case of a work like the German composer Weber's opera *Oberon*, where centrally Romantic concerns – the creation of Keatsian (▷ Keats) alternative worlds of fancy from the medieval, the oriental and the faery – has to be fitted to the mixed form of an English musical entertainment, as dictated by the taste of Madame Vestris's regime at Covent Garden, and realized in a libretto of spectacular numbers sketchily linked by Planché's doggerel rhyme. It is ironic then that the major aesthetic impulse towards European Romantic form in theatre and music came from English dramatic texts, largely through the rediscovery of the plays of ▷ Shakespeare, seen as combining a powerful appeal to feeling, a broadly democratic (in the sense of non-aristocratic) representation of history, and an apparently 'natural' flexibility of form. British writers, writing for or about the theatre, are just as frustrated and exacerbated by the limits and problems of theatrical representation as they are excited by its possibilities. But the reasons for this are as much internal to the impulses and attitudes of English Romanticism as they are attributable to the contemporary state of theatrical practice. The second might as well be seen as a result of the first. To understand English Romantic theatre we should look first at the phenomenon of the anti-theatrical, not as opposition to the theatre as an institution, from a political and religious point of view (like that of the sixteenth- and seventeenth-century Puritans), but as a creative response that problematizes theatrical representation. British Romanticism turns theatre inside out, to find new theatrical forms, or to take over the formal and philosophical opportunities made visible in this process into other media.

Theatre and Anti-theatre

Charles Lamb gives the classic statement of the anti-theatrical position in his *On the Tragedies of Shakespeare, considered with reference to their Fitness for Stage Representation* (1812):

> *It may seem a paradox, but I cannot help being of opinion that the plays of Shakspeare [sic] are less calculated for performance on a stage, than those of almost any dramatist whatever. Their distinguishing excellence is a reason that they should be so. There is so much in them, which comes not under the province of acting, with which eye, and tone, and gesture, have nothing to do.*
>
> *The glory of the scenic art is to personate passion; and the more coarse and palpable the passion is, the more hold upon the eyes and ears of the spectator the performer obviously possesses . . . The sublime images, the poetry alone, is that which is present to our minds in the reading.*
>
> *So to see Lear acted, – to see an old man tottering about the stage with a walking-stick, turned out of doors by his daughters in a rainy night, has nothing in it but what is painful and disgusting. We want to take him into shelter and relieve him. That is all the feeling that the acting of Lear ever produced in me. But the Lear of Shakespeare cannot be acted.*

For Lamb the problem is the contrast between the means the stage uses to communicate a feeling or an idea, and the immensity of that idea or the intensity of that feeling. As he says later of costume and scenery:

> *I remember the last time I saw Macbeth played, the discrepancy I felt at the changes of garment which he varied . . . if things must be represented, I see not what to find fault with in this. But in reading, what robe are we conscious of? Some dim images of royalty – a crown and sceptre, may float before our eyes, but who shall describe the fashion of it? . . . This is the inevitable consequence of imitating everything, to make all things natural. Whereas the reading of a tragedy is a fine abstraction.*

'Dim images . . . fine abstraction . . .' Lamb values reading above theatrical spectatorship for its very freedom from the specific and the material.

A split response to theatre is typical of English Romanticism, an emotionally and intellectually irreconcilable split between the limitations of theatre as a material and social phenomenon, and the transcendant possibilities, the metaphysical sublimity or psychological intensity which can be produced by certain theatrical texts or the powers of certain performers. The first is often characterized in terms of its inadequacy to the second, and that inadequacy can be presented as grotesquely comic, pitiful, sinister, or in its way rather charming. The idea that the written is of a subtlety superior to the visual seems at first almost commonsensical to us, which suggests how influential Romantic anti-theatricalism is in British culture. But to a pre-Romantic spectator, these sentiments would seem maladroit or eccentric. To make a broad contrast to eighteenth-century perceptions of theatre, one might point to the moment in Henry Fielding's *Tom Jones* (1749) when Tom and his companion Partridge go to see *Hamlet* performed by David Garrick, the great actor who above all others raised the perceived aesthetic and social status of acting, but whose revered memory is also under attack in Lamb's polemic:

> *. . . Partridge was all attention, nor did he break silence till the entrance of the ghost; upon which he asked Jones, 'What man that was in the strange dress; something,' said he, 'like what I have seen in a picture. Sure it is not armour, is it?' Jones answered, 'That is the ghost.' To which Partridge replied with a smile, 'Persuade me to that, sir, if you can. Though I can't say I ever actually saw a ghost in my life, yet I am certain I should know one, if I saw him, better than that comes to. No, no sir, ghosts don't appear in such dresses as that neither.' In this mistake, which caused much laughter in the neighbourhood of Partridge, he was suffered to continue, 'till the scene between the ghost and Hamlet, when Partridge gave that credit to Mr Garrick, which he had denied to Jones, and fell into so violent a trembling, that his knees knocked against each other, Jones asked him what was the matter, and whether he was afraid of the warrior upon the stage? 'O la! sir,' said he, 'I perceive it is now what you told me . . . but if that little man there upon the stage is not frightened, I never saw any man frightened in my life . . .'*

The difference between Lamb and Fielding is that the joke here is on Partridge, not on the actors. Here it is the inept, not the aesthetically super-sensitive spectator who can't find the necessary mind-set, the necessary ability to be simultaneously moved by a performance and to retain a sense of its medium. A more adept pre-Romantic spectator would be able to contain his or her participation in the imaginative transaction within an acceptance of the material facts of theatrical communication. Samuel Johnson gives the most cogent expression of the pre-Romantic perception of theatre in his *Preface to The Plays of William Shakespeare* (1765):

> *The truth is, that the spectators are always in their senses, and know, from the first act to the last, that the stage is only a stage, and that the players are only players. They come to hear a certain number of lines recited with just gesture and elegant modulation. The lines relate to some action, and an action must be in some place.*

Within these terms, the disjunction between the means of representation and the thing represented is acceptable, non-problematic, and often exploited confidently for theatrical effect.

If Romantic writers worry at the validity of theatrical representation, they never do so in quite so crude a way as to simply reject the stage altogether. Hazlitt, Keats, and ▷ De Quincey, to give just three examples, wrote powerfully of the impact on them of stage performances of Shakespeare. When Keats writes on the star Shakespearian actor ▷ Edmund Kean (in 'Mr Kean', a review in *The Champion*, 21 December 1817), he celebrates just that importation of the body into performance through the written text, which for Lamb and others is disruptive of the seriousness of theatrical texts:

> *There is an indescribable gusto in the voice, by which we feel that the utterer is thinking of the past and the future while thinking of the instant. When he says in 'Othello' 'put up your bright swords for the dew will rust them,' we feel that his throat has commanded where swords were as thick as reeds. From eternal risk, he speaks as though his body were unassailable.*

The actor's voice and presence here flesh out, literally, the written verse, in ways that parallel Keats's straining after a sense of the physical in his own writing. Hazlitt's response is not simply to an intensity of aesthetic effect and psychological insight as, when he writes of *Coriolanus*, to the immediate relevance of the politics of the plays to the public unrest of the times.

> *Shakespear [sic] has in this play shewn himself well versed in history and state-affairs. 'Coriolanus' is a store-house of political common-places. Any one who studies it may save himself the trouble of reading Burke's 'Reflections', or Paine's 'Rights of Man', or the debates in both Houses of Parliament since the French Revolution or our own. The arguments for or against aristocracy or democracy, on the privileges of the few and the claims of the many, on liberty and slavery, power and the abuse of it, peace and war, are here very ably handled . . .*

For De Quincey, in 'On the Knocking on the Gate in *Macbeth*', from the
▷ *London Magazine* of October 1823, the imaginative power of *Macbeth* allows
us to share the world of the murderer, while Shakespeare's attention to the
theatrical effect of the mundane ensures that the effect of the play lies in
that conjunction of the imaginative and the material which, being at the
heart of theatrical representation, is for Lamb the very reason for disowning
the medium:

> ... *when the deed is done, when the work of darkness is perfect, then the world
> of darkness passes away like a pageantry in the clouds: the knocking at the gate is
> heard; and it makes known audibly that the reaction has commenced; the human
> has made its reflux upon the fiendish; the pulses of life are beginning to beat again;
> and the re-establishment of the goings-on of the world in which we live, first makes
> us profoundly sensible of the awful parenthesis which had suspended them.*

This access to heightened experience, in a kind of retreat from, and subsequent
return to the real, can be a quintessentially Romantic pursuit of intense and even
forbidden feeling, but its meaning can be reversed as pure escape. Lamb himself
writes engagingly of the charms of stage comedy, though in ways that neutralize
it as a social event, depriving it of any critical or political force:

> *I am glad for a season to take an airing beyond the diocese of the strict consciense,
> – not to live always in the precincts of the law-courts, – but now and then, for a
> dream-while or so, to imagine a world with no meddling restrictions – to get into
> recesses, whither the hunter cannot follow me ... I come back to my cage and my
> restraint the fresher and more healthy for it.*

> ('On the Artificial Comedy of the Last Century', 1822)

Theatre here has lost any power of its own, becoming instead the vehicle of a
kind of pathos. Its flimsiness and evanescence are an appeal to the Romantic
sensibility, through which it acquires a beauty and a meaning it does not in itself
possess.

Spectacle and Meaning; Wordsworth at the Theatre

In his ▷ autobiographical poem ▷ *The Prelude* (1805), ▷ Wordsworth tracks
the growth of his own poetic powers against the itinerary of his life to the
date of writing. His 'Residence in London', the subject of Book Seven, takes
him through a progression of 'spectacles'; life itself is a random and confusing
sort of theatre. His description of the city moves from the drama of London
street life –

> ... *the quick dance
> Of colours, lights, and forms; the Babel din;
> The endless stream of men, and moving things* ...

– through 'raree shows', 'troops of wild beasts, birds and beasts/ of every nature', panoramas in paint or modelling

> *By scale exact, in model, wood or clay,*
> *From shading colours also borrowing help,*
> *Some miniature of famous spots and things . . .*

to more established forms of theatre,

> *. . . where living men,*
> *Music, and shifting pantomimic scenes,*
> *Together joined their multifarious aid*
> *To heighten the allurement. Need I fear*
> *To mention by its name . . .*
> *Half rural Sadlers Wells?*

Wordsworth leads us through this maze with constant injunctions to 'see' – so establishing the continuity of theatrical spectatorship with our response to the wider scope of London life; so setting us up, with him, as a wondering audience. The theatre itself is an enchanting concentration of instances of human ingenuity and credulity, and the end to which it points is a loving acknowledgement of the weakness of mankind, of our need for representations of the outside world, in 'imitations, fondly made in plain/ Confession of man's weakness and his loves'. As with Lamb, the inadequacy of theatre is its charm – more than charm in this case, as it points towards a human truth.

This then is one Romantic attitude to theatre – its flimsiness is a token of our own, and recuperable by the imagination as a symbol of transience, a kind of pathos. Wordworth offers examples which identify that pathos with the feminine:

> *. . . I am crossed*
> *Here by rememberance of two figures, one*
> *A rosy babe . . . child as beautiful*
> *As ever sate upon a mother's knee;*
> *The other was that parent of that babe;*
> *But on the mother's cheek the tints were false,*
> *A painted bloom. 'Twas at a theatre*
> *That I beheld this pair . . .*

This falseness and frailty of this 'fallen woman' has been brought to his mind by his memory of a play about another, but that was

> *. . . too holy theme for such a place,*
> *And doubtless treated with irreverence*
> *Albeit with their very best of skill,*
> *I mean, o distant friend! a story drawn*
> *From our own ground, – the Maid of Buttermere.*

The theme may be too easily profaned in its shocking transposition from private contemplation to the public stage, but its place on that stage, and the train of thought that it sets on, is typical of one Romantic association – of the fragility and falseness of theatre, and the frailty of the feminine. One might think of the centrality of the fallen woman, Verdi's eponymous *La Traviata*, for example, or its source, Dumas's *La Dame aux Camélias*, to nineteenth-century opera and to the 'well-made play' of the French and English theatre of the mid- to late century; also of the nineteenth-century cult of the ballerina, a cult that depended on the dancer's use of her own athletic ability to transcend the body in the representation of the ethereal, while at the same time inevitably offering to the spectator the spectacle of her own physical vulnerability,.and/or, in certain contexts, her sexual availability. There was an appalling death rate among the star teenage ballerinas of the Paris stage caused by the vulnerability of their gauze costumes to the gas used to light the theatres, a fact that increased their star status in a morbid overlap with the roles of sylphs, butterflies and willi into which their femininity was idealized. The frailty of theatrical illusion is also the frailty – moral and physical, untrustworthy and desirable – of woman.

But this characterization of theatre can be elided with another; theatre can crystallize the troubled relation of sights to words, and thus can lead back to the problem of human knowledge. Wordsworth notes:

> *The champion, Jack the Giant-killer; Lo!*
> *He dons his coat of darkness; on the stage*
> *Walks, and achieves his wonders, from the eyes*
> *Of living mortal safe as is the moon*
> *'Hid in her vacant interlunar cave'.*
> *Delusion bold! and faith must needs be coy;*
> *How is it wrought? His garb is black, the word*
> *'Invisible' flames forth upon his chest.*

Because it relies on both spectacle and words and because, more crucially, it opens up that cultural, post-Enlightenment, shift in which the relation between the two cannot be taken for granted, theatre can make available to the Romantic writer the mystery and problems of belief inherent in our relation to other beings and to the universe. Jack jokily anticipates a moment later in the book which Wordsworth introduces with a metaphor linking London street-life back to the theatre:

> *Amid the moving pageant, 'twas my chance*
> *Abruptly to be smitten with the view*
> *Of a blind Beggar, who, with upright face,*
> *Stood, propped against a wall, upon his chest*
> *Wearing a written paper, to explain*
> *The story of the man, and who he was.*
> *My mind did at this spectacle turn round*
> *As with the might of waters, and it seemed*

> *To me that in this label was a type,*
> *Or emblem, of the utmost that we know,*
> *Both of ourselves and of the universe;*
> *And, on the shape of the unmoving man,*
> *His fixed face and sightless eyes, I looked,*
> *As if admonished from another world.*

The blind man poses the problem of reading spectacle in a more serious context than does Jack. ▷ Byron's Cain, in the play of the same name (1821), falls prey to Lucifer in his attempt to make sense of the received word in terms of his own visionary experience:

> *Thou speaks't to me of things which long have swum*
> *In visions through my thought: I never could*
> *Reconcile what I saw with what I heard.*

Cain rebels against the restriction of 'the word' in that it can only tell him of a reality defined by God's law or the narrative of his father's fall. Lucifer operates in the gap between words and vision – the space of theatre, and of an ineluctable mystery. Poems in Wordsworth's ▷ *Lyrical Ballads* (1798) turn on a similar problem of knowledge, opened up by the gap between what we see in human beings or on the landscape, and what we hear, read or say. Knowledge of the other may always be beyond our grasp. Here the sense of the failure of theatre is presented as the irreconcilable demands of word and spectacle, whose paradoxical conjunction can lead us to a more profound idea, that of the mystery that conditions our being in the world.

A third version of theatre, of spectacle given meaning in attention to its inevitable aesthetic failure, is animated at the end of the book in the description of Bartholomew Fair, the great annual summer fair that had been a London institution since the Middle Ages:

> *What a Hell*
> *For eyes and ears! what anarchy and din*
> *Barbarian and infernal, – 'tis a dream,*
> *Monstrous in colour, motion, shape, sight, sound!*

Wordsworth goes on to list:

> *. . . buffoons against buffoons*
> *Grimacing, writhing, screaming, – him who grinds*
> *The hurdy-gurdy, at the fiddle weaves,*
> *Rattles the salt-box, thumps the kettle-drum,*
> *And him who at the trumpet puffs his cheeks,*
> *The silver-collared negro with his timbrel,*
> *Equestrians, tumblers, women, girls, and boys,*
> *Blue breeched, pink-vested, and with towering plumes.*

This chaos, to be contrasted with the orderly rural celebration that starts the next book, is an image of Hell. We can find similar ideas of violent and chaotic carnival in many Romantic artists. Theatre, spectacle, masquerade, all are potentially sinister, in that nothing, or some evil violent impulse, may lurk behind masks and role play. Theatre is the domain of the monstrous, in Goya, Ensor or Poe. Perhaps there is an intuition here of the closeness of carnival and revolution. Simon Sharma in his book *Citizens* points out that many activists in the French Revolution were theatre people. Revolution is in itself a theatrical act, in that it must convince, proselytize or terrify through acts that are witnessed and have been calculated for their emblematic concision and their powerful impact. Carlyle, in *The French Revolution*, presents events visually, in a flamboyantly decorative style that suggests a kind of phantasmagoria or violent pantomime, from which the English reader is protected by the Channel, as a kind of orchestra pit. More domestically, but just as subversively, theatre in ▷ Jane Austen's ▷ *Mansfield Park* (1814) provides the outlet for anti-social energies seen, however limited their scope to work, as disruptively libidinous.

So in these three instances, reading Wordsworth for what he shares with a wider Romantic culture, we encounter a perception of theatre in which a sense of the inadequacy of dramatic representation, the uncertain relation of material means to transcendent ends, can paradoxically be recouped by the Romantic imagination as a source of pathos and charm, of epistemological mystery, or as the threat of chaos and transgressive impulse.

Poets in the Theatre

For a while Byron was a member of the sub-committee of management of the ▷ Drury Lane Theatre:

> – the number of plays upon the shelves were about five hundred; ... the Scenes I had to go through! – the authors – and the authoresses – the Milliners – the wild Irishmen – the people from Brighton – from Blackwell – from Chatham – from Cheltenham – from Dublin – from Dundee – who came in upon me! – to all of whom it was proper to give a civil answer – and a hearing – and a reading – Mrs Glover's father an Irish dancing Master of Sixty years – called upon me to request to play 'Archer' – drest in silk-stockings on a frosty morning to show his legs – (which were certainly good & Irish for his age) – & had been still better – Miss Emma Somebody with a play entitled the 'Bandit of Bohemia' – or some such title or production – Mr O'Higgins – then resident at Richmond – with an Irish tragedy in which the unities could not fail to be observed for the protagonist was chained by the leg to a pillar during the chief part of the performance . . .

The Dickensian exuberance of this description – written in Byron's self-imposed exile – has something of Wordsworth's mixture of relish and distrust for the theatrical enterprise. It must be set against Byron's panic when he heard that one of his plays, the Venetian tragedy *Marino Faliero* (1821), was to be given a London performance:

I have nothing more at heart – (that is in literature) than to prevent this drama from going upon the Stage; – in short – rather than permit it – it must be suppressed altogether . . . What damned fools these speculating buffoons must be not to see that it is unfit for their Fair or their booth.

There is an aristocratic disdain here for the compromised business of theatrical production, masking a real fear of exposure to a judging audience (a fear that motivates Faliero, a victim of slander and its obsessive avenger, within the play). The incident highlights the paradoxical conjunction of theatricality and intense privacy in Byron's own self-presentation. Like Wordsworth's worries about theatre, it raises the immediate question – then why write plays? Why do the complete works of almost any nineteenth-century poet end with a sequence of obscure, largely unread, dramas?

One answer lies in the growing reverence for Shakespeare, and the rediscovery of his contemporaries, as shown in Lamb's *Specimens of English Dramatic Poets, who lived about the time of Shakespeare* (1808). The acting of Garrick and Macklin in the mid-eighteenth century, and Garrick's interest in visually powerful stagings, aiming at a maximum of emotional impact, helped to create a cult of Shakespeare as the great dramatist of character, of individuals forced to confront metaphysical and emotional extremes. Shakespeare becomes the writer to emulate, as a genius whose imaginative powers transcend the limits of individual selfhood. As Keats puts it in a famous letter of 1817, implicitly comparing himself to Shakespeare:

As to the poetical character itself (I mean that sort, of which, if I am anything, I am a member; that sort distinguished from the Wordsworthian, or egotistical sublime; which is a thing per se, and stands alone), it is not itself – it has no self – it has every thing and nothing – it has no character – it enjoys light and shade – it lives in gusto, be it foul or fair, high or low, rich or poor, mean or elevated, – it has as much delight in conceiving an Iago as an Imogen; what shocks the virtuous philosopher delights the chameleon poet.

But in emulating Shakespeare by employing dramatic form, Romantic writers tackle what they already perceive as the near-insoluble problem of imitating a supreme genius who managed to be the greatest poet *and* the greatest dramatist in one. Their aim becomes decisively unattainable – the aim of creating the art-work that combines both language and action at their highest intensity to create something which seems to transcend the material means of both. Keats achieves what he sees as the Shakespearian quality much more convincingly in his non-dramatic verse than in his plays *King Stephen* or *Otho the Great*.

It is ironic that an impetus to bardolatry that came from the theatre, particularly from Garrick, should then – as for Lamb – act towards the marginalization of theatre. But at the same time, the presence of powerful actors provided a major stimulus for writing. The Romantic theatre is a theatre of stars; Edmund Kean, William Charles Macready and ▷ Sarah Siddons all stimulated writers like Hazlitt and Keats to vivid response and reaction. Performing in large, gaslit theatres, they promoted a style of playing in which plays are conceived of as a collection of individual roles, and in which those roles are thought of as a series of moments of high-impact emotion, developed through the actors' larger-than-life presence as the unfolding of an intense, if monolithic, character. The actors were stars in that their personal charisma became part of the material through which they created characters, and through which, in a broader sense, the human and the transcendent could be linked in an event whose transience was part of its Romantic meaning. Lamb writes dismissively of 'Mrs S's . . . thrilling tones' and '. . . impressive looks'. But for Hazlitt, in 'On Mrs Siddons' and in 'Mr Kemble's Retirement' (from *A View of the London Stage*, 1818), such personal attributes point to 'something above nature':

> *She raised Tragedy to the skies, or brought it down from thence . . . Power was seated on her brow, passion emanated from her breast as from a shrine. She was tragedy personified. She was the stateliest ornament of the public mind. She was not only the idol of the people, she not only hushed the tumultuous shouts of the pit in breathless expectation, and quenched the blaze of surrounding beauty in silent tears, but to the retired and lonely student, through long years of solitude, her face has shone as if an eye had appeared from heaven; her name has been as if a voice had opened the chambers of the human heart, or as if a trumpet had awakened the sleeping and the dead. To have seen Mrs Siddons, was an event in every one's life.*

Hazlitt's praise of Kemble points to those qualities of Romantic acting which shaped a contemporary conception of Shakespeare, and which dictated the structure and emphasis of plays inevitably conceived as star vehicles:

> *His person was moulded to the character. The weight of sentiment which oppressed him was never suspended . . . So in Coriolanus, he exhibited the ruling passion with the same haughty dignity of demeanour, the same energy of will, and unbending sternness of temper throughout. He was swayed by a single impulse . . . in such characters, Mr Kemble had no occasion to call to his aid either the resources of invention, or the tricks of the art: his success depended on the increasing intensity with which he dwelt on a given feeling, or enforced a passion that resisted all interference or control.*

Romantic writers wanted to tap this kind of power – ▷ Shelley wrote ▷ *The Cenci* (1819) for Eliza O'Neill, ▷ Coleridge rewrote *Osorio* (1797), initially commissioned through Byron's agency as *Remorse*, after it was then rejected by ▷ Sheridan; it was performed successfully at the Drury Lane Theatre in 1813. The actors inspire the creation of an intense, internalized, often deliberately obscure vein of feeling in the central character, whose unfolding and realization in action is the dynamic of the piece. Less happily, the hierarchies of the star system ensure that other figures are more sketchily and stereotypically conceived.

Whatever level of achievement is represented by these two plays – for *The Cenci* is perhaps the most theatrically powerful of English Romantic plays, and in *Remorse* Coleridge makes intriguing use of a scenic and narrative form that is romantic in the older sense (the sense in which Shakespeare's late plays are called romances) to track his psychological and ethical interests – the most impressive body of dramatic work was produced by a writer who stayed deliberately aloof from the two overwhelming influences of the genius of Shakespeare and the charisma of the Romantic actor. Byron marks a deliberate distance not only from the English stage of his time, but from Shakespeare and his contemporaries, 'the mad old English dramatists', whom he sees as equally inimical to the creation of an aesthetically satisfying and philosophically serious theatre. Instead his models are the Italian dramatist Alfieri, and, in the case of *The Deformed Transformed* (1824), Goethe's ▷ *Faust*. But neo-classical English plays – Dryden's *All For Love* in the case of *Sardanapalus* (1821) and Otway's *Venice Preserv'd* in relation to *Marino Faliero* – allow him to place himself in an alternative tradition to the Shakespearean.

The most immediately striking feature of his dramatic *oeuvre* is the extreme energy, the voraciousness for subject matter, which shape a sequence varied in form but closely interlinked in essential concerns. Byron wrote most of the plays at Ravenna, between 1821 and 1823, in parallel to a spate of self-searching journal writing. An obsession with time, a fascination with the individual as defined against its passing, and his attempt to piece together some token against it, in fame or memory, is common to both. The protagonists of the drama are often presented as literally or figuratively 'on the brink', caught facing obliteration, but in that fact, in that moment, the more clearly defined as irreducibly individual. The two biblical plays, or 'Mysteries', show Byron at his most revolutionary in form and argument. *Cain* presents an archetypal Romantic protagonist, impelled by his dissatisfaction with the word of the father, the word of God as received by Adam; rejecting the patriarchal order that that imposes, he seeks knowledge in dialogue with Lucifer, and a flight into 'the abyss of space'. At the end, after his murder of Abel, his identity is marked ineradicably on him, 'the mark of Cain' which will protect him from human violence, but show him also as an outsider, condemned to wander the earth, exiled both by God and by the curse of his mother Eve. This individuating alienation, the expulsion not simply from society, but from 'natural' human relations, as represented here by a mother-child relationship, is repeated in other plays by Byron, and is visible too in figures like the 'Daemon' in ▷ Mary Shelley's ▷ *Frankenstein* (1817), or Coleridge's *Rime of the Ancient Mariner* (1798). In *Heaven and Earth* (1822), Byron takes up the story of Cain's descendants, as rebels against and victims of the biblical word; Anah and Aholibamah are loved by rebel angels, who rescue them from the deluge by taking them to some other planet, to form an alternative world; but the play ends with Japhet, the son of Noah who also loves Anah, contemplating the flood that has swept away all other human life except for that contained within the Ark, which, as the curtain falls, sails towards him, offering unwanted rescue.

The confident apocalyptic vision of these plays is matched by the forging of a new dramatic language, a kind of beginning-of-the-world style, transparent, flexible, and carefully freed from the conventional pseudo-Shakespearian linguistic gestures that can bring so many other Romantic plays dangerously close to pastiche. The push of the play is towards the protagonist's discovery of a language through which he can confront his universe in his own terms, and free himself from those that build oppressive imaginative structures around him. The historical plays ground a similar conflict in 'the labyrinth of statecraft'; in *The Two Foscari* (1821), a doge of Venice is forced to preside over the torture and death of his son, and in *Marino Faliero*, another elderly doge is impelled by his inability to gain legal redress for a slander on his young wife to join a rebellion against the state of which he is nominally head, and is punished not only by death, but by the official obliteration of his memory. In both plays the male characters are rendered powerless within the apparent exercise of power, by their own inability to think outside the terms that power sets for them. By contrast, the women, Marina and Angiolina, respectively, like the women in the Mysteries, stand outside these structures, are fluid and active where the men are trapped, but end unable to resist the processes they oppose. Myrrha, in *Sardanapalus*, is another of the strong, centrally placed woman characters who distinguish Byron's plays from those of most English dramatists of any period. Sardanapalus himself refuses to engage with the historical role set down for him as Assyrian emperor, preferring to exist within the unchronicled life of drink, appetite and a freely-indulged bisexuality, but in his love for Myrrha, and in his out-facing of palace revolution, he shapes a historic role for himself in the lyrical act of a flamboyant Romantic suicide.

> *He mounts the pile*
> Now, Myrrha!
> *Myr.*　　Art thou ready?
> *Sar.* As the torch in thy grasp.
> 　　*MYRRHA fires the pile.*
> *Myr.*　　'Tis fired! I come.
> *(As MYRRHA springs forward to throw herself into the flames, the Curtain falls)*

The unfinished *Deformed Transformed* runs ironic, magical variations on some of those themes, in its Faustian tale of a hunchback who is granted a beautiful heroic body by a dark stranger and transported by him to fulfil an historic role in the Bourbon siege of Rome. The sardonic, puppet-like style of the play, with its casually spectacular action and arch games of historic and sexual identity, make it a kind of cartoon-strip version of Byron's most personal concerns, an improvisation for which an infinite number of endings, and therefore none at all, can be projected.

In complete contrast to Byron's practice, Shelley in *The Cenci* works consciously from within a Shakespearean and ▷ Jacobean tradition, seeking to combine this with the sacred sense of tragedy and taboo that informs his two favourite Greek plays, Sophocles's *Antigone* and *Oedipus Tyrannos*. The two lead roles, Beatrice Cenci and the Count her father – a Sadean figure whose infinite cruelty and capacity for evil is a perverse expression of his sense of himself as God's substitute within the patriarchal family – are conceived of in terms of the charisma and sustained emotionally intensity of the star Romantic actor. The subject – the Count's rape of his daughter and her parricidal revenge – again encapsulates an archetypal Romantic conflict, at the end of which Beatrice, proclaiming her innocence, becomes a radical image of idealistic revolution: 'what a world we make of it,' she says, 'the oppressor and the oppressed'. Though father-daughter incest was not representable on the London stage, the play (with *Cain*, the most frequently revived of the period) is crucially *of* the stage, in that Beatrice's appeal across time and through memory to the sympathy of an audience is close to what Shelley thinks tragedy is *for*, as he describes it in ▷ *A Defence of Poetry* (1821). Sympathy both redeems the injustices of history, and improves its audiences in an extension of their capacity for pity and love. Shelley makes sympathetic and creative use of his Jacobean precedents – particularly Webster's *The Duchess of Malfi* and Shakespeare's *Othello* and *Antony and Cleopatra* – to create a tragic heroine whose victory is her remaking of herself into a kind of icon for future generations. To that extent the sense of the past that colours the verbal style is as much a part of the effect of the play as the questioning simplicity and freshness of Byron's language in *Cain*.

There was of course a vast amount of new writing for the Romantic stage coming from outside this group of major poets; but though our interest is inevitably focused on writers we know from their work in other genres, the context of their work can be supplied from elsewhere. Questions of power are paramount in the theatre of the period. ▷ Walpole's pioneering play *The Mysterious Mother* (1768), like his Gothic novel ▷ *The Castle of Otranto*, situates power witin the family, and uses a half-serious Gothic fiction to explore the Oedipal relation of family, power, and sexuality, within a flamboyantly visual theatrical mode. Milman's *The Destruction of Jerusalem* takes on historical and biblical themes in terms of an implicitly anti-semitic Christian providentialism. Both plays are Romantic in their investment in revolutionary change, and the polarity of the two – Walpole's investment in the subversion of the family, as opposed to Milman's in the expression of an epochal moment – represents interests that Byron and Shelley were able to combine, creating dramas where familial conflict and personal crises of identity are expressions of rifts and eruptions in a social and cosmic order perceived as patriarchal; in the strict biblical sense in the case of Byron's Mysteries, in Shelley's, in the creation of a ▷ Renaissance world-view informed by his fascinated if atheistical interest in the structures of the Catholic church.

Wordsworth and Coleridge, like Shelley, create villainous protagonists who represent in some sense the opposite of their project for the play. In *The Borderers* (1797), Wordsworth centres the play on Rivers (Oswald in the 1842 revision), a character of mysterious motives, Iago-like in the terms of Coleridge's conception of Iago – a figure of 'motiveless malignancy'. Wordsworth's characters are borderers in a literal sense, living on the Anglo-Scottish borders, but they are 'borderers' in a figurative sense also. As an ex-Crusader, Oswald exists between the occidental, Christian world, and another more mysterious life. He impels the other characters towards liminal states of mind, a process that climaxes in his involving Mortimer/Marmaduke in the motiveless murder of a virtuous old man. Wordsworth denied that the play in general, and this character in particular, had anything to do with his sense of the French Revolution. It is nevertheless hard to escape a sense that new psychological and moral possibilities – particularly in relation to a perverse idealism or to an abstract villainy of self-convinced integrity – are made available to these dramatists by their own attempts to come to terms with the Revolution, the Terror, and the rise of ▷ Napoleon.

Drama by Negatives: Closet drama and the Legacy of Experiment

The Borderers is structured deictically – that is, its scenes, dialogues and narrations point to, rather than enact, an event. It is thus more like the semi-dramatic form of sections of *Lyrical Ballads* than it is like *The Cenci* or *Cain*. It points to events in the past, or to psychological events whose relation to action one has simply to take for granted. Although this builds towards a compellingly original dramatic form, it also raises the same issue as Byron's worry about performances of *Faliero*. How far are these plays *of* the stage? The term 'closet drama' seems appropriate not only to Romantic plays, but to the form Shakespeare takes in Romantic reading. Coleridge is reported to have said in a lecture that:

> He had seen Mrs Siddons as Lady, and Kemble as Macbeth – *these might be the Macbeth's of the Kembles, but they were not the Macbeth's of Shakespear; he was therefore not grieved at the enormous size and monopoly of the theatres, which naturally produced many bad and but few good actors; and which drove Shakespear from the stage, to find his proper place, in the heart and in the closet . . .*

In the 1805 version of *The Prelude* 'the imaginative power . . . slept' at the theatre despite Wordsworth's passionate response 'to the changes of the scene':

> . . . yet all this
> Passed not beyond the suburbs of the mind;
> If aught there were of real grandeur here
> 'Twas only then when gross realities,
> The incarnation of the spirits that moved
> Amid the Poet's beauteous world, called forth
> With that distinctness which a contrast gives
> Or opposition, made me recognize
> As by a glimpse, the things which I had shaped,
> And yet not shaped, had seen and scarcely seen,
> Had felt, and thought of in my solitude.

In the 1850 version that last line becomes:

> When, having closed the mighty Shakespeare's page,
> I mused, and thought, and felt, in solitude.

This serves to clarify some very abstract reasoning, but at the same time it marks a displacement of the theatrical experience by the 'page', a decisive appropriation of Shakespeare for private 'musing'. Shakespeare's place for many of the Romantics is somewhere between stage and page, in private recitation. Wordsworth and his sister ▷ Dorothy read Shakespeare aloud in their garden at Grasmere, and readings from Shakespeare are much more acceptable at Mansfield Park than a full-scale performance of ▷ Mrs Inchbald's translation of *Lovers' Vows* (1798). The key Shakespeare texts are those that lend themselves to the solitary imagination. *A Midsummer Night's Dream, Romeo and Juliet* and *Hamlet* generate fantasies that colour decisively the visual arts and music of the period. All three plays are plays of fancy and introspection where the theatre, in *A Midsummer Night's Dream* and *Hamlet* especially, is as unstable an amalgam of the compelling and the inadequate as it is for the Romantics.

The term closet drama is more usefully applied to texts in dramatic form which none the less explore the unstageable, visionary imagination. In Byron's *Manfred*, the hero's solitary encounters with a spirit world, as well as the mysteries of his melancholic temperament and necromantic powers, invite us to visualize for ourselves, but baffle any attempt to fix our ideas in physical form. Byron thus exploits the half-pictorial conjuring of the imagination which Lamb found preferable to the materiality of the stage. The spirit voices are created as lyrical interventions, somehow outside the text, but not given any clear identity or placing. Shelley's *Prometheus Bound* again exploits the visionary potential of closet drama, with an aptness to an action that is essentially the action of language itself, in the shift from a tragic discourse to a language of love and liberty; the tragedy dissolves into an ideal action, as physical and mental suffering are transcended. But it would be a mistake to use this as a convenient category for plays that are simply unconventional in their theatrical demands. Even Byron's impossibly extravagant stage directions (like Wagner's) are theatrical, if in the perverse sense of the theatrically anti-theatrical, of theatre against itself. They are best seen as experimental, as attempts to remake theatre, to operate at its limits. *Cain* was admired and staged by Stanislavsky and Grotowski, *The Cenci* by Antonin Artaud; indeed these practitioners of the twentieth-century avant-garde can be seen to be the heirs of Romantic theatre. The push towards new forms in which theatre transcends itself, in which the material is somehow consumed in a spiritual or metaphysical force, is most powerfully developed in Artaud's *The Theatre and Its Double*, his manifesto for a 'theatre of cruelty':

> In the anguished, catastrophic period we live in, we feel an urgent need for a theatre which events do not exceed, whose resonance is deep within us, dominating the instability of the times.
>
> Our long habit of seeking diversion has made us forget the idea of a serious theatre, which, overturning all our preconceptions, inspires us with the fiery magnetism of its images and acts upon us like a spiritual therapeutics whose touch can never be forgotten.
>
> Everything that acts is a cruelty. It is upon this idea of extreme action, pushed beyond all limits, that theatre must be rebuilt.

Keats, writing of Kean, and quoting Coleridge's formulation in *Christabel* (1816) of an hallucinatory exploration of sexual nightmare, celebrates the intensity of theatrical representation, its mysterious agency, its acting on its audience, in strikingly Artaudian term:

> *The spiritual is felt when the very letters and prints of charactered language show like the hieroglyphics of beauty; – the mysterious signs of an immortal freemasonry! 'A thing to dream of, not to tell!'*

The tension between material means and transcendent ends that is at the core of Romantic theatre has a double outcome – on the one hand a struggle to achieve intensity by redefining the relation of word and image ('It is not a question of suppressing the spoken language,' Artaud writes, 'but of giving words approximately the importance they have in dreams'), and on the other an acknowledgement of the inadequacy of theatre, or rather of the gap between the semiotics it employs, in costume, set acting and so on, and the ideal – spiritual, political, sexual – to which it points. This gap can be expressed as nostalgia or charm, or it can be articulated more challengingly as camp, as a deliberate subversion of style and sexuality. In either case, the force of Romanticism is more intensely present in current theatrical experiment than the obscurity of many of the texts would suggest.

What then is the legacy of Romantic theatre? If we judge the validity of plays from the past in terms of their potential for revival on the modern stage, then a handful of these plays have proved their worth. *The Cenci* and *Cain* have each had several successful recent revivals, and a notable revival of *Marino Faliero* has confirmed the theatrical power of Byron's dramatic writing. But this is a limiting criterion. Tennyson and Browning, for example, wrote plays more professionally tailored for performance, but these scarcely work, as can even the most awkward of the earlier Romantic dramas, at the edge of Romantic aims and concerns. A work like Thomas Lovell Beddoes's *Death's Jest Book* (1825–48), a shapeless, self-generating fantasia on the themes of Jacobean drama, is much more compelling in its exploration of the twilit area between stage and page, word and vision, of the Gothic imagination in which the 'dead' text becomes 'live' fantasy. In terms of theatre, the main legacy of the Romantic period is the double-edged one of a split perception of theatre, as both transcendent and ludicrous, no longer to be taken for granted, but always an insistent question where spectacle problematizes the relation of language to perception. In terms of theatrical practice, we have the enshrinement of the actor, the star Shakespearean, whose cultural status validates the low standing of the profession as a whole. But we have also the idea, however inconsistently or implausibly realized, of a theatre that can be in some sense revolutionary. By putting the value of theatre in doubt, while simultaneously participating in a highly theatrical culture, British Romanticism forces a redefinition of the aims and means of theatre, and sows the seeds of the twentieth-century avant-garde.

Reference section

Abolition literature

Literature directed towards the abolition of slavery. In Britain slave trading became a *cause célèbre* in 1788, was outlawed in 1807, and made a capital offence in 1824. While most people are aware of the anti-slavery writing in America, Harriet Beecher Stowe's *Uncle Tom's Cabin* (1852) being a prime example, similar literature in England is often neglected. The most important abolitionist in Britain during this period was ▷ William Wilberforce. Amongst other writers the most notable to write abolitionist texts are ▷ Mary Wollstonecraft, Elizabeth Benger, ▷ Hannah More, ▷ Henry Brougham, and ▷ Susannah Watts.
  ▷ Prince, Mary.

Acrostic

A literary game in which the initial letters of the lines of a poem spell a word when read downwards in order.

Kind sister! aye, this third name says you are;
Enchanted has it been the Lord knows where.
And may it taste to you like good old wine,
Take you to real happiness and give
Sons, daughters and a home like honied hive.

The initial letters spell 'Keats'; and it is the third verse of an acrostic poem to Georgiana Augusta Keats, by her brother-in-law ▷ John Keats. A double acrostic can also be read downwards with the last letters of each line.

Adonais (1821)

An elegy in ▷ Spenserian stanzas by ▷ Percy Bysshe Shelley, mourning the death of ▷ John Keats, which had been attributed to a violent attack on Keats's poem ▷ *Endymion* in the ▷ *Quarterly Review* (1818). In his preface, Shelley compares the brutal insensitivity of the reviewer to that of the wild boar which killed the mythical Adonis – hence the poem's title. Shelley was not well acquainted with Keats and the inspiration of the poem is fundamentally literary. It is based on the *Lament for Adonis* by the Sicilian-Greek poet, Bion (first century BC), and its style is elaborately rhetorical, Keats being presented as a symbol of poetic creativity in a hostile world.
  ▷ Greek Literature.

Aeolian

From Aeolus, god of the winds in ancient Greek myth (▷ Classical Mythology). An Aeolian harp is a stringed instrument, placed across a window or outside a house, so that the wind causes the strings to vibrate and make music; an example may be seen at Dove Cottage in the Lake District. The poet ▷ Samuel Taylor Coleridge possessed one; hence his poem *The Eolian Harp* (1795) and references to the instrument in *Dejection* (1802). For him, it symbolized his conception of the poet 'played upon' by Nature.

Aeschylus (525–456 BC)

One of the great tragic poets of ancient Greece. Only seven of his 70 plays survive; of these the best known are *Agamemnon*, *Choephori* and *Eumenides*, making up the *Oresteia* trilogy. Aeschylus is the great starting point of all European tragedy. Shelley's masterpiece ▷ *Prometheus Unbound* (1820) was written as a sequel to Aeschylus's *Prometheus Bound*, but without pretensions to Greek form.
  ▷ Greek Literature.

Agnes, St

A Christian martyr in the reign of the Roman Emperor Diocletian (AD 284–313). She became the patron saint of virgins; her day of celebration is 21 January. It was a popular belief that ceremonies performed on the night before this day would cause a girl to dream of the man she was destined to marry. This is the idea behind Keats's ▷ *Eve of St Agnes*.

Aikin, Lucy (1781–1864)

Poet, biographer and children's author. Aikin lacked self-confidence as a creative writer, classifying herself as an editor or translator rather than as an author of original works. However, her *Epistles on Women* (1810) and *Memoirs of the Court of Queen Elizabeth* (1818) reveal that she was, respectively, a fine poet and adept political allegorist. She was acquainted with many other women authors of her age, and wrote a memoir of ▷ Joanna Baillie.
  ▷ Translation; Allegory.
Bib: Todd, J., *Dictionary of British Women Writers*.

Ainsworth, William Harrison (1805–82)

Novelist. His best novels are historical: *Jack Shepherd* (1839), *The Tower of London* (1840), *Guy Fawkes* (1841), *Old St Paul's* (1841), *Windsor Castle* (1843). He tended to idealize the heroic criminal, for example Dick Turpin in *Rookwood* (1834) and Jack Shepherd; this was a literary fashion in the 1830s and 1840s and censured by the ▷ Victorian novelist William Thackeray (1811–63) in his

early reviews under the designation 'The Newgate School of novelists'. Ainsworth edited *Bentley's Magazine* 1840–2, *Ainsworth's Magazine* 1842–53 and *New Monthly Magazine* from 1853.
Bib: Ellis, S. M., *W. H. Ainsworth and his Friends*; Worth, G. J., *William Harrison Ainsworth*.

Akenside, Mark (1721–70)
Poet. Son of a butcher in Newcastle-upon-Tyne, and a physician by profession. He wrote the influential *The Pleasures of Imagination* (1744), a philosophical poem in Miltonic blank verse (▷ Milton, John). The assured reflective modulations of the poem influenced ▷ William Wordsworth's style in ▷ *The Prelude*, the subject matter of which – childhood impressions, the moral influence of landscape – is often the same. Akenside also wrote lyric poems and ▷ odes.
Bib: Houpt, C. H., *Mark Akenside: A Biographical and Critical Study*.

Albion
The most ancient name for Britain, used in Greek by Ptolemy and in Latin by Pliny. The word possibly derived from Celtic, but it was associated by the Romans with the Latin *albus* = white, referring to the white cliffs of Dover. From the Middle Ages on it has often been used poetically to stand for Britain, notably by ▷ William Blake.

Alexandrine
A 12-syllable line of verse, possibly owing its name to the French medieval work, the *Roman d'Alexandre* (▷ medieval literature). It is common in French poetry particularly of the classical period but unusual in English, where the commonest line length is of ten syllables. Its most famous use is in the last line of the ▷ Spenserian stanza, invented by Edmund Spenser for his *Faerie Queene* (1590–6), and it was this form that was revived by the Romantic poets. One of the best examples is from ▷ Keats's ▷ 'The Eve of St. Agnes':

> *Anon his heart revives: her vespers done,*
> *Of all its wreathed pearls her hair she frees;*
> *Unclasps her warmed jewels one by one;*
> *Loosens her fragrant boddice; by degrees*
> *Her rich attire creeps rustling to her knees:*
> *Half-hidden, like a mermaid in sea-weed,*
> *Pensive awhile she dreams awake, and sees,*
> *In fancy, fair St. Agnes in her bed,*
> *But dares not look behind, or all the charm*
> *is fled.*

Allegory
From the Greek, meaning 'speaking in other terms'. A way of representing thought and experience through images, by means of which (1) complex ideas may be simplified, or (2) abstract, spiritual, or mysterious ideas and experiences may be made immediate (but not necessarily simpler) by dramatization in fiction.

Alliteration
▷ Figures of Speech.

Althusser, Louis (b 1918)
One of the most influential French Marxist philosophers of the 1960s, whose work began to appear in English translation from 1965 onwards: *For Marx* (1965), *Reading Capital* (with Etienne Balibar; 1968), and *Lenin and Philosophy* (1971). Althusser's ideas have been influential in the area of cultural studies, where his particular brand of structural ▷ Marxism has led to a radical rethinking of all social institutions, and the place of the human subject within their structures. His essay 'Ideology and Ideological State Apparatuses' (*Lenin and Philosophy*) lays the foundation for a reconsideration of literature and its relationship to ▷ ideology, and has far-reaching effects also in the area of media studies.

Amphimacer
A verse foot deriving from Greek, also known as the cretic foot, it uses one short syllable between two long ones, as in the phrase 'going mad'. Rarely used in English verse, its pattern of one unstressed syllable between two stressed may be heard in ▷ Blake's poem 'Spring': 'Sound the flute!/ Now it's mute;/ Birds delight/ Day and night.' Its opposite, amphibrach (one accented foot between two unaccented ones), is even more rare.

Anacoluthon
▷ Figures of Speech.

Anacreontics
Any kind of melodious verse, lyrical, and concerned with love and wine. From the Greek poet Anacreon (6th–5th centuries BC). ▷ Byron called his friend ▷ Thomas Moore 'Anacreon Moore', because he translated the Odes of Anacreon into English.
▷ Greek literature.

Anacrusis
The use at the beginning of a line of verse of a syllable additional to the number required

by the given metrical pattern, as in the 'and' used by ▷ Thomas Campbell, in the second of these lines from 'Ye Mariners of England': 'The danger's troubled night depart/ And the star of peace return.'

Anapaest

A metrical foot having two short or unaccented syllables followed by a long or accented one. It is usually mixed with iambics. Originally a Greek marching beat, its use in English poetry frequently retains a martial resonance, as in this line from ▷ Byron's 'The Destruction of Sennacherib': 'And the sheen of their spears was like stars on the sea.'

Ancien Régime

A French phrase, commonly used in English, to signify the political and social order in France before the Revolution of 1789, and more loosely to indicate a former state of order.
▷ French Revolution.

Ancient Mariner, The Rime of the (1798)

A literary ▷ ballad by ▷ Samuel Taylor Coleridge first published in ▷ *Lyrical Ballads*. The mariner kills a friendly albatross for no stated reason, and he and the crew of his ship are subjected to punishment by the Polar Spirit. The members of the crew die in agonies of thirst, while the mariner himself lives on in a state of 'life-in-death', until he 'unawares' blesses some water snakes and is absolved of his guilt. The dead albatross which the crew have hung round his neck falls into the sea, and the ship is magically driven to the mariner's home port where he is given absolution by a hermit. Thereafter he wanders the world, compulsively telling his story, and recommending a holy life in communion with all God's creatures. The story appears naively didactic: the mariner has sinned against the 'One Life' and has done penance for his sin. But the poem's moral scheme is deeply ambiguous. If the theme is one of Christian sin and redemption, it seems strange that the destinies of the mariner and the crew are determined by a game of dice played between Death and Life-in-Death. And it is unclear why the rest of the crew are punished so harshly. The mariner ends with an apparently orthodox and banal message of religious consolation: 'He prayeth best who loveth best/ All things both great and small.' But this consolation is belied by his sinister unease, as he holds the wedding guest with his 'glittering eye', preventing him from attending the

marriage ceremony, and leaving him 'A sadder and a wiser man'. The poem dramatizes Coleridge's sense of irredeemable guilt, and his inability at this time to find consolation in orthodox religion or in the pantheism of his friend ▷ William Wordsworth.

Anspach, Elizabeth, Princess of (1750–1828)

Dramatist, poet and letter-writer. Elizabeth Berkeley's first marriage was to Lord Craven, during which period she challenged convention by publishing her own poetry and allowing her play *The Miniature Picture* (1780) to be staged at ▷ Drury Lane Theatre. Although ostracized by polite society, she was accepted by other writers, and her work was admired by ▷ Horace Walpole who printed one of her early dramatic pieces, *The Sleep-Walker* (1778), and to whom she dedicated *Modern Anecdote* (1779). She was widowed in 1791 and embarked upon her second marriage, to Ansbach, in the same year; after this, the remainder of her plays were acted privately. She is also known for a series of letters discussing her journeys to Russia and Constantinople (1785–6), which rival those of Lady Mary Wortley Montagu (▷ Orientalism). Her *Memoirs* offer a lively account of the age, but hardly display the proto-feminism (▷ Feminism) with which she is credited; for example, she writes that, 'whenever women are indulged with any freedom, they polish sooner than man'.
Bib: Rodgers, K.M., *Feminism in Eighteenth-century England*.

Anstey, Christopher (1724–1805)

Minor poet and author of *New Bath Guide* (1766), an extremely successful book containing letters in verse form supposedly sent by people in ▷ Bath. The letters describe in a humorous fashion the exploits of the fictitious Blunderbuss family.
Bib: Powell, W.C., *Anstey: Bath Laureate*.

Anti-Jacobin, The

▷ Jacobin.

Antiquary, The (1816)

A novel by ▷ Walter Scott, the third of his ▷ 'Waverley Novels', set in Scotland in the 18th century. The main story is an ordinary romance. A young officer, Major Neville, falls in love with Isabella Wardour, whose father rejects him on account of his supposed illegitimacy. Neville follows the father and daughter to Scotland, where the three have sundry adventures; Neville saves their lives and rescues Sir Arthur Wardour from impending ruin. He also turns out to be the son and heir of a Scottish nobleman. Thus the objections to the union between Neville and Isabella are removed. The distinction of the novel arises from the subsidiary characters: Jonathan Oldbuck, a learned antiquarian scholar (like Scott himself), and Edie Ochiltree, a wandering beggar who epitomizes the feelings and traditions of the Lowland Scottish peasantry. Scott states in his preface that he agrees with ▷ Wordsworth's opinion (expressed in the Preface to the ▷ *Lyrical Ballads*) that the peasantry have an eloquence in expressing the basic and most universal passions which is lost to the educated classes.

Apocalypse

From Greek 'disclosure'. A kind of visionary literature, especially *Revelation* in the ▷ Bible. The essence of such literature, for instance, the visionary poetry of ▷ William Blake, is that it expresses in symbolic terms truths and events which surpass the ordinary reach of the human mind.

Aristotle (384–322 BC)

A Greek philosopher, born at Stageira, and so sometimes called the Stagirite. He was first a pupil of ▷ Plato, later developing his thought on principles opposed to those of his master. He was tutor to the young Alexander (the Great). His thought covered varied fields of knowledge, in most of which he has been influential. His best known works are his *Ethics*, *Politics*, and *Poetics*.

The difference between Aristotle and Plato has been described as follows: Plato makes us think in the first place of an ideal and supernatural world by turning our minds to ideal forms which are the truth in terms of which imperfect earthly things can be known and judged; Aristotle turns us towards the natural world where things are what they are, perfect or imperfect, so that knowledge comes through study and classification of them in the actual world. It can thus be seen that whilst Plato leads in the direction of mysticism, Aristotle leads towards science. Until the 13th century, Christian thought tended to be dominated by Plato, but medieval Christian thought, owing to the work of the medieval philosopher Thomas Aquinas (c 1225–74), found Aristotelianism more acceptable.

The *Poetics* is based on the study of imaginative literature in Greek from which Italian critics of the 16th century, and French dramatists and critics of the 17th century constructed a system of rules, which were respected by ▷ Augustan writers, but strongly rejected by Romantic authors.

Atheism

Disbelief in God. In the ▷ Middle Ages and the 16th and 17th centuries, atheism was abhorrent; it was equivalent to a denial of conscience, although atheism during these periods differed from the systematic belief that man's reason suffices for his welfare. This belief grew in the 18th century and emerged in the ▷ French Revolution, influencing such English intellectuals as ▷ William Godwin and through him ▷ P. B. Shelley, whose atheism caused him to be expelled from Oxford, and for whom Platonism sufficed (▷ Plato). Different, but still 18th-century in its sources, was the atheism of ▷ Utilitarians such as James Mill (1773–1836) and John Stuart Mill (1806–73), who were less naïve about Reason than Godwin but, as practical men, saw religion as unnecessary in their scheme for human betterment.

Athenaeum, The

Founded in 1828, it was one of the most enlightened periodicals of the 19th century. It was honest and independent in literary criticism, and a leader of the movement to spread education among the working classes. In 1831 it reduced its price by half in order to reach this wider public, and in consequence increased its circulation six times. It was also very progressive in social reform. In 1921 it was incorporated in the *Nation and Athenaeum*, which in turn was merged in 1931 with the socialist weekly *The New Statesman*.

Augustanism

There are two aspects to 'Augustanism', one political, the other more strictly literary.
1 *Political Augustanism* In the decades following the ▷ Restoration a more or less fanciful parallel between recent English history and that of early imperial Rome was developed. Both the Emperor Augustus (27 BC–AD 14) and King Charles II could be felt to have restored order to the state as legitimate successors to rulers who had been assassinated by Republicans (Julius Caesar, Charles I). Both preserved the forms of constitutionality, and kept at least the appearance of a balance of power between Senate or Parliament and the head of state. Both rulers, and their successors, presided over an expansion of imperial power which

extended their own civilization over more barbarous peoples, by means of military power – the army in the case of Rome, the navy in the case of Britain. Where there had previously been the *Pax Romana* there would now be a *Pax Britannica*. Both Tories and ▷ Whigs could feel reassured by this parallel, though naturally a Whig would tend to stress the constitutionality of the new order, while a Tory such as the poet Alexander Pope (1688–1744) stressed its Stuart legitimacy: 'And Peace and Plenty tell, a *Stuart* reigns' (*Windsor Forest*). Political Augustanism is concerned essentially with society and with public issues, and is optimistic about British civilization and its role in the world as imperial power. It is detectable in such diverse works as Daniel Defoe's (1660–1731) *Robinson Crusoe* and James Thomson's (1700–48) *Castle of Indolence.*

2 *Literary Augustanism* The reign of Augustus coincided with the golden age of Roman culture and literature, and Roman writers of the time, such as ▷ Horace and Virgil, explicitly celebrate the Roman imperial destiny (▷ Latin literature). During the period of stability and growing prosperity following the Restoration, the somewhat naive adulation of the classics found in Tudor literature is replaced by a growing understanding of, and sense of equality with, the great Latin writers. At last English literature was coming of age in terms of self-conscious theoretical confidence, technical sophistication and diversity of genre and metrical form. The foundation of the ▷ Poet Laureateship as a regular court office is a sign of this new confidence. In his essays, John Dryden (1631–1700) constantly parallels the achievements of modern English writers with their classical ancestors. The young Alexander Pope picked up the spirit of the age very young and was promoted by his friends as an English Virgil. The true poet, it was vaguely felt, would follow Virgil in writing first ▷ pastorals (which require only technical skill and little experience of life), then would move on to Georgics, or longer discursive compositions, and would crown his life's work with an epic. With a little licence this pattern could be read into the careers of earlier English writers, such as ▷ John Milton, who were achieving classic status at this time. Ornamental, courtly forms, such as the ▷ sonnet and ▷ Spenserian stanza, were now despised as childishly ▷ 'Gothic', or employed with a conscious sense of their quaint primitiveness. The 'heroic' ▷ couplet emerged as the most dignified ▷ metre of which English verse was felt to be capable.

Since the English language, lacking the sounding mellifluousness of classical Latin, could not support lines the length of the Latin hexameter, nor dispense with the 'barbarous' ornament of rhyme, then the best recourse, it was felt, was to regularize and dignify the pentameter couplet. (Blank verse is of course a much more natural English parallel to the Latin hexameter, but the best poets were wisely unwilling for the time being to risk comparison with the recent example of Milton.) Alongside the cultivation of the couplet a doctrine of 'kinds' grew up which prescribed specific 'high' or noble vocabulary for epic writing, and specific vocabularies for the other genres. This notion, which reflects the class consciousness of the new bourgeoisie, as much as any purely literary doctrine, is seen at its most rigid in Thomas Parnell's (1679–1718) *Essay on the Different Stiles of Poetry* (1713). The neo-classical style which resulted from this regulation of metre and language could hope to appeal both to the traditional Aristotelian classicist of the time who required an 'imitation' of permanent nature, and the Lockean rationalist who could see ▷ Sir Isaac Newton's 'laws' of nature reflected in the couplet's combination of formal exactitude and infinite variety.

It is important to stress that such Augustanism is, like ▷ Romanticism, the artificial construction of literary historians, and never constituted a systematic programme or manifesto for poetry. The summary above lends it a coherence and exactitude which it never achieved in the work of any poet. Like most literary movements Augustanism was only defined after it was virtually over.

The dramatist Oliver Goldsmith (1730–74) seems to have been the first to use the adjective 'Augustan' in regard to English literature, applying it in *The Bee* (1759) to the reigns of William III and Queen Anne. The noun Augustanism seems not to have come into use until the early 20th century. In 1904 Theodore Watts-Dunton accused ▷ Thomas Gray of being 'a slave to 'Augustanism'', a judgement that Gray himself would have found quite bewildering. In the later 19th and early 20th century all 18th-century poetry tended to be characterized as overformal and emotionless, and the terms 'Augustan', 'Augustanism' and 'The Augustan Age', frequently served to obscure rather than illuminate the poetry of the period.

Bib: Ford, B. (ed.), *New Pelican Guide to English Literature, Vol. 4: From Dryden to Johnson*; Rogers, P., *The Augustan Vision*;

Rogers, P., *Hacks and Dunces*: *Pope, Swift and Grub Street*; Novak, M., *Eighteenth-Century English Literature*; Sambrook, J., *The Eighteenth Century*; Doody, M. A., *The Daring Muse*: *Augustan Poetry Reconsidered*.

Austen, Jane (1775–1817)

Novelist. Her novels in order of publication are as follows: ▷ *Sense and Sensibility* (1811), ▷ *Pride and Prejudice* (1813), ▷ *Mansfield Park* (1814), ▷ *Emma* (1816), ▷ *Northanger Abbey* and ▷ *Persuasion* (1818). The last two, published posthumously, are her first and last work respectively in order of composition. Fragments and early drafts include: *Lady Susan* (pub 1871), *The Watsons* (1871) and *Sanditon*, on which she was working when she died, published in 1925.

She restricted her material to a narrow range of society and events: a prosperous, middle-class circle in provincial surroundings. However, she treated this material with such subtlety of observation and depth of penetration that she is ranked among the best of English novelists. A French critic, Louis Cazamian, writes of her method that it is 'so classical, so delicately shaded ... that we are strongly reminded of the great French analysts'. Her classicism arises from respect for the sane, clear-sighted judgement of the ▷ Augustan age that had preceded her, but its vitality is enhanced by the ▷ Romanticism of her own period, so that her heroines acquire wisdom by a counter-balancing of the two. She brought the English novel, as an art form, to its maturity, and the wide range which that form covered later in the 19th century owed much to the imaginative assurance which she had given it.

Her life as a clergyman's daughter was outwardly uneventful but it is probably not true that this accounts for the absence of sensationalism in her novels; her circle of relatives and friends was such as could have given her a wide experience of contemporary society. The restriction of the subject matter of her fiction seems to have been dictated by artistic considerations. D. W. Harding's essay 'Regulated Hatred: An Aspect of the Work of Jane Austen' (*Scrutiny*, 1940) credits her with being a caustic satirist and critic of society. Bib: Austen-Leigh, J. E., *A Memoir of Jane Austen*; Butler, M., *Jane Austen and the War of Ideas*; Greg, J. D., *The Jane Austen Handbook*; Lascelles, M., *Jane Austen and her Art*; Mudrick, M., *Jane Austen: Irony as Defence and Discovery*; Southam, B. C. (ed.), *Jane Austen: The Critical Heritage*; Tanner, T., *Jane Austen*.

Austin, Sarah (1793–1867)

Translator. Primarily important for facilitating access to French and German ▷ medieval literature during a period in which the influence of ▷ Gothic literature was of primary importance. She published her translations in *Lays of the Minnesingers* (1825), with Edgar Taylor (▷ lay). She also translated: from German, Prince Puckler-Muskau's *Tour in England, Ireland and France* (1832), *Characteristics of Goethe* (1833) and *Fragments from German Prose Writers* (1841); and from French, several political and biographical works. Although committed to the education of women, she deemed it sensible to refrain from airing her feelings too strongly in her works. Nevertheless, she may have influenced J. S. Mill (1806–73) in his campaign for women's equality (▷ Women, Status of), as it was Austin who taught him the German language.

▷ French literature in England; German Influence on English literature.
Bib: Hamburger, L. and J., *Troubled Lives: John and Sarah Austin*.

Autobiography

The word came into English at the very end of the 18th century. In the 19th and 20th centuries the writing of the story of one's own life has become a common literary activity. However, the practice already had an ancient history, and English autobiography may be divided into three overlapping historical segments: 1 the spiritual confession; 2 the memoir; 3 the autobiographical novel.

1 The spiritual confession has as its basic type the Confessions of St Augustine of Hippo (345–430) who described his conversion to Christianity. Such records of the inner life were mostly written in the ▷ Middle Ages and the ▷ Renaissance, although an example from the Roman period is ▷ Mary Prince's account of her life as a slave, dictated to an amanuensis.

2 The memoir, on the other hand, of French derivation, originates largely in the 17th century and owes much to the practice of extensive letter-writing which then developed, *eg* the letters of Madame de Sévigné (1626–96) (▷ French literature in England). An example from 18th-century England is the fragmentary *Memoirs* (pub 1796) by the historian ▷ Edward Gibbon. But the objective memoir and the subjective confessions came together in the *Confessions* of the French-Swiss ▷ Jean-Jacques Rousseau, and this is the most prevalent form of the outstanding English autobiographies of the 19th century and that

which was most important to romantic writers. The varieties of this form are extensive: they may be a record of emotional struggles and experiences, *eg* ▷ *The Confessions of an English Opium Eater* by ▷ Thomas de Quincey; *Memoirs* by ▷ Rachel Despenser; as well as the racy life story of ▷ Harriette Wilson. They may also be essentially a history of growth of ideas, convictions, and the strengthening of vocation, in the life of the writer. In any case, an autobiographical element becomes prominent in works which are not strictly autobiographies from the early 19th century on; *eg* ▷ Wordsworth's ▷ *Prelude, or Growth of a Poet's Mind* (first version 1805); the

periodical essays of ▷ Charles Lamb in ▷ *Essays of Elia* (1820–3) and ▷ S.T. Coleridge's mixture of autobiography with philosophy and literary criticism in *Biographia Literaria* (1817). It may be said that from 1800 it becomes the instinct of writers of many kinds to use autobiographical material, or to adopt from time to time an autobiographical standpoint.

3 Finally we come to the autobiographical novel which predominated in the ▷ Victorian period, as for example in the novels of ▷ Charlotte Brontë (*Jane Eyre*, 1847, and *Villette*, 1853).

B

Baillie, Joanna (1762–1851)
Friend of ▷ Sir Walter Scott and prolific
author of plays based on the ▷ Shakespearean
model (*Plays of the Passions*; 1798, 1802, 1812),
five of which were acted. She also wrote poems
in couplets, and lyrics on sentimental and
patriotic themes (*Fugitive Verses*, 1790; *Metrical
Legends*, 1821; *Poetic Miscellanies*, 1823).
▷ Aikin, Lucy
Bib: Uphaus, R.W. and Foster, G.M., *The
"Other" Eighteenth Century*.

Ballad
Traditionally the ballad has been considered
a folkloric verse narrative which has strong
associations with communal dancing, and
support for that link has been found in the
derivation of the word 'ballad' itself (from
the late Latin verb *ballare* – to dance). More
recently scholars have viewed the association
between ballads and dance forms rather more
sceptically. Generally, the term is used of a
narrative poem which uses an elliptical and
highly stylized mode of narration, in which
the technique of repetition with variation may
play an important part. Often ballads contain
repeated choral refrains but this is not a
universal feature.

From the 18th century onwards, collections
of folk/'popular ballads' began to be made
and the form was taken up by some of
the most influential poets of the late 18th
century as a folkloric form of expression.
▷ Wordsworth's and ▷ Coleridge's collection
of poems ▷ *Lyrical Ballads* (1798) does not
contain many poems in ballad form (apart
from the brilliant balladic composition ▷ *The
Ancient Mariner*) but the function of the title
seems to be to arouse associations of oral,
non-literary poetic forms. In this collection,
art is used to conceal art. ▷ Walter Scott
produced many adaptations and imitations
of traditional Scots ballads and published a
collection of ballads entitled *The Minstrelsy of
the Scottish Border*.
Bib: Bold, A., *The Ballad*.

Balzac, Honoré de (1799–1850)
French novelist. His *La Comédie humaine*
is a panorama of French society from the
▷French Revolution to the July Monarchy
(1830). It is bound together by the use of
recurrent characters (Vautrin is one notable
instance, Rastignac another) and recurrent
motifs (notably the necessity of moral and
social order contrasted with the pressures
of the individual ego). Among the one
hundred novels which Balzac completed,
drafted or projected are *Eugénie Grandet*
(1833), *Illusions perdues* (1837–43), *La Cousine
Bette* (1846), *Le Cousin Pons* (1847), *Le
Père Goriot* (1835), *Splendeurs et misères des
courtisanes* (1847).

'French society was to be the historian,'
Balzac wrote, 'I had only to be the scribe'.
His ways of depicting French society are
geographical, historical, political and even
geological insofar as all social strata find a
place. These different representations, taken
individually or in combination, bring into play
a dynamic explained in *La Peau de chagrin*
(1831) as the product of desire and power,
with knowledge enlisted to restrain them.
But such a restraint is rare or non-existent,
and society in the *Comédie humaine* is driven
by a restlessness which tends to exhaustion
as it competes for the fulfilment of desire.
Like society, character too is open to multiple
descriptions, as a machine driven by abstracts
(passion, ambition, penury, for instance) or
as a representative of a human or social type.
In that respect, character has a potential for
expansion. It is always ready to merge into
symbol (more than just the performance of
symbolic actions) or be exaggerated into ▷
melodrama. Indeed, melodrama is a central
Balzacian ingredient and, just as characters
are actors, buildings and places too are
subject to mutation into a theatre or a scene
in which the novelistic events unfold. In its
liking for myth and melodrama, Balzac's social
realism is correspondingly more than the
accumulation of surface detail, since the detail
acts as an indicator of underlying causes. In
turn, understanding of these causes is open
only to the novelist defined by his capacity
for 'second sight', the capacity to perceive
pattern as well as pattern destroyed. And it is
considerations of this kind which distinguish
Balzac from other ▷*feuilleton* novelists such as
Eugène Sue (1804–57) and help account for
his pervasive influence on 19th century fiction,
particularly in England where Balzac shaped
the already strong vein of social ▷realism.
Bib: Prendergast, C., *Balzac: Fiction and
Melodrama*; Bellos, D., *Balzac: Le Père Goriot*.

Bannerman, Anne (1765–1829)
Poet. She lived in penurious circumstances
in Edinburgh, and her poor health and
nervous condition was commented on by
all those who came into contact with her.
Her first book, *Poems* (1800) contains
▷ odes and ▷ sonnets translated from
Goethe (▷ German influence on English
literature), while her second, *Tales of
Superstition and Chivalry* (1802) uses the
▷ ballad form to tell ▷ Gothic tales of

ghosts and prophets. Other themes include nostalgic and sentimental praise for Scotland and admiration for her contemporary ▷ Joanna Baillie.

▷ Scottish Literature in English.

Barbauld, Anna Laetitia (1743–1825)
Poet, editor and writer of children's books. Her first book, *Poems* (1773), was an immediate success. It adopts an ▷ Augustan tone, imitating Samuel Johnson's (1709–84) attack on ▷ Romantic literature. She became a friend of ▷ Joanna Baillie who inspired her to turn to political writing, which resulted in the Abolitionist tract *A Poetical Epistle to Mr Wilberforce, on the Rejection of the Bill for Abolishing the Slave Trade* (1790) (▷ Abolition literature). Barbauld is rightly renowned for her fifty-volume editions of the works of English novelists (1810), for which she wrote an interesting preface on novel writing. Her *The Female Speaker* (1811), which provides selections of literature suitable as reading matter for young ladies, has generally been mocked, but she does include ▷ Coleridge's poem ▷ 'The Ancient Mariner' and refers it its 'queer, wizard-like quality'. She was also a prominent member of the ▷ Bluestocking circle and a friend of ▷ Elizabeth Montagu.
Bib: Moore, C.E., *Fetter'd or Free? British Women Novelists. 1670–1815*; Rodgers, B., *Georgian Chronicle: Mrs Barbauld and Her Family*; Schlueter, P. and J., *An Encyclopedia of British Women Writers*.

Bard
A member of the privileged caste of poets among the ancient Celtic peoples, driven by the Romans and then the Anglo-Saxons into Wales and ▷ Ireland and, legend has it, exterminated in Wales by Edward I. The term became known to later English writers from references in ▷ Latin Literature. Poets such as ▷ Shakespeare and ▷ John Milton refer to any serious poet as a 'bard'. In the 18th century, partly as a result of the growing antiquarian interest in druidism, the term came to designate a mysteriously or sacredly inspired poet, as in ▷ Thomas Gray's famous ▷ ode ▷ *The Bard* (1757).

Bard, The (1757)
One of ▷ Thomas Gray's two famous 'Pindaric Odes' (the other being 'The Progress of Poesy'). The last surviving Celtic ▷ bard stands on a mountain-top and calls down curses upon King Edward I and the English army, as they march below,

prophesying the end of his royal house and its ultimate replacement by the (Welsh) house of Tudor. He concludes by throwing himself into the River Conway beneath. There is a stagey wildness about the work which irritated the ▷ Augustan author Samuel Johnson (1709–84), though its failure to 'promote any truth, moral or political' did not prevent if from being very popular at the time.

Barham, Richard (1788–1845)
Poet and miscellaneous prose writer. Barham is primarily known for one work: *The Ingoldsby Legends: or Mirth and Marvels* (three series collected in 1840). This collection of stories and poems was immensely successful at the time and continues to be read and valued today. The tales are often comic, but perhaps it is their ▷ Gothic quality and sexual subtext which make them enjoyable as well as intriguing.
Bib: Horne, R.H., *A New Spirit of the Age*.

Barnard, Lady Anne (1750–1825)
Poet, artist, travel writer and prolific correspondent. Anne Lindsay, (her maiden name) was a Scottish author, descended from a ▷ Jacobite family, and acquainted with ▷ Sir Walter Scott who published several of her poems. She is known for her reworking of a Scottish ▷ ballad, 'Auld Robin Gray', and a melancholy ballad of her own composition, *Lays of the Lindsays* (▷ lay). This latter poem is reproduced in ▷ Mary Wollstonecraft's *Wrongs of Women*. In 1793 she married Andrew Barnard and in 1797 they moved to South Africa where he became the colonial secretary at the Cape of Good Hope. Her ▷ travel writings, which are accompanied by drawings, show her to have been a careful and sensitive recorder of the places she visited.

▷ Scottish Literature.
Bib: Masson, M., *Lady Anne Barnard: The Court and Colonial Service under George III and the Regency*.

Barthes, Roland (1915–80)
Probably the best known and most influential of all the ▷ Structuralist and ▷ Post-structuralist critics. In books such as *Writing Degree Zero* (1953), *Mythologies* (1957), and *S/Z* (1970), Barthes undertook to expose how language functioned, and its relationship with ▷ ideology. Moreover, he was also concerned to uncover the distinctions between literary texts which operated on the basis of a stable relationship between signifier and signified (▷ sign), and those for whom the act of signification (establishing meaning) itself was

of primary importance. The terms he uses to distinguish between the two types of text are 'readerly' (*lisible*) and 'writerly' (*scriptible*). In later works, such as *The Pleasure of the Text* (1975), he went on to investigate the sources of pleasure which the text affords to the reader, and distinguished between 'the text of pleasure' which does not challenge the cultural assumptions of the reader and which is therefore comforting, and 'the text of bliss' where the reader experiences a *'jouissance'* from the unsettling effect elicited from the text's representation of the crisis of language. In addition to offering penetrating analyses of literary texts, Barthes concerned himself with the structural analysis of all cultural representations, including topics such as advertising, film, photography, music and wrestling.

Bath
A city in the west of England with hot springs whose mineral properties will afford relief to those with rheumatic diseases. In the 18th century, largely owing to the energies of Richard (Beau) Nash (1674–1762), the city became a brilliant social centre; nearly everyone of eminence in politics, literature or the arts at some time visited or lived there. Hence its prominence in the literature of the time. Nash, who virtually ruled Bath, was a civilizing influence on fashionable society: by his discipline he improved the manners of the rich but ill-bred country gentry, and by refusing to allow the wearing of swords in public assemblies he helped to reduce the practice of duelling.

▷ Anstey, Christopher; Austen, Jane; Graves, Richard.

Baudelaire, Charles (1821–67)
French poet. His best known work, *Les Fleurs du mal* (1857), points the way out of ▷ Romanticism towards modernism. Formally, it draws on the tradition of ▷ sonnet and song which Baudelaire inherited from the ▷ Renaissance. Conceptually, it springs from the perception of 'two simultaneous feelings: the horror of life and the ecstasy of life', periods of heightened sensitivity and sensibility alternating with the monotony of existence without meaning. Baudelaire is rich in suggestion, allowing sensation to transfuse the object as though the object were the source of the sensation rather than the occasion for it; and equally powerful value is bestowed upon the metaphorical expression of sense-experience. When the poet uncovers, invested with desire, an exotic and erotic universe in

a woman's hair ('La Chevelure'), this moment is also an uncovering of the possible resonances which the hair triggers in the poet. The contrasting condition of 'Ennui' is a state of torpor which saps intellectual and emotional vigour and induces creative sterility. Everyday objects are here commonly used to embody feelings of failure, dejection, horror and despair. The book's five sections explore these twin conditions, in art and love (*Spleen et Idéal*), in city life (*Tableaux Parisiens*), in stimulants (*Le Vin*), in perversity (*Fleurs du mal*) and in metaphysical rebellion (*La Révolte*), ending (in the poem 'Le Voyage') with man's yearning unsatisfied but finding in death a new journey of discovery.

Baudelaire also wrote fine music and art criticism (he championed Wagner and Delacroix); his translations of Edgar Allan Poe (1809–49) helped confirm, in France, interest in tales of the fantastic; and he was the first to investigate extensively the new genre of prose poetry. In England, his influence has been constant, though at the outset it raised moral controversy.

Beattie, James (1735–1803)
Schoolteacher and later Professor of Philosophy at Aberdeen University. His pseudo-medieval (▷ medieval literature) poem in ▷ Spenserian stanzas, *The Minstrel: or the Progress of Genius* (1771–4), popularized the mystique of the poet as solitary figure, growing to maturity amid sublime scenery. He also wrote a prose *Essay on Truth*, attacking the scepticism of the ▷ Augustan philosopher David Hume (1711–76) from a position of orthodox piety.

▷ Bard; Romanticism.

Beauclerc, Amelia (c 1810–20)
Novelist. Little is known of Amelia Beauclerc's life and her novels have occasionally been wrongly ascribed to another author. Of her eight novels, *Alinda, or The Child of Mystery* (1812) is notable for its carefully balanced scenes of transvestism and homoerotic encounters between women. Although her female characters often triumph over difficulties encountered in their dealings with men it would however be wrong to endow too radical or feminist a note to Beauclerc's writing, since much of her work is conventional and uninspired, as for example her ▷ Gothic novel, *Husband Hunters* (1816).

▷ Feminism.

Beckford, William (1759–1844)
Novelist and travel writer. Chiefly remembered for his ▷ Gothic novel *Vathek*, Beckford also wrote travel books, and was an extravagant collector of Gothic curiosities. Son of a Lord Mayor of London, Beckford's substantial family wealth enabled him to create Fonthill Abbey, where he lived in eccentric and scandalous seclusion.
▷ Hervey, Elizabeth.

Beddoes, Thomas Lovell (1803–49)
Poet and dramatist. Nephew of the novelist ▷ Maria Edgeworth, and son of a physician, Thomas Beddoes. He spent most of his adult life in Germany and Switzerland, repeatedly in trouble for his revolutionary ideas. His first published work was a collection of tales in verse, *The Improvisatore* (1821). He shared the Romantic interest in the ▷ Jacobean dramatists, and sought to revive drama in their spirit with *The Bride's Tragedy* (1822). He continued to revise his second play, *Death's Jest-Book* until his death, and it was published posthumously in 1850, as were his *Collected Poems* (1851). Despite occasional intensities his plays are unexciting dramatically, and his reputation rests chiefly on his lyric verse in the tradition of ▷ Percy Bysshe Shelley, such as *Dream Pedlary*. Beddoes died by suicide.
Bib: Thompson, J. R., *Thomas Lovell Beddoes*.

Belshazzar (6th century BC)
In the ▷ Bible (*Daniel* V) the son of Nebuchadnezzar and King of Babylon. He gave a great feast where he and his nobles 'praised the gods of gold, and of silver . . .', when mysterious words suddenly appeared on the wall. Only the Hebrew prophet-in-exile Daniel could interpret that they foretold Belshazzar's overthrow, at the hands of Cyrus, King of Persia. The feast has been the subject of poems and dramas in English, including a poem by ▷ Byron.

Bennett, Anna Maria (c.1750–1808)
Novelist. Anna Bennett (she is sometimes mistakenly known as Agnes Bennett) was a Welsh writer about whose early life little is certain – mainly because she herself offered so many variations. However, in 1785 two verifiable events occurred: first the death of her lover and father to two of her children, Admiral Sir Thomas Pye, and secondly the publication of her first novel, *Anna, or memoirs of a Welch Heiress*, whose success made her economically independent. The novel's bawdy satire set the tone for her other five works, making her a ▷ Minerva best-selling

author. Her most interesting work is *The Beggar Girl and Her Benefactors* (1797), which ▷ S.T. Coleridge described a 'the best novel since Fielding'. She was influenced more by the ▷ Augustan writers Samuel Richardson (1689–1761) and Henry Fielding (1707–54) than by her contemporary ▷ Romantic authors whose ▷ Gothic writings she often mocked. As a result of these allegiances her popularity, not surprisingly, waned quite quickly, although she was much admired by ▷ Scott as well as Coleridge.
▷ Welsh Literature in English.
Bib: Blakey, D., *The Minerva Press 1790–1820*; Rodgers, K. M., *Feminism in Eighteenth-century England*; Todd, J., *Dictionary of British Women Writers*.

Bentham, Jeremy (1748–1832)
An extremely influential thinker, founder of the school of thought called ▷ Utilitarianism. The basis of his thought was: **1** that human motives are governed by the pursuit of pleasure and avoidance of pain; **2** that the guiding rule for society should be the greatest happiness of the greatest number; **3** that the test of value for human laws and institutions should be no other than that of usefulness. These views he expounded in *Fragment on Government* (1776) and *Introduction to Principles of Morals and Legislation* (1780). His principal associates were James Mill (1773–1836) and John Stuart Mill (1806–73); collectively they were known as the Philosophical Radicals, and together they established a practical philosophy of reform of great consequence in 19th-century Britain. But their excessive rationalism frustrated sympathy and imagination in education and the relief of poverty. Bentham's thought derived from the sceptical 18th-century French 'philosophes' such as Helvetius and 18th-century English rationalists such as David Hartley (1705–57) and Joseph Priestley (1733–1804). It was, in fact, the outstanding line of continuity between 18th-century and 19th-century thinking.
Bib: Stephen, L., *The English Utilitarians*; Pringle-Patterson, A. S., *The Philosophical Radicals and other essays*; Atkinson, C. M., *Life*.

Beppo: A Venetian Story (1818)
A poem in ▷ *ottava rima* by ▷ Lord Byron. During the Venetian carnival Laura and her *cavaliere servente* (lover) are confronted by her long-absent husband, Beppo, who has turned Turk after being shipwrecked. The three of them discuss matters amicably over coffee, and the men remain friends thereafter. The

poem reflects Byron's own position at the time as *cavaliere servente* to Teresa Guiccioli.

Berry, Mary (1763–1852)

Dramatist and philosophical prose writer. Mary Berry and her sister Agnes (1764–1852) were brought up by their grandmother and allowed to educate themselves. They were much admired by ▷ Horace Walpole who dedicated books to them and allowed Mary Berry to edit several of his manuscripts, although she published these editions under her father's name, rather than her own. Mary was also friendly with several contemporary female authors, including ▷ Harriet Martineau and ▷ Joanna Baillie; indeed, the latter wrote the epilogue and prologue for Berry's play, *Fashionable Friends* (1801). The sexual freedom condoned by this play, together with Mary's own rejection of marriage, suggests that in terms of gender politics she was somewhat radical (▷ Feminism). However, her history *A Comparative View of the Social Life of England and France from the Restoration of Charles II* (1828–31) reveals a more conservative attitude.

▷ Women, Status of.
Bib: Moers, E., *Literary Women*.

Betham, Mary Matilda (1776–1852)

Poet, diarist and artist. Mary Betham's family attempted to make her relinquish literary activity for the more socially acceptable activity of sewing, but she persevered, and in 1797 published her first book of poems, *Elegies*. This is hardly a sophisticated work, but marks her out as writing within a feminine tradition through, for example, her poetic indebtedness to ▷ Ann Radcliffe and the ▷ Ladies of Llangollen. Her attempt to lay claim to a genealogy of women writers continued in her finest work, the *Lay* of Marie de France (▷ lay), in which she takes on the voice of the ▷ medieval writer who, it is supposed, tells her life-story through her poetry. The poem reveals the contemporary fashion for ▷ Gothic narratives and descriptions, but is well-researched and finely done, avoiding some of the excesses of the Gothic novel. Betham was still having to fight against her family's prejudice, however, and in the 1820s they placed her in an institution for the mentally ill from which she wrote accusatory letters, as well as continuing her poetic output. Despite her family's censorious attitude, during her lifetime Betham was recognised as a fine poet, by ▷ Coleridge for example, and continued to write until her death in 1852.

Bible in England

The Bible falls into two parts:

1 Old Testament

The first and larger part of the Bible, consisting of the sacred writings of the Jews. It concerns the peculiar, divinely ordained destiny of the Jewish race from earliest times, and it is considered by Christians to expound the divine promise which the New Testament fulfils not merely for the Jews but for the whole of mankind. The Old Testament is divided into books which are grouped by Jews into three main sections, as follows:

1 The Torah ('law', otherwise called the Pentateuch), consisting of five books as follows: *Genesis, Exodus, Leviticus, Numbers, Deuteronomy*. They are called 'the five books of Moses'. The first two are narrative and descriptive, and move from the creation of the world to the escape of the Jews from slavery in Egypt. The remainder contain laws and discourses.

2 The Prophets. This section is divided into two in the Hebrew Bible: the 'Former Prophets', consisting of *Joshua, Judges*, the two books of *Samuel* and the two books of *Kings*; and the 'Latter Prophets', consisting of *Isaiah, Jeremiah, Ezekiel*, and the Minor Prophets. The books of the Former Prophets tell the story of the establishment of the Jews in the kingdom of Israel, and their subsequent history. The Latter Prophets contain history together with prophetic discourses.

3 The Sacred Writings, or Hagiographa, which are divided into three sections: (i) the Poetical books, consisting of *Psalms, Proverbs, Job*; (ii) the five 'Rolls', which are read at special seasons in the Jewish year: *Song of Songs, Ruth, Lamentations, Ecclesiastes, Esther* – of these *Esther* and *Ruth* are narratives, the other three are poetic meditations; (iii) *Daniel, Ezra, Nehemiah*, and *Chronicles*, all consisting mainly of historical narrative.

2 New Testament

The second and shorter part of the Bible, containing the sacred books of the Christians. It is divided into books, on the pattern of the Old Testament, and dates as a whole collection from the end of the 2nd century AD. It is customary to divide the books into four groups.

1 The three Synoptic (*ie* 'summary narrative') Gospels of Saints Matthew, Mark and Luke, and the *Acts of the Apostles*. The Gospels are narratives about Jesus Christ, and *Acts* is the narrative of the missionary careers of the apostles (including St Paul) after Christ's death.

2 The Epistles (letters) of St Paul. The four

shortest of these are addressed to individuals: two to Timothy, and one each to Titus and to Philemon. The remainder are addressed to various early Christian communities. These are the Epistles to the Romans, Galatians, Ephesians, Philippians, Colossians, two to the Corinthians, and two to the Thessalonians. The Epistle to the Hebrews has been ascribed to Paul, but is nowadays considered to be by a disciple of his.

3 The Catholic Epistles, so called because they were directed to Christians generally. Two of these are ascribed to St Peter, and one each to James and Jude.

4 The Johannine writings, ascribed to the Apostle John. These are the Gospel of St John, distinguished from the Synoptic Gospels as probably not intended as a historical narrative, the Epistles of John, and the poetic, visionary narrative called the *Apocalypse*, or *Revelation*.

In the ▷ Middle Ages the only version of the Bible authorized by the Church was the Vulgate, *ie* the translation into Latin by St Jerome, completed in 405. Partial translations were made into Old English before the 11th century. From the 14th century translations were made by reformers, who believed that men without Latin should have the means of seeking guidance from divine scripture without dependence on Church authority. The main translators were these: Wycliffe (14th century); Tyndale, and Coverdale (16th century). The last-named was the producer of the *Great Bible* (also called Cranmer's Bible after the Archbishop of the time), but Henry VIII, concerned for his intermediate position between Catholics and Prostestants, ended by restricting its use. Under the Catholic Mary I (1553–8) English reformers produced the *Geneva Bible* abroad, with annotations suited to Puritan Calvinist opinion (▷ Calvin); and in 1568 the so-called *Bishop's Bible* was issued by the restored Anglicans to counteract Puritans influence. Finally, in 1611 the Authorized Version was produced with the approval of James I (1603–25). For three centuries it was to be the only one in general use, and it is still the prevailing version. In the 19th century it was revised (Revised Version) and recently a new translation has been authorized and produced (New Testament 1961: Old Testament Aporcrypha 1970). A Catholic translation the (Douai Bible) was issued at about the same time as the Authorized Version.

In spite of various other translations, Catholic and Protestant, in the 19th and 20th centuries the Authorized Version is by far the most important for its literary and social influence. It was based on previous translations, especially that of Tyndale, so that the cast of its prose is characteristically more 16th than early 17th century in style. Nonetheless much of it is of supreme eloquence, *eg* the Book of *Job*, and last 15 chapters of *Isaiah*. It was for many people in the 17th and 18th centuries the only book that was constantly read, and it was familiar to all from its use in church and education. **Bib:** Daiches, D., *The King James' Version of the Bible.*

Biographia Literaria (1817)

A miscellaneous work of ▷ autobiography, philosophy, and literary criticism, by ▷ Samuel Taylor Coleridge. Its psychological approach to creativity, influenced by the German philosophers Schlegel and ▷ Kant, foreshadows the ▷ Freudian concept of the unconscious, and its theory of imagination is central to the development of literary critical theory. The famous distinction between primary imagination, secondary imagination and fancy occurs in Chapter XIII. Primary imagination is seen as 'the living power and prime agent of all human perception'. Secondary imagination is the creative power to synthesize and re-express experience in new forms: 'It dissolves, diffuses, dissipates, in order to recreate; or where this process is rendered impossible, yet still, at all events, it struggles to idealize and to unify.' Fancy, on the other hand, simply juxtaposes memories and impressions and 'has no other counters to play with but fixities and definites'. Primary perception is thus not the mere passive holding of a mirror up to nature of classical literary theory, but involves an interaction between subjectivity and objective reality.

Much of the literary criticism in the book is devoted to detailed analysis and appreciation of ▷ William Wordsworth's artifice, and to pointing out that his language is not simply, as he asserted in the Preface to the *Lyrical Ballads*, 'the real language of men', but a highly individual artistic construct of his own. The 'critical analysis' of poems by ▷ Shakespeare and Wordsworth which occupies much of the second volume, displays a very modern sophistication in its treatment of metre and diction.

Biography

The chief source of inspiration for English biographers was the Greek, Plutarch (1st century AD), whose *Parallel Lives* of Greek and Roman great men was translated into English

by Sir Thomas North in 1579 and was widely read. Biography had been practised before in England; there had been the lives of the saints in the Middle Ages, and in the 16th century Cavendish's life of the statesman Cardinal Wolsey had appeared. The regular practice of biography, however, starts with the 17th century, not merely owing to the influence of North's translation of Plutarch, but as part of the outward-turning, increasingly scientific interest in many kinds of people (not merely saints and rulers) which in the 18th century was to give rise to the novel. Biography is a branch of history, and the art of historical writing advanced with biography: Edward Hyde, Earl of Clarendon, included fine biographical portraits in his history of the Great Rebellion, written between 1646 and 1670. Izaak Walton's lives of John Donne (1640), Sir Henry Wotton (1951), Richard Hooker (1665), George Herbert (1670) and Bishop Sanderson (1678) are closer to our modern idea of biography, and they are landmarks, if not originals, in the form, inasmuch as the subjects, though eminent men, were humble enough to lead ordinary lives in touch with usual experience. In the 18th century the writing of biographies became habitual; and also biography, or autobiography, became a way of disguising pure fiction (*eg* the novels of Defoe). Influential examples from the Romantic period include ▷ Wordsworth's ▷ *The Prelude* and ▷ Thomas De Quincey's ▷ *Confessions of an English Opium Eater*. In the last ten years, biography has become one of the fastest growth areas in publishing, Michael Holroyd and Richard Ellman being two of the major biographers of the 1980s.
Bib: Gittings, R., *The Nature of Biography*.

Blackwood's Magazine

Founded in 1817 by the publisher William Blackwood as the *Edinburgh Monthly Magazine*, it was particularly influential in the first 15 years of its existence. Like the ▷ *Quarterly Review* it was intended as a Tory rival to the liberal ▷ *Edinburgh Review*, but called itself a 'magazine' to indicate a lighter tone than that of the 'Reviews'. It attacked ▷ Lord Byron and ▷ Percy Bysshe Shelley on political grounds, and was, like the *Quarterly*, particularly hostile to ▷ John Keats, because of his association with the radical journalist ▷ Leigh Hunt. Hunt, Keats, ▷ Charles Lamb and ▷ William Hazlitt were stigmatized as the 'Cockney School' of literature. *Blackwood's Magazine* began with a brilliant group of contributors, especially ▷ Sir Walter Scott,

John G. Lockhart (known because of his fierce criticism as 'the Scorpion'), ▷ James Hogg, and ▷ John Wilson, who wrote under the pen-name of Christopher North. Between 1822 and 1835 the magazine ran a series of brilliant dialogues, *Noctes Ambrosianae*, 'Nights at Ambrose's' (a well-known inn).

Blair, Robert (1699–1746)

Scottish clergyman and author of *The Grave* (1743), a ▷ blank verse genre piece blending ▷ Gothic sinisterness, banal piety and a pseudo-Shakespearean sublimity, deriving from *Hamlet*. Its enjoyable imaginative gusto ensured that it retained its popularity throughout the century, and beyond, and played an important part in the development of the Gothic novel.

Blake, William (1757–1827)

Poet and artist. The self-educated son of a London hosier, Blake earned his living by engraving illustrations for books. His own poems are engraved rather than printed, and he wove into his text pictures which elaborated the poetic theme. His earliest poems, *Poetical Sketches* show the influence of earlier lyric writers and ▷ Macpherson's ▷ Ossianic writings. His next works, the ▷ *Songs of Innocence* (1789), and ▷ *Songs of Experience* (1794) are startlingly original. Intended, on one level, for children, they are simple but symbolically resonant lyrics 'Shewing the Two contrary States of the Human Soul'. In *Innocence* the world is unthreatening and without morality, and God is trusted implicitly. The *Experience* poems, which often parallel those of the earlier volume in setting or title, depict with fierce moral indignation, a fallen world of repression and religious hypocrisy. There is no simple relation of progression or superiority between the 'contrary states', and Blake makes no attempt to reconcile their contradictions. They remain in unresolved dialectical opposition to each other.

In later works Blake elaborates his revolutionary interpretation of Christian theology using invented characters representing psychological or spiritual forces. In *Thel* (etched c 1789), in rhythmical, unrhymed lines, usually of seven stresses, the protagonist, confronted with the interdependence of life and death, creation and destruction, flees back to the shadowy world of the unborn. *Tiriel* was written at about the same time. *The French Revolution* (1791), *America* (1793) and *Visions of the Daughters of Albion* (1793) show Blake's reaction to the American and French revolutions, which he saw as releasing the energies of humanity, so long repressed by the forces of absolutism, institutionalized religion and sexual inhibition. In ▷ *The Marriage of Heaven and Hell* (etched c 1793) Blake expressed in a series of prophetic statements and 'Memorable Fancies', mainly in prose, his contempt for 18th-century rationalism and institutionalized religion.

Because his works remained virtually unknown and he developed no lasting relationship with an audience, his later prophecies became increasingly formless and obscure. He was also unwilling to be too explicit in case he should invite trouble from the authorities. *The Book of Urizen* (1794) focuses on the tyrannical figure of Urizen, ('your reason' or 'horizon'?) who symbolizes the inhibiting powers of control and restriction. Urizen is in constant war with Orc, a Satanic force of revolutionary energy. *The Book of Ahania, The Book of Los* (1795) and *Vala* (1797), subsequently rewritten as *The Four Zoas* (1804) develop similar themes with increasing intricacy and elusiveness. His last two prophetic books *Milton* (1804) and *Jerusalem* (1804) are often impenetrable, but include some striking passages. They show a new emphasis on Christian humility and self-sacrifice. In *Milton* he elaborates on his famous observation that ▷ Milton was 'of the Devil's party without knowing it'. Milton is shown returning to earth in the form of Blake himself, in order to correct his earlier mistake. Blake is one of the most intellectually challenging of English poets, with a unique insight into the pieties and ideological deceptions of his time. **Bib:** Ault, D., *Narrative Unbound*; Davis, M., *William Blake: A New Kind of Man*; Bronowski, J., *William Blake and the Age of Revolution*; Glen, H., *Vision and Disenchantment: Blake's Songs and Wordsworth's Lyrical Ballads*; Bottrall, M. (ed.), *William Blake: Songs of Innocence and Experience* (Macmillan Casebook); Paley, M. D., *William Blake*; Erdman, D. V., *Blake: Prophet Against Empire*; Bloom, H., *Blake's Apocalypse*.

Blank verse

Verse which is unrhymed, and composed of lines which normally contain ten syllables and have the stress on every second syllable, as in the classical iambic pentameter.

The first user of the iambic pentameter in English was Geoffrey Chaucer (1340–1400) and he used it in rhyming couplets, *eg The Prologue* to *The Canterbury Tales*. The first user of blank verse was Henry Howard, Earl of Surrey (1517–47), who adopted it for a translation of the second and third books of Virgil's *Aeneid* in order to get closer to the

effect of the metrically regular but unrhymed Latin hexameters (▷ Latin literature).

The important phase for Romantic literature is the epic use of blank verse by ▷ Milton in ▷ *Paradise Lost* (1667), who gave the weight of Latin syntax to the long sentences and accordingly moved away from speech rhythms. ▷ Wordsworth and ▷ Coleridge at the beginning of the 19th century lightened the Miltonic effect back towards colloquialism, while retaining a quasi-Miltonic gravity in order to convey the pulse of sustained meditation. Examples include Wordsworth's ▷ *Lines Composed a Few Miles Above Tintern Abbey* ... (1798) and his epic of introspection ▷ *The Prelude* (1805; 1850).

Blank verse continued to provide the metrical basis for most drama of the Romantic period.

▷ Metre.

Blessington, Marguerite, Countess of (1789–1849)

Journalist and novelist. Marguerite Blessington's life was characterized by brutality and hardship, yet her beauty, vivacity and intelligence ensured that she was one of the most renowned literary hostesses of the day. She received no formal education and was sold by her father as a wife to Captain Maurice Farmer when she was fifteen, but ran away after only three months. She eventually found shelter with Charles, Earl of Blessington and, when her husband died in 1817, they married. This was the happiest period of Blessington's life and she travelled on the continent, becoming acquainted with some of the most renowned literary figures of her day. It is from this period that her witty and fast-moving work *Conversations of Lord Byron* (▷ Byron) comes, of whom she wrote just before she met him: 'Am I indeed in the same town with Byron? ... I hope he may not be fat ... for a fat poet is an anomaly in my opinion'. It was also at this time that she made an enduring friendship with ▷ Count Alfred d'Orsay, for whom she acted as patron. She had no children by Blessington and this resulted in her rejection by his family when he died in 1829, after which she had to work hard in order to support herself, often undertaking hack journalism, although she also wrote several novels. In 1849 she was declared bankrupt and died penniless in Paris a month later.

▷ Silver-fork novels.
Bib: Marshall, W.K., *Byron, Shelley, Hunt and the Liberal*; Todd, J., *Dictionary of British Women Writers*.

Bloom, Harold (b 1930)

One of the leading members of the so-called Yale school of literary criticism, along with the late ▷ Paul De Man, ▷ Geoffrey Hartman and J. Hillis Miller. In books such as *The Anxiety of Influence* (1973), *A Map of Misreading* (1975), and *Poetry and Repression* (1976) Bloom seeks to offer a revisionary account of poetry, based especially on a ▷ Freudian model of the relationship between the aspiring poet and his literary predecessors. In this way Bloom moves away from the tenets of American new criticism in his suggestion that all poetry seeks, but fails, to exclude 'precursor' texts, with which it enters into a struggle, both destructive and creative, in order to achieve its particular identity. Other books by Bloom relevant to a study of the Romantic period include: *Shelley's My Mythmaking* (1959), *The Visionary Company* (1961), *Blake's Apocalypse* (1963), *The Ringers in the Tower* (1971), *Poetry and Repression* (1976) and *The Breaking of The Vessels* (1982).

Bloomfield, Robert (1766–1823)

Poet. Bloomfield was a working-class writer who persevered in the face of great hardship, writing and publishing his poetry. His most famous work is *The Farmer's Boy* (1800), which traced the life of an orphan rustic through the natural cycle of the seasons (▷ nature). Although this book sold around 26,000 copies, the income was insufficient to live on and Bloomfield died in poverty.

Bluestocking

The 'Blue Stocking Ladies' were a group of intelligent, literary women in the mid-18th century who held evening receptions for serious conversation. As a setting for discussions in which both sexes were included, the evenings were a deliberate attempt to challenge the social stereotypes which confined intellectual debate to male gatherings and relegated the female sex to trivial topics. By bringing men and women together in this atmosphere, it was hoped that the 'polite' codes of gallantry could be disposed of. The chief hostesses included ▷ Elizabeth Montagu, Elizabeth Carter, Mary Delany, and, later, ▷ Hannah More.

The name 'bluestocking' is thought to derive from the stockings of Benjamin Stillingfleet, who, too poor to buy evening dress, attended in his daytime blue worsteds. Hannah More's poem *Bas Bleu* (1786) helped to establish the use of the term as referring to the society women, although Admiral Boscawen is traditionally credited with coining the collective noun.
Bib: Myers, S. H., *The Bluestocking Circle*.

Boadicea (d AD 61)

A Celtic queen (also Bonduca, Boudicea) who is a national heroine because of her rising against the Roman occupying forces. Her people were the Iceni of what is now the county of Norfolk; she was defeated by Suetonius Paulinus and killed herself. Poetically she has been celebrated by ▷ William Cowper in *Boadicea: an Ode*.

Boccaccio, Giovanni (?1313–75)

Italian humanist scholar and writer, born near Florence. His literary studies began in Naples where he wrote his first works but he later returned to Florence and was employed on diplomatic missions for the Florentine state. He publicly lectured on ▷ Dante's ▷ *Divina Commedia*, was a friend of Petrarch (1304–74) and the centre of a circle of humanist learning and literary activity. His works included a wide range of courtly narratives, a vernacular imitation of classical epic and a number of important encyclopaedic works in Latin which occupied the last years of his life. Boccaccio's vast narrative compilations in Latin and in the vernacular provided narrative sources for many later English writers including ▷ Keats and ▷ Tennyson.

Boileau, Nicolas (1636–1711)

French critic and poet. Through his *Art Poetique (The Poetic Art)* (1674), based on ▷ Horace's *Ars Poetica*, and his translation of the Greek treatise *On the Sublime*, he fostered in ▷ French literature the ideals of classical urbanity and regularity of form. He influenced John Dryden (1631–1700), who revised a translation of his *Art Poetique*, and Alexander Pope (1688–1744) whose *Essay on Criticism* was partly based on it, and whose *Rape of the Lock* owes something to the French poet's mock-epic, *Le Lutrin.* In the Romantic period Boileau's name became synonymous with stifling (and foreign) neo-classical decadence. The youthful ▷ John Keats abuses the French critic in splendid but callow rhetoric in *Sleep and Poetry*.

Bonhote, Elizabeth (1744–1818)

Novelist and poet. Bonhote was an unadventurous novelist and it was perhaps the very conservative nature of her narratives and themes which made her one of ▷ Minerva's best-selling authors. The settings are often rural and, in *Bungay Castle* (1796), historicized; in addition, there is always a strong ▷ didactic moral at the end of the tale. Her unquestioning acceptance of traditional and conventional values is emphasized in her collection of essays, *The Parental Monitor* (1788), which contains advice for her children. Interestingly, however, while she advocates that women should stay at home and look after their families, she encourages them to write and not to be diverted from literary pursuits.

Bib: Todd, J., *Dictionary of British Women Writers*.

Bowdler, Henrietta Maria (1753–1830)
Religious writer and editor. Henrietta, or Harriet as she is better known, came from a literary family and was encouraged to write from an early age. Although her *Sermons on the Doctrines and Duties of Christianity* (1801, ▷ Sermons) were published anonymously they ran to almost fifty editions and so impressed the Bishop of London that he attempted to find out the identity of the author so as to offer 'him' a parish. Although Harriet can hardly be commended for her editorial activity, she has the singular honour of expurgating ▷ Shakespeare's plays *before* her more famous brother, ▷ Thomas Bowdler. Her most interesting fictional work is the novel, *Pen Tamar, or The History of an Old Maid* (1831) which is a curious combination of praise and harsh ridicule of women who have chosen not to marry. She may be linked with the ▷ Bluestockings and attacked Hester Piozzi (▷ Mrs Thrale) for marrying.

Bowdler, Thomas (1754–1825)
Famous for *The Family Shakespeare*, 1818; an edition in which 'those words and expressions are omitted which cannot with propriety be read aloud in a family'. He later published an edition of ▷ Gibbon's ▷ *Decline and Fall of the Roman Empire* similarly expurgated. From these we get the word 'bowdlerize' = to expurgate.
▷ Bowdler, Henrietta Maria; Shakespeare.

Bowles, Caroline (1787–1854)
Poet and prose writer. Bowles was fortunate enough to have sufficient private income to enable her to devote her life to literature, and she initially consolidated this freedom by refusing to marry. Her poetry was published anonymously for over twenty years, sometimes in ▷ *Blackwood's Magazine*, where she was commonly known only as 'C'. Her poetic works consist of *Ellen FitzArthur: a metrical tale* (1820), *The Widow's Tale* (1820), *Tales of*

the Factories (1833) and *The Birthday* (1836), and she is also well-known for her prose tales, *Chapters on Churchyards* (1829). The titles of these works reflect their sentimental nature, which gained her a reputation as a 'pathetic' writer. Her literary output ceased, however, in 1839 when she married ▷ Robert Southey and simultaneously lost her annuity, which had been dependent upon her remaining single. Bowles and Southey had, however, built a strong friendship based on a twenty-year correspondence, and when he became seriously ill in 1839 she married him and acted as his nurse until he died in 1843.

Bowles, William Lisle (1762–1850)
Poet and clergyman; ultimately chaplain to the Prince Regent. His *Sonnets* (1789), sentimental effusions delivered in the person of 'the wanderer', were extremely popular, and revived interest in the ▷ sonnet form. ▷ Samuel Taylor Coleridge and ▷ Robert Southey were impressed by them. The preface to his edition of the work of the ▷ Augustan poet Alexander Pope (1806) took its critical stance from his former teacher at Winchester, ▷ Joseph Warton, and prompted ▷ Lord Byron's 'Letter on W. L. Bowles's Strictures on Pope' (1821).

Bromley, Eliza (d 1807)
Novelist. Interesting as an early colonialist writer whose childhood in the West Indies provided her with a genuine love for the vigour and mysteries of the place, but at the same time she often presents a stereotypical and patronizing view of the indigenous Indians and negro slaves. Her most noted work in this respect was *Louisa and Augustus, An Authentic Story in a Series of Letters* (1784), which was mocked by ▷ Jane Austen in *Love and Friendship*.

Brontë, Anne (1820–49)
Novelist and poet. The younger sister of ▷ Charlotte and ▷ Emily Brontë. She was very close to Emily as a child and together they invented the imaginary world of Gondal, the setting for several poems and a prominent feature in their lives. She wrote under the name of Acton Bell, contributing to the volume of poems by all three sisters. Her two novels are *Agnes Grey* (1847) and *The Tenant of Wildfell Hall* (1848).
Bib: Gérin, W., *Anne Brontë*.

Brontë, Charlotte (1816–55)
Novelist; the third among five daughters of Patrick Brontë, a Yorkshire clergyman of Irish

origin. All the daughters died with their single brother before their father; their mother died in 1821.

In 1846 Charlotte, with ▷ Emily and ▷ Anne Brontë, published a volume of poetry under the pen-names of Currer, Ellis and Acton Bell; only Emily's verse is particularly noteworthy. Charlotte's first novel, *The Professor*, was not published until after her death; her second, *Jane Eyre* (1847), was immediately successful. Her third novel, *Shirley*, came out in 1849, *Villette*, based on her period of teaching in Brussels, in 1853. *Villette* is her most mature. The impressiveness of her writing comes from the struggle – experienced by herself, related through her heroines in *Jane Eyre* and *Villette* – to preserve her independence of spirit in circumstances which are overwhelmingly adverse. Her novels are often seen to be autobiographical ones. *Jane Eyre* continues to be successful, and *Villette* is increasingly esteemed. *The Professor* is really *Villette* in an earlier and more imperfect form; and *Shirley*, the only one not to have autobiographical form, is less admired. Like Anne and Emily, Charlotte has been the focus of attention for modern ▷ feminist critics and the confined and restless imagery of their novels is often seen as representative of the anger of suppressed and misrepresented women.
Bib: Gaskell, E., *Life*; Cecil, D., *Early Victorian Novelists*; Ratchford, F., *The Brontës' Web of Childhood*; Hanson, L. and E. M., *The Four Brontës*; Gérin, W., *Charlotte Brontë: The Evolution of Genius*; Peters, M., *Unquiet Soul: A Biography of Charlotte Brontë*.

Brontë, Emily (1818–48)

Novelist and poet. She has been described as the finest woman poet in English literature. It is, however, for her only novel, ▷ *Wuthering Heights* (1847), that she is chiefly famous. Located firmly in the rainswept Yorkshire landscape in which the Brontë family lived, *Wuthering Heights* also develops ideas and images drawn from the more wild and dramatic aspects of Romantic poetry, particularly ▷ Byron's. Indeed, a Byronic darkness may be seen not only in the character of Heathcliff but in the real-life dissipation of Emily's brother Branwell. The novel is unique in its structure and its vision; the former is so devised that the story comes through several independent narrators. Her vision is such that she brings human passions (through her characters Heathcliff and Catherine Earnshaw) against society (represented by the households of Wuthering

Heights and Thrushcross Grange) with extraordinary violence, while at the same time retaining a cool artistic control. This enables the reader to experience a highly intelligent criticism of society's implicit claim to absorb all the energies of the individual, who potentially is larger in spirit than society ever can be. Initially received as morbid and too violent, it has grown in critical stature.
Bib: Kavanagh, C., *The Symbolism of Wuthering Heights*; Sanger, C. P., *The Structure of Wuthering Heights*; Gérin, W., *Emily Brontë: A Biography*; Mengham, R., *Wuthering Heights*.

Brooke, Charlotte (d 1793)

Poet, dramatist and translator. Brooke was educated at home by her father, Henry Brooke, a noted Irish dramatist, and remained dedicated to his welfare throughout her life, especially after the death of her mother and sister in 1772. She painstakingly edited his works in 1792. She also published several of her own poems (although she destroyed most of her early work), a tragedy (*Belisarious*, now lost), and a novel (*Emma, or the Foundling of the Wood*) which was published posthumously in 1803. However, she is best known for her defence of early ▷ Irish literature and culture, published as *Reliques of Irish Poetry Translated into English Verse with the Originals* (1788). Brooke, who had taught herself old Irish in two years, had been outraged by ▷ James Macpherson's ▷ *Ossian* and intended to show English readers that there was a considerable wealth of Irish poetry corresponding to that which had been found in Old English.
Bib: Schleuter, J. and J., *Dictionary of British Women Writers*.

Brougham, Henry Peter, Lord (1778–1868)

Lawyer, journalist, and slave-trade ▷ abolitionist. He defended Queen Caroline brilliantly in the divorce proceedings brought against her by George IV in 1820, and later became Lord Chancellor. He was one of the founders (1802) of the ▷ *Edinburgh Review* and may have been the author of the satirical essay on ▷ Lord Byron's *Hours of Idleness* which appeared in the *Review* in January 1808 and provoked Byron to write *English Bards and Scotch Reviewers* (1809).

Brunton, Mary (1778–1818)

Novelist. She married Revd Alexander Brunton in 1798 and, although she had only a meagre education, they set about studying history and philosophy together. In 1811 she published anonymously her first novel *Self-Control* with a dedication to ▷ Joanna

Baillie. Brunton was particularly keen to show how ▷ Romantic stereotypes often acted to the detriment of women; for example, at the beginning of *Self-Control* she states that her purpose is: 'to shew the power of the religious principle in bestowing self-command: and to bear testimony against a maxim as immoral as indelicate, that a reformed rake makes the best husband'. She only completed one more work, *Discipline* (1814), before dying in childbirth, although she did leave an unfinished text, *Emmeline*. The novels focus upon the psychological development of central female characters, who are in some way made to rethink their presuppositions because of outside forces. The quality of her long-neglected novels has only recently been acknowledged, and it is now accepted that *Self-Control* influenced the work of ▷ Jane Austen.

Bib: Moers, E., *Literary Women*; Springer, M., *What Manner of Woman?*

Burke, Edmund (1729–97)
Statesman and political philosopher; described by the ▷ Victorian writer, Matthew Arnold (1822–88) as 'our greatest English prose-writer'. Born in Dublin, he pursued his political career in England, and was a Member of Parliament for much of his life. Although never attaining high office, his political status was considerable, due mainly to his formidable powers of oratory and polemical argument. His early work *A Philosophical Inquiry into the Origin of our Ideas of the Sublime and the Beautiful* (1756) marks a transition in aesthetic theory from the neo-classicism of the ▷ Restoration and ▷ Augustan writers John Dryden (1631–1700) and Alexander Pope (1688–1744). Influenced by Milton, it emphasizes the sense of awe inspired by both art and nature. His most celebrated work, ▷ *Reflections on the Revolution in France* (1790), argues for the organic, evolutionary development of society, as opposed to the brutal surgery and doctrinaire theories of the French revolutionaries.

Burke's character reveals a number of paradoxes. His writings combine the cautious, pragmatic instincts of a conservative politician with a passionate rhetorical style. He regarded all forms of political innovation with suspicion, yet defended the cause of the American rebels in *On Conciliation with the Colonies* (1775). He attacked the corrupt practice of court patronage and the exploitative activities of the East India Company, yet retained for himself many benefits of the systems he deplored.

Bib: S. Ayling, *Edmund Burke: His Life and Opinions*; Cone, C, B., *Burke and the Nature of Politics* (2 vols); Stanlis, P. J. (ed.), *Edmund Burke: The Enlightenment and the Modern World*; Wilkins, B. T., *The Problem of Burke's Political Philosophy*.

Burney, Fanny (Frances, Madame D'Arblay) (1752–1840)
Daughter of the musical historian Dr Charles Burney (1726–1814), Fanny grew up in the distinguished company of Dr Johnson (1709–84), ▷ Sir Joshua Reynolds, Garrick and the ▷ Bluestockings. In 1786 she was appointed as an attendant upon Queen Charlotte, wife of George III, and in 1793 she married a French exile, General D'Arblay. From 1802–12, interned by Napoleon, she and her husband lived in France.

Burney's major novels are ▷ *Evelina* (1778), *Cecilia* (1782) and *Camilla* (1796). Their common theme is the entry into society of a young girl, beautiful and intelligent but lacking experience of the world; during subsequent adventures the girl's character is moulded. Burney was a great admirer of Samuel Richardson (1689–1761), and his influence is apparent in her use, in her first novel, of the epistolary form. Burney was well aware, however, of the difficulties facing a woman novelist; for example, in her diary entry for 18 June 1778 she comments on the reception of her novel *Evelina*:

> *In a private confabulation which I had with my Aunt Anne, she told me a thousand things that had been said in its praise, and assured me they had not for a moment doubted that the work was a man's. I must own I suffered great difficulty in refraining from laughing . . .*

Burney was also well known for her diaries and letters. Her *Early Diary* (1889) covers the years 1768–78, and contains many sketches of Johnson and Garrick; her *Diary and Letters . . . 1778–1840* (published 1842–6) is a lively account of life at court. Amongst her admirers, ▷ Jane Austen shows Burney's influence.

Bib: Henlow, J., *The History of Fanny Burney*; Kirkpatrick, S., *Fanny Burney*; Simons, J., *Fanny Burney*; Todd, J., *The Sign of Angelica*.

Burney, Sarah (1772–1844)
Novelist. Overshadowed by her half-sister ▷ Fanny Burney, Sarah was a successful novelist in her own right, earning her living mainly from her writing. Her life seems to have been conventional (for example she accepted jobs as a governess and paid

companion), with the exception of a five year interlude as a young adult, during which she and her half-brother left their respective homes (he was married) to live together. Sarah Burney's first novel *Clarentine* (1796), although published anonymously, received great acclaim, and a number of others followed, the most noteworthy being: *Geraldine Fauconberg* (1808), *The Shipwreck* and *Country Neighbours* (1816–20), and *The Renunciation* (1839). The novels focus upon the psychological reactions of their young heroines when confronted by some calamitous occurrence or mysterious revelation.

Bib: Hemlow, J., *The History of Fanny Burney*; Kirkpatrick, S., *Fanny Burney*.

Burns, Robert (1759–96)

Scottish poet. He was born in poverty, the son of a peasant or 'cottar', but nevertheless became well-read in the Bible, ▷ Shakespeare, 18th-century English poetry, and also learnt some French. His best work, in the Lowland Scots dialect, was precipitated by his reading of the poet Robert Fergusson (1750–74), and was written between 1785 and 1790, during most of which time he was working as a farmer, an occupation which undermined his health. He intended to emigrate to Jamaica with Mary Campbell, but she died in childbirth in 1787. In the same year his *Poems Chiefly in the Scots Dialect* were published in Kilmarnock, and made him famous. He moved to Edinburgh where a new edition of the volume appeared in the following year, and where he was lionized as a 'natural' genius. He was a hard drinker and womanizer, and two years after Mary Campbell's death he took as his wife Jean Armour, who had already borne children by him. He leased a farm and secured preferment in the excise service in Dumfries, despite his earlier sympathies for the French and American Revolutions. He devoted himself to reworking Scottish songs, which appeared in James Johnson's *The Scots Musical Museum* (1793–1803) and George Thomson's *Select Scottish Airs with Poetry*. But he became further impoverished, and succumbed to persistent ill health.

Perhaps Burns's best-known poems are sentimental lyrics, such as *Auld Lang Syne* or love songs like *Ae fond Kiss*, *Highland Mary*, and 'O my love's like a red, red rose'. His *Cotter's Saturday Night* celebrates Scottish peasant life in Spenserian stanzas, and other poems express a keen sympathy with the downtrodden and oppressed. But it is his comic satires which are now considered his best work: *To a Mouse*; *The Twa Dogs*; *Tam O'Shanter*; *The Jolly Beggars*. It is significant that those poems which attack Calvinism and the hypocrisy of kirk elders, such as *The Twa Herds* and *Holy Willie's Prayer*, were omitted from the Kilmarnock *Poems* of 1786. Even during his lifetime Burns was beginning to be viewed as a kind of Scottish ▷ Poet Laureate, with all the distortions which this inevitably involved. Over the past two centuries, this status, together with the patriotism of Burns Night, have served to promote a glamorized myth, at the expense of a true appreciation of Burns's poetry.

▷ Scottish literature in English.

Bib: Daiches, D., *Robert Burns*; Jack, R. D. S., and Noble, A. (eds.), *The Art of Robert Burns*; Spiers, J., *The Scots Literary Tradition*.

Bury, Charlotte (1775–1861)

Poet, novelist and diarist. Charlotte Bury was a glittering success as a literary hostess in Edinburgh, but this masked her actual poverty and she wrote because she needed to, rather than for pleasure or through dedication. Her circle included ▷ Sir Walter Scott, ▷ Susan Ferrier and Matthew Lewis; indeed, she was said to be the model for the heroine in Lewis's novel *The Monk* (▷ 'Monk' Lewis). Her own writings include *Poems on Several Occasions* (1797), seventeen unremarkable novels, and the sensational *Diary Illustrative of the Times of George IV* (1838). It was this last work, based upon her experiences as lady-in-waiting to the Princess of Wales (1810–15), that made her name, combining as it did astute political observation with salacious scandal.

▷ Diaries; Silver-fork novels.

Bib: Rosa, M. W., *The Silver-fork School*.

Byron, George Gordon, Lord (1788–1824)

Poet. His childhood was dominated by a sternly ▷ Calvinist mother, a nurse who sexually abused and beat him, and painful medical treatment for his club foot. His incestuous relationship with his half-sister, Augusta Leigh, developed into a close friendship. In compensation for his deformity he prided himself on his physical prowess, particularly in swimming. While at Harrow and Cambridge he gained a reputation for atheism, radicalism and loose-living, keeping a bear as a pet for a time. At the age of 19 he published a collection of unremarkable lyrics, *Hours of Idleness* (1807). *English Bards and Scotch Reviewers*, a vigorous but immature heroic couplet poem in imitation of Pope, followed in 1809.

He travelled across Europe to Greece in

1810, involving himself in self-consciously romantic adventures. He swam across the Hellespont like Leander in the Greek legend, and dressed in Albanian costume. He wrote in a letter, 'I smoke, and stare at mountains, and twirl my mustachios very independently.' After his return in 1811 he published Cantos I and II of ▷ *Childe Harold's Pilgrimage* (1812), a moody, self-dramatizing poem in ▷ Spenserian stanzas. It was an immediate success and he followed it with several hastily-written verse tales: *The Bride of Abydos* (1813) and *The Giaour* (1813), mainly in tetrameter couplets, *The Corsair* (1814) and *Lara* (1814), in loose heroic couplets. Each focuses on the characteristic Byronic hero: glamorous, haunted by the guilt of mysterious crimes, which he seeks to forget in violent and dangerous adventure. Lionized in society and pursued by various women, Byron ended by marrying the naive and inexperienced Anne Isabella (Annabella) Milbanke. Her intention to reform him failed, and the marriage broke up shortly after she had given birth to a daughter.

Byron left England for the last time in 1816, and met up with ▷ Percy Bysshe Shelley and ▷ Mary Wollstonecraft Godwin in Switzerland. Claire Clairmont, Mary's half-sister, gave birth to a daughter by Byron, but she died in infancy. About this time he wrote *Childe Harold* Canto III (1816) which he called 'a fine indistinct piece of poetical desolation', also ▷ *The Prisoner of Chillon* (1816), and the gloom-laden drama, ▷ *Manfred* (1817). He travelled to Italy where, after a period of sexual promiscuity with all kinds of women, he eventually fell in love with Teresa Guiccioli, the 19-year-old wife of an elderly Italian nobleman. His uncomfortable role of *cavaliere servente* or tolerated lover, is indirectly reflected in ▷ *Beppo* (1818), his first poem in *ottava rima*, a form which he made peculiarly his own, employing its rattling rhymes and concluding couplet to superb effect. It is also used in ▷ *Don Juan* (1819–24) and *The Vision of Judgement* (1822). He became restless, and after Shelley had drowned in 1822, he decided to throw himself into the cause of Greek independence.

As he had remarked in a letter of 1820:

> *When a man hath no freedom to fight for at home,*
> *Let him combat for that of his neighbours;*
> *Let him think of the glories of Greece and of Rome,*
> *And get knock'ed on the head for his labours.*

In Greece he suffered further frustrations, including a disappointed passion for a Greek youth, Loukas. He began to feel his age, and expressed this poignantly in the lyric 'On this Day I Complete my Thirty-Sixth Year'. He contracted malaria, was bled several times by his doctors, and died at Missolonghi in 1824.

Byron's popular romantic reputation, based on the first cantos of *Childe Harold*, *Manfred* and the verse tales, is important in literary historical terms. On the Continent Byron has been regarded as a significant philosopher of ▷ Romanticism. However, Byron himself was dismissive of his 'Byronic' exercises in 'poetical desolation'. He preferred the brilliant wit of Pope to what he called the 'wrong poetical system' of his Romantic contemporaries. The real value of his poetry lies in his evocation of past civilizations in the fourth canto of *Childe Harold*, and in his brilliantly casual poems in *ottava rima*. Byron's letters are often more vivid than his verse. His ▷ autobiographical journal was destroyed after his death, and many of his letters were expurgated before being published by his friend ▷ Thomas Moore in 1830. However the correspondence with his publisher ▷ John Murray has survived intact, and shows the same vitality as the later poetry, but expressed in less inhibited language.

Bib: Marchand, L. A., *Byron: A Portrait*; Quennell, P., *Byron*; Leavis, F. R., 'Byron's Satire' in *Revaluation*; Knight, G. W., *Poets of Action*; Read, H., *Byron*; Rutherford, A., *Byron: A Critical Study*; Rutherford, A. (ed.), *Byron*: The Critical Heritage; Calder, A., *Byron*; Kelsall, M., *Byron's Politics*; Beatty. B. and Newey, V., *Byron and the Limits of Fiction*; Beatty, B., *Don Juan*.

C

Cain

In the ▷ Bible (*Genesis* 4:1) the eldest child of Adam and Eve. Cain's sacrifice to God of the fruits of the earth was rejected, while the beast-offerings by his shepherd brother Abel were accepted. In a rage Cain killed Abel, so becoming the first murderer.

In *Cain: A Mystery* (1821), a verse drama by ▷ Lord Byron, the episode was dramatized with Cain in the role of tragic hero, questioning the justice of the Almighty.

Callcott, Maria (1785–1842)

Travel writer and author of children's books. Callcott's most interesting work is based on her own extensive travels, which began with her journey to India with her family in 1808. These were published as *Journal of a Residence in India* (1812) and *Letters on India* (1814). In these books Callcott shows a clear attempt to challenge her own 'European' prejudices, as well as to recount honestly the racial injustices which she witnessed (▷ nationalism). Her travels to Italy in 1818–19 also resulted in an illustrated travel book, although it was never published and remains in manuscript form in the British Library. In 1821 Callcott and her husband moved to South America; a year after their arrival, however, her husband died leaving Maria to fend for herself. The resulting *Journals* (1824) contain a fascinating account of the people she met in Brazil and Chile, in which she seems to recognize their powerful need for national independence. Back in London she earned her living as an editor and journalist, making most money from *Little Arthur's History of England* (1835), a bland historical account for children.

▷ Diaries; Travel literature.

Calvin, John (1509–1604)

French religious reformer and author of the *Institutes of the Christian Religion* (1535). He settled in Geneva, which was to become, under Calvin's influence, an important centre of one of the most disciplined and militant branches of Protestantism.

Calvin's teachings were widely influential in England, Scotland, France and Switzerland in the 17th century and later. Out of the *Institutes* and his book on predestination (published in 1552) emerged the five chief points of 'Calvinism', namely its belief in: (1) 'predestination', which holds that God determined in advance who shall be 'elected' to 'eternal life' and who shall be condemned to everlasting damnation; (2) 'particular redemption', or the choosing of a certain predetermined number of souls redeemed by Christ's death; (3) 'original sin', which holds that the infant enters the world in a state of sinfulness, carrying with it the burden of Adam's fall; (4) 'irresistible grace', which argues that those chosen to be of the 'elect' have no means of resisting that choice; and (5) the final perseverance or triumph of the 'elect'.

Taken with Calvin's views on Church government and the relation between state and ecclesiastical power, 'Calvinism' was to be of enormous influence on the ▷ Church of England in the 16th and 17th centuries. From the early 17th century onwards his doctrines became those of the established church. Calvin's *Institutes* became a recognized textbook in the universities, and it was not until the rise of Arminianism under Archishop William Laud in the pre-Civil War years that an effective opposition to Calvin's influence was mounted.

Bib: Knappen, M. M., *Tudor Puritanism*; Dickens, A. G., *The English Reformation*.

Calvinism

▷ Calvin, John.

Cambridge University

One of the two oldest English universities. Its origins are obscure, but it was in existence early in the 13th century, and was probably founded by students emigrating from ▷ Oxford. Like Oxford, it is famous for the organization of its students and scholars into colleges, these being independent self-governing bodies whose governing members usually, though not necessarily, hold office in the university as well. It achieved importance equal to Oxford only in the 15th century. From then onwards the two universities have liked to think of themselves as rival leaders of English intellectual life, a habit they retain in spite of the founding of many other universities in the 19th and 20th centuries. In literature, it has been noted for the number of outstanding English poets educated there, *eg* ▷ Wordsworth, ▷ Coleridge, ▷ Byron, ▷ Tennyson.

Campbell, Thomas (1777–1844)

Author of the reflective poem *The Pleasures of Hope* (1799), which includes the well-known couplet: ''Tis distance lends enchantment to the view,/ And robes the mountain in its azure hue' (ll 7–8). He also wrote narrative poems such as *Gertrude of Wyoming* (1809) in ▷ Spenserian stanzas, and *Theodoric* (1824) in couplets.

Canning, George (1770–1827)
Politician and poet. Although Canning
is chiefly known for his roles as foreign
secretary (1822) and prime minister (1827),
he was also a fine writer of speeches and
a minor poet. He was the founder of and
contributor to the short-lived anti-liberal
paper *The Anti-Jacobin* (1797).
  ▷ Jacobin
Bib: Rolo, P.J.V., *Canning: three biographical
studies.*

Carlyle, Thomas (1795–1881)
Scottish essayist, historian, philosopher. The
term 'philosopher' is inappropriate to him
if it implies the use of the reason for the
logical investigation of truth; his friend John
Stuart Mill, who was a philosopher in this
sense, called Carlyle a poet, meaning that
he reached his conclusions by imaginative
intuition. In his old age he became known
as 'the sage of Chelsea'; this is the kind
of admiration that he received in England
between 1840 and his death. He hated
spiritual mediocrity, mere contentment with
material prosperity, moral lassitude and
the surrender to scientific scepticism and
analytic reasoning. All these he regarded as
characteristic of British civilization in the
mid-19th century. Part of their cause was the
overwhelming technical advances resulting
from the ▷ Industrial Revolution; he also
considered the immense popularity of the
poet ▷ Byron had helped to disintegrate
spiritual wholeness because of the cynicism
and pessimism of his poetry, and he
distrusted equally the influence on the
English mind of the coldly logical French
philosophers. To counter Byron, he pointed
to the spiritual health which he found in
▷ Goethe, and to counter the French he
advocated the more emotional and intuitive
18th and 19th century German thinkers like
Richter and Goethe.
  Carlyle's influence derives even more,
however, from his own character and the
environment from which he sprang. His
father had been a Scottish stonemason, with
the moral energy and intellectual interests
which comes partly from the influence of
Scottish Calvinism (Presbyterianism). This
religious tradition in Scotland had much
in common with 17th-century Puritanism
which had left such a strong mark on the
English character; the resemblance between
the two traditions helps to account for
the hold which Carlyle established on the
English imagination. His own personality
was strong and individualistic; this, combined

with his intention of counteracting the
abstract intellectual thought of writers
like ▷ Bentham, caused him to write
in an eccentric prose style, distorting
natural word order and using archaic
language. His ▷ *Sartor Resartus* ('Tailor
Repatched', 1833–4) is a disguised spiritual
▷ autobiography in which he faces the
tendencies to intellectual scepticism and
spiritual denial in himself, and dedicates
himself to a life of spiritual affirmation. He
is unable to base this affirmative spirit on
the traditional religious beliefs that had
supported his father, so that he has to base
it on his own will, his imaginative response
to nature and the inspiration provided by the
lives of great men.
  History was for Carlyle the storehouse of
example of these great men, his 'Heroes'
– and it is in this spirit that we have
to approach his historical works: *French
Revolution* (1837), *On Heroes and Hero
Worship* (1841), *Oliver Cromwell's Letters and
Speeches* (1845) and *Frederick II of Prussia*
(1858–65). In *Signs of the Times* (1829),
Chartism (1839) and *Past and Present* (1843)
he criticized the mechanistic philosophy
which he saw underlying contemporary
industrial society, and in *Latter-Day Pamphlets*
(1850) he attacked the quasi-scientific
treatment of social questions by the
rationalist political economists. In 1867
Shooting Niagara – and After?, written at the
time of the Second Parliamentary Reform
Bill, reflects his total disbelief in the efficacy
of mere political reform.
  As a historian, Carlyle wanted history to
be related to the life of the ordinary human
being; as a social thinker, his advocacy of
the imaginative approach to man in society
relates him to the thought of ▷ Coleridge,
whom he knew through his friend John
Sterling (*Life of John Sterling*, 1851), and also
to his own disciple, John Ruskin.
  ▷ Utilitarianism; Scottish literature in
English.

Cary, Henry (1772–1844)
Translator. Cary's ▷ translation of ▷ Dante's
▷ *Divina Commedia* (1805–14) was immensely
influential on the ▷ Romantic poets, in
particular ▷ Coleridge.
Bib: King, R.W., *The Translator of Dante: the
life, work and friendships of Cary.*

Castle of Otranto, The **(1764)**
One of the first so-called ▷ Gothic novels,
by ▷ Horace Walpole. The fantastic events
are set in the Middle Ages, and the story is

full of supernatural sensationalism. The story concerns an evil usurper, a fateful prophecy about his downfall, a mysterious prince disguised as a peasant, and his eventual marriage to the beautiful heroine whom the usurper had intended as his own bride.

Castlereagh, Viscount (1769–1822)

Statesman, and Secretary of State for Foreign Affairs during and after the downfall of Napoleon, from 1812 to 1822. This period coincided with a phase of political reaction in Britain, and to the radicals of the time he represented the oppressiveness of the government. Hence the attack on him by ▷ Shelley in the ▷ *Mask of Anarchy*.

Cave, Jane (1757–1813)

Poet. A devout Anglican with ▷ Methodist inclinations, Cave constantly battled against the sense of duty which called her away from her poetry. She published her witty and fast-moving collection, *Poems on Various Subjects* (including an ▷ elegy on her maiden name) in 1783 and revised it in 1786 when she married Thomas Winscom, in an attempt to expunge any material in danger of being considered impious. While the 1786 version contains interesting material in relation to gender, as she focuses on the importance of marriage and motherhood, its tone is heavier and less spirited than the 1783 edition. In later editions she added some ▷ abolitionist writing.

Cenci, The (1819)

A tragedy by ▷ Percy Bysshe Shelley which symbolically depicts the political oppression of his own day in terms of historical events which took place in 1599. Count Francesco Cenci, a Roman nobleman, conceives an incestuous passion for his daughter Beatrice, and in desperation Beatrice, her brother Bernard, and her stepmother Lucretia conspire to kill the Count. They are discovered, tortured, condemned to death, and executed on the orders of the Pope. Like all the dramas of the ▷ Romantic poets, Shelley's play is an artificial, literary composition. Its ▷ blank verse is highly derivative of that of the ▷ Jacobean playwrights, particularly John Webster (*1578–1632*).

Chapbooks

The name for a kind of cheap literature which flourished from the 16th to the 18th century, after which they were replaced by other forms. They were so called because they were sold by 'chapmen' or travelling dealers. Their contents consisted commonly of traditional romances retold, often from the French, in crude form. The works of several best-selling ▷ Romantic authors were adapted in this manner, including ▷ 'Monk' Lewis, ▷ Ann Radcliffe and ▷ Sir Walter Scott. Some of them, such as *Dick Whittington*, about the poor boy who ended up as Lord Mayor of London, have survived as children's stories to the present day, and are often the theme of Christmas pantomines.
▷ Wilkinson, Sarah.

Chapone, Hester (1727–1801)

Author of miscellaneous writing. Hester Mulso (married to John Chapone in 1760) was a precocious child, writing a romance at nine years of age, and became one of the most intelligent and influential of the ▷ Bluestockings. She wrote to the *Rambler* complaining about the treatment of women, and argued with Samuel Richardson (1689–1761) about the character of Clarissa, advising him to reduce the powerful influence the character's father has on her life. She is quoted in Johnson's *Dictionary* (1755), wrote favourably about ▷ Mary Wollstonecraft, and dedicated her *Letters on the Improvement of the Mind* (1773) to ▷ Elizabeth Montagu.
Bib: Moers, E., *Literary Women*; Myers, S.H., *The Bluestocking Circle*.

Characters, Theophrastian

In the early 17th century a form of ▷ essay devoted to the description of human and social types grew up, and collections of such essays were known as 'Characters'. The origin of the fashion is in the brief sketches by one character of another in the comedies of the time and in the verse satires. The tone was always light and often satirical, the basic pattern deriving from the *Characters* of the ancient Greek writer ▷ Theophrastus (3rd century BC); hence the designation 'Theophrastian'.

The fashion continued, though it became less popular, throughout the 17th century and into the 18th. It was eventually superseded by the more elaborate and individualized studies and by the growth of the 18th-century novel.

Chartist movement

A working-class political movement which flourished between 1837 and 1848. It arose because the Reform Bill of 1832 had reformed Parliament in favour of middle-class political rights but had left the working-class without them. The Chartists wanted Parliament to be closely responsible to the nation as a whole and to reform an electoral system according to which the poor were excluded from membership of Parliament and denied the right to vote others into membership by their lack of the necessary property qualification. Some regions were more heavily represented in Parliament than others and all voting was subject to bribery or intimidation because votes had to be declared publicly. Consequently they put forward their Charter containing Six Points: **1** votes for all males; **2** annually elected Parliaments (instead of general elections every seven years); **3** payment of Members of Parliament (so that poor men could have political careers); **4** secret voting (voting 'by ballot'); **5** abolition of the property qualification for candidates seeking election; **6** electoral districts equal in population. The movement seemed to be a complete failure, but all these points became law between 1860 and 1914 except the demand for annually elected parliaments. The Chartists attracted an ardent following but they were badly led.

Chatterton, Thomas (1752–70)

Poet. Chatterton's father, a schoolmaster in Bristol, died before he was born, and he was educated at a charity school, then apprenticed to an attorney. He wrote precociously in all the genres of the day: mock-heroic couplets, ▷ Hudibrastics, political satire imitative of Charles Churchill (1731–64) oriental eclogues in the manner of ▷ William Collins (1721–59) and elegiac poetry in the manner of ▷ Thomas Gray. But his most original compositions were pseudo-medieval (▷ medieval literature) concoctions concerned with 15th-century Bristol. Influenced by the fashionable medievalism of ▷ James Macpherson, ▷ Thomas Percy, and ▷ Horace Walpole, Chatterton claimed to have discovered lyric poems and a 'tragycal enterlude' by a 15th-century monk, Thomas Rowley, among the documents of the church of St Mary Redcliffe, where his uncle was sexton. The publisher Dodsley rejected the pieces, but they deceived Walpole for a time, and the poet was encouraged to move from Bristol to London. He published some non-medieval poems in journals under his own name, and a burletta (comic opera) by him was accepted for performance at Drury Lane. Then, at the age of 17, in a fit of despondency, he poisoned himself with arsenic.

It was not until seven years later that the Rowley poems were definitively unmasked by the Chaucerian scholar, Thomas Tyrrwhitt. Their language is an artificial amalgam of medieval, Elizabethan and contemporary elements, typical of the omnivorous eclecticism of the period. But occasionally, as in 'An Excelente Balade of Charitie', Chatterton succeeds in evoking a unique exotic world of his own. During the Romantic period Chatterton's reputation lost all associations with hackwork and only the 'medieval' lyrics were remembered. His early death took on a mythical quality, making him a symbol, even a stereotype, of youthful poetic genius neglected by a prosaic world. ▷ William Wordsworth referred to Chatterton as a 'marvellous Boy' in *Resolution and Independence*. ▷ Samuel Taylor Coleridge wrote *A Monody on the Death of Chatterton*. ▷ John Keats dedicated his ▷ *Endymion* to his memory, and ▷ Percy Bysshe Shelley compared him with Keats in ▷ *Adonais*.

Bib: Kelly, L., *The Marvellous Boy: The Life and Myth of Thomas Chatterton*.

Childe Harold's Pilgrimage (1812–18)

A semi-autobiographical poem in ▷ Spenserian stanzas by ▷ Lord Byron, describing the wanderings of a young man seeking escape from the *ennui* caused by over-indulgence at home. Cantos I and II (1812) describe his wanderings around the Mediterranean, ending with a lament for Greece enslaved by the Turks. The writing is sometimes very slapdash. Cantos III (1816) and IV (1818) are poetically superior, being less concerned with an affectation of solitude and mystery, and focusing on what really interested the poet: social activity and the stir of great events. In the third canto occurs the famous description of the interrupted ball in Brussels on the eve of the battle of Waterloo (stanzas xxi–xxv). In the fourth canto Byron abandons the fictional protagonist and writes in the first person, evoking the large reversals of history, as he contemplates the great Italian cities of Venice, Rome and Florence. The long meditation in the Coliseum at night, with its evocation of the dying gladiator, is very moving in a broad, rhetorical way. The poem was very popular at the time, not least for its 'Byronic' protagonist – self-regarding, proud and mysterious. Today, with the partial exception of Canto IV, it is less highly regarded than Byron's comic works in ▷ *ottava rima*.

Christabel (1816)

An unfinished narrative poem by ▷ Samuel Taylor Coleridge, the first part written in 1797 and the second in 1800. The story derives from the popular folk-ballad tradition. Christabel, daughter of Sir Leoline, finds a distressed lady, Geraldine, in the woods and takes her back to the castle, unaware that she is really an enchantress. Though she discovers Geraldine's nature, Christabel is forced by a spell to keep silent before her father. There is a strange confusion of sympathies in the author's treatment of the relationship between the two women, and between them and Sir Leoline. The poem is in a metrically experimental form reminiscent of Anglo-Saxon alliterative metre, each line having four stresses but a varying number of syllables. Even in its fragmentary state it achieves a compulsively anxious, but at the same time exhilarating, effect.

Church of England

The history of the Church of England is closely bound up with the political and social history of England.

In the ▷ Middle Ages the Church of England was merely a division of the Catholic Church of western Europe governed from Rome. It became independent in 1534 through the Act of Supremacy which made the English monarch head of the church. Two centuries of radical religious dissent followed which involved bloody purges of both Catholics and Protestants. By the early 18th century, however, the Church of England had settled into a self-contented apathy, which was only briefly shaken by the religious revival led by ▷ John Wesley, who worked mainly among the poorer classes. Although Wesley was forced to form a separate ▷ Methodist Church, his example inspired the ▷ Evangelical Movement within the Church of England, which by the 19th century was an important force towards social reform. A different sort of revival was led by a group of Anglicans at ▷ Oxford University, resulting in the Oxford (or Tractarian) Movement, which affirmed the spiritual independence of the Church and its continuity with the medieval Catholic Church.

Circulating libraries

A library from which books may be borrowed. Such libraries were in private hands in the 18th century and subsisted on subscriptions from clients. The first circulating library started in 1740 and as the institution spread so the reading habit greatly increased. It was the more important since, apart from ▷ chapbooks, books were very expensive in the 18th century.

Bib: Leavis, Q. D., *Fiction and the Reading Public*.

Clare, John (1793–1864)

Poet. The son of a farm labourer in the Midlands, he was self-educated, early influences being the ▷ Bible and James Thomson's (1700–48) *Seasons*. He was unable to settle down or marry because of his poverty, and hoped that his verse might bring him security. His *Poems, Descriptive of Rural Life and Scenery*, described as being by 'a Northamptonshire Peasant' appeared in 1820, and were a great success. In that year he married, and began work on *The Village Minstrel, and Other Poems*, which appeared in 1821. This volume disappointed his hopes, despite his attempts to adjust his fresh, spontaneous style to the vagaries of literary taste. He visited London several times and made the acquaintance of ▷ Samuel Taylor Coleridge, ▷ William Hazlitt and Charles Lamb. *The Shepherd's Calendar* was published in 1827, in a version much edited by his publisher, John Taylor. (The original version of the poem, as Clare submitted it to Taylor, was published in 1964.) Under the pressure of apparent literary failure, the demands of his growing family and grinding poverty, Clare became insane in 1837. He spent the remainder of his life in lunatic asylums, periodically imagining that he was Napoleon or ▷ Lord Byron. The works which he wrote during the period of his madness were not published until the 20th century.

Clare is remarkable for his interest in nature for its own sake, rather than, as is the case with most poets, as a key to some philosophical or aesthetic illumination. During his lifetime, and since, this quality has led to the criticism that his work is merely descriptive. In his best poems however, such description conveys, in itself, a celebration of the joy of the natural scene and the changing seasons. Moreover Clare, being a farm labourer, lacks the literary idealization of nature common in other poets. In his anguished poem 'I Am' he abandons description, laments the desertion of his friends, and longs for death.

Bib: Martin, F., *The Life of John Clare*; Storey, M. (ed.), *Clare: The Critical Heritage*;

Storey, M., *The Poetry of John Clare*;
Howard, W., *John Clare*.

Classic, Classics, Classical

These words are apt to cause confusion.
The term 'classic' has been used to denote a
work about whose value it is assumed there
can be no argument. The word particularly
implies a changeless and immutable quality;
it has sometimes been used to deny the
need for reassessment, reinterpretation and
change. Because only a few works can be
classics, it may be argued that the term
is synonymous with the best. This is not
necessarily the case, especially with regard
to changes in literary taste and a constantly
moving canon of texts.

'Classics' is the study of ancient Greek
and Latin literature. 'Classic' is used as an
adjective as well as a noun. 'Classical' is
mainly used as the adjective for 'classics', *eg*
classical scholarship.

Classical education and English literature

Classical education is based on the study
of the 'classics', *ie* the literature of ancient
Greece and Rome, principally from
▷ Homer to the great Latin poets and prose
writers of the 1st century BC – 1st century
AD. Latin is more closely bound up with
western history and culture, and is the easier
language for English speakers to study;
consequently it has been more widely used in
schools than Greek, and it has been studied
at earlier stages of education. Roman literary
culture was, however, based on that of the
Greeks.

Classical and native traditions of
literature rivalled and nourished each
other until the middle of the 17th century,
and so did Protestant biblical and secular
classical philosophies of life. But after the
▷ Restoration in 1660, religious passions
declined and sceptical rationalism began
to take their place. Thus began the most
classical period of English art and literature,
the so-called ▷ Augustan age of the 18th
century. Yet within their neo-classical
horizon, the best English writers even of
this period retained strong elements of
native idiom; this is true of the poets, John
Dryden (1631–1700) and Alexander Pope
(1688–1744) and of the prose writer Samuel
Johnson (1709–84).

The ▷ French Revolution of 1789
was, at one level, the outcome of 18th
century reason, criticism and scepticism,
but it challenged the 18th-century classical
qualities of order, intellectual proportion and

balance, and the view of man as fulfilled
only in a civilized structure of society. The
English ▷ Romantic movement was partly
an outcome of the French Revolution; it
challenged many of the classical values,
attaching more importance to the cultivation
of the feelings of the individual than to the
cultivation of the reason of man in society;
it rediscovered the ▷ Middle Ages, which
for three centuries had been despised as
▷ 'Gothic', *ie* barbarous.

▷ Greek literature; Latin literature.

Classical mythology

Ancient Greek mythology can be divided
between the 'Divine Myths' and the 'Heroic
Myths'.

The divine myths are known in differing
versions from the works of various Greek
poets, of whom the most notable are
▷ Homer and Hesiod. Hesiod explained the
origin of the world in terms of a marriage
between Earth (Ge or Gaea) and Sky
(Uranus). Their children were the 12 Titans:
Oceanus, Crius, Iapetus, Theia, Rhea,
Mnemosyne, Phoebe, Tethys, Themis, Coeus,
Hyperion, and Cronos. Cronos overthrew
his father, and he and Rhea (or Cybele)
became the parents of the 'Olympian gods', so
called from their association with the sacred
mountain Olympus. The Olympians, in their
turn, overthrew Cronos and the other Titans.

The chief Olympians were Zeus and his
queen Hera. The other gods and goddesses
were the offspring of either, but as Zeus was
usually at war with Hera, they were not the
joint parents. They seem to have been seen
as male and female aspects of the sky; their
quarrels were the causes of bad weather and
cosmic disturbances. The principal offspring
of Zeus were Apollo, Artemis, Athene,
Aphrodite (sometimes represented as a
daughter of Uranus out of the sea), Dionysus,
Hermes, and Ares. Zeus had three sisters,
Hestia, Demeter (the corn goddess) and Hera
(also his wife), and two brothers, Poseidon
who ruled the sea, and Hades who ruled
the underworld. In the 3rd century BC the
Olympian gods were adopted by the Romans,
who used the Latin names more commonly
known to later European writers. Uranus,
Apollo, and some others remained the same.
Gaea became Tellus; Cronos = Saturn; Zeus
= Jupiter (or Jove); Hera = Juno; Athene
= Minerva; Artemis = Diana; Hermes
= Mercury; Ares = Mars; Hephaestus =
Vulcan; Aphrodite = Venus (and her son Eros
= Cupid); Demeter = Ceres; Poseidon =
Neptune. There were numerous minor deities

such as nymphs and satyrs in both Greek and Roman pantheons.

The Olympian deities mingled with men, and rivalled one another in deciding human destinies. They concerned themselves particularly with the destinies of the heroes, *ie* those men, sometimes partly divine by parentage, who were remarkable for the kinds of excellence which are especially valued in early societies, such as strength (Heracles), or cunning (Odysseus). Each region of Greece had its native heroes, though the greatest heroes were famous in legend all over Greece. The most famous of all was Heracles (in Latin, Hercules) who originated in Thebes. Other leading examples of the hero are: Theseus (Athens); Sisyphus and Bellerophon (Corinth); Perseus (Argolis); the Diocuri, *ie* Castor and Pollux (Laconia); Oedipus (Thebes); Achilles (Thessaly); Jason (Thessaly); Orpheus (Thrace). Like the Greek gods and goddesses, the Greek heroes were adopted by Roman legend, sometimes with a change of name. The minor hero of Greek legend, Aeneas, was raised to be the great ancestral hero of the Romans, and they had other heroes of their own, such as Romulus, the founder of Rome, and his brother Remus.

After the downfall of the Roman Empire of the West, classical deities and heroes achieved a kind of popular reality through the planets and zodiacal signs which are named after them, and which, according to astrologers, influence human fates. Otherwise their survival has depended chiefly on their importance in the works of the classical poets, such as Homer, Hesiod, Virgil and Ovid, who have meant so much to European culture. In Britain, important poets translated and thus helped to 'naturalize' the Greek and Latin poems; *eg* John Dryden (1631–1700) in the 17th century translated Virgil's *Aeneid*; and Alexander Pope (1688–1744) in the 18th century translated Homer's epics. In the 16th and 17th centuries, poets used major and minor classical deities to adorn and elevate poems intended chiefly as gracious entertainment, and occasionally they added deities of their own invention.

While European culture was understood as a more or less distinct system of values, the poets used classical deities and heroes deliberately and objectively. In the 19th century, however, the deep disturbance of European beliefs and values caused European writers to use classical myth more subjectively, as symbols through which they tried to express their personal doubts, struggles, and beliefs. Thus John Keats in the unfinished epic ▷ *Hyperion* to emulate Milton's great Christian epic, ▷ *Paradise Lost*, but instead of Christian myth he used the war of the Olympian gods and the Titans to embody his sense of the tragedy of human experience. ▷ Tennyson wrote dramatic monologues in which personifications of Greek heroes (*eg* Ulysses, Tithonus, Tiresias in eponymous poems) recounted the experiences associated with them in classical (or, in the case of Ulysses, medieval) legend, in such a way as to express the emotional conflicts of a man from the ▷ Victorian age like Tennyson himself.

▷ Greek literature; Latin literature.

Cobbett, William (1762–1835)

Journalist and political leader of the working class, especially of the rural labourer. The son of a small farmer and self-educated, he remained identified with country pursuits and interests; he was always a peasant, but a fully articulate one. The work by which he is especially known is ▷ *Rural Rides*, an account of tours through England on horseback, written for the enlightenment of a working-class public, and published between 1820 and 1830 in his periodical ▷ *Political Register*, which he edited from 1802 until his death. The *Rides* are famous for their racy, vigorous description of the countryside. His language is always clear, plain and lively; in an autobiographical fragment he declares that his first inspiration in the writing of prose was the work of Jonathan Swift (1667–1745), though he is completely without Swift's ironical suavity. His next most famous work is his *Advice to Young Men* (1829); his *Grammar of the English Language* (1818) is an outstanding guide to the writing of vigorous English.

Apart from the still appreciated vividness of his writings, Cobbett has remained a hero of forthright, independent political journalism. When he was in America (1792–1800) his *Porcupine's Gazette* and various pamphlets were in defence of Britain against the prejudices of the newly independent Americans; once back in England, he refused offers of government patronage, and though he started his *Political Register* in support of the Tories, then in power, in a few years he moved over to radical opposition, and spent two years in prison. In 1832 he was elected Member of Parliament in spite of his refusal to use the corrupt methods for influencing electors common at the time; in Parliament he went into opposition to the Whig government as an extreme left radical. He was excessively quarrelsome and prejudiced, but also exceedingly brave and eloquent in support of the cause of justice as, at any given time, he saw it.

▷ Paine, Thomas; Whig and Tory.
Bib: Cole, G. D. H., *Life; Opinions of William Cobbett*; Lobban, J. H. (ed.), *Rural Rides*, Hughes, A. M. D., *Selections*; Hazlitt, W., in *Spirit of the Age*; Carlyle, E. I., *Cobbett*; Wilson, D. A., *Paine and Cobbett: The Transatlantic Connection*.

Cobbold, Elizabeth (c 1764–1824)

Poet. Cobbold was a northern poet, spending most of her life in Liverpool and Manchester. She began publishing when she was nineteen with *Poems on Various Subjects* (1783), and followed this with *Six Narrative Poems* (1787). The poetry is bold and energetic, but the subject matter simply repeats the conventional interest in the mysterious and exotic. Her fascination with the sensational continued in her novel *The Sword, or Father Bertrand's History of His Own Times* (1791), a ▷ medieval romance which was published under her married name, Clarke. Her first marriage was to last only six months, but she soon met and in 1792 married John Cobbold, a wealthy Liverpool brewer. Her writing continued and she published several pieces of poetry including an ode on the Battle of ▷ Waterloo. Perhaps, however, her most interesting work is *The Mince Pye* (1800), a satire of contemporary ▷ nationalistic feeling. In this later work the energies of her youthful poetry remain, but are directed with a sharp and intelligent wit.

▷ Gothic novels.

Coleridge, Hartley (1796–1849)

Poet and miscellaneous author. Hartley was the disreputable son of ▷ Samuel Taylor Coleridge and is generally considered to have squandered his talents and artistic inheritance. His father wrote two poems about him: ▷ *Frost at Midnight* and *The Nightingale*. Hartley's own *Songs and Sonnets* (▷ sonnet) were published in 1833 to some acclaim, and his editions of the plays of Ford and Massinger, and Ascham's *The Scholemaster* (▷ Renaissance) are well thought-out. He spent the last part of his life in the Lake District and several of his personal effects may still be seen at Dove Cottage.
Bib: Hartman, H., *Hartley Coleridge: poet's son and poet*.

Coleridge, Samuel Taylor (1772–1834)

Poet and critic. Son of a Devon clergyman, he was educated in London and at Jesus College Cambridge. He left Cambridge to enlist in the Dragoons under the pseudonym Silas Tomkyn Comberbache, and although he returned after a matter of months he never completed his degree. His early religious leanings were towards Unitarianism. In 1794 he made the acquaintance of ▷ Robert Southey, with whom, under the influence of the ▷ French Revolution, he evolved a communistic scheme which they called ▷ 'Pantisocracy', and together they wrote the tragedy, *The Fall of Robespierre*. In 1795 he married Sara Fricker, Southey marrying her sister. His *Poems on Various Subjects* were published in 1796, at about the time he met ▷ Wordsworth. The two poets became friends, and lived close to each other for a time in Somerset. ▷ *Kubla Khan* and the first part of ▷ *Christabel* were written at this period, though they were not published until later. The joint publication, ▷ *Lyrical Ballads*, which included Coleridge's ▷ *The Rime of the Ancient Mariner*, appeared in 1798. Coleridge expressed his loss of faith in the French Revolution in *France, An Ode* (1798).

In 1798–9 he travelled in Germany and came under the influence of the transcendental philosophy of Schlegel and ▷ Kant, which dominates his later theoretical writing. During 1800–4 he moved near to Wordsworth in Keswick, and fell unhappily in love with his sister-in-law, Sarah Hutchinson, a relationship referred to in ▷ *Dejection: An Ode* (1802). Early in his life he had become reliant on opium and never succeeded in fully controlling the addiction. He began to give public lectures and became famous for his table talk. In 1809 he founded a periodical, *The Friend*, which was later published as a book (1818). In 1817 appeared ▷ *Biographia Literaria*, his autobiographical apologia and a landmark in literary theory and criticism. He quarrelled with Wordsworth in 1810, and in later life he lived in the homes of various benefactors, including the surgeon, James Gillman, who helped him to cope with his addiction. He became increasingly Tory in politics and Anglican in religion, developing an emotionalist conservatism in the tradition of Burke.

Coleridge's poetic output is small, diverse, but of great importance. His ▷ 'conversation poems', such as *Frost at Midnight* (1798), *This Lime-Tree Bower, My Prison* (1800), continue and deepen the reflective tradition of Gray and Cowper, culminating in the poignant *Dejection: An Ode* (1802). On the other hand his major symbolic works, such as *The Rime of the Ancient Mariner* (1798), *Kubla*

Khan (1816) and *Christabel* (1816), plumb new psychological and emotional depths, and can be seen to develop along similar lines as his famous theoretical definition of imagination in *Biographia Literaria*, Chapter XIII. His perspectives are consistently more intellectually alert than those of his friend Wordsworth, though the expression of his philosophical ideas is sometimes confused. His sympathetic but discriminating analysis of Wordsworth's work in *Biographia Literaria* is a model of unfussy analytical method. As both practitioner and theorist, Coleridge is central to ▷ Romanticism.

▷ Coleridge, Hartley

Bib: House, H., *Coleridge*; Lowes, J. L., *The Road to Xanadu*; Coburn, K., *In Pursuit of Coleridge*; Holmes, R., *Coleridge*; Jackson, J. R. de J. (ed.), *Coleridge: The Critical Heritage*; Jones, A. R., and Tydeman, W., *Coleridge: The Ancient Mariner and Other Poems* (Macmillan Casebook); Fruman, N., *Coleridge: The Damaged Archangel*; Cooke, K., *Coleridge*; Hamilton, P., *Coleridge's Poetics*; Wheeler, K. M., *The Creative Mind in Coleridge's Poetry*; Sultana, D. (ed.), *New Approaches to Coleridge*; Magnuson, P., *Coleridge's Nightmare Poetry*; Holmes, R., *Coleridge: Early Visions*.

Collins, William (1721–59)

Poet. The son of a hatter in Chichester, he published his *Persian Eclogues* in 1742 while he was still an undergraduate at Oxford. Their elegant exoticism and musical use of the pentameter couplet (▷ metre) made them popular, and they were reissued in 1757 as *Oriental Eclogues*. However his *Odes on Several Descriptive and Allegorical Subjects* (1746), which includes much of his best work, achieved little success at the time. The romantic *Ode on the Popular Superstitions of the Highlands of Scotland Considered as a Subject of Poetry* was written about 1749 but not published until 1788. In 1750 he suffered a mental breakdown and wrote no more verse before his death nine years later in Chichester. Collins's small output shows a fragile combination of exquisite classical control and intense lyricism. In such poems as *Ode* ('How sleep the Brave'), *To Evening* and *The Passions* he develops his own distinctive rococo idiom, involving the constant use of pretty personifications and classical abstraction, reminiscent of the friezes on Wedgewood pottery. His rhythms and tone are peculiarly original, and often quite haunting, though the influence of ▷ Thomas Gray, James Thomson and ▷ John Milton is often evident.

Bib: Johnson, S., *Lives of the Poets*; Garrod, H. W., *Collins*; Carver, P. L., *The Life of a Poet: A Biographical Sketch of William Collins*.

Colman, George, the Elder (1732–94)

Dramatist, essayist, theatre manager. He controlled first Covent Garden, and then the Haymarket Theatre and was responsible for staging the earliest productions of Oliver Goldsmith's (1730–74) plays, as well as writing dozens of plays, masques, and operas himself. He began writing poetry while still a pupil at Westminster School, and after receiving a degree at ▷ Oxford University and being called to the bar, he still retained his literary interests. Through his friendship with the actor David Garrick (1717–79), he became involved in the theatre, and eventually abandoned law as a career. In 1760 his first play, the farcical *Polly Honeycombe*, billed as 'a dramatic novel', was produced at ▷ Drury Lane. Six years later he collaborated with Garrick on ▷ *The Clandestine Marriage*, his most successful work.

After inheriting a fortune from his mother, Colman purchased a major interest in the Covent Garden Theatre which came under his joint management in 1767. Among his ventures there were productions of Goldsmith's *The Good-Natur'd Man*, and *She Stoops to Conquer*. In 1776 Colman acquired the Little Theatre in the Haymarket, where in 1781 he successfully staged John Gay's (1685–1732) *The Beggar's Opera* (1728), with women cast as the men and vice versa.

▷ Colman, George, the Younger.

Bib: Burnim, K. A., *The Plays of George Colman the Elder*; Wood, E. R. (ed.), *The Plays of David Garrick and George Colman the Elder*.

Colman, George, the Younger (1762–1836)

Dramatist, miscellany writer, and theatre manager. Son of ▷ George Colman, the elder. He was educated at Westminster School, and at Oxford, like his father. Again like his father, he was intended for the law, but preferred the stage, and had a musical farce, *The Female Dramatist*, produced at the Haymarket Theatre in 1782. In 1784 he underwent a clandestine marriage with the actress Clara Morris, of whom his father disapproved, and re-married her in open ceremony in 1788. In 1789, his father having been stricken with paralysis, and suffering from mental deterioration, he took over management of the Little Theatre in the Haymarket. He proved an effective manager, despite a penchant for personal extravagance which, among other factors, involved him in a series of quarrels and lawsuits. As a dramatist

he was prolific, contributing more than 20 plays and musical entertainments, including several which became firm favourites, such as the comic opera, *Inkle and Yarico* (1787). In 1824 he was appointed Examiner of Plays, a title he retained to his death. He proved a fastidious censor, excising all supposedly blasphemous and indecent references, even though some of his own productions skirted close to the margins of propriety.
Bib: Tasch, P. A. (ed.), *The Plays of George Colman the Younger*, Sutcliffe, B. (ed.), *Plays by George Colman the Younger and Thomas Morton*.

Combe, William (1741–1823)
Humorist, prose writer and poet. Combe is associated with the cult of the ▷ Picturesque through his most well-known works. In 1790 he published *The Devil Upon Two Sticks*, a continuation of the French comic author Alain-René Lesage's *Le Diable Boiteaux* (1707). This is a witty picturesque narrative which predates the more sentimental ▷ Romantic versions. Some time later, in 1809, he provided the poetry to accompany the comic illustrations of Thomas Rowlandson in the first of the 'Dr Syntax' series, which were crude parodies of the picturesque travel books of the day. They continued this collaboration through three works, finally collected as *The Three Tours of Dr Syntax* (1826). Syntax is a clergyman and a school teacher who is confronted with a series of strange and grotesque events which leave him open to ridicule. The character of Syntax was based on the author ▷ William Gilpin.
▷ French literature in England.
Bib: Hamilton, H.W., *Doctor Syntax: a silhouette of Combe*.

Comte, Auguste (1798–1857)
French philosopher. He sought to expound a scientifically based philosophy for human progress called Positivism, which deduced laws of development from the facts of history and excluded metaphysics and religion. His chief works were translated into English. In them he sought to establish a system that would be the scientific equivalent of the Catholic system of philosophy. In this he failed, but his work led to the modern science of sociology. In England, his chief disciple was Frederick Harrison (1831–1923). The character of his beliefs suited radically reformist and religiously sceptical English intellectuals; on the other hand, his systematization of ideas was alien to English habits of mind. His emphasis on the science of social phenomena, sociology,

was intended to lay the foundations of a social and political system geared to the new age of industry. This, combined with his vision of an educational role for the priesthood, marks him as an antagonist to the dominant strains of thought in the Romantic period.

Confessions of an English Opium-Eater (1822: enlarged ed. 1856)
An ▷ autobiography, and the most famous work of ▷ Thomas De Quincey. Like ▷ Coleridge, De Quincey began taking opium to ease physical suffering, and eventually increased the dose until he became an addict. The book contains eloquent, prose-poetic accounts of his opium dreams and also graphic descriptions of his life of poverty in London. In the former aspect the prose evokes the high musical rhetoric of the 17th-century masters, such as ▷ John Milton; in the latter, it is typical of the 19th-century mode of transmitting intimate, minute personal experience, resembling the increasingly close-textured psychology of the novel. In his tenderness for and understanding of childhood suffering, De Quincey represents a development that was new in the history of literature, and came to fruition in the ▷ Victorian novelists.

Consciousness
In its most general sense consciousness is synonymous with 'awareness'. In a more specifically ▷ Freudian context it is associated with the individual's perception of reality. For Freud, of course, the impression which an individual has of his or her experience is partial, since awareness is controlled by the processes of the unconscious, which are never recognized in their true form. More recently 'consciousness' has been associated with the ▷ Enlightenment view of individualism, in which the individual is conceived of as being distinct from society, and is also held to be the centre and origin of meaning. Following from this, what distinguishes humanity is its alleged capacity for autonomy, and hence freedom of action. The ▷ Romantic equivalent of this philosophical position is that literature is the expression of the pre-existent 'self' of the writer, and that the greatest literature is that which manifests the writer's consciousness most fully. These views of consciousness should further be distinguished from the ▷ Marxist version, in which the self is 'produced' through 'material practices', by means of which social relations are generated. Theories of consciousness affect notions of the relationship between writer and reader,

and it is in working out such relationships that the concept of 'consciousness' is important in current literary critical debate.

Conversation poem

A reflective poem, usually in ▷ blank verse, in which the poet meditates aloud, ostensibly, talking to a friend. It adopts a more intimate, introspective tone than its predecessor, the 18th-century verse epistle. The term is especially associated with ▷ Samuel Taylor Coleridge, who first used it. His *Eolian Harp* (1795), *This Lime-Tree Bower* (1800), *The Nightingale* (1798) and ▷ *Frost at Midnight* (1798) are often termed 'conversation poems'.

Cornwall, Barry

▷ Proctor, Bryan Waller.

Corsair, The (1814)

A narrative poem in heroic ▷ couplets by ▷ Lord Byron. Conrad, who has become a pirate for some mysterious reason, disguises himself as a dervish in order to gain entry to the palace of the pasha, Seyd. In the fight which ensues he insists that his men must not invade Seyd's harem ('wrong not on your lives/ One female form'), and Seyd's wife Gulnare, described decorously as 'the trembling fair', consequently falls in love with him. All his men are killed and Conrad is thrown into a dungeon to await a slow death next day. Gulnare sets him free, but when he realizes that she has murdered her own husband, Conrad is filled with revulsion. He returns to his island to find that his faithful consort Medora has died in his absence, upon which he himself mysteriously disappears. The poem's self-indulgent blend of escapist adventure, condescending sexism and glamorous exoticism, made it one of the most popular of Byron's poems.

Couplet

A pair of rhymed lines of verse of equal length. The commonest form is the so-called heroic couplet of 10 syllables and 5 stresses in each line. ▷ Blank verse was a derivative of the couplet. ▷ Leigh Hunt's 'Abou Ben Adhem' provides a good example of the couplet:

Abou Ben Adhem (may his tribe increase!)
Awoke one night from a deep dream of peace.

The 8-syllable (octosyllabic) couplet gives a lighter, less stately rhythm. It was used by ▷ Keats for *The Eve of St Mark*:

All was silent, all was gloom,
Abroad and in the homely room;
Down she sat, poor cheated soul!
And struck a lamp from the dismal coal.

Cowley, Hannah (1743–1809)

Poet, novelist and dramatist. The story goes that Cowley began writing plays after being mocked by her husband, who accused her of never actually undertaking any of the projects she planned. The result was thirteen published plays, although since she was very careless of her own writing there may well have been more. Cowley's skill was in comedy and she was adept at turning themes which had centred upon men into plots about women; examples of this gender inversion are *The Belle's Stratagem* (1780) and *A Bold Stroke For a Husband* (1783). Her awareness of the precarious role of the female dramatist is made clear in the ironic prologue to *The Belle's Stratagem*, where a male character complains about the lines she has given him:

> *. . . on affairs of state*
> *I might hold faith – yet in her cursed play,*
> *The deuce a word am I allow'd to say;*
> *Or rather coop'd, like other folks we know,*
> *Between two barren adverbs – Ay and no.*
> *Tis thus we're served, when saucy women*
> *write –*

Cowley also wrote a ▷ Gothic novel, *The Italian Marauders* (1810), and several long poems. In all Cowley's works the heroines are intelligent and independent women, perfectly able to control the situations in which they find themselves.
Bib: Uphaus, R.W. and Foster, G.M., *The 'Other' Eighteenth Century*.

Cowper, William (1731–1800)

Poet and letter-writer. Son of the rector of Great Berkhampstead in Hertfordshire, he was called to the bar in 1754, and through family connections was offered the post of Clerk of the Journals in the House of Lords. However, the early death of his mother, his experiences of bullying at public school and a thwarted love affair, had caused severe neurosis which led him to contemplate suicide at the prospect of the clerkship examination. He spent a year in an asylum and thereafter led a retired life on his own private income, first in the home of Morley and Mary Unwin in Huntingdonshire and then after Morley's death with Mary Unwin in Olney. They planned to marry in 1773, but Cowper's conviction of his own personal damnation prevented this.

In Olney he came under the influence of the evangelical Rev. John Newton with whom he published *Olney Hymns* (1779), including 'Hark my soul! it is the Lord', and 'God moves in a mysterious way'. In 1780 Newton left Olney for London and Cowper's life became less spiritually strenuous. Mary Unwin encouraged him to write, in order to counteract his religious melancholia. His *Poems* (1782) contain *Table Talk*, and eight moral satires in heroic ▷ couplets which, though uneven in quality, display a distinctive unforced sententiousness which is one of his most attractive poetic characteristics. The volume also includes *Boadicea: an Ode* and *Verses supposed to be written by Alexander Selkirk* ('I am monarch of all I survey'). In the same year Cowper published his famous comic ballad *John Gilpin*. He made the acquaintance of Lady Austen, who suggested the scheme of the ▷ mock-heroic, discursive poem ▷ *The Task: A Poem in Six Books*, which appeared in 1785, and is in the more 'natural' medium of ▷ blank verse, rather than couplets. He followed this with an undistinguished translation of ▷ Homer (1791). In 1794 Mary Unwin died, and Cowper's only subsequent work is the introspective and despairing *Castaway*, published after his death, as were his *Letters* (1803), which are among the most famous in the language.

Cowper's work illustrates the movement away from the public themes of ▷ Augustanism towards a more domestic and personal poetry of sensibility. His work eschews brilliance or technical virtuosity, and can be banal. But at their best his ▷ lyrics are delicately moving, and his couplet and blank verse writing achieves an unassuming lucidity of tone, which evokes profound resonances.

▷ Romanticism.
Bib: Cecil, D., *The Stricken Deer*; King, J., *William Cowper: A Biography*; Hutchins, B., *The Poetry of William Cowper*; Priestman, M., *Cowper's Task: Structure and Influence*; Newey, V., *Cowper's Poetry: A Critical Study and Reassessment*.

Crabbe, George (1754–1832)

Poet. Crabbe was born at Aldeburgh in Suffolk and his work is intimately associated with the region. He practised medicine before taking orders in 1781. Crabbe's earliest works, *The Library* (1781) and the anti-pastoral *The Village* (1783) have an heroic ▷ couplet metre and public, discursive tone already distinctly old-fashioned at the time.

Samuel Johnson (1709–84) gave advice on the composition of the second poem, and in his grimly stoical vision of life and his distrust of pretension and excess, Crabbe resembles Johnson in temperament. *The Village* is relentless in its rejection of the conventions of literary pastoralism, showing nature with bitter realism as it was known to the poor. In his later works – *The Parish Register* (1807), *The Borough* (1810), *Tales in Verse* (1812), *Tales of the Hall* (1819) – he depicts the diverse lives of his parishioners in a series of highly original short stories in couplets, a form which he made peculiarly his own. His best work treats social outcasts and extreme psychological states, as do a number of poems by ▷ William Wordsworth. But where Wordsworth's approach is transcendental and contemplative, Crabbe's involvement with his characters is compassionate in a more down-to-earth and intimate way. In ▷ *Peter Grimes* (Letter XXII of *The Borough*) the landscape of coastal East Anglia becomes an evocative symbol for the protagonist's breakdown and despair. Crabbe's narrative artistry, and uncompromising realism were admired by ▷ Jane Austen who remarked half-seriously that he was the only man she could ever think of marrying.
Bib: Crabbe, G. (junior), *Life*; Pollard, A. (ed.), *Crabbe: The Critical Heritage*; Bareham, T., *George Crabbe*; New, P., *George Crabbe's Poetry*.

Craik, Helen (c 1750–1825)

Poet and novelist. A ▷ Scottish writer who was encouraged by ▷ Robert Burns, Craik's poetry is now hardly read and recent criticism has focused upon her ▷ Minerva novels. Her prose writing tends towards the gloomy and fantastic, but her characters are well-drawn and introduce a realistic element into the otherwise far-fetched nature of the narrative. Among her novels are: *Julia de Saint Pierre* (1796), *Henry of Northumberland, or The Hermit's cell* (1800) and *The Nun and Her Daughter* (1805).

▷ Scottish literature in English.

Crotchet Castle (1831)

A novel by ▷ Thomas Love Peacock. The plot is unimportant, and the novel consists mainly of witty talk, burlesquing and satirizing contemporary attitudes and ideas. A crotchet is an eccentric and frivolous notion or prejudice. Some of the characters are representatives of intellectual tendencies, *eg* MacQuedy, a Scots economist whose name suggests 'Q.E.D.' (*quod erat demonstrandum*), stands for the excessive rationalism of the political economists and utilitarians of the age. On the other hand, Mr Skionar stands for the poet, critic and philosopher, ▷ S. T. Coleridge, and burlesques his transcendental mysticism. Mr Chainmail stands for the sentimental cult of the 'Gothic', *ie* the romance and sensationalism of the cult of the Middle Ages, familiar from the historical novels of ▷ Walter Scott and from the ▷ Gothic novels of the previous generation. Sanity is represented by Dr. Folliott, a clergyman, a character of robust and cheerful common sense.

Cultural Materialism

The most important book in the formation of cultural materialism is Jonathan Dollimore and Alan Sinfield's collection of essays *Political Shakespeare* (1985), whose foreword acts as a manifesto for this radical ▷ Marxist criticism. The authors themselves trace the origins of the theory to general dissatisfaction in the British academic world with the traditional essentialist humanism of existing criticism and the rise of numerous alternative approaches (▷ feminism, ▷ structuralism, ▷ psychoanalytic criticism). Apart from a debt to the political commitment to change, derived from Marxism, cultural materialism also draws upon Raymond Williams's cultural analysis which 'seeks to describe the whole system of significations by which a society or a section of it understands itself and its relations with the world' (*Political Shakespeare*). Thus, cultural materialism rejects any notion of 'high culture', and sets material values in the place of the idealism of conventional criticism, looking instead at texts in history. Cultural materialism also has links with ▷ new historicism (particularly the work of Stephen Greenblatt) in its emphasis upon the nature of subjectivity and the decentring of man, and with feminism, where the exploration of the gendered human subject is an overlapping interest. Antagonistic to the (allegedly) ahistorical and dangerously apolitical

conclusions of ▷ deconstruction, a sceptical and combative tone, together with an interest in decentring, is nevertheless common to both, suggesting an increased disillusion with traditional, this is to say, humanist, literary criticism.

Cumberland, Richard (1732–1811)

Dramatist, poet, novelist, translator, essayist, associated with the rise of sentimental domestic comedy on the English stage. He began writing poetry while still a pupil at school in Bury St Edmunds. After further education at Westminster School and ▷ Cambridge University he published his first play, *The Banishment of Cicero* in 1761. Disappointed in his career aspirations in government, he turned to writing for the stage in earnest. He continued this activity even after his political fortunes improved, eventually completing over 50 plays, operas, and adaptations of plays. His first success of any consequence was with the comedy, *The Brothers*, in 1769. In 1770 he wrote his most famous play, generally considered his best, *The West Indian*, which the actor and impresario David Garrick (1717–79) staged in the following year. Even so his work was often under attack for its supposed sentimentality. However, Cumberland was sympathetic to the causes of others, especially outcast and vilified groups. He defended the Jews in *The Jew* (1794), which was translated into several languages, including Yiddish and Hebrew, and remained popular well into the 19th century. *The Jew of Mogadore* (1808) again portrays a Jew in a kindly light, and Cumberland also defended Jews in articles in *The Observer*, written under a Jewish pseudonym. His efforts did much to rescue Jews from the villainous anti-Semitic image hitherto afforded them on the stage. In addition to plays, he wrote two novels, translations of Greek plays, ▷ epic poetry, and pamphlets expressing his views on controversial topics of the day.
Bib: Borkat, R. F. S. (ed.), *The Plays of Richard Cumberland.*

Dacre, Charlotte (c 1782–?)
Novelist and poet. Dacre and her sister, the writer ▷ Sophia King, dedicated their first work *Trifles From Helicon* (1798) to their notorious father, John King, who had just been arrested for bankruptcy. She adopted the name 'Rosa Matilda' when visiting ▷ Rachel Despenser and in publishing her first book *The Confessions of the Nun of St Omer* (1805), which she dedicated to Matthew ▷ 'Monk' Lewis; it was also under this name that ▷ Byron chose to ridicule her. Her most famous work is *Zofloya, or the Moor* (1806), a ▷ Gothic novel indebted to *The Monk*, which supposedly warns against the dangers of lust and passion, though Dacre's obvious fascination in depicting these sentiments belies the stated ▷ didactic purpose. The final scene is a *tour de force* in which the heroine is thrown to her death from a cliff by the devil. *Zofloya* influenced ▷ Shelley's *Zastrozzi* and was published in ▷ chapbook format as *The Daemon of Venice* (1810). Dacre wrote several other novels, poetry, and the lyrics for popular stage songs. No evidence remains as to how she spent her later life.

Dante Alighieri (1265–1321)
Poet and philosopher. Very little is known about the early life of Dante. He was born in Florence, a member of the Guelf family, and married Gemma Donati in 1285. His involvement in Florentine politics from 1295 led in 1300 to his exile from Florence, to which he never returned. He died at Ravenna in 1321. According to his own report, he was inspired throughout his life by his love for Beatrice, a woman who has been identified as Beatrice Portinari (d 1290).

It is difficult to date Dante's work with any degree of precision. The *Vita Nuova* (1290–4) is a lyric sequence celebrating his inspirational love for Beatrice, linked by prose narrative and commentary sections. His Latin treatise *De Vulgari Eloquentia*, perhaps begun in 1303–4 but left unfinished, is a pioneering work of literary and linguistic commentary. Here Dante considers the state and status of Italian as a literary language, and assesses the achievements of earlier French and Provençal poets in elevating the status of their vernacular media. The *Convivio* (1304–7) is an unfinished philosophical work, a 'banquet of knowledge', composed of prose commentaries on allegorical poetic sequences. Dante's political ideas, specifically on the relationship between the Pope, Emperor, and the universal Empire, are explored in *De Monarchia* (c 1310). Dante may not have begun his principal work, the

▷ *Divina Commedia*, until as late as 1314. This supremely encyclopaedic work, which encompasses a discussion of every aspect of human experience, knowledge and belief, recounts the poet's journey, with Virgil as his guide, through Hell and Purgatory and finally, through the agency of Beatrice herself, to Paradise.

▷ Boccaccio (1313–75) composed an account of Dante's life and was the first to deliver a series of public lectures on the text of the *Divina Commedia*, thus confirming the literary authority, prestige and influence of the work and its author. Dante has been read and admired by English poets through the centuries, one of the earliest English translations (of part of the *Inferno*) appearing in 1719. 19th-century poets, especially ▷ Byron and ▷ Shelley, much admired Dante's work and thus revived interest in the ▷ medieval poet.

Darley, George (1795–1846)
Poet, dramatic critic and art historian. Darley was a reclusive Irish author whose sharp dramatic criticism often angered the authors of the plays he reviewed for ▷ *The London Magazine*. As a creative writer, he wrote several volumes of poetry including *Sylvia* (1827), as well as plays. His most famous work is *Nepenthe* (1835) which undertakes an allegorical description of the imagination and which is indebted to ▷ Keats and ▷ Shelley.

▷ Irish literature in English.
Bib: Heath-Stubbs, J., *In His Darkling Plain: a study of the later fortunes of romanticism in English poetry from Darley to W.B. Yeats*; Ridler, A. (ed), *Selected Poems of George Darley*.

Darwin, Erasmus (1731–1802)
Poet and physician; grandfather of the zoologist Charles Darwin (1809–82). He wrote a lengthy poem in grotesquely elaborate ▷ couplets, *The Botanic Garden*, on the subject of the scientific classification of plants (Part II: *The Loves of the Plants*, 1789; Part I: *The Economy of Vegetation*, 1791).
▷ Garden in Romantic literature, The.

Declaration of Independence (1776)
The assertion of independence by the American colonists, starting-point of the United States. It was signed by 13 states. Although the Committee that ordered the drafting of the Declaration included such hard-headed, 18th-century rationalists as Benjamin Franklin, their document (and the Constitution of 1787) may be seen

as essentially Romantic in its idealization of freedom for the individual. The new nation demanded a new literature, and the emergence in the mid-19th-century of a truly American philosophy (promulgated by Emerson) and its corollary in poetry (supplied by Walt Whitman) may be seen as a perpetuation of Romanticism in its hospitality to experience and its emphasis on freedom of conscience, and consciousness.

Decline and Fall of the Roman Empire, The (1776–88)

By ▷ Edward Gibbon; the most eloquent and imposing historical work in the English language. It begins at the height of the Roman Empire in the 1st and 2nd centuries AD – an age with which Gibbon's own era, so deeply imbued with Latin scholarship, felt strong kinship. He then proceeds to record the successive stages of Roman decline, the rise of Christianity, the struggle with the Eastern Roman Empire (the Byzantine) centred on Constantinople (Byzantium), and that empire's eventual extinction by the capture of Constantinople in 1453. As an account, it has of course been somewhat outdated in consequence of later research, but as an imaginative epic (still regarded as substantially true) and an expression of the background to modern Europe as understood in the 18th century, it remains a much read and very important work. Its structure is as spacious as the subject, and is sustained by the energy of Gibbon's style. The attitude is one of 18th-century truth-seeking, and of urbane irony towards the Christian religion, whose growth he sees as one of the agents of destruction of classical civilization. Gibbon's sceptical mind is at the same time constantly critical of human pretensions to self-sufficiency, the attainment of wisdom, and integrity of motive; in such respects he is in the tradition of the great satirists of his century.

Deconstruction

A concept used in critical theory. It has a long philosophical pedigree, but is usually associated with the work of the French philosopher ▷ Jacques Derrida. It is a strategy applied to writing generally, and to literature in particular, whereby systems of thought and concepts are dismantled in such a way as to expose the divisions which lie at the heart of meaning itself. If interpretation is a process designed to reduce a text to some sort of 'order', deconstruction seeks to undermine the basis upon which that order rests. Deconstruction challenges the notion that all forms of mental and linguistic activity are generated from within an autonomous 'centre', advancing the more disturbing proposition that such centres are themselves to be grasped textually only as rhetorical constructions.

Bib: Derrida, J., *Speech and Phenomena*; *Writing and Difference*; *Of Grammatology*; *Positions*; Norris, C., *Deconstruction: Theory and Practice*.

Defence of Poetry, A (1840)

A prose essay by ▷ Percy Bysshe Shelley written as an 'antidote' to *The Four Ages of Poetry* by ▷ Thomas Love Peacock, which appeared in 1821. Shelley sent his *Defence* to Peacock in the same year, but it was not published until 1840. Peacock had argued that with the growth of scientific knowledge, the primitive metaphorical 'visions' of the poet were out of date: 'A poet in our times is a semi-barbarian in a civilized community'. Poetry only wasted time that would be better spent on 'some branch of useful study'. Shelley answered that poetry is not only useful, but essential, in enlarging 'the social sympathies' of humankind. The 'vitally metaphorical' language of the poet is the key to all morality: 'A man, to be greatly good, must imagine intensely and comprehensively; he must put himself in the place of another and of many others; the pains and pleasures of his species must become his own.' In the aftermath of the failure of the ideals of the ▷ French Revolution, Shelley is eager to envisage a political role for the poet, though inevitably this is expressed in rhetoric of an abstract and ideal kind: 'Poets are the unacknowledged legislators of the world'; 'Poetry is a sword of lightning, ever unsheathed'. However, Shelley's analysis of the totalitarian tendency of Peacock's ▷ utilitarianism anticipates ▷ Marx and post-Marxist thinking. Only 'anarchy and despotism' he asserts, can be expected from 'an unmitigated exercise of the calculating faculty'.

Deism

A form of religious belief which developed in the 17th century as an outcome of the Reformation. Edward Herbert (1583–1648) evolved the idea that, while the religion revealed in the Gospels was true, it was preceded by ▷ 'natural' religion, according to which by his own inner light a man could perceive all the essentials of religious truth. Herbert's deism was further expounded in the 18th century by others (often in such a way as to suggest that the Christian revelation as presented in the Gospels was redundant), and it suited the 18th-century cool and rational habit of mind which tended to see God as abstract and remote. Bishop Butler among the theologians and Hume and ▷ Kant among the philosophers, exposed the unsoundness of deistic arguments in the 18th century, and in the 19th century the growth of the genetic sciences demolished the basic assumptions of deism, *ie* that human nature and human reason have always been constant, in a constant environment.

▷ Blake, William.

Dejection: An Ode (1802)

A poem by ▷ Samuel Taylor Coleridge. The earliest version was addressed to Sara Hutchinson ('O Sara'), with whom the unhappily married Coleridge was in love. In a subsequent version this becomes 'O Wordsworth', and in the published text Sara is reinstated, but anonymously ('O Lady'). As these changes suggest, the poem reflects a complex personal unhappiness, but it was also influenced by ▷ William Wordsworth's expression of flagging inspiration in the first part of the ▷ *Immortality Ode*, written at this time. Coleridge watches a beautiful sunset, but finds that in his 'wan and heartless mood' the objective beauty of the clouds, stars and moon, inspire no response in him: 'I see them all so excellently fair,/ I see, not feel, how beautiful they are!' He reflects on the subjectivity of experience, concluding that 'we receive but what we give/ And in our life alone does Nature live'. He thus rejects the idea of the ministering benevolence of nature which was so important to Wordsworth. It is subjective imagination not objective nature which is the 'shaping spirit'. He is ambiguously cheered by reminiscences from other poets, conjured up by the wind blowing through an ▷ Aeolian harp, and the work ends, as midnight approaches, with a poignantly selfless prayer that his beloved be sleeping, safe from the storm. His love for her restores the meaning which nature had lost, but on a strictly metaphorical level: 'May all the stars hang bright above her dwelling,/ Silent *as though* they watched the sleeping Earth!'

De Loutherbourg, Philip James (Philippe Jacques) (1740–1812)

Painter, set designer, of noble Polish descent. In 1771 after a successful exhibition in Paris De Loutherbourg moved to London, where he met the actor and theatre manager David Garrick (1717–79), and presented him with proposals for co-ordinated improvements to the lighting, scenes, costumes and mechanical effects at ▷ Drury Lane.

Engaged at the theatre, De Loutherbourg 'astonished the audience', according to one observer, by his skilful and innovative use of various translucent coloured silks, lit from behind and mobile, to give changing effects of richness, subtlety, and depth to the sets. His detailed and naturalistic cut-out scenery was likened to fine paintings of contemporary and fantastic views. In 1781 he also became a member of the Royal Academy.

Admired in his day by Thomas Gainsborough (1727–88), De Loutherbourg is now considered one of the most influential designers for the English stage, bringing both imagination and technical abilities to bear, so as to create scenes and spectacles of unprecedented realism and magnificence. Much of his work can be seen as an important early contribution to the ▷ Romantic movement in literature and art.

De Man, Paul (1919–83)

Arguably the most rigorous of the so-called Yale School of criticism, and by the time of his death the foremost exponent in the U.S.A. of ▷ deconstruction as applied to Romantic, and other, poetry. His crucial essay of 1969, 'The Rhetoric of Temporality' (collected in *Blindness and Insight*, 1983) used texts by ▷ Wordsworth, ▷ Coleridge, ▷ Rousseau and others, in order to establish the undoing of Romantic ambition, expressed in ▷ rhetorical terms such as the 'symbol', by what de Man calls 'allegory'. His approach was extended in books such as *Allegories of Reading* (1980) and *The Rhetoric of Romanticism* (1984). De Man reflected on the whole of this process, and upon the resistance to certain sorts of theoretical enquiry, in a collection of essays, *The Resistance to Theory* published posthumously in 1986.

Paul de Man remains a controversial figure, not only because of the nihilistic conclusions of his mature work, but by the rediscovery after his death of certain pieces of 1940s journalism that express hospitality towards the intellectual consequences of Nazi occupation.

Demogorgon

In early Christian mythology, a terrible deity of the underworld; according to ▷ Boccaccio, a primaeval pagan god. In ▷ Shelley's ▷ *Prometheus Unbound* a spiritual principle superseding false gods.

De Quincey, Thomas (1785–1859)
Essayist and critic. Most famous for his
autobiography ▷ *Confessions of an English
Opium-Eater*. His work was mostly for
periodicals and is voluminous, but only a
few pieces are now much read. His strong
points as a writer were his exceptionally
sensitive, inward-turning imagination and his
breadth of understanding. The first produced
not only his autobiography but a fragment
of exceptional literary criticism, 'Knocking
at the Gate in Macbeth'. The English Mail
Coach (1849) and 'Murder Considered as
One of the Fine Arts' (1827) show the quality
of an exceptional psychological novelist. His
second gift produced studies of German
philosophy (▷ Kant, Lessing, Richter) and
able translations of German tales, besides
some original historical criticism. He was very
much a representative of the first generation
of English ▷ Romanticism and as the poets
of that generation found new ranges of
expression for their medium, so De Quincey
expanded the poetic range of prose, partly by
recapturing some of the quality of the early
17th-century prose writers.
Bib: Abrams, M. H., *The Milk of Paradise*;
Barrell, J., *The Infection of Thomas De Quincey:
the Psychopathology of Imperialism*; Clapton,
G. T., *Baudelaire et De Quincey*; Eaton, H. A.,
Life; Jordan, J. E., *Thomas De Quincey, Literary
Critic*; Saintsbury, G., in *Essays in English
Literature*; Sackville-West, E., *A Flame in
Sunlight*; Lindop, G., *The Opium Eater*.

Derrida, Jacques (b 1930)
Although he is primarily a philosopher, the
influence of Derrida's work on the study
of literature has been immense. He is the
originator of a mode of reading known as
▷ 'deconstruction', the major strand in
what is now regarded as the general area
of ▷ post-structuralism. His main works
are *Speech and Phenomena* (trans. 1973), *Of
Grammatology* (trans. 1974), and *Writing
and Difference* (trans. 1978). For Derrida, as
for ▷ Saussure, language is composed of
differences, that is, a series of non-identical
elements which combine with each other
to produce linguistic ▷ signs which are
accorded meaning. Traditionally, this process
is anchored to an organizing principle, a
centre, but Derrida questions this concept
and rejects the idea of a 'presence' in which
authority resides, thereby lifting all restrictions
upon the 'play' of differences. But, in addition
to the idea that language is composed of
'differences', Derrida also deploys the
term '*différance*' to indicate the continual

postponement of 'presence' which is located
in all signifiers. Thus, signs are produced
through a relatively free play of linguistic
elements (difference), but what they signify
can never be fully present since meaning is
constantly 'deferred' (*différance*). Derrida's
influence has been greatest in the U.S.A.
where after his visit to Johns Hopkins and his
teaching at Yale, deconstruction has become
the successor to American new criticism. The
thrust of literary theory in Derrida's writing
bears on the question of literature itself, and
opposes a traditional scholarly attachment to,
and privileging of, poetry. Commissioned as
an essay on Shelley, his piece 'Living On' (in
Bloom (ed.) *Deconstruction and Criticism*, 1979)
rapidly becomes a freewheeling meditation on
death, absence and writing. *Acts of Literature*
(1992) does however collect a number of
essays explicitly concerned with the literary.
▷ Grammatology; De Man, Paul.

**Despenser, Rachel Fanny Antonina
(1773–1829)**
Political writer and autobiographer. Despenser
was an illegitimate child who, on her father's
death, was sent away to a French convent
where she received a ▷ classical education.
She returned to Britain when the ▷ French
Revolution began. Despenser's education
had encouraged her democratic beliefs and
she became one of the more radical writers
of her day. ▷ De Quincey compared her to
▷ Shelley, and ▷ Wordsworth admired her
Essay on Government (1808), which asserted
the rights of women and the lower classes
(▷ Women, Status, of). Her personal life
was, however, more complicated: she had
eloped in 1794 with Matthew Lee, but left
him the following year to pursue her political
endeavours uninterrupted. In 1804 she either
eloped with or was abducted by two brothers
from the Gordon family; the stories vary,
and although a case was brought against
them for abduction they were cleared of the
accusation. Despenser subsequently retired to
the country to escape public hostility resulting
from the trial. She retaliated by publishing
her own version of events, *Vindication* in 1807.
Her *Memoirs* (c 1812) reveal an increasingly
unstable mentality and her developing
paranoia led her to accuse her family of
attempted murder.

Diaries
As a form of literature in English, diaries began
to be significant in the 17th century. The spirit
of criticism from the ▷ Renaissance and the
stress on the individual conscience from

the Reformation combined with the political and social turbulence of the 17th century to awaken people to a new awareness of personal experience and its possible interest for general readers. The private nature of the diary form also led to many women taking up this form of writing. Thus the art of the diary arose with the art of biography and ▷ autobiography. Diaries may first be divided into the two classes of those clearly meant to be strictly private and those written more or less with an eye to eventual publication. A further division may be made between those which are interesting chiefly as a record of the time in which the writer lived and those which are mainly a record of his personality. In the 18th and early 19th century the most famous diary is that of the novelist ▷ Fanny Burney, considered as a record of the time ingenuously imbued with her own personality. The diary of the great religious reformer ▷ John Wesley is comparable to that of Fox as a spiritual record, with a wider outlook on his time. In the 19th century the diaries of Thomas Creevey (1768–1838) and Charles Greville (1794–1865) are famous as records of public affairs, and that of ▷ Henry Crabb Robinson for impressions of the leading writers who were his friends.

Dibdin, Charles (1745–1814)
Song-writer, dramatist and actor. Dibdin the elder is best known for his popular songs about the sea and his ▷ dramatic monologues. He also wrote an ▷ autobiography, *The Professional Life of Mr Dibdin* (1803), which contains interesting details about life in the theatre at the time and which includes transcriptions of 600 fashionable songs. One of his sons followed him into the world of entertainment, Charles Dibdin (1768–1833), who became a dramatist. His nephew ▷ Thomas Dibdin was the renowned bibliographer.

Dibdin, Thomas Frognall (1776–1847)
Bibliographer. The nephew of the actor and song-writer ▷ Charles Dibdin, Thomas had a very different career. He was the librarian to Lord Spencer of Althorp, the first secretary of the ▷ Roxburghe Club, and an erudite bibliographer. His most important works include *Bibliomania* (1809), *Bibliophobia* and *Reminiscences of a Literary Life* (1836). As the secretary of the Roxburghe Club he also supervised the editing and reissue of a number of important literary works, mainly from the ▷ Renaissance period.

Didactic literature
Literature designed to teach, or to propound in direct terms a doctrine or system of ideas. In practice, it is not always easy to identify; so much literature is didactic in intention but not in form; sometimes writers renounce didactic intentions but in practice use didactic forms. The Romantic poets of the early 19th century (▷ Wordsworth, ▷ Coleridge, ▷ Shelley, ▷ Keats) reacted against the 18th-century Augustans (▷ Augustanism), and since then there has been a persistent prejudice against explicit didacticism. In fact much of Wordsworth (*eg* ▷ *The Excursion*, 1814) and of Shelley (*eg* ▷ *Queen Mab*, 1813) was highly didactic, though the undisguised passion to some extent conceals the fact.

Difference
A term introduced by ▷ Ferdinand de Saussure in his study of linguistics and used in literary theory. It is the means whereby value is established in any system of linguistic signs whether it be spoken or written. Saussure's *Course in General Linguistics* (1915) argues that in speech it is 'the phonetic contrasts' which permit us to distinguish between one word and another that constitute meaning. In writing the letters used to form words are arbitrary ▷ signs, and their values are therefore 'purely negative and differential' (Saussure). The result is that the written sign becomes important only insofar as it is different from other signs within the overall system of language. The notion of difference as a principle of opposition has been extended beyond the limits of structuralist thinking laid down by Saussure. For example, the ▷ Marxist philosopher Mikhail Bakhtin in a critique of Saussurean ▷ structuralism argued that 'the forms of signs are conditioned above all by the social organization of the participants involved and also by the immediate conditions of their interaction' (*Marxism and The Philosophy of Language*; 1930). Thus the clash of opposites through which meaning and value emerge is determined by the social positions of those who use the language. This means that secreted at the very heart of the form of the linguistic sign is a series of dialectical opposites whose interaction refracts the struggle taking place within the larger framework of society itself. For Bakhtin these oppositions can be defined in terms of the struggle between social classes, but the dialectical structure of these conflicts makes the notion of difference suitable for any situation which can be analysed in terms of

binary opposites. For example, for ▷ feminism this would be an opposition between 'masculine' and 'feminine' as the basis upon which sexual identity is constructed. ▷ Jacques Derrida has adapted the term to form the neologism '*différance*', which denotes the deferral of meaning whereby no sign can ever be brought into direct alignment with the object that it purports to recall. This means that meaning is always *deferred*, and can never be final.

Discourse

A term in critical theory. Especially in the writings of ▷ Michel Foucault, 'discourse' is the name given to the systems of linguistic representations through which power sustains itself. For Foucault discourse manifests itself only through concrete examples operating within specific areas of social and institutional practice. He argues that within individual discourses a series of mechanisms are used as means of controlling desire and power, which facilitate 'classification . . . ordering [and] distribution' (Foucault). In this way a mastery is exerted over what appears to be the randomness of everyday reality. It is thus possible to investigate those discourses which have been used to master reality in the past *eg* discourses concerned with questions of 'sexuality', criminality and judicial systems of punishment, or madness, as Foucault's own work demonstrates.

Bib: Foucault, M., *The Order of Things*; *Power/Knowledge: Selected Interviews and Other Writings* (ed. C. Gordon).

Dissociation of Sensibility

A critical expression made famous by T.S. Eliot (1888–1965), and used in his essay *The Metaphysical Poets* (1921), included in his *Selected Essays*). He states: 'In the seventeenth century a dissociation of sensibility set in, from which we have never recovered; and this dissociation . . . was aggravated by the influence of the two most powerful poets of the century, ▷ Milton and Dryden.' Eliot's argument is that before 1660 poets, in particular the Metaphysical poets, were 'engaged in the task of trying to find the verbal equivalent for states of mind and feeling', and that after that date 'while the language became more refined, the feeling became more crude'. Poetry, henceforward, is put to more specialized purposes: ▷ Tennyson and Browning are poets, and they think; but they do not feel their thought as immediately as the odour of a rose. A thought to Donne was an experience;

'it modified his sensibility.' The implication behind the argument is that poets (with exceptions) ceased to bring all their faculties to bear upon their art: 'Racine or Donne looked into a good deal more than the heart. One must look into the cerebral cortex, the nervous system, and the digestive tracts.'

The theory has had great influence. Those who uphold it support it with the evidence provided by the rise of modern prose after 1660, and the gradual displacement of poetry from its centrality in literature thereafter; poetry either subjected itself to the rational discipline of prose, or, in the 19th century, it tended to cultivate areas of feeling to which this rational discipline was not relevant. However, the theory has been attacked for various reasons. Eliot himself came to feel that he had used the expression in too simplified a way, and that the causes of the process were more complicated than his earlier essay had implied. Eliot's relative lack of enthusiasm for Romantic literature was also largely shared by his generation of Modernist poets and critics, and the reassessment of Romanticism in a positive light would only begin in the post-1945 period. It has been suggested that such a dissociation did not happen; or that it happened in different ways at different periods; or that, if it did happen, no deterioration in imaginative writing can be attributed to it. See Frank Kermode, *Romantic Image* and F. W. Bateson in *Essays in Criticism*, vol. 1.

***Divina Commedia* (*Divine Comedy*)**

The principal work of the Italian poet ▷ Dante (for an account of its contents, see his entry).

Bib: Cunningham, G. F., *The Divine Comedy in English, 1090–1966*; Sinclair, J. N. (trans.), *The Divine Comedy*.

Don Juan

The hero of legends from various European countries. His exploits were the subject of the Spanish play *El Burlador de Sevilla* by Tirso de Molina (1571–1641), who gave him his distinctive character of sensual adventurer. Plays and stories were woven round him in French and Italian, and he is the protagonist of an opera by Mozart (*Don Giovanni*). In English literature by far the most important work about him is the satirical epic ▷ *Don Juan* (1819–24) by ▷ Lord Byron.

***Don Juan* (1819–24)**

▷ Lord Byron's unfinished satirical epic in ▷ *ottava rima*, based very freely on the legendary figure of ▷ Don Juan. After a love affair in Spain (Canto I), Juan is sent abroad by his mother, but is shipwrecked and washed ashore on a Greek island where he is cared for by a Greek maiden, Haidee. Cantos III and IV describe their love and the destruction of their relationship by Haidee's pirate father, Lambro. In Canto V Juan has been sold as a slave to a Turkish princess who loves him; and in Cantos VI, VII and VIII he escapes and serves the Russian army against the Turks in the siege of Ismail. In Canto IX he attracts the attention of the Russian Empress, Catherine the Great, who in Canto X sends him on a mission to England, the setting for Cantos XI–XIII. Juan's affair with a duchess, and his deeper emotion for an English Catholic girl, are used as foci for a free-ranging satire on contemporary society. Juan has fewer mistresses in Byron's poem than in earlier versions of the legend, and is portrayed essentially as an *ingénu*, more often seduced by women than the seducer. The story-line is however subordinated to the philosophizing commentary of the poet himself, which ranges from flippant witticism ('What men call gallantry, and gods adultery,/ Is much more common where the climate's sultry'), through the moving rhetoric of the inserted lyric 'The isles of Greece', to harsh satire on 'the best of cutthroats', the Duke of Wellington ('And I shall be delighted to learn who,/ Save you and yours, have gain'd by Waterloo?'). The greatness of the poem derives from its flexible and informal metrical form which, unlike the ▷ Spenserian stanzas of ▷ *Childe Harold's Pilgrimage* and the couplets of his verse tales, allows Byron to give full expression to his complex and contradictory personality.

D'Orsay, Alfred Guillaume Gabriel, Count (1801–52)

Artist and dandy. A Frenchman who came under the patronage of ▷ Marguerite, Countess of Blessington, with whose entourage he travelled on the continent, meeting ▷ Byron, of whom he made a now famous pencil sketch.

Dramatic monologue

A poetic form in which the poet invents a character, or, more commonly, uses one from history or legend, and reflects on life from the character's standpoint. The dramatic monologue is a development from the ▷ conversation poem of ▷ Coleridge and ▷ Wordsworth, in which the poet reflects on life from his own current situation.

Drury Lane Theatres

The first was an old riding school in Bridges Street, converted by Thomas Killigrew to form the original Theatre Royal, Drury Lane, also known as the King's Theatre.

In 1682 the King's Company was absorbed by the Duke's, and the resulting United Company continued to stage plays at Drury Lane, and the larger spectacles and operas at Dorset Garden. After a difficult period under Christopher Rich, the theatre prospered with Colley Cibber, Robert Wilks, Thomas Doggett (c 1670–1721), and various other managers jointly in charge, and then again under ▷ David Garrick, who took over in 1747.

In 1776, upon Garrick's retirement, Drury Lane was taken over by ▷ Sheridan, who continued to run it until its destruction by fire in 1809. The present theatre opened in 1812.

Dyer, John (?1709–58)

Poet and painter. Born in Carmarthenshire, Dyer studied painting under Jonathan Richardson and visited Italy in 1724–5. In 1741 he entered the church. His most important work, *Grongar Hill* (1727), is a topographical landscape poem in the tradition of Sir John Denham's *Cooper's Hill* (1642) and Alexander Pope's *Windsor-Forest* (1713), but its fluent use of tetrameter rather than pentameter (▷ metre) couplets gives it a lyrical *élan* all of its own. Moreover Dyer's painterly eye leads him to focus, in a most original way, on the transient visual effects which succeed each other as he climbs up from the valley of the Towy. Dyer's feeling for the picturesque, rooted in his study of the paintings of Claude and Poussin, was influential on later poetry until well into the Romantic period. In 1740 appeared *The Ruins of Rome*, and in 1757 *The Fleece*, long discursive and didactic poems in Miltonic ▷ blank verse. The second emulates the example of John Philips's *Cyder* (1708), in its celebration of British scenery and British industry. It attempts to encompass all aspects of the wool trade, from the techniques of sheep-farming, modern and ancient, to the growing prosperity of Leeds and Sheffield and the growth of trade which promises to distribute British woollen manufactures 'over the whole globe'.

▷ Picturesque.

Bib: Humphrey, B., *John Dyer*.

E

Edgeworth, Maria (1767–1849)
Novelist. Her tales are commonly set in
Ireland. Her work is minor but still read for
its vivacity, good sense and realism. *Castle
Rackrent* (1800) and *The Absentee* (1812) are
two of her works still in print. She was also
an excellent writer for children (see *Tales* ed.
by Austin Dobson). She collaborated with
her father, a noted educationist, in *Practical
Education* (1798), influenced by the French-
Swiss thinker ▷ Rousseau. She was admired
by ▷ Jane Austen, William Thackeray
(1811–63) and ▷ Walter Scott, whom she
influenced. She has recently been re-evaluated
by ▷ feminist critics as a liberal contributor to
women's social history. In her satirical *Letters
for Literary Ladies* (1795) she parodies those
men who opposed the education of women
(▷ Women, education of), and in 'Letter from
a Gentleman to his friend upon the birth of a
daughter' she writes:

> *Literary ladies will, I am afraid, be losers
> in love as well as in friendship, by their
> superiority – . . . gentlemen are not apt to
> admire a prodigious quantity of learning and
> masculine acquirements in the fair sex.*

Bib: Clarke, I. C., *Life*; Newby, P. H., *Maria
Edgeworth*; Butler, M. S., *Maria Edgeworth*.

Edinburgh Review
A quarterly periodical founded by ▷ Francis
Jeffrey, Sydney Smith and ▷ Henry Brougham
in 1802. It introduced a new seriousness
into literary criticism and generally took a
moderate ▷ Whig position in politics. Jeffrey's
literary taste was rigidly classicist and he
had little sympathy with the 'Lake Poets',
▷ William Wordsworth, ▷ Samuel Taylor
Coleridge and ▷ Robert Southey. The term
originates in the *Edinburgh Review*, Oct. 1807.
    ▷ Augustanism; *Blackwood's Magazine*.

Education
Until the later 19th century, upper-class
education was commonly pursued for the
general cultivation of the mind and manners;
it included knowledge of the ancient cultures
and the arts; increasingly, it required travel.
The lower a boy (or a girl) stood in the social
scale, the more practical and vocational his
training had to be. It was not, however, until
the reign of Queen Anne (1702–14) that
much was done, apart from the increasingly
expensive apprenticeship system, for the really
poor. In that reign, the Church of England
began the establishment of large numbers
of Charity Schools which, by the end of
the reign, were giving free or nearly free
elementary education to about 25,000 children
throughout England. The education included
religious instruction. At the end of the 18th
century, children in industrial areas were
employed so extensively in factories that even
charity schools were not available to them.
For such children, after 1780, there were
the Sunday Schools, which again were partly
religious and partly concerned to inculcate the
beginnings of literacy and numbers.

The Dissenting Academies were started
by the large minority of the English Puritans,
who came to be called Dissenters or
Nonconformists in the 18th century, because
they 'dissented from', or refused to conform
with, the Thirty-nine Articles of Anglican
belief, and were thus excluded both from the
universities and from most of the grammar
and public schools. The Academies were
often of high quality, since it was natural
to the earnestness of the Dissenting mind
to take education with deep seriousness.
Since the Dissenters were particularly strong
among the commercial classes, the tendency
of their education was more scientific and
technical than that of the public schools and
the universities, and capable of throwing up a
major scientist.

The distinction of the Dissenting Academies
was the more noticeable because the
universities were in a state of decadence.
The historian ▷ Gibbon describes in his
▷ autobiography the complete indifference
of the ▷ Oxford authorities to whether he
was present or absent as a student, although
they awoke into indignation and expelled him
when he underwent his temporary conversion
to Catholicism. Both universities developed
fine schools of mathematics in the 17th
century, and ▷ Cambridge produced the most
distinguished scientist of the age in ▷ Isaac
Newton (1642–1727), but the intellectual
complacency which was characteristic of
the weaker side of 18th-century civilization
reduced them to apathy as teaching centres.
The young men of fashion who attended them
often learned more from the Grand Tour of
Europe which they made after, or sometimes
instead of, their university careers, in the
company of a tutor.

In the 19th century, partly owing to
the breakdown of sectarian restrictions
in education, much of which was under
Dissenting control, partly owing to the
establishment of the non-denominational
universities, the Dissenting Academies
declined. However, the ▷ Industrial

Revolution brought into being a new class of skilled worker: the 'mechanic' of the iron, steel and engineering industries. Such men needed brains for their skills, and their natural intelligence caused them to seek further education to advance their knowledge. This was provided by the growth of the voluntarily established Mechanics' Institutes. They began in ▷ Scotland, where education in general, since the Reformation, was more widely extended and popularly sought than in England. It was the Scottish lawyer, statesman, and man of letters, ▷ Henry Brougham, who brought the movement to England. By 1824, the London Institute had 1,500 artisans subscribing one guinea a year for their instruction, which was conducted in the evenings. It was the beginning of the movement of education in technology which has led to the enormous expansion of technical colleges under the control of local government authorities in the 20th century, especially since 1945.

In the 19th century, however, the state was much more timid in undertaking national systems of education of any sort, and Britain was well behind the most advanced European countries, especially Prussia, in this respect. The principal reason for this slow development was the religious divisions of public opinion. The medieval assumption that education must fundamentally be the concern of the Church has faded very slowly in England. Even today, 'Religious Instruction', taught non-denominationally, is often the only compulsory subject in state schools. The schools for the children of the mass of the people in the first part of the 19th century were controlled by rival Anglican and Dissenting movements: the National Society for the Education of the Poor, and the British and Foreign School Society respectively. Since the Church of England was the established Church of the state, it claimed that it should have a monopoly of religious instruction in any state system, a claim that was strongly resisted by the Dissenters. In 1833, the government for the first time acknowledged some responsibility independent of the Churches by granting a subsidy of £20,000 for school buildings, whichever society chose to build them. But it was not until Forster's Act of 1870 that state education was provided for all at primary level, to the age of 11.

Elegy

An elegy is usually taken to be a poetic lament for one who has died, or at least a grave and reflective poem. In ancient ▷ Greek and ▷ Latin literature, however, an elegy was a poem written in a particular ▷ metre (line of six dactylic feet alternating with lines of five feet) and it had no necessary connection with death or gravity; the Latin poet Ovid used it for love poetry. Most of the famous elegies in English, however, follow the narrower and more widely accepted definition: ▷ Milton's *Lycidas* is inspired by the death of his friend Edward King and ▷ Shelley's ▷ *Adonais* laments that of the poet ▷ Keats; Both of these are in the ▷ pastoral convention, in imitation of a 3rd-century BC Greek elegy called the *Lament of Moschus for Bion*.

Elegy Written in a Country Churchyard (1751)

A poem by ▷ Thomas Gray, in iambic pentameter quatrains, rhyming *abab* (▷ metre). Its quiet subtlety of tone raises the platitudes of conventional graveyard musing to a unique intensity, and several of its eloquent generalizations and phrases have become proverbial: 'Some mute inglorious Milton', 'the madding crowd's ignoble strife', 'Melancholy mark'd him for her own', 'Full many a flower is born to blush unseen,/ And waste its sweetness on the desert air.'

Samuel Johnson (1709–84), though contemptuous of Gray's more inspirational experiments such as the ▷ Pindaric Odes, had high praise for this poem: 'The *Churchyard* abounds with images which find a mirror in every mind, and with sentiments to which every bosom returns an echo.'

▷ Elegy; Sensibility.

Elgin Marbles

Greek statues and friezes, once belonging to the temple of the Parthenon in Athens, by the sculptor Pheidias (5th century BC). They are now in the British Museum and were brought to England by Thomas Bruce, Earl of Elgin. He was British ambassador in Constantinople from 1799 to 1802 and it was then that he conceived the purpose of removing them. He was accused of vandalism and defended himself in the pamphlet *Memorandum on the Earl of Elgin's Pursuits in Greece* (1810). The collection was purchased by the nation for £36,000 and placed in the museum in 1816. Lord Elgin had spent over £50,000 on removing them. They are amongst the finest sculptures in Europe and made a deep impression on contemporary artists and poets, especially ▷ John Keats and his friend Haydon. ▷ Byron expresses his indignation at Elgin's action in ▷ *Childe Harold* (II, st.11–15). The Greek nation continues to demand their return.

Elia

▷ *Essays of Elia*.

Elizabethan period of English literature

The term 'Elizabethan' is used confusingly in regard to literature.

1 It is generally applied accurately to the lyric poetry and prose (*eg* Elizabethan novels) which flowered during the reign of Elizabeth I and especially during the last half of it.

2 On the other hand the term 'Elizabethan drama' is sometimes made to cover not only the beginnings of the great poetic drama (roughly 1588–1600) but also the greater period that succeeded this in the reign of James I and even to include the period of its final decline under Charles I, *ie* until the closing of the theatres in 1642. But critics usually distinguish the mature phase as ▷ Jacobean and the decline as Caroline. By this more accurate designation, an Elizabethan dramatist would be such as Christoper Marlowe (1564–93) and the early ▷ Shakespeare; the Jacobean drama would include mature and late Shakespeare and Webster (1578–1632) and the Caroline drama, the later work of John Ford (1586–1640) and James Shirley (1596–1666).

3 In literary terminology, 'Elizabethan' has further to be distinguished from Tudor. The Queen was herself the last of the House of Tudor, but Tudor drama, the Tudor lyric, Tudor prose, etc. commonly refer to work during the previous reigns, *ie* between the accession of Henry VII in 1485 and her own accession in 1558.

Elliott, Ebenezer (1781–1849)

Poet. Often called the 'Corn Law Rhymer', Elliott is best known for his political poetry, especially his attack upon unpopular Corn Laws in *Corn Law Rhymes* (1830). *The Village Patriarch* (1829) was another work which attempted to raise social consciousness with its description of a poverty-stricken old man. He was admired by Thomas Carlyle (1795–1881). Bib: Briggs, A., *Ebenezer Elliott, the Corn Law Rhymer*.

Emma (1816)

A novel by ▷ Jane Austen. The heroine, Emma Woodhouse, has wealth, social prestige, good looks and intelligence. But her good fortune and the admiration she elicits are in reality her greatest disadvantage: they blind her to the need for self-knowledge and self-criticism. In what she imagines to be pure generosity of heart, she sets about trying to control the fate of her orphan friend of illegitimate birth and insignificant character, Harriet Smith, imagining her to be the daughter of an aristocrat and deserving a marriage socially worthy of her paternity. Later she also becomes involved with a young man, Frank Churchill, who unknown to her is secretly engaged to a girl, Jane Fairfax, who is superior to Emma in talent but much inferior in worldly fortune. Jane Austen is in fact expanding the theme of the way in which romantic fantasy can blind a character to the realities of experience, more overtly used in earlier novels, ▷ *Northanger Abbey* and ▷ *Sense and Sensibility*. Emma, who has imagination and ability but nothing on which to employ them, is first trying to make a real-life novel with Harriet Smith as heroine and then participating in a mysterious drama, which she misconceives as her own fantasy wants it to be, with Jane Fairfax as main protagonist. But Harriet decides that she is to marry the man, George Knightley, with whom Emma herself has long been unconsciously in love; Emma also discovers that Churchill, with whom she has been conducting a flirtation, has merely been using her as a tool to mask his secret engagement. She realizes, in fact, that she has caused herself to be a victim of the first of her romances and has been made to play an ignominious and unworthy role in the second. Duly repentant, Emma is ultimately rewarded by Mr Knightley's proposal of marriage. The novel is perhaps Jane Austen's finest, displaying her irony at its most subtle.

Encyclopaedists

The collaborators in the production of the great French encyclopaedia (▷ *L'Encyclopédie*) of the 18th century. The enterprise began with a translation of the English *Cyclopaedia* by Ephraim Chambers but the French version was intellectually altogether more impressive. Its editors were two leaders of the 'philosophers' – D'Alembert and Diderot – and its contributors were the leading male minds of France, such men as Voltaire (1694–1778) and ▷ Rousseau (▷ French literature in England). The inspiration was faith in reason and the desire to destroy superstition and beliefs thought to arise from it. The movement contributed to the influences which later led to the ▷ French Revolution, and it reinforced rationalism throughout Europe. In England the movement influenced ▷ Jeremy Bentham and through him the ▷ Utilitarians of the 19th century.

Encyclopédie, L'
An encyclopedia published in 35 volumes
between 1751 and 1776, under the editorship
of Diderot (1713–84) and (until 1758) the
mathematician D'Alembert (1717–83). Its
contributors included Voltaire (1694–1778),
▷ Rousseau, Montesquieu (1689–1755),
Buffon (1707–88) and Turgot (1727–81).
The work originated in a translation of
the English *Cyclopaedia* (1728) of Ephraim
Chambers (d 1740), but the French version
was intellectually more ambitious and more
impressive. It was guided by a trust in reason
and rationalistic explanation, and the desire to
destroy superstition and the beliefs thought
to arise from it. The work's fierce attacks
on Church and state proved potent criticism
of the ▷ Ancien Régime (it was suppressed
at various stages of its composition) and
heralded the overthrow of the monarchy in the
▷ French Revolution. It reinforced European
rationalism and in England influenced
▷ Jeremy Bentham and through him the
19th-century Utilitarians (▷ Utilitarianism).

Endymion (1818)
Poem by ▷ John Keats. It is based on an
ancient Greek myth about a shepherd with
whom the moon goddess fell in love. The
poem has passages of great freshness and
beauty, but, as Keats soon came to realize, it
is immature. Its classicism is a resource for
the free embroidering of fanciful stories; and
the theme, the indulgence of the senses, is
one that Keats quickly outgrew.
▷ Classical mythology; Greek literature.

Enlightenment
The term was originally borrowed into English
in the 1860s from German (*Aufklärung*), to
designate the spirit and aims of the French
philosophers of the 18th century (▷ French
literature in England). But as historical
perspectives have changed, the word has
come to be used in a much wider sense,
to denote the whole period following the
▷ Renaissance, during which scepticism
and scientific rationalism came to dominate
European thinking. Enlightenment grew out
of Renaissance at different times in different
countries. In Britain, the empiricism of
Francis Bacon (1561–1626) and the secular
pragmatism of Thomas Hobbes (1588–1679)
mark its early stages. Its golden age began
however with John Locke (1632–1704)
in philosophy, and ▷ Sir Isaac Newton
(1642–1727) in science, and it reached its
height in the first half of the 18th century.
Locke argued that 'Reason must be our last

judge and guide in everything', and rejected
medieval philosophy as superstition. Newton's
theory of gravitation seemed to explain the
mysteries of the solar system. The fact that
Newton had also worked on optics was
ingeniously alluded to in Alexander Pope's
(1688–1744) couplet: 'Nature, and Nature's
Laws lay hid in Night./ God said, *Let Newton
be*! and All was *Light*'.
The onset of the Enlightenment in Britain
coincided with the bourgeois revolution
and many of its values reflect the optimistic
temper of the newly dominant class, as
much as any abstract philosophical system.
In contrast to the previous ideology of static
hierarchy, appropriate to a landowning
aristocracy and its peasant underclass, the
new ideology of merchants and professional
men places its emphasis on understanding
and dominating the environment. God loses
his numinousness, becoming a kind of divine
mathematician, and the ▷ Deist thinkers of
the time rejected the dogmas of the scriptures
in favour of ▷ 'natural religion' based on an
understanding of God's laws through science.
Pope expresses this idea in classic form in his
Essay on Man (1733–4), cleverly blending it
with the older hierarchical idea of the Great
Chain of Being. Pope's *Essay* stands as a
compendium of popular Enlightenment ideas,
expressing the expansive confidence of the
middle class that 'Whatever *is*, is *right*.' It was
easy for the middle-class reader of the day to
feel that British philosophy, science, trade,
and imperialism were all working together to
advance civilization throughout the world. It
is a myth projected in many of the works of
Pope, James Thomson (1700–48) and other
writers of the time.
As the 18th century developed, the
bourgeoisie's confidence in its progressive
destiny faltered, reaching a crisis after the
▷ French Revolution in what we now call
the ▷ Romantic movement. ▷ William Blake
attempted to restore the pre-Enlightenment
numinousness of God and nature, rejecting
Newton's 'particles of light', and the idea
of inert matter or empty space. Imagination,
not science, was for him the key to nature:
'Every thing possible to be believ'd is an
image of truth.' ▷ Percy Bysshe Shelley, using
politically resonant imagery, asserted that
'man, having enslaved the elements, remains
himself a slave' and warned of the dangers
of 'an unmitigated exercise of the calculating
faculty' (one of the characteristic institutions
of the Enlightenment period was, of course,
the slave trade). Even the fundamentally
materialist ▷ John Keats complained

about the prosaic nature of Enlightenment philosophy:

> *There was an awful rainbow once in heaven:*
> *We know her woof, her texture; she is given*
> *In the dull catalogue of common things.*
> *Philosophy will clip an Angel's wings.*
>   (*Lamia*; 231–4)

More recently 'Enlightenment' has been given a yet wider historical application by the German philosophers Theodor Adorno and Max Horkheimer, whose book, *Dialectic of Enlightenment* (1944) sees the manipulative, calculating spirit of Enlightenment as the identifying characteristic of Western civilization (▷ German influence on English literature). They trace its manifestations from Odysseus's tricking of the primitive bumpkin Polyphemus, to the treatment of people as means rather than ends which characterizes both modern totalitarian politics and consumer capitalism. Recent ecological movements, which advocate a respect for nature, rather than an exploitation of it, continue the same dialectic.
▷ Augustanism.
Bib: Willey, B., *The Eighteenth-Century Background*; Redwood, J., *Reason, Ridicule and Religion: The Age of Enlightenment in England*.

Epic

1 A narrative of heroic actions, often with a principal hero, usually mythical in its content, offering inspiration and ennoblement within a particular cultural or national tradition.

2 The word denotes qualities of heroism and grandeur, appropriate to epic but present in other literary or even non-literary forms.

Epics occur in almost all national cultures, and commonly give an account of national origins, or enshrine ancient, heroic myths central to the culture. For European culture at large, much the most influential epics are the *Iliad* and the *Odyssey* of ▷ Homer and the *Aeneid* by Virgil. C. S. Lewis in *Preface to Paradise Lost* makes a helpful distinction between primary and secondary epics: primary ones, such as Homer's, are composed for a society which is still fairly close to the conditions of society described in the narrative; secondary epics are based on the pattern of primary epics but written for a materially developed society more or less remote from the conditions described, *eg* Virgil's *Aeneid*. In English literature the Old English *Beowulf* may be counted as a primary epic. A number of attempts at secondary epic have been made since the 16th century, but

▷ John Milton's ▷ *Paradise Lost* is unique in its acknowledged greatness and its closeness to the Virgilian structure. An example of the ▷ Romantic use of epic is ▷ Wordsworth's ▷ *The Prelude*.

Epipsychidion (1821)

▷ Shelley's turbulent poem concerning the relationship between the intellectual flights of metaphor and the felt reality of love, composed in Pisa and triggered by the incarceration of 'the noble and unfortunate lady', Emilia Viviani, in a convent. The degree to which the poet's relationship with Emilia was flirtatious or ▷ platonic is not clear to us now, and may not have been so then. What is more clear is that the imprisonment of a beautiful girl (by parents in search of a suitable husband) was a gift to Shelley as a poet, enabling him to attack favourite targets such as marriage and the church with passionate and trenchant oratory. Indeed, ▷ Romantic ▷ rhetoric in this poem begins to become its own subject, and the unfortunate Emilia becomes less a woman than a fecund figure of speech, 'A Metaphor of Spring and Youth and Morning; A Vision like Incarnate April, warning/ With smiles and tears, Frost the Anatomy/ Into his summer grave'. At once fiery and self-questioning, *Epipsychidion* not only bears on those themes that ▷ Deconstructionist critics such as ▷ Paul de Man have detected in Romantic poetry, but appears through the complexities of its language to deconstruct itself.

Essay, The

'Essay' derives from the French *essai*, meaning 'experiment', 'attempt'. As a literary term it is used to cover an enormous range of composition, from school exercises to thorough scientific and philosophical works, the only quality in common being the implied desire of the writer to reserve to himself some freedom of treatment. But the essay is also a recognized literary form in a more defined sense: it is understood to be a fairly short prose composition, in style often familiarly conversational and in subject either self-revelatory or illustrative (more or less humorously) of social manners and types.

During the 19th century the essay form flourished in the work of ▷ Charles Lamb, ▷ William Hazlitt, ▷ Leigh Hunt and ▷ De Quincey. In these writers, social comment combines with a confessional, autobiographical element which had never been so prominent in the English essay before. This was true to the autobiographical spirit of so much

19th-century literature. These essayists were links between the early ▷ Romantic poets – especially ▷ Wordsworth – and the mid-Victorian novelists; they shared the close interest in material surroundings characteristic of those poets, and their essays often contained character delineations related to such environmental settings.

Essays of Elia (1823; 1833)

A series of essays by ▷ Charles Lamb, published in ▷ *The London Magazine* and then in a collected edition. They emulate the essays of Joseph Addison (1672–1719) and Sir Richard Steele (1672–1729) in the *Spectator* and *Tatler* of a century before, but depend less on their content than on Lamb's attempt to win the affection and interest of the reader for himself as a person. The style is whimsical and self-conscious, owing something to the musical and humorously eccentric appeal of Robert Burton's (1577–1640) *Anatomy of Melancholy* which to some extent it emulates. However, there are passages of witty observation and acute character sketches.
▷ Essay.

Evangelical Movement

A movement for Protestant revival in the Church of England in the late 18th and early 19th century. It was stimulated partly by ▷ John Wesley's ▷ Methodist revival and the activities of other sects (especially among the lower classes) outside the Church of England; it was also a reaction against the ▷ rationalism and scepticism of the 18th-century aristocracy, and against the ▷ atheism of the ▷ French Revolution. Politically, the movement tended to be conservative and was therefore strong among the Tories, whereas the ▷ Whigs (especially their aristocratic leaders such as ▷ Charles James Fox) retained more of the 18th-century worldliness and scepticism. In doctrine the Evangelicals were inclined to be austere, to attach importance to strength of faith and biblical guidance, and to oppose ceremony and ritual. Socially they developed a strong sense of responsibility to their fellow human beings, so that one of their leaders, ▷ William Wilberforce, devoted his life to the cause of abolishing slavery and the slave trade in British dominions, and later Lord Shaftesbury (1801–85) made it his life-work to alleviate the social and working conditions of the working classes. The leaders of the movement were laymen rather than clergy, and upper class rather than lower class, amongst whom the ▷ Nonconformist sects were more actively influential. As the Nonconformists were to contribute to English socialism later in the century a religious rather than a ▷ Marxist inspiration, so the Evangelicals later led to generations of highly responsible, independent-minded intellectuals such as the historians Thomas Babington Macaulay and Trevelyan.

Eve of St Agnes (1820)

The 18th-century fashion for pseudo-medieval poetry in ▷ Spenserian stanzas culminated in ▷ John Keats's masterpiece of sensuous aestheticism. Madeline retires to bed on St Agnes' Eve hoping to be granted a vision of her lover by the saint. Meanwhile her lover Porphyro, an enemy to her family, steals into her chamber, aided by an aged servant woman, and watches his beloved undress from a closet. When the girl wakes she finds that Porphyro has prepared a sumptuous banquet of 'cakes and dainties'. They make love before fleeing into the storm. The poet employs every extreme of verbal artifice to transform this flimsy escapist fantasy into a pattern of archetypal contrasts: youth and age, fire and ice, security and danger. The interwoven rhyme scheme and the final ▷ alexandrine of each stanza are each made to yield the maximum ornamental and musical effect. Dense, tactile imagery abounds ('the tiger-moth's deep-damask'd wings'). There are crowded alliterations ('the silver, snarling trumpets 'gan to chide'); inventive archaisms ('carven imag'ries', 'blue affrayed eyes'); neologisms ('jellies soother than the creamy curd'); transferred epithets ('azure-lidded sleep', 'silken Samarkand'); exotic compounds ('flaw-blown sleet', 'palsy-twitch'd'); and synaesthetic constructions ('warm gules', 'perfume light'), all designed to overwhelm and delight the reader's senses.

Evelina (1778)

A novel in letters by ▷ Fanny Burney. Evelina has been abandoned by her aristocratic father, and her socially much humbler mother is dead. She has been brought up by her guardian, a solitary clergyman. As a beautiful, well-bred, and intelligent young girl, she pays a visit to a friend in London, where she falls in love with a handsome aristocrat, Lord Orville, is pursued by an unscrupulous rake, Sir Clement Willoughby, and is much embarrassed by vulgar relatives, especially her grandmother, Madame Duval. The convincing and delightful part of the novel consists in its acute and lively social observation, in many ways superior to anything of the sort yet accomplished in the 18th-century novel, and anticipating the maturer art of ▷ Jane Austen in the early 19th century.

Examiner, The

A weekly periodical founded by John and ▷ Leigh Hunt in 1808, famous for its radical politics. It had no party allegiance, but criticized public affairs, in the words of Leigh Hunt's friend ▷ John Keats, 'from a principle of taste'. In 1813 the Hunts were sent to prison for two years for exposing the gross flattery in another paper of the Prince Regent (later George IV).

Excursion, The (1814)

A long ▷ didactic poem in ▷ blank verse by ▷ William Wordsworth. It was intended to be the middle part of a three-part philosophical poem, to be called *The Recluse*, but the other two parts were never written. ▷ *The Prelude*, intended as an introduction to *The Recluse*, was completed in 1805, but was not published until after Wordsworth's death in 1850. Book I of *The Excursion*, which contains the most enduring poetry in the work, comprises a piece written some years before: *Margaret or the* ▷ *Ruined Cottage*. Books II–IV contain discussion between the poem's protagonist, the Wanderer, and his friend, the Solitary, who lacks faith in man and God. In Books V–VII a new character, the Pastor, relates the histories of some of his former parishioners buried in the churchyard. The last two books are concerned with the degradation of the poor by industrial expansion, and proposes educational reforms.

▷ Education.

Experience, Songs of

▷ *Songs of Innocence and Experience*.

Fanshawe, Catherine (1765–1834)

Poet and letter-writer. Fanshawe came from
a genteel background, which encouraged the
education and cultural activity of women. In
some ways perceptions of Fanshawe resemble
those of ▷ Jane Austen, for during the 19th
century she was considered a feminine,
refined and respectable author, whose poetry
was suitable for young women. However, on
reading her work now it seems impossible
that anyone could miss the sharp and
incisive irony. Fanshawe parodies different
▷ discourses, satirizes political conventions
and displays a worldly and somewhat cynical
view about women's position in polite society.
She and her sisters are also accredited with
editing the memoirs of Lady Ann Fanshawe,
who was an important ▷ Renaissance woman.

Faust

The Faust myth is much older than those
legends which crystallize round the historical
figure of Faust and form a part of it. The
myth of men seeking great earthly power from
demons at the cost of their immortal souls
goes back to the ancient Jews at about the
time of Christ, and centres on several figures
of medieval European Christendom. In the
16th century the myth received new vitality
through the influence upon it of various
bodies of ideas: ▷ Renaissance humanism,
in its sceptical and critical spirit; neo-Platonic
mysticism, in its conception of the potentially
immense reach of the human mind; and the
Protestant Reformation, in its adherence
to the pure Word of God as opposed to
humanist claims for reason and Catholic
claims for authority alike. The historical
Faust was an early 16th-century German
philosopher who was ridiculed by other
intellectuals for his extravagant pretensions
to magical powers. Nonetheless, pamphlets
and plays built up a widespread, partly comic
and partly serious image of him as the pattern
of human arrogance eternally damned for
his preference of human learning over the
Holy Word. Mephistopheles, the devil with
whom Faust made his bargain, was himself
condemned to eternal suffering and regarded
himself in this light.

▷ Wolfgang Goethe's masterpiece *Faust*
(Pt. 1 1808; 11 1832) gives an entirely new
turn to the myth. Mephistopheles is no
longer the evil spirit in eternal torment,
but 'the spirit that denies', *ie* that refuses to
acknowledge the intrinsic reality of any human
or spiritual value. Thus Goethe's version
of the myth became itself one of the great
myths of modern man. The struggle is no
longer between earthly power and spiritual
holiness: it is between the cynicism of those
who deny that there is goodness in the search
for goodness, and the dedication of those who
make the search.

▷ German influence on English literature.

Feminism

In literary criticism this term is used to
describe a range of critical positions which
argues that the distinction between 'masculine'
and 'feminine' is formative in the generation
of all discursive practices. In its concern to
bring to the fore the particular situation of
women in society 'feminism' as a focus for the
raising of consciousness has a long history,
and can be taken to embrace an interest
in all forms of women's writing throughout
history. In its essentialist guise, feminism
proposes a range of experiences peculiar
to women, which are, by definition, denied
to men, and which it seeks to emphasize in
order to compensate for the oppressive nature
of a society rooted in what it takes to be
patriarchal authority. A good example would
be the recent highlighting of ▷ Dorothy
Wordsworth's diaries and their importance
to the poetry of her brother ▷ William. A
more materialist (▷ Materialism) account
would emphasize the extent to which gender
difference is a cultural construction, and
therefore amenable to change by concerted
political action. Indeed, the Romantic author
▷ Mary Wollstonecraft was an early exponent
of such criticism. Traditional materialist
accounts, especially those of ▷ Marx,
have placed the issue of 'class' above that
of 'gender', but contemporary feminism
regards the issue of 'gender' as frequently
cutting across 'class' divisions, and raising
fundamental questions about the social
role of women in relations of production
and exchange. Insofar as all literature is
'gendered', then feminist literary criticism
is concerned with the analysis of the social
construction of 'femininity' and 'masculinity'
in particular texts. One of its major objectives
is to expose how hitherto 'masculine' criticism
has sought to represent itself as a universal
experience, and in the Romantic period this
has led to an increased awareness of female
authors such as ▷ Mary Berry, ▷ Catherine
Gore and ▷ Amelia Opie. Similarly, the
focus is adjusted in order to enable literary
works themselves to disclose the ways in
which the experiences they communicate
are determined by wider social assumptions
about gender difference, which move beyond
the formal boundaries of the text. To this

extent feminism is necessarily the focus of an interdisciplinary approach to literature, psychology, sociology and philosophy.

Psychoanalytic feminism, for example, often overlaps with socialist feminism. It approaches the concept of gender as a problem rather than a given, and draws on ▷ Freud's emphasis on the instability of sexual identities. The fact that femininity – and masculinity – are never fully acquired, once and for all, suggests a relative openness allowing for changes in the ways they are distributed. Literature's disturbance and exploration of ways of thinking about sexual difference have proved a rich source for feminist critics.

Traditional criticism of Romantic literature has tended to be dominated by masculine ideology, and it is only recently that critics have recognized the importance of a 'feminine Romanticism', with its claims to independence, assertion of female identity and valuing of private experience.

▷ Minerva Press; Women's movement.
Bib: de Beauvoir, S., *The Second Sex*; Greene, G. and Kahn, C. (eds.), *Making a Difference: Feminist Literary Criticism*; Millett, K., *Sexual Politics*; Spender, D., *Feminist Theorists*; Wollstonecraft, M., *Vindication of the Rights of Women*; Rogers, K.M., *Feminism in Eighteenth-century England*; Mellor, A., *Romanticism and Feminism*.

Fenwick, Eliza (c 1760–c1840)
Novelist and children's author. Fenwick may be associated with the development of radical women's writing at the end of the 18th century. She was friendly with ▷ Mary Wollstonecraft and ▷ Mary Lamb, and she left her alcoholic husband in 1800, supporting herself, without regrets, for the remaining 40 years of her life. Fenwick's most important and, indeed, compelling piece of work is her novel, *Secresy, or The Ruin on the Rock* (1795). It focuses on the lives of two women, Sibella and Caroline, who grow in self-awareness and recognize the ills of their society. The ending is tragic, with both women losing what they love, but the sexual openness of the work, together with its praise of female friendship, ensure that the overall tone of the book remains challenging rather than depressing (▷ Feminism). Fenwick believed that education was the answer to social problems, a theme which she takes up in her didactic children's book, *Visits to the Juvenile Library* (1805). Her last years were spent running ▷ Godwin's library and travelling the world as a governess.
Bib: Wedd, A.F., *The Fate of the Fenwicks*.

Ferrier, Susan Edmonstone (1782–1854)
Novelist. The youngest of ten children, Susan Ferrier was born in Edinburgh. Her father was a lawyer, a principal clerk of session along with ▷ Sir Walter Scott, so Ferrier was early introduced to literary society. Through visits to Inverary Castle she also became acquainted with the fashionable world. After her mother died in 1797 her three sisters married and she kept house for her father who died in 1829. She later insisted on the destruction of correspondence with a sister, thus destroying much biographical material. Her novels of Scottish life included portraits of known people. *Marriage* (1818) was written in 1810 with a minimal contribution from her friend Miss Clavering, *The Inheritance* in 1824 and *Destiny, or the chief's daughter* in 1831. Her aim was didactic and her method keen observation, comedy and clear writing.
▷ Silver-fork novels.
Bib: Grant, A., *Susan Ferrier of Edinburgh: a Biography*.

Feuilleton
In French, a leaflet. Also used in French for that part of a newspaper devoted to literature, non-political news and gossip. In English the term was once used for the instalment of a serial story: it was the French newspaper *Le Siècle* which was the first to commission a serial novel specifically for part publication, in 1836. They were called *romans feuilletons*.
▷ Balzac, Honoré de.

Figures of Speech
Alliteration The beginning of accented syllables near to each other with the same consonantal sound, as in many idiomatic phrases: 'safe and sound': 'thick and thin'; 'right as rain'. Alliteration is thus the opposite of ▷ rhyme (below), by which the similar sounds occur at the ends of the syllables: 'near and dear'; 'health and wealth'. Alliteration dominated the pattern of Old English poetry; after the Conquest, French influence caused rhyme to predominate. However, in the 14th century there seems to have been an 'alliterative revival'. Alliterative verse was accentual, *ie* did not depend on the regular distribution of accented syllables in a line, but on the number of accented syllables in the lines.

After the 14th century, rhyme and the regular count of syllables became the normal pattern for English verse. Alliteration, however, continued to be used unsystematically by every poet. For example,

▷ Burns uses it to comic effect in 'The Twa Dogs':

*His locked, letter'd, brawbrass collar
Shew'd him the gentleman and scholar.*

Anacoluthon From the Greek: 'not following on'. Strictly speaking, this is not a figure of speech, but a grammatical term for a sentence which does not continue the syntactical pattern with which it starts. It may be used deliberately with the virtue of intensifying the force of a sentence *eg* by the sudden change from indirect to direct speech. Its capacity for dramatic fragmentation is used repeatedly for comic effect by ▷ Byron in ▷ *Don Juan*, *eg*:

*Sooner shall heaven kiss earth – (here he fell sicker)
Oh, Julia! What is every other woe?*
(Canto I)

Anti-climax
   ▷ *Bathos* (below).
Antithesis A method of emphasis by the placing of opposed ideas or characteristics in direct contrast with each other.
Apostrophe A form of direct address often used by a narrator in the middle of his narrative as a means of emphasizing a moral lesson. Apostrophe frequently addresses a real person, living or dead, as in the opening of ▷ Wordsworth's sonnet on Milton: 'Milton! Thou shouldst be living at this hour!'
Assonance The rhyming of vowel sounds without the rhyming of consonants.
Bathos From the Greek: 'death'. The descent from the sublime to the ridiculous. This may be the result of incompetence in the writer, but may also be used skilfully as a method of ridicule. Among the canonical Romantic poets, ▷ Byron is the absolute master of bathos, as in the lines written on the back of his manuscript of ▷ *Don Juan*, Canto I:

*I say – the future is a serious matter –
And so – for God's sake – hock and soda-water!*

Climax From the Greek: 'a ladder'. The climb from lower matters to higher, with the consequent satisfying of raised expectations.
Euphemism A mild or vague expression used to conceal a painful or disagreeable truth, *eg* 'he passed on' for 'he died'. It is sometimes used ironically.
Euphuism A highly artificial quality of style resembling that of the ▷ Renaissance writer John Lyly's *Euphues* (1578–80).

Hyperbole Expression in extreme language so as to achieve intensity, *eg* ▷ Shelley's exclamation at the apparent failure of his own poem to achieve its target, towards the end of ▷ *Epipsychidion*: 'I pant, I sink, I tremble, I expire!'
Innuendo A way of expressing dislike or criticism indirectly, or by a hint; an insinuation.
Irony From the Greek: 'dissimulation'. A form of expression by which the writer intends his meaning to be understood differently and less favourably, in contrast to his or her overt statement:

It is a truth universally acknowledged, that a single man in possession of a good fortune must be in want of a wife.

This opening sentence of ▷ Jane Austen's *Pride and Prejudice* is to be understood as meaning that the appearance of such a young man in a neighbourhood inspires very strong wishes in the hearts of mothers of unmarried daughters, and that these wishes cause the mothers to behave as though the statement were indeed a fact.
Dramatic irony occurs when a character in a play makes a statement in innocent assurance of its truth, while the audience is well aware that he or she is deceived. Tragedies by ▷ Byron, or ▷ Shelley's *The Cenci*, are indebted to Elizabethan and Jacobean drama in this area.
Irony in Romantic poetry tends frequently to complicate meaning to a degree which makes the stable interpretation of a particular poem hard to establish. This is particularly true of ▷ William Blake and ▷ P. B. Shelley.
Litotes Emphatic expression through an ironical negative, *eg* 'She's no beauty', meaning that the woman is ugly.
Malapropism A comic misuse of language, usually by a person who is both pretentious and ignorant. The term derives from the character Mrs Malaprop in Sheridan's play *The Rivals* (1775). This comic device had in fact been used by earlier writers, such as ▷ Shakespeare in the portrayal of Dogberry in *Much Ado About Nothing*.
Meiosis Understatement, used as a deliberate method of emphasis by irony, *eg* 'Would you like to be rich?' – 'I should rather think so!'
Metaphor A figure of speech by which unlike objects are identified with each other for the purpose of emphasizing one or more aspects of resemblance between them. A simple example: 'the camel is the ship of the

desert'. Romantic poetry abounds in more complex examples, as in the opening of ▷ Keats's 'Ode on a Grecian Urn', which employs humanized metaphor to treat an inanimate object:

> *Thou still unravish's bride of quietness,*
> *Thou foster-child of silence and slow time.*

The opposite approach to metaphor is adopted by ▷ Shelley in ▷ *Epipsychidion*, when the human addressee of a poem, Emilia, is called:

> *A metaphor of Spring and Youth and*
> *   Morning;*
> *A Vision like Incarnate April, warming,*
> *With smiles and tears, Frost the Anatomy*
> *Into his summer grave.*

('Anatomy' here means 'skeleton'.)

Mixed metaphor is a confused image in which the successive parts are inconsistent, so that (usually) absurdity results: 'I smell a rat, I see it floating in the air, but I will nip it in the bud', *ie* 'I suspect an evil, and I can already see the beginnings of it, but I will take action to suppress it.' However, mixed metaphor is sometimes used deliberately to express a state of confusion.

Dead metaphor is one in which the image has become so familiar that it is no longer thought of as figurative, *eg* the phrase 'to take steps', meaning 'to take action'.

Metonymy The naming of a person, institution or human characteristic by some object or attribute with which it is clearly associated, as when a king or queen may be referred to as 'the Crown';

> *Sceptre and Crown*
> *Must tumble down,*
> *And in the dust be equal made*
> *With the poor crooked scythe and spade.*
> *   ('The Levelling Dust', James Shirley)*

Here 'Sceptre and Crown' refer to kings, and perhaps more broadly to the classes which control government, while 'scythe and spade' stand for the humble peasantry. Metonymy has taken on additional meanings since the advent of ▷ structuralism. One of the originators of Russian Formalism, ▷ Roman Jakobson, draws a distinction between 'metaphor' – the linguistic relationship between two different objects on the grounds of their similarity – and 'metonymy' as a means of establishing a relationship between

two objects in terms of their contiguity. Where metaphor is regarded as a major rhetorical device in *poetry*, metonymy is more usually associated with *prose*. The critic and novelist David Lodge (b 1935) takes up this distinction in his book *The Modes of Modern Writing* (1977), and suggests that 'metaphor' and 'metonymy' constitute a structurally significant binary opposition that enables the distinction to be made between poetry and drama on the one hand, and prose on the other. Lodge emphasizes, however, that these terms are not mutually exclusive, but rather contribute to 'a theory of dominance of one quality over another'. Hence it is possible for a novel to contain 'poetic' effects and vice versa. Among the most important essays on metaphor and metonymy in Romantic poetry is J. Hillis Miller's 'The Critic As Host' in Bloom (ed.) *Deconstruction and Poetry*, (1979).

Oxymoron A figure of speech formed by the conjunction of two contrasting terms in a compressed paradox, such as ▷ Coleridge's 'Life-in-Death' from ▷ *The Rime of the Ancient Mariner.*

Palindrome A word or sentence that reads the same backwards or forwards, *eg*

> *Lewd did I live; evil I*
> *   did dwel*
> *   (Phillips, 1706)*

Paradox A statement that challenges the mind by appearing to be self-contradictory.

Pathetic fallacy A term invented by the ▷ Victorian critic John Ruskin (1819–1900; *Modern Painters*, Vol. III, Pt. iv, Ch. 12) to denote the tendency common especially among poets to ascribe human emotions or qualities to inanimate objects, *eg* ▷ Coleridge's line 'As if this earth in fast thick pants were breathing' from ▷ *Kubla Khan.*

Personification A kind of metaphor, by which an abstraction or inanimate object is endowed with personality, As for example in ▷ Keats's 'To Autumn', where Autumn is described as a human being:

> *Who hath not seen thee oft amid thy store?*
> *   Sometimes whoever seeks abroad may find*
> *Thee sitting careless on a granary floor,*
> *   Thy hair soft-lifted by the winnowing wind;*

Play on words A use of a word with more than one meaning or of two words which sound the same in such a way that both meanings are called to mind. In its simplest form, as the modern pun, this is merely a joke. In the 16th and 17th centuries poets frequently played upon words seriously; this is especially true of ▷ Shakespeare and dramatists contemporary with him.

This very serious use of puns or plays upon words decreased in the 18th century, when Samuel Johnson (1709–84) censured Shakespeare's fondness for puns (or, as Johnson called them, 'quibbles'). The reason for this disapproval of the serious 'play upon words' was the admiration of educated men for 'mathematical plainness of meaning', a criterion emulated by poets as well as by prose writers. Poetry of the Romantic period is however characterized by daring or subtle play on words, as in Keats's reckless punning in his 'Ode on a Grecian Urn':

> *O Attic shape! Fair altitude! with brede*
> *Of marble men and maidens overwrought*

'Brede' and 'overwrought' are here puns, and 'Attic' calls up the word 'altitude'. ▷ Byron and ▷ Shelley play continuously on words for comic and philosophical effect respectively, and ▷ Blake's play on words in even such brief lyrics as 'The Sick Rose' and 'London' becomes so intense as to make it impossible for a reader to find less than a multitude of interpretations for them.

The revival of a play on words in modern poetry is partly due to the rise of another science, that of psychoanalysis, especially the school of ▷ Freud, with its emphasis on the interplay of conscious and unconscious meanings in the use of language.

Pun
   ▷ Play on words (above).

Rhyme A verbal music made through identity of sound in the final syllables of words. Several varieties of rhyme exist:
   End-rhyme When the final syllables of lines of verse are rhymed.
   Internal rhyme When one at least of the rhyming words is in mid-line.
   Masculine rhymes are single stressed syllables as in the following example from ▷ Anna Barbauld's 'Life':

> *Life! I know not what thou art,*
> *But know that thou and I must part.*

Feminine rhymes are on two syllables, the second of which is unaccented. As in the following from ▷ Coleridge's ▷ Dejection: an Ode:

> *Mad lutenist! who in this month of showers,*
> *Of dark brown gardens, and of peeping*
> *flowers.*

Half-rhymes (pararhymes) are the rhyming of consonants but not of vowels (contrast ▷ Assonance above). They are sometimes used as an equivalent for full rhymes, since consonants are more noticeable in rhyme music than vowels. Change in pronounciation sometimes has the effect of changing what was intended as full rhyme into half-rhyme, as in the final stanza of ▷ Blake's poem 'The Crystal Cabinet':

> *A Weeping Babe upon the Wild*
> *And Weeping Woman pale reclin'd,*
> *And in the outward air again*
> *I filled with Woe the passing Wind.*

The pronunciation of 'wind' has clearly changed.

Simile Similar to metaphor, but in similes the comparison is made explicit by the use of a word such as 'like' or 'as'.

Syllepsis A figure of speech by which a word is used in a literal and a metaphorical sense at the same time, *eg* 'You have broken my heart and my best china vase'.

Synecdoche A figure of speech by which a part is used to express a whole, or a whole is used to express a part, *eg* 'fifty sail' is used for fifty ships, or the 'smiling year' is used for the spring. In practice, synecdoche is indistinguishable from ▷ metonymy (above). Like metonymy this figure depends upon a relationship of contiguity, and is regarded as one side of the opposition between 'poetry' and 'non-poetry'. Both metonymy and synecdoche operate by combining attributes of particular objects, therefore they are crucial rhetorical devices for the representation of reality, and are closely related to ▷ realism as a literary style insofar as they function referentially.

Transferred epithet The transference of an adjective from the noun to which it applies grammatically to some other word in the sentence, usually in such a way as to express the quality of an action or of behaviour, *eg* 'My host handed me a hospitable glass of wine', instead of 'My hospitable host handed me . . .'.

Zeugma A figure similar to ▷ syllepsis (above); one word used with two others, to only one of which it is grammatically or logically applicable.

Flodden, Battle of (1513)

The invading Scottish forces under King James IV, fighting in alliance with France which had been invaded by a Henry VIII of England, were heavily defeated by the English general, the Earl of Surrey. James himself was killed, as well as large numbers of his nobility. The battle was commemorated by a famous dirge *The Flowers of the Forest*, the best-known version of which is by Jean Elliott (1727–1805). *Marmion, A Tale of Flodden Field* (1808) is the most celebrated of the narrative poems by ▷ Sir Walter Scott.

Flowerdew, Alice (1759–1830)

Poet. After the death of her husband, Flowerdew published her spiritual and ▷ didactic work, including some interesting ▷ hymns, in *Poems on Moral and Religious Subjects* (1803), probably from financial need. The third edition (1811) of this collection carries a new preface in which the education of women (▷ Women, education of) is discussed. By this time Flowerdew was teaching in a London school and the practical nature of her argument clearly stems from personal experience. She forthrightly asserts that men and women have equal intellectual potential, but that women have been repressed by the lack of a proper education.

▷ Feminism.

Foucault, Michel (1926–84)

Along with ▷ Louis Althusser and ▷ Jacques Derrida, Foucault is one of the most influential of French philosophers, and one whose work has been taken up by the practitioners of other disciplines. Foucault rejects the totalizing explanations of human development in favour of a more detailed analysis of how power functions within particular ▷ discourses. In *Madness and Civilization* (1965) he explored the historical opposition between 'madness' and 'civilization', applying ▷ Saussure's notion of differentials (▷ Difference) to the various ways in which society excludes the behaviour which threatens it. He later took this issue up in *Discipline and Punish* (1977), and *I Pierre Riviere* (1978). In *The Order of Things* (1971) and *The Archaeology of Knowledge* (1972) he investigated the ways in which human knowledge is organized, and the transition from discourses which rely upon a notion of 'self-presence', to those which operate differentially to produce the kind of linguistic self-consciousness characteristic of postmodernism. In essays such as those translated in *Language, Counter-memory, Practice* (1977), he sought to clarify specific areas of opposition through which discourse is constructed. At the time of his death he had embarked on an investigation of the discourses of sexuality through the ages, and

the three volumes of *The History of Sexuality* (1978–87) have now been published.

Fox, Charles James (1749–1806)

Principal leader of the ▷ Whig party from 1775 (the beginning of the American War of Independence) until his death. The Crown was not then above politics and the Tories, almost continuously in power during the same period, had the support of George III. Fox's fearless opposition in the House of Commons to the policies of the government in America, in ▷ Ireland and in regard to the ▷ French Revolution caused the king to refuse his offer of participation in the government in 1804, when he became convinced of the rightness of the war against France. Fox was dissolute in private life but set a high standard of political independence of mind. His principal political opponents were the Prime Ministers Lord North during the American war and ▷ William Pitt the Younger during the French one. Though powerful in opposition, he was less effective in office; but his service as Foreign Secretary in the Whig governments of 1782 and 1806 was too brief to show results.

Francis, Anne (1738–1800)

Poet and translator. Anne Francis was a distinguished scholar; she had a ▷ classical education, learning Latin, Greek and Hebrew. After her marriage to Revd Robert Francis, she published a translation of the *Song of Solomon* (1781) which she also edited, and in 1785 she brought out *The Obsequies of Demetrius Poliorcetes*, which reworked some of Plutarch's writing. Francis was also an admirer of ▷ Goethe and wrote *Charlotte to Werther: A Poetical Epistle* (1787) as a vehicle for defending him against what she felt were unjust accusations. Several more personal works remain, for example the elegies and odes to her family published in *Miscellaneous Poems* (1790). In light of this detailed and scholarly activity, it is surprising that Francis should think that such work was 'an *improper* undertaking for a *woman*' (Preface to the *Song of Solomon*).

Frankenstein, or the Modern Prometheus (1817)

A philosophical romance which is also a tale of terror, by ▷ Mary Shelley. It belongs in part to the 'Gothic' tradition popular at the time and partly to a philosophical tradition going back to ▷ Rousseau, concerned with themes of isolation, suffering and social injustice. Mary Shelley originally wrote it to compete with the tales of terror being

composed for their own amusement by her lover and later husband, ▷ P. B. Shelley and their friend, the poet ▷ Lord Byron. Frankenstein is a Swiss student of natural philosophy who constructs a monster and endows it with life. Its impulses are benevolent, but it is everywhere regarded with loathing and fear; its benevolence turns to hatred, and it destroys its creator and his bride.
▷ Gothic novels.
Bib: Hammond, R., *The Modern Frankenstein: Fiction Becomes Fact.*

French literature in England

Perhaps the most important French work in the 18th century in relation to its influence in English literature was the result of a collective enterprise rather than an individual piece: the ▷ *Encyclopédie*. It provided a focus for the *philosophes*, Diderot, Voltaire and ▷ Rousseau, and a forum larger than that which Voltaire, for example, enjoyed with John Locke (1632–1704). More famously, its criticisms of the ▷ Ancien Régime prefigured the ▷ French Revolution. It might be possible to see Wordsworth's ▷ *Prelude* as a transposed re-enactment of this yoking of *Encyclopédie* and revolution, the political upheaval described in 'Residence in France' here conducive to 'Imagination and Taste, How Impaired and Restored', politics now harnessed to the service of the imagination. The cutting-edge of the early ▷ Romanticism occurs in poetry rather than prose, in England rather than in France, with Wordsworth and ▷ Byron rather than with Lamartine (1790–1869) and ▷ Hugo. France was to experience revolution three times in the course of the 19th century, but for a comparable dramatizing of revolution and imagination such as Wordsworth articulates here in the *Prelude*, France needed more than its Romantic poets could offer.

In the work of Charles Baudelaire, however, French poetry shows a vibrant new Romanticism of exotic locations and experiences, combined with an urban anti-Romanticism. *Les Fleurs du Mal* (1857) – the Flowers of Disease, or Evil – is the first European poetry of the city, interested in drugs, crime and nocturnal adventure in a Parisian setting, and alert to the ways in which poetry would soon be marginalized in an age of mechanical reproduction. Baudelaire was a major influence on ▷ A.C. Swinburne, and the 'Decadent' poets of 1890s London.

However, 20th-century French literary theory has provided one of the most interesting adjuncts to Romantic English

literature. The writings of ▷ Roland Barthes, ▷ Jacques Lacan and the ▷ post-structuralists have revised the literary canon (reintroducing writers such as the ▷ Marquis de Sade and ▷ Comte de Lautréamont), as well as providing the instrumental forces of disruption which unsettle rather than confirm assumptions about the world (narrative or real). Thus current French objections to realism are not simply objections to a world view taken as paradigmatic for literature, they are equally objections to a type of critical view which sponsors such a world view as natural, co-extensive with the order of things.

French Revolution (1789–94)

The immediate effect of the French Revolution was to abolish the French monarchy, to reduce forever the rigid class divisions of French society, and to begin wars (lasting till 1815) which for the time being extensively altered the map of Europe. Its lasting effect was to inspire the European mind with the belief that change is historically inevitable and static order unnatural, and to imbue it with modern ideas of democracy, nationalism and equality, at least of opportunity.

The immediate effect on England was confusing, for many of the changes being brought about in France had already occurred here in the 17th century, especially the establishment of the sovereignty of the elected representatives of the people in Parliament in 1688. Such changes had occurred here, however, without the same upheavals, partly because English society and politics had always been more fluid than in the other larger states of Europe, and though unjustified privileges and inequalities existed, there were few definable differences between the ▷ Whigs on the left who were neutral or sympathetic to the Revolution, and the Tories on the right who feared it from the start. Only when General Bonaparte took increasing charge of France and became Emperor ▷ Napoleon I in 1804 did Britain become united in fear of French aggression. However, ▷ Edmund Burke published in 1790 his ▷ *Reflections on the Revolution in France*, one of the most eloquent documents of English political thinking, foretelling the disasters which the Revolution was to bring, and condemning it as ruthless surgery on the living organism of society. His opponent ▷ Tom Paine answered him with *The Rights of Man* (1791), and the younger intellectuals agreed with Paine. ▷ Wordsworth wrote later in ▷ *The Prelude* 'Bliss was it in that dawn to be alive', and ▷ William Blake wore a revolutionary cockade in the streets; ▷ Southey and ▷ Coleridge planned the ideal communist society, ▷ Pantisocracy; the philosophic novelist ▷ William Godwin published *Political Justice* and *Caleb Williams* to prove that reason was the only guide to conduct and society needed by man. Later Wordsworth and Coleridge came round to a view closer to Burke's, and the younger generation, ▷ Byron and ▷ Shelley, saw them as traitors; the more so because the defeat of Napoleon at Waterloo (▷ Waterloo, Battle of) introduced a phase of political and social repression everywhere. But the older generation (except perhaps Southey) did not so much go back on their earlier enthusiasms as think them out more deeply; the philosophical conservatism of the older Coleridge was as radical in its thinking as the ▷ Utilitarianism of philosophical radicals such as ▷ Bentham.

▷ French literature in England.

Bib: Deane, S., *The French Revolution and Enlightenment in England 1789–1832*; Grossley, C. and Small, I., *The French Revolution and British Culture*.

Frere, John Hookham (1769–1846)

Friend of the statesman ▷ George Canning and British envoy in Lisbon and later Madrid in the first decade of the 19th century. He collaborated with ▷ Robert Southey on his translation of *The Chronicles of the Cid* (1808) contributed extensively to *The Anti-Jacobin* (▷ Jacobin) and was one of the founders of ▷ *The Quarterly Review*. His mock-romantic Arthurian poem, *The Monks and the Giants* (1817–18), written under the pseudonym 'Whistlecraft' introduced ▷ Lord Byron to the ▷ *ottava rima* style in which he wrote ▷ *Beppo* and ▷ *Don Juan*. In the 1830s and 40s Frere produced lively verse translations of four plays by the Greek dramatist Aristophanes (▷ Greek literature).

Freud, Sigmund (1856–1939)

The founder of psychoanalysis, and one of the seminal figures of 20th-century thought. Born in Moravia, then part of the Austro-Hungarian Empire, he settled in Vienna. He began his career as a doctor specializing in the physiology of the nervous system and, after experimenting briefly with hypnosis, developed the technique of free association for the treatment of hysteria and neurosis. His work is based on a number of principles. The first is psychic determinism, the principle that all mental events, including

dreams, fantasies, errors and neurotic symptoms, have meaning. The second is the primacy of the unconscious mind in mental life, the unconscious being regarded as a dynamic force drawing on the energy of instinctual drives, and as the location of desires which are repressed because they are socially unacceptable or a threat to the ego. The third is a developmental view of human life, which stresses the importance of infantile experience and accounts for personality in terms of the progressive channelling of an initially undifferentiated energy or libido. Important aspects of ▷ psychoanalytical theory and practice arising from these principles include the theory of infantile sexuality and its development, centred on the Oedipus Complex, the techniques of free association and dream interpretation as means of analysing repressed material, and the beliefs that much behaviour is unconsciously motivated, that sexuality plays a major role in the personality, and that civilization has been created by the direction of libidinous impulses to symbolic ends (including the creation of art). Freud regarded neurotic and normal behaviour as differing in degree rather than kind.

Despite his scientific orientation, Freud's thought had affinities with that of the Romantic poets, and several features of modern literature which show his influence also have Romantic antecedents. These include a particular interest in the quality and significance of childhood experience, a fascination with memory and with what is buried in the adult personality, and a concern with disturbed states of consciousness. The writings of ▷ Coleridge and ▷ De Quincey in particular are forerunners of Freud, in their shared conviction that the mind remembers all personal experience, but locks it in hidden chambers of memory that may only find their key in dreams, visions, or unexpected thought-associations. The Romantics' interest in madness also anticipate psychoanalysis.

In Modernist literature, the stream of consciousness technique and other experimental narrative techniques which have gained acceptance abandon external realism in favour of the rendering of consciousness, of dreams or of fantasies and owe much to Freud's belief in the significance of these areas of experience, which had been relatively neglected by scientific thought. Furthermore, the technique of free association revealed a tendency of the mind, when rational constraints were lessened, to move towards points of psychic conflict, and this discovery helped to validate new means of structuring literary works, through association, symbol, and other forms of non-rationalistic patterning. The view that the individual's unconscious life is as important as his or her public and social self is crucial to much 20th-century literature, especially Surrealist poetry. The Freudian unconscious is in particular the realm of fantasy, and Freudian thought has encouraged the belief that fantasy is of profound significance in our lives, with considerable consequences for literary forms and modes.

Psychoanalysis has developed very considerably since Freud, and continues to interact with literary practice and theory. In the field of theory, those who have studied but radically revised Freud's ideas, such as ▷ Jacques Lacan and ▷ feminist theorists, have been especially important.
Bib: Brown, J. A. C., *Freud and the Post-Freudians*; Freud, S., *Introductory Lectures on Psychoanalysis*.

Frost at Midnight (1798)

▷ Samuel Taylor Coleridge's ▷ conversation poem issues from the first phase of English ▷ Romantic poetry, characterized by its emphasis on spiritual ▷ autobiography, memory and the workings of the intellect and imagination, and the idealistic projection of a life of freedom for the poet's child, ▷ Hartley, under the benign tutelage of ▷ Nature. The idealism of the poem is shadowed not only by the dissipation of energies shown by the real Hartley Coleridge in later life, but by a discrepancy between what the poet desires or imagines, and what he can occupy with certainty. If this melancholy divergence reflects aspects of Coleridge's personality, as a dreamer and an opium addict, it may also express a more general truth about the fall from linguistic illusionism to to a darker existential reality. ▷ Deconstructionist critics such as ▷ Paul de Man have been particularly alert to this kind of doubleness in Romantic texts.

G

Galt, John (1779–1839)
Scottish writer of poems, travels, dramas
and novels. He is chiefly remembered for
his novels, especially *The Ayrshire Legatees*
(1821), *Annals of the Parish* (1821), *The Provost*
(1822) and *The Entail* (1823). These are
vivid, realistic, humorous accounts of Scottish
provincial society.
▷ Scottish literature in English.
Bib: Gordon, R. K., *John Galt*; Aberdein, J.
W., *John Galt*; Parker, W. M., *Susan Ferrier
and John Galt* (British Council).

The Garden in Romantic literature
Until the 18th century gardens were strictly
formal, elegant and classical in style. However,
from the early part of that century larger
gardens were designed increasingly with eyes
that appreciated the wildness of 'picturesque'
landscape, a taste formed partly by 17th-
century Italian and French painters such as
Salvator Rosa and Claude. Thus gardens
became to some extent imitations of pictures;
if the landscape were not wild enough, dead
trees might be planted, *eg* in Kensington
Gardens, London. Imitation Greek temples,
such as occur in Claude's pictures, were
erected at suitable viewpoints, for instance on
an island in a probably artificially created lake.
The poet Alexander Pope (1688–1744) was
fond of carefully constructed caves ('grottos').
Later in the century, the taste for these
architectural ornaments called 'follies' became
more exotic: Chinese pagodas were built and
imitation ruins of medieval ▷ Gothic castles
were very common.

The 18th-century taste for 'wild' gardens
was closely related to the literature of the
period; it was indeed stimulated by James
Thompson's landscape poems the *Seasons*
(1730). Later 18th-century poets, such as
▷ William Collins (1721–59), ▷ William
Cowper, ▷ Thomas Gray and others,
wrote landscape poetry; much of it gives the
impression of the poet enjoying a landscape
from a distance or from a sheltered spot, as
the landed gentry enjoyed their landscape
gardens from their drawing-room windows.
Designers of landscape gardens became
artists with great prestige. The most famous
designer was Lancelot Brown ('Capability'
Brown, 1715–83), who refused to allow any
merely useful building, such as stables, to
remain in sight of the house. But comfort, if
not convenience, was maintained: 18th- and
early 19th-century novels frequently mention
'shrubberies' – ▷ picturesque, sheltered
walks, where the ladies could walk out of the
weather. At the very end of the century, the
books on landscape gardening and on the
picturesque in landscape by ▷ Gilpin were
widely read and coincided with the rise of
the English school of landscape painters such
as Cotman and Crome. Though the novelist
▷ Jane Austen described surroundings very
little, references to the taste for landscape
recur in her books, and the whole fashion for
landscape-gardening is satirized in ▷ Thomas
Love Peacock's witty discussion novel,
▷ *Headlong Hall*.

Garrick, David (1717–79)
Actor, theatre manager, dramatist, whose
genius as an actor greatly enhanced the
theatrical profession in social prestige, and
who was also responsible for far-reaching
innovations in the theatre.

In 1737 he came to London with Samuel
Johnson who had been his tutor at Lichfield
and entered Lincoln's Inn, but his career
there did not last. He had shown a taste for
theatricals early in his youth, and in 1740
he put together a burlesque play based on
characters of Henry Fielding, *Lethe: or Aesop
in the Shades*, which was performed at a
benefit night for Henry Giffard.

In 1741 Giffard took a small company
including Garrick to Ipswich, and here the
actor performed regularly for the first time,
making his debut as Aboan in Thomas
Southerne's *Oroonoko* before returning to
Giffard's Theatre at Goodman's Fields.
Garrick, still unknown, played Richard III,
to a rapturous reception. In 1742 Garrick
travelled to Dublin with Peg Woffington,
who became his mistress, and together
they joined the Smock Alley Theatre. They
returned to London and in 1742 Garrick
opened his first season at Drury Lane.
Denied their salaries by the irresponsible
manager Charles Fleetwood, Garrick, Charles
Macklin, and several other actors rebelled
in 1743. Eventually, after a series of further
disruptions, including several riots at the
theatre, and a season at Covent Garden
(1746–47), Garrick became a joint manager
at Drury Lane in 1747. Two years later he
married the actress Eva Maria Veigel.

Garrick proved a vigorous and creative
manager, reviving the fortunes of Drury Lane,
and adding to his own status as the leading
actor of his generation. His sensitive and
naturalistic acting style, inspired by that of
Macklin but perfected by Garrick himself,
set a standard for the period, making the
previous formal and 'stagey' methods of
acting seem outmoded. In 1763, after further
rioting at the theatre, Garrick abolished the

long practice of allowing spectators on the stage. He introduced lighting concealed from the audience which he had observed during a professional visit to Paris, and engaged the brilliant scene designer ▷ De Loutherberg who created a series of sets in naturalistic, romantic style that complemented Garrick's own style of acting. He also wrote a number of plays, and rewrote others to conform with the tastes of his time, including *The Lying Valet* (1741), *Miss in Her Teens* (1747), in which he himself played the part of the fop, Fribble, *The Clandestine Marriage* (1766) (in collaboration with ▷ George Colman the Elder), *The Country Girl* (1766) (a revision of ▷ William Wycherley's *The Country Wife*), *The Irish Widow* (1772), *Bon Ton; Or High Life Above Stairs* (1775), and reworkings of several plays of Shakespeare.

Garrick retired in 1776, and died at his home in London after a long and painful struggle with illness. He was buried at Westminster Abbey, near the monument to Shakespeare who had provided him with many of his finest tragic roles, including not only Richard III, but Hamlet (his most popular part), Macbeth, and Lear. Garrick also excelled in comedy, his best parts including Abel Drugger in Ben Jonson's *The Alchemist*, Benedick in *Much Ado About Nothing*, and Bayes in the Duke of Buckingham's *The Rehearsal*, in which he triumphed when he imitated several well-known contemporary actors.

Bib: Murphy, A., *The Life of Garrick*; Oman, C., *David Garrick*; Kahrl, G. M. and Stone, G. W., *David Garrick, A Critical Biography*; Kendall, A., *David Garrick: A Biography*; Wood, E. R. *Plays by David Garrick and George Colman the Elder*.

Genre

In its use in the language of literary criticism the concept of 'genre' proposes that particular groups of texts can be seen as parts of a system of representations agreed between writer and reader. For example, a work such as ▷ Aristotle's *Poetics* isolates those characteristics which are to be found in a group of dramatic texts which are given the generic label 'tragedy'. The pleasure which an audience derives from watching a particular tragedy emanates in part from its fulfilling certain requirements stimulated by expectations arising from within the form itself. But each particular tragedy cannot be reduced simply to the sum of its generic parts. Each play repeats certain characteristics which have come to be recognized as indispensable

features of the genre, but each one also exists in a relationship of difference from the general rule. The same kind of argument may be advanced in relation to particular sorts of poetry, or novel. The concept of genre helps to account for the particular pleasures which readers/spectators experience when confronted with a specific text. It also offers an insight into one of the many determining factors which contribute to the formation of the structure and coherence of any individual text. Key genres explored by Romantic literature include the ▷ conversation poem, developed by ▷ Coleridge from his reading of ▷ Cowper; the meditation on landscape and the self, exemplified by the poetry of ▷ Wordsworth; the anti-governmental satire, practised by ▷ Blake, the early Wordsworth, and brought to a new pitch of aggression by ▷ Shelley; and the spiritual ▷ autobiography, of which all Romantic writers may be said to offer important examples.

Gentleman's Magazine, The

Founded in 1731, it was the first to call itself a 'magazine'. It included, as later magazines were to do, a wider variety of material than the Reviews, including political reports, under the editorship of ▷ John Nichols.

Georgian

A term for the architectural style of the period 1714–1810, under George I, II and III. Georgian architecture was severe but balanced in its proportions. It was influenced partly by the Palladian style of Inigo Jones (1573–1651) and partly by the direct experience of English travellers who made the Grand Tour of Italy and admired its classical buildings. The term is not usually applied to 18th-century literature; in other arts its suggestion of elegance and proportion is often modified by a taste for satire and caricature, as in Hogarth's paintings. It was followed by the ▷ Regency style.

Georgics

Virgil's *Georgics* (from the Greek word for a farmer) comprise four poems, addressed to the Emperor Augustus, describing agriculture; they were extensively imitated in England in the 18th century, for example by ▷ William Cowper in ▷ *The Task*.
 ▷ Greek literature; Latin literature.

German influence on English literature

Unlike other European literatures, such as French or Italian, the literature of the German-speaking world did not begin to make itself felt in Britain to any great extent until relatively recent times. There are two reasons for this. The first is that the great flowering of a literature written in the *modern* form of the German language did not take place until the second half of the 18th century; the second is that German did not begin to assume the status of a major foreign language for the English until the second decade of the following century and even then it remained far behind French in importance.

In the cultural interchange between the two literatures Britain has on balance been the dominant partner. German men and women of letters during the 18th century were far more likely to have a lively awareness of current developments in English literature than were their English counterparts in developments in Germany. For example, the status of ▷ *Paradise Lost* as an epic poem was debated, and ▷ Augustan authors such as Alexander Pope (1688–1744) and Oliver Goldsmith (1730–74) were known and admired. In this way English literature was able to play a crucial role in the process by which German writers of the late 18th century succeeded in exerting their independence from the prevailing standards of neo-classical decorum which French models seemed to dictate. The writers of the *Sturm und Drang* ('Storm and Stress') movement, as later the German ▷ Romantics, looked to Britain rather than France for support and justification of their revolutionary project. ▷ Shakespeare's status as a German classic dates from this time, and the early attempts of Gothold Ephraim Lessing (1729–81), ▷ Johann Wolfgang von Goethe and Friedrich Schiller (1759–1805), who also translated *Macbeth*, to provide a repertoire for a German national theatre owed a great deal to the English dramatist. So when German theatre first made an impression in Britain, the new stimulus contained many, though unrecognized, indigenous elements. Interest in German theatre seems to have been kindled by the Scot Henry Mackenzie (1745–1831) who gave an address on the subject to the Royal Society of Edinburgh in 1788. During the 1790s the English stage experienced a vogue for German plays, but the public's taste was essentially for the ▷ Gothic, and the most performed writer was the justly forgotten August von Kotzebue (1761–1819). It was not in drama, however, that the first impact of the new German literature was felt but in the novel. Goethe's epistolary novel *Die Leiden des jungen Werthers* (*The Sorrows of Young Werther*) (1774) was a landmark for it was the

first work of German literature to achieve European recognition. It was translated into most European languages and reached Britain in 1799, significantly via a French version. The novel's apparent defence of suicide caused a storm of righteous indignation, but the huge popularity of the novel, here as elsewhere, had much to do with the fact that it appealed to a taste for 'sentimental' literature which had already been established in Germany and Britain. Other currents made themselves felt also. Bishop ▷ Percy's *Reliques of Ancient English Poetry* (1765) had stimulated Herder and, through him, Goethe to explore their own native oral tradition of 'natural' *Volkspoesie*. This interest is reflected in the novel in Werther's admiration of ▷ *Ossian*, ▷ James Macpherson's collection of supposed fragments of lost Celtic epics, which had appeared in 1765.

This discovery of German literature by an English audience unfortunately soon met an insurmountable obstacle in the form of war. In the wake of the ▷ French Revolution a climate of opinion was created which was deeply and indiscriminately suspicious of all mainland European influence as ▷ Jacobin, subversive and unpatriotic. The fashion for German plays was snuffed out almost instantly, and it was not until the ending of the Napoleonic wars, with England and Prussia as victorious allies, that a new climate favourable to the reception of German writers could be created. The publication of Madame de Staël's *De l'Allemagne* (1813) is rightly regarded as a crucial event in this process. When English interest was reawakened, it was once again Goethe who was at the centre of controversy. It is easy to smile now at the response to the first part of *Faust* (1808), but the work was then felt to be deeply shocking. Quite apart from a degree of frankness in sexual matters unthinkable in an English work, there were features which were regarded as highly offensive to orthodox Christian sentiment. Goethe's reputation as an immoral author was revived, and it seems likely that fear for his own reputation played some part in ▷ Samuel Taylor Coleridge not undertaking a commissioned translation of the work. It is one of the imbalances in the relations between English and German literature that while English classics found immensely talented translators in Germany – the Tieck-Schlegel version of Shakespeare, for example – many great German works have been either completely overlooked or ill-served by their English translators.

Of the first generation of English Romantic

poets only Coleridge, if we discount ▷ William Blake's idiosyncratic relationship to the mystic and visionary Jakob Böhme (1575–1624), was deeply influenced by German culture. A cautious admirer of Goethe, translator of Schiller's *Wallensteins Tod* (*Wallenstein's Death*), Coleridge visited Göttingen in 1798. His thought was deeply indebted to ▷ Immanuel Kant, Johann Gottfried von Herder (1744–1803) and the *Naturphilosophie* of Friedrich Schelling (1775–1854). ▷ William Wordsworth, who in his view of nature was far closer to Goethe than he realized, shared the opinion of many in dismissing him as an immoral and irreligious writer, but ▷ Byron and ▷ Shelley had no sympathy with such small-mindedness. Shelley valued *Faust* highly, and it is a loss to English culture that his efforts at translation never extended beyond a few small fragments of the work. As for Byron, his admiration was genuine, if not matched by any great depth of response. His esteem, however, was reciprocated. Sadly Byron, whose works, ▷ *Childe Harold's Pilgrimage* and ▷ *Don Juan* especially, were widely read and admired in Germany as in the rest of Europe, did not live to see the tribute Goethe paid him in the second part of *Faust* (1832), where the English poet is represented as the child of Faust and Helen.

For the ▷ Victorian thinker Matthew Arnold (1822–88) Goethe and Heine were great modern spirits in comparison with whom the English Romantics were insular and intellectually deficient. However, it is now appreciated that the profound influence of the so-called 'Higher Criticism' in Britain does not commence with the publication in 1846 of George Eliot's translation of Strauß's *Das Leben Jesu* (1835) but has roots which reach back into the last quarter of the 18th century, and that Coleridge was ahead of his time in his appreciation of the significance to religion and philosophy of the German school of biblical criticism. Arnold had recognized in Goethe a figure who was working to 'dissolve' the dogmatic Christianity which had once been the bedrock of European civilization. It is now clear, however, that it was the Higher Criticism which, by mythologizing Christianity, undermined its own claims. From this it is clear that when considering the massive response of English writers to German literature at this time, no sharp line can be drawn between works of imagination on the one hand and works of historical scholarship, cultural history and philosophy on the other.

Bib: Jasper, D., *The Interpretation of Belief: Coleridge, Schleiermacher and Romanticism*.

Giaour, The (1813)

A verse tale by ▷ Lord Byron in tetrameter couplets (▷ metre) interspersed with quatrains. The word was used by the Turks as a general term for non-Muslims, especially Christians. The poem is about the love of a Turkish slave Leila for a giaour; her master causes her to be thrown into the sea, and her lover avenges her death.
   ▷ Orientalism.

Gibbon, Edward (1737–94)

One of the greatest English historians, author of ▷ *The Decline and Fall of the Roman Empire* (1776–88). His reputation rests almost entirely on this work, but his *Memoirs* (1796), put together from fragments after his death, are one of the most interesting biographies of the 18th century. In 1761 he published in French his *Essai sur l'Etude de la Littérature*, translated into English in 1764; it was more successful abroad than at home. He was also a Member of Parliament, 1774–81.
Bib: Low, D. M., *Edward Gibbon*; Young, G. M., *Gibbon*; Sainte-Beuve, C.-A., in *Causeries dy Lundi* vol viii.

Gifford, William (1756–1826)

Journalist. He began as a shoemaker's apprentice, and rose to be an influential writer and editor of the right-wing press. He edited *The Anti-Jacobin* (1797–8) to counteract opinion sympathetic to the ▷ French Revolution, and became editor of the famous Conservative ▷ *Quarterly Review* in 1809.
   ▷ Jacobin.

Gilbert, Ann (1782–1866)

Poet, reviewer, children's author, diarist and autobiographer. Gilbert's writing equalled that of her more famous sister, ▷ Jane Taylor, and both were precocious and prolific authors. Her first book of poems, *Original Poems* (1804–5), was immediately successful and led to her undertaking the editorship of *The Eclectic Review*. In this capacity she reviewed contemporary novels. After her marriage to Revd Joseph Gilbert in 1813, she moved to Sheffield and Nottingham and turned her literary skills to more political matters, writing against slavery (▷ Abolition literature), in favour of temperance, and offering general advice on government legislation. Gilbert had kept a diary from an early age and at 66 she began to transform some of the material into an ▷ autobiography; it was never finished, but the extant material was published posthumously in 1874.

Gilpin, William (1724–1804)

Theorist. Gilpin's work was very important in establishing the cult of the ▷ Picturesque, as well as in heralding certain themes valued by the ▷ Romantic poets. He based his ideas upon journeys he undertook to the most 'picturesque' parts of Britain, including the Lake District and the Scottish Highlands, and published his theories in *Three Essays: On Picturesque Beauty; On Picturesque Travel; and On Sketching Landscapes* (1792). His efforts were not universally praised, and he was satirized in the figure of Dr Syntax by ▷ Coombe.

Gipsies

A nomadic race, dark-skinned, speaking their own language related to the Indian Hindi. They spread across Europe in the 15th century and seem to have reached Britain about 1500. Owing to a belief that they came from Egypt, they were known as Egyptians, corrupted to Gipsies (Gypsies), but they called themselves Romanies. They commonly lived in caravans and moved from place to place, making a living (in the English countryside) as tinkers and by begging. Among country people they had a bad reputation for lawlessness and stealing, including the kidnapping of children; but their exoticism caused them to be romanticized in the 19th century, *eg* the gipsies in the novel *Guy Mannering* (1815) by ▷ Walter Scott.

Godwin, William (1756–1836)

Philosopher and novelist. His central belief was that reason was sufficient to guide the conduct, not merely of individuals but also of all society. His principal work was *The Inquiry concerning Political Justice* (1793). Man he believed to be innately good and, under guidance of reason, capable of living without laws or control. Punishments he declared (at a time when the English penal system was one of the severest in Europe) to be unjust; as were the accumulation of property and the institution of marriage. The Prime Minister, ▷ William Pitt (the Younger), decided that the book was too expensive to be dangerous. Godwin's best-known novel came out in 1794: *Caleb Williams* was written to demonstrate the power for injustice accessible to the privileged classes. Godwin was a brave man, not merely with the pen; but his naivety as a thinker would have left him without influence if his opinions had not agreed so well with the more extreme currents of feeling provoked by the contemporary ▷ French Revolution. As it was, he influenced a number of better minds, including, for a very short time, the poet ▷ Coleridge and, for a much longer period, ▷ Shelley, who became his son-in-law. Godwin's wife was ▷ Mary Wollstonecraft, an early propagandist for the rights of women and authoress of *A Vindication of the Rights of Woman* (1792).

Goethe, Johann Wolfgang von (1749–1832)

German poet; the greatest European man of letters of his time. His fame was due not only to the wide scope of his imaginative creation, but to the many-sidedness and massive independence of his personality. From 1770 to 1788 he was an inaugurator and leader of the passionate outbreak known in German as the *Sturm und Drang* – 'storm and stress'– movement, but from 1788 (after his visit to Italy) he represented to the world a balanced harmony inspired by the classicism he had found there. But he did not lose his sense that the spirit is free to find its own fulfilment according to its own principle of growth. At the same time, from 1775 he was prominent in the affairs of the German principality of Weimar (whose prince was his friend), concerning himself with practical sciences useful to the state, and thence with a serious study of botany and other natural and physical sciences to the point of making significant contributions to scientific thought. His commanding mind was admired in France, England, and Italy, with whose literatures Goethe was in touch; he corresponded with ▷ Byron, and ▷ Walter Scott translated his *Goetz von Berlichingen*, which dated from the romantic phase of Goethe's career.

Goethe is most famous for his double drama of ▷ *Faust*, but other works that became famous in England include the romantic drama already mentioned; the epic *Hermann and Dorothea*; a study in Romantic sensibility *The Sorrows of Young Werther*; the novel *Wilhelm Meister*, and a large body of ▷ lyrical verse.

▷ German influence on English literature.

Gooch, Elizabeth Sarah (b 1756)

Novelist, poet and autobiographer. Elizabeth Gooch's most fascinating work is her ▷ autobiography, *Life* (1792), partly because of the difficulties she encountered and the sordid world she was forced to live in, but mainly because of the rapid-paced narrative and her penchant for vivid sensationalism. She was the daughter of a Portuguese Jewish father who died when she was three, and her stepfather never fully accepted her into his family. She was sent to school at Fountains Abbey where she entered into a romance, which was thwarted. Following this she was 'married off' to William Gooch who was more interested in her dowry than in showing her any real affection. It was not long before Gooch accused her of adultery and sent her to France, where she became a prostitute. The subsequent years saw a series of escapades in which she acted on stage, fled from debtors, disguised herself as a man so as to follow her lover into battle, and persistently tried to wring money out of her embarrassed family. By 1788 she was in prison, from where she wrote *Appeal to the Public*. Gooch's later life is obscure, but several novels and a biography of Thomas Bellamy, all written between 1795 and 1800, remain.

Gore, Catherine (1799–1861)

Novelist and dramatist. Catherine Gore (née Moody) married in 1823, had ten children and supported her family through writing. She produced nearly seventy novels of the ▷ Silver-fork school in which fashionable and dashing men wooed fashionable and submissive women. What marks out Gore's novels is her close attention to the details of women's daily household activities, and her work is an invaluable source for women's history rather than appealing to today's literary tastes, although it is only fair to note that she was perfectly aware of the quality of her own work, commenting that she was a writer of 'rubbish'. Gore's best known work is *Cecil: or Adventures of a Coxcombe* (1841) which was published anonymously, and which was supposed to be a biography of one of ▷ Byron's friends. The character displays all the traits of an aristocratic and decadent dandy, and it is believed that Gore obtained the details for the description from her friend ▷ William Beckford. Her other novels include *Theresa Marchmont or the Maid of Honour* (1824), *Manners of the day, or Woman as the game* (1830), which was praised by George IV, *Mothers and Daughters* (1830), *Mrs Armytage: or female domination* (1836), and *The banker's wife, or court and city* (1843), which was dedicated to Sir John Dean Paul, portrayed as a swindler, as he in fact turned out to be in 1855 when Gore lost £20,000 She also wrote some fine poetry which remains unpublished, but which was admired by ▷ Joanna Baillie. Gore also set some of ▷ Robert Burns's poetry to music,

and had considerable success as a dramatist, including the popular *The School for Coquettes* (1831) and the acclaimed *Quid Pro Quo* (1843).
Bib: Moers, E., *Literary Women*; Rosa, M.W., *The Silver-fork School*.

Gothic

A term for the style of architecture which dominated western Europe in the Middle Ages. Its main features were the pointed arch and the ribbed vault. In England, this period is divided into three: Early English (13th century), Decorated (14th) and Perpendicular (15th–16th). A fine example of the last is King's College Chapel, Cambridge.
▷ Gothic revival.

Gothic novels

A genre of novels dealing with tales of the macabre and supernatural, which reached a height of popularity in the 1790s. The term 'Gothic' originally implied 'medieval', or rather a fantasized version of what was seen to be medieval. Later, 'Gothic' came to cover all areas of the fantastic and supernatural, and the characteristics of the genre are graveyards and ghosts.
▷ Walpole's ▷ *The Castle of Otranto* is generally seen as the earliest Gothic novel. ▷ Monk' Lewis, ▷ William Beckford and ▷ Mrs Radcliffe are notable exploiters of the genre. The vogue for Gothic novels soon produced parodies; ▷ Thomas Love Peacock's ▷ *Nightmare Abbey* and ▷ Jane Austen's ▷ *Northanger Abbey* are among the best examples.
In the 19th century, ▷ Mary Shelley and the ▷ Brontës show the influence of the tradition.
Bib: Baldick, C., *In Frankenstein's Shadow*; Ellis, K.F., *The Contested Castle: Gothic Novels and the Subversion of Domestic Ideology*; Meade, T., *The English Gothic Novel*; Milbank, A., *Daughters of the House*.

Gothic revival

An architectural style now chiefly associated with the reign of Queen Victoria (1837–1901). However, a taste for Gothic had in fact started in the 18th century with ▷ Horace Walpole's design of his home, Strawberry Hill (1747). The taste for Gothic spread between 1750 and 1830; as an artistic style it remained a minority cult, but as a sentiment it grew with the popularity of the sensationalism of the ▷ Gothic novels and with the rise of the romantic cultivation of the ▷ sensibility. In the 18th century, the taste for Gothic tended to be fanciful and sensational rather than deeply serious, although it gained seriousness from such a publication as ▷ Thomas Percy's *Reliques*; the 19th-century ▷ Romantic revival, especially the novels of ▷ Walter Scott, produced a deeper and much more genuine feeling for the ▷ Middle Ages. In poetry and fiction, ▷ Tennyson's revival of Arthurian legend in *Idylls of the King*, can be ascribed to a prevailing neo-Gothic appeal to the imagination. But in the 1870s, a reaction set in: neo-Gothic architectural styles were succeeded by a return to classicism, generally known as the new 'Queen Anne' style, though it was often much more eclectic and exuberant.

▷ Medieval literature.

Grammatology

This term is used by the French philosopher ▷ Jacques Derrida to denote 'a general science of writing'. As a scientific practice, its objective is to disturb the traditional hierarchical relationship between 'speech' and 'writing' where the latter is regarded as an instrument of the former. Derrida's 'science of writing' is an attempt to deconstruct (▷ Deconstruction) the metaphysical assumptions upon which the hierarchical relationship between speech and writing is based. He takes to the limit the ▷ Saussurean notion of the arbitrariness of the linguistic ▷ sign, arguing against a natural relationship between the spoken word and what it signifies.

Grant, Anne (1755–1838)

Poet, historian and letter-writer. Anne Grant (née Macvicar) was born in Glasgow, spent her childhood and teenage years in America, and returned to Britain in 1768 when she married Revd James Grant and retired with him to the Scottish Highlands. Most of Grant's work contains ▷ autobiographical elements, her *Memoirs of an American Lady* (1808) being the most clearly indebted to her own experiences of colonial life. Her *Poems* appeared in 1803 and focus on her observations of the Highland countryside and its society. Similar material emerged regularly in later works, such as *The Highlanders* (1808). There has been an attempt to reclaim Grant as an early feminist, though she herself attacked ▷ Mary Wollstonecraft in 1794 for claiming that women had equal intellectual powers, asserting vehemently the conventional view that women were clearly inferior to men.

▷ Scottish literature in English.

Graves, Richard (1715–1804)

Novelist. Graves was the rector of Claverton and a well known figure in ▷ Bath society. He is best remembered for his novel *The Spiritual Quixote, or the Summer Rambles of Mr Geoffrey Wildgoose* (1773), which recounts the comic journeys of a ▷ Methodist preacher. The figure of Wildgoose satirizes the Methodist, George Whitefield (1717–70), whom Graves had met during their student days at Oxford.
Bib: Hill, C.J., *The Literary Career of Graves*.

Gray, Thomas (1716–71)

Poet and prose-writer. The sole survivor of 12 children, Gray was born in Cornhill, London. His father, a scrivener, was mentally unbalanced and Gray was brought up by his mother, who sent him to Eton where he made friends with ▷ Horace Walpole. He went on to Peterhouse, ▷ Cambridge, and gained a high reputation for his ▷ Latin poetry, though he failed to take a degree. In 1739 he embarked on a tour of the continent with Walpole, but in 1741 they quarrelled and Gray returned alone. He turned to the study of law, and began a tragedy *Agrippina*, which remained unfinished. The death of Richard West, a close friend from his Eton days, in 1742, precipitated a period of poetic activity, in which he produced his *Ode on a Distant Prospect of Eton College* (published 1747), *Sonnet on the Death of Richard West* and *Ode to Adversity* (published in Dodsley's *Collections*, 1748). Also in 1742 he began ▷ *Elegy written in a Country Churchyard*, while staying with his mother and aunt at their retirement home in Stoke Poges. The poem was carefully revised over a long period and eventually appeared in 1751, achieving instant recognition as a masterpiece.

From 1742 Gray lived in Peterhouse and later Pembroke College, Cambridge, except for a period (1759–61) in London where he pursued his studies in the British Museum. Relations with Walpole were soon restored and it was the death of Walpole's cat which inspired Gray's delightful mock-heroic *Ode on the Death of a Favourite Cat* (1748). The *Odes by Mr Gray* (1757), comprising his two Pindaric Odes, *The Progress of Poesy* and ▷ *The Bard*, was the first book published by Walpole's Strawberry Hill press. In the same year he was offered the laureateship, but refused. In 1761 he wrote a number of poems reflecting a mixture of bookish scholarship and romantic primitivism, very characteristic of the period: *The Fatal Sisters*.

An Ode, The Descent of Odin. An Ode (*From the Norse-Tongue*), *The Triumphs of Owen. A Fragment* (from the Welsh). They were published in 1768 in Dodsley's collected edition of his works, *Poems by Mr Gray*. In the same year Gray was appointed Professor of Modern History at Cambridge, though he never delivered a lecture. In 1769 he travelled in the Lake District and his *Journal* (1775), relates his reactions to its sublime scenery. His letters reveal a profoundly learned, but witty and entertaining personality.

Gray's reflective works, in particular the *Elegy*, are masterpieces of the hesitant, personal poetry of ▷ sensibility. His odes, although not so successful, reflect the restless experimentalism of his period. It has been too easy to cast Gray either as a half-hearted ▷ Augustan or a timid pre-romantic, both tendencies being encouraged by ▷ William Wordsworth's dogmatic strictures on the language of his *Sonnet on the Death of Mr West*, and ▷ Samuel Taylor Coleridge's corrective follow-up in ▷ *Biographia Literaria*, Chapter XVIII. It is better to see him in his own right. His particular poetic strengths are an ease of personification and abstraction (shared by his contemporary Samuel Johnson (1709–84) and emulated by ▷ John Keats in his ▷ Odes), and a restrained but eloquent felicity of phrasing, which places some of his lines among the best-remembered in the language: 'where ignorance is bliss/ 'Tis folly to be wise'; 'And Melancholy mark'd him for her own.'

▷ Bard; Romanticism.

Bib: Johnson, S., in *Lives of the Poets*; Arnold M., in *Essays in Criticism* (2nd series); Ketton-Cremer, R. W., *Thomas Gray: A Biography*; Leavis, F. R., in *Revaluation*; Tillotson, G., in *Augustan Studies*; Powell Jones, W., *Thomas Gray, Scholar*; Starr, H. W. (ed.), *Twentieth-Century Interpretations of Gray's Elegy*.

Greek literature

Until Greece was conquered by the Romans in 146 BC, it was a country of small states, mixed racial stock and cultural origins from all round the eastern Mediterranean. These states attained a high level of self-conscious political and artistic culture, which later enriched the Roman Empire and was thence transmitted to medieval and modern Europe.

The beginnings of Greek literature cannot be dated but its first period ended about 500 BC. The period contains ▷ Homer's epics, the *Iliad* and the *Odyssey*, and the poems of Hesiod. Homer's epics are the real starting-point of European imaginative literature; Hesiod's *Theogony* is one of the principal sources of our knowledge of the Greek religious system. In English literature since the 18th century, the term ▷ elegy has implied narrower limits of subject and treatment than it had for the Greeks and the Romans, but the Greek evolution of the elegy and the ▷ lyric in this period has shaped our ideas of the character and resources of the short poem. An important variety of the lyric (whose principal characteristic was originally that it was intended to have musical accompaniment) was the 'Pindaric ode', so called after its most famous practitioner, ▷ Pindar; this was much imitated by English poets from the 17th to 19th centuries.

The second period (500–300 BC) is called the 'Attic Period' because it centred on the greatest of the Greek cities, Athens, capital of the state of Attica. The outstanding imaginative achievement of the Athenians was the creation of dramatic literature. The 'choral lyric', sung by choirs on religious occasions and especially on the festival of the wine-god Dionysus, was developed into a dialogue by Thespis in the 6th century. In the 5th century this was further developed into dramatic tragedy by three writers whose works have a fundamental influence on all our ideas of the theatre: ▷ Aeschylus, Sophocles and Euripides. The primitive religion of the Greeks, based on the worship of the gods as the all-powerful forces of nature, was the origin of Greek tragedy; it was also the origin of comedy, of which the greatest Greek writer was Aristophanes. Athens, in this period, also developed Greek prose literature, in the works of the first of the historians, Herodotus, in the immensely influential philosophies of Plato and ▷ Aristotle, and in political oratory, especially that of Demosthenes.

Demosthenes achieved fame by his efforts to sustain the Greeks in their wars (357–338 BC) against Philip of Macedon, a state to the north of Greece. The war ended with the Macedonians making themselves the dominant power in Greece. They did not actually destroy the independence of the states, but the intensity and many-sidedness of Greek city life diminished. However, Philip's son Alexander the Great (ruled 336–323 BC) took Greek culture with him in his rapid conquests round the eastern Mediterranean and as far east as north-west India. The result was the 'Hellenistic Period' lasting until the Roman conquest, after which it did not cease but went into a new phase. The culture of Greece now became a climate of civilization shared by many lands; it was no longer even centred in Greece but in the university city of Alexandria in Egypt. The price paid for this expansion was that without the sustenance of the vigorous Greek city life, the literature lost its force, depth and originality, though it retained its secondary qualities such as grace and sophistication. The best known imaginative works of this period are the 'pastoral' poems by Theocritus and others; they influenced the Roman poet Virgil, and were extensively used as models by ▷ Renaissance poets in the 16th and 17th centuries.

In the Graeco-Roman period (146 BC–AD 500), the Greeks were the teachers and cultural allies of their conquerors, the Romans. ▷ Latin literature written under Greek influence now excelled what continued to be written in Greek. Yet Renaissance Europe felt so much closer to the Romans than to the Greeks that it was the Greek writers of this period who influenced it more deeply than the earlier Greeks did. The historian and biographer Plutarch, for instance was widely read in England in the age of ▷ Shakespeare, who used him as a sourcebook for his plays.

In considering the influence of Greek literature on European, and in particular on English, literature, we have to distinguish between the influence of Greek philosophy and that of Greek imaginative writing. Plato and Aristotle had profound effects on Christian thought. Plato was made dominant by St Augustine of Hippo (4th–5th century), until St Thomas Aquinas replaced his influence by that of Aristotle. In the 16th century, Plato again became most important, but now as a source of humanist as well as of religious ideas. Aristotle remained dominant as the first philosopher of literature for three centuries, and together they are still regarded as the important starting-points of European philosophy. Greek imaginative writing, on the other hand, made its impression on European, and especially English, imaginative writing chiefly through its assimilation by Roman writers. It was not, for example, the unexcelled Greek dramatists who impressed themselves on the equally unexcelled English dramatists of the age of Shakespeare, but the comparatively inferior Roman ones, Plautus in comedy and Seneca in tragedy. Only in the 30 years of the ▷ Romantic revival that followed the ▷ French Revolution did English writers (partly under ▷ German influence) really discriminate between Greek and Roman literature, and value the Greeks more highly.

Even then, such a poet as ▷ Shelley valued Greek culture as sentiment rather than as a deep influence. For such as him, the Greeks stood for freedom of spirit and of intellect, whereas Latin culture was associated with the pre-revolutionary authoritarian 'old regime' to which he and others of his generation were so much opposed. It must not be forgotten that Greek culture was based on maintaining slaves and that their women were excluded from public life and restricted to the household (▷ Women, Status of). Neither class was considered as capable of full humanity as free Greek males. The extraordinary privilege accorded to Greek culture in Western thought has often obscured these details.

▷ Classical education; Classical mythology.

Green, Sarah (c 1790–1825)

Novelist and prose writer. Little is known about Sarah Green's personal life, but it is possible to trace through her novels a development from quiet docility to sharp feminist ▷ satire (▷ Feminism). Her *Mental Improvement for a Young Lady* (1793) is a ▷ didactic text aimed at teaching her niece correct feminine behaviour which, unsurprisingly, amounts to being chaste and obedient. Interestingly, novels are forbidden reading for the well brought-up young lady. After this incursion into print, *The Private History of the Court of England* (1808) comes as somewhat of a shock, since it describes the scandals of contemporary court life, especially the notorious affairs of the Prince of Wales, under the meagre ▷ allegorical veil of a historical setting. The actress and novelist, ▷ Mary Robinson, who was one of the Prince's many mistresses, is depicted in the novel as an intelligent woman oppressed by a misogynistic husband. Green took up this last theme again in her novel *Gretna Green Weddings, or The Nieces* (1823) which attempts to show that the abuse of women is true villainy, rather than an acceptable, although repugnant, social trait. The other butt of her satiric wit was the romance, which she attacked ruthlessly in her criticism *Romance Readers and Romance Writers* (1810–11), and which she fictionalized in the hilarious *Scotch Novel Reading, or Modern Quackery* (1824). In this latter book a father tries to save his two daughters from mental instability which has been brought on by reading ▷ Byron and ▷ Sir Walter Scott. Their madness takes the form of attempting to live out fiction in their lives; the younger daughter who is obsessed with Scott is saved, but the Byronic daughter dies tragically.

Grimm's Fairy Tales
German folk-tales collected by the brothers
Jacob (1785–1863) and Wilhelm (1786–1859)
Grimm, and published 1812–15. They first
appeared in English in a volume illustrated
by George Cruickshank and containing
such stories as 'Snow White', 'Hansel and
Gretel' and 'Rumpelstiltskin'. They were the
first collectors to write down the stories just
as they heard them, without attempting to
improve them.

▷ German influence on English literature.

Gunning, Elizabeth (1769–1823)
Novelist and translator. Daughter of the
▷ Augustan novelist Susannah Gunning
and the cousin of ▷ Charlotte Bury, the
sensational nature of Elizabeth's family life led
▷ Walpole to entitle them the 'Gunningiad'.

Elizabeth herself rejected the husband her
father chose for her to pursue a relationship
with a somewhat reluctant suitor. However, it
was when she was accused of forging letters
that her father disowned her and she was left
dependent upon the bounty of her mother,
which she also came close to losing. Her
novels are reminiscent of her mother's writing,
both following the traditions of sentiment
and ▷ melodrama, and concerning mainly
aristocratic families who encounter strange
and sensational events; examples of these
include *The Orphans of Snowdon* (1797)
and *The Gipsy Countess* (1799). Her most
interesting work is *Family Stories* (1802), which
purports to be a collection of magic tales
for children, but which retells the traditional
material from a darker and more adult
perspective.

H

Hallam, Arthur Henry (1811–1833)
Poet and miscellaneous writer. The son of ▷ Henry Hallam, but better known as the friend of ▷ Tennyson and famously commemorated in that poet's ▷ *In Memoriam* (1833–50). Hallam showed great promise as a scholar and was primarily influenced by the ▷ Romantic poets. His works were edited posthumously by his father as *Remains in Verse and Prose of A. H. Hallam* (1834).

Hallam, Henry (1777–1859)
Historian. Henry Hallam was the father of ▷ Arthur Henry Hallam, whom ▷ Tennyson commemorated in ▷ *In Memoriam* (1833–50). He is well known for his thorough and influential *Constitutional History of England* (1827) and his comprehensive *An Introduction to the Literature of Europe during the Fifteenth, Sixteenth and Seventeenth Centuries* (1837–9), and he edited his son's works in *Memoir of A. H. Hallam* (1834).

Hamilton, Elizabeth (1758–1816)
Essayist and satirist. Elizabeth Hamilton is known to have predicted her fate as 'one cheerful, pleased, old maid', and although she became ill during the last years of her life, this proved to be a very apt prophecy. Her many publications include *Translation of the Letters of a Hindoo Rajah* (1796), which is not a translation but a satire of contemporary British society through the eyes of the fictional character of the titular Indian Rajah, and *Memoirs of Modern Philosophers* (1800), which attacks contemporary society for its treatment of women, but simultaneously exposes the ludicrousness of women who believe they can alter anything, and in which she attacked contemporary philosophers as 'men who, without much knowledge, either moral or natural, entertain a high idea of their own superiority from having the temerity to reject whatever has the sanction of experience and common sense'. She also wrote on education and undertook historical character sketches.
▷ Nationalism.
Bib: Butler, M., *Jane Austen and the War of Ideas*.

Hands, Elizabeth (fl 1785)
Poet. A neglected writer of great skill and variety, Hands had to contend with contemporary prejudice against her class (she was a servant) as well as her sex. She was sharply aware of both social barriers, writing the ▷ satirical 'Ode on a Dishclout' (▷ ode), and inverting conventional gender roles in her pastorals, where she makes the female nymphs sing in competition describing the beauty of their lovers, the male shepherds. Her most ambitious work, *The Death of Amnon* was published in 1789 and focuses upon incest and rape.
Bib: Landry, D., *The Muses of Resistance*.

Hanway, Mary Ann (c 1775–1815)
Novelist. Little is known about Hanway's life, and she is memorable mainly for her ▷ Minerva novels. The plots of her works are predictable – beautiful, orphaned heroines discover their long-lost parents and marry happily – and the ▷ didacticism advocating unadulterated moral virtue is cloying and repetitive. But Hanway's figurative language, although unsophisticated, is passionate and ornate, and some of the passages describing physical details appear darkly obsessive. These preoccupations are coupled with an odd, but clearly stated, intention of writing so that her female readers could expunge their own emotional and bodily disorders through the process of reading. Apart from seeing novels as a form of therapy, Hanway had other ideas in advance of her time, attacking contemporary society for the way in which it treated black people, and perceiving that the education system was biased towards men (▷ Women, Education of).
▷ Psychoanalytical criticism.
Bib: Schlueter, P. and J., *An Encyclopedia of British Women Writers*.

Harcourt, Mary (c 1750–1833)
Diarist. Mary Harcourt married a commander in the British army, William Harcourt, in 1778, and travelled with him when he was on active duty. Her accounts of what she saw during these periods reflect the horrors of war, show the small, and often neglected, acts of pity and heroism, as well as uncovering the political motivations behind the objectives. Her work was published by the *Harcourt Papers* in 1792–5.
▷ Diaries; Nationalism.

Hartman, Geoffrey (b 1929)
American critic. Following early essays on ▷ Wordsworth, Hopkins, Rilke, Valéry and André Malraux, Hartman produced one of the most cogent and incisive critical books on Wordsworth to date, *Wordsworth's Poetry, 1787–1814* (1964). His writing at this stage was essentially located in ▷ new criticism, with an admixture of phenomenology. Hartman's openness to continental European

influences in the areas of philosophy and literary theory, combined with his continued engagement with English Romantic poetry, led him into a key role in the establishment of the 'Yale School' of ▷ deconstruction. His books include *Beyond Formalism: Literary Essays, 1958–70* (1970), *The Fate of Reading and other Essays* (1975), *Criticism in the Wilderness* (1980), *Saving the Text: Literature, Derrida, Philosophy* (1981) and *Easy Pieces* (1985).

Harvey, Jane (1776–c 1841)
Poet and novelist. A northern writer, Harvey was born in Newcastle-upon-Tyne and often included sentimental descriptions of her home town and its impoverished inhabitants in her works, as for example in *Poems on Various Subjects* (1797), written in ▷ Spenserian stanzas, and in the late *Fugitive Pieces* (1841). Otherwise, Harvey is mainly known as a ▷ Minerva novelist, whose skill lies in ingenious plots and amusing characterizations.

Hatton, Ann (1764–1838)
Novelist. Ann Hatton (née Kemble) was the sister of the acclaimed actress ▷ Sarah Siddons, but lacking her sister's looks and build – Ann had a squint and a limp – she was apprenticed to a mantua maker by her family. Bad luck or ill-judgement seemed to dog Ann: her first husband proved to be a bigamist, she was accidentally shot in the face while in a bath house (probably one of ill-repute), and she chose to stage a suicide attempt in Westminster Abbey. However, in 1792 she married William Hatton and they began a new, and more successful, life in America, where she wrote several popular librettos. By 1806 she was once more in Britain and, having been widowed, began to write ▷ Minerva novels to make a living. Hatton took every ingredient of the ▷ Gothic novel and reproduced it in faithful stereotype; she was, as a result, one of the most popular novelists on the Minerva lists. An early work, *Poems on Miscellaneous Subjects* (1783), shows that her style was both sentimental and Gothic, but also reveal a youthful promise that was never to be fulfilled.

Hawkins, Laetitia-Matilda (1759–1835)
Novelist, autobiographer and travel writer. Hawkins's early years shadowed her creative output for most of her life. Her father was the ▷ Augustan scholar John Hawkins, who produced one of the first histories of music as well as a life of Dr Johnson (1709–84). Johnson, who appointed Hawkins as his

executor, found him difficult, and this is certainly the experience of his daughter who felt that her spirit had been broken by his incessant condemnation and criticism. Her first works were published anonymously, but she used her own name for *The Countess and Gertrude, or Modes of Discipline* (1811) which was dedicated to ▷ Harriet Bowdler. The narratives of her fictions often depict a repressed and self-deprecating heroine, who battles to assert herself over her male relatives. She produced a somewhat amorphous ▷ autobiography with general comments, *Anecdotes, Biographical Sketches and memoirs* (1823), which was mocked by ▷ De Quincey. Her novels, however, were admired by ▷ Jane Austen. Her ▷ travel writings remain in manuscript form.
Bib: Todd, J., *Dictionary of British Women Writers*.

Hayley, William (1745–1820)
Poet and biographer. Hayley was a popular poet, but was generally dismissed by other writers of the period, including ▷ Byron and ▷ Southey. He was befriended by ▷ Blake, however, who illustrated two of his works, *Little Tom the Sailor* (1800) and *Ballads Founded on Anecdotes Relating to Animals* (1805). Hayley also published the lives of several literary figures including ▷ Cowper and ▷ Milton.
▷ Ballad.

Hays, Mary (1760–1843)
Radical writer. Hays was born into a family of Rational Dissenters and her early writings are concerned with religious matters; for example, in *Cursory Remarks* (1791) she attacks the prejudices of the established church. Then, in 1792 she met ▷ Mary Wollstonecraft and the main thrust of her writing became feminist (▷ Feminism). For example, in *Appeal to the Men of Great Britain in Behalf of Women* (1798; published anonymously), she wrote:

> But for a woman to be obliged to humour the follies, the caprice, the vices of men of a very different stamp, and to be obliged to consider this as their duty; is perhaps as unfortunate a system of politics in morals, as ever was introduced for degrading the human species.

Hays also wrote advocating vocational training for women and demanding the right to independent economic means, and she attempted to redress the pro-male balance of historical evidence by writing *Female Biography* (1803) and *Memoirs of Queens* (1821). While respected in this capacity, Hays's fictional work was ridiculed by her contemporaries, for example by ▷ Coleridge and ▷ Elizabeth Hamilton, mainly because her novels are unrepentantly ▷ autobiographical. *Memoirs of Emma Courtney* (1796) is a particularly honest and sometimes disconcertingly personal account of a woman who fails to win the love of the man she desires (in real life, William Frend).

▷ Histories and Chronicles; Women, Education of.

Bib: Moers, E., *Literary Women*; Todd, J., *The Sign of Angelica*.

Hazlitt, William (1778–1830)

Essayist and critic. He was the son of a ▷ Unitarian minister with strong radical views, and himself took the liberal side in politics throughout his life; though he wrote for many papers and periodicals, he is most associated with John and ▷ Leigh Hunt's radical weekly, ▷ *The Examiner*. He was the early admirer and friend of ▷ Coleridge and ▷ Wordsworth (see one of his best essays, *My First Acquaintance with Poets*; 1823), and though he later resented what he considered their betrayal of the liberal cause, he continued to admire especially Wordsworth's early poetry for its integrity and disinterestedness, qualities which he exemplified in his own life. However, he did not share the simplifying, materialistic outlook of many of the radicals *eg* the ▷ Utilitarians; his best work, *The Spirit of the Age* (1825) – studies of the leading minds of the time, including ▷ Bentham and Wordsworth – shows his feeling that rational theorists like the former were really remoter from reality, though they claimed to base all their thought on experience, than were the poets who gave form to their experience directly. This regard for whole truth shows in his most perceptive criticism, especially of ▷ Shakespeare (*Characters of Shakespeare's Plays*, 1817–18). Other critical works: *Lectures on the English Poets* (1818–19); *English Comic Writers* (1819); *Dramatic Literature of the Age of Elizabeth* (1820); *Table Talk, or Original Essays on Men and Manners* (1821–2).

Though nowadays best known for his criticism, Hazlitt has always had a larger public for his miscellaneous essays, such as *On Going a Journey*, *Going to a Fight*, etc. His graphic, terse, energetic style often gives this part of his work strong character.

▷ Essay.

Bib: Howe, P. P., *Life*; Baker, H., *Life*; Schneider, E., *The Aesthetics of Hazlitt*;

Brinton, C., *The Political Ideas of the English Romantics*; Stephen, L., in *Hours in a Library*; Saintsbury, G., in *Essays in English Literature*.

Headlong Hall (1816)

A novel by ▷ Thomas Love Peacock. It is his first and shows the main characteristics of his maturer work: witty, burlesque conversations and, innovatively, very little plot. The narrative is interspersed with attractive ▷ lyrics and songs. As in his other novels, the characters are caricatures of contemporary types.

Heart of Midlothian, The (1818)

A novel by ▷ Sir Walter Scott. Midlothian is a county in Scotland in which Edinburgh, the Scottish capital, is situated. The title refers to the old Tolbooth prison in Edinburgh, so nicknamed. The central part of the story is Jeanie Deans's journey on foot to London in order to appeal to the Duke of Argyle – a Scottish nobleman high in royal favour – on behalf of her sister Effie who has been wrongfully charged with child murder. Argyle was a historical character, and the events are linked up with the attack on the Tolbooth – known as the Porteous Riot – which actually took place in 1736. As in other novels by Scott about 18th-century Scotland, the characterization is vigorous, *eg* of Madge Wildfire who has abducted the child whom Effie is supposed to have murdered, and Dumbiedikes, the silent suitor of Jeanie. It is often regarded as the best of Scott's novels.

Heber, Reginald (1783–1826)

Poet and religious writer. Heber's most famous works are probably the hymns 'Hark the Herald Angels Sing' and 'Holy, Holy, Holy' (*Hymns, Written and Adapted to the Weekly Church Service*, 1827), although he published several more extensive works including, *Poems and Translations* (1812) and *The Lay of the Purple Falcon: a metrical romance* (1847). In 1822 he was appointed Bishop of Calcutta, a role which inspired him to write *Narrative of a Journey through India* (1828).

▷ Hymns; Lay.

Bib: Smith, G., *Bishop Heber: Poet and Missionary*.

Hellas

In Greek, the name of Greece. Hellenes were the Greeks. Hellenism: the influence of ancient Hellenic or Greek culture, especially in what was understood as its ideals of intellectual enlightenment and the cultivation of beauty.

Hellas is also the title of a poetic drama

by ▷ Shelley, it was published in 1822
and inspired by the proclamation of Greek
independence in 1821.
  ▷ Greek literature.

Hemans, Felicia Dorothea (née Browne) (1793–1835)
Poet. After being deserted by her army
captain husband in 1818, Felicia Hemans
turned to writing to support her family,
living first in Wales and then in Dublin. She
published many volumes of verse, including
Translations from Camoens and other Poems
(1818), *Welsh Melodies* (1822), *Records of
Women* (1828) and *Hymns on the Works of
Nature* (1833). Her combination of liberalism
and piety made her very popular. Her best
remembered poems today are *Casabianca*
('The boy stood on the burning deck') and
The Homes of England ('The stately Homes of
England,/ How beautiful they stand!').
Bib: Hickok, K., *Representations of Women*:
Nineteenth-century British Women's Poetry;
Trinder, P. W., *Mrs Hemans*.

Hermeneutics
Used in literary criticism to denote the science
of interpretation as opposed to commentary.
Hermeneutics is concerned primarily with
the question of determining meaning,
and is based upon the presupposition of
a transcendental notion of understanding,
and a conception of truth as being in some
sense beyond language. Hermeneutics
also postulates that there is one truth, and
is therefore opposed on principle to the
notion of 'pluralism' that is associated with
▷ deconstruction and ▷ materialist readings.

Heroic couplet
  ▷ Couplet; Augustanism.

Heroic, Mock
A literary mode in which large and important
events are juxtaposed with small and
insignificant ones for a variety of comic,
satirical or more profoundly ironic effects. In
its narrow sense mock heroic is the product
of the ▷ Augustan, neo-classical age. As the
bourgeoisie wrested cultural hegemony from
the aristocracy in the late 17th century, a
new, more complex attitude to the ancient
aristocratic ideals of honour and nobility
developed. A new irony infused their literary
expression in the ▷ classical forms of ▷ epic
and tragedy. Epic retained the respect of the
reading public, but it was too archaic and
primitive to satisfy the modern imagination
in its traditional form. ▷ John Milton's

▷ *Paradise Lost*, the only significant literary
epic in English, has about it much of the
complexity of the novel, and its more atavistic
heroic elements (the war in heaven, the vision
of future history) seem mechanical. In the
generations following Milton, the Augustan
poets, John Dryden and Alexander Pope
translated the ancient epics, but their own
original work took the more complex form of
mock epic.

Hervey, Elizabeth (c 1748–c1820)
Novelist. Hervey was the half-sister of
▷ William Beckford, who is thought to
have had her in mind when he attacked
sentimental novels in *Modern Novel Writing*,
although his attack could equally well be
directed at ▷ Hannah More or ▷ Mary
Robinson. Whatever the intention, Hervey
appears to have been genuinely upset, partly
because the accusation was not particularly
just. Her works exhibit some of the plot
characteristics of sentimental novels, for
example in *Louisa* (1789) where the heroine
is selflessly devoted to the illegitimate child
of her betrothed, but her character sketches
and descriptive passages are sharper and
more self-consciously witty than Beckford's
summation suggests.

Histories and Chronicles
Histories and chronicles are important in the
study of literature in two ways: as sources for
imaginative material and as literature in their
own right.
  The 18th century was a period in which
antiquarian scholarship became thoroughly
established; the antiquarians were interested
by the nature of their studies in the detailed
life of the past. ▷ Walter Scott was one of
them and his historical novels, though very
uneven in quality, are important as a new kind
of history as well as a new kind of imaginative
literature. It was his re-creation of the daily
life of the past that was one of the influences
upon the Victorian writer Thomas Carlyle
(1795–1881), whose historical works (the
most notable of which is his *French Revolution*,
1837) are more imaginative than factual. ▷ T.
B. Macaulay was a better historian and not
inferior as an imaginative writer; ▷ *Macaulay's
History of England* is the only historical work
which comes near ▷ Gibbon's ▷ *Decline
and Fall* in reputation, and Macaulay was
responsible for the so-called 'Whig view of
history' as steady progress in material welfare
and political advance. It was, however, in the
19th century that the controversy about history
as an art or as a science developed, and other

distinguished historians of the latter part of
the century tended to become comparatively
specialized scholars without the breadth of
appeal of such men as Gibbon and Macaulay.

Women writers of the ▷ Romantic period
began an attempt, still going on today,
to reverse the patriarchial domination of
histories; for example, ▷ Mary Hays.

Hofland, Barbara (1770–1844)

Poet and novelist. Hugely prolific northern
writer, Hofland was widowed only two years
after her marriage to Thomas Hoole and
was forced to write in order to keep herself
and her baby. Her first book, *Poems* (1805),
was successful and, although she ran a
boarding school in Harrogate, she continued
publishing, moving from poetry to the more
lucrative novel form. In 1808 she married
the young, self-centred artist, Thomas
Hofland, and was forced to provide for the
family by writing at night, so as not to disturb
his daytime creative activities. There is an
interesting portrait of an egotistical artist in
Hofland's ▷ didactic text, *Son of a Genius*
(1812). On the whole her work is intelligent
and carefully presented, with some lighter
touches in the later, more psychologically
involved novels such as *Katherine* (1828).

Hogg, James (1770–1835)

Poet and novelist. Hogg was nicknamed
'the Ettrick Shepherd' because he had been
a shepherd in Ettrick Forest in southern
Scotland until his poetic talent was discovered
by ▷ Sir Walter Scott. He is now best
known for his powerful work of Calvinist
guilt and ▷ Gothic supernaturalism, *The
Private Memoirs and Confessions of a Justified
Sinner* (1824).
Bib: Groves, D., *James Hogg: the Growth of
a Writer*.

Holcroft, Thomas (1745–1809)

Dramatist, novelist and autobiographer.
Holcroft was a self-made man and remained
deeply committed to the principle of self-
improvement. He was politically radical and
much influenced by ▷ Godwin, whose *Caleb
Williams* (1794) he attempted to imitate in his
own social novels, *Anna St Ives* (1792) and *The
Adventures of Hugh Trevor* (1794). He wrote
several plays and some poetry. Holcroft's
most important and interesting work, however,
is his ▷ autobiography, *Memoirs of the Late
Thomas Holcroft* (1816), which was edited by
his friend ▷ Hazlitt.
Bib: Baine, R.M., *Holcroft and the Revolutionary
Novel*.

Holford, Margaret (1761–1834) and Holford, Margaret (1778–1852)

Mother and daughter. The elder Holford
was a poet, dramatist and novelist, while her
daughter is known for her poetry and prose.
Holford senior's novels have predictable
plots which rely heavily on the contemporary
vogue for sensationalism and exotic mystery.
Her first novel, *Fanny* (1785), is dramatic
and lively, ending with the reformation of the
hero from rake into model husband. Her two
plays, *Neither's The Man* (1798) and *The Way
to Win Her* (1814), are more challenging; they
recall ▷ Restoration comedy and advocate
the superiority of female 'wit'. Holford junior
turned her talents towards poetry and was
heavily influenced by ▷ Sir Walter Scott. Her
published work, *Wallace, or The Fight of Falkirk*
(1809) and *Poems* (1811) were very popular at
the time, but they are too sentimental to be
popular with a 20th-century readership. She
also wrote a novel *Warbeck of Wolfstein* (1820),
which was influenced by ▷ Shelley.
▷ Gothic novels.

Homer

Ancient Greek epic poet, author of the *Iliad*
and the *Odyssey*, basic works for ▷ Greek
literature. Ancient traditions exist about
Homer, for instance that latterly he was
blind and that seven cities claimed to be his
birthplace, but nothing is conclusively known
about him. Archaeological investigation
has disclosed that the destruction of Troy,
following the siege described in the *Iliad*,
took place in the 12th century BC; linguistic,
historical and literary analysis of the poems
show them to date as artistic wholes from
perhaps the 8th century BC. That they are
artistic wholes is in fact the only evidence
for the existence of Homer; efforts to show
that they are compilations by a number of
poets have proved unconvincing, though it is
clear that Homer himself was using the work
of other poets between the Trojan war and
his own time. The Victorian critic Matthew
Arnold (1822–88) in his essay *On Translating
Homer* (1861) says that Homer is rapid in
movement, plain in diction, simple in ideas
and noble in manner; and that the translations
of three eminent English poets, George
Chapman (1559–1634), Alexander Pope
(1688–1744) and ▷ William Cowper all fail in
one or more of these qualities, however fine
their verse is in other respects.

Hood, Thomas (1799–1845)

Poet. His serious poetry shows strongly the
influence of ▷ John Keats, but he is known

chiefly for his comic and topical verse; the latter includes grim but haunting poems about contemporary social abuses, *eg The Song of the Shirt* (1843), a kind of poetic poster art which does not bear close examination but is extremely effective on first reading. In his comic verse, he was notorious for his puns which he used obtrusively but often wittily.
Bib: Jerrold, W., *Life*; Reid, J. C., *A Critical Study*.

Hook, Theodore Edward (1788–1841)

Novelist, poet and dramatist. Hook is primarily remembered as a ▷ Silver-fork novelist; his works include *Sayings and Doings* (1824–8) and *Gilbert Gurney* (1836). He was intimately acquainted with the aristocratic world which he describes, and his books were often used as behavioural guides for those who wished to enter polite society. Their narratives and characters, however, lack distinction.
Bib: Brightfield, M.F., *Hook and His Novels*.

Horace (Quintus Horatius Flaccus, 65–8 BC)

Roman poet of the ▷ Augustan age. His work divides into three classes; his ▷ Satires, ▷ Odes and Epistles. The last includes the *Art Poetica* or *De Arte Poetica* (Concerning the Art of Poetry) which became an important critical document for Europe – for England particularly in the 18th century. It emphasizes the importance of cultivating art in poetry; he lays down the principle that if you do not understand poetry it is better to leave it alone. Art means above all the cultivation of alert judgement: expression and form must be appropriate to theme characterization and form must be consistent with the subject and with themselves; conciseness is a virtue in didacticism; adaptation of a writer is allowed but plagiarism is not; the poet must study to be wise as a man, and he must be his own severest critic; a just critic is a severe one.
The English Augustans' concern was to cultivate proportion and balance. Criticism and satire thus became important to them as correctives of inborn human tendencies, and they cultivated the congenial spirit of Horace as Horace himself had sought to practise the virtues of the Greeks.
▷ Smith, Horatio; Smith, James.

Hudibrastics

Term deriving from *Hudibras* (1663, 1664 and 1678), a mock-heroic ▷ satire in tetrameter ▷ couplets by Samuel Butler (1612–80). The Presbyterian Sir Hudibras, and his

Independent Squire Ralpho, undergo various adventures designed to expose the hypocrisy of the Puritans, interspersed with satire on various scientific and intellectual follies.
▷ Heroic, mock.

Hugo, Victor(-Marie) (1802–85)

French poet, playwright and novelist. Born in Besançon, he lived in Spain and Italy as a child, where his father, a General, followed ▷ Napoleon. Despite nostalgia for the Napoleonic age, Hugo was a confirmed democrat and was elected to the Assembly in 1848 and again in 1870. He lived in exile in the Channel Isles between 1851 and 1870 after the *coup d'état* of Louis Napoleon. As a young man he refused a military career in favour of literature; he gained favour through poetry and was made Chevalier de la Legion d'Honneur by 1825. He read and admired Chateaubriand, a proto-Romantic influence, and after the publication of his play *Cromwell* (1827) with its famous Preface, became a spearhead of the French Romantic movement. He married Adèle Foucher, and was much affected by the death of his daughter in 1845. He was made a peer and became an important figure, being buried with great ceremony in the Panthéon. His plays have lasted less well than the novels and poetry which are remarkable not for intellectual content so much as beauty, faith and feeling. Hugo's output was prolific: the plays include *Hernani* (1830) and *Ruy Blas* (1838); the novels *Notre Dame de Paris* (1831), the celebrated *Les Misérables* (1862), *Les Travailleurs de la Mer* (1866), *L'Homme qui Rit* (1869). His many collections of poems include *Les Odes* (1822), *Odes et Ballades* (1826), *Les Orientales* (1829), *Les Feuilles d'Automne* (1831), *Les Chants du Crépuscule* (1835), *Les Voix Intérieures* (1837), *Les Rayons et les Ombres* (1840), *Les Châtiments* (1853), *Les Contemplations* (1856) and *La Légende des Siècles* (1859, 1877, 1883).
▷ French literature in England.

Hunt, Leigh (1784–1859)

Journalist and poet. With his brother John, he edited the boldly radical weekly periodical ▷ *The Examiner* until he gave up his share in it in 1821. His outspoken attack on the Prince Regent in 1813 brought two years' imprisonment for the brothers, but they continued to edit the journal in prison. He was joint editor with ▷ Lord Byron of the short-lived quarterly, the *Liberal*, and he edited or had a hand in several other periodicals, doing much to publicize the work of both ▷ John Keats and ▷ Percy Bysshe

Shelley. His essays, popular at the time, are mostly effusions on trivial topics, though his busy and active life makes his autobiography (1850) one of his most memorable works. Later in life he was caricatured as the genial sponger, Mr Skimpole, in Charles Dickens's *Bleak House* (1852–3).

The Hunt literary circle was nicknamed the 'Cockney School' by the critic John G. Lockhart, indicating a certain vulgarity. Hunt's own poetry does indeed display a facile cosiness of tone, reminiscent of the suburban drawing-room. However, its most prominent technical features: a cloying physicality of imagery, and double or triple rhymes with feminine endings, were enthusiastically adopted by his protégé, Keats. Keats's early poem 'I stood tiptoe upon a little hill' is dedicated to Hunt and closely imitates the manner of Hunt's best work, *The Story of Rimini* (1816), from which it borrows such vocabulary as 'blisses', 'tresses', 'bower', 'blushes'. The characteristic rhyme 'blisses'/'kisses' occurs in both poems, and other rhymes of Keats ('posy'/'rosy', 'flitting'/'quitting', 'ever wrestle'/'ever nestle') recall such rhymes as 'flushes'/'blushes', 'dissemble'/'in a tremble' in *The Story of Rimini*.

Bib: Blunden, E., *Leigh Hunt's Examiner Examined*; Blunden, E., *Life*.

Hunter, Rachel (1754–1813)

Novelist. Hunter became a novelist in her 40s, and at the time her novels appeared to be somewhat self-conscious of their narrative form, and were mocked by ▷ Jane Austen. Today, however, we might call them 'metafictional' (▷ Metalanguage), that is, writing which deliberately questions the relationship between fiction and reality by drawing attention to its own status as a linguistic construct. For example, in Hunter's *The Unexpected Legacy* (1804) the Preface is written by an author who quotes an attack on novels by a friend; both characters are fictitious, although coming in the Preface the reader expects them to be real. Similarly, in *Lady Maclairn, The Victim of Villainy* (1806) the author is supposedly only the editor of the letters, and, adding to the complexity, she places herself within the novel as a character, ending up as a governess to the heroine's family. In addition to the adoption of multiple authorial voices, Hunter also layers plot and time to create a complex interweaving of stories, each creating a different relationship between 'fiction' and 'reality'. Thematically, she seems to have been fascinated by the idea

of mixed racial marriages; this is the concern of *Lady Maclairn* and her first published novel, *Letitia, or The Castle without a Spectre* (1801), the latter of which may also be classed as a ▷ Gothic novel.

Hymns

The word 'hymn' is of ancient Greek origin; it meant a song of praise to the gods. Such songs have been important in all the religions that have lain behind European culture; Latin hymns were composed and sung in the Christian churches from the earliest days of Christianity, and the Jewish hymns, or Psalms, are shared by the Jewish and the Christian religions.

English hymns date from the Reformation and were firmly established by the 18th century, a period which is characterized by Dissenting hymn-writers such as Isaac Watts (1674–1748). His language combines the homeliness of the broadside ballads of the city streets with the dignity and musical cadence of biblical English. ▷ Charles Wesley, the brother of the ▷ Methodist leader ▷ John Wesley, had greater versatility than Watts, and was very prolific; his best hymns are impressive though without the power of the best by Watts. Other notable 18th-century hymn-writers were ▷ Reginald Heber, ▷ Alice Flowerdew, John Newton (1725–1807) and ▷ William Cowper. All these had at least some of the force of common speech and spontaneous emotion in their hymns. Beside them, the hymns of the orthodox Anglican, Joseph Addison (1672–1719), are cold, though dignified and sincere.

Hyperion

In Greek myth, a Titan, son of the sky god Uranus and the earth goddess Ge. He was one of the greatest of the Titans, and often identified with the sun, of whom in the original myth he was the father; the sun-god was Helios.

▷ *Hyperion* by Keats.

Hyperion (1820)
The Fall of Hyperion (1856)

Two fragments of an epic poem in blank verse by ▷ John Keats, written in 1818–19, the second (*The Fall of Hyperion*) unrevised. Keats's aim was to rival ▷ John Milton's philosophical profundity by treating a theme of divine conflict. The Greek myth of the war of the Olympian Gods and the primal Titans is adapted to the aestheticist idea that 'first in beauty should be first in might'. *Hyperion* (published in 1820) opens with a magnificent scene in which Saturn, chief of the Titans, mourns his lost power, while Hyperion, the only Titan as yet unfallen, roams uneasily round his palace. Apollo, the destined Olympian successor to Hyperion is confronted by Mnemosyne who begins to initiate him into godhead. At this point the fragment breaks off, Keats's explanation being that it was too Miltonic: 'I prefer the native music . . . to Milton's cut by feet.' However it is difficult to imagine how the approaching beauty-contest between Hyperion and Apollo could have been related in terms of epic conflict without absurdity, or how the moral difficulties of the theme could have been overcome. It is indeed,

the highly Miltonic passages concerning the suffering of the Titans which are the most poetically moving parts of the surviving fragment.

The Fall of Hyperion (not published until 1856) escapes from narrative problems into personal preoccupations, opening with a dream in which the poet finds himself undergoing a symbolic test of dedication in the temple of (Juno) Moneta, the Counsellor. After a powerful discussion of the nature of the poetic calling, containing some of Keats's most mature verse, the story is retold as before, in the same Miltonic manner, breaking off even earlier than the previous version, as the same narrative problems loomed ahead.

I

Idealism

In philosophy, any form of thought which finds reality not in the mind of the perceiver (the subject), nor in the thing experienced (the object) but in the idea in which they meet. In its earliest form idealism was developed by the ▷ Greek philosophers Socrates and his disciple Plato. Their influence was important in the 16th-century Europe of the ▷ Renaissance.

In ordinary usage, idealism means the ability to conceive perfection as a standard by which ordinary behaviour and achievement is to be judged. This view is really an inheritance from Plato, who believed that earthly realities were imperfect derivatives of heavenly perfections. To 'idealize' a thing or person is to present the image of what ought to be, rather than what experience knows in ordinary life. In imaginative art we have come to consider this as a fault, but to a 16th-century critic such as Sir Philip Sidney (1554–86) poetry existed for just such a purpose.

In modern critical theory idealism is associated with the anti-materialist (▷ Materialism) impulse to denigrate history and social context. The meaning of this term is complicated by its history within the discipline of philosophy, and by its common usage as a description of human behaviour not susceptible to the 'realistic' impulses of self-interest. The term is sometimes used in critical theory to denote the primacy of thought, and to indicate a particular kind of relationship between writer and text where it is a sequence of ideas that act as the deep structure for events and relationships.

Ideology

This term is defined by ▷ Karl Marx and Friedrich Engels (1800–95) in *The German Ideology* as 'false consciousness'. A further meaning, which the 20th-century critic Raymond Williams traces to the usage initiated by ▷ Napoleon Bonaparte, denotes a fanatical commitment to a particular set of ideas, and this has remained a dominant meaning in the sphere of modern right-wing politics, especially in relation to the question of dogmatism. The term has come to the fore again in the ▷ post-structuralist Marxism of ▷ Louis Althusser, where it is distinguished from 'science'. Ideology here is defined as the means whereby, at the level of ideas, every social group produces and reproduces the conditions of its own existence. Althusser argues that 'Ideology is a "representation" of the imaginary relationship of individuals

to their real conditions of existence' (*Lenin and Philosophy*; 1971). In order to ensure that political power remains the preserve of a dominant class, individual 'subjects' are assigned particular positions in society. A full range of social institutions, such as the Church, the family and the education system, are the means through which a particular hierarchy of values is disseminated. The point to emphasize, however, is that ideology disguises the real material relations between the different social classes, and this knowledge can only be retrieved through a theoretically aware analysis of the interrelationships that prevail within society at any one time. A ruling class sustains itself in power, partly by coercion (repressive apparatuses), but also by negotiation with other subordinate classes (hegemony; Althusser's ideological state of apparatuses).

Social change occurs when the ideology of the dominant class is no longer able to contain the contradictions existing in real social relations. The function of literary texts in this process is complex. In one sense they reproduce ideology, but also they may offer a critique of it by 'distancing' themselves from the ideology with which they are historically implicated. Since all language is by definition 'ideological', insofar as it is motivated by particular sorts of social relationship, the language of a literary text can very often be implicated in an ideology of which it is not aware. The text's implication in ideology can only be excavated through a critical process which seeks to uncover the assumptions upon which it is based.

Bib: Althusser, L., *For Marx*; Thompson, J. B., *Studies in the Theory of Ideology*.

Imaginary

When used in contemporary literary theory, this term originates in ▷ Jacques Lacan's re-reading of ▷ Freud, where it refers generally to the perceived or *imagined* world of which the infant sees itself as the centre. In other words, this is the first opportunity that the child has to construct a coherent identity for itself. But in Lacan's view this image is a myth; it is an imaginary subjectivity that allows the ego to speak of itself as 'I', but which represses those fragmentary energies which constitute the unconscious. ▷ Louis Althusser uses the term 'imaginary', which he takes from Lacan, in a very different way, while retaining the concept of a constellation of forces which contribute to the formation of the human subject. In Althusser the subject *misrecognizes* his or her place in the social order through an ideology which posits as 'natural' a fixed relationship between social classes. What is at issue for both Lacan and Althusser is the way in which individual human subjects are constituted by an order which extends beyond the images through which that order is represented to them. In Lacan's psychoanalytical theory the realm of the 'imaginary' is contained within that of the ▷ 'symbolic order', and it is the function of psychoanalysis to uncover the 'real' relations which exist beneath this series of representations. In Althusser, the 'mirror' phase can be equated with 'ideology' in that this is the means through which individual human subjects *misrecognize* themselves and their position in the social order.

▷ Psychoanalytical criticism.

Inchbald, Mrs Elizabeth (1753–1821)
Novelist, dramatist and actress. Among other plays she translated Kotzbue's *Lovers' Vows* from the German, and this is the play rehearsed in ▷ Jane Austen's ▷ *Mansfield Park*. This, and some of the other 19 plays she wrote or adapted, were popular successes: Jane Austen assumes knowledge of it by the reader. However, her best works are her two novels: *A Simple Story* (1791) and *Nature and Art* (1796).

▷ German influence on English literature.
Bib: Littlewood, S. R., *Elizabeth Inchbald and her Circle.*

Industrial Revolution, The
An industrial revolution has been defined as 'the change that transforms a people with peasant occupations and local markets into an industrial society with world-wide connections' (*Encyclopaedia Britannica*). Clearly then many countries have industrial revolutions, and more than one; for example it is currently said that Britain is undergoing a new industrial revolution in high-technology processes. However, we understand *the* Industrial Revolution to mean the succession of changes which transformed England from a predominantly rural and agricultural country into a predominantly urban and manufacturing one in the 18th and 19th centuries, and especially between 1750 and 1850. It was, moreover, the first such revolution in the modern world.

Although not, apart from London, a country of great towns, England at the beginning of the 18th century was already a great trading nation, with much private capital ready for investment. Not only was trade free to move throughout the British Isles but there

was considerable freedom of movement between the social classes, which were not rigidly defined almost into caste systems as in other European countries, *eg* France. English middle-class religion had emphasis on the individual conscience as the guide to conduct and also on the moral excellence of sober, industrious employment; these values encouraged self-reliance and enterprising initiative. Although some of this middle class (the Nonconformist or Dissenting sects which rejected the Church of England) were barred from political rights, and Parliament, controlled by the aristocracy, was far from truly representative, the political leaders of the country were extremely interested in commerce, which they were ready to participate in and profit from. The bent of the whole nation, from the early days of the 17th century, had been increasingly practical and the steadily growing population provided a market which invited exploitation by various methods of improved production. Once the process started, it gathered its own momentum, which was increased by the existence of large supplies of convenient fuel in the country's coalfields. Agriculture also contributed to industrial growth: the landowners were zealous farmers and their improved methods of cultivation not only freed much labour, which then became available for employment in the town factories, but increased the food supplies available for the towns. Finally, the 18th century (in contrast to 17th) was a time of peace and stability in Britain, undisturbed by the wars in which her armies and money were engaged across the sea.

In the textile industry, already established since the 15th century as the principal industry, a number of machines were invented which increased production and reduced labour but were too large for the cottages where the processes had hitherto been carried out. They therefore had to be housed in factories and mills where large numbers of employees worked together. These machines were at first operated by water power. In the iron industry, the principal fuel used hitherto had been charcoal, the supply of which was becoming exhausted. However, improved methods of smelting by coal were discovered and ironmasters set up their blast furnaces in the neighbourhood of the coalfields in the north midlands and north of England.

Most important of all, in 1769, James Watt patented an adaptation of his steam-engine to the machines used in the textile industry; this consequently ceased to depend on water power and concentrated itself in the north of England to be near the coalfields. An important result was the immense expansion in manufacture of cotton cloth. An extensive system of canals was constructed in the 18th century for the transport of goods and fuel, and the modern methods of road and bridge building were introduced, but the decisive advance in communications was the invention of the steam rail locomotive by George Stephenson (1814); by 1850 a railway system covered the country. We cannot understand the process of the British Industrial Revolution if we do not appreciate that it was a period of epic excitement, especially in the development of rail transport. It produced inventors and engineers such as Isambard Brunel (1806–59) who had to force their projects against established prejudice and ignorance. The other side of the epic story was the meteoric emergence of great financial speculators such as George Hudson (1800–71), the 'Railway King', who rose from being a York draper to control of a third of the railway system, and ended in disgrace. The social changes were unprecedentedly dramatic, in the rapid growth of the midland and northern industrial towns and the opening of new opportunities for wealth among humble but ambitious men and women. This individualistic aspect of industrialism has been recorded as one of the powerful motivations behind 19th-century culture.

In Memoriam A. H. H.

A sequence of poems by ▷ Alfred Tennyson inspired by the death of ▷ Arthur Henry Hallam, at 22, in 1833. He was a brilliant young man of great promise and hopefulness; Tennyson, a year or two older, had found in friendship with Hallam a strong resource against his own disposition to despondency and scepticism. Hallam's death crystallized for him the difficulty of spiritual affirmation in an age of upheaval in established ideas. Science was already shaking traditional certainties and contributing to the feeling that the reality of nature itself was perpetual flux: there are echoes in *In Memoriam* of Lyell's *Principles of Geology* (1830–3).

The poem was written between 1833 and 1850, and is structurally loose or fragmented – it was to be called 'Fragments of an Elegy'. It consists of 130 sections, each section being a ▷ lyric in stanzas of four eight-syllable lines rhyming *abba* – a form used by Ben Jonson (1572–1637) in his ▷ elegy 'Though Beauty be the Mark of praise'. The sequence is a single poem arranged in three sections

divided by Christmas Odes, and the whole concluded by a marriage-song for the wedding of Tennyson's sister; another sister, Emily, had been engaged to Hallam. Various moods of grief are expressed, and a reaching out to restored confidence and hope; in places Tennyson engages in debate between religion and science. Despite much disagreement about the work as a whole, *In Memoriam* is usually acknowledged to be Tennyson's finest achievement.

Innocence, Songs of
▷ *Songs of Innocence and Experience.*

Intertextuality
A term first introduced into critical theory by the French ▷ psychoanalytical writer Julia Kristeva (b 1941), relating specifically to the use she makes of the work of the Russian ▷ materialist theorist Mikhail Bakhtin (1895–1975). The concept of intertextuality implies that literary texts are composed of dialectically opposed utterances, and that it is the function of the critic to identify these different strands and to account for their oppositions within the text itself. Kristeva notes that Bakhtin's '"dialogism" does not strive towards transcendence . . . but rather towards harmony, all the while implying an idea of rupture (of opposition and analogy) as a modality of transformation' (*Desire and Language*; trans. 1980). Similarly, no text can be entirely free of other texts. No work is written or read in isolation, it is located, in Kristeva's words, 'within the totality of previous . . . texts'. This is a second important aspect of intertextuality.
▷ Feminism.

Intimations of Immortality from Recollections of Early Childhood, Ode: (1807)
An ▷ ode by ▷ William Wordsworth in stanzas of varying length. The first four stanzas were composed in 1802; the rest of the poem was completed in 1806, and the whole was published in 1807. The first part laments that nature no longer appears to the poet as it did in his youth: 'Apparelled in celestial light,/ The glory and the freshness of a dream'. Wordsworth explains this in terms of the ▷ Platonic myth that the soul pre-exists the body in a perfect world of oneness with nature. At birth we come 'trailing clouds of glory . . ./ From God, who is our home'. But soon 'Shades of the prison-house begin to close/ Upon the growing Boy'. The poem thus expresses a radical Romantic reversal

of accepted values: dream is more real than waking, youth is the period of wisdom and true insight. As the poem progresses, the poet's confidence revives, and he asserts a continuing oneness with nature despite his age: 'To me the meanest flower that blows can give/ Thoughts that do often lie too deep for tears'. The upbeat rhetoric is splendid, but many readers are left with the impression that Wordsworth is unnaturally forcing up his spirits towards the end of the poem, in a way which ▷ Samuel Taylor Coleridge is unable to do in his related work, ▷ *Dejection: An Ode*.

Ireland

English attempts to rule Ireland up to the 18th century were characterized by intolerance and the savage subjection of its Catholic inhabitants. However, towards the end of the 18th century, partly owing to the Irish patriotism of Anglo-Irish Protestants the penal laws were reduced in severity, and in 1782 an Irish constitution was promulgated, by which the Irish Protestants were given political rights and limited powers in an Irish Parliament freed from Privy Council control. The experiment was a failure, and in 1801 Ireland was united politically and in all other respects with England and Scotland, Irish Protestants receiving for the first time representation in the English Parliament.

The 19th century was the age of steady emancipation of Irish Catholics and mounting Irish patriotism. The population at the beginning of the century was four and a half million, fewer than one and a half million being of English or Scottish Protestant descent. The Anglo-Irish were the social leaders of the country; the Scots were a middle class of businessmen and farmers; the native Irish were largely peasants. In 1829 Catholic Emancipation removed all the important restrictions on Catholics, notably the political ones. Henceforward there was a growing party of Irish Catholics in the British House of Commons, in the last quarter of the century known as the Home Rule Party from its intention to win national independence for Ireland. In the middle of the century reform was concentrated on land matters; this was the more necessary for the misery of the Irish peasantry whose sufferings were increased by the severe famines of the 1840s, leading to deaths on a massive scale and to massive emigration to the U.S.A. In 1841 the population was over eight million, and it is now about three million; Ireland is thus one of the very few countries in the world whose population has actually diminished in the last

100 years. Attempts to obtain Home Rule through the English Parliament failed. A brief rebellion in 1916 was put down, but a severe one in 1919–21 resulted in independence within the Commonwealth, and the Irish Free State was formed in 1922, taking the name Eire in 1937. Northern Ireland, consisting of six counties of Ulster, remained within the United Kingdom and is represented in the British Parliament.

Ireland, Samuel William Henry (1777–1835)

Forger and poet. Ireland is infamous for having written several plays which he claimed were by ▷ Shakespeare. The deception was uncovered in 1796 when ▷ Malone published *An Enquiry into the Authenticity of Certain Papers Attributed to Shakespeare, Queen Elizabeth and Henry, Earl of Southampton*, at which Ireland confessed. However, before this revelation Ireland's play *Vortigern*, supposed by ▷ Kemble to be by Shakespeare, had been staged and generally disliked by the public. Ireland published several books of poems under his own name, including *The Fisher Boy* (1808), but his work was heavily derivative and unimaginative.
Bib: Grebanier, B., *The Great Shakespeare Forgery*.

Irish literature in English

Ireland – England's first and closest colony – presents a recent history of literary movements and concerns that is very differently paced from that of its colonist. From 1171, the year of Ireland's conquest by Henry II, until the latter years of the 19th century, the history of Irish literature in English is, largely speaking, part of the general history of English literature.

Throughout the 18th and 19th centuries – and into the 20th – writers from Anglo-Irish Ireland made a rich and vigorous contribution to English literature. Their writings were not primarily concerned with the matter of Ireland or their authors' own Irishness. Those who did write of Ireland, like Dion Boucicault (1820–90), who is held by many to be the inventor of the 'stage Irishman', and ▷ Thomas Moore, the purveyor to the drawing-rooms of London of an Ireland sugared by sentiment and exile, capitalized on what looks with hindsight like caricature. All these writers of the Anglo-Irish Ascendancy, coming from their background of landed privilege, seemed to be unaware of the still surviving Gaelic tradition of native Irish literature, with its long ancestry and close connections with mainland Europe.

Moreover, during this pre-Revival period

only a handful of creative writers mirrored the growing interest that folklorists like T. Crofton Croker (1798–1849), travellers (again, many of them from Europe) and diarists were taking in Irish peasant life outside the 'Pale'. ▷ Maria Edgeworth and William Carleton (1794–1869) stand almost alone in the seriousness with which they looked at their native land and its inhabitants. Edgeworth's *Castle Rackrent* (1800) and Carleton's *Traits and Stories of the Irish Peasantry* (1830–3) are isolated landmarks; and Carleton, an adopted member of Ascendancy culture who was born a Catholic peasant, has been read in recent years with renewed interest and recognition. More interest is also being shown towards less well-known Irish authors of the Romantic period, such as ▷ Charlotte Brooke, ▷ John O'Keeffe and, his daughter, ▷ Adelaide O'Keeffe.

Bib: Corkery, D., *Hidden Ireland*.

Italian influence on English literature

After the ▷ Renaissance period, it was Italy as a storehouse of the past, rather than a challenging present, that drew Englishmen. In the 18th century the English invented a sort of tourism; what was called the 'Grand Tour' formed part of the education of upper-class young men and Italy was one of its principal objectives. They were drawn to the architectural and sculptural remains of the old Roman Empire, the framework of their literary education in Latin literature.

The most important contributors to the Italian Romantic novel are probably Alessandro Manzoni (1785–1873), who influenced ▷ Sir Walter Scott, and Ugo Foscolo (1778–1827), who was himself exiled in England. Foscolo's *The Last Letters of Jacopo Ortis* (1802–14) was a major contribution to the novel form, while his poetry, which lays emphasis on his exile, *Of Sepulchres* (1807) participates in the rise of romantic poetry. Another Italian Romantic poet is Giacamo Leopardi (1798–1837) whose international renown, especially for *Canti* (1845) resides in the natural imagery and tones of despair in his poetry. ▷ Shelley, in his 'Ode to the West Wind' and the unfinished 'Triumph of Life' adapts the Italian *terza rima* for use in English poetry. ▷ Byron, partly through his extended residence in Venice, shows a lively awareness of Italian culture and settings, particularly in ▷ *Beppo*, portions of ▷ *Childe Harold's Pilgrimage* and ▷ *Don Juan*, which resurrects the *ottava rima* form pioneered by Boccaccio in the 14th century.

Ivanhoe (1819)

A historical novel by ▷ Sir Walter Scott. It is set in the reign of Richard I, who is one of the characters; the story concerns rivalry between the king and his wicked brother John (King, 1199–1216), and between Saxons and the ruling Norman aristocracy. Locksley (the legendary outlaw, Robin Hood) aids Richard against the rebellious Normans, and helps to bring about the union of the Saxon hero, Wilfred of Ivanhoe, and the heroine Rowena. It was the first novel by Scott to deal with an English (as distinct from a Scottish) subject, and was very popular in the 19th century. This popularity is partly due to its being one of the first attempts to write a novel about the Middle Ages with a genuine regard for history.

Jacobean

Used to indicate the period of James I (1603–25) and applied especially to the literature and style of architecture of his reign. In literature, it is most commonly a way of distinguishing the style of drama under James from the style that prevailed under Elizabeth. Strictly, ▷ Elizabethan drama is experimental, expansive, sometimes ingenuous, in fairly close touch with medieval tradition but energetic with Renaissance forces. It includes the work of the University wits – Christopher Marlowe (1564–93), Thomas Kyd (1558–94), Robert Greene (1558–92), George Peele (1556–96) – and also earlier ▷ Shakespeare. Jacobean drama is thought of as critical, sombre, disillusioned. It includes mature and late Shakespeare, Ben Jonson (1572–1637), Cyril Tourneur (1575–1626), John Webster (1578–1632), Thomas Middleton (1580–1627), Francis Beaumont (1584–1616). and John Fletcher (1579–1625). The Caroline period is associated with such figures as Philip Massinger (1583–1640), John Ford (1586–1640) and James Shirley (1596–1666). Courts were the centre of culture, and depended largely on the circumstances of monarchs; while the reign of Elizabeth was prosperous at home and (mainly) triumphant overseas, that of James saw increasing disagreement at home, and the course of events abroad was negative or even nationally humiliating. The reign of Charles I was yet more bitter in home dissensions but his court was one of distinction and refinement. The tone of the drama varied with these differences in national fortune and court conduct. However the labelling of literary periods is always to some extent simplifying and even falsifying.

The Jacobean period was the first that was really rich in prose, with writers like Francis Bacon (1561–1626), John Donne (1572–1631) and Lancelot Andrewes (1555–1626). Their work contrasts especially with ▷ Restoration prose, which sacrificed the poetic qualities of the Jacobean writing for the sake of grace and lucidity.

▷ Seventeenth-century literature.

Jacobin

Originally a name given to Dominican friars in France, because their first convent was in the Rue St Jacques in Paris. The name was transferred to a political society which rented a room in the convent in the first year of the ▷ French Revolution. The society developed into a highly organized political party, led by ▷ Robespierre, who became practically dictator of France in 1793. The club was closed after the fall of Robespierre in 1794. The Jacobins were extreme in asserting the principle of equality and in their opposition to privilege. Later, when conservative reaction had set in, 'Jacobin' was used loosely for anyone with political liberal tendencies in England as well as in France; *eg* the paper *The Anti-Jacobin* was founded by ▷ George Canning to combat English liberal opinion in 1797.

Jacobite

From Jacobus, the Latin form of James. James II, of the House of Stuart, was deposed in 1688 because, as a convert to Catholicism, he was considered to be conspiring against the established Protestant religion and against Parliament. His supporters were called Jacobites and this name continued for the supporters of his Catholic son and grandsons.

After the crown passed to the House of Hanover, a German Protestant family, in 1714, British Jacobites conspired to restore the House of ▷ Stuart. The Jacobite Rebellions of 1715 and 1745 were the two most formidable attempts; both had principally Scottish support, partly because the Stuarts had originally been a Scottish royal family. The 'Forty-five' rebellion quickly became a romantic legend chiefly because of the supposed gallantry and charm of its leader, Charles Edward Stuart, grandson of James II – 'Bonnie Prince Charlie' to his Scottish supporters and the 'Young Pretender' to his opponents. After the failure of the 'Forty-five' Jacobitism became increasingly a matter of sentiment which even persists to the present day, though the direct line of the Stuarts died out in 1807.

▷ *Rob Roy*; Scott, Sir Walter.

Jakobson, Roman (1896–1982)

Born in Moscow where he was educated. He worked in Czechoslovakia for almost 20 years, between 1920 and 1939, and after the German invasion he escaped to Scandinavia, before going to the U.S.A. where he taught in a number of universities, and became Professor of Russian Literature at the Massachusetts Institute of Technology. During his formative years he was heavily influenced by a number of avante-garde movements in the Arts, but in his own work he laid specific emphasis upon the formulation of a 'poetics' which took into account the findings of ▷ structuralism, and the work of the Russian formalists. He was an active member of the Society for the

Study of Poetic Language (OPOYAZ) which was founded in St Petersburg in 1916, and in 1926 he founded the Prague Linguistic Circle. His wife Krystyna Pomorska notes, in a recent collection of his writings, that poetry and visual art became for Jakobson the fundamental spheres for observing how verbal phenomena work and for studying how to approach them (Roman Jakobson, *Language and Literature*, 1987). Jakobson's work on the relationship between metaphor and metonymy (▷ Figures of speech) has been taken up and developed by a number of critics, with fruitful results for the understanding of Romantic poetry. The work of ▷ Paul de Man, ▷ Geoffrey Hartman, J. Hillis Miller and ▷ Harold Bloom is especially noteworthy.
Bib: Hawkes, T., *Structuralism and Semiotics*; Jakobson, R., *Language and Literature* and *Verbal Art, Verbal Sign, Verbal Time*; Bennett, T., *Formalism and Marxism*; Erlich, V., *Russian Formalism: History-Doctrine*.

James, George Payne Rainsford (1799–1860)
Novelist and biographer. James was a diplomat and the historiographer of King William IV. He wrote numerous novels in the style of ▷ Walter Scott, as well as some useful historical material such as *The Life of Edward the Black Prince* (1836). His novels are predictable and often focus upon fearless and daring horsemen, for which he was justly ridiculed.
▷ Histories and Chronicles.
Bib: Ellis, S.M., *The Solitary Horseman: or the Life and Adventures of James*.

Jameson, Anna Brownell (1794–1860)
Essayist, travel writer, art historian, critic and biographer. Jameson is one of the most renowned Irish writers of her day, and she was friendly with many of her literary contemporaries, including ▷ Harriet Martineau, ▷ Mary Mitford, and Catherine Sedgwick, as well as the ▷ Victorian authors Elizabeth Barrett (1806–61) and Robert Browning (1812–89). Her work is known on two accounts: first for her book on Shakespeare's heroines, *Characteristics of Women* (1832), for which she read Samuel Johnson (1709–84), ▷ Hazlitt, ▷ Coleridge and ▷ Lamb. This book has recently been revived by ▷ feminist criticism and seen more as a vindication of the imaginative and independent women of the early 19th century than as homage to a patriarch of English literature. However, Jameson herself reported that her writing would please only those women who were 'fair, pure-hearted,

delicate-minded, and unclassical'. Secondly, Jameson was praised for her travel writings which include *Winter Studies and Summer Rambles in Canada* (1838) and *Pictures of the Social Life in Germany* (1840). These are more lively and exciting than conventional ▷ travel literature and may be classified as ▷ picaresque writing.
Bib: Nestor, P., *Female Friendships and Communities*; Sherman, C., *Women as Interpreters of the Visual Arts*; Thomas, C., *Love and Work Enough: The Life of Anna Jameson*.

Jeffrey, Francis (1773–1850)
Critic and editor (1803–29) of the influential ▷ *Edinburgh Review* which he helped to found in 1802. His poetic taste was conservative, and he was unsympathetic to the ▷ Lake Poets, ▷ Wordsworth and ▷ Coleridge. However, in 1820 he judiciously encouraged ▷ Keats for his ▷ *Endymion*, which had been condemned by ▷ *Blackwoods* and the ▷ *Quarterly*. His weakness as a critic was not his conservatism but his susceptibility to verse of second-rate appeal such as that of Thomas Campbell and of Samuel Rogers.

As editor, Jeffrey gave the *Edinburgh* authority proportionate to its intellectual independence, and its sales reached nearly 14,000 in 1818 – a high figure at any time for a periodical of such intellectual seriousness. In politics, Jeffrey was a ▷ Whig and his journal was the mouthpiece of responsible Whig opinion.

His profession was the law, in which he excelled and was eventually made a judge.

Jewsbury, Maria Jane (1800–33)
Poet. The eldest sister of the ▷ Victorian novelist Geraldine Jewsbury, Maria suffered from general ill-health, although her early death was due to an attack of cholera she suffered in India. Her first published work, *Phantasmagoria* (1825), consists of poems and some prose sketches which attack contemporary literary tastes. She dedicated the book to ▷ Wordsworth, whose daughter, Dora, was one of her friends. *Lays of Leisure Hours* (1829) was dedicated to another acquaintance, ▷ Felicia Hemans, to whom she wrote: 'the ambition of writing a book, being praised publically and associating with authors, siezed me'.
▷ Lay.
Bib: Howe, S., *Geraldine Jewsbury, Her Life and Errors*.

Jones, Sir William (1746–94)

Translator. Jones occupied the post of high
court judge at Calcutta for eleven years
(1783–94) and during this period learned
Sanskrit and embarked upon translating
Indian literature into English. His most
famous work of this period is *Sacontala, or
the Fatal Ring: an Indian Drama by Calidas*
(1779). Before Jones travelled to India, he
had learned Arabic, translating several poems
which were published as *The Moullakat* (1782).
His works contributed to the fashion for
oriental culture and he influenced ▷ Byron,
▷ Southey and ▷ Moore.
  ▷ Orientalism; Translation.
Bib: Cannon, G.H., *Oriental Jones: A
Biography*; Mukherjee, S.N., *Jones: A Study In
Eighteenth-century British Attitudes to India*.

Julian and Maddalo (1818)

▷ Shelley's troubled and oblique narrative
poem, set in Venice, concerning his relationship
with ▷ Lord Byron. The poem analyses their
differences of approach to religion,
politics and ethics, through the characters
of Julian (Shelley) described self-mockingly
in the Preface as 'rather serious', and Count
Maddalo (Byron) a more worldly and sceptical
figure. A long portion of the poem is taken
up with their meeting, or rather overhearing
the tortured outpourings of, an unnamed
'Maniac', whose tale of losing his reason
through a broken love relationship may be
read as a standing rebuke to both Shelley's
lofty ▷ idealism, and Byron's cynical wit.
Neither can offer a remedy for the intractable
recurrence of human pain, though both,
as poets, must articulate it; as Maddalo is
made to remark, 'Most wretched men/ Are
cradled into poetry by wrong,/ They learn in
suffering what they teach in song'. Although
Shelley was to be misrepresented by the ▷
Victorians and critics early this century as
the purely lyrical voice of Romantic ardour,
both *Julian and Maddalo* and ▷ *Epipsychidion*
(1821) are Romantic poems about the limits
of ▷ Romanticism, filled with complex
misgivings and self-interrogation.

K

Kant, Immanuel (1724–1804)
German philosopher of Scottish descent. His
most important works include: *Critique of Pure
Reason* (1781 and 1787); *Prolegomena to every
future Metaphysic* (1783); *Foundation for the
Metaphysic of Ethic* (1785); *Critique of Practical
Reason* (1788); *Critique of Judgement* (1790).
He counteracted Leibnitzian rationalism and
the scepticism of David Hume (1711–76)
by asserting the 'transcendence' of the
human mind over time and space (hence
'transcendental philosophy'). Time and space
are forms of our consciousness: we can know
by appearances but we cannot know 'things
in themselves'. On the other hand, it is in the
nature of our consciousness to have inherent
in it an awareness of design in nature, and of
moral and aesthetic value under a Divine moral
law. His philosophy, continued and modified
by other German philosophers (Fichte,
Schelling, Hegel), profoundly influenced the
poet and philosopher ▷ Coleridge; through
Coleridge, it provided a line of thought which,
in 19th century England, rivalled the sceptical
materialistically inclined tradition stemming
from John Locke (1632–1704), Hume and
▷ Bentham.

> ▷ German influence on English literature.

Kean, Edmund (?1787–1833)
One of the greatest actors of the early 19th
century. He was the illegitimate son of a
hawker and itinerant actress, Anne Carey.
He began acting as an infant, and trained at
▷ Drury Lane so vigorously, it is said, that he
had to wear irons to prevent deformity. This
disadvantage was aggravated by a later fall
during a circus performance in which he broke
both his legs. He remained small in stature,
and the actress ▷ Sarah Siddons once referred
to him as 'a horrid little man'. He received
some education through charity, at a school
in Leicester Square, and again at a school
in Soho, paid for by an aunt. Despite some
early recognition as an actor, Kean long led a
precarious existence, as strolling actor, singer,
and tumbler, during which period he married
Mary Chambers, an actress.

In 1814 Kean made his famous debut as
Shylock (▷ Shakespeare's *The Merchant of
Venice*), discarding the traditional red wig and
playing him as a violent and tragic figure, after
which his career blossomed, bringing him
fame and financial reward. He followed his
first success with other triumphs as Macbeth,
Othello, Iago, Richard III, Lear, Barabas
in Christopher Marlowe's *The Jew of Malta*
(c 1590) Jaffeir in Thomas Otway's *Venice
Preserv'd* (1682) and Sir Giles Overreach in

Philip Massinger's *A New Way to Pay Old
Debts* (1625). He toured America and Canada,
receiving tumultuous acclaim. Much of his
personal behaviour attracted gossip and
censure; he had numerous love affairs, and
drank excessively. At one time he appears to
have been locked up as a lunatic. In 1829 he
broke down during a performance of *Henry V*,
and apologized to the audience for losing his
memory. His last performance was as Othello,
with his son Charles as Iago, at Covent Garden
and he died a few weeks later. The most
famous judgment of Kean is ▷ Coleridge's:
'To see him act, is like reading Shakespeare by
flashes of lightning'.
Bib: Cornwall, B., *Life of Edmund Kean* (2
vols); Hawkins, F. W., *Life of Edmund Kean*
(2 vols); Hillebrand, H. N., *Edmund Kean*;
Fitzsimmons, R., *Edmund Kean: Fire from
Heaven*.

Keats, John (1795–1821)
Poet. The son of a livery-stable keeper in
London, he was apprenticed to an apothecary,
and for a time intended to be a surgeon, but
abandoned this career in his determination to
be a poet. He became the protégé of ▷ Leigh
Hunt, and adopted many of the older man's
attitudes and literary mannerisms, though
he was never, like Hunt, politically active.
Through Hunt he met ▷ Percy Bysshe
Shelley who helped him with the publication
of *Poems by John Keats* (1817), which include
his exhilarating if callow statement of poetic
ambition, *Sleep and Poetry*. The volume was not
a success and Keats set himself to improve his
art by writing a long poem in couplets – almost
as a kind of technical exercise. *Endymion*
appeared in 1818, and though its rambling
allegory fails to sustain narrative interest and
its poetry is of uneven quality, it performed its
function in developing Keats's style and ideas.
It was severely criticized in the ▷ *Quarterly
Review* and ▷ *Blackwood's Magazine*, partly
with justification and partly because of their
opposition to Hunt's radicalism. Its first lines
show in an early immature form the aesthetic
creed which preoccupied Keats throughout
his short career: 'A thing of beauty is a joy
forever:/ Its loveliness increases'.

Early in 1818 Keats composed *Isabella*, a
macabre Italian romance in ▷ *ottava rima*,
superficially similar to Hunt's work but with
a sensuous complexity of Keat's own. In the
same year he began work on ▷ *Hyperion*, a
'philosophical' poem in Miltonic ▷ blank
verse, which remained unfinished at his death.
During much of 1818 Keats was nursing
his brother Tom as he died of consumption,

an experience which complicated his later expressions of faith in the permanence of beauty. Towards the end of 1818 he fell in love with Fanny Brawne, and from this point on his work shows a leap in emotional depth and maturity. ▷ *The Eve of St Agnes* (1820), is a 'medieval' romance fragment in ▷ Spenserian stanzas. In 1819 Keats wrote his ▷ Odes, *To Psyche, To a Nightingale, On a Grecian Urn, On Melancholy, On Indolence, To Autumn*, and ▷ *Lamia*, a narrative romance in pentameter couplets (▷ metre). On 3 February 1820 Keats began coughing blood, and at once realized its meaning: 'That drop of blood is my death warrant. I must die.' He had consumption and knew that he would soon follow his brother. It seems that he wrote nothing from this point onwards. He travelled to Italy in September 1820 with his friend Joseph Severn and died in Rome in February 1821, directing that the epitaph on his grave should read 'Here lies one whose name was writ in water.'

Keats felt that the deepest meaning of life lay in the apprehension of material beauty, and his works are the most important embodiment in poetry of the philosophy of Aestheticism. His mature poems confront the implications of this belief in a world of disease and decay, and their most characteristic effect is the evocation of poignant transience. He is remarkable also for his intelligent awareness of his own poetic development, which enabled him to reach maturity so early in his short career. His letters are among the finest in English, not only for their discussion of his aesthetic ideas ('negative capability', 'the chameleon poet') but also simply for their human quality, their spontaneity and humour.
Bib: Gittings, R., *John Keats*; Leavis, F. R., in *Revaluation*; Ridley, M. R., *Keats's Craftmanship*; Hill, J. S. (ed.), *Keats: Narrative Poems. A Selection of Critical Essays*; Fraser, G. S., *Keats: Odes. A Selection of Critical Essays*; Jones, J., *John Keats's Dream of Truth*; Ricks, C., *Keats and Embarassment*; Van Ghent, D., *Keats: The Myth of the Hero*; Hirst, W. S., *John Keats*; Allott, M., *John Keats*; Levinson, M., *Keat's Life of Allegory: The Origins of a Style*.

Kelly, Isabella (c1758–1857)

Poet and novelist. Scottish author, whose first published work was a series of confessional poems and short satirical pieces, *Collection of Poems and Fables* (c 1794). However, she soon began writing ▷ Gothic novels for ▷ Minerva Press and these followed the conventional, but highly popular, pattern, containing ruined abbeys, ghosts, ancient manuscripts and illegitimate children. *The Abbey of St Asaph*

(1795) is the most accessible to 20th-century readers.
▷ Autobiography; Scottish literature in English.
Bib: Summers, M., *A Gothic Bibliography*; Tompkins, J.M.S., *The Popular Novel in England 1770–1800*.

Kemble, John Philip (1757–1823)

Actor, singer, manager, dramatist. Kemble was the son of the theatrical manager Roger Kemble and actress Sarah (née Ward). His sister became known as the actress ▷ Sarah Siddons, and six other siblings also went on to the stage, with the exception of the author ▷ Ann Hatton.

In 1777 he began acting at Liverpool, and the following year his first play, *Belisarius; or Injured Innonence* was staged there.

He began the first of many seasons at ▷ Drury Lane in 1783, where his roles included Hamlet, Richard III, Shylock, and King John. Three of his sisters acted there during this time, and he played Othello to Sarah Siddons' Desdemona in 1785. In 1788 he took over management of Drury Lane, whose patent was held by ▷ Richard Sheridan, and soon introduced elements of 'theatrical realism' into his productions, such as providing what he considered authentic Roman costumes for some of ▷ Shakespeare's Roman plays.

After 1791 when Drury Lane was declared unsafe, Kemble moved his company to the King's Theatre in the Haymarket, Covent Garden and several provincial theatres. In 1816 the advent of ▷ Edmund Kean to the stage drew from Kemble much of the public respect and admiration he had enjoyed throughout his career and he retired the following year.

Throughout his life, Kemble was admired for his good looks, elegance, and charm, and respected for his forceful professional abilities as an actor and as a manager. He had a rigorous, classical approach to acting, excelling in parts, especially those of Shakespeare, to which a grand manner and style were suited, and, like many of his period, had a prodigious memory enabling him to retain many long roles in his repertoire. He lacked the emotional range of David Garrick (1717–79), and later Edmund Kean, and suffered from a tendency to drink to excess, which occasionally interfered with his ability to perform. Some 58 plays, most of them alterations, are attributed to his authorship.
Bib: Baker, H., *John Philip Kemble*; Child, H., *The Shakespearean Productions of John Philip Kemble*; Donohue, J., *Dramatic Character in the English Romantic Age*; Joseph, B., *The Tragic Actor*; Kelly, L., *The Kemble Era: John Philip, Sarah Siddons and the London Stage*.

King, Sophia (c 1782–?)

Novelist and poet. Sister to ▷ Charlotte
Dacre and, like her, overawed by their
powerful and infamous father, John King.
Her ▷ melodramatic novels centre upon
repressed heroines and dark destructive fathers
and lovers. *Cordelia, or The Romance of Real
Life* (1799), published by ▷ Minerva, has a
daughter who devotes her life to her wicked
father; *The Fatal Spectre, or Unknown Warrior*
(1801) has a male protagonist who ruins his
mistress and is discovered to be the devil; and
The Adventures of Victor Allen (1805) has a hero
who displays biting cruelty towards women,
even though the psychological reasons for this
are later uncovered. This latter work is seen
to anticipate ▷ *Frankenstein*. King described
her writing as a place where, 'the fantastic
imagination roves unshackled'.

Bib: Tompkins, J.M.S., *The Popular Novel in
England 1770–1800*.

Kubla Khan: or, A Vision in a Dream: A Fragment (1816)

An ▷ ode by ▷ Samuel Taylor Coleridge,
written in 1797, when he was living in
Somerset. Coleridge recorded that he fell
asleep after reading a description in *Purchas
his Pilgrimage* (1613) of the pleasure gardens
constructed in Xanadu by the 13th-century
Mongol king of China, Khan (king) Kublai.
While he was asleep 'from two to three
hundred lines' came to him, which upon
waking he hastened to write down. However he
was interrupted by 'a person on business from
Porlock', and afterwards could recall nothing
of the remainder, 'with the exception of some
eight or ten scattered lines and images'.
It is difficult to know how much of this
account to believe. One element Coleridge
suppresses is his addiction to opium, which is
certainly relevant to the hallucinatory clarity
of the poem's exotic images. Because of the
oddness of Coleridge's account 'a visitor from
Porlock' has become a byword for any kind of
intriguing, possibly evasive, excuse.

Despite its designation 'A Fragment' the
work is artistically complete. The first three
sections rework phrases from the ▷ Jacobean
travel book, to describe a strangely primal
landscape. An awesome 'mighty fountain'
forms the source of the 'sacred river' Alph, on
the banks of which Kubla has built a 'stately
pleasure-dome' surrounded by orchards
and gardens. After watering the garden the
river continues its course, entering 'caverns
measureless to man' and sinking 'in tumult to
a lifeless ocean'. The clarity and primitiveness
of these images gives the poem an archetypal
resonance. The river can be seen as the river of
life or creativity; the fountain symbolizes birth
(of an individual, civilization, poetic inspiration),
and the 'lifeless ocean' death or sterility. The
dome stands for the precarious creative balance
between. It is possible that the final fourth
section of the poem, which seems to be a
commentary upon the preceding lines, were 'the
eight or ten lines or images' written after the
departure of Coleridge's visitor, if he or she ever
existed. The poem ends by imputing magical
qualities to the poem itself and its bardic author:
'Weave a circle round him thrice,/ And close
your eyes with holy dread,/ For he on honey-dew
hath fed,/ And drunk the milk of Paradise.'

▷ Bard; Romanticism.

Lacan, Jacques (1901–81)

French psychoanalyst whose re-readings of ▷ Freud have become influential within the area of literary criticism. Lacan's *The Four Fundamental Concepts of Psychoanalysis* (trans. 1977), and his *Ecrits: A Selection* (trans. 1977) outline the nature of his revision of Freudian psychoanalytic method. A further selection of papers has appeared under the title of *Feminine Sexuality* (trans. 1982). It is to Lacan that we owe the critical terms ▷ 'imaginary' and ▷ 'symbolic order'. Similarly, it is to his investigation of the operations of the unconscious according to the model of language – 'the unconscious is structured like a language' – that we owe the notion of a 'split' human subject. For Lacan the 'imaginary' is associated with the pre-Oedipal and pre-linguistic relationship between mother and child (the 'mirror' stage) where there appears to be no discrepancy between identity and its outward reflection. This is succeeded by the entry of the infant into the 'symbolic order', with its rules and prohibitions centred around the figure of the father (the phallus). The 'desire of the mother' is then repressed by the child's entry into language and the 'symbolic order'. The desire for 'imaginary' unity is also repressed to form the unconscious, which the interaction between analyst and patient aims to unlock. Some of the fundamental divisions that Lacan has located in the 'subject' have proved highly adaptable for a range of ▷ materialist literary criticisms, including (more controversially) ▷ feminism. As a young man, Lacan was a member of the ▷ Surrealist group in Paris, whose activities restated in modern terms a number of key Romantic interests, for example in dreams, madness and the hidden workings of the mind, all topics that his theoretical works deal with in a style frequently as opaque and challenging as poetry.

Lady of the Lake, The (1810)

A narrative poem by ▷ Sir Walter Scott set in the Scotland of James V (1513–42).

Lake Poets

A term coined by ▷ Francis Jeffrey in the ▷ *Edinburgh Review* (October 1807) to describe ▷ Samuel Taylor Coleridge, ▷ Robert Southey and ▷ William Wordsworth, who for a time lived in close association in the Lake District. The community of literary and social outlook in their earlier work made it natural to speak of them as a group, but in fact only Wordsworth was profoundly identified with the locality.

Lamb, Lady Caroline (1785–1828)

Novelist and poet. The only daughter of the 3rd Earl of Bessborough, she was taken to Italy at the age of three and brought up mostly in the care of a servant. Educated at Devonshire House School, she was then looked after by her maternal grandmother, Lady Spencer, who worried about her instability and 'eccentricities'. She married the statesman William Lamb (later the 2nd Viscount Melbourne), but in 1812, just after her marriage, became desperately infatuated with ▷ Byron, of whom she wrote in her diary that he was 'mad, bad and dangerous to know'. After he broke with her, she became increasingly unstable and violent-tempered, and her husband sued for separation becoming temporarily reconciled, however, on the day fixed for the execution of the deed. Meeting Byron's funeral cortège seems to have hastened her disintegration and she ended up living with her father-in-law and only surviving son, an invalid. Her first novel, *Glenarvon* (1816), had a significant, though brief success, due no doubt to its portrayal of Byron and herself in a wild and romantic story. It was published anonymously, though she courted notoriety, being impulsive, vain and excitable to the point of insanity, as well as highly original. She wrote two further novels, *Graham Hamilton* (1822) and *Ada Reis* (1823), and poetry, some of which has been set to music.
Bib: Jenkins, E., *Lady Caroline Lamb*.

Lamb, Charles (1775–1834)

Essayist and critic. His best-known work is his two volumes of the ▷ *Essays of Elia* (1823 and 1833), in which he discourses about his life and times. His *Specimens of English Dramatic Poets who lived about the Time of Shakespeare* directed interest towards ▷ Shakespeare's contemporaries, who had been somewhat neglected in the 18th century, although perhaps not so much ignored as Lamb thought. His friends included many writers of his time, and this fact gives a special interest to his letters. He collaborated with his sister ▷ Mary in adapting Shakespeare's plays into stories for children – *Tales from Shakespeare* (1807). His poems are unimportant but one or two, *eg The Old Familiar Faces* (1798) and the prose-poem, *Dream Children*, recur in anthologies. Lamb seems to have been a man of unusual charm and of gifts which he never allowed himself to display fully and energetically, perhaps because he was haunted by the fear of insanity, to which both he and his sister were subject.

Bib: Lucas, E. V., *Life*; Tillyard, E. M. W. (ed.), *Lamb's Criticism;* Blunden, E., *Charles Lamb and his Contemporaries*; Cecil, D., *A Portrait of Charles Lamb*.

Lamb, Mary Ann (1764–1847)

Sister to ▷ Charles Lamb and daughter of a lawyer, she was brought up in poor circumstances, helping her mother, who worked as a needlewoman. In 1796, overworked and stressed, she pursued her mother's apprentice round the room with a knife in a fit of irritation, and when her mother interposed she killed her. The verdict was one of insanity and she was given into the custody of her brother Charles who took charge of her, finding suitable accommodation for her during her periodic bouts of illness and maintaining a close and affectionate relationship. With Charles, she wrote *Tales from Shakespeare* (1807), designed to make ▷ Shakespeare's stories accessible to the young; *The Adventures of Ulysses* (1808), which was an attempt to do the same for ▷ Homer; and *Mrs Leicester's School* (1809), a collection of short stories.

Lamia (1820)

A poem in pentameter ▷ couplets (▷ metre) by ▷ John Keats, based on a story in Robert Burton's *Anatomy of Melancholy* (1621–51). In ancient myth a lamia was a female demon, one of whose practices was to entice young men in order to devour them. In Keats's poem a serpent is transformed into a beautiful girl who fascinates a young Corinthian, Lycius. He takes her into his home and makes a bridal feast which is attended by the philosopher Apollonius. Apollonius recognizes the lamia and calls her by her true name, whereupon she vanishes and Lycius dies. The poem, with its rich, fluently enjambed couplets, is an ambiguous plea in favour of aestheticism and sensual escapism. Lamia should be the villain of the poem, but in fact it is Apollonius. The world to which she introduces the young Greek is one of ravishing beauty and magic, and the final triumph of philosophical truth is accompanied by the death of the imagination: 'Do not all charms fly/ At the mere touch of cold philosophy?'

Landon, Letitia Elizabeth
▷ L.E.L.

Landor, Walter Savage (1775–1864)

Poet. Of upper-class background he was expelled from Oxford University for his intemperate radicalism, and lived for many years in Florence. He wrote the ▷ blank verse epic, *Gebir* (1798), the tragedy *Count Julian* (1812), and collections of verse: *Hellenics* (1847), *Italics* (1848), *Heroic Idylls* (1863). He was a fine classical scholar, producing a ▷ Latin version of *Gebir*, and his imagination was essentially literary in its inspiration. He is now chiefly remembered for his prose *Imaginary Conversations* (1824, 1828, 1829) between such figures of the past as Dante and Beatrice, and Elizabeth and Mary Tudor. His quarrelsome but generous personality was caricatured by Charles Dickens as Boythorn in *Bleak House* (1852–3).

Bib: Pinsky, R., *Landor's Poetry*.

Langue

This term appears throughout ▷ Ferdinand de Saussure's *Course in General, Linguistics* (1915) to denote the system of ▷ signs which makes up any language structure. According to Saussure, individual utterances (▷ parole) are constructed out of elements which have no existence 'prior to the linguistic system, but only conceptual and phonetic differences arising out of that system'. This observation is fundamental to ▷ structuralism, which is concerned with the positioning of particular elements within a nonvariable structure. 'Langue' is the term used to denote the linguistic structure itself, that is the rules which lie behind particular linguistic events.

Latin literature

Rome began as a small Italian city state, and grew to an empire that surrounded the Mediterranean and extended as far north as the borderland between England and Scotland. Politically, it established the framework out of which modern Europe grew. Culturally, in part by native force and in part by its assimilation and transmission of the older and richer culture of Greece, its literature became the basis of European values, and especially those values that arise from the individual's relationship to his society.

Between 300 and 100 BC, Rome began to produce literature, and at the same time, after its conquest of the rich Greek colonics in southern Italy, to expand its imaginative and intellectual vision and to increase and refine the expressiveness of the Latin language through the study of ▷ Greek literature.

Primitive Roman literature had been of two kinds: that of the recording and examination of public life and conduct in annals of eminent men and in oratory, and that of the distinctively Roman art of satirical comedy (▷ satire). These centuries saw the production of the comic dramas of Plautus and of Terence. The orator and historian Cato the Censor upheld the virtues of Roman severity against Greek sophistication and luxury; the dominant figure, however, was the poet Ennius (239–169) who preserved a balance between Greek and Latin values by emulating ▷ Homer in a patriotic epic in Latin idiom and Greek metre, the *Annales*.

The first half of the first century BC was the last great period of the Roman Republic. Active participation in politics was still one of the principal concerns of Roman aristocrats, and by this time Romans had studied and profited from lessons in depth and force of thinking from Greece. Cicero was the great persuasive orator of public debate; such was the power of his eloquence that the period is often known as the Ciceronian age. Julius Caesar's terse, practical account of his wars in Gaul and invasion of Britain shows a different kind of prose excellence, and the vividness of Sallust's histories of episodes in recent Roman history is different again. It was thus an age of prose, but it included one of the finest of all philosophical poems, the *De Rerum Natura* ('Concerning the Nature of Things') of Lucretius, who expounded the thought of the Greek philosopher Epicurus. It included also the passionate love poems of Catullus, who gave new vitality to Greek mythology.

Julius Caesar's great-nephew, Augustus Caesar, became the first Emperor in 27 BC, and he ruled till his death in AD 14. The Republic ended, and with it the kind of moral thought and eloquence which had made Cicero so famous. Roman literature, however, entered upon its most famous period – the Augustan Age (▷ Augustanism). If the Empire had not quite reached its greatest extent, its power was nonetheless at its peak; the old traditions of austerity and energy were not yet extinct; civilization, wealth and sophistication had not yet overbalanced into decadence resulting from excessive luxury. Augustus himself was a patron of letters. In prose, the outstanding writer was the historian Livy, but it was above all an age of poetry. The most famous of Roman poets, Virgil, celebrated great traditions, looked back to by a stable society, in which active political participation had become difficult or unimportant. His contemporary, ▷ Horace, celebrated the

values of civilized private life. Tibullus, Propertius, and above all Ovid were poets of pleasure appealing to the refined taste of an elegant society. .

The last period of Roman literature lasted approximately a hundred years from the death of Augustus. The Emperors were bad, the idea of Rome was losing much of its force, society was showing symptoms of decadence. The best writers became more detached from and more critical of Roman society. In the philosophy and drama of Seneca, the heroic poetry of Lucan, the satire of Persius (34–62), the Greek philosophy of Stoicism seemed the strongest defence of human dignity against social oppression and distress. The most powerful work, however, was the savage satire of Juvenal and the sombre history of his time by Tacitus.

Literature in Latin did not of course end here, nor did it end with the Roman Empire in the 5th century AD. Latin became the language of the Roman Catholic Church, and therefore of the early medieval educated classes. It remained a living, growing language till its style was fixed by ▷ Renaissance scholars in the 16th century. Even in the 17th century, Francis Bacon wrote much of his philosophy in Latin, and ▷ Milton wrote Latin poetry. Classical Latin was read and admired in medieval England, but knowledge of it was incomplete and inaccurate; much of this knowledge was obtained from contemporary French and Italian writers whose traditions were closer to classical Latin. Virgil retained great prestige, and Terence was studied in the monasteries for the purity of his style. After 1500, the Renaissance caused English writers to study and emulate the classical writers. Writers modelled themselves on styles of classical prose; the terse manner of Seneca and Tacitus was imitated by Bacon, whereas the eloquent flow of Cicero was emulated by Edmund Burke. More important than the study of styles was the way in which English writers again and again measured themselves against their own society by placing themselves in the position of Roman writers, and then assessed their society from a Roman standpoint. So, in the late 16th century Donne modelled his elegies on those of Ovid, and a little later Ben Jonson rewrote the lyrics of Catullus; in the 17th century Milton emulated Virgil as Virgil had once emulated Homer; in the 18th century Pope took the standpoint of Horace, and Samuel Johnson adopted that of Juvenal.

Lautréamont, Comte de (pseudonym of Isidore-Lucien Ducasse) (1846–70)
French writer of lyrical prose pieces which appeared under the title *Les Chants de Maldoror* in 1868, with a slightly expanded posthumous version in 1890. The hero, Maldoror, is a demonic figure and his world is one of delirium and nightmare interspersed with blasphemy and eroticism. The hallucinatory quality of this work attracted the interest of the Surrealists (▷ Surrealism), who claimed Lautréamont as one of their own and promoted his work. Their interest has been carried forward into contemporary French criticism.
▷ French literature in England.

Lay
A term in use from the medieval period for a lyrical or narrative composition, especially one recited or sung to music. The 19th-century revival of interest in the Middle Ages stimulated a revival of the lay form, which may be exemplified in poems such as ▷ Walter Scott's *Lay of the Ancient Minstrel and* ▷ Mary Betham's *Lay of Marie de France*.

Leadbetter, Mary (1758–1826)
Poet and story-writer. Leadbetter was an Irish Quaker who wrote poetry and short prose pieces which pictured the country life she saw about her. Her writing is often ▷ didactic, for example, she wrote against slavery (▷ Abolition Literature) and class prejudice. ▷ Maria Edgeworth wrote the notes for her *Cottage Dialogues Among the Irish Peasantry* (1811).
▷ Irish literature in English.

Leavis, Frank Raymond (1895–1978)
Critic. From 1932 till 1953 he edited *Scrutiny*, a literary review with high critical standards, and pervaded by his personality. It maintained that the values of a society in all its activities derive from its culture, and that central to British culture is English literature; that a literature can be sustained only by discriminating readers, and therefore by a body of highly trained critics working together, especially in the collaborative circumstances of a university (*Education and the University*; 1943). The need for the testing of judgements by collaborative discussion is important in Leavis's view of criticism. Unfortunately, collaboration may become uncritical discipleship, and this was one of the two unfortunate consequences of the exceptional force of Leavis's personality. The other unfortunate consequence was

the hostility which this force of personality aroused in many critics who were not among his collaborators and followers. He maintained that true critical discernment can be achieved only by a total response of the mind – intellectual, imaginative and moral; thus a critical judgement reflects not only the work of literature being judged, but the worth of the personality that makes the judgement, so that Leavis's censure of critics with whom he strongly disagreed was sometimes extraordinarily vehement, as in his *Two Cultures?: The Significance of C. P. Snow* (1962). However this vehemence was a price he paid for his determination to sustain a living tradition of literature not only by assessing contemporary writers with the utmost rigour, but also by reassessing the writers of the past, distinguishing those he thought had a vital relevance for the modern sensibility from those that stand as mere monuments in academic museums. Such evaluative treatments caused him to be widely regarded as a destructive critic; his attack on the three-centuries-long prestige of ▷ Milton (*Revaluation* 1936 and *The Common Pursuit* 1952) gave particular offence.

Leavis's intense concern with the relationship between the kind of sensibility nourished by a literary culture and the quality of a society as a whole has a historical background that extends to the beginning of the 19th century. It first appears in ▷ Wordsworth's *Preface to the* ▷ *Lyrical Ballads* (1800), is to be felt in the writings of the 19th-century philosopher John Stuart Mill (1806–73; see *Mill on Bentham and Coleridge*, ed. by Leavis, 1950), and is explicit in Matthew Arnold's (1822–88) writings, especially *Culture and Anarchy* (1869). The outstanding importance of novels in connection with the theme has caused Leavis to be above all a critic of the novel; perhaps his most important single book is *The Great Tradition: George Eliot, Henry James, Joseph Conrad* (1948), but this should be read in conjunction with his books on Lawrence and (with Q. D. Leavis) on *Dickens the Novelist* (1971). Although his attack on ▷ Shelley for imprecision (in *Revaluation*) now seems itself hopelessly imprecise, his own criticism stands in a Romantic tradition of opposition to unbridled commercialism and industrialization, with their dehumanizing consequences for work and creativity. Although still influential, Leavis must now be considered together with more contemporary literary theory, such as ▷ post-structuralism which has tended to challenge radically and contradict vehemently his criticism.

Lee, Harriet (1757–1851)

Novelist and playwright. The sister of
▷ Sophia Lee, with whom she wrote
Canterbury Tales (12 tales, two by Sophia,
which ran from 1797–1805). The tales
cover predictable material, for example one
is a ▷ Gothic romance and another offers
a sensational account of the ▷ French
Revolution. One story, however, *Kruitzer,
The German's Tale* (1801), depicts the
suffering of a woman unable either to escape
her weak husband, or to reform her evil,
but romantic son, and was acknowledged
by ▷ Byron as the source of his *Werner*
(1821). In addition to this brief success,
Lee's prose works won some acclaim, but
she achieved much less recognition for her
dramatic output. *The New Peerage, or Our
Eyes may Deceive Us* (1787) and *The Mysterious
Marriage, or the Heirship of Roselva* (1795–8)
are unremarkable in their plots, and the
characters are somewhat flat and stereotyped.
She rejected a proposal of marriage by
▷ Godwin.
Bib: Punter, D., *The Literature of Terror:
A History of Gothic Fictions from 1765 to
the Present Day*; Rodgers, K., *Feminism in
Eighteenth-century England*.

Lee, Sophia (1750–1824)

Novelist and dramatist. Sister of ▷ Harriet
Lee, with whom she collaborated in the series
of *Canterbury Tales* (1797–1805), contributing
the ones for 1798 and 1799, both of which
were unremarkable. Sophia, however, had
more success than her sister in the literary
world; her play *The Chapter of Accidents*
(1780) was staged regularly, and her novel,
The Recess, or A Tale of Other Times (1783–5)
ran to five editions over the following nine
years. The latter is particularly interesting
since it deals with two women who are the
unacknowledged daughters of Mary Queen
of Scots, and attempts to show how history
ignores the roles that women have played
in important political events (▷ Histories
and Chronicles). She earned a considerable
amount of money from *The Chapter* and set
up a school at ▷ Bath with her sister on the
proceeds.
Bib: Punter, D., *The Literature of Terror:
A History of Gothic Fictions from 1765 to
the Present Day*; Rodgers, K., *Feminism in
Eighteenth-century England*.

Leech-Gatherer, The

Sometimes used as an alternative title for
▷ William Wordsworth's poem ▷ *Resolution
and Independence*.

Le Fanu, J. (Joseph) S. (Sheridan) (1814–73)

Novelist and journalist. Born in Dublin of
an old Huguenot family related by marriage
to the family of the dramatist ▷ Sheridan,
he wrote poetry as a child, including a long
Irish poem at the age of 14. After education
by his father and tutors, he went to Trinity
in 1833, writing for the *Dublin University
Magazine* and in 1837 joining the staff. He
later became editor and proprietor. In 1837
he published some Irish ▷ ballads and in
1839 was called to the bar, although he did
not practise, soon turning to journalism. He
bought *The Warden, Evening Packet* and part of
the *Dublin Evening Mail*, later amalgamating
the three into the *Evening Mail*. In 1844 he
married Susan Bennett and withdrew from
society after her death in 1858, when he wrote
most of his novels, many in bed, on scraps
of paper. His writing is ingeniously plotted,
shows an attraction to the supernatural and
has been increasingly well received this
century. The novels include *The House by
the Churchyard* (1863), *Wylder's Hand* (1864),
Uncle Silas (1864), *Guy Deverell* (1865), *The
Tenants of Malory* (1867), *A Lost Name* (1868),
The Wyvern Mystery (1869), *Checkmate* (1871),
The Rose and the Key (1871) and *Willing to Die*
(1873), which was finished a few days before
his death. The short stories, *In a Glass Darkly*,
appeared in 1872 and a collection of neglected
stories, *Madam Crowl's Ghost and Other Tales
of Mystery*, in 1923.

L.E.L., Letitia Elizabeth Landon (1802–38)

Poet and novelist. One of the most popular
and prolific authors of her day, Landon
published under the initials 'L.E.L.'. Her
poetry was influenced by ▷ French literature,
rather than English, although she is clearly
regarded as a ▷ Romantic poet; collections
include, *The Fate of Adelaide* (1821), *The
Improvisatrice* (1824), *The Troubadour* (1825),
and *The Golden Violet* (1827). Landon wrote of
her own tendency towards sentiment:

> *Aware that to elevate I must first soften, and
> that if I wish to purify I must first touch, I
> have ever endeavoured to bring forward grief,
> disappointment, the fallen leaf, the faded
> flower, the broken heart, and the early grave.*

Her first novel, *Romance and Reality*, appeared
in 1831; it is a personalized view of London
society and includes thinly disguised portraits
of the ▷ Victorian novelist, Edward Bulwar
Lytton and his wife. This provided salacious

information for contemporary readers, since Landon's name was linked romantically with Lytton's, as well as to the journalist William Maginn's, and when rumours of an abortion followed, her engagement with John Forster was broken off. Landon wrote of her own misfortunes:

> Alas! that ever
> Praise should have been what praise has
>   been to me –
> The opiate of the mind.

Landon eventually married George Maclean, the governor of Cape Coast Castle on the Gold Coast in 1838, but died four months after reaching Africa supposedly from an overdose of prussic acid.
Bib: Aston, H., *Letty Landon*; Showalter, E., *A Literature of Their Own*.

Lennox, Charlotte (?1727–1804)
Charlotte Lennox was probably born in America, and grew up in New York. From an early age she is known to have been in London trying, unsuccessfully, to make a career on the stage. In 1747 she published *Poems on Several Occasions*, and in 1750, the year in which her appearance on the stage is last reported, she brought out her first novel, *The Life of Harriot Stuart*.

Lennox's literary talent was enthusiastically supported by Samuel Johnson and Henry Fielding. In 1752 *The Female Quixote* established her name as a writer; the novel tells of a naive heroine, Arabella, whose view of the world is foolishly filtered through the romances she reads. Lennox uses this framework to satirize sexual stereotypes and the social conventions of courtship.

Johnson's help in finding publishers for Lennox was probably partly motivated by his knowledge of her circumstances as well as her literary achievements. Her husband, Alexander, was a constant drain on the family's finances, and Lennox's writing provided their only support. She worked on translations and adaptations to supplement their income, and produced three volumes of Shakespeare's sources, with Johnson's encouragement. Her final novel *Euphemia* (1790) explores the position of women in marriage, reflecting her own experience with the spendthrift husband she eventually left.
▷ Women, status of.

Letter-writing
This is clearly an important branch of literature even when the interest of the letters is essentially historical or ▷ biographical. Letters may also be, by intention or by consequence of genius, works of intrinsic literary value. The 18th century (the age of the epistolary novel) was more than any other the period when letter-writing was cultivated as an art: see, above all, the letters of ▷ Horace Walpole and those to his son by Lord Chesterfield (1694–1773) – the former a record of events and the latter consisting of moral reflections. Earlier than the 18th century, postal services were not sufficiently organized to encourage regular letter-writing, and the art of familiar prose was inadequately cultivated; by the mid-19th century, communications had improved enough to make frequent and full letter-writing redundant. By then letters had intrinsic, literary interest chiefly by virtue of the writers' talent for literary expression in other modes of writing, added to the accident that they found letters a congenial means of communication. In the first 30 years of the 19th century the Romantic habit of introspection resulted in a quantity of extremely interesting letters: those of ▷ Keats, ▷ Byron, ▷ Coleridge and ▷ Lamb are outstanding.

Lewes, George Henry (1817–78)
Philosopher and critic. He wrote on a wide variety of subjects but his most remembered work is his *Life of Goethe* (1855), researched with George Eliot's (1819–80) help. Other works include *The Biographical History of Philosophy* (1845–6), studies in biology such as *Studies in Animal Life* (1862), two novels, *Ranthrope* (1847) and *Rose, Blanche and Violet* (1848), critical essays on the novel and the theatre, and, his most important philosophical book, *Problems of Life and Mind* (1873–8), the last volume of which was completed by George Eliot after his death. He collaborated with ▷ Thornton Leigh Hunt in founding the *Leader* and was first editor of the *Fortnightly Review* 1865–6. In 1854 he left his wife, who had had three sons by Hunt, and lived with Mary Ann Evans (George Eliot) until his death.
Bib: Ashton, R., *G.H. Lewes*; Kitchell, A. T., *George Lewes and George Eliot*.

Lewis, Alethea (1750–1827)
Novelist. A ▷ didactic writer whose works are thoughtful but often heavily moralistic and naive in style. Her novels include *Plain Sense* (1795) for ▷ Minerva, and the ▷ Gothic *The Nuns of the Desert, or The Woodland Witches* (1805). She also wrote a philosophical treatise

under the pen-name 'Eugenia De Acton',
Essays on the Art of Being Happy (1803).

Lewis, Matthew Gregory (1775–1818)
▷ 'Monk' Lewis.

Llangollen, the Ladies of
The 'Ladies of Llangollen' were Lady Eleanor
Butler (1739–1829) and Sarah Ponsonby
(1755–1831); they were close friends for ten
years before pressure from their families
– Butler was encouraged to become a nun
and Ponsonby to accept the attentions of a
male suitor – drove them to elope, and they
set up house together at Plas Newydd in
Llangollen. Their writings were published in
*The Hamwood Papers of the Ladies of Llangollen
and Caroline Hamilton* (1930), edited by
G.H.Bell. It is clear from Butler's diary that
they saw their retreat as a rural idyll which
gave them the opportunity to study and
appreciate ▷ nature. As such, they belong to
the ▷ Romantic tradition. ▷ Wordsworth and
▷ Anna Seward came to visit them at Plas
Newydd, the former writing them a sonnet
and the latter a poem called 'Llangollen Vale'
(1795). Their house, an interesting example of
the ▷ Gothic Revival in architecture, may still
be visited.

London Magazine, The
Three periodicals of this name have existed:
the first ran 1732–85; the second, 1820–29;
and the third, founded in 1954, still exists.
The second is the most famous. It was
founded as the political opponent of the
right-wing ▷ *Blackwood's Magazine*, and its
first editor, John Scott, was killed in a duel
in consequence of the rivalry. It had unusual
literary distinction, with ▷ Lamb, ▷ Hazlitt,
▷ Hood and ▷ De Quincey on its staff; it
published the first version of De Quincey's
▷ *Confessions of an English Opium-Eater*.

Lotos-Eaters, The
A poem by ▷ Alfred Tennyson, first
published in the 1833 volume, which contains
much of his most distinguished work. Its
subject is the ancient Greek myth of the
lotophagi ('lotus-eaters' – Tennyson used
the Greek spelling, 'lotos') who occur in
▷ Homer's *Odyssey*. Those who visit the land
where the lotus fruit grows and eat some of it
lose all desire to return home. The theme of
Tennyson's poem is the temptation to reject
the world of activity, change and stress, in
favour of a trancelike existence measured only
by the more languorous rhythms of nature.
It is in the tradition of Edmund Spenser

(1552–99) and the more luxuriant ▷ Keats:
the rhythms have hypnotic music, and the
imagery is strongly and unsettlingly sensuous.
Tennyson's pre-Victorian poems may be
viewed as an important part of the Romantic
bequest to the later 19th century.

**Lucretius (Titus Lucretius Carus) (1st
century BC)**
Roman poet; author of the great didactic
poem *De Rerum Natura* ('Concerning the
Nature of Things'). It outlines the philosophy
of the ▷ Greek thinker Epicurus, which is
based on the atomic theory of Democritus.
The poet seeks to expound that all reality
is material. The gods exist but they also are
material, though immortal, and they are not
concerned with the affairs of men; the soul,
too, is material and mortal like
the body, dissolving into its original atoms
after death. Lucretius is not, however, a
cynical poet; he testifies to the beauty of the
natural world and this love together with
his reverence for reason caused him to be
greatly admired by English poets including
▷ Tennyson.
  Lucretius is a late ▷ dramatic monologue
by Tennyson, in which the poet philosopher
expounds his dying vision of the world.

Lucy Poems
A group of five ▷ lyrics by ▷ William
Wordsworth, composed between 1799 and
1801. There is no clear evidence that the
figure of Lucy represents any actual person,
though her ambiguity may be an expression
of the poet's intense relationship with his
sister ▷ Dorothy. In 'Strange fits of passion
I have known' the lover approaches Lucy's
cottage as the moon sinks behind it, and
suddenly imagines, for no apparent reason,
that she might be dead. In 'Three years she
grew' Lucy is a child who has died young,
and in 'A slumber did my spirit seal' the
poet consoles himself with the idea that the dead
Lucy is now part of inanimate nature, 'Rolled
round in earth's diurnal course,/ With rocks,
and stones, and trees'. The sublime, almost
mystical, simplicity of style of these poems has
incurred parody. The poem which begins 'She
dwelt among the untrodden ways/ Beside the
springs of Dove,/ A Maid whom there were
none to praise/ And very few to love', was
delightfully rewritten by ▷ Samuel Taylor
Coleridge's son, ▷ Hartley, to apply to the
poet himself: 'He lived amidst th'untrodden
ways/ To Rydal Lake that lead;/ A bard
whom there were none to praise,/ And very
few to read'.

Lyric

In Ancient Greece the name given to verse
sung to a lyre (from the Greek 'lurikos' –
'for the lyre'), whether as a solo performance
or by a choir. In English usage, the term
has had different associations in different
historical/literary periods. Elizabethan critics
first used the term in England: George
Puttenham (d 1590), for example, describes
a lyric poet as someone who composes
'songs or ballads of pleasure to be sung
with the voice, and to the harpe'. From the
illustrative quotations in the O.E.D. (s.v.
lyric), it is clear that in later usage musical
accompaniment was no longer considered
essential to the definition of the form. By
the 19th century John Ruskin (1819–1900)
defined lyric poetry as 'the expression by the
poet of his own feelings': a definition which
has the virtue of drawing attention to the
personal and emotional focus of many lyric
poems, but rather obscures any recognition
of the highly stylized modes of mediating
between personal experience and its public
expression employed in lyric texts, which, like
all literary conventions, may change over time.
Ruskin's definition owes a good deal to the
personalization of the lyric in the Romantic
period, eg ▷ Keats's 'When I have fears that
I may cease to be', and ▷ Shelley's 'To a
Skylark'. In modern English, the term lyric
has a very general range of reference: it may
be used to cover most forms of short poetry,
especially that which has a personal focus of
some kind, or is non-narrative. But the very
generality of its reference undermines its
value as a critical term since it may refer to
many different kinds of poetic genres and sub-
genres (as modern collections of lyric poetry
reveal). The term 'lyrics' now describes verbal
arrangements for musical accompaniment.
Bib: Lindley, D., Lyric.

Lyrical Ballads, with a Few other Poems (1798)

A collection of poems by ▷ William
Wordsworth and ▷ Samuel Taylor Coleridge,
often seen as the starting point of the
Romantic movement, the term 'lyrical
ballad' indicating the combination of
primitive simplicity (▷ ballad) and literary
elevation (▷ lyric) at which Wordsworth in
particular aimed. The volume first appeared
anonymously in 1798. Most of the poems were
by Wordsworth, Coleridge's contributions
being The Rime of the ▷ Ancient Mariner, The
Foster Mother's Tale, To the Nightingale, and
The Dungeon. The second edition (1800)
appeared under Wordsworth's name only,
and included the famous Preface and his poem
▷ Michael. Coleridge's poem Love was added
in place of Wordsworth's The Convict. In the
third edition of 1802 the Preface was enlarged.
The fourth and final edition appeared
in 1805.

In Chapter XIV of his ▷ Biographia Literaria,
Coleridge describes how the collaboration
came about. He and Wordsworth had been
discussing 'two cardinal points of poetry,
the power of exciting the sympathy of the
reader by a faithful adherence to the truth of
nature, and the power of giving the interest
of novelty by the modifying colours of the
imagination'. They projected a volume in
which Coleridge should direct himself to
characters 'supernatural' or at least romantic;
yet so as to transfer from our inward nature
a human interest . . . sufficient to procure
. . . that willing suspension of disbelief for
the moment, which constitutes poetic faith'.
Wordsworth's object would be to 'excite a
feeling analogous to the supernatural' for
everyday things the beauty of which was
normally concealed by the 'film of familiarity'.

Wordsworth's Preface (1800) is a poetic
manifesto attacking the 'gaudiness and inane
phraseology' of poets such as ▷ Thomas
Gray, who attempt to separate the language
of poetry as far as possible from that of
real life. Wordsworth proposes instead to
fit 'to metrical arrangement a selection of
the real language of men in a state of vivid
sensation'. 'Humble and rustic life' is the
chosen subject 'because in that condition, the
essential passions of the heart find a better
soil in which they can attain their maturity,
are less under restraint, and speak a plainer
and more emphatic language'. It is important
not to oversimplify Wordsworth's aims or
practice here. His language in the volume
does sometimes affect the flat plainness of
prose (in The Thorn for example), and at
other times he employs the sing-song metre
and artless repetitions of the primitive ballad
('Her eyes were fair, and very fair,/ – Her
beauty made me glad'). Sometimes however,
as in the non-ballad ▷ blank verse poem
Lines Composed a Few Miles Above Tintern
Abbey, the philosophical, literary vocabulary of
earlier reflective verse is in evidence ('tranquil
restoration', 'somewhat of a sad perplexity').
At first Coleridge felt entirely at one with
Wordsworth's Preface, but later, in Biographia
Literaria, Chapters XVII–XX, he subjected
Wordsworth's theories of poetic language to
incisive analysis.

Macaulay, Thomas Babington (1800–59)
Historian, ▷ essayist, politician and poet. He
was actively on the ▷ Whig side politically;
that is to say, without being a radical
reformer, he had strong faith in the virtue
of British parliamentary institutions. He was,
from the publication of his essay on ▷ Milton
in 1825, a constant contributor to the main
Whig periodical, the ▷ *Edinburgh Review*,
and his *History of England* (1848 and 1855) is
strongly marked by his political convictions.
He was trained as a lawyer and became an
eloquent orator; his writing has corresponding
qualities of persuasiveness and vividness.
As a historian he was best at impressionistic
reconstruction of the past, and the same
gift served him in his biographical essays on
John Bunyan (1628–88), Oliver Goldsmith
(1730–74), Samuel Johnson (1709–84), and
▷ Fanny Burney. He represented the most
optimistic strain of feeling in mid-19th-century
England – its faith in the march of progress.

Macaulay's *Lays of Ancient Rome* (1842)
were an attempt to reconstruct legendary
Roman history in a way that might resemble
the lost ▷ ballad poetry of ancient Rome.
Though not major poetry, they are very
vigorous verse with the kind of appeal that is
to be found in effective ballad poetry.

Macaulay was raised to the peerage in 1857.
▷ Histories; *Macaulay's History of England*.
Bib: Trevelyan, G. M., *Life and Letters*;
Bryant, A., *Macaulay*; Firth, C., *A Commentary
on Macaulay's History of England*; Trevelyan,
G. M. in *Clio: a Muse;* Stephen, L., in *Hours
in a Library*; Clive, J., *Thomas Babington
Macaulay: The Shaping of the Historian*.

**Macaulay's History of England from the
    Accession of James II**
The history (Vols. 1 & 2, 1848; 3 & 4, 1855;
5, 1861) is a thorough, detailed account of
two reigns: James II and William III. It is
unfinished and was originally intended to
extend to the time of George I (1714–27) and
further. The period covered is perhaps the
most crucial for English political development.
James II, a Catholic, tried to enforce his will
in the Catholic interest against Parliament,
which frustrated him and expelled him
from the throne in the Revolution of 1688.
Parliament then summoned William from
Holland to reign jointly with his wife, who
was also James's daughter, Mary II (1689–94).
William was the champion of the Protestant
cause in Europe, and Mary was also
Protestant.

Macaulay's politics were strongly in the
▷ Whig parliamentary tradition and his history

is an epic of the triumph of the ideas which
to him gave meaning to English history.
Considered as history, the work is accordingly
one-sided, much more a work of historical
art than of historical science; it represents
what historians have come to call 'the Whig
interpretation of history'.

Macpherson, James (1736–96)
The son of a farmer, educated in Aberdeen
and at Edinburgh University. In 1760 he
published 16 prose poems under the title
*Fragments of Ancient Poetry, Collected in the
Highlands of Scotland, and translated from the
Gaelic or Erse Language*. He attributed them to
the 3rd-century poet ▷ Ossian, an attribution
which was accepted by most readers at the
time, though some scholars were sceptical.
After travelling in the Western Isles in 1760–1
at the expense of his supporters in Edinburgh,
he published 'translations' of two complete
epics by Ossian: *Fingal* (1762) and *Temora*
(1763), which he claimed to have similarly
'collected'. The cloudy rhetoric and dramatic
character simplification of Macpherson's
prose-poetry caught the mood of the moment.
▷ Thomas Gray was enraptured by 'the
infinite beauty' of the *Fragments*, ▷ William
Blake was adulatory about them, and
Macpherson's *Ossian* retained its popularity
throughout the Romantic period, particularly
on the continent. ▷ Goethe admired it:
▷ Napoleon carried a copy of Macpherson on
his campaigns and took it into exile with him
to St Helena. Samuel Johnson (1709–84) was
amongst those who attacked the authenticity
of Macpherson's sources, replying when
asked if he believed that any modern man
could have written such works: 'Yes Sir,
many men, many women, and many children.'
The indignant poet threatened him with
physical violence. In later years Macpherson
became a political journalist, wrote history
with a Jacobite bias, and was elected M.P.
for Camelford. After his death the Highland
Society of Scotland undertook an inquiry
into his work and in 1805 declared it to be an
amalgam of freely adapted Irish ballads and
original compositions by Macpherson himself.

Maid Marian (1822)
▷ Thomas Love Peacock's parody of
▷ medieval romances (such as ▷ Scott's
▷ *Ivanhoe*, 1819) fashionable in the early 19th
century. It contains very good songs in comic
opera style.

Mallarmé, Stéphane
▷ Symbolism.

M

Malone, Edmund (1741–1812)

The greatest early editor of ▷ Shakespeare's works, many of whose textual emendations and editorial principles are still widely used. His greatest work remains his posthumously published edition of the complete Shakespeare (1821) and his research on the order in which Shakespeare's plays were written. He was also the first to denounce the Shakespearean forgeries of ▷ William Henry Ireland (1775–1835), one of whose fake plays, *Vortigern* and *Rowena*, was performed as Shakespeare's at ▷ Drury Lane.

Malthus, Thomas Robert (1766–1834)

Economist; particularly famous for his *Essay on Population* (1798), which he reissued in an expanded and altered form in 1803. Its original title was: *An Essay on the Principle of Population as it affects the Future Improvement of Society, with Remarks on the Speculations of Mr Godwin, M. Condorcet, and other Writers.*

The essence of his view was that social progress tends to be limited by the fact that population increases more rapidly than means of subsistence, and always reaches the limits of subsistence, so that a substantial part of society is doomed to live beyond the margin of poverty. The 'natural checks' which prevent population increase from exceeding the means of subsistence are war, famine, and pestilence, to which he added human misery and vice. In the second edition he added a further possible check by 'moral restraint', *ie* late marriages and sexual continence. These arguments made a strong impression on public opinion; an important practical consequence of them was the replacement of the existing haphazard methods of poor relief by the harsh but reasoned and systematic Poor Law system of 1834.

Malthus's relentless and pitiless reasoning led to political economy becoming known as the 'gloomy science'. His conclusions were contested by humanitarians, and later seemed belied by factors he did not foresee, such as cheap imports of food from newly exploited colonies like Canada. Since 1918 'Malthusian' theories of the dangers of over-population have revived.

Manchester Massacre, The

▷ Peterloo Massacre, The.

Manfred (1817)

A dramatic poem in ▷ blank verse by ▷ Lord Byron, set in the Alps. It focuses on the typical Byronic hero, outcast from society and haunted by the guilt of unnamed crimes. Manfred conjures up the Spirits of earth and air, the Witch of the Alps, the Destinies and Nemesis, and beseeches them in vain for oblivion. He eventually dies absolved, however, saved from the clutches of the evil spirits who claim his soul by the intervention of Astarte, the spirit of the woman whom he had loved. The poem, reminiscent of ▷ Goethe's *Faust*, was very popular throughout the 19th century, Schumann and Tchaikovsky basing major musical compositions upon it. Byron himself referred to it in a letter as 'a sort of mad drama'.

Mansfield Park (1814)

A novel by ▷ Jane Austen. The theme is the conflict between three different styles of moral feeling. The first is that of Sir Thomas Bertram, owner of Mansfield Park; it stands for a system of conservative, orderly principle, a tradition inherited from the 18th century, emphasizing stability and discounting the feelings. The second style of moral feeling is embodied in Fanny Price, Sir Thomas's niece whom he takes into his household because her parents are poor and their family too large; although she is timid, withdrawn and overawed by her new surroundings, she possesses a highly developed sensibility and capacity for affection both of which are foreign to the Bertrams, except to the younger son, Edmund, who to some degree appreciates her. The third style is represented by Henry and Mary Crawford, half-brother and half-sister to the wife of the village parson. They are rich, independent, attractive; they do not share Sir Thomas's cold theories, and they do possess Fanny's capacity for ardent feeling; on the other hand, they are without Sir Thomas's dedication to conscience and without Fanny's reverence for consistency of moral with affectionate and aesthetic sensibilities. The difference between the three styles of life becomes overt while Sir Thomas is absent in the West Indies; the Crawfords virtually take over Mansfield Park in order to rehearse, with the Bertram children and two guests, a performance of Kotzebue's *Lovers' Vows*. Henry Crawford is by this time conducting a flirtation with Maria Bertram, who is engaged to one of the guests, Mr Rushworth, and Mary Crawford is in love with Edmund; these relationships are in effect parodied in the play (popular in Jane Austen's time) so that the characters can perform on the stage what they desire to enact in real life. Fanny, knowing that Sir Thomas would disapprove of amateur acting, refuses to take part, but the situation is painful to her because she is secretly in love with Edmund herself. The rehearsals are stopped by Sir Thomas's sudden return, but a new crisis occurs in Fanny's life when Henry, awakened to the reality of her diffident charms, proposes marriage to her. She refuses him, much to Sir Thomas's uncomprehending disapproval, and is not in a position to explain to him the grounds of her refusal: that she disapproves of Henry morally and is in love with his son. She is exiled to her own family at Portsmouth, where disorder and strong emotion, often reduced to callous bad temper by poverty and overcrowding, are the rule. Henry is for a time constant, but he disgraces himself, the Bertrams and his sister by eloping with Maria after she has married. By degrees, both Sir Thomas and Edmund came to appreciate Fanny at her true value, and at the end of the novel she is to become Edmund's wife.

Of Jane Austen's completed works *Mansfield Park* is the most direct criticism of the ▷ Regency style of sensibility (represented by the Crawfords), with its tendency to reject continuity with the best elements of the past; at the same time the criticism is balanced by a recognition of the importance of the sensibility if morality is to receive true life from the feelings. It is also a bold challenge to the romantic style of fiction: Mary Crawford, antagonist to the heroine Fanny, is not only shown as friendly to her and in all but the deepest sense appreciative of her; she is also the possessor of genuine social attractions which Fanny lacks. The reader is made to like both her and her brother, and at the same time obliged to acknowledge Fanny's ultimate human superiority.

Marmion, A Tale of Flodden Field (1808)
An historical romance in tetrameter ▷ couplets (▷ metre) by ▷ Sir Walter Scott, set in 1513, the year of the catastrophic defeat of James IV of Scotland by the English. The story concerns the attempts of Lord Marmion to marry the rich Lady Clare, and to dispose of her lover by making false allegations of treason against him. Marmion is eventually killed in the battle and the lovers are reunited. The poem contains the famous lyrics 'Where shall the lover rest', and 'O, young Lochinvar is come out of the west'.

Marriage of Heaven and Hell, The (c 1793)
A composition mainly in poetic prose by ▷ William Blake. It was engraved, with designs woven into the text in the early 1790s, at the time he was working on ▷ *The Songs*

of Experience. The text consists of a series of symbolic, caustically·humorous anecdotes, and terse aphorisms. Blake's thesis, influenced by the thought of the mystic ▷ Emanuel Swedenborg, is that the rationality of John Locke (1632–1704) and ▷ Sir Isaac Newton, and the piety of established hierarchical religion, are repressive and sterile. He thus presents Hell as a region of dangerous but vital energies, and Heaven, without them, as a lifeless, ▷ Deistic abstraction. The most famous section of the work is the 'Proverbs of Hell', 70 aphorisms asserting flux and creativity against the stasis and hierarchy of Heaven: 'The road of excess leads to the palace of wisdom', 'The tygers of wrath are wiser than the horses of instruction', 'Sooner murder an infant in its cradle than nurse unacted desires.'
▷ *Songs of Innocence and Experience*.

Marryat, Frederick, Captain (1792–1848)
Novelist. He was a Captain in the Royal Navy and his novels are chiefly about the sea. The best known of them are: *Frank Mildmay* (1829); *Peter Simple* (1834); *Jacob Faithful* (1834); *Mr Midshipman Easy* (1836). *Japhet in Search of a Father* (1836) is the story of a child of unknown parents who eventually achieves prosperity. Others of his books were intended for boys; the best-known of these is *Masterman Ready* (1841). Marryat continued the 18th-century realistic tradition of narrative, the most famous examples of which are the novels of Tobias Smollett (1721–71).
▷ Realism.
Bib: Marryat, F., *Life and Letters of Captain Marryat*; Conrad, J., 'Tales of the Sea' in *Notes on Life and Letters*; Warner, O., *Captain Marryat: a Rediscovery*.

Martineau, Harriet (1802–76)
Critic and ▷ essayist; also biographer and novelist. The sixth of eight children of a manufacturer of camlet and bombazine, she was born in Norwich where she was educated, at home and later in school. She had no sense of taste or smell and was a sickly child, gloomy, jealous and morbid, suffering from her parents' discipline and domestic scrimping, necessitated by their desire to educate their children to earn their own living. She supported herself initially partly by needlework and partly by writing reviews for the *Monthly Repository*. A devout ▷ Unitarian, she first published *Devotional Exercises* (1823), and in 1830 and 1831 won all three prizes in a competition set by the Central

Unitarian Association for essays intended to convert the Roman Catholics, Jews and Mahommedans. Between 1832 and 1834 she wrote *Illustrations of Political Economy*, social reformist stories influenced by ▷ Jeremy Bentham and John Stuart Mill (1806–73) along with stories for 'Brougham's Society for the Diffusion of Useful Knowledge', of which some 10,000 copies were sold. She became a celebrity, living with her mother and aunt in Westminster, dining out every day except Sunday with friends such as ▷ Malthus, Sydney Smith, Milnes and politicians whom she advised; she suggested and managed Thomas Carlyle's (1795–1881) first course of lectures in 1837. In 1834 she visited the U.S. partly for her health, supporting the Abolitionists despite threats and difficulties, publishing in 1837 *Society in America* and, a lighter and more popular product of her trip, *A Retrospect of Western Travel*. In 1839 she toured abroad again, but had to return quickly from Venice and was ill for some six months. In 1843 she published *Life in the Sick Room*, which she came to despise when her views on religion developed. She was cured of a serious illness by mesmerism in 1844 and went on to practise it herself, giving an account in *Letters on Mesmerism* (1845). She travelled in Egypt and Palestine in 1846–7. By now she had rejected all religion.

She wrote numerous articles in the *Daily News* and some for the ▷ *Edinburgh Review*. Her other works include: *Deerbrook* (1839), her first novel and her favourite, *The Hour and The Man* (1840) on Toussaint l'Ouverture, a popular volume of children's stories *The Playfellow* (1841), *The History of England During the Thirty Years' Peace* (1849) and *Laws of Man's Social Nature*. She was influenced by ▷ Comte, of whose philosophy she produced a free translation and condensation, *The Philosophy of Comte* (1853). She wrote a hurried ▷ autobiography in 1855 when diagnosed terminally ill, *An Autobiographical Memoir*, published eventually in 1876. Martineau never married, writing that, 'thus, I am not only entirely satisfied with my lot, but I think it the very best for me – I am probably the happiest single woman in England'. She attributed her power to 'earnestness and intellectual clearness within a certain range', although she had 'no approach to genius' due to her lack of imagination.

Bib: Pichanick, V. K., *Harriet Martineau, the Woman and Her Work*; Spender, D. and Todd, J., *Anthology of British Woman Writers*; Webb, R. K., *Harriet Martineau, a Radical Victorian*.

Marxism
Founded on the school of thought espoused by Karl Marx (1818–83). Marx was born in Trier of German-Jewish parentage, and attended university in Berlin and Bonn where he first encountered Hegelian dialectic. He met Friedrich Engels (1820–95) in Paris in 1844, and in 1848, the Year of Revolutions, they published *The Communist Manifesto* together. In that year Marx returned to Germany and took part in the unsuccessful revolution there before fleeing to Britain where he was to remain until his death in 1883. In 1867 he published *Capital*, the voluminous work for which he is best known. Marx is justly renowned for his adaptation of the Hegelian dialectic for a materialist account of social formations, which is based upon an analysis of the opposition between different social classes. He is, arguably, the most prolific thinker and social commentator of the 19th century whose work has had far-reaching effects on subsequent generations of scholars, philosophers, politicians and analysts of human culture. In the political ferment of the 1960s, and especially in France, his work has been subject to a series of extraordinarily productive re-readings, especially by philosophers such as ▷ Louis Althusser which continue to affect the understanding of all aspects of cultural life. In Britain Marx's work is what lies behind a very powerful literary and historical tradition of commentary and analysis, and has informed much work in the areas of sociology, and the study of the mass media. *Capital* and a range of earlier texts have come to form the basis of the materialist analysis of culture.

▷ New historicism.

Mask of Anarchy, The (1832)
A poem by ▷ Percy Bysshe Shelley, written in 1819, after he had heard news of the ▷ 'Peterloo Massacre' in Manchester, when soldiers fired on a peaceful demonstration in favour of parliamentary reform. He sent the poem to ▷ Leigh Hunt for publication in his radical periodical ▷ *The Examiner*, but Hunt dared not print it at the time, and withheld publication until 1832. The poem was intended for popular reading, and Shelley used quatrains and five-line stanzas, similar to those of the popular ▷ ballad. He identifies Anarchy with the lawless tyranny of the British government, and exhibits its leaders in a garish pageant of Anarchy's minions: 'I met Murder on the way – / He had a mask like Castlereagh – / Very smooth he looked, yet grim; / Seven blood-hounds followed him.'

Shelley ends with a magnificent address to the 'Men of England, heirs of Glory', exhorting them to throw off their chains: 'Ye are many – they are few.' Its rough, angry style and passionate rhetoric give the poem a prophetic resonance which anticipates the *Communist Manifesto* of Karl Marx and Friedrich Engels (1848) (▷ Marxism).

Mason, William (1725–97)
Poet and biographer. A minor poet, Mason was heavily influenced by his friend ▷ Gray, whose poems he edited with an appended ▷ biography, *The Poems of Gray with Memoirs* (1775). Mason's own works, *Elfrida* (1751) and *Caractacus* (1759) use ▷ Pindaric odes (▷ Ode). He was also interested in the ▷ Picturesque, publishing a three volume poem on gardening called *The English Garden* (1771–81), which despite its uninspired poetry reveals an understanding of design and form. He had numerous friends in the literary world, including ▷ Walpole.

Materialism
The philosophical theory that only physical matter is real and that all phenomena and processes can be explained by reference to it. Related to this is the doctrine that political and social change is triggered by change in the material and economic basis of society.
   ▷ Cultural Materialism; Marxism.

Maturin, Charles Robert (1782–1824)
Irish novelist and dramatist. Like ▷ 'Monk' Lewis and ▷ Mrs Radcliffe he belonged to the school of writers who exploited the emotions of terror and love of mystery among readers in the late 18th and early 19th centuries. *The Fatal Revenge, or The Family of Montorso* (1807), *The Wild Irish Boy* (1808) and *The Milesian Chief* (1812) were ridiculed but admired for their power by ▷ Walter Scott. Scott and ▷ Byron secured the production of Maturin's tragedy *Bertram* in 1816, which was a great success. His other tragedies were less successful, and he returned to the novel. The best of his later novels is *Melmoth the Wanderer* (1820), to which the French novelist ▷ Balzac wrote a sequel *Melmoth réconcilié à l'église* (1835).
   ▷ Irish literature in English.

Maud (1855)
One of the best-known poems by ▷ Alfred Tennyson. It is called 'A Monodrama', and is in fact an example of the ▷ dramatic monologue, a form particularly characteristic of ▷ Victorian poetry.

It is in three parts. Part I tells of the mysterious death of the narrator's father, who has been ruined by the contrivances of 'that old man, now lord of the broad estate and the Hall'. But the narrator gradually falls in love with the old lord's daughter, and here occurs the famous lyric 'Come into the garden, Maud'. The young lord, her brother, treats him with contempt, however, and Part II opens with their duel and the death of the brother. The narrator flies abroad, and falls into the depths of morbid despair. In Part III he recovers, and seeks salvation through the service of his country in war: the poem was written in the year in which the Crimean War broke out.
   Maud exemplifies the versatility of Tennyson's craftsmanship by the variety of its metrical (▷ metre) and stanzaic form, and the brilliant distinctness of his vision in some of the imagery. It contains bitter criticism of the temper of the age. The poem has been held to betray Tennyson's confusion about his age; criticizing it, yet swimming with its tide. *Maud* is a ▷ Gothic conflation of images of disease, mental aberration and sexual repression.

Medieval literature
The literature produced in England between (roughly) 1300 and 1500 (Edward I established the Model Parliament in 1295 and Henry VII became king, founding the Tudor dynasty, in 1485). Within this period a vast amount of widely diverse texts were produced, which may roughly be divided into five groups:
   1 *Medieval English lyrics* These were songs, both religious and secular in theme, which belong to popular tradition; many were discovered in manuscript form during the ▷ Romantic period (▷ Percy).
   2 *Narrative* Long tales, both in verse and prose, contain some of the most moving and powerful passages of medieval literature, including some of Chaucer's *The Canterbury Tales* (1373–93), the anonymous *Gawain and the Green Knight* and Thomas Malory's *Morte D'Arthur* (1469–70). Malory's great prose retelling of Arthurian legend was very popular in the late Romantic period and ▷ Tennyson drew from it extensively.
   3 *Pastoral literature and drama* While these religious and ▷ didactic works were very important during the medieval period, they had little influence on the Romantic writers, although there has more recently been a revival of interest in the morality and miracle plays.
   4 *Chaucer, Gower and Langland* The three major authors of the period have been read

and enjoyed consistently since their texts were first produced. Geoffrey Chaucer's (1340–1400) works include his compilation of narratives *The Canterbury Tales* and his verse romance *Troilus and Criseyde* (1380–88). John Gower's (1330–1408) *Confessio Amantis* is also a collection of tales, though with a move devotional and moralistic tone. Little is known about William Langland (1330–81), but his long spiritual ▷ allegory, *Piers Plowman* contains material of great social and historical interest.

The Romantic period saw the beginning of a revived interest in the ▷ Middle Ages and medieval literature, which is often associated with the ▷ Gothic revival. Several writers including ▷ Sir Walter Scott, ▷ John Keats, ▷ Thomas Chatterton and ▷ Horace Walpole employ themes and linguistic forms from this earlier period. Others, such as ▷ Byron and ▷ Shelley, were more indebted to the 13th and 14th-century Italian writers ▷ Boccaccio and ▷ Dante. The popularity of medieval material at this time is parodied in ▷ Peacock's ▷ *Maid Marian*.

▷ Macpherson; Ossian; Tristan and Iseult.
Bib: Mitchell, J., *Scott, Chaucer and Medieval Romance*.

Melincourt, or Sir Oran Haut-ton (1817)

A novel by ▷ Thomas Love Peacock. Sir Oran Haut-ton is an orang-outang of delightful manners and a good flute-player for whom the young philosopher, Mr Sylvan Forester, has bought the title of baronet and a seat in Parliament. 'Haut ton' is a French phrase then used in English for 'high tone', *ie* fashionable, refined, and aristocratic. Peacock is developing the idea of Lord Monboddo (1714–90), an early anthropologist, who describes such a creature in his books, as an example of 'the infantine state of our species'; Peacock's ape, however, compares favourably with the aristocracy. The book is a satire on the right-wing (Tory) establishment, and especially those writers who had once been Radicals but now favoured it: ▷ Southey (Mr Feathernest); ▷ Wordsworth (Mr Paperstamp); ▷ Coleridge (Mr Mystic). Mr Vamp and Mr Killthedead are Tory reviewers, and Mr Fax may represent ▷ Malthus. Sylvan Forester may be the poet ▷ Shelley; and Simon Sarcastic, Peacock himself.

Melodrama

The prefix 'melo-' derives from the Greek 'melos', music. Originally, melodrama was a play in which there was no singing but the

dialogue had a musical accompaniment; the first example is said to be ▷ Rousseau's *Pygmalion* (1775). The musical accompaniment gradually ceased; the word came to denote romantic plays of extravagantly violent action, and it is now applied to sensational action without adequate motivation, in any work of fiction.

The word has also been used to denote popular ballad operas in which spoken dialogue is used extensively. This use, however, is much less common.

Metalanguage

A term coined by the linguist L. Hjelmslev to describe a language which refers to *another language* rather than to non-linguistic objects situations or events. In the words of ▷ Roland Barthes it is 'a second language in which one speaks about the first' (*Mythologies*). In this sense, metalanguage can be used as a means of reflecting on language itself.

Methodism

A religious movement founded by ▷ John Wesley. The name was at first applied derisively to himself and his associates when he was a student at Oxford in 1729, referring to the strict rules that they made for themselves in order to follow a religious life; however, he early accepted the designation. From 1739 a time when the Church of England was particularly apathetic, the movement spread rapidly among the poor all over England, and it became especially strong in the industrial towns. Wesley himself had no desire to separate Methodism from the Anglican Church, but the demands on his energies forced him to ordain preachers whom the Church felt it could not accept as clergymen; consequently the Methodists developed an independent organization.

The later movement divided into a number of distinct organizations. It spread abroad, especially to the U.S.A. where the membership numbers about 13 million, as compared with rather more than half a million in Britain.

Metre

From the Greek word meaning 'measure'. In poetry, metre is the measure of the rhythm of a line of verse, when the line is rhythmically systematic, *ie* can be divided into units of 'metrical feet'. The names for these feet all derive from ancient Greek verse. The

commonest feet in use in English are as
follows:

Iambus   *eg* the words 'again', 'revenge',
            'delight'.
            'Iambics march from short to
            long.'

Trochee   *eg* the words 'never', 'happy',
            'heartless'.
            'Trochee trips from long to
            short.'

Anapest   *eg* the words 'entertain',
            'supersede', 'engineer'.
            'With a leap and a bound the
            swift anapaests throng.'

Spondee   *eg* the words 'maintain',
            'heartbreak', 'wineglass'
            'Slow spondee stalks, strong
            foot ...'

Dactyl   *eg* the words 'melody',
            'happiness', 'sorrowful'.
            '... yet ill able
            'Ever to come up with dactyl
            trisyllable.'

The illustrative lines are taken from
▷ Coleridge's mnemonic rhyme 'Metrical
Feet' (the dactyl example in particular being
a joke).

It is important to remember three
points when analysing ('scanning') English
verse:

1 Despite Coleridge's use of 'long' and
'short' for iambic and trochaic feet, these
words are inappropriate to English metrical
feet, which are composed of accented and
unaccented syllables (two accented ones
in the case of the spondee) irrespective of
their length.

2 Except in the case of the iambus, it is
unusual to find lines of verse composed
entirely of the same foot; this is especially true
of the spondee and the dactyl.

3 It is unwise to think of metre at all
when reading a great deal of English verse.
Old and Middle English alliterative verse

(▷ Figures of speech) was not metrical at all.
Although the skilful deployment of metre is an
important component of Romantic poetry (*eg*
▷ Wordsworth's use of blank verse in ▷ *The
Prelude* and elsewhere, or ▷ Byron's use of
▷ *ottava rima* in ▷ *Don Juan*), poets were in
general dissatisfied with the excessive metrical
tightness of much 18th-century poetry, which
seemed to them to emphasise verse-form at
the expense of impassioned thoughts and
feeling.

Verse lines have names according to
the number of feet they contain; much
the commonest English line is the iambic
pentameter (five feet). The hexameter has
six feet, and is called an ▷ Alexandrine
when they are iambic. Other lengths:
monometer = one foot; dimeter = two feet;
trimeter = three feet; tetrameter = four
feet; heptameter = seven feet; octameter =
eight feet.
   ▷ Blank verse; Ode; Sonnet.

Michael (1800)

A poem in ▷ blank verse by ▷ William
Wordsworth concerning the austere life of
a shepherd in the Lake District, whose
only son Luke goes away to work in town,
meets disgrace, and then disappears. The
emptiness of Michael's life without his son
is symbolized, in an image of characteristic
simplicity, by the unbuilt sheepfold, whose
first stone Luke had laid before his departure
as a covenant between them. Michael spends
the last seven years of his life brooding over it
and leaves it still unfinished at his death.
   ▷ Lake Poets.

Middle Ages, The

A term used by historians to cover the
period between the fall of the Roman
Empire of the West (end of the 5th century)
and the beginning of the ▷ Renaissance,
conventionally dated from the extinction of
the Roman Empire of the East (Byzantine
Empire) in 1453. The expression dates from
the 16th century when it is found in the Latin
writings of a number of humanists – 'media
aetas', 'medium aevum'. The conception in
the 16th century was that civilization was
renewing itself by rediscovery of the ancient
civilizations of Greece and Rome; scholars
considered that the centuries between the
5th and 15th were a relatively dark period of
ignorance and cultural backwardness. For long
after the 16th century modern history was
commonly assumed to have begun with the
15th-century Renaissance. Some scholars are
inclined to think this view mistaken; many of

them also consider that the so-called Middle Ages had much more continuity with classical history than the men of the Renaissance supposed. The term Middle Ages is thus a misleading and erroneous one but its use has become habitual and cannot be dispensed with. Moreover the Renaissance of the 15th–16th centuries did herald an important change, however one interprets it, and it is still useful to have a term to designate the centuries which preceded it.

In English history, it is common to think of the Middle Ages as extending from the Norman Conquest of 1066 until the end of the Wars of the Roses and the accession of Henry VII (first of the House of Tudor) in 1485. The period from the 5th to the 11th century is called loosely the Old English period. The term Middle Ages was first used by John Donne in a sermon in 1621.

Milton, John (1608–74)

Poet and prose polemicist. Milton was born in London, the son of a scrivener and musician, and educated at St Paul's School and Christ's College Cambridge. After leaving Cambridge, in 1632, Milton lived for the next five years at his father's house in Horton. During this, his early poetic career, he wrote the companion pieces *L'Allegro* and *Il Penseroso*, two masques *Arcades* and *Comus*, and the ▷ elegy *Lycidas*. From 1638 to 1639 Milton travelled abroad, chiefly in Italy. His Italian journey was to have a lasting influence on his later development, not least in the contact he established amongst Florentine intellectuals. But more than that, it re-affirmed his distaste – loathing even – for Roman Catholicism, and focussed his intense opposition to the Laudian regime in England.

Milton's continental journey was interrupted early in 1639 at Naples, where he claims to have first heard news of the political crisis in England. He was later to claim that he thought it 'base that I should travel abroad at my ease for the cultivation of my mind while my fellow citizens at home were fighting for liberty' (*Defensio secunda*). Returning to England, Milton embarked upon what has now come to be seen as the second phase of his career – that of a political prose writer, and propagandist for the anti-Royalist cause in the English Civil War. Between 1640 and 1655, Milton was to write little poetry. His energies and his sympathies were now to be engaged fully on the side of the republican forces in England – though he was a not uncritical supporter of the new experiment in government. From this period can be dated the series of great prose declarations dealing with political and religious questions – *Of Reformation* (1641), his attack on episcopacy in the *Apology for Smectymnuus* (1642), his statement on personal liberty contained in *The Doctrine and Discipline of Divorce* (1643). These works were followed by *Areopagitica* (1644), *Tenure of Kings and Magistrates* (1649), *Eikonoklastes* (1649), the two 'defences' of the English people (1651 and 1654), *A Treatise of Civil Power* (1659) and, almost at the moment when Charles II returned to England to re-establish the claims of monarchy, *A Readie and Easie Way to Establish a Free Commonwealth* (1660). The list of topics upon which Milton wrote in this period is bewildering, but running through all his prose writings is a stable belief that the English people have been chosen, by God, to perform a necessary political act – the establishment of a state based on principles of choice and, within certain bounds, freedom.

▷ *Paradise Lost*, Milton's great religious and political poem, was begun at some point in the mid-1650s – perhaps in the growing awareness that, though political choices had been made in England, the wrong choice had been made. The poem was not published, however, until 1667, with a second (revised) edition appearing in 1674, shortly before Milton's death in November of that year. But the period after 1660 is usually recognized as the third and final phase of Milton's career. It is the period of the publication of ▷ *Paradise Regained* and *Samson Agonistes*. Though it has long been claimed that Milton's absorption in the task of writing these works marked an end to his career of political engagement, it is probably truer to say that these works signal a renewed, and possibly deeper, investigation of the themes which had occupied him for most of his life – the questions of political and religious liberty, the problems associated with choice and rule, and the problematic nature of government and obedience. Milton exerted an enormous influence on the ▷ Romantic poets, including ▷ Blake, ▷ Wordsworth, ▷ Keats and ▷ Shelley; their poetry bears the imprint of Miltonic language and metre, as well as overtly displaying a constant revaluation and re-visioning of *Paradise lost*.

Bib: Carey, J. and Fowler, A. (ed.), *The Complete Poems of John Milton*; Wolfe, D. M. (ed.), *Complete Prose Works of John Milton*; Parker, W. R., *Milton: A Biography*; Hill, C., *Milton and the English Revolution*; Nyquist, M. and Ferguson, M. (ed.), *Re-membering Milton*; Goslee, N. M., *Uriel's Eye: Miltonic*

Stationing and Statuary in Blake, Keats and Shelley.

Mimesis

In ▷ Plato's *Republic* 'mimesis' is used to designate 'imitation', but in a derogatory way. The term is given a rigorous, positive meaning in ▷ Aristotle's *Poetics* where it is used to describe a process of selection and representation appropriate to tragedy: 'the imitation of an action'. Literary criticism from Sir Philip Sidney (1554–86) onwards has wrestled with the problem of the imitative function of literary texts, but after ▷ structuralism with its questioning of the referential function of all language, the term has taken on a new and problematic dimension. Mimesis has frequently been associated with the term ▷ 'realism', and with the capacity of language to reflect reality. This debate has been carried on vigorously at a theoretical level, in the exchanges earlier this century between the Hungarian critic Georg Lukács, and the dramatist Bertolt Brecht. The nub of the debate between these two ▷ Marxist thinkers was how best to represent 'the deeper causal complexes of society' (Brecht). Brecht rejected the view propounded by Lukács that the novel was the literary form which pre-eminently represented social process, arguing that realism was a major political, philosophical and practical issue and should not be dealt with by literature alone. Such a view rejected the metaphysical implications which lay behind the Aristotelian notion of mimesis, in favour of a more historical analysis which saw literature as part of the process of social change.

Debate about the capacity language does or does not possess to imitate reality had been an important feature of Romantic poetry and literary theory. In the Preface to the second edition of ▷ *Lyrical Ballads*, ▷ Wordsworth wrote of the close relation between poetry and 'powerful feelings', in 'a language really used by men'. Mimesis in Romantic poetry would henceforth be yoked to psychological realism. However, the new interest in psychology and the subjective goes hand in hand with an interest in the accurate depiction of external scenes and landscapes. Romantic poetry is full of *tours de force* of observation, ranging from Wordsworth's writings on the Lake District (in prose, as well as verse) to the ominously desolate coastline painted by ▷ Shelley at the beginning of ▷ *Julian and Maddalo*, or the accounts of battle in the 'Siege of Ismail' section of ▷ Byron's ▷ *Don Juan*. In short, the question of mimesis is explored freely in the Romantic period, in contrast to the anxious debate of the 20th century.

Minerva Press

Established in London in 1790 by William Lane, it combined a press with a ▷ circulating library, and published mainly women authors for a primarily female readership. It is often identified with the worst kind of ▷ Gothic and sentimental excess, and probably equates most closely to the Mills and Boon pulp novels published in the late 20th century. Yet Minerva did produce some interesting work, perhaps more by accident than design, and certainly provided the means for many women to earn their living as authors.
Bib: Blakey, D., *The Minerva Press 1790–1820.*

Mitford, Mary Russell (1786–1855)

Poet, dramatist, letter-writer, autobiographer and sketch-writer. Mary Mitford remained living with her parents in the country, supporting her family, especially her father who was laden with gambling debts, by her prolific writing. Her first publication, *Miscellaneous Poems* (1810), was well received and she was encouraged by ▷ Coleridge to continue writing. She produced several acclaimed and lucrative dramas, *Julian* (1823), *Foscari* (1826) and *Rienzi* (1828). Even more successful were her prose sketches of country life, in particular *Our Village* (1824–32). Her style was lucid and direct, and Mitford herself stated that she 'always wrote on the spot and at the moment and in nearly every instance with the closest and most resolute fidelity to the place and the people'. While rightly lauded for her work, Mitford felt isolated with her family in the country and entered into correspondence with some of the other well-known authors of her day; these included Elizabeth Barrett Browning (1806–61), ▷ Felica Hemans, ▷ Charles Lamb, ▷ Harriet Martineau, and ▷ Amelia Opie. Today it is these letters which provide the most valuable insight into Mitford's own life and work, as well as presenting us with a picture of the literary world at the beginning of the 19th century. More formal ▷ autobiographical material may be found in her *Recollections of a Literary Life*, (1857).
Bib: Astin, M., *Mary Russell Mitford*; Edwards, P.D., *Idyllic Realism from Mary Russell Mitford to Hardy.*

'Monk' Lewis (1775–1818)

Matthew Gregory Lewis, whose sensational novel *The Monk* (1796) had such success in its day that he was nicknamed after it.

▷ Gothic novels.

Montagu, Elizabeth (1720–1800)

An eminent ▷ Bluestocking and famous epistolarist, Montagu's early intellectual abilities were widely remarked upon, and Samuel Johnson (1709–84) hailed her as 'Queen of the Blues'.

Montagu began to hold her formal receptions in the early 1750s, and she boasted to the actor David Garrick (1717–79) that, whatever the social status of the guests, 'I never invite idiots'. Her patronage of young authors aided James Beattie (1735–1803) and Richard Price (1723–91).

In 1769 her *Essay on the Writings and Genius of Shakespeare*, challenging Voltaire's theories, was widely admired, though Johnson perceived its critical failings.
▷ Shakespeare.

Mont Blanc (1816)

Poem by ▷ Shelley, inspired by the view from the Bridge of Arve in the valley at Chamouni, Switzerland. It was first printed at the end of his *History of a Six Week's Tour* (1817), in which the poet describes this work as 'composed under the immediate impression of the deep and powerful feelings excited by the objects it attempts to describe; and, as an undisciplined overflowing of the soul'. This emphasis on a subjective and emotional reaction to a turbulent landscape scene recalls the work of the first-generation ▷ Romantic poets ▷ Wordsworth and ▷ Coleridge, vividly present in the poem's evocation of the human mind, which 'renders and receives fast influencings,/ Holding an unremitting interchange/ With the clear universe of things around'. Equally important however is *Mont Blanc's* revisionary and antagonistic relationship to Coleridge's *Hymn Before Sun-rise in the Vale of Chamouni* (1802), which describes the same landscape. Where Coleridge attributes the splendours of the scene to the workings of divinity, the atheist Shelley views the significance of landscape as produced by the human mind alone.

Montrose, James Graham, Marquess of (1612–50)

Scottish patriot, general and statesman. He was one of the noblest and most gifted of Charles I's supporters in and after the Civil War. After spasmodic but brilliant successes, he was caught by Parliament forces and executed. ▷ Walter Scott's novel *A Legend of Montrose* (1819) concerns his career. John Buchan wrote a biography of him.

Moore, Thomas (1779–1852)

Born in Dublin, Moore studied law at the Middle Temple and became a popular drawing-room singer. Later he was for a time Admiralty Registrar in Bermuda. His early pseudonymous volume, *The Poetical Works of the late Thomas Little Esq.* (1801) was referred to by ▷ Lord Byron in *English Bards and Scotch Reviewers* (1809), and the two poets became close friends. Moore received many letters from Byron, though he shamefully expurgated them after Byron's death, and agreed to destroy the *Memoirs* which Byron had left to him. Moore's own writings range from ▷ lyric to satire, from prose romance to history and biography. The extremely popular *Irish Melodies*, which contain his most enduring work, appeared in ten parts between 1807 and 1835, and in 1813 he published a group of satires aimed at the Prince Regent, *The Twopenny Post Bag*. His long narrative poem in the Byronic mode, *Lalla Rookh: An Oriental Romance* (1817), achieved an international reputation, but in his next work *The Fudge Family in Paris* (1818) he returned to satire, aiming his shafts against the Englishman abroad. His *Loves of the Angels* (1823) became notorious for its eroticism. He also wrote a prose romance set in 3rd-century Egypt, *The Epicurean* (1827), a *History of Ireland* (1835–46), and biographies of Thomas Sheridan (1825), and (ironically in view of his destruction of his friend's own autobiographical work) of Byron (1830).
Bib: White, T. de V., *Tom Moore: The Irish Poet*.

More, Hannah (1745–1833)

An eminent ▷ Bluestocking, More settled in London in 1774, where she became the friend of David Garrick (1717–79), Johnson (1709–84), ▷ Percy and ▷ Montagu. She was a conservative Christian ▷ feminist who opposed ▷ Mary Wollstonecraft on women's rights. Her tragedy *Percy* was produced by Garrick in 1777, and established both her literary reputation and her social status. A tragedy, *The Fatal Falsehood*, appeared in 1779. ▷ Horace Walpole became her great admirer, printing *Bishop Bonner's Ghost* at the Strawberry Hill press in 1789. In 1784 her earlier poem *Bas Bleu* was published.

More used her writing to express concern about social reform. *Village Politics* appeared in 1793, and the *Cheap Repository Tracts* of 1795–8 sold two million copies. *Thoughts on the Importance of the Manners of the Great* (1788) also ran into several editions. In 1809 More published *Coelebs in Search of a Wife*, a

novel which, despite hostile reviews, proved an immense success. Her correspondence is lively and entertaining.
Bib: Jones, M. G., *Hannah More*.

Morgan, Sydney (1776–1859)
Novelist. Lady Sydney Morgan (née Owenson) was a prolific Irish author, whose ▷ nationalist politics were reflected in her fictional recreations of Irish history and legend. Her novels, which include *St Clair* (1803) and the popular *Wild Irish Girl* (1806), did much to establish the idea of Ireland's past as fashionable and romantic both in her own country and in England. Moreover, she contributed to the Celtic revival of the mid-19th century. Her novel *The Missionary* (1811) influenced both ▷ Byron and ▷ Shelley.
▷ Macpherson, James; Ossian; Irish literature in English.
Bib: Spender, D and Todd, J., *Anthology of British Women Writers*; Stevenson, L., *The Wild Irish Girl: the life of Sydney Owenson, Lady Morgan*.

Morier, James Justin (1780–1849)
Travel writer and novelist. Morier was a diplomat stationed in Persia and his ▷ travel books, *A Journey Through Persia* (1812) and *A Second Journey Through Persia* (1818) describe his experiences while there. In 1817 he resigned his post and devoted himself to writing novels, including *The Adventures of Hajji Baba of Ispahan* (1824), a ▷ picaresque tale of an ordinary Persian artisan, which made an important contribution to the growing popularity of ▷ Orientalism.

Morning Chronicle
A London ▷ Whig ▷ newspaper founded in 1769; its contributors included ▷ Sheridan and ▷ Lamb. It came to an end in 1862.

Morning Herald, The
A London ▷ newspaper, 1780–1869. It had a large circulation, and published police cases, illustrated by the famous artist George Cruikshank, illustrator of Dickens's novel *Oliver Twist*.

Morning Post, The
A conservative but highly independent London newspaper, founded 1772, ceased 1936. ▷ Wordsworth, ▷ Coleridge and ▷ Southey contributed to it.

Murphy, Arthur (1727–1805)
Dramatist. Murphy's prolific output includes tragedies, comedies and farces. He adapted the works of the French dramatists Molière and Voltaire (▷ French literature in England), and his own plays include the witty ▷ satire, *Three Weeks After Marriage* (1764). Murphy is also known for writing biographies of Fielding (*An Essay on the Life and Genius of Henry Fielding*, 1762), Garrick (*The Life of David Garrick*, 1801), and his friend Dr Johnson (*An Essay on the Life and Genius of Samuel Johnson*, 1792).
Bib: Dunbar, H.H., *The Dramatic Career of Murphy*.

Murray, John (1778–1843)
Publisher. He founded the ▷ *Quarterly Review* in 1809, and published works by ▷ Lord Byron, ▷ Jane Austen and ▷ George Crabbe, among others. Alone among Byron's correspondents he refused to cooperate with the conspiracy to destroy the poet's *Memoir* and expurgate his letters after his death. Byron's correspondence with Murray thus provides our best insight into Byron's actual language in informal contexts. Murray's father (1745–93) and his son (1808–92), both named John, were also publishers of note.

Musgrave, Agnes (fl 1800)
Novelist. Almost nothing is known of Musgrave's life, but she was a best-selling ▷ Minerva novelist from 1795 to 1801. Intriguingly, her first work purports to be a history of the Musgrave family through the female line from ▷ medieval times to her own age; it is supposedly discovered and recounted by the author. *Edmund of the Forest* (1797), *The Solemn Injunction* (1798) and *The Confession* (1801) followed Musgrave's first novel, but they are all rather predictably sensational and quasi ▷ Gothic.

***Mysteries of Udolpho, The* (1794)**
A novel by ▷ Mrs Ann Radcliffe. It achieved great fame in its own day, and is often cited as the typical ▷ Gothic novel. It is mainly set in a sombre castle in the Apennine mountains in Italy. The atmosphere is of secret plots, concealed passages, abductions, and the supernatural. ▷ Jane Austen satirized the taste for such sensational literature in ▷ *Northanger Abbey*.

N

Napoleon I (Napoleon Bonaparte, originally Buonaparte, 1769–1821)

A Corsican whose unique career began in the ▷ French Revolution, when he joined the French army defending the first French Republic against European alliances. His military successes brought him to dictatorship in 1799, with the title of First Consul, and in 1804 he became Emperor. His armies dominated the greater part of Europe until 1812, when his campaign against Russia failed. His final defeat at the hands of the British and the Prussians under ▷ Wellington and Blucher at ▷ Waterloo (1815) led to his exile on the Atlantic island of St Helena, where he died.

His unprecedented success aroused contrasted feelings amongst the British. For the great majority he was a nightmare figure; mothers used his name to frighten naughty children into discipline. To a man like ▷ Wordsworth he was the tyrant who revealed the illusoriness of the ideals of universal freedom which the Revolution had seemed to express. For ▷ Byron and ▷ Shelley he was the first man in Europe to have risen to the summit of power by intrinsic merit and not at least partly through privilege; his downfall and the restoration of the traditional kinds of government that he had overthrown was for them a defeat of the new hopes for mankind. Byron described him memorably in ▷ Child Harold Canto III, stanzas 36–44.

▷ French literature in England.

Nationalism

The emotion or the doctrine according to which human egotism and its passions are expanded so as to become identical with the nation state. As a widespread phenomenon it is usually dated from the American War of Independence (1775–83) and from the ▷ French Revolution and the wars that followed it. This makes it an especially 19th- and 20th-century phenomenon, which it undoubtedly is, but on the other hand intense national self-consciousness existed among the older European nations before, though without the fanaticism which has been characteristic of it since 1790. Thus strong national feeling arose in England and France, in consequence of the Hundred Years War in the 15th century; it arose again in the 16th and 17th centuries under the English queen Elizabeth I and the French king Louis XIV respectively. Possibly these earlier emotions should be distinguished as patriotism, but the distinction is vague.

Natural Religion

A belief first taught by Lord Herbert of Cherbury (1583–1648); according to him, belief in God and right conduct are planted in human instincts. This Christian doctrine was the basis for deistic thought (▷ Deism) in the later 17th and 18th centuries, and contributed to the growth of religious toleration, though also to passivity of religious feeling and hence to indifference. Herbert's aim was to resolve the doubts arising out of the religious conflicts of his time. For the reaction against Deism, see ▷ William Blake's proposition *There is No Natural Religion* (1788).

Nature

The word is used throughout English literature with meanings that vary constantly according to period or to mode of expression, *eg* philosophic, religious or personal. This note is intended to guide the student by showing some of the basic approaches to the idea.

1 *Creation and the Fall*. Fundamental to all conceptions of Nature is traditional Christian doctrine (▷ Bible). This influences English writers even when they are using a more or less agnostic or atheistic approach. The doctrine is that Nature is God's creation, but by the fall of man, symbolized by the story of Adam's disobedience in the book of *Genesis*, earthly nature is self-willed and destructive though not to the extent that the Divine Will and Order is obliterated in it.

2 *All-embracing Nature*. Nature is sometimes seen as the whole of reality so far as earthly experience goes. This use of the word had a particular significance in the 18th century when scientific Reason had replaced the religious imagination as the familiar vehicle for the interpretation of reality. See 4 *Nature and Truth*.

3 *Nature and God*. In line with traditional Christian doctrine, Natural Law is linked to Human Law and Divine Law as a manifestation of the Divine Will, in such works as Hooker's *Laws of Ecclesiastical Polity* (1597). However, from the beginning of the 17th century, there was a new interest in the function of human reason as an instrument for the acquisition of knowledge independently of religious feeling. Men like Ralegh (*History of the World*, 1614) and Bacon (*The Advancement of Learning*, 1605) began to ask what, given that God was the Primary Cause of Nature, were the Secondary, or Immediate, Causes of natural phenomena. ▷ Newton's work on gravitation (*Principia Mathematica*, 1687) and Locke's *Essay Concerning Human Understanding* (1690) seemed to solve the problem, causing people

to see God as the Divine Artificer whose Reason could be discerned in the government of even the smallest phenomena, as well as in the great original act of Creation.

4 *Nature and Truth.* Nature is in the 18th century Truth scientifically considered. 'To follow Nature' (*eg* in works of imaginative literature) may mean: (i) to present things and people (*eg* an imagined character) as they really are; (ii) to reveal truths that lie beneath appearances; (iii) to follow rational principles. It was the attempt to 'follow Nature' in these ways that constituted the main discipline of novelists such as Daniel Defoe (1660–1731) and Samuel Richardson (1689–1761).

5 *Nature as Moral Paradox.* The Christian conception of Nature as both God-created and spoilt by the fall of man led at various times to the problem that Nature is both good and evil. According to the medieval conception, maintained until the middle of the 17th century, human society was itself the outcome of the Divine Natural Order, so that it was by Natural Law that children should honour their parents, subjects their sovereigns, etc. On the other hand, the natural passions of men and beasts, unrestrained by reason, were the source of rapacity and ruin. Thus ▷ Shakespeare's King Lear begins by relying on the former conception of Nature, but he is exposed to the reality of the latter.

19th-century natural science revived the feeling that Nature was essentially destructive, and hostile or at best indifferent to men; this is the 'Nature red in tooth and claw' image of ▷ Tennyson's ▷ *In Memoriam*, set against the idea of the love of God.

6 *Nature for Man's Use.* Implicit in Christian doctrine was the belief that Nature was created *for* man; that it was his birthright to exploit and use it. This begins with the conception of Nature as the Great Mother, originating in pre-Christian times but pervasive in medieval verse and later, *eg* in much Elizabethan ▷ pastoral poetry. It took a more active significance when the 17th- and 18th-century 'natural philosophers' sought methods by which man could increase his power over Nature; 18th-century poetry commonly shows Nature as beautiful when she is productive under the ingenuity of human exploitation.

7 *Nature and Art.* 'Art' in earlier contexts often includes technology, *eg* in Polixenes's remarks on cultivation to Perdita in *The Winter's Tale* IV. iii; here art is seen as itself a product of nature. But art was often set against nature in Shakespeare's time and afterwards.

8 *Nature opposed to Court and City.* 'Art', however, was not necessarily an improvement. The city and the court, in Shakespeare's time, were the centres of new financial forces generating intrigue and 'unnatural' (*ie* inhuman) behaviour. There was also a kind of pastoral made by idealizing the life of the great country houses. In the 18th century poets like James Thomson (1700–78) wrote about natural surroundings for their own sake, and sometimes included wild nature as their subject, but it was ▷ Wordsworth who gave to wild nature its importance as the principal subject of what later came to be known as 'nature' poetry.

9 *Nature in Communion with the Individual.* Wordsworth was to some extent anticipated in the 18th century by the poet ▷ William Cowper, and the philosopher ▷ Jean-Jacques Rousseau. It was Wordsworth above all, however, who gave to Nature its modern most familiar sense – as the non-urban, preferably wild environment of man, to which the depths of his own nature always respond. Here he finds a communion which refreshes the loneliness of his spirit in a relationship which underlies and gives meaning to his human relationships.

Nelson, Horatio, Viscount (1758–1805)
English admiral, and a national hero. His naval successes against ▷ Napoleon culminated in the Battle of Trafalgar (1805) at which he lost his life in gaining victory over the combined French and Spanish fleets, thus saving England from French invasion. As an officer he was strongly independent and unconventional; one of the famous anecdotes about him tells how he put his telescope to his blind eye at the battle of Copenhagen in 1801 in order not to see his superior officer's signal ordering him to withdraw. Equally famous are the signal to his ships before Trafalgar: 'England expects every man to do his duty', and his dying words: 'Now I am satisfied; thank God I have done my duty.' His love affair with the beautiful Lady Hamilton was a notorious romance. In 1813 the poet ▷ Robert Southey published his life, one of the best known of English biographies.
▷ Nationalism.

Neo-classicism
This term can be understood for the purposes of English literary culture in two senses: first, the broad sense, which refers to the ▷ Renaissance of ▷ Classical culture and its influence on English literature down to the end of the 18th century. This influence

operated mainly by the cultivation of ▷ Latin culture, and was mediated first by Italy and later by France. Secondly, the narrow sense of neo-classicism refers to a European artistic movement which originated in Germany and lasted approximately from 1750 until 1830.

In the first sense, neo-classical culture affected English literature in two phases. The first phase, which emerged in 16th century England, developed a fine school of classical scholars, including Thomas More and Sir Thomas Wyatt. The second phase, which began in 1660 and lasted throughout the 18th century, was much influenced by contemporary French literature, which was marked by distinguished achievement. English culture was entering a relatively aristocratic period in reaction to the Republican decade of the 1650s; it was also undergoing an increasingly strong revulsion against religious and political passions such as produced the Civil War. The result was admiration for philosophy, reason, scepticism, wit and refinement – all qualities conducive to neo-classic culture. Significantly this was also the first important period of English criticism. Yet thoroughly neo-classic critics like Thomas Rymer (1641–1713) were the exception. The restlessness of English society, the increasing importance of the middle class, the difficulty of making such a large exception to neo-classical principles as Shakespeare, and the hostility the English literary tradition has always shown to authoritarian doctrines, all help to explain the refusal of the leading critics, John Dryden (1631–1700) and Samuel Johnson (1709–80) to adopt neo-classic theory unquestioningly. Nonetheless, such a figure as the French neo-classicist ▷ Boileau was deeply respected, and the best poets and essayists (though hardly the novelists) all exhibited the neo-classic virtues of clarity, order, reason, wit and balance.

Neo-classicism in the narrow sense was the cultivation of Greek culture in opposition to Roman culture, and originated partly in the German movement to emancipate ▷ German culture from France. It can be said that whereas Renaissance classicism sought to emulate the culture of Rome, this 'New Humanism' sought inspiration in the originality of the Greeks. This difference enabled the new neo-Classicism to merge with ▷ Romanticism, whose progenitor was above all ▷ Rousseau. In England, it is thus impossible to distinguish neo-classic from Romantic writers in the period 1790–1830. It is clear, however, that ▷ William Blake shows neo-classic inspiration in his graphic

art, and that the poems by ▷ Keats on classical themes (▷ *Endymion* and the two ▷ *Hyperions*) are in a romantic-classical style, very different from ▷ Augustan classicism of the previous century. Neo-classicism is more distinguishable in the architectural style known as ▷ Regency, and in the sculpture of an artist such as Flaxman, than in imaginative literature.

▷ French literature in England; Italian influence in English literature.
Bib: Honour, H., *Neo-classicism*.

New criticism

This term is given to a movement which developed in the late 1940s in the U.S.A., and which dedicated itself to opposing the kind of criticism that is associated with ▷ Romanticism, and 19th-century realism. The 'practical criticism' of ▷ I. A. Richards was an influential stimulus to this movement in which emphasis was placed upon the self-contained nature of the literary text. In the work of 'new' critics such as Cleanth Brooks, W. K. Wimsatt, John Crowe Ransom, Allen Tate, and R. P. Blackmur, concern with the 'intention' of the writer was replaced by close reading of particular texts, and depended upon the assumption that any literary work was self-contained. New criticism placed a particular emphasis upon poetry, and asserted that the individual poem 'must not mean but be'.

Although the methods of new criticism now seem insufficiently historical, the tradition of close reading is perpetuated in ▷ Deconstruction (though hardly in a form which the 40s generation would have relished). Since its inception, English Literature as a university discipline has been marked by alternating fashions for either close reading or historicization.

New historicism

A theoretical movement which developed in America in the 1980s and which has had an enormous influence on English studies, especially in the field of ▷ Shakespeare criticism. It developed its identity partly against the ahistorical approaches of ▷ new criticism and the unselfconscious historicism of earlier critics. New historicism draws upon ▷ Marxist criticism in its emphasis upon political and social context and rejection of individual aspiration and universalism, but at the same time it insists that historical context can never be recovered objectively. New historicists do not assume that literature reflects reality and that these 'reflections' enable the reader to recover without distortion the past presented in the texts. Rather, they look for an interplay between text and society, which can never be presented neutrally. Moreover, readers must be aware of their *own* historical context: we read texts from the perspective of our own age and can never perfectly recreate history. For example, we should be aware that late 20th-century ▷ feminism may make us overly critical of ▷ Romantic women writers, such as ▷ Anne Grant who asserted that women were inferior to men, when in fact they were simply voicing conventional or dominant opinions of their own period.

▷ Cultural materialism; Materialism; Marxism.

Bib: Greenblatt, S., *Renaissance Self-fashioning*; Howard, J. E. and O'Connor, M. F., *Shakespeare Reproduced*; Tennenhouse, L., *Power on Display*; Veeser, H. A., *The New Historicism*.

Newspapers

Periodicals resembling newspapers began in a small way in the reign of James I; in the decades of the Civil War and the Interregnum they increased in number owing to the need of either side to engage in propaganda. From 1695 press censorship was abandoned; newspapers and weekly periodicals began to flourish.

The first attempt to reach a mass circulation was made through this kind of periodical by ▷ William Cobbett with his *Weekly Political Register* (started 1802), and in 1808 ▷ Leigh Hunt's weekly *Examiner*, directed to a more educated public though with less remarkable literary merit, began to rival Cobbett's paper as a medium of radical comment and criticism.

Of daily papers founded in the 18th century, the ▷ *Morning Post* (started 1772) survived until 1936, and ▷ *The Times* (started 1785) is today the daily with the greatest prestige, though it has a comparatively small circulation. Other important dailies with a shorter life were the ▷ *Morning Chronicle* (1769–1862), and the ▷ *Morning Herald* (1780–1869). Both reached peak circulations of about 6,000. To reach the very large circulations of today, newspapers had to await the abolition of the stamp duty – a tax on newspapers – in 1855. The Stamp Tax was started in 1712. It was a method of restricting circulations by raising the prices of newspapers. The government of the day resented criticism of its policies but did not dare revive the Licensing Act, the lapsing

of which in 1695 was really the start of the British freedom of the press. The abolition of the tax, together with the advent of cheap paper and a nationwide potential public thanks to universal literacy, led to a new kind of newspaper at the end of the 19th century. Alfred and Harold Harmsworth, later Lord Northcliffe and Lord Rothermere, founded the *Daily Mail* in 1896; by 1901 it was selling a million copies. Other popular newspapers followed it with steadily increasing circulations.

Newton, Sir Isaac (1642–1727)

Mathematician and natural philosopher. He entered Trinity College, Cambridge, in 1661, became a fellow of the college in 1667, and Professor of Mathematics in the university in 1669. He resigned the professorship in 1701; in 1703 he was made President of the Royal Society, and was re-elected annually until his death. Queen Anne knighted him in 1705.

His principal work was *Philosophiae Naturalis Principia Mathematica* (1687). By the application of mathematical calculation, it explained the force of mathematical calculation, and explained the force of gravity in its operation through the solar system. His book on *Optics* (1704) was less important, but it aroused new interest in vision and colour and influenced descriptive writing throughout the 18th century. His scientific and mathematical discoveries did not shake his religious convictions, which were very strong, and he also wrote on theology and biblical chronology. On the other hand, he did not understand and had no use for the imaginative faculty, and like Locke (whose *Essay concerning Human Understanding* was published in 1690) he dismissed poetry as an unimportant and irrelevant activity.

Despite this indifference to poetic literature, Newton's discoveries, combined as they were with his religious piety, had a great influence on 18th-century poets. He caused them to revere Reason in both Man and God, who, seen through Newton's writings, became the Divine Artist of the Universe. Pope's *Essay on Man* was a restatement of the traditional vision of the natural order newly shaped to accord with Newton's rational harmony, and it was Pope who composed for Newton the famous epitaph:

> *Nature and Nature's laws lay hid in night:*
> *God said, 'Let Newton be!' and all was Light.*

The most famous poet of the natural scene in

the 18th century, James Thomson (1700–48) wrote his *Seasons* in accordance with Newtonian principles. In the revised ▷ *Prelude* (1850) ▷ Wordsworth wrote of the statue in Trinity College:

> *Of Newton with his prism and silent face,*
> *The marble index of a mind for ever*
> *Voyaging through strange seas of Thought,*
> *alone.*

Wordsworth thus chooses to emphasize the mysteriousness of science, whereas Pope had emphasized its power to clarify mystery. In general, 19th-century poets, having discovered the force of the irrational in human experience, lost respect for Newton; for William Blake he stood for a deathly narrowing of experience:

> *May God us keep*
> *From Single vision Newton's sleep!*
> (Letter to Butts, 1802)

Bib: Nicholson, M. H., *Newton Demands the Muse.*

Nichols, John (1745–1826)
Historian. Nichols's antiquarian activities provided a useful source for literary activity; for example, his *The Progresses and Public Processions of Queen Elizabeth* (1788–1821) were used by ▷ Scott in his novel *Kenilworth*. He also provided a fascinating account of the literary activity of his day in *Literary Anecdotes of the Eighteenth Century* (1812–16) and *Illustrations of the Literary History of the Eighteenth century* (1817–58; completed by his son). During his lifetime, however, Nichols was considered somewhat old-fashioned and his editorship of ▷ *The Gentleman's Magazine* (1792–1826) led to it being dismissed by younger writers such as ▷ Hazlitt.
  ▷ Histories and Chronicles.

Nietzsche, Friedrich Wilhelm (1844–1900)
German philosopher. He challenged the concepts of 'the good, the true, and the beautiful' as, in their existing form of abstract values, a decadent system at the mercy of the common man's will to level distinctions of all kinds. He set his hope on the will to power of a new race of men who would assert their own spiritual identities. Among his more famous works are a book on the philosopher Schopenhauer and the composer Wagner, whom he regarded as his own teachers: *Unzeitgemässe Betrachtungen* ('Thoughts out

of Season'; 1876); *Die Fröhliche Wissenschaft* ('The Joyful Wisdom'; 1882); *Also sprach Zarathustra* ('Thus spake Zarathustra'; 1891).
  Nietzsche was one of the important progenitors of Existentialism, and he had a considerable influence on some of the major English writers in the first quarter of this century. For example, D. H. Lawrence (1885–1930) wrote in the spirit of Nietzsche in his affirmation of spontaneous living from deep sources of energy in the individual – human 'disquality' (see *Women in Love*, ch. 8) as opposed to democratic egalitarianism. The Irish poet W. B. Yeats (1865–1939) also affirmed a natural aristocracy of the human spirit, and saw in Nietzsche a continuation of the message of the poet ▷ William Blake, who preached the transcendence of the human 'identity' over the 'self', which is defined and limited by the material environment. After 1930, Nietzsche's influence declined because he was seen as a prophet of fascism. However, in recent criticism Nietzsche's work has been re-evaluated by ▷ post-structuralist theory, especially with regard to his discussion of metaphor and metonymy (▷ Figures of speech) and the privileging of a rhetorical reading of philosophical texts.
  ▷ German influence on English literature.

Nightingale, Ode to a
  ▷ Odes, Keats's.

Nightmare Abbey (1818)
A novel by ▷ Thomas Love Peacock. It is a satire on the current taste for ▷ Gothic mystery and romantic despair. Mr Glowry and his son Scythrop own the Abbey; Scythrop is in love with two girls, like Peacock's friend, the poet ▷ Shelley. Mr Flosky is a satirical portrait of ▷ Coleridge in his aspect as a transcendental mystic, and Mr Cypress represents ▷ Byron's self-centredness. There are other characters of cheerful temperament to counteract the romantic sombreness of these. The plot is slight, but the comic fantasy is sustained by it and by the conversations, which are always the greater part of a Peacock novel.

Nineteenth century in English literature
The period opened with a great revival of poetic expression. The first generation of the new poets – ▷ William Blake, ▷ William Wordsworth, ▷ Samuel Taylor Coleridge – all began under the inspiration of deep spiritual and social disturbances, the historical manifestation of which was the ▷ French Revolution. Against this Wordsworth and

Coleridge reacted in disillusionment when they saw it transformed by ▷ Napoleon Bonaparte. On the other hand, the second generation of poets – ▷ Lord Byron, ▷ P. B. Shelley, ▷ John Keats (he was the least touched by politics) felt the bitterness of anticlimax after the overthrow of Napoleon in 1815 and intensely resented the restoration of the old oppressive regimes. These six poets differed from one another greatly, although all except Blake felt the influence of Wordsworth, and they were not, except for Byron, amongst the most popular. Several of the more popular ones are now almost forgotten, *eg* ▷ Thomas Moore; ▷ Walter Scott is more remembered for his novels but his poetry is important in that he did most to express the new liberation of feeling through old ▷ ballad styles and in medieval settings. ▷ George Crabbe continued 18th-century poetic style with a 19th-century awareness of the common people and sensitiveness to the influence of environment.

But a sharp change occurred in the dominant form of literary expression after 1830. Despite the popularity of the poetry of ▷ Alfred Tennyson in the mid-century and (later) that of Robert Browning (1812–89), it was the novel, particularly adapted as it was to the rapid social transformations of the ▷ Industrial Revolution, which became the representative medium. 1830 marks the beginning of the career of Charles Dickens (1812–70) and his lifetime was almost to coincide with the first phase of the English novel; in addition to himself, the leading names are George Eliot (1819–80), ▷ Emily Brontë, ▷ Charlotte Brontë and William Makepeace Thackeray (1811–63). The last quarter of the century saw the second phase of the novel in Henry James (1843–1916) and Joseph Conrad (1857–1924), who wrote with much more awareness of foreign influences; with their more radical questioning of social and cultural assumptions they became also the first important figures of the 20th-century novel. Thomas Hardy (1840–1928) is almost as prominent a figure but as a regional novelist he stands apart from the other two, who were notably cosmopolitan: his insight is profound but, in his best work, it is expressed through a specific environment.

An important aspect of 19th-century literature is its autobiographical inclination. Some outstanding works during the century were autobiographies (*eg* ▷ Thomas De Quincey's ▷ *Confessions of an English Opium-Eater*) but the tendency was even more important as a diffused approach to

imaginative art, in poetry (*eg* Wordsworth's ▷ *Prelude*) and in the novel (*eg* Charlotte Brontë's *Villette*). This may account for the increase in women novelists of the period; ▷ feminist criticism often argues for the attraction of autobiography to women writers as an expression of freedom. It was, if anything, even more important in non-fictional prose, both that of the early 19th-century periodical essayists such as ▷ William Hazlitt and ▷ Charles Lamb, and that of the Victorian 'sages' – the polemicists of the middle and later century, who commonly expressed their deep concern with society (its changes, and its dangers and potentiality for the human consciousness) in autobiographical and semi-autobiographical form. Examples are Carlyle's (1795–1881) *Sartor Resartus*, and John Stuart Mill's (1806–73) *Autobiography*. The autobiographical habit of mind is bound up with great changes in prevailing attitudes to the nature of the human personality but the literary practice derives from a French 18th-century work, the *Confessions* of ▷ Rousseau.

19th-century literary criticism also shows urgent concern with the social and spiritual questions of the age. The most important critics are Wordsworth, Coleridge (whose chief critical work is characteristically in part autobiography – ▷ *Biographia Literaria*) and Matthew Arnold (1822–88). By the end of the century, Henry James had become the first important systematic critic of the novel.

It is common to think of the 19th century as the century of ▷ Romanticism in contrast to the 18th century as the 'Age of Reason'. This is too simple, however. Firstly, Romanticism had its beginnings in the 18th century; secondly, continuity with 18th-century rationalism was an important aspect of 19th-century thought and feeling, *eg* in ▷ Utilitarianism; and finally, Romanticism is a difficult term in relation to English literature and needs separate treatment.

▷ Autobiography; Victorian period.

Nineties Poets

The group of poets centred around the Rhymer's Club in the 1890s, including Lionel Johnson (1867–1902), Ernest Dowson (1867–1900) and Arthur Symons (1865–1945). The confessional and decadent quality of their work, together with the incidence of untimely death in their lives, led W.B. Yeats to label them 'The Tragic Generation' in his *Autobiographies*. Influenced by Baudelaire (▷ French literature in England), the Nineties Poets offer in a jaded and miniaturized form the interest in selfhood, experimentation and the

exotic which had been more abundantly and energetically present in Romantic poetry.
Bib: Stanford, D., *Poets of the Nineties*; Thornton, R. K. R., *Poetry of the 'Nineties*.

Noble Savage, The
▷ Primitivism.

Northanger Abbey (1818)
A novel by ▷ Jane Austen. It was started in 1798 and incompletely revised when it was published (in 1818 after her death) with her last completed novel ▷ *Persuasion*.

The book is in part a satire on the sensational and sentimental literature of the time, particularly of the enormously popular ▷ *Mysteries of Udolpho* by ▷ Mrs Radcliffe. The heroine is an ingenuous young girl, Catherine Morland, who visits the fashionable resort of Bath and afterwards, with some friends she has made there, the country house of Northanger Abbey. She is healthy-minded and trusting but very suggestible; on the one hand she is entirely deceived by the worldly flattery of her scheming friend, Isabella Thorpe, who tries to marry Catherine's brother under the mistaken impression that he is very rich, and on the other hand she suspects (under the influence of Mrs Radcliffe's novel) that Northanger Abbey conceals terrible secrets. Its owner, General Tilney, is the father of the man she loves and is in fact almost as cold-hearted and inhumane as she suspects him of being, but in quite a different way; he has not, as she at first suspected, murdered his wife, but he turns Catherine out of the house at very short notice from purely mercenary motives. The theme of the book is partly the danger of confusing literature and life, a theme to which Jane Austen returns in ▷ *Sense and Sensibility* and ▷ *Emma*; it is also that life is as surprising and remorseless as the most romantic literature but in quite a different way.

▷ Roche, Regina Maria.

Oates, Titus (1649–1705)

An English conspirator. He was the son of a Puritan preacher, and himself professed to stand for the defence of Protestantism against supposed Catholic dangers, but he was really a disreputable adventurer who used the religious passions of the time for his personal advantage. In 1678 he fabricated the Popish Plot, by which he pretended without factual basis to expose a Catholic conspiracy against the Church of England. Popular suspicion of Charles II, and the fact that the Queen and his brother James were avowed Roman Catholics, caused a national panic, and a large number of Catholics were put to death. His evidence was eventually proved false, and he was imprisoned. He figures in ▷ Scott's novel *Peveril of the Peak* (1822).

Ode

The Pindaric Ode is modelled on the works of ▷ Pindar, a Greek poet of the 5th century BC, best known for his odes celebrating the victors at the Olympic games. These were accompanied by music and dance, and were disposed in a threefold pattern corresponding to the movements of the Greek dramatic chorus (*strophe, antistrophe, epode*). From the 17th century onwards English poets took Pindar as a model for lyric and declamatory verse expressive of high-wrought emotion. ▷ Thomas Gray's *Progress of Poesy* follows Pindar's stanza forms with scholarly exactness. 'Pindarics' remained popular throughout the 18th century and became a natural vehicle for the new ▷ 'Romantic' sensibility. Gray's use of them in ▷ *The Bard* and *The Progress of Poesy*, for all its scholarly meticulousness, is intended to sound bold and inspirational. The form remains essentially the same in such romantic works as ▷ William Wordsworth's ode: ▷ Intimations of Immortality and ▷ Samuel Taylor Coleridge's ▷ *Dejection*, though by now it has lost its classical, 'Pindaric' associations, and is fully naturalized.

The Roman poet ▷ Horace imitated Pindar, but his odes employ unvarying stanza forms. The 'regular' Horatian ode was imitated by ▷ Horatio and ▷ James Smith in *Horace in London*. ▷ John Keats's Odes, with their long and complex, but regular stanzas, lie somewhere between the Pindaric and Horatian form.

Odes, Keats's

▷ John Keats's six Odes: *On Indolence, On a Grecian Urn, On Melancholy, To Psyche, To a Nightingale*, and *To Autumn*, were all written in 1819. They are in regular stanzaic form, but the length of stanza and complexity of rhyme-scheme recalls the freer ▷ Pindaric tradition of the ▷ ode. They constitute the most complex expression of Keats's aestheticist approach to life. In each poem a celebration of sensuous beauty of the material world is rendered the more intensely poignant by an acknowledgement of transience and decay.

On a Grecian Urn and *To a Nightingale* are companion pieces, one concerned with Art, the other with Nature. Both urn and bird persuade the poet for a while that their beauty is permanent. The urn's message to Man is 'Beauty is truth, truth beauty', and the Nightingale seems an 'immortal bird', 'not born for death'. However the urn's comfort remains on its beautiful surface. Though a 'friend to man' it is a 'Cold Pastoral'. The beautiful figures depicted upon it, preserved from time by art, can never reachieve the trembling elusive life which they possessed when really alive. Their death and distance is paradoxically only accentuated by Keats's ecstatic, even hectic, celebration of its artistic immortality. Similarly, the nightingale's song, though unchanged through history, fades as the particular bird to which he is listening flies away, and Keats is returned to his 'sole self', admitting that 'the fancy cannot cheat so well/ As she is fam'd to do, deceiving elf'.

The Ode to Autumn contains no explicit philosophizing, and seems purely descriptive. It provides, however, an emotional answer to the problems of the previous odes. The images of the poem are beautiful precisely because the scene described is a transient moment in the flux of time. The poignant pleasure they give derives from their lack of permanence or stability: 'And gathering swallows twitter in the skies'. Keats is here expressing in his own way the paradox of the great prophet of ▷ Romanticism, ▷ William Blake: 'He who binds to himself a joy/ Does the winged life destroy;/ But he who kisses the joy as it flies/ Lives in eternity's sun rise.'

O'Keeffe, Adelaide (1776–1865)

Novelist and children's author. Daughter and amanuensis of the Irish dramatist ▷ John O'Keeffe, Adelaide would have certainly written down his most famous play, *Wild Oats* (1791), since she began copying for him when he became blind in 1788. O'Keeffe's father was the centre of her affections, and she wrote in order to sustain her family when he had to retire, penning a touching memoir to him after his death (published with his poems as *O'Keeffe's Legacy to his Daughter*, 1834). She is best known for her *Original Poems for Infant*

Minds (1804–5), which although ▷ didactic, are also spiced with a certain sense of disrespectful fun. Her novels are far more adventurous works for an adult readership, and include *Dudley* (1819) and *The Broken Sword* (1854), which deal with the emotional problems besetting families and are both perceptive and gently humorous.

O'Keeffe, John (1747–1883)

Actor and dramatist, who wrote many popular comedies and comic operas in the late 18th century. O'Keeffe was drawn to the stage by reading the plays of George Farquhar (1678–1707) and he wrote his first play, *The Gallant*, at the age of 15, later obtaining a post as an actor. In 1773 he took up writing seriously, and his farce, *Tony Lumpkin in Town*, based on Oliver Goldsmith's (1730–74) *She Stoops to Conquer*, was staged in Dublin, and afterwards at the Haymarket Theatre in London. His *Wild Oats, or the Strolling Gentleman* (1791) was revived by the Royal Shakespeare Company in 1976, with great success, largely because of the magnificent acting vehicle provided in the character of Rover. This play would have been written down by his daughter, the novelist ▷ Adelaide O'Keeffe, since John had become blind in 1788. O'Keeffe's autobiography was published in 1826.

Olney Hymns (1779)

A collection of religious poems by the Revd John Newton and ▷ William Cowper, so called from the village of Olney where they lived.

Opera in England

Opera, in the sense of a staged drama in which the words and music are of equal importance, began in Italy at the end of the 16th century. It was an integral part of the ▷ Renaissance, arising out of the attempt to revive what were thought to be the performance practices of ▷ Greek drama. Subjects, therefore, were tragedies drawn from classical mythology and the words were set to a declamatory style of singing known as recitative.

In the 18th century Italian opera was imported, as well as the German composer, Handel, who wrote operas in the Italian style, but the fashion for such entertainment proved to be short-lived. The romantic operas that held the stage in the first half of the 19th century are, apart from Balfe's *The Bohemian Girl*, little known nowadays.

Opie, Amelia (1769–1853)

Novelist and poet. Opie began to participate in London society in 1794 and she soon became acquainted with and admired by the more radical members of the literary groups, in particular, ▷ Elizabeth Inchbald, ▷ William Godwin and ▷ Mary Wollstonecraft (whom Opie depicts in her novel, *Adeline Mowbray, or The Mother and Daughter*, 1804). Her other novels include, *The Father and Daughter* (1801), *Valentine's Eve* (1816) and *Madeline* (1822); they are all sentimental novels set in unremarkable domestic circumstances and fully corroborate her own stated pupose in writing novels: 'I like to make people cry, indeed, if I do not do it, all my readers are disappointed'. Her ceaseless literary outpouring is of questionable quality, and this led to her being ▷ satirized as Miss Poppyseed by ▷ Peacock in his novel *Headlong Hall*. She married the painter John Opie in 1798 (her maiden name was Alderson), but at his death in 1807 moved to Norwich where, in 1825, she became a Quaker, devoting herself to spiritual writing, e.g. *Lays for the Dead* (1833).
Bib: James, A.H., *Best Sellers of Jane Austen's Age*; Menzies, J., Wilson and Lloyd, H., *Amelia: The Tale of a Plain Friend*.

Orientalism

Narratives of the East, in verse and prose, were immensely popular in the 18th and 19th centuries, ranging in style and theme from the dry analytical wit of Samuel Johnson's *Rasselas* (1759) to the galloping romance of ▷ Byron's 'Turkish Tales', ▷ *The Giaour* (1813) or ▷ *The Corsair* (1814). With their interest in lust, slavery, abduction and the exotic, the latter had a huge popular appeal related in part to the image of Lord Byron himself, variously portrayed in oils as rapaciously and broodingly ▷ Gothic, or got up to fight in Albanian costume. That such hectic and flashy adventure-poetry says more about the ▷ Romantic libido than about any real Oriental place seems to be confirmed by Captain Benwick in ▷ Jane Austen's novel ▷ *Persuasion* (1818), whose interest in the star-crossed and storm-tossed leads Anne Elliot to remark, 'that she thought it was the misfortune of poetry, to be seldom safely enjoyed by those who enjoyed it completely'.

Less self-mythologizing than Byron, ▷ Southey in *The Curse of Kehama* (1810), and ▷ Moore in *Lalla Rookh* (1817) make forays into similar territory, while in a more complex and indirect way ▷ Coleridge's ▷ *Kubla Khan* (1797) shows that the poetic associations of Oriental imagery might be paradisal and delicate, and not wholly to do with despotism and wildness. Many of the hallucinations and dream-visions recorded in ▷ Thomas De Quincey's ▷ *Confessions of an English Opium-Eater* (1822) involve the Oriental, and the author's drug-induced conflation of different periods and cultures may typify a general British reaction to the non-occidental world as there to be pillaged for its images, whether by artists, explorers, or more obvious agents of imperialism. The drug makes De Quincey temporary victim, rather than oppressor: 'I fled from the wrath of Brama through all the forests of Asia: Vishnu hated me: Seeva laid wait for me. I came suddenly upon Isis and Osiris: I had done a deed, they said, which the ibis and the crocodile trembled at.'

Despised for its illiberal forms of government, explored and exploited, the Orient fell victim to a garish literary tradition, stretching from ▷ Beckford's *Vathek* (1786) to Sax Rohmer's devilish criminal genius, Dr Fu Manchu. Yet to Western eyes it remained the geographical and racial expression of what is Other; desirable, Edenic, malleable by the individual imagination.
Bib: Barrell, J., *The Infection of Thomas de Quincey: the Psycopathology of Imperialism*; Said, E., *Orientalism*.

Ossian

James Macpherson (1736–96) was the author of a series of blank verse epics which he attributed to Ossian, son of Finn, and which he claimed to have translated from the Gaelic. There was considerable interest in ▷ Primitivism in the 1760s, and works such as *Fingal, an Ancient Epic Poem in Six Books* (1762) and *Temora* (1763) caused a great sensation, particularly among patriotic Scots. Ossian's fame also spread to the European continent, where the poetry was read with enthusiasm by ▷ Napoleon Bonaparte, and quoted by ▷ Goethe in *The Sorrows of Young Werther*. Samuel Johnson (1709–84) was among the earliest sceptics; when asked whether he thought any man 'of the modern age' could have written the poems, he replied: 'Yes, Sir, many men, many women, and many children.' Following Macpherson's death, an investigating committee concluded that the poetry was a collage of edited and newly-written material. Despite this exposure, Matthew Arnold (1822–88) defended the poetry as late as 1866 for its 'vein of piercing regret and sadness'. In the ancient legends Oisin (Ossian) bridged the gap between the heroic pagan age and Irish Christianity; his

longevity was due to an extended residence in Fairyland.
▷ Macpherson, James.

Ottava rima

An Italian stanza of 8 lines rhyming *a b a b a b c c*. It was used by ▷ Boccaccio in the 14th century. Pulci in the 15th century used it for the mock-heroic, ironic style with which the stanza is chiefly associated in English through ▷ Byron's ▷ *Don Juan* and his *Vision of Judgement*. In *Don Juan*, the form is frequently exploited for the possibilities it allows for playing off long syntactical units against the bathos (▷ Figures of speech) of the closing couplet:

> *What is the end of fame? 'tis but to fill*
>   *A certain portion of uncertain paper:*
> *Some liken it to climbing up a hill,*
>   *Whose summit, like all hills, is lost*
> *in vapour;*
> *For this men write, speak, preach, and*
> *heroes kill,*
>   *And bards burn what they call their*
> *'midnight taper',*
> *To have, when the original is dust,*
> *A name, a wretched picture, and worse bust.*
>   (Canto I, CCXVIII)

Owen, Robert (1771–1858)

Social reformer, and a leading socialist thinker in the early 19th century. He became part-owner of the New Lanark Cotton Mills in 1800, and found that its workers were living in the degraded and nearly desperate conditions common in the earlier phase of the ▷ Industrial Revolution. He set about improving their housing and working conditions, and established infant schools. His reforms were a success, but his expenditure on them caused resentment among his partners, and in 1813 he established a new firm, with ▷ Jeremy Bentham as one of his associates. In the same year he published a volume of essays, *A New View of Society*, in which he sought to prove that the human character is entirely created by its environment. In 1817, in a report to the House of Commons, Owen pointed out that the existing social misery was caused by men competing unsuccessfully with machines, and he recommended the establishment of socialist working communities in the country; they were to vary from 500 to 3,000 in size, and were to be partly industrial. His views were received favourably by, among other people, the Duke of Kent, the father of Queen Victoria, but Owen spoilt his case with public opinion in general by mixing his proposals with anti-religious propaganda. Nonetheless two experiments were attempted in 1825, one in England and one in America; both failed in under two years. Owen now became the leader of a socialist-secular movement, through which he sought to replace the emphasis on political reform by emphasis on economic action. His influence led to the Grand National Consolidated Trades Union in 1833 but this also failed owing to bad organization. The word 'socialism' originated through discussions centred on the Association of all Classes of all Nations, which Owen founded in 1835. The only permanent success among Owen's experiments was his establishment of the Cooperative Movement, which nowadays is affiliated to the Labour Party.

Oxford University

The oldest of the English Universities. It was started by students from the still older University of Paris in the 12th century, and the colleges which give it (and Cambridge) its distinctive character began to be founded in the 13th century, as a means of housing students and keeping order among them. The colleges are not controlled by the University, but are self-governing institutions, though their members usually (always in the case of senior members) hold university appointments as well. Oxford provided the students who early in the 13th century started ▷ Cambridge University, but Oxford remained of superior importance until the 15th century, by which time it was infected by Wycliffite heresies, and the major patrons (especially the Crown) began to distribute to Cambridge at least an equal share of the wealth in endowments.

Oxford produced some of the intellectual leaders of medieval Europe: in the 13th century Roger Bacon and Duns Scotus, in the 14th century Wycliffe. The New Learning of the Renaissance began in the 16th century, under the leadership of Erasmus, Thomas More, Grocyn and Colet, to oust medieval scholasticism. Since then Oxford has retained its status as one of the main channels through which persons who attain positions of power in public life receive their education.

Ozymandias (1818)

A witty sonnet by ▷ Percy Bysshe Shelley concerning the vanity of human ambition. An ancient statue stands broken and isolated in the desert, its boastful inscription now carrying an ironically different meaning from that first intended: 'My name is Ozymandias, king of kings:/ Look on my works, ye Mighty, and despair!' The ancient Greek historian Diodorus Siculus (1st century BC) calls the tomb of the great Egyptian Pharoah Rameses II the tomb of Ozymandias.

Paine, Thomas (1737–1809)
Political author. The son a small farmer, his
early career in England as an official ended
in failure, and he sailed for America in 1774.
In 1776 he published the republican pamphlet
Common Sense, which set the colonists openly
on the road to independence. After the
start of the American War of Independence,
he maintained the morale of the rebels
with a series of pamphlets called *The Crisis*
(1776–83). The opening sentence was 'These
are the times that try men's souls' – words
which became a battle-cry.

In 1787 he returned to Europe to carry
on his fight for republican democracy. When
▷ Burke published his ▷ *Reflections on the
Revolution in France* in 1790, Paine replied
with Part I of his ▷ *Rights of Man* (1791). The
Government was making the preparations
for his trial for reason in 1792 when the poet
▷ William Blake got him out of the country
to France, where the French revolutionary
government had elected him a member of
the republican Convention. In France he
published his *Age of Reason* (1793) which
defended a rational, abstract form of ▷ deism
against orthodox Christianity. This caused
him to lose his popularity in England and in
America. He also lost favour with the French
for his injudicious criticisms, and for a time
he was imprisoned, though he was later
restored to his seat in the Convention. In
1802 he returned to America to find that he
had lost his influence there and he died at
his farm in New Rochelle in 1809. Ten years
later the English radical ▷ William Cobbett
returned to England with Tom Paine's bones.
For some time his works remained a text-book
for English radicalism.
Bib: Wilson D.A., *Paine and Cobbett: The
Transatlantic Connection*; Philip, M., *Paine*.

Pantheism
A term used to cover a variety of religious
and philosophical beliefs, which have in
common that God is present in Nature,
and not separable from it in the sense in
which a cause is separable from its effect,
or a creator from his creation. Pantheism is
implicit in doctrines derived from ▷ Plato,
eg in some of the neo-Platonists of the 16th
century, and in some poetry inspired by the
natural environment. Amongst English poets,
the most famous example is ▷ Wordsworth
in his earlier phase (1797–1807), notably in
the first two books of his 1805 version of
▷ *The Prelude*. In his revised version of this
autobiographical poem, Wordsworth tried to
eliminate the pantheistic tendencies, since
they are not in accordance with most forms of
Christian doctrine.

Pantisocracy
The name given by ▷ Samuel Taylor
Coleridge and ▷ Robert Southey to the ideal
anarchistic society which preoccupied them in
1794–5 during the first phase of the ▷ French
Revolution (from the Greek: *pan* = 'all', *isos*
= 'the same', *cratos* = 'power'). They hoped
to establish a community on the banks of the
River Susquehanna in the United States in
which motives of gain would be replaced by
brotherly love. They were unable to raise
money, however, their ideas changed, and
they abandoned their plan.

***Paradise Lost* (1667)**
An epic poem by ▷ John Milton, first published
in ten books in 1667, but reorganized and
published in 12 books in a second edition of
1674. The composition of *Paradise Lost* was
possibly begun in the mid-1650s, but the idea
for an epic based on scriptural sources had,
in all probability, occurred to Milton at least
as early as 1640, when the four drafts of an
outline tragedy were composed. These drafts,
contained in a Trinity College, Cambridge,
manuscript, indicate that, in original
conception, *Paradise Lost* (or, to give the poem
its draft title – *Adam Unparadized*) was to have
been a sacred drama, rather than an epic.
This hint at a dramatic origin, on the lines of
classical Greek tragedy, helps to explain the
undoubtedly dramatic qualities to be found
in the poem – for example the soliloquizing
habits of Satan, and the *peripeteias*, or
discoveries, where new ironies in the narrative
are allowed to unfold.

The chief source of the poem is the
▷ Bible, but the Bible as glossed and
commented upon by the Patristic (early
Christian) authorities, and by Protestant
theologians. But also important to Milton's
project were the classical writers – ▷ Homer
and Virgil – from whom Milton's conception
of 'epic' was principally inherited.

However, the possible progenitors of
Milton's poem remain numberless, since
Paradise Lost draws upon the whole field of
intellectual endeavour open to a classically
trained European scholar in the 17th
century.

For all that it is a poem rooted in Milton's
literary experience, it is also a poem of, and
for, its times. The poem's chief theme is
rebellion – the rebellion of Satan and his
followers against God, and the rebellion of
Adam and Eve against divine law. Within

this sacred context, Milton sets himself the task of justifying God's creational will to his 17th-century readers. But, in confronting questions such as choice, obedience and forms of government, Milton also raises the issues of freedom, social relationships and the quality and definition of power – whether almighty, satanic or human. We can thus understand the poem as confronting political questions which, in the moment of its composition and eventual publication following the English Civil War and the Restoration of the monarchy, were of real urgency both to the republican Milton and his readers. That is not to say that, as some of Milton's commentators have claimed, the poem operates as a veiled ▷ allegory of events in mid-17th-century England. But the issues which the protagonists in *Paradise Lost* face are also issues which were at the heart of contemporary political debate. To entwine matters of theology and political theory was by no means a strange grafting to Milton's contemporaries. Religion and politics were inseparably twinned, and *Paradise Lost* confronts that conjunction at every point.

The history of the poem's critical reception since the date of its publication is itself a commentary on the history of English literary 'taste'. For all that 18th-century writers admired Milton's grand scheme, their admiration was tinged by a certain uneasiness. Both Joseph Addison (1672–1719) and Samuel Johnson (1709–84) felt that Milton's achievement was undoubtedly immense, but that it was also an achievement which could not and should not be replicated. For the poets of the ▷ Romantic period – ▷ William Blake, ▷ Percy Bysshe Shelley, ▷ John Keats, and the ▷ William Wordsworth of ▷ *The Prelude* – *Paradise Lost* was read as a significant text in the history of the individual's struggle to identify him or herself within the political and social sphere. But rather than understand the poem as a theological epic, they tended to read it as a text of human liberty, with Satan, rather than God, as the focus of the poem's meaning. In the 20th century, following the re-evaluation in poetic taste prompted by T.S. Eliot (1888–1965) and ▷ F.R. Leavis, *Paradise Lost* was seen, once more, as a masterpiece of questionable stature. Was it, perhaps, removed from what Eliot and Leavis in particular cared to identify as the 'English tradition'? The debate initiated by Leavis and his followers was to be answered in a series of important accounts of the poem by the critics C.S. Lewis, William Empson

and Christopher Ricks. From the 1970s attention has been refocused, by ▷ Marxist and ▷ feminist critics especially, on what have long been unexamined aspects of the poem: its treatment of patriarchal authority and its relationship to the continuing historical debate on the intellectual culture of the revolutionary period. At the same time, Milton's themes of language and identity have rendered the poem a fruitful text for ▷ psychoanalytic criticism. We might conclude, then, that, if perhaps the greatest achievement of the English literary ▷ Renaissance, *Paradise Lost* is also a text open to continuous re-reading and revision.
Bib: Carey, J. and Fowler, A. (eds.) *The Complete Poems of John Milton*.

Paradise Regained (1671)

An epic poem by ▷ John Milton in four books, it was first published (together with *Samson Agonistes*) in 1671. Begun after the publication of ▷ *Paradise Lost* in 1667, the poem can, in some sense, be thought of as a sequel to *Paradise Lost*. In particular, the poem's treatment of Christ, his resistance to temptation, and the redeeming nature of his ministry on earth, cast him in the theologically traditional role of the 'Second Adam' – a regenerative and redeeming force in the world.

Where *Paradise Lost*, however, was conceived of along lines inherited from classical epic, *Paradise Regained* is in the form of the 'brief epic' in the style of the book of *Job*. The chief subject matter of the poem is the temptation of Christ in the wilderness, described in the gospel of *St Luke*.

Parody

Parody consists of mocking a style of literary production through an exaggerated imitation. It is close to ▷ satire in its criticism of eccentricities, but it must always refer to literature or a way of writing, rather than satire's more open scope. For example, ▷ James and ▷ Horatio Smith's ▷ *Rejected Addresses* (1812) contains witty parodies of ▷ Wordsworth, ▷ Coleridge, ▷ Southey, ▷ Byron, ▷ Crabbe and ▷ Scott.

Parole

In the work of ▷ Ferdinand de Saussure, the founder of ▷ Structuralism, this is usually translated as 'speech' or 'speech act'. It refers to a particular instance of speech. '*Parole*' is to be distinguished from ▷ '*langue*' (language) which is the linguistic system which underpins every utterance (*parole*). Speakers of a language (*langue*) avail themselves of parts of that system and reactivate it each time they engage in speech (*parole*).

▷ Sign.

Parties, Political

The English political scene has been dominated by political parties since the mid-17th century. It was not till the 19th century that political parties became highly organized, and though there have seldom been more than two important ones, these have not always been the same. The principal phase of party development during the 18th and early 19th centuries may be summarized as follows: Tories virtually disappeared from the political scene until the accession of George III in 1760. During this period Parliament dominated the monarchy, but the Whigs divided up into a number of family alliances and political coteries. After 1760, George III tried to revive royal power by creating a party in Parliament to support it; these were called the King's Friends or New Tories. The victory of the colonists in the American War of Independence (1776–83) and the king's insanity destroyed his ambitions for reviving royal power, but other issues confirmed the Tories in power from 1783 to 1830. Chief among these new issues dividing the nation were: (i) the ▷ French Revolution, which influenced the Whigs in the direction of political reform and the Tories in the direction of resistance to change; (ii) the English ▷ Industrial Revolution which was rapidly expanding an urban middle class which lacked political rights owing to the anachronistic parliamentary electoral system; and (iii) new social problems arising from the growth of a large urban proletariat. ▷ The Reform Bill of 1832 was another Whig victory, greatly increasing the power of the urban middle class.

Pastoral

A form of literature originally developed by the ancient Greeks and Romans in the idylls of the former and the eclogues of the latter. Ancient pastoral idealized the Greek state of Arcadia which had a rustic population of shepherds and herdsmen. The ▷ Renaissance of the 16th century, deeply interested in the literature of the Greeks and Romans, revived the pastoral mode; the earliest forms of it date back in Italian literature to the 15th century, but it was the romance *Arcadia* (1504), by the Italian poet Sannazaro, which was particularly

influential throughout Europe. The appeal of the pastoral kind of literature was partly to human wishfulness – the desire to conceive of circumstances in which the complexity of human problems could be reduced to its simplest elements: the shepherds and shepherdesses of pastoral are imagined as having no worries, and they live in an ideal climate with no serious physical calamities; love and death, and making songs and music about these experiences, are their only preoccupations. Another function of pastoral, however, was as a vehicle of moral and social criticism; the shepherds and shepherdesses sought the pleasures of nature and despised or were innocent of the corrupting luxury of courts and cities. Finally, pastoral presented a means of offering, allegorically, thinly disguised tributes of praise and flattery to real people whom the poet admired or wanted to please. The satirical, moral and eulogistic functions of Renaissance pastoral all tended to make it allegorical, since it was through ▷ allegory that the poet could most safely make his criticisms felt, and could most eloquently convey his praise. Allegory also suited the neo-Platonic (▷ Plato), idealizing cast of mind so characteristic of 16th-century writers. When we remember that the tradition of romantic love was one of the most ardently pursued inheritances from the ▷ Middle Ages, and that the circumstances of pastoral lent themselves to its expression, it is not surprising that the pastoral mode was so extensively cultivated in 16th-century Europe. To England it came late, by way of influences from France, Spain and Italy, but it lasted longer; it was especially pervasive in the last quarter of the 16th century, and continued till the mid-17th; there was a minor revival early in the 18th century.

Classical pastoral has not been practised notably since the first half of the 18th century. However the 20th-century critic William Empson (*Some Versions of Pastoral*, 1935) sometimes uses the term more widely than classical pastoral denotes. Even so, pastoral – even of the non-classical kind – is not synonymous with 'nature poetry' or poetry of country life: ▷ Wordsworth, ▷ Clare, Thomas Hardy (1840–1928), and Seamus Heaney (b 1939) are not writers of pastoral in any usually accepted sense.

Peacock, Thomas Love (1785–1866)

Novelist and poet. After unsuccessful attempts in poetry and the theatre, he found his special form in the 'discussion novel': *Headlong Hall* (1816); ▷ *Melincourt* (1817); ▷ *Nightmare*

Abbey (1818); ▷ *Maid Marian* (1822); *The Misfortunes of Elphin* (1829); ▷ *Crotchet Castle* (1831); *Gryll Grange* (1861). These consist almost entirely of conversation and have very little plot; the characters represent outlooks, ideas, and attitudes such as arouse Peacock's derision, and the prevailing tone is comic and satirical. The conversations are interspersed with songs, often of great charm, and hilarious and extravagent episodes. His sceptical essay *The Four Ages of Poetry* (1820) provoked ▷ Shelley's famous ▷ *Defence of Poetry* (1821). **Bib:** Van Doren, C., *Life*; Priestley, J. B., *Life*; Able, A. H., *Meredith and Peacock – A Study in Literary Influence*; House, H., in *All in Due Time*; Brett-Smith, H. F. B. (ed.), *Life and Works*, Vol I; Mayoux, J. J., *Un Epicurien Anglais: Peacock*; Jack, I., Chap VII in *Oxford History of English Literature*.

Percy, Thomas (1729–1811)

Clergyman and antiquarian; he became Bishop of Dromore in 1782. Along with ▷ James Macpherson, ▷ Horace Walpole and ▷ Thomas Gray, Percy was a pioneer of the literary exoticism which flourished in the later 18th century. In 1761 he published *Hau Kiou Choaan*, a translation of a Portuguese version of a Chinese romance, and in 1763 *Five Pieces of Runic Poetry*, translated from Latin versions of Old Icelandic texts. His most influential work, ▷ *Reliques of Ancient English Poetry* (1765), includes poems from a 17th-century manuscript now in the British Museum and known as 'The Percy Folio'. This manuscript contains many ballads of ancient origin which Percy edited according to 18th-century taste, adding also some modern compositions in the archaic style. Although his editorial approach was not that of a modern purist, the volume marks a significant phase in the revival of interest in early poetry, and exerted a strong influence on later poets such as ▷ Thomas Chatterton, ▷ Sir Walter Scott, ▷ William Wordsworth and ▷ Samuel Taylor Coleridge.

▷ Orientalism.
Bib: Davis, B. H., *Thomas Percy*.

Perfectibilism

The optimistic doctrine that individuals and society are capable of achieving perfection in living. The ▷ French Revolution, with its reliance on reason for the solution of all human problems, encouraged perfectibilism, and the philosopher ▷ William Godwin was an English example. ▷ Peacock, in *Headlong Hall* (1816), presents a humorous version of a perfectibilist in Mr Foster.

Persuasion (1818)

The last completed novel by ▷ Jane Austen; it was published, incompletely revised, in 1818, the year following her death. The theme is the coming together of the heroine, Anne Elliott, and the hero, Captain Wentworth, in spite of social obstacles, the selfishness and foolishness of her father (Sir Walter) and sisters, and the rival attraction of the more obviously seductive Musgrove sisters. Anne, before the novel begins, had already refused Wentworth on the counsel of Lady Russell, who stands in place of mother to her; Lady Russell had misunderstood Wentworth's character and feared his poverty. Anne's personality is diffident and humble but at the opening of the story she has begun to realize that the refusal was a mistake, likely to ruin her happiness. The renewal of Wentworth's love and his eventual marriage to Anne is a victory: their strong and distinctive but quiet and reticent qualities overcome the cruder and shallower social characteristics of their circumstances.

Peter Bell: A Tale (1819)
Peter Bell the Third (1939)

The first is a 'lyrical ballad' by ▷ William Wordsworth, written in 1798 but not published until 1819. Peter, a hard-hearted hawker of earthenware, finds an ass gazing down at its drowned master in the River Swale. He seeks out the man's widow, and on his journey is reformed by the spiritual influence of nature. The poem possesses that deliberate flatness which characterizes some of Wordsworth's most original early works. ▷ Percy Bysshe Shelley, in his *Peter Bell the Third* (1819; published 1839), having read a review of the poem, used its title (somewhat inappropriately) in a ▷ satire on the older poet's descent into respectability and conservatism. As Shelley says in his Dedication: 'He was at first sublime, pathetic, impressive, profound; then dull; then prosy and dull; and now dull – oh so very dull! it is an ultra-legitimate dulness.'

Peter Grimes

A tale in heroic couplets (▷ metre) by ▷ George Crabbe, Letter XXII in the series composing *The Borough* (1810). Peter is the son of a poor fisherman who tries to bring him up kindly and religiously. However, the boy is violent and wilful, and causes the death of his father by ill-treatment. He then lives a solitary life, distrusted and feared by the neighbourhood, with only a boy from an orphanage for company. He treats the boy brutally and finally causes his death, after which he misuses two other boys in the same way. The magistrates forbid him to employ any more pauper boys as apprentices, and his life becomes increasingly solitary, until he is found drifting distractedly along the desolate coast in his boat. As he dies he tells how he has been haunted by the ghosts of his dead father and the three boys, who never leave him, and ceaselessly condemn him to an eternity of lonely drifting. The poem is remarkable for its social realism and psychological power. It was made into an opera by Benjamin Britten (1945).

Peterloo Massacre, The

At a political meeting advocating the reform of parliamentary elections at St Peter's Field, Manchester, in 1819, the magistrates took alarm and ordered soldiers to attack the crowd. A small number of people were killed, and a large number were injured. The event caused intense resentment against the government of the time, and was nicknamed 'Peterloo' in ironic reference to the Anglo-Prussian victory over Napoleon at ▷ Waterloo in 1815. It provoked ▷ Shelley's fierce poem ▷ *The Mask of Anarchy*. It was also one of the causes of the establishment of the Metropolitan Police Force by Robert Peel in 1829, so that there should be a possibility of keeping order among crowds without the use of soldiers and firearms.
  ▷ Reform Bills, Parliamentary.

Picaresque

From the Spanish *picaro*, 'rogue'. The term is especially applied to a form of prose fiction originating in Spain in the 16th century, dealing with the adventures of rogues.
  ▷ Jameson, Anna Brownell.

Picturesque, The Cult of the

A term used in the late 18th and early 19th centuries to describe a certain kind of scenery, where cultivation was employed to produce artificially 'wild' nature. Landscape gardeners incorporated 'wildernesses' into their prospects, often with fake ruins suggesting the decay of classical civilization. The writer most identified with the 'picturesque' was ▷ William Gilpin, who wrote a series of illustrated picturesque tours. ▷ Jane Austen in ▷ *Mansfield Park* parodies the cult, and ▷ Thomas Love Peacock's *Headlong Hall* satirizes a contemporary dispute about its qualities.

Pindar (5th century BC)

Greek poet. He is famous for his lyrical ▷ odes, *ie* poems to be sung to the accompaniment of musical instruments and dancing. The odes had a strong religious tone and were designed for solemn occasions, including sporting celebrations. The fact that their composition was influenced by their musical and dance accompaniment gives the odes an appearance of irregularity. This, and the loftiness of their emotion, made them tempting models, from the 17th to 19th centuries, for English poets when they were writing on themes of deep emotional power and felt the need of an ample form which would allow them considerable licence in the treatment of the subject. Pindar's odes were not really as unsystematic as they seemed, however, and many English poems in 'Pindarics' have only a superficial resemblance to the kind of ode that Pindar wrote.

Pindaric Ode
  ▷ Ode.

Pitt (the Younger), William (1759–1806)

Politician. The son of William Pitt, Earl of Chatham. He led the government from 1783 to 1801, and again in the years 1804–6. He first became Prime Minister when he was only 24, at a time when George III's government had been deeply discredited by defeat in the American War of Independence, brought to an end by the Treaty of Versailles, 1783. Moreover, politics were thoroughly corrupted by various systems of bribery, and Parliament represented only the interests of various sections of the privileged classes. Pitt was as prudent a statesman as his father had been a dynamic one, and he was famous for his strict integrity. His first ministry was one of cautious reconstruction such as Britain needed for the long wars with France (War of the ▷ French Revolution, 1793–1801, and the Napoleonic War, 1803–15). Politically conservative, he was the first political leader to rely on public opinion as expressed in the electoral constituencies instead of on more or less bribed backing among Members of Parliament.

Plato (?428–?348 BC)

Greek philosopher. He was a follower of the Athenian philosopher Socrates, and his dialogues represent conversations in which Socrates takes the lead. The most famous of these 'Socratic' dialogues are *Protagoras, Gorgias, Phaedo, Symposium, Republic, Phaedrus,*

Timaeus. His longest work, the *Laws*, does not include Socrates as a character. His central conception is that beyond the world of transient material phenomena lies another eternal world of ideal forms which the material world represents in the form of imitations. His figure for this in the *Republic* is that men in the material world are like people watching shadows moving on the wall of a cave; they see only these shadows and not the realities which cast the shadows. Plato is one of the two most influential philosophers in European thought, the other being ▷ Aristotle, who was at first his pupil.

Platonic Love

A term which has come to possess three distinct, if related, senses: 1 A love between individuals which transcends sexual desire and attains spiritual heights. This is the most popularly understood sense of the term. 2 The complex doctrine of love which embraces sexuality, but which is directed towards an ideal end, to be found discussed in ▷ Plato's *Symposium*. 3 A reference to homosexual love which is derived from the praise of homosexual love to be found in the *Symposium*.

Plumptre, Anne (1760–1818) and Annabella (1761–1838)

Translators and novelists. The two Plumptre sisters were well educated and were prolific authors, usually in tandem, for most of their lives. They probably began by sending poems to periodicals, but the first certain works by them are two ▷ Minerva novels. Anne wrote *Antoinette* (1796), the story of a beautiful and intelligent woman philosopher, while Annabella (commonly known as Bell) published *Montgomery, or Scenes in Wales* (1796). Shortly afterwards they began translating from German, Anne undertaking seven plays by Kotzebue and Bell, Iffland's play, *The Foresters* (1799) and Kotzebue's *The Guardian Angel* (1802). They then returned to novels, producing Bell's *The Western Mail* (1801) and Anne's *Something New* (1801). It was only in 1802, when Anne travelled to France to see the effects of the ▷ French Revolution with ▷ Amelia Opie that the two sisters parted ways, Anne to commence writing ▷ travel and ▷ autobiographical works (*Narrative*, 1810, and *History of Myself and My Friends*, 1813), and Bell to concentrate on children's stories and domestic material (*Stories for Children*, 1804, and *Domestic Management, or the Healthful Cookery Book*, 1804). They collaborated once again just before Anne's death in 1818 writing the strange and fascinating collection, *Tales of Wonder, of Humour, and of Sentiment*.

Poet Laureate

The laurel, also known as the bay (*Laurus nobilis*), was sacred to Apollo, the god most associated with the arts. The Greeks honoured Olympic victors and triumphant generals, by crowning them with a wreath of laurel leaves. In the 15th century the universities of Oxford and Cambridge gave the title 'laureate', meaning worthy of laurels, to various poets and it was later given to court poets like Ben Jonson (1582–1637). In 1668 the title gained its modern status when John Dryden (1631–1700) was granted a stipend as a member of the royal household charged with writing court odes and celebrating state occasions in verse. Since the time of Dryden the laureateship has been awarded to a few poets of lasting worth and to many of mediocre talent, chosen for reasons of fashion or political acceptability. The list is as follows: Thomas Shadwell, Nahum Tate, Nicholas Rowe, Laurence Eusden, Colley Cibber, William Whitehead, ▷ Thomas Warton, Henry James Pye, ▷ Robert Southey, ▷ William Wordsworth, ▷ Alfred Tennyson, Alfred Austin, Robert Bridges, John Masefield, Cecil Day Lewis, John Betjeman and Ted Hughes. Poets who were offered the laureateship but declined it include ▷ Thomas Gray, ▷ Sir Walter Scott, Samuel Rogers, William Morris and Philip Larkin. Wordsworth was the first Poet Laureate to make his acceptance of the office conditional on his not being obliged to honour official occasions with specially composed poems, though some later laureates have continued the practice, notably Tennyson, Betjeman and Hughes.

Polidori, John (1796–1821)

Polidori emerged from a literary background in Soho's Italian community, his father Gaetano having translated the complete works of ▷ Milton and ▷ Walpole's ▷ *Castle of Otranto* into Italian. He studied medicine at the University of Edinburgh, graduating at the age of 19: his dissertation, on such topics as somnambulism and mesmerism, showed an interest in the ▷ Gothic as well as the medical, a combination that may have been peculiarly appropriate to his next spell of employment, as ▷ Lord Byron's physician. Their relationship was volatile and short-lived. Polidori was however a crucial member of the 'Pisan Circle' whose shared enthusiasm for horror and the fantastic was to produce, most famously, ▷ Mary Shelley's novel ▷ *Frankenstein* (1817). Scarcely known to modern readers, Polidori's short tale *The Vampyre* (1819) was hugely popular, and is the first text to fuse the hitherto disparate features of the vampire myth into a coherent literary whole. Bram Stoker's novel *Dracula* (1897) shows that the influence of Polidori's 'Lord Ruthven' was still powerful many decades later. Indeed, the presentation of Count Dracula in, for example, the Hammer films of the late 1950s and 1960s is closer to Polidori's version of the suavely aristocratic vampire than it is to the bewhiskered, Slavic ancient of Stoker's novel. It is possible to see the image of Lord Byron in Polidori's Lord Ruthven, and it was falsely assumed at the time of first publication that Byron was the author of *The Vampyre*. Its real author, troubled not only by debt but by brain damage sustained in a carriage accident, died (perhaps by his own hand) at the age of 25.

Political Register, The
A weekly journal started by ▷ William Cobbett in 1802, and continued until the year of his death, 1835. It was singularly bold and independent in opinion, and had a wide circulation especially among the poor of rural England. In 1803, Cobbett was fined £500 for his criticism of the government's Irish policy, and in 1809 he was sent to prison for two years for his criticism of military punishments. He continued to edit the paper from prison. From 1821 it included serial publication of ▷ *Rural Rides*.

Post-structuralism
At first glance, the term post-structuralism seems to imply that the post-structuralists came after the structuralists and that post-structuralism was the heir of ▷ structuralism. In practice, however, there is not a clear-cut division between structuralism and post-structuralism. Although the two have different focuses of interest and preoccupations, many of their concerns bind them together. Structuralism encompasses approaches to criticism which use linguistic models to enable critics to focus not on the inherent meaning of a work but on the structures which *produce* or generate meaning. Post-structuralism focuses on the ways in which the texts themselves subvert this enterprise. Leading post-structuralists include ▷ Derrida, ▷ Lacan, J. Hillis Miller and ▷ Paul de Man.
   ▷ Deconstruction; Feminism; Reception theory.

Bib: Culler, J. *On Deconstruction*.

Prelude, or Growth of a Poet's Mind, The (1805: 1850)
A ▷ blank verse ▷ autobiographical poem by ▷ William Wordsworth. The first version, in 13 books, was written between 1799 and 1805, but remained unpublished. Wordsworth continued to revise the poem at intervals throughout his life, and a version in 14 books appeared in 1850, after his death. With the encouragement of ▷ Samuel Taylor Coleridge, Wordsworth originally hoped to achieve a great philosophical poem (provisionally entitled *The Recluse*) 'on man, on nature, and on human life', to which *The Prelude* was intended as an introduction. Only one further part of the project, the vastly inferior ▷ *Excursion*, was completed. In *The Prelude* Wordsworth takes stock of his experience and resources, and traces the events of his early life. Books I–II, which concern 'Childhood and School-Time' contain some of his best-known work, illustrating the interaction between his growing mind and nature, as he climbs up to a raven's nest, rows a boat out on to a lake at night, or skates under the stars. Later books concern his time at Cambridge, in London and in revolutionary France (▷ French Revolution). The heading of Book VIII sums up a constant theme: 'Love of Nature Leading to Love of Man'.
   In a sense the work is a continuation of the ▷ epic tradition in a bourgeois form, the heroic adventures of the aristocratic warrior hero being replaced by the inner adventures of the individual poet. This helps to explain the epic grandeur of the poem's tone and scope, though this is not always sustained in practice. The revisions in the 1850 version, though they frequently improve the phrasing and pace of the 1805 text, impose upon it a Christian orthodoxy which muffles the immediacy of Wordsworth's original idiosyncratic ▷ pantheism.

Pre-Raphaelite Brotherhood
A movement of painters and poets which began just before 1850; it was more important in painting than in poetry, but one of its leading members, Dante Gabriel Rossetti, was equally famous in both arts. The essence of the movement was opposition to technical skill without inspiration. This made it anti-Victorian, inasmuch as industrial techniques (illustrated by the Great Exhibition of 1851) were producing vast quantities of work which were products of engineering. Technical skill without inspiration was deemed to be

an aspect of the neo-classical art of the 18th century, against which the Romantics had already reacted.

The principal painters of the Brotherhood were Rossetti, John Millais and Holman Hunt; its poets were Rossetti and his sister Christina Rossetti, and, a little later, William Morris.

The movement drew for its poetical inspiration on the ardour of the Romantic poet, ▷ John Keats, who had also cultivated the Middle Ages, and it greatly revered the contemporary poet, Alfred Tennyson, whose art owed much to Keats. But Pre-Raphaelitism was not merely an aesthetic movement; a great influence upon it was the work of the art critic John Ruskin, who had a strong social conscience about the duty of art to society, and especially of the duty of redeeming the squalid life of the urban working classes.

However, Keats had not been dismayed by the world of his time so much as by the inevitability of desperate suffering as part of the human lot in every age. Arnold and Tennyson, in their poetry, were dismayed by the surface hideousness and the apparently irremediable injustices of their society. They had tended to write a 'poetry of withdrawal', creating an inner world of unassailable dreams (Tennyson) or a transcendent fortress of lofty feeling (Arnold). The Pre-Raphaelites followed this example. The poetry of Rossetti and of Morris is a 'literary' art, *ie* it depends on the proved poetic stimulus of a special 'poetic' language and imagery which was alien to the ordinary man of the age, and had no relationship to the economically productive drive of the age itself. Thus, whatever the social consciences of Rossetti and Morris, they tended to take poetry to be an autonomous activity, largely independent of the political and social issues of the time. The poet ▷ A.C. Swinburne had the courage to take this autonomy seriously; with him, 'art for art's sake' was born, and the aesthetic movement. In general, however, Pre-Raphaelite writing may be viewed as a residue of the Romantic period, and as limited by escapism; the generation of Keats had been more open to experience and confrontation. **Bib:** Stanford, D. (ed.), *Pre-Raphaelite Writing*.

Pride and Prejudice (1813)

A novel by ▷ Jane Austen. Mr and Mrs Bennet belong to the minor gentry and live at Longbourne near London. Mr Bennet is witty and intelligent, and bored with his foolish wife. They have five daughters, whose marriage prospects are Mrs Bennet's chief interest in life, since the estate is 'entailed' – *ie* by the law of the period it will go on Mr Bennet's death to his nearest male relation, a sycophantic clergyman called Mr Collins. The main part of the story is concerned with the relationship between the witty and attractive Elizabeth Bennet and the haughty and fastidious Fitzwilliam Darcy, who at first considers her beneath his notice and later, on coming to the point of asking her to marry him, finds that she is resolutely prejudiced against him. His friend Charles Bingley is in love with the eldest daughter, Jane, but they are kept apart by the jealous snobbishness of his sisters and (at first) the fastidious disapproval of Darcy. Meanwhile, Elizabeth is subjected to an insolent offer of marriage by Mr Collins and the arrogant condescension of his patroness, Lady Catherine de Bourgh, Darcy's aunt. Those who regard the Bennet family as foolish and vulgar have their opinion justified when Lydia Bennet elopes with an irresponsible young officer, George Wickham. By this time, however, Darcy and Elizabeth have been chastened by finding in one another a fastidiousness and pride that equal their own and, despite the family scandal, they are united.

The novel has always been one of the most liked of Jane Austen's, and it contains excellent social comedy, but in some respects it stands apart. She herself said of it 'The work is rather too light, and bright, and sparkling; it wants to be stretched out here and there with a long chapter of sense.' Elizabeth Bennet was, however, her own favourite heroine.

Priestley, Joseph (1733–1804)

A Nonconformist minister, scientist and teacher. He was partly educated at a nonconformist academy at Daventry; such academies existed in the 18th century to give a university education to Non Conformists, who for their religious views were not admitted to the recognized universities of Oxford and Cambridge. They were commonly more advanced scientifically than the real universities; Priestley eventually became the first chemist to isolate oxygen. In 1768 he published his *Essay on the First Principles of Government*, advocating 'the happiness of the majority' as the criterion by which government must be judged. This line of thought was developed by ▷ Jeremy Bentham and his 19th-century followers, the ▷ Utilitarians. Priestley's house in Birmingham was destroyed by a mob in 1791, owing to his well-known sympathy with the ▷ French Revolution, and in 1794 he emigrated to the United States.

Primitivism

From a literary viewpoint, the concept of primitivism revolves around the figure of the 'noble savage'. Descended from the classical notion of a Golden Age, the concept gains most popularity and intellectual resonance in the 18th century, anticipated by the figure of Man Friday in Defoe's *Robinson Crusoe* (1719) and Aphra Behn's novel *Oroonoko, or the History of the Royal Slave* (1688), successfully adapted for the stage by Thomas Southerne in 1695. Based partly on the author's experiences of Surinam, the latter is one of the earliest examples of protest-literature against the slave-trade, describing primitive people in 'the first state of innocence, before men knew how to sin': the whole primitivist tradition may be read as a varied series of laments for, and objections against, the myth of *Genesis* and the Fall of mankind. Primitivism expresses an optimistic belief in the essential goodness of human beings, corrupted and deformed by so-called civilization. The chief conduit for debate in this area was the philosopher ▷ Rousseau. His writings of the 1750s contrast the harmonious existence of primitive man in a 'state of nature' with the indolence, profligacy, and selfish obsession with the concept of private property experienced by Europeans. *Emile* (1762) attempted to establish the principles of a new educational system, through which a child could develop rational independence of mind, while preserving a natural innocence, while the *Social Contract* of the same year argued for equality before the law, a more fair distribution of wealth, and a democratic subscription to the common good. While the resonance of these ideas for ▷ the French Revolution is self-evident, their influence on ▷ Romantic literature runs deep, persisting well beyond a point when the Revolution itself had been compromised by slaughter. ▷ Blake's perception of the corruption of individual desire by institutional diktat, ▷ Wordsworth's and ▷ Coleridge's early interest in the child, the inarticulate and the marginalized, Coleridge's ▷ conversation poems, ▷ Shelley's political idealism and ▷ Byron's evocation of island paradises in ▷ *Don Juan* and other poems, all bear witness to the continuation of primitivist speculation in the imaginative literature of the period. It formed a significant portion of the bequest

of European Romanticism to American literature; the most complex and poignant expressions of primitivism are perhaps to be found in the novels of Herman Melville (1819–91), particularly *Typee* (1846), *Omoo* (1847), and the character of Queequeg in *Moby Dick* (1851). The resurgence of Edenic rusticity, sexual permissiveness and equality in ▷ Nature that characterized American radicalism in the Cold War years suggests a domesticated and introspective modification of the prelapsarian strain in Romantic thought.
Bib: Tinker, C.B., *Nature's Simple Plan*, Fairchild, H.N., *The Noble Savage*, Whitney, L., *Primitivism and the Idea of Progress*, Roszak, T., *Towards a Counter-Culture*.

Prince, Mary (c 1788–c 1833)

Autobiographer. Mary Prince was a slave who, on being abandoned in London in 1831, was befriended by Susannah Moodie (one of the first Canadian women writers) who acted as her amanuensis, and by Thomas Pringe who campaigned for her emancipation. Her story was published in that year as part of the campaign, and makes for dispiriting, although compelling, reading. Prince was born in Bermuda in the household of a kindly family, but she was sold separately from her family when she was 11 and her new owners were savagely cruel to her. Over the next 18 years Prince was flogged, put to work at salt production (particularly harsh), and probably sexually abused. But by 1826 she was in Antigua, had converted to ▷ Methodism, had learned to read and had married Daniel Jones, a free man. Her owners appeared to have attempted to break this new sense of independence by taking her to London, but when that failed they simply threw her out on to the streets. Prince's narrative is part of a tradition of slave narratives which began at the beginning of the 18th century and were an important contribution to the political movement against slavery.
   ▷ Abolition literature; Autobiography.

Prisoner of Chillon, The (1816)

A poem by ▷ Lord Byron in tetrameter ▷ couplets (▷ metre) interspersed with quatrains. It is based on the story of François de Bonnivard (1496–1570), prior of the monastery of St Victor, near Geneva, who participated in a revolt against the Duke of Savoy and attempted to set up a republic in Geneva. He was imprisoned from 1530 to 1536 in the castle of Chillon. Byron's work is prefaced by a facile sonnet extolling Liberty as the 'Eternal Spirit of the chainless

Mind!' The poem itself, however, contradicts this optimism, describing the slow pining away of the narrator's two brothers, and the disintegration of his own mind under the strain of solitude: 'It was at length the same to me,/ Fetter'd or fetterless to be,/ I learn'd to love despair.' The historical Bonnivard was given a pension after his release, and was married four times.

Proctor, Bryan Waller (1787–1874)
Poet, dramatist and biographer. Proctor, a lawyer, wrote under the pseudonym of 'Barry Cornwall'. His work, including *Dramatic Scenes* (1819) and *Marcian Collona* (1820), was very popular with the public, but generally dismissed by other poets, such as ▷ Keats and ▷ Shelley. He was, however, on friendly terms with ▷ Lamb, who had admired *Dramatic Scenes*, and Proctor undertook his biography, *Charles Lamb: A Memoir* (1866).

Prometheus
In Greek myth, one of the Titans.

In the war between the gods and the Titans, he remained neutral, and was still on terms with Zeus when the gods were victorious. He was, however, very cunning and skilful.

According to legend Zeus was angry at a deception practised on him by Prometheus and deprived mankind of fire. Prometheus, however, stole fire from the gods, and gave it to man. Zeus then tried to punish man by sending the first woman (Pandora) with her jar of misfortunes; Hope, however, was left to man when the misfortunes were released to plague humanity. Zeus now tried to drown the human race in a great flood, but again Prometheus came to the rescue. To punish Prometheus for repeatedly outwitting him, Zeus had him bound to Mount Caucasus, and sent an eagle which gnawed incessantly at his liver. Prometheus, however, refused to ask pardon, and withheld a secret affecting Zeus's destiny. Eventually, Zeus allowed Heracles to free the Titan, who told the secret, and enabled Zeus to save himself. Prometheus was mortal, and on his death descended to the underworld. However, at the prayer of the centaur, Cheiron, he was eventually released, and permitted by Zeus to join the company of the gods. ▷ Shelley's lyrical drama ▷ *Prometheus Unbound* completes the Promethean trilogy by the Greek poet ▷ Aeschylus, and places the figure of Prometheus in a contemporary political context.

Prometheus Unbound (1820)
A 'lyrical drama in four acts' by ▷ Percy Bysshe Shelley, written to correspond to the final lost play of the Promethean trilogy by the Greek poet, ▷ Aeschylus. The demigod Prometheus, having stolen the secret of fire from the gods and given it to man, is punished by being chained to a rock and subjected to everlasting torture. Nevertheless, comforted by his mother, the Earth, and consoled by thoughts of his bride, Asia, the Spirit of Nature, he remains defiant against Jupiter, king of the gods. At the appointed hour Demogorgon, the primal life-force, defeats Jupiter, frees Prometheus, and an era of love dawns, in which all cruelty and oppression are banished: 'the man remains/ Sceptreless, free, uncircumscribed, but man/ Equal, unclassed, tribeless, and nationless,/ Exempt from awe, worship, degree, the king/ Over himself'. The original Greek myth in which Zeus (Jupiter) and Prometheus are reconciled, is thus transformed into a political allegory of modern revolution. The style is elaborately abstract, and the play is to be read rather than acted. In his Preface the poet refers to his desire 'to familiarize the highly refined imagination of the more select classes of poetical readers with beautiful idealisms of moral excellence'. Despite its cloyingly consistent elevation of tone, it is a strangely powerful work.

Psyche
In Greek myth, a personification of the human soul. Eros fell in love with her, and kept her in a magnificent palace where he visited her only at night, warning her that should she try to see him or discover who he was, he would leave her for ever. However, one night she lit a lamp to see him; he awoke, and departed. The palace vanished, and Psyche became the victim of a series of terrible ordeals imposed on her by Aphrodite – which she survived, thanks to the invisible protection of Eros, who finally persuaded Zeus to allow Psyche to be admitted among the gods. Psyche has been the subject of a number of poems in English, the most famous of which is the *Ode to Psyche* (1819) by ▷ John Keats.
　▷ Odes, Keats's.

Psychoanalytical criticism
Psychoanalysis and literary criticism both seek to interpret their respective objects of enquiry, and both involve the analysis of language. In its early manifestations psychoanalytical criticism (*eg* Ernest Jones's *Hamlet and Oedipus*; 1949) sought to apply the methods

of psychoanalysis to particular texts, in order to uncover their 'unconscious'. Jones's claim was to reveal the causes of Hamlet's behaviour beginning from the assumption that 'current response is always compounded partly of a response to the actual situation and partly of past responses to older situations that are unconsciously felt to be similar'. The French psychoanalyst ▷ Jacques Lacan's re-reading of ▷ Freud has sought to render problematical this relationship between patient and analyst, and, by implication, between text and reader. Lacan's description of the unconscious as being structured 'like a language' raises fundamental questions for the authoritative role usually ascribed to the literary critic. To this extent the 'unconscious' of the literary text is brought into confrontation with the unconscious of the critic.

Many of the terms taken from psychology which are associated with Lacan's reading of Freud have been incorporated into the language of literary criticism; for example the decentred subject of psychoanalysis, condensation, displacement, the realm of the ▷ 'imaginary', the ▷ symbolic order, all refer in some way to textual mechanisms.

Certain of the discoveries or tendencies of psychoanalytic literature were anticipated in the writings of the Romantic period, particularly in the emphasis on the importance of memory and dream that we find in the work of ▷ Coleridge and ▷ De Quincey. **Bib:** Laplanche, J. and Pontalis, J-B., *The Language of Psychoanalysis*; Lacan, J., *The Four Fundamental Concepts of Psychoanalysis*; Wright, E., *Psychoanalytical Criticism*.

Purbeck, Elizabeth and Jane (c 1789–1802)
Novelists. The Purbeck sisters wrote collaborative novels which balanced romantic narratives with gentle social and political comment. *History of Sir George Warrington, or The Political Quixote* (1797) and *Neville Castle* (1802) show a certain sympathy for the ideals of equality and use characters from real life, such as ▷ Tom Paine, and historical backdrops, like the ▷ French Revolution, in order to test their protagonist's devotion to their political and philosophical commitments. The latter novel also provides interesting critical material on ▷ Fanny Burney, Henry Fielding (1707–54), ▷ Sophia Lee, and Samuel Richardson (1689–1761).

Quarterly Review, The
Founded by ▷ John Murray in 1809 as a moderate Tory rival to the ▷ *Edinburgh Review*. The first editor was the irascible traditionalist ▷ William Gifford, and later editors included ▷ Samuel Taylor Coleridge's nephew, Sir J. T. Coleridge, and John Lockhart. ▷ Sir Walter Scott, ▷ Robert Southey, and ▷ Samuel Rogers were early contributors. Scott's approving review of ▷ Jane Austen's ▷ *Emma* appeared in the *Quarterly* in March 1816, and a hostile article by John Wilson Croker on ▷ John Keats's

▷ *Endymion* (Sept. 1818) provoked ▷ Lord Byron's squib (written in 1821):

> *Who kill'd John Keats?*
> *'I,' says the* Quarterly,
> *So savage and Tartarly;*
> *'Twas one of my feats.'*

Queen Mab
▷ A name for the queen of the fairies used in Shakespeare's *Romeo and Juliet* (I. iv) and ▷ Shelley's polemical poem *Queen Mab* (1813).

Q

R

Radcliffe, Mrs Ann (1764–1823)

Novelist. She was one of the most famous of the writers of ▷ Gothic novels, which sought to gain their effect through mystery and the supernatural in a setting of grand scenic description. She was immensely popular in her own day for her four novels: *The Sicilian Romance* (1790); *The Romance of the Forest* (1791); ▷ *The Mysteries of Udolpho* (1794), and *The Italian* (1797). *Udolpho* is the most remembered, partly owing to satirization through an account of its effect on a young girl in ▷ Jane Austen's ▷ *Northanger Abbey*.
Bib: Todd, J., *The Sign of Angelica*.

Radicalism

The political views of Radicals, who believe in the need for thorough reform going right to the roots (the etymological basis of 'radical') and origins of undemocratic abuses. The term probably originated in 1797 with the declaration of Charles James Fox that 'radical reform' was necessary. In the early 19th century it had the pejorative connotation that 'extremist' has today.

Reader-response criticism

▷ Reception theory.

Realism

A term used in various senses, both in philosophy and in literary criticism. Three principal meanings, two of them philosophical and one literary, are particularly worth distinction.

1 In medieval philosophy, the realists were opposed to the nominalists. Realism here means that classes of things ('universals') have reality whereas individuals have not, or at least have less: *eg* individual birds take their reality from the classification 'bird'. The nominalists considered that only the individual bird has reality, and that the classification 'bird' is only a formulation in the mind.

2 Since the Middle Ages, realism has become opposed to ▷ idealism. Here realism means that reality exists apart from ideas about it in the mind, and idealism represents the view that we can know nothing that is not in our minds.

3 Literary realism is a 19th-century conception, related to 2 and coterminous with industrial capitalism. In general, it means the use of the imagination to represent things as common sense supposes they are. 19th-century realism in literature arose, however, from a reaction against 19th-century Romanticism, and it is related to naturalism.

It might be said that Romantic poetry (particularly that of ▷ Blake, ▷ Wordsworth, ▷ Coleridge and ▷ Shelley), aspires to enact what is real through an evocation of the workings of the mind, rather than simply attempting to depict external reality.

Reception theory

This movement is associated pre-eminently with the German contemporary literary theorists Wolfgang Iser and Hans-Robert Jauss, and is often linked with reader-response criticism. Reception theory emphasizes the reader's consumption of the literary text over and above the question of the sum total of rhetorical devices which contribute to its structure as a piece of literature. The work of reception (*Rezeptionästhetik*) causes the reader constantly to rethink the canonical value of texts, since it involves noting the history of a text's reception as well as the current value which it may possess for the critic. Insofar as reception theory concerns itself with larger historical questions, it emphasizes histories of response which help to account for the reception of particular texts in the present. The approach to 'history' outlined here is pragmatic, and the emphasis is laid firmly on the matter of the interaction between text and reader and on the way cultural context is required to make sense of literature.
Bib: Fish, S., *Is There a Text in this Class?*; Iser, W., *The Act of Reading*; Tomkins, J.P., *Reader-Response Criticism*.

Recluse, The

▷ *Excursion, The*

Reeve, Clara (1729–1807)

Novelist. Important for her contribution to the ▷ Gothic novel, Reeve wrote *The Champion of Virtue* in 1777, revised and republished as *The Old English Baron* in 1778. This book was hugely successful, catching the tone of ▷ Walpole's popular ▷ *The Castle of Otranto* (1764), to which she was directly and self-confessedly indebted. Reeve wrote that in *The Old English Baron* she had tried to unite 'the most attractive and interesting circumstances of ancient Romance and modern Novel'. However, she criticized Walpole's excessive violence and he retaliated by calling her work insipid. The female characters in the novel appear incidental, and indeed Reeve's writing became increasingly conservative as she grew older. For example, she commented that ▷ women's education should consist of, 'virtue, modesty and discretion'. Nevertheless, in her critical volume, *The Progress of Romance* (1785), she claims that ▷ romantic novels are ideally suited to women writers and she deals in some detail with those female authors she considers interesting. Reeve's other novels follow similar Gothic or sentimental patterns and include: *The Two Mentors* (1783), *The Exiles* (1788), and *The School for Widows* (1791). Her early work includes the unjustly neglected *Original Poems on Several Occasions* (1769).

Bib: Punter, D., *The Literature of terror: A History of Gothic Fiction from 1765 to the Present Day*.

Reflections on the Revolution in France (1790)

A political treatise by ▷ Edmund Burke. Burke attacks the principles on which the ▷ French Revolution was being conducted, denies that the English Revolution of 1688 was based on the same principles, and insists that a society is an organic growth like a tree, requiring the same kind of careful surgery in accordance with its principles of growth. The book was provoked by a sermon in praise of the French Revolution, preached by a Nonconformist minister, Dr Price; Burke is in effect not merely attacking the French revolutionaries, but the reverence for abstract, rational, scientific enlightenment which during the 18th century, had increasingly transformed the 17th-century Puritans into the 18th-century rationalistic Dissenters or Nonconformists, and had found disciples among many others of the educated classes. The *Reflections* is a great work of conservative political philosophy, as well as a masterpiece of polemical prose. It represents the French Revolution as a turning-point in history: 'The age of chivalry is gone. That of sophisters, economists and calculators has succeeded; and the glory of Europe is extinguished for ever.'
▷ Paine, Thomas.

Reform Bills, Parliamentary

In English history, a succession of laws passed in the 19th and 20th centuries for the reform of the system of election of Members of Parliament. The system has always been based on towns and rural districts, grouped into constituencies, each electing one or (until recently) sometimes more than one candidate as Member. The most important Reform Bill was the first, passed through Parliament in 1832, because it reduced the electoral confusion into a rational system. Most constituencies had remained unchanged since the ▷ Middle Ages; in consequence, some towns had grown to great size with inadequate representation in Parliament, or none at all, while others were represented by more than one Member although they had sunk into insignificance or even, in a few cases, had ceased to exist. This meant great power for the landed aristocracy, and great deprivation of power for the large and growing middle class. Some boroughs ('towns' – but often mere villages) were called 'pocket boroughs' because they were virtually owned by one landlord, who had them 'in his pocket', *ie* caused them to elect the Members of his choice; others were called 'rotten boroughs' because few inhabitants possessed the right to vote, and they were easily and habitually bribed. The law of 1832 redistributed Members of Parliament so as to correspond to the great centres of population, but limited the franchise (right to vote) to those who possessed a level of income such as ensured that electors belonged at least to the middle class.
▷ *Mask of Anarchy, The*; Peterloo Massacre.

Regency

In English history, the period 1811–20 when George, Prince of Wales, later George IV (1820–30), took the title of Prince Regent during the final illness of his father, George III (1760–1820). In British cultural history, the term is often applied to cover the first 20 years of the 19th century during which a certain style of taste in art and architecture prevailed. It was inspired by the taste of the first French Empire (▷ Napoleon I) which itself arose from French revolutionary cultivation of ancient Greece, especially the republic of Athens. Architecture was austerely classical (the 'Greek style'), and dress was similarly modelled on long, graceful lines suitable for men and women with slender figures.

In literature, the term covers the working life of the second generation of Romantic poets (▷ Byron, ▷ Shelley and ▷ Keats), the work of the essayists ▷ Lamb and ▷ Hazlitt, and that of the novelists ▷ Jane Austen and ▷ Walter Scott. The best work of the essentially Augustan poet ▷ Crabbe also comes into the Regency period. The word is applied, however, more to architecture, dress and furniture than to literature, the principal architects being John Nash (1752–1835) and John Soane (1753–1837), architect of the Bank of England.

Rejected Addresses (1812)

When the ▷ Drury Lane theatre was rebuilt after having been destroyed by fire, the committee in charge, which included ▷ Lord

Byron, advertised for an address to be recited at the reopening. None of those submitted was judged suitable, and Byron himself composed the lines which were actually delivered. *Rejected Addresses*, by ▷ James and ▷ Horace Smith, purports to include the unsuccessful submissions of all the major poets of the day. It contains often brilliant ▷ parodies of ▷ William Wordsworth, ▷ Samuel Taylor Coleridge, ▷ Robert Southey, ▷ Lord Byron, ▷ George Crabbe and ▷ Sir Walter Scott, among others.

Reliques

▷ Thomas Percy's *Reliques of Ancient English Poetry* (1765) contains a mixture of genuine and ancient ballads, edited to conform to the tastes of the later 18th century, and contemporary offerings in an archaic style. Although Percy's approach to editing lacked stringency, it is important to distinguish his important labour of retrieval from the element of fakery and fantasy to be found in the ▷ Ossian poems of ▷ James Macpherson.

Renaissance in England, The

'Renaissance' (or 'Renascence') derives from Latin 'renascentia' = 'rebirth'. The word was first used by Italian scholars in the mid-16th century to express the rediscovery of ancient Roman and Greek culture, which was now studied for its own sake and not used merely to enhance the authority of the Church. Modern scholars are more inclined to use the term to express a great variety of interdependent changes which Europe underwent politically, economically and culturally between 1450 (although the starting-points were much earlier) and 1600. The religious outcome of these changes is expressed through the terms Reformation and Counter-reformation, a sequence of events which were closely bound up with the Renaissance.

In England, the Renaissance is usually thought of as beginning with the accession of the House of Tudor to the throne in 1485. Politically, this marks the end of the period of civil war amongst the old feudal aristocracy (the Wars of the Roses) in the mid-15th century, and the establishment of something like a modern, efficient, centralized state; technically, the date is close to that of the introduction of printing into England – an invention without which the great cultural changes of the Renaissance could not have occurred. Culturally, the first important period in England was the reign of the second Tudor monarch, Henry VIII. This was the period of the English humanist Thomas More, (1478–1535) and the poet Sir Thomas Wyatt (1503–42).

Several distinctive features characterize the English Renaissance. The first is the lateness of its impact; Italian, French, German, Dutch and Spanish scholars had already worked on the ancient Greek and Latin writers, and had produced works of their own inspired by the classics; in consequence, English culture was revitalized not so much directly by the classics as by contemporary Europeans under the influence of the classics. Castiglione's *The Courtier* (1528), Machiavelli's *The Prince* (1513), Ariosto's *Orlando* (1532), were as important in the English Renaissance as the works of ▷ classical authors such as Virgil's *Aeneid*, or the plays of Seneca, and it was characteristic that North's 1579 translation of Plutarch's *Lives* was not from the original Greek but from a French version. A further characteristic of English Renaissance literature is that it is primarily artistic, rather than philosophical and scholarly, and another is the coinciding of the Renaissance and the Reformation in England, in contrast to the rest of the Europe where the Reformation (or, in countries that remained Roman Catholic, the Counter-reformation) succeeded the Renaissance.

The English Renaissance was largely literary, and achieved its finest expression in the so-called Elizabethan drama which began to excel only in the last decade of the 16th century and reached its height in the first 15 years of the 17th; its finest exponents were Christopher Marlowe (1564–93), Ben Jonson (1572–1637), and ▷ William Shakespeare. Non-dramatic poetry was also extremely rich, and reached its peak in the same period in the work of Edmund Spenser (1552–99), Philip Sidney (1554–86), Shakespeare and John Donne (1572–1631), but it is typical of the lateness of the Renaissance in England that its most ambitious product, ▷ John Milton's epic ▷ *Paradise Lost*, was published as late as 1667. Native English prose shaped itself more slowly than poetry; More wrote his *Utopia* in Latin, which was the vehicle of some other writers including Francis Bacon (1561–1626) in much of his work owing to its advantages (for international circulation) over English, at a time when the latter was little learned in other countries. Nonetheless English prose developed with vigour in native English writers such as Roger Ascham (1515–68), Thomas North (1535–1601), Richard Hooker (1553–1600) in the English works of Francis Bacon, and in the translators of the ▷ Bible.

Resolution and Independence (1807)

A poem by ▷ William Wordsworth, sometimes known as *The Leech-Gatherer*, composed in 1802, published in 1807, and subsequently revised. It uses a reduced version of ▷ Spenserian stanzas, rhyming *ababbcc*, the first six lines being pentameters and the last an Alexandrine (▷ metre). Travelling across the moor the poet finds that the freshness of nature fails to raise his spirits. He reflects on ▷ Thomas Chatterton and ▷ Robert Burns, and the 'despondency and madness' to which the poetic vocation seems to lead. In his reverie he encounters the portentous figure of 'a Man', 'in his extreme old age', standing 'Beside a pool bare to the eye of heaven'. At first he seems part of inanimate nature, like a 'huge stone', but when approached he explains that he earns 'an honest maintenance' by roaming from pond to pond collecting leeches (much in demand by doctors of the day for blood-letting). The man's equanimity dispels the poet's moodiness: 'I could have laughed myself to scorn to find/ In that decrepit Man so firm a mind'. Despite its elements of conventional piety, the poem is remarkable for its sense of awe and spiritual humility before a man who in social terms is of no account.

Restoration, The

The word is used in two senses: the reestablishment of the Stuart monarchy in the person of King Charles II after the republican experiment of 1649–60; and as a period designation, often to cover the last 40 years of the 17th century, *ie* not only the reign of Charles II but that of his brother James II, and that of William III and Mary II. This period was marked by special cultural characteristics which were promoted by the political fact of the restoration of the monarchy. In this sense the term is most commonly used to identify three principal literary products: **1** Restoration prose; **2** Restoration drama (especially comedy); **3** Restoration poetry.

1 Restoration prose is marked by a very conscious determination by leading writers to use prose as a vehicle of reason. It had of course already been used in this way by, for instance, Francis Bacon (1561–1626), but even Bacon did not distinguish the virtues of prose for such a vehicle. It was one of the aims of the new Royal Society to cultivate these virtues, which were described by Thomas Sprat in his *History of the Royal Society* (1667): 'a close, naked, natural way of speaking; positive expressions; clear

senses; a native easiness; bringing all things as near the Mathematical plainness, as they can: and preferring the language of Artisans, Countrymen, and Merchants before that of Wits, or Scholars'. The Restoration period is indeed the first age of modern English prose writing. Its master was the poet, John Dryden (1631–1700), in his prose criticism, for instance his *Essay on Dramatic Poesy* (1668).

2 Restoration drama. This period is sometimes described as 'the silver age' of English drama, by comparison with the 'golden' age of ▷ Shakespeare. Owing to the hostility of the Puritans to drama, the art had practically ceased to be practised in the period of their power, 1642–60 when the public theatres were closed; it was then continued with ardour, but in less promising circumstances than in the 'golden' age. The decline had indeed already been evident before the close of the theatres in 1642, and a dramatist such as James Shirley (1596–1666), writing in the 1630s, exhibits many of the characteristic virtues and weaknesses of the Restoration. The audience had already ceased to be one drawn from all classes, and was restricted to people of fashion and refinement; wit, elegance of speech, skilful stage technique were the qualities which were sought after, and they implied a drama different from that of Shakespeare and his contemporaries, which had been intended to please alike the learned and the simple, the profound and the frivolous. After 1660, the French drama of Molière in comedy and of Corneille and Racine in tragedy were the dominating influences of the English stage (▷ French literature in England), but English society was not so constructed as to be able to emulate the French 'golden' age. English 'heroic' tragedy, with the exception of a few plays by Dryden, lacked the conviction of French tragedy in a comparable style, and the comedy of Sir George Etherege (1634–92), William Wycherley (1640–1716), Sir John Vanbrugh (1664–1726), George Farquhar (1678–1707), and even of William Congreve (1670–1729), is slight and superficial by comparison with that of Molière. However, Restoration comedy is in prose, unlike most of the tragedy, and the virtues of Restoration dramatists are especially in the wit, grace and poise of their prose dialogue; the comedies are still successful and even popular on the English stage, whereas few of the tragedies are ever performed.

3 Restoration (non-dramatic) poetry. This, especially the poetry of Dryden, is really the beginning of ▷ Augustan poetry. The virtues admired in the prose of the time reigned also over the poetry, so that a 'close, naked, natural way of speaking' is as evident in the verse as in the prose of Dryden. Besides him, Samuel Butler (1612–80) and the Earl of Rochester (1647–80) are the principal names classifiable as 'Restoration poets', but the foremost poet of the reign of Charles II, ▷ John Milton, cannot be so classified. The Restoration poets excelled in satire whereas Milton, in his epics and his one tragedy in so different a style from the neo-classic French tragedies, is a late product of the English Renaissance, profoundly modified by Puritanism.

Resurrection man; Resurrectionist

A term in use in the late 18th and early 19th centuries for one who made a living by digging up dead bodies and selling them to anatomists to use for dissection; such a person is Jerry Cruncher in Dickens's novel about the French Revolution, *A Tale of Two Cities* (1859).

Reynolds, John Hamilton (1796–1852)

Recipient of some of ▷ John Keats's most important letters, and of the verse epistle *To J. H. Reynolds Esq.* He published several volumes of poetry, including *The Garden of Florence and Other Poems* (1821).

Reynolds, Sir Joshua (1723–92)

One of the leading portrait painters of the 18th century, the age of English portrait painting. He was the first President of the Royal Academy, and the author of *Discourses*, *ie* lectures, delivered to its students between 1760 and 1790, on the principles of art. The friend of Samuel Johnson (1709–84) he was a founder-member of the Literary Club of which Johnson was the centre. Reynolds was strongly representative of 18th-century aristocratic taste, and in the opinion of ▷ William Blake, writing about 1808, 'This man was Hired to Depress Art'. However, his *Discourses* were admired by the greatest 19th-century English art critic, John Ruskin.

Rhetoric

Rhetoric in the medieval period was a formal skill of considerable importance. It was taken to mean the effective presentation of ideas with a set of rules or style, and was founded in the ▷ classical tradition of ▷ Aristotle and Cicero. It was taught in monastic schools as part of the *trivium*, Rhetoric, Logic and Grammar, which used as its basic text Geoffrey de Vinsauf's *Poetria Nova* (1200). Rhetoric not only formed patterns in which

texts should be written, but it also governed how the works should be received, and allocated them to particular categories, *eg* epic, debate or sermon. The system of rhetoric was paramount to the operation of literature in the medieval period.

Similarly, almost all of the practice or theory of writing in the ▷ Renaissance period was touched by what became known as the 'Art of Rhetoric'. Rhetorical theory formed an important part of the educational syllabus at the universities, and almost every major writer of the 16th and 17th centuries would have undergone some training in rhetoric. Rhetoric was learned first through reading the classical text-books on rhetoric, in particular the works of Quintilian (especially the *Institutio Oratore*) and Cicero. Secondly, practical rhetorical exercises were performed by the student in which a particular topic was debated. In these debates, the student was expected to be able to organize an argument according to set formulae, producing examples with which to sustain the analysis which themselves would be derived from a suitable store of words, images, fables and metaphors discovered in reading classical texts.

But the production of arguments was only one part of the rhetoricians' skills. Rhetoric also involved the classification of language – in particular the classification and analysis of ▷ figures of speech. Further, it was understood as an enabling tool by which ▷ discourse could be reproduced. In essence, therefore, it offered a system for producing both speech and writing. This system can be considered under five distinct parts: 1 'invention', which signifies the discovery of arguments applicable to a given case; 2 'arrangement' or 'disposition', which governed the ordering of the arguments to be used; 3 'style' or the actual choice of words and units of expression; 4 the important area of 'memory', which helped the rhetorician develop skills in recalling the order and substance of the argument being deployed; 5 'delivery', which was applicable mainly to spoken discourse but which governed such details as the appropriate facial expressions or gestures which might be used.

Whilst rhetoric was understood as a way of facilitating the classification of the various parts of an argument it was also a powerful tool in the analysis of discourse and it can thus be understood as a form of literary criticism. It was, however, in its abiding influence on stylistic forms that it was of most importance to the Renaissance writer. Numerous text-books on rhetoric were published throughout the 16th century in England. Perhaps the most important were: Leonard Cox, *The Art or Craft of Rhetoric* (1624); Richard Sherry, *A Treatise of Schemes and Tropes* (1550); Thomas Wilson, *Art of Rhetoric* (1553); Henry Peacham, *The Garden of Eloquence* (1577); and Abraham Fraunce, *Arcadian Rhetoric* (1584). But many other texts were written with the art of rhetoric either governing the structure or informing the language. Sir Philip Sidney's *An Apologie for Poetrie* (1595), for example, is structured according to rhetorical principles of organization.

Recent developments in critical theory have sought to re-emphasize rhetoric as a form of critical practice, particularly in relation to the *effects* that any verbal construction may have on those to whom it is addressed. In this respect rhetoric is closely associated with some of the larger issues which surface in relation to the theory of 'discourse'. The recent emphasis upon the *structure* of discourse draws attention away from language as a means of *classifying* to one of examining the way discourses are constructed in order to achieve certain effects. Here the emphasis would be on the different *ways* in which particular figures are presented in language, and what that presentation may involve. This form of rhetorical analysis has been undertaken by ▷ Jacques Derrida in volumes such as *Of Grammatology* (1974), by ▷ Paul De Man in his *Blindness and Insight* (1971), by Terry Eagleton in *Criticism and Ideology* (1976), and in a whole range of texts by ▷ Michel Foucault.

Richards, I. A. (1893–1979)

Critic. His approach to poetry was philosophic, linguistic and psychological. One of his important insights was that we are inevitably influenced by some kind of 'poetry', even if it is only that of bad films and magazine covers, or advertisements. In *Principles of Literary Criticism* (1924) and *Science and Poetry* (1926) he discusses what kind of truth is the subject-matter of poetry, the place of poetry in the context of the rest of life, and what is the nature of critical judgements of poetry. He worked to his conclusion on Benthamite (▷ Utiliarianism) lines, of asking what is 'the use' of poetry, but his conclusion was not far from that of Matthew Arnold (1822–88) that poetry's function in the modern world is that formerly provided by religion – to provide a 'touchstone' of value, and hence, if only indirectly, a guide to living (see Arnold's 'Study of Poetry', in *Essays in Criticism*, 2nd Series, 1888). Richards's *Practical Criticism*

(1929) is a teaching manual for the study of poetry with the aim of training students to judge poems presented anonymously, without being influenced by the author's reputation; its ideas have been extensively followed in English and American schools and universities. Much of his later work was purely linguistic, *eg Basic English and its Uses* (1943). Other works: *The Meaning of Meaning* (with Ogden, 1923); *Coleridge on Imagination* (1934); *The Philosophy of Rhetoric* (1936); *Speculative Instruments* (1955); *Goodbye Earth and other poems* (1959); *The Screens* (1961).
▷ New criticism.
Bib: Hyman, S., *The Armed Vision*.

Rights of Man, The (1791–2)

▷ Thomas Paine's *The Rights of Man* is a political treatise in two parts, first published in 1791 and 1792 respectively. Part I is essentially a reaction to ▷ Edmund Burke's ▷ *Reflections on a Revolution in France* of 1790. Burke is attacked for indulging in dramatic writing at the expense of truth: 'Mr Burke should recollect that he is writing history, and not *plays*.' Part II makes a comparison between the new constitutions of France and America, and the hidebound British attachment to hereditary succession. Paine's progressive and egalitarian proposals were labelled seditious, and Paine, who had already escaped to France with the assistance of ▷ William Blake, was convicted of treason and sentenced to banishment.

Rime of the Ancient Mariner, The
▷ *Ancient Mariner, The Rime of the*

Ritson, Joseph (1752–1803)

Editor and literary scholar. Joseph Ritson was an idiosyncratic scholar who suffered from ill health and who eventually went mad. He produced, however, important editions of early English poetry, including *A Select Collection of English Songs* (1783) and *Ancient English Metrical Romances* (1802). His demanding editorial standards led him to dismiss the works of ▷ Warton and ▷ Percy, but he remained a close and admiring friend of ▷ Walter Scott.
Bib: Johnston, A., *In His Enchanted Ground*.

Roberts, Emma (c 1793–1840)

Poet and travel writer. Roberts's most interesting writing focuses on India where she travelled for three years after moving there with her married sister in 1828. On her return to London, she published her first book of poems, *Oriental Scenes, Sketches and Tales* (1832) and dedicated it to ▷ L.E.L. with whom she had lived before travelling abroad. A prose work, *Scenes and Characteristics of Hindostan, with Sketches of Anglo-Indian Society* (1835), followed, and in both works Roberts shows herself to be an acute and impartial observer of injustice and cruelty. She attacked both Indian and English bigotry and intolerance, especially where women were the victims. In 1839 she returned to India and began editing *The Bombay United Service Gazette*. Two further travel books on India followed before her death in 1840.

▷ Nationalism; Orientalism; Travel literature.

Robespierre, Isidore Maximilien de (1758–94)

A leader of the extremist ▷ Jacobins during the ▷ French Revolution. He exercised virtual dictatorship from July 1793 to July 1794, during which he conducted the Reign of Terror and tried to establish the worship of the deistic Supreme Being in opposition to Catholicism on the one side and atheism on the other. His reputation for fanatical integrity caused him to be known as the Incorruptible. Represented in Anthony Trollope's *La Vendée* (1850), where considerable emphasis is placed on his integrity.

▷ Deism.

Robinson, Henry Crabb (1775–1867)

Diarist. Robinson studied at Jena University where he met ▷ Goethe and Schiller. He was one of the first foreign ▷ newspaper correspondents, becoming foreign editor of ▷ *The Times*. In later life he practised as a barrister, and helped found the Athenaeum Club and University College London. His extensive diaries and correspondence throw much light on the literary scene of his time, in particular on ▷ William Blake, ▷ William Wordsworth, ▷ Samuel Taylor Coleridge, ▷ Charles Lamb and ▷ William Hazlitt. They were partly published in 1869, and since then further selections have appeared.

Robinson, Mary (1758–1800)

Novelist, poet and actress. Although Mary Robinson is now known for her ▷ Gothic novels, during her lifetime she was infamous for her affair with the Prince of Wales. He saw her in the role of Perdita in 1779–80 and became enamoured with her. The relationship lasted just over a year, leaving Robinson the butt of crude satire and with

the lasting nickname 'Perdita'. In 1783 she became paralysed from the waist down after a miscarriage and from then on she was forced to earn her living by writing. Her poetry was never very original, picking up populist sentiment in relation to current events, such as the storming of the Bastille, and when her collection *Lyrical Tales* (1800) was published ▷ Wordsworth considered changing the title of his own work. In comparison her novels are sharp and witty, tinged with liberal sentiment; they include, *Vancenza* (1792), *Angelina* (1795) and *Hubert de Sevrac* (1796).

Bib: Bass, P., *The Green Dragon*; Rodgers, K., *Feminism in Eighteenth-century England*.

Rob Roy (1817)

A novel by ▷ Sir Walter Scott, giving a picture of Scotland just before the first ▷ Jacobite rebellion of 1715. The plot concerns the rivalry in love of the cousins Francis and Rashleigh Osbaldistone for Diana Vernon. Rashleigh, the villain, is involved in Jacobite intrigue. Their adventures are interwoven with the fortunes of Rob Roy Macgregor, a historical character whom Scott romanticizes. He is the chief of the Clan Macgregor in the Scottish Highlands, and a convicted outlaw who lives by plunder. In the novel he acts on the side of the hero, Francis, at Diana's earnest appeal. As usual in Scott's novels, the notable parts are those which concern Scottish common life, and such characters as Bailie Nicol Jarvie and Francis's servant Andrew Fairservice.

Roche, Regina Maria (1764–1845)

Novelist. Prolific Irish novelist, Roche wrote sentimental tales about the injustices done to her various protagonists and their families. The tone, however, was predictably ▷ Gothic, and she became one of the stalwarts of the ▷ Minerva Press. Her novels include *The Vicar of Lansdowne, or Country Quarters* (1789), *The Children of the Abbey* (1796) and *Clermont* (1798). This last work was satirized by ▷ Jane Austen in ▷ *Northanger Abbey*.

▷ Irish literature in English.

Rogers, Samuel (1763–1855)

Poet. The wealthy son of a banker from Stoke Newington, he wrote an *Ode to Superstition* (1786) (▷ Ode) and the popular reflective poem, *The Pleasures of Memory* (1792). *Columbus*, a fragment of an ▷ epic, appeared in 1810, and a narrative poem, *Jacqueline*, was published together with ▷ Lord Byron's *Lara* in 1814. He was offered the ▷ Poet

Laureateship on the death of ▷ William Wordsworth in 1850, but declined.

Romanticism

Two phases in the development of this concept need to be distinguished:

1 *'Romantick' taste* (c 1650–c 1789) The adjective 'romantic' came into use in the mid-17th century, at the point when the romance form, which had dominated secular literature during the Middle Ages and the ▷ Renaissance, fell from prominence. As ▷ Enlightenment philosophy and neo-classical taste developed, the romance form was subjected to self-conscious analysis and criticism. In its early stages the word took various forms: 'romancy', 'romancical', 'romantique', 'romantick'. Its meaning, 'like a romance', carried a number of different connotations, related to the various features of romance: the archaic rituals of chivalry, magic, superstition, improbable adventures, idealistic love, and wild scenery. Samuel Pepys used the word in 1667: 'These things are almost romantique, and yet true'. And the *Oxford English Dictionary* cites a 1659 reference to 'An old house in a romancey place'.

During the 18th century romantic wildness was disapproved of by the more puritanical, rational and enlightened reader. Some thinkers, however, such as the third Earl of Shaftesbury, self-consciously boasted of their emotional idealism and enthusiasm for wild scenery. Also most readers enjoyed the 'romantick' alternatives to neo-classicism indulged in at times by the poets and prose writers. Sometimes poets employed imitations of ornamental, medieval or ▷ 'Gothic' forms, such as the ▷ Spenserian stanza and the ▷ ballad, though romantic sensibility could also be expressed in the heroic ▷ couplet. Alexander Pope's (1688–1744) *Eloisa to Abelard* and *Elegy to the Memory of an Unfortunate Lady*, James Thomson's (1700–48) *Castle of Indolence*, ▷ Thomas Gray's translations of Norse and Welsh ballads and his ode, ▷ *The Bard*, and ▷ James Macpherson's ▷ Ossian, illustrate the range of romantic taste in the 18th century. The subjects of these works: passionate love, religious enthusiasm, laziness, medieval history, suicide, lie outside the mainstream of ▷ Augustanism, and they all share (with different degrees of seriousness) a sense of daring literary excess.

2 *The Romantic Movement* (1789–1824) The six great poets of what is now generally called the Romantic Movement, are in many ways extremely diverse. ▷ William Blake,

the pioneer of the group, was (in however complex and idiosyncratic ways) a Christian, who felt that ▷ William Wordsworth's ▷ pantheistic 'natural piety' made him 'a Heathen Philosopher at Enmity against all true Poetry'. ▷ Lord Byron emulated the wit and urbanity of Alexander Pope, whereas ▷ John Keats was contemptuous of neo-classical couplet writers who 'sway'd about upon a rocking horse,/ And thought it Pegasus'. ▷ Percy Bysshe Shelley was an atheist, ▷ Samuel Taylor Coleridge became an apologist for the Church of England. However, despite their differences, these poets show essential similarities in their response to the same historical situation, and do form a coherent group. It will be best to begin by describing their characteristics, leaving the label, 'Romanticism', to be explained afterwards.

The ▷ French Revolution dispelled the literary self-consciousness of the period of ▷ Sensibility. On the political level, the bourgeois complacency of the earlier period was suddenly lost. Even conservative writers at this time, such as ▷ Edmund Burke and ▷ Sir Walter Scott were forced to find new arguments in favour of the *status quo*, based on appeals to ancient tradition and emotional prejudice, rather than the authority of Reason and the natural order. The major poets were less inhibited. Blake was morally indignant about the institutions of State and Church. Wordsworth and Coleridge began their careers as fervent proponents of social revolution, while the second generation Romantics, Byron, Shelley, and (less prominently) Keats, remained true to the original revolutionary spirit through the succeeding period of reaction. The Romantics rejected the rigid social and literary hierarchy of the 18th century. Where Pope in the *Essay on Man* condescendingly conceded 'the poor Indian' his Natural Religion, Wordsworth feels profoundly shamed by that of the lowly leech gatherer in ▷ *Resolution and Independence*. The feelings of the individual take precedence over Reason and social convention, and particularly in the works of Wordsworth, outcasts, the very young, the very old, the poor and the mad, are seriously attended to. In the work of both Blake and Wordsworth youth becomes the fountain of wisdom rather than age. In a similar way dreams take on a new significance as the key to the unconscious depths of our being. Coleridge in his ▷ *Biographia Literaria*, gives a new, more complex meaning to the key Romantic term 'imagination'.

Fundamental to Romanticism is a new attitude towards the role of man in nature. The writers of the Enlightenment period, the Earl of Rochester (1647–80), John Dryden (1631–1700) and Pope had shared with the ancients a certainty as to what nature was, and a confidence about their place in it. For them *human* nature was an integral part, even the greatest glory, of 'Nature', and (like gravity) obeyed 'Nature's laws'. In the early stages of Enlightenment it seemed easy to reconcile the new exploitative science and technology with a traditional piety about God's creation. But by the end of the century a crisis had developed. Enlightenment had finally robbed nature of its authentic, primitive awesomeness. More practically its manipulative exploitation by man seemed in danger of destroying nature itself. ▷ William Cowper expressed this new mood of diffidence and alienation in his aphorism: 'God made the country, and man made the town', while Shelley declared more boldly that 'man, having enslaved the elements, remains himself a slave'. Newton's light had reduced nature to a manipulable material system. It had become either a useful recreational facility (Wordsworth wrote a guidebook to the picturesque Lakes), or – in atavistic reaction – a mystical substitute for religion. Shelley's proposed answer to the crisis of Enlightenment, like that of all the Romantic poets, was to cultivate the 'imagination' and 'the poetical faculty'.

Nature thus ceases to be an objective intellectual concept for the Romantics, and becomes instead an elusive metaphor. The brisk clarity of Pope's: 'First follow *Nature* . . . which is still the same', is replaced by the anxious emotive rhetoric of Wordsworth's: 'And I have felt/ A sense sublime/ Of something far more deeply interfused'. Nature is often approached indirectly – seen from afar, or not *seen* at all: 'I cannot see what flowers are at my feet,/ Nor what soft incense hangs upon the boughs,/ But, in embalmed darkness, guess each sweet' (*Ode to a Nightingale*, stanza V). The relation between the poet and nature becomes ambiguous and insecure: 'I see, not feel, how beautiful they are!' (▷ *Dejection: An Ode*, stanza II); 'Whither is fled the visionary gleam?/ Where is it now, the glory and the dream?' (*Ode:* ▷ *Intimations of Immortality*, ll. 56–7); 'The wilderness has a mysterious tongue/ Which teaches awful doubt' (Shelley, *Mont Blanc*, ll. 76–7). From being the middle term in the Great Chain, 'The glory, jest, and riddle of the world!' (*Essay on Man*, II, l. 17), or – less buoyantly but equally definitively – a 'reas'ning *Engine*'

inevitably destined for the dirt (Rochester, *Satyr on Reason*, ll. 29–30), the human being has become a dubious subjectivity, constantly redefining his or her identity.

The Romantic poets continued to employ the 'romantick' forms of the earlier period: Spenserian stanzas, ballad, and irregular ode. They cultivated medievalism and imitated Elizabethan and ▷ Jacobean playwrights. They also revived the neglected ▷ sonnet form. However, their designation 'Romantic Poets' derives less from their development of previous romantic taste, than from the growing popularity of German aesthetic categories in England. In the late 18th century ▷ Goethe and Schiller had developed the contrast between romantic (emotional, inspirational) art, and classical (serene, balanced) art, into a theoretical opposition between aesthetic absolutes, and the German critic Schlegel and the French essayist Mme de Staël had popularized this distinction. At first, observers in England saw this debate as a strictly foreign phenomenon. Byron in a letter of 1820 remarked 'I perceive that in Germany as well as in Italy, there is a great struggle about what they call *Classical* and *Romantic*', and he went on to hope that such disputes would not spread to England. However, such a polarity does seem to underlie some of Keats's work. His ▷ *Hyperion*, and his *Ode on a Grecian Urn* (written after he had seen the Parthenon or 'Elgin' marbles in London), can be seen as 'classical', while his ▷ *Eve of St Agnes* and *Ode to a Nightingale* are 'romantic' (▷ *Odes*, Keats's).

The abstract noun 'Romanticism', did not come into use in England until the mid-19th century; early citations in the *Oxford English Dictionary* are in reference to the music of Liszt, and in the phrase 'German Romanticism'. By the time readers began to see these six English poets as forming a single 'movement' it seemed natural to simplify their work in accordance with this categorization. Romanticism thus stands as an emotional reaction against the rational classicism of 18th-century Augustanism. It is important to remember that all these terms embody large simplifications. If they are used without a sense of the historical complexities which lie behind them, they can distort the literature to which they refer, rather than illuminating it.
Bib: Abrams, M. H., *The Mirror and the Lamp*; Praz, M., *The Romantic Agony*; Ford, B. (ed.), *New Pelican Guide to English Literature*, *Vol. 5: From Blake to Byron*; Bloom, H., *The Visionary Company*; Watson, J. R., *English*

Poetry of the Romantic Period: 1789–1830;
Butler, M., *Rebels and Reactionaries: English
Literature and its Background: 1760–1830*;
McGann, J., *The Romantic Ideology*; Mellor, A.
K., *Romanticism and Feminism*.

Roscoe, William (1753–1831)
Poet. Famous for his children's book, *The
Butterfly's Ball and the Grasshopper's Feast*
(1806). He also wrote other poems, and
biographies of Lorenzo de Medici (1796) and
Pope Leo the Tenth (1805).

Ross, Mrs (c 1811–25)
Novelist and writer of short stories. Published
by ▷ Minerva among others, Mrs Ross is one
of few prose writers to balance rationalism
and ▷ Romanticism, 'sense and sensibility'
as it were, and combine them with relatively
direct descriptions of sexuality. Her plots
and characters are ingenious and she clearly
expects her readers fully to appreciate her
novels' tough moral conclusions. Her work
includes: *The Cousins, or A Woman's Promise
and A Lover's Vow* (1811), *The Balance of
Comfort, or The Old Maid and Married Woman*
(1817), and *The Woman of Genius* (1821).

Rousseau, Jean-Jacques (1712–78)
French-Swiss thinker. His chief works were:
Discourse on the Influence of Learning and Art
(1750), in which he argues that progress
in these has not improved human morals;
Discourse on Inequality (1754), in which society
is considered to have spoilt the liberty and
virtue natural to primitive peoples; a novel,
The New Héloïse (1761), in which the return
to primitive nature is considered in relation
to the relationships of the sexes and the
family; *The Social Contract* (1761), a political
treatise with the theme that the basis of
society is artificial, not binding on individuals
when society ceases to serve their interests;
Emile (1762), advocating education through
the evocation of the natural impulses and
interests of the child, and the *Confessions*,
an autobiography which was self-revealing
without precedent, published after his death.

Rousseau was immensely influential,
not only in France but throughout Europe.
His praise of nature and protests against
society were significant contributions to the
creation of a revolutionary state of mind,
culminating in the ▷ French Revolution of
1789. Education from nature, his conception
of nature as a life-giving force, was of
great importance in the background of
▷ Wordsworth, and through Wordsworth,
of much of English 19th-century imaginative

thinking. Linked with his devotion to nature
was his equally influential reverence for
childhood. As an autobiographer, Rousseau
was one of the first to base the importance
of individual experience on its uniqueness,
not on its moral excellence or intellectual
attainment. This was quite contrary to the
characteristic 18th-century view, expressed
in works like Samuel Johnson's (1709–84)
Rasselas, in which the valuable experience was
conceived to be only that which was true of
and for humanity at large.

Roxburghe Club
Book Club. The Roxburghe was the first
book club and took its name from John Ker,
third Duke of Roxburghe (1740–1804), who
had acquired a vast collection of antiquarian
books. When his 1471 edition of ▷ Boccaccio
was sold for £2,260, a phenomenal sum in
those days, several book enthusiasts celebrated
the event with a dinner during which the
club was initiated. Its first president was Lord
Spencer of Althorp and its first secretary was
his librarian, ▷ Thomas Frognall Dibdin.
The Roxburghe Club continues to this day,
each member financing the production of an
important and unjustly neglected work.

Roxburghe, John Ker, Third Duke of
▷ Roxburghe Club.

**Ruined Cottage, The, or The Story of
Margaret (1814)**
A poem in ▷ blank verse by ▷ William
Wordsworth, written in 1797, and included in
Book I of ▷ *The Excursion* (1814). It tells the
poignant story of a woman whose husband is
driven by grinding poverty to join the army.
He never returns, and eventually grief and
poverty take Margaret's life. Contemplating
her cottage, now derelict and overgrown, the
narrator is overcome by 'the impotence of
grief', and reflects on:

*That secret spirit of humanity
Which 'mid the calm oblivious tendencies
Of nature, 'mid her plants, and weeds, and
    flowers,
And silent overgrowings, still survived.*

Rural Rides (1820–30)
Reports of rural conditions by ▷ William
Cobbett. He disapproved of certain remedies
proposed by an official body to the Government
for agricultural distress resulting from the
Napoleonic War. He decided to make a number
of tours on horseback in order to find out the
facts for himself, and published his impressions

in his journal, the ▷ *Political Register*, between 1820 and 1830, when they were collected into book form. The essays are in vivid, direct prose, full of acute comments, lively incident, and strong if prejudiced argument. They are early examples of direct journalistic reporting and are raised to permanent value as literature by the energy of Cobbett's conviction and the simplicity and vigour of his prose, which he had modelled on the writings of Jonathan Swift (1667–1745).

Sade, Donatien Alphonse, Marquis de (1740–1814)

French novelist and poet. His belief that his destructive impulses were part of his nature, and yet uncontrollable, counterbalanced the doctrine of ▷ Rousseau, according to whom man undistorted by social forces was naturally good. Sade's ideas profoundly influenced the dark side of ▷ Romanticism but, with the exception of ▷ Swinburne, were less pervasive in England. Sade has recently received renewed attention in France (eg ▷ Roland Barthes, Sade, Fourier, Loyola; 1971), where he has fed into a ▷ Nietzschean strain of literary and theoretical thinking.

Saladin (1138–93)

Sultan of Egypt. His conquest of the Christian Latin Kingdom of Jerusalem (1187) provoked the Third Crusade under Richard I of England and Philip II of France, with whom he made a truce. He was famous for his fierce piety compounded with chivalrous generosity; in English history and legend these qualities are made to represent him as a suitable antagonist to Richard, himself a legend for his courage and chivalry. Their rivalry is the subject of ▷ Scott's novel The Talisman (1825). Historically, Saladin is important for halting the invasion of the East by the Christian West, and starting a counter-movement against the West which lasted until the 17th century.

Sand, George (1804–76)

Pseudonym of Amandine-Aurore Lucille Dupin, baronne Dudevant, she was born in Paris and brought up at her paternal grandmother's country property at Nohant (later hers), following the death of her father, in an atmosphere of quarrels between her mother and grandmother. After a convent education in Paris, she ran wild again at Nohant, reading avidly ▷ Rousseau, ▷ Byron, ▷ Shakespeare and Chateaubriand among others. She married the baron Dudevant, a retired army officer, and had two children, but by 1831 was living an independent life in Paris, writing to earn her living. Her work reflected the men and ideas in her personal life, and her catholic enthusiasm for humanitarianism, Christian socialism, Republicanism, etc. She also wrote idealized romances of rustic life, set around Nohant. Indiana (1832) was the first of many successes and was followed by Valentine (1832), Lélia (1833), Jacques (1834) and Mauprat (1837). These championed the rights of women to follow their desires and ignore convention. Spiridion (1839) and others reflect her ideas, and the country tales include La Mare au Diable (1846) and La Petite Fadette (1848). Her relationship with the poet Alfred de Musset is fictionalized in Elle et lui (1859) and incidents in her nine-year liaison with the composer Chopin are portrayed in Un hiver à Majorque (1841). She also wrote some political articles, biographical and critical essays, unsuccessful drama and an autobiography in four volumes, Histoire de ma vie (1854–5).

Sardanapalus (7th century BC)

In Greek legend, the last king of Assyria, famous for his luxury and effeminacy. He threw off his self-indulgence to defeat formidable rebels in a succession of battles. Eventually he had to face total defeat, and burnt up his wives and himself in his palace. This (with variations) is the subject of ▷ Byron's tragedy Sardanapalus (1821).

Sartor Resartus: The Life and Opinions of Herr Teufelsdröckh

A disguised spiritual ▷ autobiography by Thomas Carlyle (1795–1881). It was serialized (1833–4) in Fraser's Magazine and published in book form in Boston, U.S.A., in 1836 and in Britain in 1838. Carlyle was under the influence of the German Romantics, eg Jean Paul Richter. The title is Latin for 'the tailor re-patched': Carlyle offers the fable that human beliefs and institutions are like clothes and need renewing. Against ▷ Byron's attitude of doubt, isolation and suffering, Carlyle calls for the affirmativeness of the German poet ▷ Goethe; heroic qualities such as sacrifice and devotion to duty must redeem the inner man and, through men, the directionless age in which Carlyle felt himself to be living – the age of flux and the decay of unquestioning religious faith. Besides the drive of German influence, Carlyle felt the force of the old-fashioned Scottish Calvinism such as had animated his father. The three crucial chapters are 'The Everlasting No', 'Centre of Indifference' and 'The Everlasting Yea'. Despite the difficulty he had in getting the book published in Britain, it marks the beginning of his exposition of the creed of heroism, which made Carlyle an inspiring figure in commerce-dominated mid-19th-century Britain.

▷ German influence on English literature; Victorian period.

Satan

A Hebrew word meaning 'adversary'; in the Christian tradition, one of the habitual names for the Devil. In *Job* (Old Testament), an older tradition is evident in I:6–12 and II:1–6. Satan is a servant of God, and his special function is to test the virtue of men by trials and suffering.

▷ Milton, John; *Paradise Lost*.

Satire

A form of attack through mockery, it may exist in any literary medium, but is often regarded as a medium in itself. The origins of the word help to explain the manifestations of satire. It derives from the Latin 'satura' = a vessel filled with the earliest agricultural produce of the year, used in seasonal festivals to celebrate harvest; a secondary meaning is 'miscellany of entertainment', implying merry-making at such festivals, probably including verbal warfare. This primitive humour gave rise to a highly cultivated form of literary attack in the poetry of ▷ Horace, Persius (1st century AD) and Juvenal. Thus from ancient Roman culture two ideas of satire have come down to us: the first expresses a basic instinct for comedy through mockery in human beings, and was not invented by the Romans; the second is a self-conscious medium, implying standards of civilized and moral rightness in the mind of the poet and hence a desire on his or her part to instruct readers so as to reform their moral failings and absurdities. The two kinds of satire are inter-related, so that it is not possible to distinguish them sharply. Moreover, it is not easy to distinguish strict satire in either of its original forms from other kinds of comedy.

1 Strict satire, *ie* satire emulating the Roman poets. This was one of the outcomes of ▷ Renaissance cultivation of ancient ▷ Latin literature. The great age of the strict satire was the 18th century, notably in the work of Alexander Pope (1688–1744) who emulated the relatively genial satire of Horace, and Samuel Johnson (1709–84) who emulated the sombre style of Juvenal. Satire of this sort makes its object of attack the social forms and corruptions of the time, and its distinctive medium is the 10-syllable rhymed couplet, perfected by Pope and used with different force by Johnson.

2 Comedy of Humours and Comedy of Manners. These are the most easily distinguishable forms of dramatic satire. The former is associated chiefly with the Renaissance dramatist Ben Jonson (1572–1637), and has its roots in the older Morality drama, which was only intermittently satirical. The 'humours' in Jonson's conception are the obsessions and manias to which the nature of human beings invites them to abandon themselves; they have a close relation to the medieval Seven Deadly Sins, such as lust, avarice and gluttony. The Comedy of Manners belongs to the period 1660–1800, and, especially, to the first 40 years of it. Its most notable exponent is ▷ Sheridan at the end of the 18th. This comedy is less concerned with basic human dispositions and more with transient social ones; rational social behaviour is the standard in the mind of the dramatist. Both these forms of satire were taken over by novelists; indeed, the 18th-century novelist Henry Fielding (1707–54) began as a writer of dramatic comedies of manners.

3 Satire of ▷ Parody and Irony (▷ Figures of Speech). This includes the most skilful and powerful satire in the language; its most productive period is between 1660 and 1750. Parody at its most powerful implies the writer's complete respect for the serious form which he is using in a comic way; thus in this period (which included the very serious ▷ epic ▷ *Paradise Lost*) the prestige of the epic form was still high, and John Dryden (1631–1700) (*Absalom and Achitophel*) and Pope (*The Rape of the Lock* and *The Dunciad*) used their appreciation of epic to make ironic contrast between the grandeur of its style and the pettiness, meanness and destructiveness of their chosen subject.

Irony does not necessarily use parody, but even when it does not, it operates in a similar way, by addressing the reader in terms which he or she has learnt to receive as acceptable at their face value, and then shocking him or her into recognition that something quite unacceptable is the real subject. One of the most incisive ironists in English Literature is the novelist ▷ Jane Austen.

4 Flytings, and other traditional forms. The Middle Ages took from its popular festivals a strong tradition of verbal combat (flytings) and sardonic criticism of the established social order. One aspect of this emerges in popular ▷ ballads (especially in the printed form of broadsides which developed after the medieval period).

5 Novelistic satire. Much satire in novels from the 18th to the 20th century cannot be summed up under comedy of manners. The novels of ▷ Peacock, for example, establish a tradition of comic discussions mocking at contemporary trends of thought.

Saussure, Ferdinand de (1857–1913)

Swiss linguist, generally regarded as the founder of ▷ Structuralism. Saussure's

Course in General Linguistics was published two years after his death, in 1915, and represents a reconstruction of three series of lectures which he gave at the University of Geneva during the years 1906–7, 1908–9, and 1910–11. It was Saussure who pioneered the distinction between ▷ 'langue' and ▷ 'parole', and who sought to define the operations of language according to the principles of combination and ▷ difference. Although ▷ deconstruction has done much to undermine the Structuralist base of Saussure's thinking, the concept of 'difference' as a determining principle in establishing meaning ('signification') remains one of the key concepts in modern critical theory. Moreover, Saussure's work provided the foundation for the methodological analysis of ▷ sign systems (▷ semiotics), and the types of linguistic investigation which he undertook have been successfully appropriated by literary critics, as well as by social anthropologists such as Claude Lévi-Strauss (b 1908).

Scotland
The northern kingdom of Great Britain. Geographically, racially, linguistically and culturally, it has two parts.

The northern and north-western half, known as the Highlands and the Islands, is Celtic in race, with a Norse admixture. The native language was originally the Celtic one called Gaelic, but this is now spoken only by a small minority. Until the middle of the 18th century its social structure was of the semi-tribal clan system under hereditary chieftains. Its culture was chiefly oral and Gaelic-speaking, and much of it has been lost. The so-called Scottish national dress, of the kilt woven into chequered designs known as tartans, was peculiar to this region; it was forbidden after the second ▷ Jacobite rebellion of 1745, when the British government started its policy of colonizing the Highlands, but it was revived in the 19th century as a sentimental fashion for the upper classes and is now an extremely profitable export item. This region of Scotland, though extremely beautiful, has had a torn history; centuries of clan warfare were followed by century and a half of economic neglect and depopulation, during which the small farms of 'crofts' were steadily replaced by 'grouse moors', preserved by rich landlords for hunting and shooting. In the 20th century the economy has to some extent revived, thanks to the tourist industry and efforts by successive governments to cultivate forests.

The southern and eastern half of the country is called the Lowlands, and contains all the important cities including the capital, Edinburgh, and the largest, Glasgow. These two cities are respectively at the east and west ends of the narrowest part of the country, and the plain between them was a rich coal-mining area. The Lowlands are geographically hilly, in spite of their name. Racially, the population is as Germanic in origin as that of most of England, and with small exceptions it has always been English-speaking. It has never been subjected to the clan system of the Highlands, although the great families along the border with England had, until the 17th century, an influence comparable to that of the clan chieftains of the Celtic north. Economically and politically, the Lowlands have always been the richer and more important part of the country. When we speak of Scottish culture, we are nearly always thinking of the literature of the Lowlands; this has had its distinctive tradition, but it has become increasingly absorbed into English culture since the 16th century.

Scott, Sir Walter (1771–1832)
Scottish poet and novelist. The son of an Edinburgh lawyer, he was descended from famous families on the Scottish side of the border with England. This ancestry early attracted him to the drama and tragedy of Anglo-Scottish border history; he became an antiquarian, and a very Romantic one. His ▷ Romanticism was stimulated further by reading the poetry of the contemporary Germans, Bürger and ▷ Goethe; he hoped to do for the Scottish border what they had done for the German Middle Ages, and make its past live again in modern romance. A widespread taste was already developed for the ▷ Middle Ages and was manifesting itself in the ▷ Gothic novel. He collaborated with the most famous of the Gothic novelists – ▷ 'Monk' Lewis – in producing *Tales of Wonder* in 1801. A little later ▷ S. T. Coleridge's poem ▷ *Christabel* inspired him to write poems in the same metre, and between 1805 and 1815 he produced the succession of narrative poems which made him famous. He began to feel himself outdone as a narrative poet by ▷ Byron, however, and from 1815 he devoted himself to the novels for which he is now better known. Publishing enterprises in which he had begun to involve himself in 1809 left him with a debt of £130,000 to pay off, when the London publisher Constable went bankrupt. Scott was immensely proud, and determined to pay off the debt by his own literary efforts. By writing very prolifically for

the rest of his life, he nearly succeeded; he was by then a very sick man, and his efforts are a legend of literary heroism.

Scott's most famous poems are *The Lay of the Last Minstrel* (1805); ▷ *Marmion* (1808), and ▷ *The Lady of the Lake* (1810). The first two are from Anglo-Scottish border history and legend; the third is about the equally bitter enmity of Scottish Highlander for Scottish Lowlander. The readability of these poems makes it easy to account for their popularity, but the kind of interest they offer – the dramatization of the life of a whole society – was not such as Scott was able to work out in the verse-narrative medium.

His novels show a double interest: he was the first novelist in English to present characters as part of a society, and not merely against the background of a particular society, the nature of which is taken for granted; he was also the inventor of the true historical novel. His best work is contained in the Waverley novels and in the first three series of *Tales of My Landlord*: ▷ *Waverley* (1814), *Guy Mannering* (1815), *The Antiquary* (1816), *Old Mortality* (1816), ▷ *Rob Roy* (1817), ▷ *The Heart of Midlothian* (1818), *The Bride of Lammermoor* and *The Legend of Montrose* (1819). All these concern 17th- and 18th-century Scotland, and the religious and dynastic struggles that shaped the nation as Scott knew it. From then onwards he was writing with excessive haste in order to pay off his debts, and he commonly chose English and medieval subjects, *eg* ▷ *Ivanhoe* (1819), *Kenilworth* (about English Elizabethan times – 1821), *Quentin Durward* (1823) and some 16 others, only one of which, *St Roman's Well* (1823), was set in Scott's own time.

Not only was Scott's influence, both in Britain and Europe, very large in shaping literary taste, but he had an extensive influence in encouraging non-literary taste, such as that for wild landscape (especially of the Highlands) and more intelligent interest in the past. As a critic he was among the first to recognize the genius of ▷ Jane Austen. In politics he was strongly right-wing (Tory), and he helped to found the great Tory review, the ▷ *Quarterly*, in 1809.

Bib: Buchan, J., *Life*; Davie, D., *The Heyday of Sir Walter Scott*; Hayden, J. O., *Scott: The Critical Heritage*; Hillhouse, J. T., *The Waverley Novels and their Critics*; Lewis, C. S., in *They Asked for a Paper*; Lockhart, J. G., *Memoirs*; Muir, E., *Scott and Scotland*; Goslee, N. M., *Scott the Rhymer*.

Scottish literature in English
This belongs above all to the Lowlands (▷ Scotland); it is a distinctive branch of literature in the English language, the Lowland Scottish form of which had originally a close resemblance to that spoken in the north of England. Racially, linguistically and culturally, Lowland Scottish ties with England were close, despite the constant wars between the two countries between the late 13th and mid-16th centuries. In contrast, until the 18th-century destruction of Highland culture, the Lowlanders had little more than the political bond of a common sovereign with their Gaelic-speaking fellow-countrymen of the north. While it is not true to say that Scottish literature is a branch of English literature, the two literatures have been closely related.

The flowering of high Scottish poetry was halted by the Scottish religious Reformation, and all the political troubles attendant on it from 1550 till 1700. Such poets in this period as deserve attention (e.g. Drummond of Hawthornden, 1585–1649) were generally thoroughly anglicized. The native culture remained alive at popular level, however, especially in its fine ballad and folksong tradition of which *Sir Patrick Spens* is one of the most notable examples. In the 18th century a revival took place, the first noteworthy example being Allan Ramsay's *The Gentle Shepherd* (1725). ▷ Robert Burns is perhaps the first famous Scottish poet since the 16th century. By now, however, the tide of English influence had moved strongly into Scotland; ▷ Walter Scott collected Scottish ▷ ballads, and produced a few fine examples in the ballad tradition, but his longer poems belong to the history of English verse narrative, though their subject was often Scottish history and legend.

Gaelic literature of the Highlands had what is said to be a 'golden age' in the later 18th century, just at the time when Gaelic culture was being destroyed by the English and the Lowland Scots for political reasons. The work in it (*eg* that of Alexander Macdonald, Dugald Buchanan) is little known outside the comparatively small number of Gaelic speakers in the Highlands, and does not belong to English literature. For the alleged translations of the Ossianic poems by ▷ James Macpherson (1736–96) see under ▷ Ossian.

Scottish prose literary tradition may be seen in medieval philosophers and in the great Scottish writers (especially from the 18th century) who were mainly anglicized in their prose expression, such as ▷ Adam Smith in the 18th century and Walter Scott in the 19th.

Bib: Gifford, D., *The History of Scottish literature*.

Semiology, Semiotics
The term 'semiology' was used in ▷ Ferdinand de Saussure's *Course in General Linguistics* (published 1915) to describe 'a science of ▷ signs', whose objective is 'to investigate the nature of signs and the laws governing them'. The more current term, semiotics, was associated originally with the American philosopher C. S. Peirce. Peirce's tripartite division of signs into 'icon' (a sign possessing a similarity to its object), 'symbol' (a sign arbitrarily linked to the object), and 'index' (a sign physically associated with its object), has more recently been revised in Umberto Eco's *A Theory of Semiotics* (1976) where the emphasis throughout is upon the complex mechanisms and conventions which govern the production of signs.

Sennacherib
King of Assyria, 705–681 BC. He made extensive conquests, but one of the most eloquent narratives of the Old Testament of the Bible describes how his attempt to capture Jerusalem from Hezekiah, king of the Jews, was prevented by a sudden pestilence among his army (2 *Chronicles* 32). This is the subject of ▷ Byron's poem, 'The destruction of Sennacherib' in *Hebrew Melodies* (1815).

Sense and Sensibility (1811)
A novel by ▷ Jane Austen. A youthful version, *Elinor and Marianne*, has been lost. The revised novel was published in 1811.

The two heroines, Elinor and Marianne Dashwood, are fatherless sisters who live with their mother in comparative poverty, having been defrauded of more substantial income by their stepbrother, John Dashwood, and his arrogant and selfish wife. The title of the novel indicates the difference between the sisters: Elinor is practical and watches after the family affairs with sober good sense, and Marianne prides herself on the strength of her feelings and her contempt for material interests. Elinor is in love with a depressed and apparently dull young man, Edward Ferrars (brother of Mrs John Dashwood), while Marianne loves the handsome and glamorous John Willoughby. The superficial contrast between the sisters and their lovers is shown to be deceptive: Elinor's feelings are as deep as Marianne's but her sense of responsibility is greater and she keeps her sorrows to herself, whereas Marianne makes almost a virtue of the public exhibition of her grief, thus becoming a burden on her sister and her mother. In the end, the romantic-seeming Willoughby turns out to have given up Marianne from fear of losing a legacy, while the prosaic Edward gladly sacrifices the favour of a rich relative for the sake of marriage to Elinor.

Sensibility
The term 'sensibility', indicating the tendency to be easily and strongly affected by emotion, came into general use in the early 18th century. At this time writers and thinkers, such as the third Earl of Shaftesbury (1671–1713), in reaction against the practical, materialist philosophy of Thomas Hobbes (1588–1679) began to promote an idealistic, spiritual alternative, based on personal feeling. The essayist Joseph Addison (1672–1719) in 1711 defined modesty as 'an exquisite Sensibility', 'a kind of quick and delicate Feeling in the Soul'. By the middle of the 18th century the word 'sensibility' had grown in stature, indicating the capacity for compassion or altruism, and also the possession of good taste in the arts. The critic Joseph Warton (1722–1800) in 1756 declines to explain a subtle point since 'any reader of sensibility' will already have taken it. Laurence Sterne (1713–68) in his *Sentimental Journey* (1768) eulogizes 'Dear Sensibility! source unexhausted of all that's precious in our joys or costly in our sorrows!' The word remained fashionable in this sense in the early 19th century when ▷ Jane Austen used it in the title of her novel ▷ *Sense and Sensibility* (1811).

Recently critics have begun to refer to the period from about the time of the death of Alexander Pope in 1744 until the publication of ▷ *Lyrical Ballads* in 1798 as the 'Age of Sensibility'. This label is preferred to 'late Augustanism' or 'pre-Romanticism', since it stresses the distinctive characteristics of the period rather than relating it by negative contrast to a different one. The poets of this time, ▷ Thomas Gray, ▷ William Collins and ▷ William Cowper, share a distinctive emphasis on feeling as an end in itself, rather than as part of some larger philosophical scheme. This can be seen both in the resonant truisms of Gray's ▷ *Elegy* and *Eton College Ode*, and in the descriptive delicacy of Collins's *To Evening* or Cowper's *The Poplar-Field*. Even the conservative neo-classicist Samuel Johnson (1709–84) shows something of this sensibility in the emotional intensity of his Christian stoicism.

However, the cultivation of sensibility

also led to experiment and restlessness in poetic form. Emotional novelty was sought in exoticism and medievalism. The oral ▷ ballad was given respectability by ▷ Thomas Percy's ▷ *Reliques*, while ▷ James Macpherson, ▷ Thomas Chatterton, and ▷ Thomas Warton all adopted various medieval, ▷ 'Gothic' tastes or literary forms. These developments in poetry were paralleled in the 'Gothic story', ▷ *The Castle of Otranto* (1765) by ▷ Horace Walpole. The new intensity of feeling took a less exotic form in the profuse sentiment of Samuel Richardson's (1689–1761) novels, and also in the cult of sentimentalism promoted by Sterne's *A Sentimental Journey* and Henry Mackenzie's *The Man of Feeling* (1771).

Bib: Todd, J., *Sensibility*; Hilles, F. W., and Bloom, H. (eds.), *From Sensibility to Romanticism*; Frye, N., *Towards Defining an Age of Sensibility*.

September Massacre

An episode of the ▷ French Revolution, when fear of foreign invasion caused revolutionaries to massacre political prisoners between 2 and 5 September 1795.

Sermons

The word 'sermon' is used in English to denote a speech from a church pulpit for the edification of the audience, always in this context called a 'congregation'. The sermon considered as a means of communication had a central importance in English life until the 19th century, when universal literacy and the rise of the mass-circulation newspaper tended to eclipse it. At a popular level, it reached a larger audience than any other form of public communication. Chaucer's Pardoner in the *Canterbury Tales* demonstrates the power that a medieval preacher felt that he had over an ignorant and superstitious audience, but *The Pardoner's Tale* is partly a satire about how the sermon could be abused. The sermon was a means of religious and governmental (*eg* Elizabethan *Book of Homilies*) propaganda. Doctrine, speculative philosophy, social criticism, and ethical problems of daily life were all within the sphere of the sermon, and interested all ranks of society in one way or another.

During the 18th century however, there was a tendency for sermons to lose touch with the common people. The sermons of William Paley (1743–1805) owed their fame to his talents as a teacher, but they show mediocrity of thought and tepidity of feeling. Those of the novelist Laurence

Sterne (1713–68) (*Sermons of Mr Yorick*, 1760) of the poet ▷ George Crabbe and the editor ▷ Henrietta Maria Bowdler have merit (especially Sterne's) as literary essays in ethics, but that is what they are, rather than spiritual discourses. It was left to those outside the Anglican tradition, ▷ John Wesley, the founder of ▷ Methodism, and George Whitefield (1714–70) to address themselves to the less educated.

Bid: Henson, H. (ed.), *Selected English Sermons* (World's Classics); Sampson, A. (ed.), *Famous English Sermons*.

Serres, Olivia (1772–1834)

Miscellaneous writer and artist. Olivia Serres claimed to be the daughter of the Duke of Cumberland by a secret marriage, and in 1822 published *Statement to the English Nation* setting out her evidence for this declaration. Nothing came of it, however, and she died penniless leaving a vast collection of manuscripts on numerous subjects. Her published work includes a collection of poems, *Flights of Fancy* (1805), which is ostensibly sentimental but often idiosyncratically radical. *St Julian* (1808) is also sentimental in tone, but interesting for its indebtedness to ▷ Rousseau.

Seventeenth-century literature

The 17th century was one of the richest periods in the history of English literature, both for achievement and for variety. It also saw a revolution in the human mind, not only in Britain but elsewhere in Europe – a revolution which constitutes the birth of the modern outlook. The century begins with writers like ▷ William Shakespeare and John Donne (1572–1631) whose language fused thought and feeling in both poetry and prose; it ends with John Dryden (1631–1700) and John Locke (1632–1704), writers whose language was shaped by a new ideal of prose, who opposed 'judgement' to 'wit' – that is to say, the analytic to the synthetic powers of the mind. Another way of putting it is to say that the century opens with one of the most exciting periods of poetic drama in the whole history of Europe, and it closes with the most influential period of English ▷ satire, and the prose of fact which in the next century was to find its most ample form of expression in the novel.

We are in the habit of using the term 'Elizabethan drama' for this period of the English theatre, but in fact it was in the reign of James I, the ▷ Jacobean period, that this type of drama came to fruition. By 1600,

Shakespeare was only approaching his best work and Ben Jonson (1572–1637) was just beginning his career. The finest of this drama was the result of a precarious balance, which kept the long medieval past in mind together with the social and intellectual changes of the present, and communicated with the populace as well as with the court. Already by 1610, this balance was being upset; the elegant but superficial taste of the younger dramatists, Francis Beaumont (1584–1616) and John Fletcher (1579–1625), was turning a national drama into an upper-and middle-class London theatre, which has remained dominant to the present day. By the time of the Caroline drama of the reign of Charles I, this transformation was nearing completeness in the plays of Philip Massinger (1583–1640) and John Ford (1586–1640). But in the meantime, the peculiar genius of the best dramatists, especially Shakespeare, had helped to produce among the lyric poets the school now so much admired under the name of the Metaphysicals. The great Metaphysical poets (notably John Donne, George Herbert, 1593–1633, and Andrew Marvell, 1621–78) owe their name to the possession of a quality which is central to Shakespeare's genius: the capacity to unite oppositions of thought and of feeling under the control of a flexible, open, but poised intelligence; their poetry, like Shakespeare's work, thus expresses a peculiarly rich body of experience, united from different levels of the mind.

But the Metaphysicals were not the only fertile school of poets in the first half of the century, nor was Shakespearean drama the only kind from which poets could learn. Shakespeare's rival, Ben Jonson, was, as a dramatist, in isolated opposition to the Shakespearean drama. The difference lay partly in conceptions of form. Jonson imposed his form upon his matter; the confusion and violence of experience is shaped by a selective process which is a disciplining of the mind as well as a critical analysis of the subject. In his lyric poetry as well as in his dramas, this discipline shows itself in irony, proportion, and a union of strength with elegance. Jonson's example influenced the later Metaphysicals, notably Marvell, but it also led to a different school, not always to be sharply distinguished, which we know as the Cavalier Poets, such as, Thomas Carew (1594–1640) and Robert Herrick (1591–1674). Above all, Jonson's criteria anticipated the 'classicists' of the later part of the century, especially Dryden.

But yet another poet left an important legacy to the 17th century. This was Edmund Spenser (1552–99) who had perfected those qualities of musical cadence and sensuous imagery which many readers think of as essentially 'poetic'. He had his followers in the first 30 years of the 17th century, though none of note, but it is to him that ▷ John Milton owes most among his predecessors. In Milton, we have two very different 17th-century outlooks uneasily united: the love of all that is implied by the ▷ Renaissance, that is to say the revaluation of classical literature and the discovery of the glories of earthly civilization as opposed to those of a heavenly destiny, and devotion to Puritanism, implying the extreme Protestant belief that not only is all truth God's truth, but that the sole ultimate source of it is the Bible. This uneasy union produced in Milton the determination to impose on his society a Judaic-Christian conception of human destiny so grand that it compelled acceptance, and to use as his medium what was considered to be the grandest of all the ancient artistic forms, the ▷ epic.

▷ *Paradise Lost* (1667) was so impressive as an attempt to realize this impossible ambition, and so imposing in its union of the classical form and the biblical subject, that it has retained its power through three centuries. But Milton's sonorous eloquence, like Spenser's sensuous music, was a kind of magic that subdued the intellect rather than persuaded it. The unfortunate consequence was the common belief among 18th- and 19th-century poets that 'sublime' poetry should elevate the emotions while passing the intellect by. This Miltonic influence no doubt encouraged the exponents of reason like Locke (*Essay concerning Human Understanding*, 1690) to believe that poetry belongs to an immature stage of mental development, before the mind has acquired reason and respect for facts, the best medium for which is prose.

From the beginning of the century, prose writers showed signs of seeing their function as clarifying the reason as opposed to enlarging the imagination. This turning away from the imagination went naturally with a gradual relegation of religion. Francis Bacon (1561–1626), in his *Advancement of Learning* (1605), treats religion with respect and then ignores it, and he ends his few remarks on poetry with the sentence: 'But it is not good to stay too long in the theatre.' ▷ Shelley (in his *Defence of Poetry*, 1821) was nonetheless to consider Bacon himself to be a poet, but the vivid imagery which strikes out of his terse style is more functional than that of earlier prose writers. Bacon's main theme is the inductive method of acquiring knowledge through experiment, and all his prose, including his *Essays*, is essentially practical. Although the imaginative connotations are preserved, the dominant tendency in the first half of the century is to use prose descriptively and analytically. Thomas Browne's *Religio Medici* (1642–3) is written, like his other works, in the most sonorous prose in the English language, but Browne is defending his religious faith just because it exceeds his reason, and his poetic style (in contrast to that of the great sermon writers like John Donne) is partly a conscious contrivance. (In the Romantic period, it would have had some influence on ▷ Thomas De Quincey).

In the middle of the century, Thomas Hobbes published his treatise on political philosophy, *Leviathan* (1651) in which, with pungent ruthlessness, he forced his readers to face the 'facts' of human nature in their grimmest interpretation. After the ▷ Restoration of the Monarchy (1660), the historian of the Royal Society, Bishop Sprat, laid down the new standards that were to guide the prose writer: 'a close, naked, natural way of speaking; positive expressions; clear senses; a native easiness'. This is the prose we find in the dialogue of Restoration comedy, in the literary criticism of Dryden, and above all in the sceptical, reasonable philosophy of Locke. However, the spiritual life of the middle and lower classes was not yet permeated by this rationalism. The spirit of Puritanism, still biblical and poetic, is expressed in the spiritual autobiographies of the Puritan leaders, such as the Quaker George Fox (*Journal*, 1694), and, at its most impressive, that imaginative work *The Pilgrim's Progress* (1678), by the Baptist tinsmith, John Bunyan. In this work, the old ▷ allegories of the Middle Ages reach forward into the field of the novel, the new form which was to come into being in the 18th century.

Seward, Anna (1747–1809)

Poet and letter-writer. She was nicknamed 'The Swan of Lichfield', and James Boswell consulted her in the composition of his *Life of Samuel Johnson* (1791). Her poetical works were published by ▷ Sir Walter Scott in 1810, and her *Letters* appeared in 1811.

Shakespeare, William (1564–1616) – biography

Dramatist and poet. He was baptized on 26 April 1564; his birth is commemorated on 23 April, which happens also to be St George's Day, the festival of the patron saint of England. His father, John Shakespeare, was a Stratford-on-Avon merchant who dealt in gloves and probably other goods; his grandfather, Richard Shakespeare, was a yeoman, and his mother, Mary Arden, was the daughter of a local farmer who belonged to the local noble family of Arden, after whom the forest to the north of Stratford was named. John Shakespeare's affairs prospered at first, and in 1568 he was appointed to the highest office in the town – High Bailiff, equivalent to Mayor. A grammar school existed in Stratford, and since it was free to the sons of burgesses, it is generally assumed that William attended it. If he did, he probably received a good education in the Latin language; there is evidence that the sons of Stratford merchants were, or could be, well read and well educated. He married Anne Hathaway in 1582, and they had three children: Suzanna, born 1583, and the twin son and daughter, Hamnet and Judith, born 1585.

Thereafter Shakespeare's life is a blank, until we meet a reference to him in *A Groatsworth of Wit* (1592), an autobiographical pamphlet by the London playwright Robert Greene, who accuses him of plagiarism. By 1592, therefore, Shakespeare was already successfully embarked as a dramatist in London, but there is no clear evidence of when he went there. From 1592 to 1594, the London theatres were closed owing to epidemics of plague, and Shakespeare seems to have used the opportunity to make a reputation for himself as a narrative poet: his *Venus and Adonis* was published in 1593, and *The Rape of Lucrece* a year later. Both were dedicated to Henry Wriothesley, Earl of Southampton. He continued to prosper as a dramatist, and in the winter of 1594 was a leading member of the Lord Chamberlain's Men with whom he remained for the rest of his career. In 1596 his father acquired a coat of arms – the sign of a Gentleman – and in 1597 William bought New Place, the largest house in Stratford. There he probably established his father, who had been in financial difficulties since 1577. In 1592, John Shakespeare had been registered as a recusant; this might mean that he was a Catholic, but is more likely to show that he was trying to escape arrest for debt.

In 1598, Francis Meres, in his literary commentary *Palladis Tamia, Wit's Treasury*, mentions Shakespeare as one of the leading writers of the time, lists 12 of his plays, and mentions his sonnets as circulating privately; they were published in 1609. The

Lord Chamberlain's Men opened the Globe Theatre in 1598, and Shakespeare became a shareholder in it. After the accession of James I the company came under royal patronage, and were called the King's Men; this gave Shakespeare a status in the royal household. He is known to have been an actor as well as a playwright, but tradition associates him with small parts: Adam in *As You Like It*, and the Ghost in *Hamlet*. He may have retired to New Place in Stratford in 1610, but he continued his connections with London, and purchased a house in Blackfriars in 1613. In the same year, the Globe theatre was burnt down during a performance of the last play with which Shakespeare's name is associated, *Henry VIII*. His will is dated less than a month from his death. The fact that he left his 'second-best bed' to his wife is no evidence that he was on bad terms with her; the best one would naturally go with his main property to his elder daughter, who had married John Hall; his younger daughter, who had married Thomas Quiney, was also provided for, but his son, Hamnet, had died in childhood. His last direct descendant, Lady Barnard, died in 1670.

Owing to the fact that the subject-matter of biography was restricted until the mid-17th century to princes, statesmen and great soldiers, the documentary evidence of Shakespeare's life is, apart from the above facts, slight. His contemporaries, Christopher Marlowe and Ben Jonson are in some respects better documented because they involved themselves more with political events. Many legends and traditions have grown up about Shakespeare since near his own day, but they are untrustworthy. He was certainly one of the most successful English writers of his time; his income has been estimated at about £200 a year, considerable earnings for those days. After the death of Marlowe in 1593, his greatest rival was Ben Jonson, who criticized his want of art (in *Discoveries*, 1640), admired his character, and paid a noble tribute to him in the prefatory poem to the First Folio collection of his plays (1623).

Bib: Chambers, E. K., *William Shakespeare: A Study of Facts and Problems*, 2 vols.; Schoenbaum, S., *Shakespeare's Lives*; *William Shakespeare: A Documentary Life*.

Shakespeare – criticism

As with any author of the first greatness, different ages have appreciated different aspects of Shakespeare. In his own day, popular taste, according to Ben Jonson, particularly enjoyed *Titus Andronicus*, now regarded as one of the least interesting of his plays. John Dryden (1631–1700) (*Essay on Dramatic Poesy*), picked out *Richard II*; Samuel Johnson (1709–84) (*Preface to Shakespeare*, 1765) admired the comedies. It is possible to understand these preferences: *Titus* is the most bloodthirsty of all the plays, and suited the more vulgar tastes of an age in which executions were popular spectacles. Dryden and Johnson both belonged to neo-classical periods. Johnson, like Dryden, was troubled by the differences in Shakespeare's tragedies from the formalism of ancient Greek and 17th-century tragedy which the spirit of their period encouraged them to admire, and Johnson's warm humanity caused him to respond to the plays which displayed wide human appeal while their mode permitted some licence of form. Both Johnson and Dryden rose superior to the limitations of their period in according Shakespeare such greatness. The inheritor of Johnson's mantle as the most perceptive critic of Shakespeare in the 19th century is ▷ S. T. Coleridge, whose seminal lectures on Shakespeare were inspired by German ▷ Romanticism. In his letters ▷ John Keats offers some of the most enduringly valuable comments on Shakespeare's works before A. C. Bradley published *Shakespearean Tragedy* in 1904, which was to prove the most influential text on Shakespeare for two generations.

If the 20th century has not produced a Johnson, or Coleridge or Bradley in Shakespeare studies, Wilson Knight (*The Imperial Theme*, *The Crown of Life*), Harley Granville-Barker (*Preface to Shakespeare*) and others such as D. A. Traversi (*An Approach to Shakespeare*) and H. C. Goddard (*The Meaning of Shakespeare*) have all contributed to our deeper understanding of the plays and poetry. Shakespeare's education has been closely scrutinized by T. W. Baldwin in two volumes, *Shakespeare's Smalle Latin and Lesse Greeke*, and Geoffrey Bullough's eight volumes on Shakespeare's sources, *Narrative and Dramatic Sources of Shakespeare*, are indispensable to Shakespearean critics. Increasingly the critical debate has been conducted in a number of specialized journals, particularly the long-established *Shakespeare Jahrbuch*, *Shakespeare Survey*, *Shakespeare Studies*, and *Shakespeare Quarterly*. A few books are outstanding in their focus on particular aspects of Shakespeare, such as C. L. Barber's influential essay on Shakespearean comedy and the rituals of English folklore and country customs, *Shakespeare's Festive Comedy*, and Northrop Frye's archetypal study of comedy and romance, *A Natural Perspective*. Howard Felperin's distinguished book on Shakespeare's last plays, *Shakespearean Romance* and Janet Adelman's thought-provoking study of *Antony and Cleopatra* and its mythopoeic imagery in *The Common Liar* both reflect the influence of Frye in their sober and formally predicated approaches.

Of a more radical bent is Jan Kott's famous essay on *King Lear* in '*King Lear*, or *Endgame*' (1964) which argued the case for Shakespeare as our contemporary, with his finger imaginatively on the pulse of a dark, modern human predicament. On the same lines Peter Brook's famous production of *A Midsummer Night's Dream* in 1970 emancipated the play from its putative operatic and conformist frame and irretrievably altered our perception of it. By thus indicating the extent to which the theatre can influence interpretation of plays, Brook materially contributed to redirecting critical attention back to the stage.

Modern social and critical movements have made their impact felt in the field of Shakespeare studies: deconstruction, in the guise of a creative disintegration of the texts' organic status, and feminism provide the impetus for some of the most controversial writing on Shakespeare in the 1980s, as do 'cultural materialism' and particularly 'new historicism'. The latter in particular seems set to command a wide audience in the works of Stephen Greenblatt and Louis Montrose, whose work combines the scholarly scruples of the older tradition with an acute sceptical and self-critical awareness of the historical and epistemological contexts of literary criticism in society.

Bib: Bate, J., *Shakespeare and the English Romantic Imagination*. Bradley, A. C., *Shakespearean Tragedy*; Barber, C. L., *Shakespeare's Festive Comedy*; Coleridge, S. T., *Shakespearean Criticism*; Dollimore, J., *Radical Tragedy*; Dryden, J., *Essays*; Frye, N., *A Natural Perspective*; Greenblatt, S., *Renaissance Self-Fashioning*; Jardine, L., *Still Harping on Daughters*; Johnson, S., *On Shakespeare*.

Shakespeare – history of textual study
Apart from a scene sometimes ascribed to Shakespeare in the play *Sir Thomas More* (1596), none of Shakespeare's work has survived in manuscript. In his own lifetime, 18 of his plays were published in separate volumes, but this was probably without the author's permission, and therefore without his revisions and textual corrections. His non-dramatic poems, including the sonnets,

were also published during his lifetime. After his death, his fellow-actors, Heminges and Condell, published his collected plays (except *Pericles*) in the large, single volume known as the First Folio, and this was succeeded by the Second Folio (1632), and the Third (two editions), and Fourth in 1663, 1664 and 1685. The Second Folio regularized the division of the plays into Acts and Scenes, and the second issue of the Third added *Pericles*, as well as other plays which are certainly not by Shakespeare. In several important respects the Folio editions were unsatisfactory:

1 The texts of some (though not all) of the smaller quarto volumes of the plays published during the poet's lifetime differed materially from the text of even the First Folio, which in turn differed from the later folios.

2 The First Folio arranged the plays according to their kinds (Comedies, Histories, or Tragedies) and gave no indication of the order in which the plays were written.

3 There was no evidence that even the first editors had had access to the best manuscript texts, and there were evident errors in some passages, the fault of either the editors or their printers, and editors of the later Folios made alterations of their own. Consequently, there was plenty of work during the next two centuries for scholars to re-establish, as nearly as possible, Shakespeare's original text. Work also had to be done on the chronological order of the plays, discovery of the sources of their plots, philological investigations of linguistic peculiarities, and research into the conditions in which the plays were originally acted.

Two of the most eminent 18th-century writers published editions of the plays; these were Alexander Pope (in 1725 and 1728), and Samuel Johnson (in 1765). Neither, however, was a sound scholarly edition, though Johnson's was important for its critical Preface and annotations. Lewis Theobald (1688–1744) attacked Pope's poor scholarship in his *Shakespeare Restored* (1726), and published his own edition in 1734. He was the first enlightened editor, and did permanently useful work both in removing post-Shakespearean additions and alterations and in suggesting emendations of corrupt passages. After him came Steevens and Capell, who compared the original Quarto texts with the Folio ones, and ▷ Edmond Malone (1741–1812), the most eminent of the 18th-century Shakespeare scholars. In 1778 he made the first serious attempt to establish the chronological order of the plays, and in 1790 he brought out the best edition of them yet established.

Shakespearean scholarship in the 18th century was more the work of individuals than a collaborative enterprise. They saw many of the problems involved in estimating the relative values of the early texts, the possibilities of scholarly emendation of corrupt passages, and the necessity of eliminating the errors of unscholarly 17th- and 18th-century editors. This work culminated in the publication of 'Variorum' editions of the plays, 1803–21. But the establishment of a really sound text required the study of wider subject-matter: Shakespeare's work had to be estimated as a whole so that his development could be understood; philological study of the state of the language in his time was needed; historical events had to be examined for their possible relevance; many sources for the plots remained to be discovered; theatrical conditions and the relationship of Shakespeare to dramatists contemporary with him needed exploration; even handwriting was important, for the detection of possible misprinting. All this was the work of the collaborative scholarship of the 19th century. It was carried out by German scholars, by the English Shakespeare Societies led by Halliwell and Furnivall, and by the universities.

In the later 18th century Shakespeare became an inspiration to the movement in Germany for the emancipation of German culture from its long subjection to French culture, represented by the very different genius of Racine. A. W. Schlegel's remarkable translations (1797–1810) were fine enough to enable Germans to adopt Shakespeare as something like a national poet. German scholars such as Tieck, Ulrici, Gervinus and Franz adopted Shakespearean studies with thoroughness and enthusiasm. They stimulated the foundation of Shakespeare Societies in England, and in 1863–6 the Cambridge University Press was able to publish an edition of Shakespeare's works, which, in its revised form (1891–3), is substantially the text now generally in use.

There has been considerable editorial activity in the 20th century, and it was to be expected that the 'New Bibliography', spearheaded by A. W. Pollard, R. B. McKerrow and W. W. Greg would produce a major reconsideration of the Shakespearean text. In the end the fruit of their research, and particularly of McKerrow's brilliant *Prolegomena for the Oxford Shakespeare* (1939), needed to wait for nearly 40 years before they

were put to use by the editors of the *Oxford Shakespeare*, Gary Taylor and Stanley Wells. In the meantime Charlton Hinman produced two seminal volumes on the collations of the extant Folios in *The Printing and Proof-Reading of the First Folio* and incorporated his findings in *The Norton Facsimile: The First Folio of Shakespeare*, which remains a standard work of reference. All the major university and other presses turned their attention to re-editing Shakespeare in the late 1960s and early 1970s. At a time when Oxford University Press were printing two complete one-volume Shakespeares (one old spelling and another modern spelling) as well as a huge textual companion and the entire works in separate editions for the Oxford English Texts, Cambridge University Press published the first volume of Peter Blayney's exhaustive survey of the 'origins' of the First Quarto of *King Lear: The Texts of 'King Lear' and their Origins*. Cambridge, Methuen (New Arden), Macmillan and Longman have pursued similar goals: updating and editing afresh Shakespeare's works, each bringing to the canon a different approach. Whereas most of the editions have followed basically conservative principles, most have embraced to a greater or lesser degree the Oxford view of the plays as primarily works for the theatre. Increasingly Oxford's view of Shakespeare as a dramatist who regularly reshaped his plays in line with theatrical and aesthetic demands is gaining ground. The particular focus for this hypothesis has become the two-text (Quarto and Folio) *King Lear* which most editors now agree reflects two different versions of the play. The same editorial principles are being applied to other texts which reflect similar source situations such as *Richard III*, *Hamlet* and *Othello*. Among Oxford's most radical proposals are the printing of two versions of *King Lear*, the calling of Falstaff 'Oldcastle' in *Henry IV, Part I*, as well as boldly recreating the text of *Pericles*.

The history of Shakespeare editing in Britain towards the end of the 20th century is ultimately one of the creative disintegration of the shibboleths of traditional editorial policy, even if all the changes proposed by contemporary scholars do not find favour with posterity.

Bib: Bowers, F., *On Editing Shakespeare*; Greg, W. W., *The Shakespeare First Folio: Its Bibliographical and Textual History*; Honigmann, E. A. J., *The Stability of Shakespeare's Text*; McKerrow, R. B., *Prolegomena for the Oxford Shakespeare*;

Wells, S., *Re-Editing Shakespeare for the Modern Reader*.

Shakespeare's plays
Earliest publications. The first collected edition was the volume known as the First Folio (1623). This included all the plays now acknowledged to be by Shakespeare, with the exception of *Pericles*. It also includes *Henry·VIII*. Stationers (the profession then combining bookselling and publishing) were glad to bring out individual plays in quarto editions in his lifetime, however, and since there was no law of copyright these were often 'pirated', *ie* published without the permission of the author. On the whole, Shakespeare's company (the Lord Chamberlain's Men) did not want such publication, since printed editions enabled other acting companies to perform the plays in competition. 18 of Shakespeare's plays were published in this way, sometimes in more than one edition, and occasionally in editions that varied considerably. Since none of the plays has survived in the original manuscript, the task of modern editors is often to reconcile different quartos (where they exist) with each other, and any quartos that exist with corresponding versions in the First Folio. The following is a list of the separate editions of the plays, published while Shakespeare was alive or soon after his death, with dates of different editions where they substantially disagree with one another:

Titus Andronicus (1594)
Henry VI, Part II (1594)
Henry VI, Part III (1595)
Richard II (1597, 1608)
Richard III (1597)
Romeo and Juliet (1597, 1599)
Love's Labour's Lost (1598)
Henry IV, (Part I) (1598)
Henry IV, (Part II) (1600)
Henry V (1600)
A Midsummer Night's Dream (1600)
The Merchant of Venice (1600)
Much Ado About Nothing (1600)
The Merry Wives of Windsor (1602)
Hamlet (1603, 1604)
King Lear (1608)
Troilus and Cressida (1609)
Pericles (1609)
Othello (1622)

Order of composition. The First Folio does not print the plays in the order in which they were written. Scholars have had to work out their chronological order, on three

main kinds of evidence: **1** external evidence (*eg* records of production, publication); **2** internal evidence (*eg* allusions to contemporary events); **3** stylistic evidence. The following is an approximate chronological arrangement, though in some instances there is no certainty:

1590–91	Henry VI, Parts II and III
1591–92	Henry V, Part I
1592–93	Richard III
	The Comedy of Errors
1593–94	Titus Andronicus
	The Taming of the Shrew
	Two Gentlemen of Verona
1594–95	Love's Labour's Lost
	Romeo and Juliet
1595–96	Richard II
	A Midsummer Night's Dream
1596–97	King John
	The Merchant of Venice
1597–98	Henry IV, Parts I and II
1598–99	Much Ado about Nothing
	Henry V
1599–	
1600	Julius Caesar
	The Merry Wives of Windsor
	As You Like It
	Twelfth Night
1600–1	Hamlet
	Measure for Measure
1601–2	Troilus and Cressida
1602–3	All's Well that Ends Well
1604–5	Othello
	King Lear
1605–6	Macbeth
1606–7	Antony and Cleopatra
1607–8	Coriolanus
	Timon of Athens
1608–9	Pericles
1609–10	Cymbeline
1610–11	The Winter's Tale
1611–12	The Tempest

Shakespeare is now believed to have written all of *Henry VIII* and to have collaborated with Fletcher on *Two Noble Kinsmen*.

Shakespeare – Sonnets
First published in 1609, but there is no clear evidence for when they were written. They are commonly thought to date from 1595–9; Francis Meres in *Palladis Tamia* (1598) mentions that Shakespeare wrote sonnets. There are 154 sonnets; numbers 1–126 are addressed to a man (126 is in fact not a sonnet but a 12-line poem) and the remainder

are addressed to a woman – the so-called 'dark lady of the sonnets', since it is made clear that she is dark in hair and complexion. There has been much speculation about the dedication: 'To the only begetter of these ensuing sonnets Mr W.H. all happiness and that eternity promised by our everliving poet Wisheth the well-wishing adventurer in setting forth T.T.' 'T.T.' stands for Thomas Thorpe, the stationer (*ie* bookseller and publisher of the sonnets); speculation centres on what is meant by 'begetter' and who is meant by 'W.H.' W.H. may stand for the man (William Hughes?) who *procured* the manuscript of the sonnets for Thorpe, if that is what 'begetter' means. But if 'begetter' means 'inspirer', it has been conjectured that W.H. may be the inverted initials of Henry Wriothesley, 3rd Earl of Southampton, to whom Shakespeare had dedicated his *Venus and Adonis* and *The Rape of Lucrece*, or they may stand for William Herbert, Earl of Pembroke, or for someone else. Guesses have also been made as to the identity of the 'dark lady', who has been thought by some to be Mary Fitton, a Maid of Honour at Court who was a mistress of William Herbert. There is too little evidence for profitable conjecture on either subject.

Critics and scholars disagree about the extent to which the sonnets are autobiographical (and if so what they express) or whether they are 'literary exercises' without a personal theme. A middle view is that they are exploratory of personal relations in friendship and in love, and that some of them rehearse themes later dramatized in the plays – for instance 94 suggests the character of Angelo in *Measure for Measure*, and the recurrent concern with the destructiveness of time seems to look forward to *Troilus and Cressida* and the great tragedies. Since it is unknown whether the edition of 1609 is a reliable version, there is also some doubt whether the order of the sonnets in it is that intended by Shakespeare; most scholars see little reason to question it.

One of the most valuable recent editions of the *Sonnets* is Stephen Booth's which uses the 1609 text, rightly accepting its ordering of the poetry as binding. Booth's edition compares the modern text with the Quarto versions at each stage. But if his extensive notes are instructive, they also tend to be too comprehensive in their suggestions of infinite and ultimately meaningless ambiguities in the text. John Kerrigan's edition of *The Sonnets and A Lover's Complaint* provides a sensitive text, informative notes and does justice to the often neglected *A Lover's Complaint*. Kerrigan authoritatively attributes the poem to

Shakespeare and offers the best commentary on it to date.
Bib: Leishman, J.B., *Themes and Variations in Shakespeare's Sonnets*; Schaar, C., *Elizabethan Sonnet Themes and the dating of Shakespeare's Sonnets*; Smith, H., *The Tension of the Lyre: Poetry in Shakespeare's Sonnets*.

Shelley, Mary Wollstonecraft (1797–1851)
The only daughter of feminist ▷ Mary Wollstonecraft and radical philosopher ▷ William Godwin, her mother having died a few days after her birth. Her father remarried in 1801 but Mary found her stepmother unsympathetic and remained rather close to her father despite his cold manner. She idolized her own mother, and educated herself through contact with her father's intellectual circle and her own hard study. She met ▷ Percy Bysshe Shelley in 1812 and on return from an extended visit to friends in 1814 became very close to him. He was in the midst of separating from his wife Harriet, and within a couple of months he and Mary left England together, marrying in 1816 after Harriet's suicide. They had a devoted but difficult relationship, only one of their children surviving childhood, Godwin pressing them for loans and Shelley's father Timothy making only a small allowance for the child, Percy. After Shelley's death in 1822 Mary stayed a short while in Italy, then returned to London where she continued to write novels, produced an account of her travels with Percy in Europe and edited Shelley's poetry and prose, but proved too exhausted to write his biography, which she abandoned.
▷ *Frankenstein, or the Modern Prometheus* (1817) was her first and most famous novel, apparently inspired by a dream. *The Last Man* (1826) has characters based on Shelley and ▷ Byron, and *Lodore* (1835) contains much that is autobiographical. *Mathilda* (1819) and *Valperga* (1823) are among her other novels; *Rambles in Germany and Italy* (1844) was well received; she also published many short stories in annuals like *The Keepsake*. Her ▷ diary, recently published as *The Journals of Mary Shelley*, provides a fascinating account of her life and her attitudes to writing.
▷ Feminism.
Bib: Jones, F. L. (ed.), *Mary Shelley's Journal* and *The Letters of Mary Shelley*; Lyles, W. H., *Mary Shelley: An Annotated Biography*; Nitchie, E., *Mary Shelley*; Poovey, M., *The Proper Lady and the Woman Writer*; Gilbert, S. and Gubar, S., *The Madwoman in the Attic*; Fleenor, J., *The Female Gothic*.

Shelley, Percy Bysshe (1792–1822)
Poet. He was born into an aristocratic family in Sussex, and was educated at Eton and ▷ Oxford, from which he was expelled in 1811 for circulating a pamphlet, *The Necessity of Atheism*. He eloped with and married Harriet Westbrook, who was then only 16, and whom he left after three years. He travelled abroad in 1814 with Mary Wollstonecraft Godwin, daughter of the ▷ feminist ▷ Mary Wollstonecraft and the philosopher ▷ William Godwin, whose extreme rationalism had attracted the young poet. At one point, in accordance with his idealistic notions of free love, Shelley proposed that both Harriet and Mary should live together with him. Accompanied by Mary's step-sister, Claire Clairmont, he and Mary travelled to Switzerland where they joined ▷ Lord Byron, with whom Shelley made a close friendship. Harriet drowned herself in the Serpentine in 1816 and Shelley married Mary, though he continued to develop intense platonic relationships with other women. They moved to Lerici in Italy and in 1822 he was drowned while sailing, in circumstances which suggested that he made no attempt to save himself.

Shelley's earliest writings, produced while he was at Eton and Oxford, are ▷ Gothic romances in the style of ▷ 'Monk' Lewis. His first important poem was the atheistic *Queen Mab* (1813) in the tradition of the irregular ▷ ode. In 1816 appeared the ▷ blank verse *Alastor; or the Spirit of Solitude*, in which an exquisitely sensitive young poet is drawn by a highly erotic vision, representing 'truth and virtue . . . And lofty hopes of divine liberty', across exotic eastern landscapes, only to die, disappointed. *The Revolt of Islam* (1817) in ▷ Spenserian stanzas, preaches bloodless revolution, and has a similar beautiful youth as its protagonist. ▷ *Mont Blanc*, published in the same year, is a less self-indulgent work, in which Shelley turns his intellectual scepticism on the conventional piety of such poems as ▷ Samuel Taylor Coleridge's *Hymn Before Sun-rise in the Vale of Chamouni* (1802), which describes the same landscape. Where Coleridge attributes the sublime beauty of nature to a 'Great Hierarch', the atheist Shelley attributes it (like Coleridge himself in ▷ *Dejection: An Ode*) to 'the human mind's imaginings'. In ▷ *Julian and Maddalo* (written 1818, published 1824), he describes in irregularly rhyming ▷ couplets a visit to a madhouse in Venice in the company of Byron, who appears in the guise of an Italian nobleman.

In 1819 Shelley published *The Cenci*, a play in the Elizabethan style, and composed the 'lyrical drama', ▷ *Prometheus Unbound* (1820). He also wrote the *Ode to the West Wind* in which his abstract symbolism is, for once, brilliantly controlled, and makes the natural force of the wind into a convincing metaphor for political revolution. The news of the ▷ 'Peterloo Massacre' in Manchester on August 16, 1819, prompted ▷ *The Mask of Anarchy* (published 1832), a poem of superb rhetoric, calling upon the men of England to overthrow their oppressors. This was followed by *To a Skylark* (1820), the famous elegy on ▷ John Keats, ▷ *Adonais* (1821), *The Witch of Atlas* (published 1824), and another 'lyrical drama', *Hellas* (1822), inspired by the struggle for Greek independence from Turkey. He was working on *The Triumph of Life* when he died, a grimly garish dream-allegory in ▷ *terza rima* in which the poet contemplates the gory but awesome pageant of history, in company with the spirit of ▷ Jean-Jacques Rousseau. Shelley's prose ▷ *Defence of Poetry* (written 1821; published 1840) was written in answer to *The Four Ages of Poetry* by his friend ▷ Thomas Love Peacock, who argued that poetry was an obsolete art. Shelley retorts boldly that poets are 'the unacknowledged legislators of the world'.

Shelley can be an extremely irritating poet, particularly when congratulating himself on the exquisiteness of his own sensibility, or indulging in dreamy abstraction and elaborately theatrical symbolism. In his best work, however, he actually achieves the sublimity about which he talks so much, and when dealing with intellectual or political issues he can be eloquently lucid and incisive.
Bib: Blunden, E., *Life*; Barcus, J. E., *Shelley: The Critical Heritage*; Rogers, N., *Shelley at Work*; Webb, T., *Shelley: A Voice Not Understood*; Leighton, A., *Shelley and the Sublime*; Foot, P., *Red Shelley*; Dawson, P. M. S., *The Unacknowledged Legislator: Shelley and Politics*; Swinden, P. (ed.), *Shelley: Shorter Poems* (Macmillan Casebook); Everest, K., *The Poems of Shelley*.

Shepherd's Calender, The (1827)
▷ Clare, John.

Sheraton, Thomas (1751–1806)
Next to Thomas Chippendale (1718–79) the most famous English furniture designer. His reputation, which began about 1790, was built up on his severe and graceful style; later, under the influence of French Empire furniture, his designs became much more

elaborate. He had many imitators, and the name 'Sheraton' is usually associated with a general style rather than with the works of the original master.

Sheridan, Richard Brinsley (1751–1816)
Dramatist and politician. Like many dramatists of note writing in English during the 18th and 19th centuries, he was of Irish extraction, born in Dublin. His courtship of his future wife, Elizabeth Linley, began with his carrying her off to a French nunnery to save her from the attentions of a suitor to whom she objected; he returned to fight two duels with his rival; in 1773 his secret marriage to her in France was publicly recognized. In 1776 he became principal director and, a little later, sole proprietor of the ▷ Drury Lane Theatre in London; it was twice burnt down and rebuilt during his proprietorship. He entered Parliament in 1780, and was famous for his oratory there; his support for the Independence of the American Colonies caused the American Congress to offer him £20,000, which he refused. His most famous oratorical exploit was his impeachment of Warren Hastings in 1787. During the ▷ French Revolution, he supported the ▷ Whig leader, ▷ Fox, in opposing military intervention against France. Later he held an independent position politically, but he was influential, partly owing to his friendship with the Prince Regent (later George IV). He ended his life deeply in debt.

His memorable plays are *The Rivals* (1775), *The School for Scandal* (1777), and *The Critic* (1779); they show a reaction against the sentimental comedy which had dominated the English theatre for much of the 18th century, and the first two belong to a revival of the Comedy of Manners which had been dominant at the beginning of it. They are still appreciated for the freshness of their dialogue and the ingenuity of their comic situations. Other plays: *St Patrick's Day* (1775); *The Duenna* (a comic opera, 1775); *A Trip to Scarborough* (1777), and the tragedy *Pizarro* (1799).
Bib: Sichel, W., *Life*; Nicoll, A., *A History of Late Eighteenth-century Drama*; Sadleir, T. H., *The Political Career of Sheridan*; Danziger, M. K., *Oliver Goldsmith and Richard Brinsley Sheridan*.

Sherwood, Mary Martha (1775–1851)
Novelist, diarist, autobiographer, but mainly known as a children's author. Mary Sherwood began writing at seventeen in order to help fund the school in which she was a pupil (*The*

Traditions was published by ▷ Minerva in 1795), and she continued working on novels in order to support, first her parents and siblings, and later her husband and children. She married her cousin Henry Sherwood in 1805 and they went to India as missionaries. Her two most famous books are *Little Henry and His Bearer* (1815) and *The Fairchild Family* (1818; second and third parts were published in 1842 and 1847). This last book was immensely popular, partly because its overtly moralizing tone is neatly undercut with a delight in gruesome details and genuinely scary passages. In the later, ▷ Victorian, editions these parts were considered too unpleasant for the young and were expurgated. From then on, the book declined in popularity.
Bib: Cutt, M.N., *Mrs Sherwood and Her Books for Children*.

Siddons, Sarah (1755–1831)
Actress. The most celebrated woman on the stage in the 18th century. She was the eldest child of the actor-manager Roger Kemble and Sarah (née Ward), and was born into what became an important acting dynasty, although her sister, ▷ Ann Hutton, became estranged from the family and earned her living as writer. Siddons began acting as a child, including the part of Ariel in a performance of the Dryden/D'Avenant version of ▷ Shakespeare's *The Tempest*, in which her future husband, William Siddons (1744–1808), played Hyppolito. She fought her parents' disapproval in order to marry him, in 1773, and the couple continued acting in the provinces. David Garrick (1717–79) engaged her for a season at ▷ Drury Lane, 1775–76, but her first appearances there were poorly received. Her fortunes turned during a visit to Manchester, and her reputation as an actress was consolidated at Bristol and at ▷ Bath. In 1782 she appeared again at Drury Lane, playing Isabella in Garrick's version of Thomas Southerne's *The Fatal Marriage* (1694). Her triumph was immediate, and she went on to play a succession of major roles with the company, including Belvidera in Otway's *Venice Preserv'd* (1682). It is said that people breakfasted near the theatre, so as to be first in the queue for tickets to see her, some coming from as far away as Newcastle, and prices rose to as much as a hundred guineas. Contemporaries commented on her beauty, stately dignity, and expressiveness, as well as her articulacy, so that not a word was lost. Her capacity to convey passion and grief was legendary. But she was sometimes

criticized for her lack of variety, was poor in comic roles, and although she had many friends in high places, she had a reputation for being difficult to work with, and mean with money.

In 1785 Siddons played her most famous part, Lady Macbeth, for the first time, later performing it on occasion by royal command. She added to her repertoire Cordelia, Cleopatra, Desdemona, Rosalind in *As You Like It*, other major Shakespearian roles and many other roles, some written especially for her. Her career was interrupted only for brief intervals by the births of her seven children. In 1803 she followed her brother ▷ John Philip Kemble to Covent Garden. In old age she became fat and had to be helped out of a chair, the fact disguised by other actresses being similarly treated. Widowed in 1805, Siddons retired in 1812, afterwards appearing only at special benefits.

Bib: Boaden, J., *Memoirs of Mrs Siddons* (2 vols); Campbell, T., *Life of Mrs Siddons*; Manvell, R., *Sarah Siddons*; Kelly, L., *The Kemble Era: John Philip and the London Stage*.

Sign

This is the term used by ▷ Ferdinand de Saussure in his *Course in General Linguistics* (1915) to refer to any linguistic unit through which meaning is produced. In Saussure's theory, the *sign* is the combination of two discrete elements, the *signifier* (form which signifies) and the *signified* (idea signified). In the phrase 'A rose by any other name would smell as sweet', the word 'rose' is the signifier and the 'concept of a rose' is the signified.

Signifier and signified are distinct aspects of the sign, but exist only within it. One important aspect of Saussure's definition of the sign is that any particular combination of signifier and signified is *arbitrary*. So a 'rose' could be called a 'chrysanthemum' or a 'telephone', but would still be as aromatic. Saussure's perceptions have been very influential in the development of ways of discussing the processes through which meaning is achieved.

▷ Langue; Parole; Structuralism; Post-structuralism; Discourse; Barthes, Roland; Derrida, Jacques.

Silver-fork novels

Novels of fashion which took as their setting the society of the wealthy upper classes and which were popular at the beginning of the 19th century. Even at the time there was debate as to whether these novels

unquestioningly praised the seemingly empty lives of their heroes and heroines (the term comes from 'silver-fork polisher', which means to compliment those wealthy enough to possess such cutlery), or whether they were in fact subtle satires revealing upper-class hypocrisy. These two aspects may seen to be represented by ▷ William Hazlitt, who referred to silver-fork novelists as 'dandy writers' (*The Examiner*, 1827), and by the ▷ Victorian novelist Edward Bulwer Lytton (1803–73) himself described as such an author, who defended his work as an exposé of the fashionable classes rather than an accolade to them. Other silver-fork novelists include: ▷ Marguerite Blessington, ▷ Charlotte Bury, ▷ Susan Ferrier, ▷ Catherine Gore, ▷ Lady Caroline Lamb, ▷ Frances Trollope.

Bib: Adburgham, A., *Silver Fork Society: Fashionable Life and Literature 1814–1840*; Rosa, M.W., *The Silver-fork School*.

Sixteenth-century literature

In the 16th century changes in English society produced an extraordinary release of radical energies, particularly in the last decade. The powerful feudal system gave place to a new aristocracy and the growth of a new class: that of the country gentlefolk and of the city merchants. The Church ceased to be part of an international organization and became part of the national polity, under the authority of the Crown, and after a struggle for survival, the nation became succinctly nationalistic.

Yet in some respects the ▷ Middle Ages died slowly in England. Lord Berners's translation (1525) of the 14th-century *Chronicles* of Froissart belongs with the prose of Malory's *Morte d'Arthur* (1469–70), and Sir Thomas More's principal work in English, *The History of King Richard III* (written 1513?), is medieval in spirit.

The language of prose made notable advances in the 16th century. It is significant that much of the finest prose was about education, such as Sir Thomas Elyot's *Governor* (1531) and Roger Ascham's *The Schoolmaster* (pub 1570), and some of it arose out of the religious changes, notably William Tyndale's (1492–1536) version of the New Testament, the Sermons of Latimer, and Cranmer's noble *Book of Common Prayer* (1549 and 1552).

In poetry, the same tentative movement away from the Middle Ages occurred. John Skelton (1460–1529) has more vitality than the English (as distinct from Scottish) poets of the 15th century. Thomas Wyatt's (1503–42) poetry has a strong individuality and his rhythms, though often subtle, seem to be suspended between the roughness of the 15th century and the smoothness which Chaucer (1340–1400) had introduced, thereby creating a tension redolent of the changing social position of the Tudor courtier.

Henry Howard, Earl of Surrey (1517–47) and Thomas Sackville (1536–1608) are less interesting than Wyatt, but their work is moving closer to the smooth handling of language which the Elizabethans prized so much in the ▷ sonnets of Sir Philip Sidney (pub 1591) and in Spenser from *The Shepherd's Calendar* (1579) to *The Faerie Queene* (1596).

The Morality Play style of drama continued into the 16th century although its content became less religious and more secular, as in Skelton's *Magnificence* (1516?) and the *Satire of the Three Estates* (1540) by the Scots poet David Lindsay. A lighter kind of play called the Interlude moved towards the first pure comedies, *Ralph Roister Doister* (written 1551?) and *Gammer Gurton's Needle* (1556). Meanwhile the Morality Play could be said to have become secular and (often) political, and tended to evolve into the historical drama, such as *Gorboduc* (1561) by Sackville and Norton, and *Cambyses* (1569) by Preston. Preston was a scholar; Sackville was an aristocrat. Now that the drama had lost its roots in the Church and the town rituals, it needed thoroughly professional writers to give it a fully developed form and life of its own. A group of just such writers – Thomas Kyd (1558–94), John Lyly (1554–1606), George Peele (1556–96), Robert Greene (1558–92) and Christopher Marlowe (1564–93), collectively known as the University Wits – began work in the 1580s. They evolved among them a self-confident art of the theatre, and ▷ Shakespeare in his first decade (from *Henry VI* to *Hamlet*) was indebted to them.

These new writers, including Shakespeare himself, formed a new social phenomenon: the professional man of letters, who was not a nobleman like Wyatt, Surrey or Sidney, practising literature as part of the aristocratic life, nor a scholar or churchman like Ascham or Tyndale, practising it as a by-product of his profession, nor a court poet as Chaucer had been and Spenser was, practising it partly with a view to receiving court emoluments, but a writer who depended on monetary 'takings' from the public theatre. They contributed to the extraordinary vitality of the 1590s, not only in the drama but in prose pamphleteering and the kind of romance known as the Elizabethan novel, in which Thomas Nashe (1567–1601), Thomas Lodge (1558–1625) and Thomas Deloney (1543–1600) were among the foremost practitioners.

In the 1590s the drama, non-dramatic poetry of all kinds but notably the sonnet and the lyric, and prose including not only pamphleteers but the great philosophical writing of Richard Hooker (*Laws of Ecclesiastical Polity*, 1593–7) developed in new ways. The poetry has an extraordinary range of style, from the highly wrought music of Spenser's *Faerie Queene* to the involved and complex thought of John Donne's (1572–1631) *Songs and Sonnets*. Literary criticism has also made its beginnings with Puttenham's *Art of English Poetry* (pub 1589) and Sidney's *Apologie for Poetry* (pub 1598). There were also a number of translations in the period; ▷ Italian and ▷ French writing and thought, as well as the ancient classics (above all, the philosophy of ▷ Plato and the critical theory of ▷ Horace and, through the Italians, ▷ Aristotle) contributed a large part of the English literary Renaissance.

Sleath, Eleanor (c 1800)

Novelist. Sleath wrote six ▷ Gothic novels for ▷ Minerva. While mocked by ▷ Jane Austen for her unsophisticated style, Sleath's novels were packed full of all the usual Gothic ingredients (ghosts, castles, disguises and villainy), have fast-paced narratives, and are altogether enjoyable, mainly because they are so utterly unpretentious. *Orphan of the Rhine* (1798) and *The Nocturnal Minstrel, or The Spirit of the Wood* (1810) have historical settings and beautiful heroines who although crossed by fate and deceived by scoundrels triumph in the end. *The Bristol Heiress, or The Errors of Education* begins slowly and seems to be a satire of polite society, but quickly improves when the plot transfers to a strange, haunted castle in Cumberland.

Smith, Adam (1723–90)

Political economist. His important work was *An Enquiry into the Nature and Causes of the Wealth of Nations* – always referred to as *The Wealth of Nations* – published in 1776, at the outbreak of the rebellion of the American colonists, who, he predicted, 'will be one of the foremost nations of the world'. The especial influence of this book comes from his discussion of the function of the state in the degree and kind of control it should exercise over the activities of society, and in particular, of trade. He concluded that the traditional mercantile system (nowadays called 'protection') was based on a misunderstanding of the nature of wealth, and that nations prospered to the extent that governments allowed trade to remain freely competitive, unrestrained by taxes intended to protect the economy of a nation from competiton from other nations. His opinions became increasingly influential and eventually dominant in British economics during the first half of the 19th century; his opposition to *unnecessary* interference by the government in trade and society became harmful in that it was interpreted by later governments as an excuse not to remedy social abuses arising from industrialism.

Smith, Charlotte (1749–1806)

Novelist and poet. Charlotte Smith wrote poetry because that was her first love and novels because, after her husband was imprisoned for debt, she needed the money for herself and her large family. The poetry, including *Elegiac Sonnets, and Other Essays* (1784) and *The Emigrants* (1793) was admired by ▷ Leigh Hunt, while her novels were praised by ▷ Sir Walter Scott and influenced ▷ Ann Radcliffe. Her ironic and spare writing was partly based on her own experiences; for example, in *Emmeline, The Orphan of the Castle* (1788), the male characters are weak in comparison to the strong and mutually supportive female protagonists, while *The Banished Man* (1794) satirizes a woman writer surmounted by difficulties. This self-irony also occurs in *Elegiac Sonnets* (▷ elegy):

The partial Muse, has from my earliest hours
  Smiled on the rugged path I'm doomed
to tread,
And still with sportive hand has snatch'd
  wild flowers,
  To weave fantastic garlands for my head:
But far, far happier is the lot of those
  Who never learn'd her dear delusive art.

Of all her novels *The Old Manor House* (1793) is considered her best work, and is the most readily accessible to a 20th-century readership. She also produced an excellent ▷ translation of Prevost's *Manon Lescaut* (1786), but this was withdrawn because it was considered immoral.
  ▷ French literature in England.
Bib: Bowstead, D., *Fettered or Free? British Women Novelists, 1670–1815*; Hillbish, F.M.A., *Charlotte Smith, Poet and Novelist*; Kelly, G., *The English Jacobin Novel*; Todd, J., *Sensibility: An Introduction.*

Smith, Horatio (1779–1849)

Poet and novelist. Horatio Smith (also known as 'Horace') collaborated with his brother ▷ James Smith on ▷ *Rejected Addresses* (1812) and *Horace in London* (1813), extremely popular imitations of ▷ Horace's ▷ odes. Horatio went on to write historical romances in the style of ▷ Scott, including *Brambletye House* (1826) and *The Tor Hill* (1846).

Smith, James (1775–1839)

Poet. James was the brother of ▷ Horatio Smith, with whom he wrote ▷ *Rejected Addresses* (1812) and *Horace in London* (1813), ▷ odes in imitation of ▷ Horace.

Songs of Innocence and Experience (1789/1794)

Two collections of lyric poems by ▷ William Blake, engraved and illuminated by hand. The *Songs of Innocence* were completed in 1789 and *The Songs of Experience* were added in an enlarged edition in 1794. They were intended to be read by children, and although frequently profound and complex, are perfectly lucid and easy to comprehend. They present 'the Two Contrary States of the Human Soul', and are thus complementary, since in Blake's dialectical view 'Without Contraries is no progression'. The world of Innocence is without morality, repression or fear, and in Blake's dynamic interpretation of Christian mythology, unfallen. Inevitably some of the *Innocence* poems, such as *The Lamb* and *A Cradle Song*, seem sentimental and oversweet to the adult, fallen reader, while others, such as *Holy Thursday* and *The Chimney Sweeper* can seem highly ironic in their trusting attitude towards corrupt parental and political authority. But irony is no part of Innocence, and the *Experience* counterparts to these poems are in no sense a debunking of the *Innocence* versions. However it must be admitted that the bitter social criticism and moral indignation of *Experience* produce more memorable verse (though again perhaps this is more the case for the adult reader than the child). *The Tyger, The Clod and the Pebble*, and *The Sick Rose*, are among the most concentrated symbolic poems in the language, remarkable for their combination of emotional complexity and intellectual clarity. It is characteristic of Blake's dialectical approach that the later poem *To Tirzah*, added to *Experience* in the 1801 edition, flatly contradicts the sexual libertarianism of the other poems in the *Experience* collection, depicting the freeing of the soul from its physical bonds.

Sonnet
A short poem of 14 lines, and a rhyme
scheme restricted by one or other of a
variety of principles. The most famous
pattern is called the 'Petrarchan sonnet',
from its masterly use by the ▷ Italian poet
Petrarch. This divides naturally into an
eight-line stanza (octave) rhyming *abba abba*,
and a six-line stanza in which two or three
rhymes may occur; the two stanzas provide
also for contrast in attitude to the theme.
The origin of the sonnet is unknown, but
its earliest examples date from the 13th
century in Europe, although it did not reach
England until the 16th century. The immense
popularity of the form perhaps derives from
its combination of discipline, musicality and
amplitude. The subject-matter is commonly
love, but after the 16th century it becomes, at
least in England, much more varied.

The first writers of sonnets in England
were Sir Thomas Wyatt (1503–42) and
Henry Howard Surrey (?1517–47); the popular
anthology *Tottel's Miscellany* (1559) made their
experiments widely known. The first really
fine sonnet sequence was Sir Philip Sidney's
(1554–86) *Astrophil and Stella*. Its publication
in 1591 set an eagerly followed fashion for
its distinctively English form. This consisted
of a single stanza of 14 lines concluding in a
▷ couplet; it is thought that the comparative
scarcity of rhyming words in the English
language may be the explanation of the
greater number of rhymes and freedom in the
rhyming scheme in contrast to the Petrarchan
form. The greatest of the succeeding
sequences was undoubtedly ▷ Shakespeare's.

The sonnet form continued to be used
after 1600, notably by ▷ John Milton, but
much less for amorous themes and more
for religious ones or for expressions of other
forms of personal experience (*eg* Milton's *On
his Blindness*) or for political declamation.
Milton used the Petrarchan rhyme scheme,
but he kept the English form of using a
single stanza. From the mid-17th to mid-18th
century the different style of thought and
feeling suggested by the heroic couplet kept
the sonnet out of use; the cult of sentiment by
poets such as ▷ Thomas Gray and ▷ William
Cowper then brought it back, but a real
revival had to wait for the first 30 years of the
19th century in the work of the ▷ Romantics
– especially ▷ William Wordsworth, who
used it freely, ▷ John Keats, who wrote
few, but some of them among his best short
poems, and ▷ Percy Bysshe Shelley whose
▷ *Ozymandias* sonnet is one of the best of
all his poems. The Romantic poets tended to
follow the Miltonic example both in form and
subject-matter.

Southey, Robert (1774–1843)
Poet and historian. He was a friend of
▷ Samuel Taylor Coleridge (they married
sisters) and also of ▷ William Wordsworth.
Southey shared their revolutionary ardour
in the 1790s, but his opinions, like theirs,
became conservative at about the turn of
the century, and when the Tory ▷ *Quarterly
Review* was founded in 1809 he became one of
its leading contributors. He was made ▷ Poet
Laureate in 1813. In 1839 he married the
poet ▷ Caroline Bowles with whom he had
been friends for twenty years; she nursed him
through his last years of ill-health. Southey
wrote long heroic ▷ epics (*Thalaba*, 1801;
Madoc, 1805; *Roderick*, 1814) which at the
time were much admired. The best known
of his shorter poems is *The Battle of Blenheim*.
He wrote several historical works in prose,
including *The Life of Nelson* (1813) and *A
History of the Peninsular War* (1823–32). His
change in political opinion, and in particular
his position as Poet Laureate, drew the fire
of the second generation of Romantic poets,
and he lacked the poetic originality which
partially redeemed Wordsworth and Coleridge
in their eyes. In 1821 his poem ▷ *A Vision
of Judgement*, describing the admission of
George III into heaven, provoked ▷ Byron's
▷ *The Vision of Judgement*, with its brilliant
caricature of Southey as servile turncoat
and bumbling hack: 'He had written much
blank verse, and blanker prose,/ And more of
both than anybody knows.' He also features
as Mr Feathernest in ▷ Thomas Love
Peacock's satirical novel ▷ *Melincourt* (1817).
▷ Pantisocracy.
Bib: Curry, K., *Southey*; Madden, L. (ed.),
Robert Southey: The Critical Heritage.

Spanish influence on English literature
The earliest translation of a Spanish
masterpiece into any language was that
of Cervantes's *Don Quixote* (1605–15) by
Thomas Shelton in 1612 (Part I) and 1620
(Part II). Of all Spanish texts, *Don Quixote*
was to have the most profound influence on
English literature: in the 17th century Francis
Beaumont's *The Knight of the Burning Pestle*
(1607) and Samuel Butler's *Hudibras* (1663)
utilize the comic elements of the novel,
while Philip Massinger's *The Renegado* (1624)
combines material from *Don Quixote* together
with Cervantes's play *Los Baños de Argel*
(1615). In the 18th century, Henry Fielding's
Don Quixote in England (1734) and Laurence

Sterne's *Tristram Shandy* (1760-7), and in the 19th century the novels of ▷ Walter Scott and Charles Dickens perpetuate English indebtedness to Cervantes.

The 16th and 17th centuries in Spain are known as the Golden Age, which paralleled in quality, but greatly exceeded in abundance of texts, the creativity of the Elizabethan and Jacobean ages in England. The plays of Pedro Calderón de la Barca (1600-81) have often been compared to those of ▷ Shakespeare, for example by ▷ Shelley, who learned Spanish in order to read Calderón's dramas and partially translated into English Calderón's famous religious drama, *El mágico prodigioso* (*The Wonder-Working Magician*, 1637). Shelley also admired *La cisma de Inglaterra* (*The Schism of England*, perf. 1627), a play dealing with the same subject as Shakespeare's *Henry VIII*.

Translation has inevitably played an important role in the interrelationship between Spanish and English literatures, but occasionally the two cultures actually converge, as in the English poetry of the Spanish romantic poet and intellectual, Joseph Blanco White (1775-1841) whose ▷ sonnet, 'To Night', appears in *The Oxford Book of English Verse 1250-1918* (ed. A. Quiller-Couch).

Spence, Elizabeth Isabella (1768-1832)

Novelist and travel writer. Spence began writing for amusement, but when she was orphaned in 1786 she gradually began to use her writing as a means of support. Her early work consists of rather banal accounts of her travels within Britain and of the people she met, including *Summer Excursions* (1809; England and Wales) and *Letters From the Highlands* (1816; Scotland). The novels which followed attempted to retain the tone of ▷ travel writing by mixing regional history and descriptions of local scenes with fictional characters and narrative, and include *A Traveller's Tale of the Last Century* (1819), *Old Stories* (1822) and *How to be Rid of a Wife* (1823).

▷ Picturesque.

Spenserian stanza

A verse form devised by Edmund Spenser for his poem *The Faerie Queene* (1590-6). It consists of eight ten-syllable lines, plus a ninth line of 12 syllables (▷ Alexandrine), an iambic rhythm and a rhyme scheme as follows: *a b a b b c b c c*.

The Romantics revived the form, *eg* ▷ Lord Byron in ▷ *Childe Harold*, though he was never quite at home with it; ▷ Percy Bysshe

Shelley in his elegy on Keats, ▷ *Adonais*; and ▷ John Keats himself in his ▷ *Eve of St Agnes*. Keats's use of the form in this poem remains perhaps the most fluent since the work of its originator:

> Anon his heart revives: her vespers done,
> Of all its wreathèd pearls her hair she frees;
> Unclasps her warmèd jewels one by one;
> Loosens her fragrant bodice; by degrees
> Her rich attire creeps rustling to her knees;
> Half-hidden, like a mermaid in sea-weed,
> Pensive awhile she dreams awake, and sees,
> In fancy, fair St Agnes in her bed,
> But dares not look behind or all the charm
> is fled.

(XXVI)

Stendhal (pseudonym of Henri Beyle) (1788-1842)

French writer, known for his novels *Armance* (1822), *La Chartreuse de Parme* (1839), *Le Rouge et le Noir* (1830) and *Lucien Leuwen* (unfinished and published posthumously in 1894). Considered the first of the French realists (▷ Realism), Stendhal is renowned for his exact depiction of milieu and for his close attention to psychological verisimilitude and motivation. However, his realism is neither a simple fidelity to detail nor does it underwrite the values and representations which aristocratic and bourgeois society makes of itself. Stendhal depicts instead the conflict of social verisimilitudes with narrative inventions which contravene such verisimilitudes; so the mainspring of *Le Rouge et le Noir* is the socially unacceptable love of the aristocratic Mathilde and the commoner Julien, while *Armance* raises the 'shocking' issue of homosexuality before its Byronic (▷ Byron) conclusion. On the author's side, irony is his means of refusing to endorse such values. Irony here is not a purely corrosive negativity. It discreetly raises the issue of the ethics of representation itself, moving outwards from the hero and society to ask whether the novel can hold together that encounter of social and individual forces it narrates.

Stendhal's interests were wide and he was likewise the author of travel books, journalism and controversial literary pamphlets (*Racine et Shakespeare*, 1823 and 1825, in which he declared his support for the Romantics). Three volumes of autobiographical writing were published after his death: his *Journal* (1888), *La Vie de Henry Brulard* (1890) and *Souvenirs d'égotisme* (1892).

Strawberry Hill
   ▷ Walpole, Horace.

Structuralism
A form of critical theory chiefly derived from
the work of ▷ Ferdinand de Saussure and
Russian Formalism. Structuralism rejects
the notion that the text expresses an author's
meaning or reflects society but treats it as
an independent unit which activates various
objective relationships with other texts.
Structuralism then, concentrates upon the
relationship between cultural elements,
especially those in binary oppositions,
without which, it is claimed, meaning cannot
exist. Thus, for structuralists, texts remain
within a self-contained and closeted world,
ignoring author, reader and any form of
external reality.
   ▷ Mimesis; Post-structuralism.
Bib: Culler, J., *Structuralist Poetics*.

Subjectivity
In its use in the language of literary criticism
this concept is not to be confused with
the notion of 'individual response' with
which it has customarily been associated.
▷ Louis Althusser and ▷ Jacques Lacan
develop the notion of human beings as
'subjects', that is points at which all of
those social, cultural, and psychic forces
which contribute to the construction of
the individual come together. Implicit
in the concept of the 'subject' is the idea
of the grammatical positioning of the
personal pronoun in a sentence: the 'I' being
referred to as 'the subject of discourse'.
Also, implicit in the concept of 'subjectivity'
is the notion of 'subjection', which raises
fundamental questions about the ways
in which the behaviour of individual
'subjects' is conditioned by external forces.
Within the boundaries of critical theory the
'subject' is never unified (except through
the functioning of an ▷ ideology which
is designed to efface contradiction), but
is in reality split, or 'decentred'. This
is part of a movement away from the
kind of philosophical humanism which
would place the individual at the centre
of attention. It would attribute to him or
her an· autonomy of action as well as an
authority arising out of the suggestion that
he or she is the origin and source of all
meaning. 'Subjectivity' is an indispensable
category of analysis for ▷ feminism,
▷ psychoanalytical criticism and for the
various kinds of ▷ materialist analyses
of texts.

Sublimation
This term is used in Freudian psychoanalysis
to describe the process whereby activities
which have their origins in the unconscious,
and which can be traced to primal issues of
sexuality, are diverted and surface in other
areas of human endeavour, as something else.
This concept is of particular use to literary
criticism, not only because it can provide an
explanation of the mechanisms of artistic
creation itself, but because it assists in the
analysis of literary representations of human
motives and actions. Implicit in sublimation
is the notion of an unconscious whose
operations, distorted as desires, rise to the
level of the conscious.
   ▷ Freud, Sigmund; Psychoanalytical
criticism.

Subversion
This is a term usually associated with the
sphere of political action, but applied to
literary texts it points towards the relationship
between a particular text, or even a part of
a text, and what is generally regarded as the
prevailing order. Individual texts are capable
of challenging dominant orthodoxies, either
at the level of literary form, or at the level
of discernible content. Thus, they may be
said to subvert expectations or dominant
values. A more complex kind of subversion
may take place within the boundaries of
a particular text which otherwise would
be accepted as conforming to prevailing
values and attitudes. Where this happens,
negotiation takes place (which can be
analysed as part of the text's structure)
whereby that which is dominant in the text
seeks to contain and control those forces
which could subvert it. Such a process is
particularly evident in relation to sexual
difference, where a potentially subversive
'femininity' is often seen to threaten the
dominant masculine discourses which
seek to contain it. Very often potentially
subversive energies are only ever permitted
to enter a text in marginalized forms,
eg female promiscuity, as various forms
of 'evil' all of which are shown to be a
danger to the status quo. An acceptance
of the judgements implied in these moral
categories is usually a precondition of
a reading which is complicit with its
dominant discourses and structures. A
more critical reading will seek to reinstate
the text's 'subversive' elements in order to
show precisely how certain values, and the
literary structures which sustain them, are
produced.

Surrealism

Inaugurated in Paris in 1924 by André Breton's first *Surrealist Manifesto* (1934), its founding members included Louis Aragon (1897–1982), Robert Desnos (1900–45) and Paul Eluard (1895–1952). The movement's ambition was a radical programme, extending beyond art and literature to embrace social and political reform. Purely within France, Surrealism's roots lay in Guillaume Apollinaire's (1880–1918) experiments with poem-objects and in the cubist poetry of Pierre Reverdy (1889–1960). More broadly, as the first *Manifesto* made clear, it was especially indebted to Freudian (▷ Freud) theories of dream and sought to overthrow rationalism in favour of unconscious mental states, so giving rise to an expanded sense of the psychic life. Such unconscious processes could best be liberated by activities such as 'automatic writing'. By this technique, a writer's faculty of conscious censorship is laid aside, allowing the chance encounter between two otherwise unrelated elements which might produce the surreal image and initiate the incursion of dream into reality.

Just as Surrealism travelled easily between forms of artistic production and ostensibly external forms such as psychology and philosophy, so its own artistic manifestations span poetry, prose and painting, though it is best known for and possibly most representatively manifested in the first and last of these. Max Ernst (1891–1976), and René Magritte (1898–1967) helped establish the movement in art and Salvador Dali (1904–89) provided dream-like work, plainly inspired by Freud; his surreal objects such as the lobster-telephone amuse, and shock our sense of the everyday propriety of such objects. World War II caused an hiatus in Surrealism's activities and despite the success of the various Surrealist Exhibitions (*eg* London, 1936) and by the 1950s the movement's force was to all intents and purposes spent.

The widespread influence of French Surrealism between the Wars gave rise to two corresponding movements, Belgian Surrealism and English Surrealism. In its interest in irrationality, dream, and the workings of desire and memory, together with its left-wing political programme, Surrealism may be viewed as a near restatement of Romantic enthusiasms in 20th-century terms.

Swedenborg, Emanuel (1688–1722)

Swedish scientist, philosopher and theologian. The earlier part of his life was dedicated to the natural sciences, and his theories anticipate important discoveries in geology, cosmology, and especially in the physiology of the brain. Later he devoted himself to religion and had mystical experiences: his religious beliefs led to the founding of the New Jerusalem Church and the English Theosophical Society. According to Swedenborg's beliefs, God is Divine Man, whose essence is infinite love; there are correspondences between spiritual nature and material nature, but the former is alive and the latter is dead; both in God and in man and nature there are three degrees, those of love, wisdom and use, or end, cause and effect; by a love of each degree man comes into relation with them, and his end is to become the image of his Creator, God. Swedenborg's *Heaven and Hell* and *True Christian Religion* were translated into English in 1778 and 1781, and amongst his followers were the father of the poet ▷William Blake, and Blake's friend, the sculptor, John Flaxman. Swedenborg's doctrines are the starting point of much of Blake's thinking. But Blake, who wrote comments on Swedenborg's doctrines, came to disagree with the philosopher in important respects.

Swinburne, Algernon Charles (1837–1909)

Poet and critic. The style of his poetry is very distinctive, and his literary sympathies were wide. Swinburne led a dissolute, wild life (his predilection for flagellation is infamous), and produced poetry which shocked those who read it carefully, and intoxicated his youthful contemporaries, especially Thomas Hardy and the ▷ Pre-Raphaelites. He read eclectically, absorbing classical literature, the ▷ Elizabethans, Walt Whitman, ▷ William Blake, the ▷ Marquis de Sade and ▷ Baudelaire ▷ (French literature in England).

Against the prejudices of his time, which declared that poets should be morally serviceable, he asserted the right to pursue the poetic vocation to express beauty, but this in itself isolated him from contemporary English culture, especially the novel, which emphasized the search for deeper moral experience. Swinburne's influence was strong on his younger contemporaries of the aesthetic movement, and the ▷ Nineties poets. In many respects his work enacts a modified continuation of the wilder side of ▷Shelley's poetry and convictions.

Symbolic order

A psychoanalytical term now frequently used in literary criticism. 'Symbolic' in this context refers initially to the notion that language itself is comprised of symbols which stand for things. But, the French psychoanalyst ▷ Jacques Lacan observes that: 'It is the world of words that creates the world of things', and in so doing introduces an 'order' into what would otherwise be disparate units. That process of ordering is motivated by a series of impulses and desires which are not usually available to the conscious mind. Thus, the symbolic order is that order of representations through whose organization the child enters into language and the social order as a gendered human 'subject'. In the case of Freudian psychoanalysis (▷ Freud) each symbol refers back to an Oedipal stage which the infant passes through on the way to maturity. In Lacan, the 'unconscious' is said to be structured like a language, already a system of representations through which the individual gendered subject realizes his or her identity. In some respect all literary texts traverse the realm of the symbolic order in that they represent and articulate those images through which reality is grasped discursively.

▷ Psychoanalytical criticism.

Symbolism

A name primarily associated with a school of French poets writing in the second half of the 19th century. The movement grew out of the work of ▷ Baudelaire (1821–67) and is above all associated with Paul Verlaine (1844–96), Arthur Rimbaud (1854–91) and Stephane Mallarmé (1842–98). In addition to Baudelaire, the American writer Edgar Allan Poe (1809–49) and the German music-dramatist Richard Wagner (1813–83) contributed to the shaping of Symbolism. It constituted a development from ▷ Romanticism inasmuch as it was poetry of the feelings as opposed to the reason, but it was a reaction against it inasmuch as it was more intellectual in its conception of the way poetry operates. This intellectualism did not imply that the content of poetry should be one of what is ordinarily called ideas: Mallarmé's affirmation was that 'Poetry is not made with ideas; it is made with words'. This looks forward to much 20th-century thought in all

the arts, requiring that the artist should above all have respect for the medium in which he has chosen to work; it also anticipates T. S. Eliot's praise of the English 17th-century Metaphysical poets that 'they were, at best, engaged in the task of trying to find the verbal equivalent for states of mind and feeling'. Since 'states of mind and feeling' are ultimately mysterious and elusive, the Symbolists emphasized the suggestiveness of poetic language, but though this emphasis on suggestiveness makes much of their poetry obscure, their care for the organization and operation of language kept it from vagueness, in the sense in which the poetry of their English contemporary, the late Romantic ▷ Algernon Swinburne, is very commonly vague. Swinburne is also much concerned with the poetic medium of words, but in such a way that his verse subdues the reader into a state of passive receptivity, whereas the French Symbolists evoke active participation; Swinburne relies for his effect on stimulating emotions already latent in the reader, whereas the Symbolists incite extension of these emotions. T. S. Eliot's essay on Swinburne (in *Selected Essays*) is a help in elucidating the distinction.

The French Symbolists are particularly important in English literature for their decisive influence on the two most important poets writing in English in the first half of the 20th century: T. S. Eliot and W. B. Yeats. Eliot's understanding of them was much the more intimate and profound, but A. Symons's *The Symbolist Movement in Literature* (1899) (▷ Nineties poets) acted on them both.

Synchronic

Adjective used by ▷ Ferdinand de Saussure to describe the analysis of the meaning of a ▷ sign in relation to the other current elements of the language system ▷ *langue*. Saussure juxtaposes the synchronic study of language with the *diachronic* study of language which looks at the historical development of language. This is one of the important polarities in Saussure's theories.

▷ Parole.

T

Tam O'Shanter (1791)

A poem by ▷ Robert Burns in Lowland Scots dialect. Tam, a drunken farmer, riding home late at night, passes 'Aloway's old haunted Kirk' which he sees lighted up. He creeps nearer to find witches and warlocks dancing to the tune of the bagpipes played by Old Nick. He admires one of the prettiest of the witches and in his excitement cries out: 'Weel done, cutty-sark!' ('short-shirt'). The witches come rushing after him, but he is able to reach the middle of the bridge over the River Doon, beyond which they cannot follow him, though they wrench off his horse's tail. The work shows an effortless adaptation of the mock heroic (▷ heroic, mock) pentameter ▷ couplet to the vigorous and earthy Scots language.

Task, The (1785)

A long ▷ blank-verse poem by ▷ William Cowper, combining ▷ mock heroic with ▷ Georgic and sentimental elements. It begins in heavily Miltonic vein with an account of the history of Cowper's own sofa. Later passages concern the joys of rural retirement, gardening, the peculiarities of various local characters, and the moral and religious corruptions of the day, which are condemned at great length. The poem manages to achieve a distinctive and engaging tone, despite the miscellaneousness of its literary elements, and its simplicity of diction foreshadows that of ▷ William Wordsworth in ▷ Lyrical Ballads.

Tasso, Torquato (1544–95)

Italian poet. He continued the tradition of the romance epic, already made famous by Ludovico Ariosto's Orlando Furioso (1532), in his two major works, Rinaldo (1562) and Jerusalem Delivered (1581). Tasso's imagination was romantic but in his literary ideal he was ▷ classical, and the thought of the second poem is elevated by the high seriousness of the Catholic Counter-Reformation. His seriousness made his work very attractive to the English romance epic poet, Edmund Spenser, whose very Protestant The Faerie Queene (1590–6) is also an attempt to rival Ariosto by a poem of similar form but imbued with strong religious feeling. Tasso's impress is strong on parts of The Faerie Queene, especially in its Platonism (▷ Plato). Jerusalem Delivered was finely translated by Sir Edward Fairfax and published under the title of Godfrey of Bulloigne or the Recovery of Jerusalem in 1600.

Tasso was locked up for insanity by Alphonso II, Prince of Ferrara, between 1579–86; subsequent legend attributed his imprisonment to a love affair with the Princess Leonara d'Este. This supposed love affair was the subject of a poem by ▷ Lord Byron, The Lament of Tasso (1817).

Taylor, Jane (1783–1824) and Ann (1782–1866)

Authors of popular children's books in verse: Original Poems for Infant Minds (1804), Rhymes for the Nursery (1806), in which appears 'Twinkle twinkle, little Star', and Hymns for Infant Minds (1810).

Tel Quel

A magazine, for many years the leading French avant-garde journal. Its name was taken from a work by Paul Valéry (1871–1945) and it was edited by Philippe Sollers (b 1936), novelist, theorist and husband of the feminist writer, Julia Kristeva. In political terms, the magazine's sympathies were Marxist-Leninist-Maoist. It welcomed the student demonstrations of May 1968 with an issue entitled 'The Revolution, here and now' and its programme for a French 'Cultural Revolution' was backed by figures such as the composer Pierre Boulez (b 1925) and the novelist and theoretician Jean Ricardou (b 1932). Tel Quel provided a forum for left-wing intellectuals and gave rise to the Tel Quel group. Their joint publication, Théorie d'ensemble (1968), contained inter alia ▷ Jacques Derrida's essay 'La Différance', ▷ Michel Foucault's piece 'Distance, aspect, origine' (discussing Alain Robbe-Grillet and Sollers) and ▷ Roland Barthes's 'Drame, poème, roman' (on Sollers). Alongside its support for radical political and theoretical positions, the magazine did much to promote the cause of a literary counter-orthodoxy, represented by ▷ Sade, ▷ Lautréamont, Georges Bataille and Robbe-Grillet.

In the late 1970s, Tel Quel began to lose its radical impetus. Sollers renounced his theoretical persuasions, sympathized with the right-wing group, Les Nouveaux Philosophes, and embraced Catholicism. From 1982, the magazine changed its name to L'Infini and found itself a new publisher.

Temple, Laura Sophia (1763–c 1820)

Poet. A neglected writer whose work was admired at the time (for example, by ▷ Coleridge) and whose poetry marks her out as central to the ▷ Romantic tradition. Three collections remain extant: Poems (1805), Lyric and Other Poems (1808) and The Siege of Zaragoza and Other Poems (1812). She and her husband became destitute towards 1820 and they appealed to the Royal Literary Fund for support, but nothing is known of them after this date. The request mentions another long poem in manuscript, but this has been lost. Temple used a wide range of forms, including ▷ ballads, ▷ sonnets, ▷ lyrics, and the ▷ dramatic monologue, and her subject matter was fittingly Romantic, in that she focused on ▷ nature, temporality, and the power of poetry, with occasional excursions into ▷ orientalism.

Tennyson, Alfred (1809–92)

Poet, usually known, after he was made a baron in 1884, as Alfred, Lord Tennyson.

Tennyson's family background does not conform to the 20th-century ideal of the family in the 19th century. He was one of 12 children, his father was a violent alcoholic rector, his mother was distressed and wretched, two of his brothers became insane and a third was also an alcoholic. Images of mental illness, doubt and conflict thus naturally fracture Tennyson's work, especially the most interesting and intense poems. He did not begin to win fame until the 1840s, but thereafter achieved popularity unequalled by any other English poet in his own lifetime. In 1850 he was made ▷ Poet Laureate (in succession to ▷ Wordsworth) and in 1884 he was made a Baron – the only English poet ever to have been ennobled purely for his poetry. This popularity arose from two facts: he had, on the one hand, exquisite poetic skill; he was, on the other hand, in his mental and emotional outlook, very representative of his age. He had a characteristically ▷ Victorian insular patriotism; he was both exhilarated and disturbed, like so many of his contemporaries, by the social and industrial changes of the age, and he was distressed by the shaking of traditional religious beliefs by science.

He countered this threat from the intellect by an emotional, sometimes sentimental, idealism which was extremely acceptable to the middle-class reading public. His idiom was that of the Romantics – Wordsworth, ▷ Shelley, especially ▷ Keats – but his formal technique was as meticulous as that of the 18th century poets; the combination was both beguiling and reassuring. Physically and in his dress, he was imposing and romantic, and with this appearance he typified the poet for the nation.

The first three books of his sole authorship (1830, 1832, 1842) include much of what is now considered his best, most disturbing and challenging work – eg *Mariana, The Lady of*

Shalott, Ulysses, Morte d'Arthur, ▷ *The Lotos-Eaters.* In 1833 his great friend, ▷ Arthur Hallam, died, and the great grief of this loss produced the series of ▷ elegies which are usually considered to be his masterpiece – ▷ *In Memoriam A.H.H.*, eventually published in 1850. Queen Victoria declared that she valued it next to the Bible; however, it was the mixture of picturesque romanticism and acceptable idealism in *The Princess* (1850) which greatly extended Tennyson's popularity with the general public. In recent years readings of Victorian poetry have freed themselves from modernist valuations, and Tennyson's work has been re-read with interest for its strong acknowledgement and analysis of problematic areas of psychic and social existence; questions of mental health, the role of women, war and economic conditions.

Bib: Sinfield, A., *Alfred Tennyson*; Nicholson, H., *Tennyson: Aspects of his Life, Character and Poetry*; Palmer, D. J. (ed.), *Tennyson*; Killham, J., *Tennyson and The Princess*; Killham, J. (ed.), *Essays on Tennyson*; Ricks, C., *Tennyson*; Ricks, C. (ed.), *Poems*.

Terza rima

The pattern used by the Italian poet ▷ Dante in his long poem the ▷ *Divina Commedia*. Each line is of 11 syllables, the last syllable unaccented, and the rhyme scheme follows the pattern *aba bcb cdc ded* etc. Examples in English are rare, and consist of 10-syllable lines. One reason for the scarce use of *terza rima* in English is the paucity of rhyming words in the language, by comparison with Italian. ▷ Shelley used the form with great success in his long poem *The Triumph of Life*, unfinished at the time of his death in 1822.

Thelwall, John (1764–1834)

Poet and essayist. Thelwall was a radical writer who published tracts and ▷ essays explaining his political views. His radicalism led to his arrest in 1794, but he was acquitted at the trial, and wrote about the experience in *Poems Written in Close Confinement in the Tower and Newgate Upon a Charge of Treason* (1795). Thelwall is also known for his acquaintance with ▷ Wordsworth and ▷ Coleridge whom he visited in the Lake District, having walked all the way from London.

Theophrastus

A Greek philosopher, follower of ▷ Aristotle, of the 4th century BC. Amongst other writings, he composed a series of descriptions of moral types called *Ethical Characters*. These were the original pattern for the minor literary form of character-writing, widely practised in England in the early 17th century. The most notable example is John Earle's *Microcosmography* (1628). Other examples: Joseph Hall's *Characters of Virtues and Vices* (1608); Thomas Overbury's *Characters* (1614).

▷ Characters, Theophrastian.

Thrale, Hester Lynch (1741–1821) (later Hester Thrale Piozzi)

Born Hester Salusbury, she married Henry Thrale in 1763. Thrale was a wealthy brewer with political ambitions, and when in the following year they made the acquaintance of Samuel Johnson (1709–84), Johnson assisted Thrale by writing election addresses. The friendship between Johnson and Hester Thrale became very close, and at various times Johnson lived with the family in their home at Streatham. When Thrale died in 1781, Hester Thrale remarried. Gabriel Piozzi, her second husband, was an Italian musician, and her friends and family vociferously disapproved. The marriage ended the friendship with Johnson, who sent her an anguished letter on the subject.

Hester Thrale's biography of Johnson, *Anecdotes of the late Samuel Johnson*, was strongly contested by James Boswell (1740–95) when it appeared in 1786; his motives in challenging her account probably stem from literary rivalry. Hester Thrale was also an energetic letter writer, and *Thraliana*, a selection of anecdotes, poems, jests and journal entries, covers the period 1776–1809. Bib: Clifford, J. L., *Hester Lynch Piozzi*.

Tighe, Mary (1772–1810)

Poet. The life of Mary Tighe (née Blachford) accords with the archetypal biography constructed for the ▷ Romantic poet. Although she had a strict religious upbringing, she married her cousin (Henry Tighe), with whom she was passionately in love, against her mother's wishes, and they moved into the social and literary London scene. Her first book of poems, *Psyche, or the Legend of Love* (1805), was an ▷ allegory in six cantos written in ▷ Spenserian stanzas and depicting Psyche's experiences in Cupid's palace. In her preface she apologizes for her focus upon passion, but when the poem begins with its languorous exploration of space and emotion, no qualms surface to halt the steady sensuous flow of the poetry. Two other works exist, *Mary, A Series of Reflections During 20 Years* (1811) and an ▷ autobiography, *Selina*, which is in manuscript

form in the National Library of Ireland. Even as *Psyche* was published, Tighe knew she was suffering from consumption, and died when she was thirty-eight.

Times, The

British newspaper. It was founded in 1785 as *The Daily Universal Register*, and took its present name in 1788. In the 19th century it took the lead in contriving new methods of collecting news (notably through the employment of foreign correspondents), and its succession of distinguished editors and contributors gave it an outstanding status among British newspapers. Though always in private ownership, it has always claimed to be an independent newspaper rather than a party one. The literary style of one of its staff writers caused it to be nicknamed 'The Thunderer' in the 19th century.

Tintern Abbey

One of the most famous remains of the medieval abbeys, dissolved by Henry VIII in 1536–39. It stands in a particularly beautiful natural setting, in the valley of the River Wye, near the border of England and Wales. The poet ▷ William Wordsworth used this setting for one of the best known of his early poems, *Lines Composed a Few Miles Above Tintern Abbey* (in ▷ *Lyrical Ballads*), in which he meditates on the influence of natural surroundings on the formation of his mind.

Tintern Abbey, Lines Composed a Few Miles Above (1798)

A reflective poem in ▷ blank verse by ▷ William Wordsworth, not itself a lyrical ballad but one of the 'few other poems' included in ▷ *Lyrical Ballads* (1798). The poet returns to a spot on the river Wye visited five years earlier, and reflects upon the moral influence its beauty has exerted upon him in the meantime, inspiring 'little, nameless, unremembered, acts/ Of kindness and of love'. He goes on to describe himself as 'A worshipper of Nature', and this is his most ▷ pantheistic work.

Tithonus

In Greek myth, the son of Laomedon, king of Troy. Such was his beauty that Eos (Aurora), goddess of the dawn, fell in love with him and made him her husband. She secured for him from Zeus the gift of immortal life, but forgot to require also immortal youth. ▷ Tennyson's poem *Tithonus* is a ▷ dramatic monologue representing Tithonus in the agony of his eternal old age.

Transference

This is the term used in Freudian psychoanalysis, along with others such as 'condensation' and 'displacement', to describe one of the mechanisms whereby unconscious desires enter into consciousness (▷ Freud). It is given a more specific meaning in the relationship between analyst and patient (analysand) in psychoanalysis, as part of the process of removing those impediments to the recollection of repressed impulses on the part of the latter. Situations and emotions are relived during the treatment and these ultimately express the indestructibility of unconscious fantasies. In the structure of a literary work, repetitions of particular situations and events, and even the duplication of 'character', can be explained as kinds of transference of the 'unconscious fantasies' of the writer. In this way desires and feelings which in psychoanalysis occur in the life of the patient, are *transferred* onto the analyst/reader, producing a repetition or re-enactment of them. For example, in ▷ Shakespeare's *Hamlet* 'madness' is transferred from the hero onto Ophelia, and an analysis of that process situates the reader/spectator within a complex process of the construction of male/female subjectivity as a result. The issue can be complicated further if the writer 'Shakespeare' is taken to be the 'analysand' projecting unconscious desires and feelings through his 'characters' onto the 'analyst' (reader/spectator).

▷ Psychoanalytical criticism.

Transgression

As a term used in contemporary literary criticism, it is generally associated with the concept of ▷ 'subversion' insofar as it denotes the act of crossing accepted boundaries. Applied to literary texts it is usually taken to refer to any form of behaviour or representation which challenges the dominant values encoded within that text.

Translation

The life of English literature has always issued from a combination of strong insular traditions and participation in wider European traditions. Translation has always been the principal means of assimilating European literatures into the English idiom, and it was particularly important before the 18th century, when the main streams of European cultural life were flowing through other languages. The aim of translators was then less to make an accurate rendering than to make the substance of foreign work thoroughly intelligible to the English spirit; the character of the translation thus proceeded as much from the mind of the translator as from the mind of the original writer. If the translator had a strong personality, the translation often became a distinguished work of English literature in its own right. Translators with less individuality often produced work of historical importance because of its contemporary influence on English writing.

During the Romantic period writers became restless under Augustan restraints, and became interested in literatures that had hitherto been ignored or despised; ▷ Thomas Gray imitated Icelandic and Celtic verse. ▷ James Macpherson's versions of Gaelic legends, which he alleged to be by the legendary poet ▷ Ossian, were more inventions and adaptations than translations, but they probably had a wider influence in other countries than any other English work going under the name of translation, with the exception of the English Bible. ▷ Sir William Jones (1746–94), the first important British Oriental scholar (▷ Orientalism), published in 1783 a version in English of the ancient Arabic poems called *Moâllakát*, as well as other work from Persian and from Sanskrit.

Some of the more distinguished translations of the first 30 years of the 19th century, such as Cary's translation in ▷ blank verse of ▷ Dante's *Divine Comedy* (1805–12), ▷ Coleridge's version of Schiller's *Wallenstein* (1800), and ▷ Shelley's fragments of ▷ Goethe and Calderón (▷ Spanish influence on English literature), show the new kinds of influence on the Romantic writers.

▷ German influence on English literature.

Travel literature

This large branch of English literature may be conveniently divided into three headings: 1 fantasy purporting to be fact; 2 factual accounts; 3 travel experiences regarded as material for art. The first group is largely confined to pre- ▷ Renaissance writers. This developed into the second group as extensive travel became more widespread. Indeed, the steady growth of English overseas trade kept alive a taste for accounts of great voyages throughout the 17th and 18th centuries. At the end of the 17th century Captain William Dampier published three books which included the imaginations of Daniel Defoe (1660–1731) and Jonathan Swift (1667–1745): *New Voyage Round the World* (1697), *Voyages and Descriptions* (1699), and *Voyage to New Holland* (1703). Dampier was an excellently direct and clear writer of his own books, but

Lord George Anson's voyage round the world (1740–44) was written up from his journals by his chaplain, R. Waters, and depends on the singularly dramatic events for its force of interest. The last of these outstanding accounts of great voyages were the three undertaken by Captain James Cook, *A Voyage Round Cape Horn and the Cape of Good Hope* (1773), *A Voyage Towards the South Pole and Round the World* (1777), and *A Voyage to the Pacific Ocean* (1784). With the discovery of the coastlines of Australia and New Zealand, the main outlines of world geography became known, and the interest of both explorers and their readers passed to the mysteries of the great undiscovered interiors of the continents. With this change in subject matter, a change also came over the style of travel literature.

The third group may be characterized by Sir Richard Burton's (1821–90) book about India, *Scinde or the Unhappy Valley* (1851), and his later books about his exploration of East and Central Africa (*First Footsteps in East Africa*, 1856; *The Lake Region of Central Africa*, 1860) bear more of the stamp of the author's personal feelings and reactions. Partly, no doubt, this arose from the new importance attached to authorial personality due to ▷ Romanticism; also the contact with strange physical environments and peoples (in contrast to the emptiness and impersonality of the ocean) inevitably drew out authorial response. At all events, travel literature began to draw nearer to ▷ autobiography.

Tristan and Iseult

There are many medieval and post-medieval versions of the tragic love affair between Tristan (Tristram/Tristrem) and Iseult (Iseut/Isolde/Isolt/Isode); however, if the lovers' tragedy is a fixed element in their history, details of why and how it happened are not. It seems likely that their love story has a source in early Celtic legendary narrative: Tristan seems to be a transfiguration of the 8th-century Pictish Prince Drust, and there are Irish analogues to the story of the erotic triangle which forms the basis of the Tristan and Iseult narrative. But there are no Celtic versions of the love story which pre-date the French versions, composed in the later 12th century.

In the mid-12th century Tristan is mentioned as an ideal lover in the lyrics of the troubadours, which suggests some version of his story was circulating at this time. Fragments of longer vernacular narratives about Tristan and Iseult are extant by Thomas (c 1175) and Béroul (c 1190). Marie de France also included an episode from the lovers' history in her collection of *Lais*, and Chrétien de Troyes claimed to have produced a version of the story too, though no trace of the text has survived (his romance, *Cligés*, contains many references to the affair between Tristan and Iseult). From the fragments by Thomas and Béroul, and from their subsequent reworkings (especially in early medieval German versions), some idea of the overall story-line may be established.

Tristan is the son of Rivalen and Blancheflor (the sister of King Mark of Cornwall). Blancheflor dies the day her son is born, and he is brought up as an orphan until he is old enough to go to Mark's court, where he kills the Irish champion, Morholt. Later he is given the task of finding a bride for Mark. Tristan travels to Ireland, is wounded in a fight against a dragon, and is nursed by the king of Ireland's daughter, Iseult. She manages to identify Tristan as the killer of her brother Morholt; however, she saves Tristan's life on condition that he rescue her from an unwanted marriage. Tristan takes Iseult back to be Mark's wife, but on the voyage to Cornwall they accidentally drink a love potion which had been designed for Iseult and her future husband, and so they fall passionately in love. Their love affair continues after Iseult's marriage to Mark (with the help of Iseult's maid), but rumours about their adultery finally reach Mark. Later, after the affair has been exposed, Tristan goes into exile in Brittany, and marries another Iseelt (of the White Hands), although the marriage is never consummated. When, at a later stage, he is wounded by a poisonous weapon, he calls for Iseult of Ireland to come to heal him: if she consents, the ship which carries her is to have white sails; if not, her message is to be carried in a ship with black sails. Although Iseult comes to Tristan's aid, Iseult of the White Hands tells Tristan that a ship with black sails is approaching. At this news Tristan dies. Iseult, realizing she has come too late, dies of grief beside Tristan.

The status of the love potion (whether it is a permanent or temporary spell, whether it is a metaphor for their love, rather than a literal love potion) is a variable element in the love story. So too is the means by which the lovers are exposed and punished by Mark: in some versions the lovers are condemned, but Tristan manages to escape and rescue Iseult from a group of lepers to whom she has been given for their pleasure; in some versions Iseult survives a truth ordeal by swearing an equivocal oath, and the lovers subsequently run away to live together for a time in a forest. The story of frustrated and passionate love arouses very different ethical responses, too, from medieval poets and prose writers: Tristan and Iseult have an equivocal status as exemplary lovers, being famous and infamous, a subject for praise and blame. Gottfried von Strassburg's *Tristan* (c 1210) provides one of the most celebratory versions of the story, which strongly affirms the metaphysical status of the bonds between these two lovers (and this, in turn, is the source for Wagner's opera of 1865, *Tristan und Isolde*).

The experience of Mark, Iseult and Tristan clearly offers a parallel to, and perhaps a prototype for, the other major erotic triangle of Arthurian romance involving King Arthur, Guinevere, and Lancelot. And in the later French prose versions of the Tristan story (dating from the 13th century), the friendship between Tristan and Lancelot is developed: in these versions, substantial accounts are added of Tristan's adventures as a Knight of the Round Table, and in these versions he is killed, finally, by King Mark himself. Malory's long 'Book of Sir Tristram' is a reworking of the French prose *Tristan* (c 1225). The 13th-century English verse romance, *Sir Tristrem* (in the Auchinleck manuscript), provides an incomplete reworking of Thomas's 12th-century *Tristan*.

▷ Tennyson, is among the later poets to take Tristan and Iseult as their subjects, but presents the least sympathetic, and most critical interpretation of the lovers' experience.

Bib: Ferrante, J., *The Conflict of Love and Honour: The Medieval Tristan Legend in France, Germany, and Italy*; Lacy, N. et al (eds.), *The Arthurian Encyclopaedia*.

Trollope, Frances (1780–1863)
Born Frances Milton in Somerset, the daughter of a vicar, she married in 1809 and had six children, including the future novelist Anthony Trollope (1815–82). She began writing when she was over 50 to support the family in the face of her husband's financial disasters and published over 40 books on travel, and novels. Despite the financial success of her first book she worked extremely hard, from before dawn each day, writing and caring for her family. She visited America for an extended period and lived in France, Austria and Italy for a few years. Her writing owed its popularity perhaps to her scathing views of Americans, also to its exuberant quality and her rather coarse, humorous women. *Domestic Manners of the Americans* (1832) brought her fame and popularity; *Paris and the Parisians* (1835), *Vienna and the Austrians* (1838) and *A Visit to Italy* (1842) were also successful. Her novels include *The Vicar of Wrexhill* (1837), portraying a mixture of vice and religion, *The Widow of Barnaby* (1838) and *The Life and Adventures of a Clever Woman* (1854).
Bib: Trollope, F. E., *Frances Trollope: Her Life and Literary Work from George III to Victoria*; Johnston, J., *The Life, Manners and Travels of Fanny Trollope: A Biography*.

U

Unitarianism

A doctrine of religion that rejects the usual Christian doctrine of the Trinity, or three Persons in one God (the Father, the Son, and the Holy Ghost), in favour of a belief in the single person of God the Father. It originated in Britain in the 18th century and was in accord with the rationalistic approach to religion of that century. The first Unitarian church opened in London in 1774; many English Presbyterians (in the 16th and 17th centuries one of the largest sects outside the Church of England) became Unitarians.

Urizen

▷ Blake, William.

Utilitarianism

A 19th-century political, economic and social doctrine which based all values on utility, *ie* the usefulness of anything, measured by the extent to which it promotes the material happiness of the greatest number of people. It is especially associated with ▷ Jeremy Bentham, at first a jurist concerned with legal reform and later a social philosopher. Followers of the movement are thus often called 'Benthamites' but Bentham's disciple John Stuart Mill (1806–73) used the term 'Utilitarians'. Owing to their habit of criticizing social concepts and institutions on strictly rational tests, the leaders of the movement were also known as Philosophical Radicals.

Utilitarianism dominated 19th-century social thinking, but it had all its roots in various forms of 18th-century rationalism. In moral philosophy, David Hume (1711–76) had a strong influence on Bentham by his assumption that the supreme human virtue is benevolence, *ie* the disposition to increase the happiness of others. Psychologically, Bentham's principle that humans are governed by the impulses to seek pleasure and avoid pain derives from the associationism of David Hartley (1705–57). But Bentham and his associates believed that the virtue of benevolence, and human impulses towards pleasure, operate within social and economic laws which are scientifically demonstrable. Bentham accepted ▷ Adam Smith's reasoning in *The Wealth of Nations* (1776) that material prosperity is governed by economic laws of supply and demand, the beneficial operation of which is only hindered by governmental interference. ▷ Malthus, in his *Essay on the Principle of Population* (1798), maintained that it is mathematically demonstrable that population always tends to increase beyond

the means of subsistence and Ricardo, a friend of Bentham's, applied Malthus's principle to wages, arguing that as the population increases wages will necessarily get lower, since the increase is more rapid than that of the wealth available to support the workers. Smith, Malthus and Ricardo were masters of what was called the science of Political Economy, and the inhuman fatalism with which they endowed it caused it to be known as the dismal science. However, it was not dismal for the industrial middle class of employers, whose interests it suited; they were already 'utilitarians' by self-interest and thus willing converts to the theory.

Thus the operation of Utilitarianism in the 19th century was paradoxical. It liberated society from laws which were inefficient survivals from the past but it replaced them by laws that often operated with cold inhumanity (*eg* the Poor Law of 1834). It reduced senseless government interference with society but its concern with efficiency encouraged a bureaucratic civil service. It liberated the employers but it was often unsympathetic to the interests of the employees. Its principle was benevolence but its faith in reason often made it indifferent to individual suffering. The inhumanity of the creed, and its indifference to cultural values unless they could be shown to be materially useful, caused it to be vigorously attacked by leading writers. But perhaps its sanest and most lucid critic was John Stuart Mill; though himself a Utilitarian to the end of his life, he saw the philosophical limitations of the movement and exposed them in his essays in 1838 on Bentham, and on ▷ Samuel Taylor Coleridge whom he admired as the father of the opposing tendency of thought. Mill's essay *Utilitarianism* (1863) emphasized that some kinds of pleasure are better than others – a distinction Bentham failed to make – and that the highest virtue in humanity is 'the desire to be in unity with our fellow creatures'. Mill was aware, as Bentham had not been, of the importance of the artistic imagination, in particular of poetry, in a civilization.

Utopian literature

Sir Thomas More's (1478–1535) *Utopia* brought into the English language the word 'utopian' = 'imaginary and ideal place', and started a succession of 'utopias' in English literature. The idea of inventing an imaginary country to be used as a 'model' by which to judge earthly societies did not, however, originate with More, but with his master the Greek philosopher ▷ Plato, who did the same in his dialogues *Timaeus* and the *Republic*.

From the 18th century on, much utopian literature is satirical, intended to give warning of vicious tendencies of society rather than to exemplify ideals. An example of this is Bernard de Mandeville's (1670–1733) *Fable of the Bees* (1714), about the downfall of an ideal society through the viciousness of its inhabitants; and Swift's *Gulliver's Travels* (1726) can be put in the same class.

A utopian strain runs through most literature of the Romantic period, though the emphasis falls more on private paradises than in the literary creation of social models. Despite ▷ Coleridge's announced intention to leave England to form a utopian community on the banks of America's Susquehanna River, it is the visionary idealism of ▷ *Kubla Khan*, with its wistful and personal note, that sustains most interest. The poetry of ▷ Byron and ▷ Shelley, particularly ▷ *Don Juan* and ▷ *Epipsychidion* respectively, contains private Edens that turn out to be transient. Shelley's ▷ *Prometheus Unbound* is more unequivocally utopian.

V

Victorian period

The period coinciding with the reign of Queen Victoria (1837–1901) is commonly divided into three.

1 *1837–1851: the Early Victorian period.* This was a time of struggle and growth; the age of the ▷ Chartist Movement and the Anti-Corn Law League, but also of the building of railways. The 'hungry forties' ended with the Great Exhibition in 1851, the culmination of the ▷ Industrial Revolution, which Britain achieved earlier than any other nation.

2 *1851–1870: the Mid-Victorian period.* Britain had passed the time of the worst popular discontents, and was at her height in wealth, power, and influence.

3 *1870–1901: the Late Victorian Period.* A less fortunate period, when other nations (especially Germany and the United States) were competing with Britain industrially. Britain had acquired much territory in consequence of her pursuit of trade; she now became imperialist in her jealousy and mistrust of other imperialist nations, and the period ended with the imperialist South African War (Boer War) of 1899–1901. Economically, Britain was becoming less the 'workshop of the world' than the world's banker. Domestically, partly in consequence of the second Parliamentary ▷ Reform Bill (enfranchising the town workers – 1867) and the Education Act (establishing a state system of education – 1870) it was a time of popular political and social movements which included the building up of trade unions and the formation of the Labour Party.

Culturally, the Victorian period was the age when change rather than stability came first to be accepted as normal in the nature of human outlook. Ancient foundations of religious belief were eroded, among intellectuals, by scientific advances, especially the biological discoveries of Charles Darwin (1809–82). The educated classes and their leaders sought to establish guiding values for living; it was the period of the 'Victorian Sage' – including J. S. Mill (1806–73) and ▷ Tennyson – educating the social conscience. The relationship of the individual to himself, to other individuals, and to society at large is the study to which the novel is admirably adapted; the English novel developed in the works of William Thackeray (1811–63), Charles Dickens (1812–70), the ▷ Brontës, and George Eliot (1819–80) into the art form of the age. Culturally and in many ways socially, the Victorian period saw the outset and display of the problems which the 20th century has had to attempt to solve.

No clear divide can be made between ▷ Romantic and Victorian literature; writers like ▷ Wordsworth (who lived until 1850) had considerable influence on younger writers.
Bib: Harrison, A. H., *Victorian Poets and Romantic Poems: Intertexuality and Ideology.*

Vision of Judgement, A (1821)
Vision of Judgement, The (1822)

▷ Robert Southey's poem *A Vision of Judgement*, which shows the soul of the dead king George III being received into heaven, provoked ▷ Lord Byron's comic masterpiece *The Vision of Judgement*. Byron's poem changes Southey's ponderous classical hexameters (▷ metre) into racy ▷ *ottava rima* stanzas, and reduces George's ascent into heaven to the familiar genre of a 'Saint Peter sat at the celestial gate' story. George arrives, 'an old man/ With an old soul, and both extremely blind' and has to wait at the gate while Satan and St Michael argue over his immortal destiny. Satan claims him, since despite his 'neutral virtues' he was the constant enemy of political liberty: 'The New World shook him off; the Old yet groans/ Beneath what he and his prepared, if not/ Completed'. The debate is interrupted by the arrival of the devil Asmodeus who, hovering over Skiddaw, has caught the ▷ Poet Laureate scribbling away at 'some libel' (Southey's *Vision*) and snatched him up to heaven to give an account of himself. After offering to write both Michael's and Satan's biographies for a good profit ('Mine is a pen of all work'), Southey insists on reading his 'grand heroics' to the assembled throng, and in the ensuing desperate scramble to escape, King George slips into heaven unnoticed.

In his poem Byron finally achieved his ambition to rival his literary idol Alexander Pope (1688–1744), and the imaginative *élan* and iconoclastic inventiveness of the earlier poet's *Dunciad* are brilliantly emulated. Byron's *ottava rima* form, however, generates a freer, looser tone than Pope's ▷ couplets, allowing for some touches of magnificent political rhetoric. Moreover, Byron's wittily blasphemous treatment of religion shows a characteristically ▷ Romantic insight. Theology is converted into politics: the angels 'all are Tories', Peter is jealous of Paul as a *parvenu*, and Satan is compared to an impoverished Castilian nobleman, wary of the 'mushroom rich civilian', Michael, who has supplanted him. Though Southey's gauchely painstaking poem is now quite unread, Byron's parody remains one of the most imaginative comic works in the language.

Walpole, Horace (1717–97)
Letter-writer, antiquarian, connoisseur. He
was son of the powerful statesman Robert
Walpole, and for a short time followed a
political career, but he abandoned it, though
he continued his interest in politics. His
father's influence procured for him three
sinecures (*ie* posts under the government
which carried salaries though they required
very little work) and these enabled him to pass
his life as an assiduous spectator and man
of pleasure. He developed a strong taste for
the Gothic style in all its forms, converting
his house (Strawberry Hill, Twickenham,
where he settled in 1747) into what he called
'a little Gothic castle', and writing the first of
the ▷ Gothic novels, ▷ *The Castle of Otranto*
(1764). He is chiefly famous for his letters,
however, and is regarded as one of the best
correspondents in the best period of ▷ letter-
writing. Their main quality is their liveliness,
humour, and vividness of observation.
Bid: Lives by Ketton-Cremer and Lewis, W.
S.; Stephen, L., in *Hours in a Library*.

Warton, Joseph (1722–1800)
Critic and poet; headmaster of Winchester
School and the brother of ▷ Thomas Warton.
His *Essay on the Genius and Writings of Pope*
(vol. I, 1756; vol. II, 1782) distinguishes
the 'true poet' from the mere 'man of
wit' and is often seen as a 'pre-Romantic'
document, though Warton himself admired
Alexander Pope (1688–1744) and edited his
works (1797).

Warton, Thomas (1728–90)
Professor of Poetry at Oxford (1757–67)
and later (1785–90) ▷ Poet Laureate. His
Poems (1777) include several ▷ sonnets,
a form neglected in previous decades.
His *The Suicide: An Ode* and *Verses on Sir
Joshua Reynolds' Painted Window* toy with
'romantick' excess and ▷ Gothic medievalism,
without ever having the courage of their
convictions, and his comic verse is perhaps
more successful. He edited the humorous
miscellany, *The Oxford Sausage* (1764). It is
in his criticism, with its scholarly approach to
early literature that his real importance lies.
His *Observations on the Faerie Queene of Spenser*
(1754) shows a sensitive historical perspective,
and his *History of English Poetry* (1774–81),
conveys his fascination with the 'Gothic'
Middle Ages more convincingly than the
dilettantism of his poems. Breaking off at the
death of Elizabeth I, it complemented Samuel
Johnson's (1709–84) *Lives of the Poets*, and
despite their aesthetic differences the two men

were on friendly terms. In 1785 he published
an edition of ▷ John Milton's early poems.
   ▷ Romanticism.
Bib: Pittock, J., *The Ascendancy of Taste: The
Achievement of Joseph and Thomas Warton*;
Rinacker, C., *Thomas Warton: A Biographical
and Critical Study*.

Waterloo, Battle of (1815)
An army of British, Dutch, Belgians and
Germans under the ▷ Duke of Wellington
and the Prussian army under Blücher finally
defeated a French army under ▷ Napoleon
and thus ended the Napoleonic War
(1803–15). Waterloo is a village in Belgium
to the south of Brussels. Wellington's
army took up its position in squares, which
the French attacked unavailingly all day,
until Blücher's army came to Wellington's
assistance. Wellington's own comment on the
battle was that 'it was a damn near thing', and
Napoleon's defeat is partly attributable to his
failing health. He surrendered to the British
and was exiled for the remainder of his life
to the island of St Helena. English history
represents this as a victory for the English
army: in Germany it is seen as an occasion
retrieved by the Prussian force from defeat.
   ▷ Nationalism.

Watts, Susanna (1768–1842)
Poet, prose writer and artist. ▷ Evangelical
writer whose humble origins and powerful
moral beliefs endowed her with an interesting
character, which combined self-depreciation
with the zeal of a crusader. Her poetry was
generally well thought of, including *Original
Poems and Translations* (1802) and the
posthumous *Hymns and Poems* (1842). She
settled in Leicester, and her *Walk Through
Leicester* was published as a guide to the town
in 1804; the City Library there still holds her
original manuscript. Watts's fictional work
always had a barely concealed ▷ didactic
purpose, from trying to help suffering animals
(*The Humming-Bird*, 1824–5) to attacking the
middle classes (*The Wonderful Travels of Prince
Fan-Feredin in the Country of Arcadia*, 1828).
   ▷ Hymns; Travel literature.

Waverley (1814)
The first of ▷ Sir Walter Scott's novels,
subtitled *'Tis Sixty Years Since*. The hero,
Edward Waverley, is a young English officer
who visits the Highlands of Scotland just
before the ▷ Jacobite Rebellion of 1745.
Here he falls in love with Flora, the Jacobite
daughter of a Highland chieftain. He joins

the Jacobite forces. When these are eventually defeated, Waverley is saved from execution by a senior English officer on the other side, whom he has saved in a battle. *Waverley* is the first historical novel of distinction in English literature, and Scott's vivid description of Scottish society and scenery caused it to be received with great enthusiasm.

Wealth of Nations
▷ Smith, Adam.

Wedgwood
The name of a firm of distinguished manufacturers of china. The founder of the firm, Josiah Wedgwood (1730–95), was the son of a potter of Burslem. He perfected an English style of pottery called cream ware, and later Queen's ware. He then developed a new style of classical designs, inspired by contemporary interest in ancient Greek pottery and by the discovery of the Roman city of Pompeii in southern Italy. The most famous of the Wedgwood designers in this style was the friend of the poet ▷ William Blake, John Flaxman. The Wedgwood factory near Hanley is called Etruria; the firm continues in production at the present day. Josiah's son, Thomas Wedgwood (1771–1805), was a generous patron to the poet ▷ S.T. Coleridge.

Wellington, Arthur Wellesley, 1st Duke of (1769–1852)
General and statesman. By origin, of Anglo-Irish aristocracy. He joined the army in 1787, and between 1796 and 1805 he had a distinguished military career in India, where his eldest brother was Governor-General. Arthur Wellesley then returned to Britain. Between 1808 and 1814 he gained fame for his resistance to the French armies of ▷ Napoleon on the Spanish Peninsula. In 1815, with the Prussian general Blücher, he inflicted the final defeat on Napoleon at ▷ Waterloo. He was created Duke in 1814.

He took part in the Congress of Vienna, which made the peace treaty with France, and his influence did much to prevent the partition of the country. Thereafter, his career was in British politics, where he was one of the principal leaders of the Tory (Conservative) party. He gave way, however, over one issue, that of Catholic Emancipation (*ie* granting Catholics full political rights) because he understood its political inevitability; he was less clear-sighted about Parliamentary reform, and was forced to resign in 1830. He again held ministerial posts, though not that of

Prime Minister, in 1834, and 1841–6, under the leadership of Robert Peel. After his death, ▷Tennyson commemorated him with one of his best poems, his *Ode on the Death of the Duke of Wellington*. He was popularly known as 'the Iron Duke', and used proudly to call his London mansion at Hyde Park Corner, 'Number One, London'.

Welsh literature in English
Before the ▷ Romantic period, Welsh literature was virtually unknown in English, since it had not not been translated from the Welsh language. However, Celtic material generally benefited from the antiquarian excavations of the ▷ Augustan period, and the later Romantic interest in myth, the ▷ Gothic and the search for literary origins (▷ Macpherson; Ossian). The first major translation of Welsh poetry, *Some Specimens of the Poetry of the Ancient Welsh Bards* (ed. Ieuan Brydydd Hir; 1764) had an important influence, on, for example, ▷ Thomas Gray's ▷ 'The Bard' (1757) and 'The Triumph of Owen' (1768). Such was the demand for similar works that Iolo Morganwg successfully passed off his own work as supposed early Welsh 'bards'. The early Arthurian tales were translated first by Dr Owen Pughe in *Relicks of the Welsh Bards* (1795–1829), and later by the English author, Lady Charlotte Guest, who gave them their, somewhat incorrect, title *The Mabinogion* (1838–49). Guest is very much an inheritor of the Romantic tradition of ▷ Scott, and in that sense, corresponds to the poet ▷ Tennyson whom she much admired. Pughe, the first translator of 'Pwyll' and 'Math son of Mathonwy' (both tales from *The Mabinogion*) also produced the first Welsh dictionary, which runs to 2 volumes and compares well with Dr Johnson's English dictionary.
Bib: Stephens, M., *Oxford Companion to the Literature of Wales*.

Wesley, Charles (1707–88)
Hymn writer. Brother of the evangelist, ▷ John Wesley, he was the poet of the ▷ Methodist movement. He wrote about 6,500 hymns of unequal merit. Some of them, such as 'Hark the herald Angels Sing', 'Jesu, lover of my soul', and 'Love divine all Loves excelling' show genuine poetic feeling, and are well known.

Wesley, John (1703–91)
Evangelist, and founder of the ▷ Methodist religious movement. At Oxford, with his brother Charles, he became the centre of

a society which regulated the lives of its members; this led to their being described as 'Methodists'. He was at first a strict Anglican, conforming rigidly to Church of England liturgies and doctrines, but on a voyage to America in 1735 he became deeply impressed by the purity and undogmatic spirit of fellow-passengers belonging to the German sect known as the Moravians. On his return to England, Wesley preached up and down Britain. Both the Church of England and the Dissenters who were heirs of the 17th-century Puritans had by now relatively little to offer to the minds of the simple people; reaction against the violent conflicts of the previous century had caused the clergy of all denominations to obscure the sense of religion as a power in individual lives. Wesley taught both that every man was naturally a sinner, and that the power of God was available to all for spiritual salvation. In this he followed the Arminian tradition of religious belief, instead of the belief in Predestination more prevalent among the 17th-century Puritans. Wesley's direct challenge to the hearts and the wills of his hearers caused deep psychological disturbances, and the Methodists were despised by many for the hysteria and emotionalism of their meetings. Nonetheless, the influence of Wesley was extensive and profound, and bore fruit in other religious revivals in the 19th century. He was courteous and had a pleasant wit. When confronted by an arrogant opponent in a narrow street who declared 'I never make way for fools!', Wesley stood aside politely, replying: 'I always do.'

▷ Sermons.

West, Jane (1758–1852)

Poet, novelist and dramatist. A prolific author, whose restrained prose style and dry sense of humour brought admiration from ▷ Jane Austen and ▷ Mary Wollstonecraft. West's self-deprecating wit may be seen in her mocking self-description:

> You said the author was a charmer,
> Self-taught, and married to a farmer;
> Who wrote all kinds of verse with ease,
> Made pies and puddings, frocks and cheese.

Her poetry and plays were published in 1791, but thereafter she concentrated upon novels. Her work includes material that is anti-sentimental (*The Advantages of Education, or The History of Maria Williams*, 1793), anti-radical (*A Tale of the Times*, 1799) and anti-feminist (*Letters to a Young Lady*, 1806). Her historical novels, *The Loyalists* (1812) and *Alicia de Lacey* (1814), are perhaps the most readable today.

Bib: Butler, M., *Jane Austen and the War of Ideas*; Rendall, J., *The Origins of Modern Feminism 1780–1860*.

Whig and Tory

Political terms distinguishing the two parties which were the forebears of the present Liberal and Conservative parties respectively. They were originally terms of abuse, provoked by the attempt of Lord Shaftesbury in 1679 to exclude James Duke of York (later James II) from succession to the throne because he was a Catholic. Shaftesbury and his party were called Whigs because their preference for the Protestant religion over the law of hereditary succession caused their opponents to liken them to the Scottish Presbyterian rebels of the time – called derisively 'whigs' from the nickname given to Scottish drovers. They retaliated by calling the supporters of James, 'tories', from the Irish term for robbers, implying that they no more cared about safeguarding the Protestant religion than did the Irish Catholic rebels. The Exclusion question was settled in favour of James, but not for long, since the Tories did in fact care greatly about the maintenance of the Church of England, and when James II was clearly seen to be acting in Catholic interests, the Tories united with the Whigs in deposing him in 1688. The political terms remained because, though not very consistently, the parties remained; and the parties survived because they represented distinct social interests in the country, though also not very consistently. The Whigs were especially the party of the landed aristocracy, who cared less for the institutions of the Crown and the Church of England than for their own power; since this was allied to the commercial interests of the country, they tended to gain support from the merchants of the towns, many of whom were Dissenters opposed to the Church of England. The principal Tory support came from the smaller landed gentry, or squirearchy, whose interests were conservative, and whose fortunes seemed best protected by introducing as little change in the established institutions, whether of Church or of State, as possible. In the major crises the Tories were generally defeated, but they had extraordinary survival capacity by virtue of their willingness to accept changes once they had become inevitable. Their first major defeat was in 1714 when the Tory party was split between Henry Bolingbroke's (1678–1751) anti-Hanoverian

faction and those loyal to the 1701 Act of
Settlement by which the throne went to the
House of Hanover and not to Anne's Catholic
half-brother.

Whigs were then supreme for 40 years
(though they disintegrated into rival groups),
until after the accession of George III in 1760.
George tried then to revive the power of the
throne by securing supporters for his politics
in Parliament; these supporters were known
as 'the King's Friends' or 'New Tories'. This
policy was also defeated, however, by their
loss of prestige as a result of the victory of
the American rebels in the War of American
Independence (1775–83). The country was
not then in a mood to see the return of
the restless and corrupt Whigs, and Tory
governments continued in power until 1832.

About 1830 the names Liberal and
Conservative began to replace Whig and
Tory in popular use, and these terms were
officially adopted some 30 years later. 'Tory'
survives, to some extent, as interchangeable
with Conservative (it is shorter for newspaper
headlines), but 'Whig' has been altogether
superseded.

White, Gilbert (1720–93)

Writer on natural history. He was born
at Selborne, a village in Hampshire. After
spending, some years as a Fellow of Oriel
College, ▷ Oxford, he became a country
curate, and spent the last nine years of his
life in the village of his birth. His *Natural
History of Selborne* (1789) is a record of the
plant, animal, and bird life there, inspired
by genuine scientific curiosity and showing
great delicacy and charm of expression. The
book has been described as the first to raise
natural history to the level of literature, and
is the fruit of the development of 17th- and
18th-century natural science, partly initiated
by the greatest of English naturalists, John
Ray (1627–1705), author *The Wisdom of God
Manifested in the Works of his Creation* (1691),
a scientist who shared ▷ Newton's intellectual
curiosity and his religious awe at the spectacle
of divine organization in the universe. Another
tradition leading to White was the newly
awakened sensibility for natural surroundings
in the poetry of ▷ William Collins (1721–59),
and ▷ William Cowper. The poetic movement
culminated in the 19th century in the work of
▷ Wordsworth and ▷ Clare.
Bib: Holt-White, R., *Life and Letters*.

White, Henry Kirke (1785–1806)

Poet. White came from a poor family but won
a scholarship to ▷ Cambridge after being
encouraged and helped by ▷ Southey. His
first book of poetry, *Clifton Grove* (1803),
showed great promise, but he died while
still at university and Southey published his
papers together with a small biography in *The
Remains of Kirke White* (1807).

Wilberforce, William (1759–1833)

Philanthropist and politician. He devoted
much of his life to the campaign to abolish
the slave trade and slavery in overseas
British territories. In 1807, the slave trade
was made illegal, and so was slavery itself in
the year of his death. He was a leader of the
▷ Evangelical movement, particularly of a
group known as the Clapham Sect because it
met in his house at Clapham.

Wilkinson, Sarah (?–c 1830)

Novelist. By Wilkinson's own account she
published a novel, *The Thatched Cottage*,
opened a school on the proceeds, and taught
intermittently after that time. Her own novels,
of which *The Spectre of Lanmere Abbey* (1820)
is perhaps the best, include all the required
▷ Gothic ingredients and she was much
influenced by ▷ Ann Radcliffe. However,
Wilkinson was unable to take the ghosts,
hauntings and other paraphernalia seriously
and a mocking irony always undercuts, quite
pleasurably, the overladen and exaggerated
tone expected of the genre. Wilkinson is also
known for her ▷ chapbooks, which consist of
condensed forms of popular works as well as
simplified ▷ translations of foreign literature.
She scrupulously acknowledged the authors of
the works she treated in this manner (Henry
Fielding, ▷ 'Monk' Lewis, Ann Radcliffe and
▷ Sir Walter Scott), but her own irrepressible
ironic tone creates a witty self-consciousness.

Williams, Helen (1762–1827)

Poet, novelist, and letter-writer. Her poetry,
especially her ▷ sonnets (1786), is vivid
and emotive, and her novel *Julia* (1790) is
an interesting reworking of ▷ Rousseau's
Nouvelle Heloise, but Williams is best known
for the letters she wrote from France during
the ▷ French Revolution. Although she was
horrified by the violence and bloodshed,
her sympathies were radical and, hence,
controversial. She specifically described the
important role of women in overthrowing the
injustices of the *ancien régime*. Williams was
acquainted with ▷ Mary Wollstonecraft and
with ▷ Wordsworth, whose first published
poem, written anonymously in 1787, was
entitled 'Sonnet on Seeing Miss Helen Maria
Williams Weep at a Tale of Distress'.

▷ French literature in England.
Bib: Todd, J., *Sensibility: An Introduction*.

Wilson, Harriette (1786–1845)

Autobiographer. Infamous for her racy ▷ autobiography, *Memoirs* (1825), in which she describes her life as a courtesan and her affairs with many of the leading figures of her day. She planned the book with her husband, William Henry Rochfort (whom she had married in 1823), as a form of blackmail and, indeed, when it was published it caused an immediate commotion amongst those mentioned (including Beau Brummel and the ▷ Duke of Wellington), as well as amongst the outraged upholders of morality. She followed this with two *romans-à-clef* which are immensely readable accounts of London life: *Paris Lions and London Tigers* (1825) and *Clara Gazul* (1830).

Wilson, John (1785–1854)

Scottish journalist, chiefly known under the pseudonym 'Christopher North' which he used when writing for ▷ *Blackwood's Magazine*, for which he was the principal writer from 1817. He wrote very lively, semi-dramatic discussions called *Noctes Ambrosianae* which became famous. In 1820 he was elected to the professorship of moral philosophy in Edinburgh University. He had no special qualifications for the post, but was backed by ▷ Walter Scott. Nonetheless he filled the post very effectively. He contributed much other journalism to *Blackwood's*, and was also a poet: *The Isle of Palms* (1812) and *The City of the Plague* (1816).
Bib: Swan, E., *Christopher North – John Wilson*.

Wolcot, John (1738–1819)

Poet. After a career as a doctor in Jamaica and Cornwall, Wolcot accompanied the painter Opie to London, intent on a career in literature. His poems, published under the pseudonym Peter Pindar are crude if vigorous ▷ satires on respectable public figures and institutions: *Lyric Odes to the Royal Academicians* (1782–5), *The Lousiad* (1785), *Instructions to a Celebrated Laureat* (1787). His *Bozzy and Piozzi* (1786) is a whimsical poem in which ▷ James Boswell and ▷ Hester Thrale are shown reminiscing about Samuel Johnson (1709–84), who had died two years earlier.

Wollstonecraft, Mary (1759–97)

Pamphleteer and novelist. Wollstonecraft is notable for her outspoken views on the role of women in society, and on the part played by education in woman's oppression. After running a school in London with her sister, she set out her ideas in the early pamphlet *Thoughts on the Education of Daughters* (1787). The following year her novel, *Mary*, developed this theme, together with a satirical perspective on the manners of the aristocracy, possibly based on her own experiences as governess with the family of Lord Kingsborough in Ireland.

Wollstonecraft's most famous work, *A Vindication of the Rights of Woman* (1792) now stands as one of the major documents in the history of women's writing. Attacking the 'mistaken notions of female excellence' which she recognized in contemporary attitudes to 'femininity' and the cult of the sentimental, Wollstonecraft argued that women were not naturally submissive, but taught to be so, confined to 'smiling under the lash at which [they] dare not snarl'. Although widely caricatured by critics for her own 'immoral' life – an affair with Gilbert Imlay, and subsequent marriage with ▷ William Godwin – Wollstonecraft's ideas are closely related to the moralist tradition of writing addressed to young women. Arguing that the true basis of marriage must be not love but friendship, she continues the rational proposals outlined by the 17th-century pamphleteer Mary Astell in such works as *A Serious Proposal to the Ladies*. The most radical of her thoughts concern the treatment by society of unmarried mothers, whom she believed were worthy of the respect and support of their families and lovers. Her novel *Maria: or, The Wrongs of Woman* (1798) remained unfinished and was published posthumously, but develops the ideas of *A Vindication* in a more complex and experimental context. The philosophical tradition behind her writings is evident in *A Vindication of the Rights of Man* (1790), a reply to ▷ Burke, and in the dedication of *Rights of Woman* to Talleyrand.
▷ Feminism.
Bib: Todd, J., *The Sign of Angelica*; Butler, M. and Todd, J. (eds.), *The Works of Mary Wollstonecraft*; Tomalin, C., *The Life and Death of Mary Wollstonecraft*.

Women, Education of

In medieval convents, nuns often learned and received the same education as monks. Thereafter, women's intellectual education was not widely provided for until the later 19th century, though much would depend on their social rank, their parents, or their husbands.

Boarding schools for girls came into existence in the 17th century and became more numerous in the 18th, but either they were empty of real educational value or they were absurdly pretentious, like Miss Pinkerton's Academy described in Thackeray's *Vanity Fair* (1848); Mrs Malaprop in ▷ Sheridan's comedy *The Rivals* (1775) is a satire on the half-educated upper class women. Upper-class girls had governesses for general education, music masters, dancing masters, and teachers of 'deportment', *ie* in the bearing of the body; lower class women were illiterate, unless they learned to read and write at 'charity schools'. On the other hand they had a much wider range of domestic skills than is usual with modern women, and among the poor, a rich store of folklore. However, in the 18th century there was already a shift in values. Swift, in his letter to a young lady about to enter marriage, points out that the way to keep a husband's affections was to grow in maturity of mind, and the ▷ bluestocking women of the middle of the century were entertainers of the intellectual elite of their society.

The big change dates from the mid-19th century. ▷ Tennyson's *The Princess* (1850), for example advocates educational opportunities for women and the eponymous heroine actually founds a university for this purpose. Actual colleges were founded for the higher education of women (beginning with Queen's College, London, 1848), and schools (*eg* Cheltenham Ladies' College) comparable to the public schools for boys were founded. The women's colleges Girton (1869) and Newnham (1875) were founded in Cambridge, and others followed at Oxford. Societies were also founded for the advancing of women's education. All this in spite of warnings from medical men that cerebral development in the female must be at the cost of physiological, *ie* child-bearing, aptitude. Since the commencement of state education in 1870, the status of women teachers has been brought equal to that of men teachers, and since 1902 equal secondary education has been provided for both sexes.

Women, Status of

Unmarried women had few prospects in Britain until the second half of the 19th century. In the ▷ Middle Ages they could enter convents and become nuns, but when in 1536–9 Henry VIII closed the convents and the monasteries, no alternative opened to them. Widows like Chaucer's (1340–1400) Wife of Bath in *The Canterbury Tales* might

inherit a business (in her case that of a clothier) and run it efficiently, or like Mistress Quickly in ▷ Shakespeare's *Henry IV, Part II* they might run inns. The profession of acting was opened to women from the ▷ Restoration of the Monarchy in 1660, and writing began to be a possible means of making money from the time of Aphra Behn (1640–89). Later the increase of interest in education for girls led to extensive employment of governesses to teach the children in private families; such a position might be peaceful and pleasant, like Mrs Weston's experience in the Woodhouse family in ▷ Jane Austen's ▷ *Emma*, but it was at least as likely to be unpleasant, underpaid, and despised, as the novelist ▷ Charlotte Brontë found. Nursing was also open to women, but nurses had no training and were commonly a low class of women like Betsey Prig and Mrs Gamp in Dickens's *Martin Chuzzlewit* (1843–4) until Florence Nightingale reformed the profession.

Wives and their property were entirely in the power of their husbands according to the law, though in practice they might take the management of both into their own hands, like the Wife of Bath. A Dutch observer (1575) stated that England was called 'the Paradise of married women' because they took their lives more easily than continental wives. Nonetheless, a middle-class wife worked hard, as her husband's assistant (probably his accountant) in his business, and as a mistress of baking, brewing, household management and amateur medicine.

The 19th century was the heroic age for women in Britain. No other nation before the 20th century has produced such a distinguished line of women writers as the novelists Jane Austen, Elizabeth Gaskell (1810–65), ▷ Charlotte and ▷ Emily Brontë and George Eliot (Mary Ann Evans; 1819–80). In addition there was the prison reformer, Elizabeth Fry; the reformer of the nursing profession, Florence Nightingale; the explorer, Mary Kingsley; the sociologist, Beatrice Webb (1858–1943), pioneers in education, and the first women doctors. The Married Women's Property Act of 1882 for the first time gave wives rights to their own property which had hitherto been merged with their husbands'. Political rights came more slowly, and were preceded by an active and sometimes violent movement, led by the Suffragettes, who fought for them. Women over 30 were given the vote in 1918 as a consequence of their success in taking over men's work during World War I, but women over 21 (the age at which men were entitled to vote or stand for Parliament) had to wait until 1928.

Women's movement, The

The women's movement – under many names – is dedicated to the campaign for political and legal rights for women. It wishes to prevent discrimination on the grounds of gender and is, generally, a movement for social change.

There is no single source, although the history of women's quest for equality is a long one. The *Querelle des Femmes* in the medieval period, Aphra Behn and Mary Astell in the 17th century, and ▷ Mary Wollstonecraft in the ▷ Romantic Age all furthered women's rights. In the ▷ Victorian period ▷ feminism became linked with other social movements such as anti-slavery campaigners, evangelical groups and Quakers. The suffragette movement (1860–1930) united women and this solidarity was to re-emerge in the radicalization of the 1960s. The important works of this later stage in the women's movement are Simone de Beauvoir's *Le Deuxième Sexe* (1949), Kate Millett's *Sexual Politics* (1969) and Germaine Greer's *The Female Eunuch* (1970). The 1970s and 1980s have witnessed the second stage of the women's movement and seen its dismemberment into separate pressure groups – *eg* lesbianism, Third World – and its partial metamorphosis into post-feminism. This latter term has become popularized and takes for granted that women now have equality with men, but the mainstream of the women's movement denies this emphatically and perseveres with its campaign.

▷ Women, Status of.

Bib: Mitchell, J. and Oakley, A. (eds.), *What is Feminism?*; Eisenstein, H., *Contemporary Feminist Thought*.

Wordsworth, Dorothy (1771–1855)

Diarist, letter-writer and poet. The sister of ▷ William Wordsworth and consequently one of the few women writers acknowledged by traditional criticism. Although Dorothy grew up with distant relatives, in 1794 she rejoined her brother and lived with him, and later his wife and children, until her death. She devoted herself entirely to William's creative genius and even her own journal was written to 'give William pleasure by it'. Her descriptions of the friendship she and William shared with ▷ Coleridge, of their long discussions and observations of nature, and of the daily routine and surroundings of Dove Cottage are valuable to literary historians. But because her own writing does not fall into a conventional literary classification, it has often been neglected by critics and biographers. Recently, however, she has been reclaimed by ▷ feminist criticism which has pointed towards the parallels between her writing and her brother's, often making it impossible to tell who originated certain phrases, vocabulary and images.

Bib: Homans, M., *Women Writers and Poetic Identity*; Levin, S.M., *Dorothy Wordsworth and Romanticism*.

Wordsworth, William (1770–1850)

Poet. He was born in Cumberland, the son of a law-agent. His mother died when he was only eight, and when his father died five years later, he was sent to school at Hawkshead, where he led a life of solitary freedom among the fells. In 1787 he went to Cambridge, but more inspiring in their influence were his two visits to revolutionary France: the first in 1790, and the second, lasting a year, from November 1791. During the second visit his love affair with a surgeon's daughter, Annette Vallon, resulted in her pregnancy, and she later bore him a daughter. Forced to leave Annette behind on his return Wordsworth underwent a period of turmoil, intensified when England went to war with France in 1793. The emotional trauma of this period in his life seems to have been displaced into the searching anxiety which underlies much of his early poetry. The love affair is not mentioned explicitly in his work but is recounted at one remove in the story of *Vaudracour and Julia* (written c 1804; published 1820).

Wordsworth's relatives intended him for the Church, but his religious views at this time tended towards an unorthodox ▷ pantheism, evolved during his strangely lonely but happy childhood. Moreover, the writings of the extreme rationalist philosopher ▷ William Godwin influenced him still further against the possibility of a career in the Church of England. Fortunately in 1795 a friend left him a legacy sufficient to keep him independent, and he settled down in Somerset with his sister ▷ Dorothy, one of the most sustaining personal influences of his life. By 1797 he had made the friendship of ▷ Samuel Taylor Coleridge, who came to live nearby, and in 1798 the two poets collaborated in producing ▷ *Lyrical Ballads*. In 1799 William and Dorothy moved to Dove Cottage, Grasmere, and in 1802 Wordsworth married Mary Hutchinson. By this time, he was disillusioned with France, now under dictatorship, had abandoned Godwinism, and was beginning to turn back to orthodox religion. He also became more conservative in politics, to the disgust of younger men such as ▷ Byron and ▷ Shelley. The great decade of his poetry ran from 1797 to 1807. Thereafter it declined in quality while his reputation slowly grew. By 1830 his achievement was generally acknowledged, and in 1843 he was made ▷ Poet Laureate.

Wordsworth's first volumes (*Descriptive Sketches, An Evening Walk*, 1793) show the characteristic tone and diction of 18th-century topographical and nature poetry. They were followed by a tragedy, *The Borderers* (not published until 1842). The *Lyrical Ballads* collection marks a new departure however, in the uncompromising simplicity of much of its language, its concern with the poor and outcast, and its fusion of natural description with inward states of mind. These qualities have often caused the volume to be viewed as the starting point of the ▷ Romantic Movement. The *Preface* to the 1800 edition of *Lyrical Ballads* also contained Wordsworth's attack on the 'gaudiness and inane phraseology' which he felt encumbered contemporary verse. With the encouragement of Coleridge, he planned a long philosophical poem to be called *The Recluse*, and in preparation for it, wrote ▷ *The Prelude*. This was completed by 1805, but not published until 1850, and then in a revised form. In 1807 Wordsworth published *Poems in Two Volumes*, and in 1814 ▷ *The Excursion*, the only part of *The Recluse* to be completed besides *The Prelude*. These were followed by *The White Doe of Rylstone* (1815); *Peter Bell* (1819); *The River Duddon* (1820); *Ecclesiastical Sketches* (1822); *Sonnets* (1838).

Wordsworth's greatness lies in his impressive, even stubborn authenticity of tone. Sometimes this is achieved through the use of primitive or simplistic literary form as in such lyrical ballads as *We are Seven* and *The Thorn*, and also the ▷ Lucy poems. Sometimes Wordsworth develops the discursive ▷ blank verse manner of the 18th-century ▷ Georgic into an original, profoundly introspective vehicle for what ▷ John Keats called his 'egotistical sublime', as in *The Prelude*, ▷ *The Ruined Cottage* and ▷ *Tintern Abbey*. Frequently he succeeds in convincing the reader that subject matter which in other poets would be merely banal or even comic, is in fact of mysterious portentousness. This technique is particularly impressive in poems which treat the poor, the mad, the senile, members of humanity generally disregarded in earlier poetry. In these works his diction

and tone brush aside the class-based doctrine of kinds, and the related conceptions of 'high' and 'low' language which dominate much 18th-century verse. Such poems as *Simon Lee, The Idiot Boy*, and ▷ *Resolution and Independence* (1807) seem to challenge the reader's humanity, by their empathy with the wretched, the abject, and the poverty-stricken.

Another characteristically Romantic idea, that 'the child is father to the man', that youth is essentially richer in wisdom and insight than age, is developed into a full-scale philosophy in the early books of *The Prelude*. It is significant however that the illustrative reminiscences of the poet's own youth are far more effective as poetry than the passages of explicit theorizing. The *Ode: ▷ Intimations of Immortality from Recollections of Early Childhood* (1807) is often thought to show Wordsworth's uneasy recognition that his inspiration was leaving him. It is a mistake, however, to suppose that he wrote no good poetry after 1807, though his spiritual earnestness increasingly declines into orthodox piety, and his bold austerity of tone into mere banality. **Bib:** Moorman, M., *Life*; Bateson, F. W., *Wordsworth, A Reinterpretation*; Knight, G. W., in *The Starlit Dome*; Sherry, C., *Wordsworth's Poetry of the Imagination*; Beer, J., *Wordsworth and the Human Heart*; Wordsworth, J., *William Wordsworth: The Borders of Vision*; Watson, J. R., *Wordsworth*; Hartman, G., *Wordsworth's Poetry 1787–1814*; Jacobus, M., *Tradition and Experiment in Wordsworth's Lyrical Ballads (1798)*; Jones, A. R., and Tydeman, W. (eds.), *Wordsworth: Lyrical Ballads* (Macmillan Casebook); Harvey, W. J., and Gravil, R., *Wordsworth: The Prelude* (Macmillan Casebook).

Wuthering Heights (1847)

The sole novel of ▷ Emily Brontë. The title of the book is the name of an old house, high up on the Yorkshire moors, occupied by the Earnshaw family, and the novel is set at the very end of the 18th century. Into this house Mr Earnshaw brings a child who has been living the life of a wild animal in the slums of Liverpool. His parents are quite unknown and Earnshaw adopts him, giving him the single name of Heathcliff. However, Mr Earnshaw treats him less like a human being than like an over-indulged pet animal; this arouses the fierce resentment of his son Hindley and it is only with the daughter Catherine (Cathy) that Heathcliff has a human relationship. After Mr Earnshaw's death, Heathcliff is maltreated by Hindley, now master of the house, and lives like a despised animal instead of a spoilt one; his strong bond with Cathy, however, remains. But Cathy marries Edgar Linton from the 'civilized' household of Thrushcross Grange in the valley. Heathcliff runs away and is heard of no more for three years. During this period Cathy and Edgar are contented together, though she has fits of depression. When Heathcliff returns, he has become a rich man but is as socially excluded as ever, as deeply identified with Cathy, and full of hatred for the Linton and the Earnshaw families, which he sets about to destroy, especially after the death of Cathy in giving birth to a daughter. He nearly succeeds in doing so but has to withhold harm from Hareton Earnshaw, the son of Hindley, and Catherine Linton, the daughter of Cathy, who are deeply in love. Heathcliff becomes detached from external reality and lives only for his union with Cathy in death. On the last page a weeping little boy declares that he has seen the ghosts of the dead Heathcliff and Cathy walking on the moor.

Emily Brontë's aim seems to have been to present an image of the feminine personality under the social constrictions of the civilization of the time. Cathy rather than Heathcliff is the central character. Women were not supposed to possess the wilder, instinctive feelings which were acknowledged in men; and girls' training, among the middle and upper classes, was a systematic inhibition of anything of the sort. Cathy, however, has this element in herself awakened by her early association with Heathcliff and, though her marriage with Edgar Linton is in many ways ideal both personally and socially, she can never afterwards be fully herself: 'Nelly, I *am* Heathcliff.' Heathcliff, on the other hand, represents the savage forces in human beings which civilization attempts vainly to eliminate, whereas it should somehow assimilate them. Much of the interest of the book lies in the brilliant complexity of the structure, the dual narrative, time shifts and flashbacks, as well as the original handling of ▷ Gothic and ▷ Romantic elements, and how they colour the evocation of houses and landscapes.

Xanadu
▷ *Kubla Khan.*

X

Yearsley, Ann (1752–1806)
Poet, playwright and novelist. Ann Yearsley is often called 'Lactilla, the Bristol Milkwoman', for she was an uneducated dairywoman who was encouraged to write poetry by ▷ Hannah More. At first the relationship worked well, but as Yearsley became more independent she demanded more control over the money she had earned, and the friendship finally ended in lasting recrimination. She appears to defend herself against More's accusations in the preface to *The Royal Captives* where she writes: 'None may condemn me; Nature herself drew delusion in the desert where

I was beloved by Fancy, before I was alive to Fame.' Her development can be traced in the difference between the naïve *Poems on Several occasions* (1785) and the politically astute material in *Poems on Various Subjects* (1787). She also wrote a play, *Earl Goodwin* (1791), and a ▷ Gothic novel, *The Royal Captives* (1795), but her income was finally to come from a very successful ▷ circulating library which she opened in 1793. ▷ Southey includes her in his *Lives of the Uneducated Poets*.
Bib: Tomkins, J.M.S., *The Polite Marriage*.

Y

Chronology

This chronology gives a breakdown of important dates, both literary and historical. The literary dates are listed in the left-hand column and the historical events in the right-hand column. The listing is necessarily selective.

1700
Congreve: *The Way of the World*

1704
Swift: *Battle of the Books*
Tale of a Tub
1707
Farquhar: *The Beaux' Stratagem*

1709
Pope: trans. of part of Books XII and XVI of
Homer's *Iliad*
Steele: *The Tatler* (Apr. 1709–Jan. 1711)
1711
Addison (and Steele): *The Spectator* (1 Mar.
1711– 6 Dec. 1712)
Pope: *Essay on Criticism*
1712
Pope: *The Rape of the Lock* (first version)
1713
Pope: *Windsor Forest*
1714
Pope: *The Rape of the Lock* (final version)

1719
Defoe: *Robinson Crusoe*

1724
Defoe: *Journal of the Plague Year*
Moll Flanders
1725
Pope: trans. of Homer's *Odyssey* (Volumes I–III;
completed 1726)
The Plays of Shakespeare (an edition)
1726
Swift: *Gulliver's Travels*

1728
Gay: *The Beggar's Opera* (first acted 29 Jan.;
published 14 Feb.)
Pope: *The Dunciad* (in three books)
1730
The Grub Street Journal (–1737)
1733
Pope: *Essay on Man* (Epistles I–III)
1734
Pope: *An Essay on Man* (Epistle IV)
Theobald: *The Plays of Shakespeare* (an edition)
1735
Pope: *Epistle to Dr Arbuthnot*
1740
Richardson: *Pamela* (Volumes I–II)
1741
Fielding: *Shamela*
Hume: *Essays Moral and Political* (Volume I)
Richardson: *Pamela* (Volumes III–IV)

1742
Fielding: *Joseph Andrews*
1747
Richardson: *Clarissa* (Volumes I–II)
1749
Cleland: *Fanny Hill*
Fielding: *Tom Jones*

1752
Adoption of the Gregorian calendar: 2 September followed by 14 September
1753
Apr. Charter granted for the foundation of the British Museum

1755
Johnson: *Dictionary of the English Language*
1760
Sterne: *Tristram Shandy* (Volumes I–II)

1760
25 Oct. Death of George II. Accession of George III.

1761
Sterne: *Tristram Shandy* (Volumes III–IV and V–VI)

1763
16 May Boswell meets Johnson

1764
Horace Walpole: *The Castle of Otranto*
1765
Johnson: *The Plays of Shakespeare* (an edition)
Percy: *Reliques of Ancient English Poetry*
Sterne: *Tristram Shandy* (Volumes VII–VIII)
1766
Goldsmith: *The Vicar of Wakefield*
1767
Sterne: *Tristram Shandy* (Volume IX)
1768
Chatterton: *Rowleyan Writings* (composed)
Gray: *Poems*

1769
Opening of the Royal Academy
1770
Lord North becomes Prime Minister
Import duties on all goods except tea removed
1772
Start of Captain Cook's second voyage of discovery
1773
The Boston Tea Party

1773
Goldsmith: *She Stoops to Conquer* (produced)
1774
Thomas Warton: *History of English Poetry* (Volume I; completed 1781)
1775
Sheridan: *The Rivals* (produced)

1775
Defeat of the British at the Battle of Lexington: start of the American War of Independence
George Washington becomes Commander-in-Chief of American forces

1776
Gibbon: *Decline and Fall of the Roman Empire* (Volume I)
1777
Sheridan: *School for Scandal* (first acted)
1778
Fanny Burney: *Evelina*
1779
Johnson: *Lives of the Poets* (Volume I)
Sheridan: *The Critic* (first acted)
1780
Bentham: *Principles of Morals and Legislation* (privately printed)
1781
Johnson: *Lives of the Poets* (Volume II)

1782
Fanny Burns: *Cecilia*
Cowper: *Poems*

1785
Cowper: *The Task*
1786
Burns: *Poems Chiefly in the Scottish Dialect*
(Kilmarnock)

1789
Blake: *Songs of Innocence* (composed)

1790
Burke: *Reflections on the Revolution in France*
Malone: *The Works of Shakespeare* (an edition)
1791
Boswell: *The Life of Johnson*
Tom Paine: *The Rights of Man* (Part I)
1792
Tom Paine: *The Rights of Man* (Part II)

1793
Godwin: *Political Justice*
1794
Blake: *Songs of Innocence and Experience* (first
combined volume)
Ann Radcliffe: *The Mysteries of Udolpho*
1796
Fanny Burney: *Camilla*
Coleridge: *Poems on Various Subjects*
M. G. Lewis: *The Monk*
1797
Coleridge: *Kubla Khan* (probably written)
1798
Wordsworth: *The Prelude* (begun)
                    (and Coleridge): *Lyrical Ballads*

1799
Hannah More: *Modern Female Education*

1802
Scott: *Ministrelsy of the Scottish Border* (Volumes I
and II)
1803
Scott: *Ministrelsy of the Scottish Border* (Volume
III)

1805
Wordsworth: *The Prelude* (completed)
1806
Scott: *Ballads and Lyrical Pieces*
1807
C. and M. Lamb: *Tales from Shakespeare*

1782
Resignation of Lord North
Preliminaries for peace between Britain and America
1783
Pitt's first ministry (−1801)
1784
John Wesley founds Methodism
William Pitt becomes Prime Minister

1788
First colony founded in Australia
The Times first published
1789
The Storming of the Bastille: Start of the French
Revolution

1792
Paris Commune established
Trial of Tom Paine
1793
Louis XVI executed

1798
The Irish rebellion
Nelson beats the French fleet at the Battle of the
Nile
1799
Newspaper Act

1800
Bill of Union of Great Britain and Ireland

1804
Napoleon crowned Emperor
1805
Battle of Trafalgar: Nelson defeats French fleet

1809
Battle of Corunna: death of Sir John Moore

1811
Jane Austen: *Sense and Sensibility*

1812
Byron: *Childe Harold* (Cantos I and II)
1813
Jane Austen: *Pride and Prejudice*
Shelley: 'Queen Mab'
1814
Jane Austen: *Mansfield Park*
Fanny Burney: *The Wanderer*
Maria Edgeworth: *Patronage*
Scott: *Waverley*
Wordsworth: 'The Excursion'
1815
Wordsworth: *Poems*

1816
Jane Austen: *Emma*
Byron: *Childe Harold* (Canto III)
Coleridge: *Kubla Khan* (published)
Scott: *Old Mortality*
1817
Blackwood's Magazine (established)
Coleridge: *Biographia Literaria*
Mary Shelley: *Frankenstein*
1818
Jane Austen: *Northanger Abbey*
             Persuasion
Byron: *Childe Harold* (Canto IV)
Hazlitt: *Lectures on the English Poets*
Keats: *Endymion*
Peacock: *Nightmare Abbey*
Scott: *Heart of Midlothian*
1819
Byron: *Don Juan* (Cantos I and II)
Keats: 'Hyperion' (written; published 1856)
Scott: *Bride of Lammermoor*
Shelley: 'The Cenci'
1820
Keats: 'Eve of St Agnes'
Lamb: *Essays of Elia* (begun)
Scott: *Ivanhoe*
Shelley: 'Prometheus Unbound'
1821
Byron: *Don Juan* (Cantos III–V)
       'Sardanapalus'
De Quincey: *Confessions of an English Opium Eater*
Scott: *Kenilworth*
1822
Shelley: 'Hellas'

1823
Byron: *Don Juan* (Cantos VI–XIV)
Hazlitt: *Liber Amoris*
Scott: *Quentin Durward*

1824
Byron: *Don Juan* (Cantos XV–XVI)
Lamb: *Essays of Elia* (second series)
Westminster Review (established)
1825
Carlyle: *Life of Schiller*

1811
The Regency Act makes the Prince of Wales Prince
Regent (George III insane)
Luddite riots

1815
Passage of Corn Law prohibiting imports when
price low
Battle of Waterloo: Wellington defeats Napoleon

1818
5 May Birth of Karl Marx

1819
The Peterloo Massacre: Manchester reform meeting
broken up
Parliament passes the Six Acts to suppress possible
disorder
1820
Death of George III: succeeded by George IV (the
Prince Regent)

1821
Greek War of Independence
Legislation regarding free trade

1822
George Canning becomes Leader of the House of
Commons and Foreign Secretary
1823
Catholic association established in Ireland by Daniel
O'Connell
Robert Peel permits transportation of convicts
The Monroe doctrine: United States refuses to
tolerate European political intervention in
American states

1826
Elizabeth Barrett Browning: *Essay on Mind and
other Poems*
1828
The *Spectator* (established)
1830
Cobbett: *Rural Rides*
Tennyson: *Poems Chiefly Lyrical*
1831
Peacock: *Crotchet Castle*
1832
Tennyson: 'The Lady of Shalott'

1833
Carlyle: *Sartor Resartus* (in *Frazer's Magazine*;
completed 1834)
Tennyson: *Poems*
1834
Dickens: *Sketches by Boz*

1836
Dickens: *Pickwick Papers* (completed 1837)
1837
Dickens: *Oliver Twist* (completed 1838)

1838
Elizabeth Barrett Browning: *The Seraphim and
Other Poems*
Dickens: *Nicholas Nickleby* (completed 1839)
1840
Browning: 'Sordello'
Dickens: *Old Curiosity Shop*
1841
Browning: 'Pippa Passes'
Dickens: *Barnaby Rudge*
1842
Browning: *Dramatic Lyrics*

1843
Carlyle: *Past and Present*
Dickens: *Martin Chuzzlewit* (completed 1844)
Macaulay: *Essays* (reprinted from *Edinburgh Review*)
Ruskin: *Modern Painters* (Volume I)
Wordsworth (becomes Poet Laureate)
1844
Elizabeth Barrett Browning: *Poems*
1845
Browning: *Dramatic Romances and Lyrics*
Benjamin Disraeli: *Sybil, or The Two Nations*
1846
C., E. and A. Brontë: *Poems*
Dickens: *Dombey and Son* (completed 1848)
1847
A. Brontë: *Agnes Grey*
C. Brontë: *Jane Eyre*
E. Brontë: *Wuthering Heights*
1848
Elizabeth Gaskell: *Mary Barton*
Thackeray: *Vanity Fair* (completed)

1828
Tory administration formed by Wellington
1830
26 June Death of George IV: William IV comes to
the throne

1832
The Reform Bill becomes law (start of electoral
reform process)
1833
29 Aug. Controls placed upon child labour by
passage of Factory Act

1834
Formation of the Grand National Consolidated
Trades Union
The Tolpuddle Martyrs sentenced to transportation
Abolition of slavery in territories governed by
Britain
1836
Chartist movement founded
1837
Death of William IV; Queen Victoria succeeds to
the throne

1841
Conservative ministry formed by Robert Peel

1842
Parliament rejects Chartist petition
Mines Act: regulates employment of women and
children underground
Chartist uprisings

1846
May Repeal of the Corn Laws

1849
C. Brontë: *Shirley*
Dickens: *David Copperfield*
Thackeray: *Pendennis* (completed 1850)
1850
Elizabeth Barrett Browning: *Sonnets from the Portuguese*
Ruskin: *Pre-Raphaelitism*
Tennyson: 'In Memoriam' (becomes Poet Laureate) 'The Princess'
Wordsworth: 'The Prelude' (written 1805)

1852
Dickens: *Bleak House*
1853
Matthew Arnold: 'The Scholar Gypsy' 'Sohrab and Rustum'
C. Brontë: *Villette*
Elizabeth Gaskell: *Cranford*
1854
Dickens: *Hard Times*

1855
Browning: 'Men and Women'
Dickens: *Little Dorrit* (completed 1857)
Tennyson: 'Maud'
Trollope: *The Warden*
1857
C. Brontë: *The Professor*
Elizabeth Barrett Browning: 'Aurora Leigh'
Trollope: *Barchester Towers*
1858
William Morris: *Defence of Guinevere and other Poems*
1859
Darwin: *Origin of Species*
Dickens: *Tale of Two Cities*
George Eliot: *Adam Bede*
Tennyson: *Idylls of the King*
1860
Wilkie Collins: *Woman in White*
Dickens: *Great Expectations* (completed 1861)
George Eliot: *Mill on the Floss*
1861
George Eliot: *Silas Marner*
D. G. Rossetti: *Early Italian Poets*
Swinburne: *The Queen Mother Rosamund*
1862
Elizabeth Barrett Browning: *Last Poems*
J. S. Mill: *Utilitarianism* (in *Frazer's Magazine*)
Christina Rossetti: *Goblin Market and Other Poems*
1863
George Eliot: *Romola*
Thomas Huxley: *Man's Place in Nature*
Kingsley: *Water Babies*
1864
Browning: *Dramatis Personae*
1865
Matthew Arnold: *Essays in Criticism*
Lewis Carroll: *Alice's Adventures in Wonderland*
Dickens: *Our Mutual Friend* (completed)

1849
Benjamin Disraeli becomes Conservative leader

1851
Palmerston resigns
1852
Lord John Russell resigns
1853
Free Trade budget introduced by Gladstone

1854
Britain and France declare war on Russia (Crimean War)
The Battle of Balaclava: the charge of the Light Brigade

1859
Benjamin Disraeli's Reform Bill
Liberal administration formed by Palmerston

1861
American Civil War starts

1865
The Confederate army surrenders at Shreveport: end of the American Civil War
Palmerston dies; Lord John Russell becomes Prime Minister

1866
Elizabeth Gaskell: *Wives and Daughters*
Swinburne: *Poems and Ballads*
1867
Matthew Arnold: *The Study of Celtic Literature*

1868
Wilkie Collins: *The Moonstone*
George Eliot: *The Spanish Gypsy*
William Morris: *Earthly Paradise* (Volumes I and II)
1869
Blackmore: *Lorna Doone*

1870
Dickens: *Mystery of Edwin Drood*
D. G. Rossetti: *Poems*
1871
George Eliot: *Middlemarch* (completed 1872)
Swinburne: *Songs before Sunrise*

1872
Hardy: *Under the Greenwood Tree*
1873
Pater: *Studies in the History of the Renaissance*
1874
Hardy: *Far from the Madding Crowd*
Swinburne: *Bothwell*

1876
George Eliot: *Daniel Deronda*
1877
Henry James: *The American*
1878
Hardy: *The Return of the Native*
Swinburne: *Poems and Ballads*
1879
Browning: 'Dramatic Idylls'
Henry James: *Daisy Miller*
Meredith: *The Egoist*
1880
Browning: 'Dramatic Idylls' (second series)
Benjamin Disraeli: *Endymion*
Swinburne: *Songs of the Spring Tides*
1881
Hardy: *A Laodicean*
Henry James: *Portrait of a Lady*
Christina Rossetti: *A Pageant and Other Poems*
D. G. Rossetti: *Ballads and Sonnets*
1882
Matthew Arnold: *Irish Essays*
Swinburne: 'Tristram of Lyonesse'
1883
Burton: trans. of *Arabian Nights Entertainments*
Stevenson: *Treasure Island*

1886
Henry James: *The Bostonians*
Stevenson: *Dr Jekyll and Mr Hyde*
           Kidnapped

1867
Fenian disturbances
The Dominion of Canada established by the British North America Act
Suffrage extended by Parliamentary Reform Act
1868
Benjamin Disraeli becomes Prime Minister
Liberal victory in General Election: Gladstone forms ministry

1869
Opening of the Suez Canal
Birth of Gandhi

1871
Religious tests for entry to universities of Oxford and Cambridge abolished by the Universities Tests Act
Trades Unions legalized by Act of Parliament
1872
Voting by secret ballot introduced by the Ballot Act
1873
Judicature Act, reforming courts of law
1874
Conservative victory in General Election
Benjamin Disraeli forms ministry
1875
Public Health Act

1877
Queen Victoria becomes Empress of India

1880
Liberal administration formed by Gladstone

1883
Karl Marx dies

1885
General Gordon dies at Khartoum
1886
Gladstone brings in Home Rule Bill for Ireland
Second reading of Home Rule Bill brings Liberal defeat
1887
The Golden Jubilee of Queen Victoria

1888
Matthew Arnold: *Essays in Criticism* (second in series)
1889
Yeats: 'The Wanderings of Oisin'

1891
Gissing: *New Grub Street*
Hardy: *Tess of the D'Urbervilles*
William Morris: *News from Nowhere*
Shaw: *The Quintessence of Ibsenism*
Wilde: *The Picture of Dorian Gray*
1892
Wilde: *Lady Windermere's Fan*
Yeats: *The Countess Cathleen*
1893
Gissing: *The Odd Woman*
Wilde: *Salome*
1894
Kipling: *The Jungle Book*
William Morris: *The Wood beyond the World*
1895
Hardy: *Jude the Obscure*
H. G. Wells: *The Time Machine*
Wilde: *The Importance of Being Earnest*
Yeats: *Poems*
1897
Henry James: *What Maisie Knew*
H. G. Wells: *The Invisible Man*
Yeats: 'The Secret Rose'
1898
Conrad: *The Nigger of the Narcissus*
Hardy: *Wessex Poems*
Henry James: 'The Turn of the Screw'
Shaw: *Arms and the Man*
    Mrs Warren's Profession
H. G. Wells: *The War of the Worlds*
Wilde: *Ballad of Reading Gaol*
1899
Henry James: *The Awkward Age*
John Cowper Powys: *Poems* (published)

1888
Local Government Act (establishes local councils)

1890
Parnell resigns as Irish Nationalist leader

1893
Jan. Independent Labour Party founded by Kier Hardy at Bradford conference

1898
19 May Gladstone dies

1899
Boer War begins